Acknowledgements

My sincere thanks to all those who contributed to the successful publication of this third edition of Living and Working in Ireland, including Kerry Laredo (research and editing), Lilac Johnston (proofreading), Di Tolland (design and desktop publishing) and Jim Watson for the superb illustrations, maps and cover design. I would also like to thank Chris Toomey (research), Stephen Jeffery (The Property Finders), Richard Ryan (An Post), Brian Sheehan (Editor, Industrial Relations News), and Tina Moisander (Vivas Health) for their help with this and previous editions. Finally, a special thank you to the many photographers (listed on page 414) – in particular Peter Farmer – whose beautiful images add colour and bring Ireland to life.

What readers & reviewers have said about Survival Books:

'If you need to find out how France works then this book is indispensable. Native French people probably have a less thorough understanding of how their country functions.'

Living France

'It's everything you always wanted to ask but didn't for fear of the contemptuous put down. The best English-language guide. Its pages are stuffed with practical information on everyday subjects and are designed to compliment the traditional guidebook.'

Swiss News

'Rarely has a 'survival guide' contained such useful advice – This book dispels doubts for first-time travellers, yet is also useful for seasoned globetrotters – In a word, if you're planning to move to the US or go there for a long-term stay, then buy this book both for general reading and as a ready-reference.'

American Citizens Abroad

'Let's say it at once. David Hampshire's Living and Working in France is the best handbook ever produced for visitors and foreign residents in this country; indeed, my discussion with locals showed that it has much to teach even those born and bred in l'Hexagone – It is Hampshire's meticulous detail which lifts his work way beyond the range of other books with similar titles. Often you think of a supplementary question and search for the answer in vain. With Hampshire this is rarely the case. – He writes with great clarity (and gives French equivalents of all key terms), a touch of humour and a ready eye for the odd (and often illuminating) fact. – This book is absolutely indispensable.'

The Riviera Reporter

'A must for all future expats. I invested in several books but this is the only one you need. Every issue and concern is covered, every daft question you have but are frightened to ask is answered honestly without pulling any punches. Highly recommended.'

Reader

'In answer to the desert island question about the one how-to book on France, this book would be it.'

The Recorder

'The ultimate reference book. Every subject imaginable is exhaustively explained in simple terms. An excellent introduction to fully enjoy all that this fine country has to offer and save time and money in the process.'

American Club of Zurich

'The amount of information covered is not short of incredible. I thought I knew enough about my birth country. This book has proved me wrong. Don't go to France without it. Big mistake if you do. Absolutely priceless!'

Reader

'When you buy a model plane for your child, a video recorder, or some new computer gizmo, you get with it a leaflet or booklet pleading 'Read Me First', or bearing large friendly letters or bold type saying 'IMPORTANT - follow the instructions carefully'. This book should be similarly supplied to all those entering France with anything more durable than a 5-day return ticket. – It is worth reading even if you are just visiting briefly, or if you have lived here for years and feel totally knowledgeable and secure. But if you need to find out how France works then it is indispensable. Native French people probably have a less thorough understanding of how their country functions. – Where it is most essential, the book is most up to the minute.

Living France

A comprehensive guide to all things French, written in a highly readable and amusing style, for anyone planning to live, work or retire in France.

The Times

Covers every conceivable question that might be asked concerning everyday life – I know of no other book that could take the place of this one.

France in Print

A concise, thorough account of the Do's and DONT's for a foreigner in Switzerland – Crammed with useful information and lightened with humorous quips which make the facts more readable.

American Citizens Abroad

'I found this a wonderful book crammed with facts and figures, with a straightforward approach to the problems and pitfalls you are likely to encounter. The whole laced with humour and a thorough understanding of what's involved. Gets my vote!'

Reader

'A vital tool in the war against real estate sharks; don't even think of buying without reading this book first!'

Everything Spain

'We would like to congratulate you on this work: it is really super! We hand it out to our expatriates and they read it with great interest and pleasure.'

ICI (Switzerland) AG

Important Note

Ireland is a diverse country with many faces, two languages and continuously changing rules, regulations (particularly regarding business, social security and taxes), interest rates and prices. In particular, a change of government in Ireland can have far-reaching effects on many aspects of life. I cannot recommend too strongly that you check with an official and reliable source (not always the same), and obtain expert legal advice before making any major decisions or undertaking an irreversible course of action. However, don't believe everything you're told or read, even, dare I say it, herein!

Useful addresses and references to other sources of information have been included in all chapters and **Appendices A**, **B** and **C** to help you obtain further information and verify data with official sources. Important points have been emphasised in bold print, some of which it would be expensive or even dangerous to disregard. **Ignore them at your peril or cost!**

Note

Contents

Authors' Notes

♦ Frequent references are made in this book to the European Union (EU) which comprises Austria, Belgium, Bulgaria, Cyprus, the Czech Republic, Denmark, Estonia, Finland, France, Germany, Greece, Hungary, Ireland, Italy, Latvia, Lithuania, Luxembourg, Malta, the Netherlands, Poland, Portugal, Rumania, Slovakia, Slovenia, Spain, Sweden and the UK. The EU countries plus Iceland, Liechtenstein and Norway comprise the European Economic Area (EEA).

♦ Times are shown using am (Latin: ante meridiem) for before noon and pm (post meridiem) for after noon, e.g. 10am and 10pm.

♦ Prices are shown in Euros and should be taken as estimates only, although they were mostly correct at the time of publication and are unlikely to change significantly overnight. Unless otherwise stated, prices quoted include value added tax (VAT) at 4.8, 13.5 or 21 per cent.

♦ His/he/him/man/men, etc. also mean her/she/her/woman/women, etc. This is done simply to make life easier for both the reader and the author, and isn't intended to be sexist.

♦ Spelling and vocabulary are British English; American English words are given in brackets where they differ significantly from British English.

♦ Key Irish (Gaelic) words and phrases are shown in italics, and warnings and important points are shown in bold type.

♦ The following symbols are used in this book: ☎ (telephone), 🖹 (fax), 🖳 (Internet) and ✉ (email).

♦ Lists of embassies and consulates, further reading and useful websites are contained in **Appendices A**, **B** and **C** respectively.

♦ For those unfamiliar with the Irish system of **Weights and Measures,** conversion tables (Imperial/metric) are included in **Appendix D**.

♦ A map of the four provinces is shown inside the front cover and a map of the counties inside the back cover.

Newport, Co. Mayo

Introduction

Whether you are already living or working in Ireland or just thinking about it – this is THE BOOK for you. Forget about those glossy guide books, excellent though they are for tourists; this amazing book was written especially with you in mind and is worth its weight in shamrocks. Furthermore, this updated and fully revised 3rd edition is printed in full colour. *Living and Working in Ireland* is designed to meet the needs of anyone wishing to know the essentials of Irish life – however long your intended stay, you'll find the information contained in this book invaluable.

General information isn't difficult to find in Ireland; however, reliable and up-to-date information specifically intended for foreigners living and working in Ireland isn't so easy to find, least of all in one volume. Our aim in publishing this book was to help fill this void, and provide the comprehensive, practical information necessary for a relatively trouble-free life. You may have visited Ireland as a tourist, but living and working there is a different matter altogether. Adjusting to a different environment and culture and making a home in any foreign country can be a traumatic and stressful experience, and Ireland is no exception.

Living and Working in Ireland is a comprehensive handbook on a wide range of everyday subjects and represents the most up-to-date source of general information available to foreigners in Ireland. It isn't, however, simply a monologue of dry facts and figures, but a practical and entertaining look at life in Ireland.

Adapting to life in a new country is a continuous process, and although this book will help reduce your 'rookie' phase and minimise the frustrations, it doesn't contain all the answers (most of us don't even know the right questions to ask). What it will do, is help you make informed decisions and calculated judgements, instead of uneducated guesses and costly mistakes. Most importantly, it will help you save time, trouble and money, and repay your investment many times over.

Although you may find some of the information a bit daunting, don't be discouraged. Most problems occur only once and fade into insignificance after a short time (as you face the next half a dozen). Most foreigners in Ireland would agree that, all things considered, they love living there. A period spent in Ireland is a wonderful way to enrich your life, broaden your horizons, and, with any luck (and some hard work) you may even please your bank manager. I trust this book will help you avoid the pitfalls of life in Ireland and smooth your way to a happy and rewarding future in your new home.

May the road rise to meet you!

Joe Laredo

September 2008

Custom House, Dublin

1.

FINDING A JOB

Ireland is one of the most open economies in the world in terms of trade in goods and services and in foreign investment, boasting a business-friendly regulatory environment, moderate tax rates and a flexible labour market. But although Ireland is one of the few countries in the world which is keen to attract new workers from abroad – most countries positively discourage them – it isn't necessarily easy to find a job there. Ireland has a relatively small labour market and there's a lot of competition for the best paid jobs; although in certain industries where skilled staff are in short supply, it's possible to pick and choose from an abundance of vacancies (see below).

ECONOMY

The Irish economy is the envy of Europe. In common with most other developed countries, Ireland suffered the ravages of unemployment in the last century and its economy went into a deep recession in the '60s, from which it only recovered in the '90s. That recovery, of course, has been nothing less than spectacular, with the result that the 'Celtic Tiger' has become the fastest growing economy in Europe and among Organisation for Economic Co-operation and Development (OECD) countries and, in terms of 'international competitiveness' is now ranked among the world's leading countries; indeed, the OECD recently described its economic performance as 'exemplary'.

Since 1994, when its unemployment rate had reached a staggering 15.7 per cent, Ireland has created hundreds of thousands of jobs, although since its all-time low of 3.8 per cent in early 2000, unemployment has risen by around 4 per cent per year and reached a nine-year high of 5.7 per cent in mid-2008, prompting fears of a recession; the Economic and Social Research Institute (ESRI) predicts that the economy will contract by 0.4 per cent in 2008 before resuming expansion – of around 2 per cent – in 2009, but that unemployment will rise by 60 per cent by the same year.

The driving forces of Ireland's growth have changed in recent years. In the mid to late '90s,

growth was driven by strong performance in exports, which grew up to 20 per cent per year. While exports have remained at a high level, growth since 2000 has largely been driven by increases in domestic spending by individuals and in construction by the government and private businesses. However, internationally-trading businesses continue to play a major role in economic growth.

In the ten years to 2004, Irish gross national product (GNP) growth averaged over 7 per cent per annum in real terms (more than double that of the US and almost three times that of countries in the euro zone). The Irish economy continued to perform well until 2007, when annual growth was 6 per cent, but the first half of 2008 saw the 'end of an era', as the country's budget deficit nearly quadrupled (to €5.6bn). The determining factor was the sudden reversal of fortunes in the construction sector, a key plank in the 'Celtic Tiger' boom that saw 70,000 homes being built annually. Only half that number are predicted in 2008, and property prices dropped by around 10 per cent in the first half of the year. The current 'crisis' is exacerbated by weakening consumer confidence and tightening credit, following the US sub-prime crisis.

Other threats to Ireland's growth include the strength of the euro against foreign currencies such as the pound and the dollar, increasing wage costs (which have risen faster since 1998 than those in any other EU country), and the price of waste management, insurance and electricity (the latter costing businesses some 40 per cent more than in the UK, for example). Improvements in social services and infrastructure have lagged behind economic development and will need to be accelerated if Ireland is to continue to attract the qualified labour force it needs to sustain growth.

Public transport, and especially bus services, are in need of improvement, and state education needs additional funding to tackle the high 'drop-out' rate (i.e. children leaving school with no qualifications) and create better out-of-school-hours care facilities and work incentives – rather than benefits and hand-outs – so that more women and single parents (of either sex) can join the workforce.

Older people also need encouragement and assistance to find jobs, as fewer than 40 per cent of over-55s have an upper-secondary school qualification compared with 75 per cent of 25- to 34-year-olds; an increase in spending on research and development (R&D) is required to foster innovation; and the plethora of funding agencies need better co-ordination to maximise their effectiveness.

Protection is another barrier to economic progress, and increased competition is particularly needed in the electricity and telecommunication markets (which are still dominated by state-owned enterprises) and the retail trade, although the recent abolition of the Groceries Order, which set minimum prices for non-perishable groceries, is a step in the right direction; the so-called Competition Authority in fact has no authority to enforce competitive practice.

> The spiralling increase in the cost of property (see page 98) must be brought under control if the economy isn't to stagnate or decline.

The government is aware of all the above shortcomings and, in 2006, took steps to rectify them, including an increase in research funding, changes to the primary school curriculum, plans to create 50,000 childcare places by 2010 and, most radically, a planned budget deficit from 2006 to 2008 in order to simulate growth.

Nevertheless, Ireland now faces an unprecedented challenge to its economic development, as many parts of China, India, South-east Asia and Central Europe are now developing the types of high-tech manufacturing and service activities – including electronics, software, financial and other services and pharmaceuticals – that have driven Ireland's growth over the last 15 years. As a result, the country is likely to specialise even more in high-value niche areas, particularly in high-tech goods, including office and telecommunication equipment, and chemicals.

JOB MARKET

Over the last decade there have been radical changes in the Irish job market. Most significantly, there has been a major shift away from agriculture (though agricultural production is increasing) towards high-tech manufacturing and, especially, service industries, which employ 900,000 people or 45 per cent of the workforce. Overall, employment in the services sector has increased by some 5 per cent annually in recent years, the largest increases being in personal services, security and other protection services, professionals and craft workers, while manufacturing has been in decline.

Until recently, the construction industry has also experienced accelerating growth: according to the Central Statistics Office, employment in construction increased by some 80 per cent in the five years to 2007, but has fallen by almost 12 per cent in the year mid-2007 to mid-2008.

A government analysis of employment trends in six key sectors – engineering, internationally traded services, IT hardware, IT software, medical devices and pharmaceuticals – published in May 2006, identified the three most 'dynamic' sectors as IT hardware and software and internationally traded services, while employment in engineering had declined from its peak in 2000; although even in the IT hardware sector, there had recently been net job losses.

Although many industrial workers have been retrained, not all have been able to make the necessary transition, and job vacancies in tele-services, software and electronics manufacturing, nursing and healthcare, pharmaceuticals and medical products, automotive and aerospace engineering, construction, retailing and, especially, engineering have multiplied in recent years, as have business and financial services, despite significant annual increases in overall employment (of around 2.5 per cent or 50,000 people).

The *FÁS/ESRI Employment and Vacancies Survey* indicates the four-year trend in job opportunities. The latest survey, published in April 2008, revealed a 3 per cent decrease (to 7 per cent) in the number of firms reporting vacancies – the lowest vacancy rate since mid-2005 – the majority of the decrease being in the industry and services sectors (both down 4 per cent) – although the services sector was the only one that recorded an improvement in employment prospects. The vacancies most difficult to fill were mechanics and sales staff (in the retail sector), quantity surveyors, managers and estimators (in construction), engineers, managers and general operators (in industry) and accounting and legal personnel (in services).

Among Ireland's top companies (in terms of their market value) are four financial institutions (Allied Irish Banks, Bank of Ireland, Anglo Irish Bank Corporation and Irish Life & Permanent),

CRH and the Grafton Group (building materials), the Elan Corporation (pharmaceuticals), Independent News and Media, the Kerry Group (food production) and Ryanair (airline).

The Great Place to Work Institute is a market research company that produces an annual review (published by *The Irish Independent*) of the 50 'best' companies (with more than 50 employees) to work for in Ireland – on the basis of a survey of employers and employees designed to ascertain how well they get on together! The 'best' company in 2007 (the latest year for which a survey has been published) was O2, followed by (in alphabetical order) Airtricity, Brightwater, the Children's University Hospital, DePuy (Ireland), Diageo Ireland, GE Commercial Aviation Services, Google Ireland, Intel Ireland and PEI. A list of all 50 companies and further details can be found on 🖳 www. greatplacetowork.ie/best/list-ie-2006.htm.

The job market is particularly attractive for graduates, among whom unemployment is only around 3 per cent, as Irish employers continue to employ significant numbers of graduates, particularly in areas such as engineering, business and IT. Statistics might suggest that it is also attractive to foreigners. According to the mid-2008 *Quarterly National Household Survey* published by the Central Statistics Office (CSO), an astonishing 90 per cent of all new jobs in Ireland are currently being filled by foreign workers, and the number of non-Irish workers reached 352,000 (up from 283,000 in 2006). This is misleading, however, as a foreigner must be highly qualified to find a job in Ireland – even more so than a native – and anyone arriving in Ireland looking for a job should expect to find stiff competition from the locals.

The Irish workforce is well educated, well trained and well motivated and you shouldn't expect employers to favour you simply because you've

uprooted yourself and your family and set up home in a foreign land; in fact the opposite may be the case, as hiring and promotion practice is somewhat old-fashioned in that the 'old boys' network still operates in a number of areas and managers have limited autonomy when it comes to recruiting staff. Even well qualified local graduates cannot always walk straight into a job.

It's also important to note that many young (and not so young) people still leave the country each year in search of better employment opportunities overseas. If an Irish person cannot find a job in his place of birth, it's bound to be more difficult for a foreigner.

On the positive side, although some people have difficulty in finding employment, there are relatively few stories of abject failure, and only a small number of new migrants with good job skills fail to find a job (the unemployment rate among skilled migrants is much lower than the national average). Most people who are prepared to work hard and adapt to the Irish way of doing things find that they do better in their job or career in Ireland than they would at home

It's essential to have a plan of action for finding a job and to do your homework before arrival and – if necessary – be prepared to change your plans as you go along.

As commuting times, costs and parking problems have increased, particularly in Dublin (where a parking space can cost an employee thousands of euros per year), there has been a big increase in the amount of tele-working (some 15 per cent of employees now work from home during normal office hours). Some employers have brought work close to their staff, or indeed prospective employees: high-tech design and consulting companies, for example, are setting up satellite offices in different parts of the country, closer to universities or industrial centres.

Whereas only a few decades ago, many young people sought a 'job for life', today people in their

'20s and '30s don't expect to stay with the same employer for much more than two years (though some employers are now offering three and five-year 'packages' in an attempt to recoup their investment in recruiting and training new staff). Ireland has also witnessed a move away from restricted job definitions to more generalised role descriptions.

Tele-services

Tele-services include technical support for computer and software customers, selling financial and marketing services or other goods, and making reservations (e.g. hotels, flights). Since 2000, Ireland has become the European leader in call centres, with over 60 companies setting up operations employing some 10,000 people.

Companies in this sector include American Airlines, AOLBertelsmann, Best Western, Citibank, Compaq, Corel Corporation, Dell, DER, Digital Equipment, Gateway 2000, Hertz, IBM, ITT Sheraton, KAO Infosystems, Korean Airlines, Lufthansa German Airlines, Oracle, Radisson Hotels, Sitel, United Airlines and UPS.

Candidates must be fluent in English and at least one other European language (German is preferred, then French, Italian and Spanish). A Diploma in Tele-Services can be taken.

Software

Ireland is the world's largest exporter of software (having overtaken the US in 2000). From a handful of companies a decade and a half ago, there are now over 900 software firms in Ireland (130 of them foreign-owned) exporting over €16 billion worth of products and services. Five of the world's ten largest software companies have development or production facilities in Ireland, and 60 per cent of all software packages sold in Europe are produced in the country.

However, the industry currently faces a number of possible threats, including the possibility of recession in the US, the largest

market for Irish software, and the fact that internet-based services are likely to become increasingly important, which will make location less of a factor, thus eroding the advantages that Ireland has built up.

> The software industry is concentrated mainly in the Dublin area, with much smaller clusters in Limerick, Galway and Cork, and very little anywhere else.

Multinational companies in this sector include IBM, Intel, Liberty IT, Microsoft, Nortel Networks, Northbrook Technologies, Openwave and SAP, and Irish companies include Baltimore Technologies, Datalex, IONA Technologies, Parthus Technologies, Riverdeep and Trintech.

Almost 80 per cent of employees in this sector are graduates. The key person in software manufacture is the developer/engineer, who creates new products. A computer-science degree isn't necessary, but maths and languages are useful, as well as technical skills and some sort of technology-related qualification. In particular, there's a huge demand for C++ and Java/DB developers, systems administrators, location software testers and IT analysts. More information is available from the Irish Software Association (💻 www.software.ie).

Electronics

Electronics manufacturing is another rapidly expanding business sector, employing over 60,000 people. Companies include Alps Electric, American Power Conversion, Analog Devices, Apple Computers, AT&T, Avid Technology, Bootstrap, Courns, Cabletron Creative Labs, Connaught Electronics, Cornel Electronics, Dovatron, EICON, EMC, Ericsson, Europlex Manufacturing, Fujitsu Isotec, General Electric, General Instruments, Hewlett Packard, Hi-Tech Electronics, Hitachi-Koki, Hormann Electronics, IBM, Intel, Irish Printed Circuits, Kostal, Lake Communications, LG Group, Lucent Technologies, Madge Networks, Matsushita Kotobuki, Maxtor, Mentec International, Mitsumi, Mitsubishi

Chemical, Motorola, Nortel, Northern Telecom, Philips, Quaestor Analytic, Quantum, SCI, Seagate Technology, Sensormatic, Siemens, Sigma Wireless Technologies, Silicon Systems Design, Stratus, Sun Microsystems, 3Com, Trintech Manufacturing, Westinghouse and Xilinx.

Ireland's seven universities and 12 institutes of technology recently increased their student intake in an attempt to cope with the expected demand for people with electrical, mechanical, production, manufacturing and engineering skills and knowledge of metals and plastics. A minimum qualification is Leaving Certificate maths (or the equivalent) and there are opportunities for specialists and multi-skilled workers.

Nursing & Healthcare

There's an acute shortage of nurses, midwives and junior doctors in Ireland, where there are over 5,000 nurses from non-EU countries (especially the Philippines). The nursing shortage is particularly acute in the Dublin area and the government recently announced measures aimed at attracting back nurses who had left the profession (11,000 nurses are registered as 'inactive') or work abroad and encouraging those who work part-time to work full-time.

In other parts of the country, doctors are in short supply and an extra 1,000 consultants are also needed. Specialist nurse training courses are being created in Cork, Waterford and Limerick, and fees for 'back to nursing' courses have been abolished (students on the four-week course are even paid a salary!). Agencies specialising in nursing recruitment include the Alliance Nursing Agency in Dublin (💻 www.alliancenurses.ie) and Kate Cowhig International Recruitment (💻 www.kcr.ie), which also recruits other healthcare workers.

Pharmaceuticals & Medical Products

Ireland is a major base for the development and manufacture of pharmaceuticals and medical products but, although it's an important sector, it represents only around 10 per cent of total industrial employment and is dominated by foreign multinationals. Nine of the world's top ten pharmaceutical companies and 13 of the world's top 15 medical products companies have plants in Ireland. The medical devices and diagnostics industry employs 19,000 people and accounts for 7.5 per cent of Ireland's manufacturing base.

Pharmaceuticals companies include Akzo Pharma, Bristol-Meyers Squibb, Elan, Eli Lilly, E. Merck, FMC, Forest Laboratories, Fujitsawa, Ivax, Johnson & Johnson, Leo Laboratories, Schering-Plough, SmithKline Beecham, Warner Lambert, Wyeth Medica and Yamanouchi. Medical products companies include Abbott, Allergan, Bausch & Lomb, Baxter, Bayer Diagnostics, Becton Dickinson, Beiersdorf, Boston Scientific, Braun, CF Bard, Hollister, Howmedica, Mallinckrodt, Millipore, Olympus, Organon Teknika, Puritan Bennett, Sherwood Medical, Welch-Allyn American Home Products and Vistakon.

> ### ⚠ Caution
>
> At the retail level, there's a ban on foreign-trained pharmacists (even if they're Irish-born) starting chemists' shops: if you're trained abroad, you must buy a business that has been trading for at least three years.

Automotive & Aerospace Engineering

Another growing sector in which designers, engineers and toolmakers are required is automotive and aerospace engineering. Companies include ABB, Alcatel Cable, Alcoa, Allied Signal, AO Smith, Beru, Betatherm, Bijur Lubrication, Bruss, Cooper Industries, Crown Equipment, Dahlstrom, Donnelly Mirrors, Elasto Metall, Emerson Electric, Fujikura, General Monitors, General Motors, General Signal, Groschopp, Henniges, Jacobs Engineering, Kostal, Kromberg & Schubert, Lapple, Legrand, Liebherr, Menvier Swaine, Mitsubishi Belting, Moog, Ohshima, Packo, Pauwels, Pratt & Whitney, Radiac Abrasives, Sifco Turbine, Simon Engineering, Snap-Tite, Thermo King, Trac Tech, Volex, Wavin, Westinghouse, Wilo and Woco.

Financial Services

The financial services sector employs almost 50,000 people, and half as many again work in associated services. More than 1,000 of the world's leading financial institutions have established operations within Dublin's International Financial Services Centre (IFSC), which was founded in 1987 and has since become one of the prime locations in the EU for the financial services industry. Activities include banking; asset, fund and corporate treasury management; financing; securitisation; insurance and leasing.

Over 7,000 people are now employed at the IFSC, and there are opportunities for junior fund administrators and fund managers as well as customer service, IT and e-commerce staff. The 'big five' financial services companies are Arthur Andersen, Deloitte & Touche, Ernst & Young, KPMG and PricewaterhouseCoopers. Competition among financial institutions for staff is intense, and salaries and perks can be generous, although there's no shortage of applicants, as financial services jobs generally offer considerable security.

Construction

Until the start of 2008, the Irish construction industry had been growing steadily since the mid-'90s and it accounts for almost a quarter of GNP.

Some 300,000 people are involved in construction – almost 12 per cent of total employment.

The industry is focusing increasingly on major projects, such as road construction and shopping centres. With planned improvements to roads, railways, airports and water treatment plants, growth is expected to continue for several more years, although it's expected to slow. Opportunities exist for school-leavers (e.g. plant operators), apprentices (e.g. electricians, joiners, plumbers, carpenters and painters) and graduates (e.g. architects and surveyors). Although the sector is suffering a relative recession, there are vacancies nationwide in some disciplines – especially for managers, quantity surveyors and estimators.

Retailing

The boom in consumer spending in the last decade has seen a record number of new retail outlets opening and jobs increasing annually, although this is expected to slow in the next few years. Recruitment in the fast moving consumer goods' (FMCG) sector is growing steadily, with particular demand for

sales and marketing professionals, principally at brand management, category management and marketing management levels, in both domestic and international markets.

Teaching

There's a demand for second-level teachers, especially of chemistry, French, Irish, IT, maths and religious studies, and for first-level teachers. Your qualifications must be acceptable to the Teaching Council (💻 www.teachingcouncil. ie). Information about vacancies may be available from the principal teachers' union, the Association of Secondary Teachers of Ireland (💻 www.asti.ie).

Other Sectors

Other areas in which growth is expected in the early part of the century, albeit at a slower rate than those listed above, are consumer products, tourism, agriculture and fishing (especially food processing, which accounts for over a quarter of Ireland's food and drink exports), telecommunications, teaching, accountancy, food production and catering. There's a particular demand for personal assistants and secretaries – especially legal secretaries. As with pharmacy (see above), there are restrictions on a number of professions, including law, medicine, dentistry and veterinary practice, e.g. regarding entry, fees, advertising, training and the recognition of foreign qualifications.

SALARY

Average salaries have been rising rapidly since the mid-'90s and in 2005 overtook the EU average increases of 4.4 per cent in manufacturing industries, 6.3 per cent in the public sector and 6.4 per cent in the construction industry; indeed, income per capita in Ireland is among the highest in the world. Larger companies generally pay higher wages than smaller businesses (which also often expect employees to work longer hours); for a similar job you might expect to earn 30 per cent more in a company with over 500 staff than in a company with fewer than 50 staff.

There are, however, exceptions – especially in the rank of middle management, where job content rather than title is the principal factor affecting earnings. Similarly, in sales jobs, the most important factor is performance, and high performers can expect generous remuneration. At representative level, salaries tend to be similar across sectors and companies, as responsibility is evenly shared.

It isn't immediately obvious what salary you should command in Ireland, as wages and salaries aren't usually quoted in job advertisements. As trade unions are still influential in Ireland, wages are often negotiated on a collective basis and are therefore broadly similar in different industries and areas. Regional differences in salary are generally smaller than differences between industry sectors. Whereas the best paid sectors used to be mining and the chemical industries, it's now IT and financial services which enjoy the highest pay, though chemical and pharmaceutical manufacturing is still well rewarded.

Other above average sectors are communications (including telecommunications and transport); food, drink and tobacco processing; medical appliance manufacturing; oil and gas exploration (there will be a particularly large bonus for the first person to find oil in Ireland!); and construction.

Among the worst paid sectors are material manufacturing (including metal, plastics, textiles, rubber, leather, glass and pottery), printing and publishing, electrical and electronic engineering, and distribution. Bigger companies tend to pay better than smaller ones. In terms of departments, the best paid managers are those in production and manufacturing, followed by those in IT, administration and marketing or sales, finance and accounting, and finally human resources (HR). The best executive jobs tend to be in marketing followed by sales, finance and technical departments.

As far as it's possible to generalise, average annual salary ranges for various positions are shown in the table below. The average public servant earns around €45,000 per year.

Average Annual Salary	
Position	**Salary (€)**
Senior Managers	40,000 to 100,000
Middle Managers	35,000 to 50,000
Junior Managers	30,000 to 40,000
Executives	25,000 to 40,000*
Sales People	20,000 to 40,000*
Non-executives	10,000 to 15,000

* excluding bonuses and commission

Starting Salaries

The average graduate starting salary is around €27,250. Generally, those with good science or technology (especially medical and paramedical) qualifications can expect higher starting salaries than those without. The highest starting salaries (over €28,000) are in the armed forces, education, engineering and IT, as well as some construction-related jobs, and positions requiring degrees in mathematics and geology/earth sciences. Then come other science and computing-related posts, and jobs requiring qualifications in humanities, social work and social care.

The lowest starting salaries for graduates (under €25,000) are associated with art and design, business studies, hospitality, information services and psychology. As far as regional variations are concerned, the highest starting salaries (averaging €27,500) are in Leinster, which includes Dublin.

According to a survey undertaken at the 2008 Graduate Recruiters' Conference (run by Graduate Careers Ireland, 🖥 www.gradireland. com), a postgraduate qualification has an effect on salary in only around 25 per cent of cases.

The average graduate is entitled to 23 days' paid holiday in his first year of employment.

Bonuses & Benefits

In areas where there are staff shortages, it has become common for companies to offer not only attractive salaries but also a range of other incentives to attract (and retain) employees. The most popular (i.e. most widely offered) benefits are company pension schemes, bonuses and private health insurance. Variable pay (i.e. a relatively low basic salary with substantial bonuses, known as risk-income) is becoming increasingly popular. Some companies will offer this kind of package only to their executives and heads of department, while others, particularly in the IT sector, apply the principle more or less across the board. In these cases, personnel at all levels will typically receive up to 40 per cent of their salary in the form of performance-related payments and ` share options.

Around 16 per cent of managers and 18 per cent of executives receive cash bonuses – up to 25 per cent of basic salary for senior managers and around 15 per cent for executives – and share options are given to 21 per cent of managers and 12 per cent of executives. In fact, share purchase schemes are cited as one of the biggest reasons for staff staying with an employer.

A common benefits package (offered by almost half of Irish companies) is a flexible or 'flex' programme, where employees can choose from a variety of benefits offered according to their circumstances, although there may be a number of 'core' benefits that apply to all.

Employers in the financial services, banking and insurance sectors offer preferential loans and mortgages, while others offer relocation assistance, which can exceed €60,000. Other benefits include pensions, holidays, insurance and company cars (though the last has declined due to increased tax penalties. Dell Computers has even resorted to an internal lottery to attract and retain staff at its manufacturing plant in Limerick; prizes are awarded weekly and range from bicycles to holidays and even cars. Peripheral perks may include free courses or personal training classes: Xerox, which has a major manufacturing centre near Dublin, has an Open Learning Centre and a Virtual Learning Environment, through which staff can teach themselves a variety of skills, from languages to driving.

Since January 2004, benefits-in-kind have been subject to PRSI and the Health Levy, and these charges should be set against the value of the benefits you're offered.

Another recent innovation in remuneration is employee referral bonuses, whereby employees are rewarded for recruiting staff. Many companies are effectively using their entire workforce as recruiters. Referral bonuses vary considerably: the minimum is generally around €1,500, while some firms have been known to pay €7,500 or more for key placements.

Many companies are so desperate to find suitably qualified and skilled staff that it isn't uncommon for graduates to ask prospective employers what the company has to offer them. The demand for middle and senior managers, especially in the financial and technology sectors, has led to annual salary increases of up to 10 per cent, without taking into account other benefits such as share options and equity stakes.

Minimum Wage

A national minimum wage was introduced in Ireland on 1st April 2000 which, far from being an April Fool, was considerably higher than the UK minimum. The current rate for 'experienced adult workers' is €8.65 per hour. Other categories of worker, including those under 18, those in their first two years of employment and those undergoing training, are subject to various other minimum rates, the lowest being the illogically named 'sub-minimum wage' of €6.06 per hour (70 per cent of the 'full' minimum wage) for workers under 18. In sectors covered by a Joint Labour Committee, higher minimum wages apply.

WOMEN

Traditionally restricted to nursing, teaching, domestic service and clerical work (if they weren't working as nuns), Irish women began to participate more fully in the labour force in the '70s (until 1977, married women were forbidden to work in the civil service), but it wasn't really until the '90s that they achieved any measure of equal representation with men. The growth in service industries in particular created additional career opportunities, and in the six years from 1991 to 1997 the number of full time working women in Ireland grew more than in the previous 20 years, while many more took up part-time employment.

The number of working mothers almost doubled between 1987 and 1997 and 65 per cent of women aged 25-54 are now in employment (which, paradoxically, has led to a national shortage of childcare facilities!). Nevertheless, despite the fact that the last two Irish Presidents have been female, women are still greatly outnumbered in senior positions.

Under EU law, discrimination on grounds of sex or marital status is illegal except in

cases where a person of one sex or the other is required for the job, e.g. the World's Strongest Man or a brassiere model! However, if there are unequal numbers of one sex in a particular job, employers are entitled to provide special training for the sex which is less well represented. When Ireland joined the EU in 1977, it failed to meet EU requirements on equality of pay for women. Typically, the Irish tried to obtain a special dispensation on the basis that many firms would go out of business if they had to pay women the same as men (!), but their appeal was rejected and equal pay became a legal requirement.

Since then much has been done to bring greater sexual equality to the workplace, which is being monitored as part of the National Development Plan by the Gender Equality Unit of the Department of Justice, Equality & Law Reform (💻 www.ndpgenderequality.ie). December 2005 saw the launch of a two year 'leadership initiative for females in trade unions' (abbreviated to 'LIFT'), whereby the government hoped to achieve a minimum of 40 per cent female representation on State Boards (the current figure is 25 per cent); and other government initiatives include Equal, Equality for Women, Gateways, Women in Business and the Equal Opportunities Childcare Programme.

Nevertheless, as in other countries, equality in theory doesn't mean equality in practice: although female participation in the workforce has increased, it's still below the OECD average (except among the under-30s); there's a pay gap between male and female workers of around 14 per cent, although this is falling annually; and a recent government report indicated that women continue to suffer inequality, and even discrimination, in the workplace, admitting that there was 'still some way to go in tackling the gaps in pay and under-representation by women at the top' due to 'negative stereotyping, biased recruitment, promotion systems and discrimination', as well as to inadequate childcare facilities (see **Economy** on page 17).

EU & NON-EU CITIZENS

As a member of the European Union (EU), Ireland distinguishes in its immigration policy between people from within and from outside the European Economic Area.

Nationals of all EEA countries have the right to enter, live and work in Ireland or any other member state without a work permit, provided they have a valid passport or national identity card and comply with Ireland's laws and regulations on employment. (EEA nationals constitute around 65 per cent of foreigners living in Ireland.) In theory, all EEA nationals are further entitled to the same treatment as Irish subjects in matters of pay, working conditions, access to housing, vocational training, social security and trade union rights, and dependants are entitled to join them and enjoy the same rights. EU legislation is designed to make it easier for people to live and work in other member states.

There are, however, still practical barriers to full freedom of movement and the right to work within the EU. For example, some jobs in Ireland require job applicants to have specific skills or vocational qualifications, and qualifications obtained in some member states aren't yet recognised (see **Qualifications** below). There are also restrictions on employment in the civil service, when the right to work may be limited in individual cases on the grounds of government policy, security or public health.

Non-EEA nationals require a permit to work in Ireland (see **Employment Permits** on page 73). Until 2003, it was up to employers to prove that they had made every effort to employ an EEA national before applying for a work permit for a non-EEA national, but they could otherwise recruit as many non-EEA workers as they wished for any job at any level. The Employment Permits Bill of 2003, however, made non-EEA nationals ineligible for permits to work in specific sectors.

A recent government report indicated that non-EEA workers suffer widespread discrimination at the hands of employers, to whom they're 'tied' by the work permit scheme, including below-minimum-wage remuneration, poor working conditions and even racial abuse. As a result, the government allowed employees as well as employers to apply for employment permits and required employees to work for the same employer for only 12 months. As non-EEA nationals are granted only temporary (though renewable) employment permits, the only way they can obtain entitlement to permanent residence is through naturalisation, possible after five years of residence.

☑ SURVIVAL TIP

Irish government policy with regard to citizens of 'new' EU member countries and non-EEA nationals is constantly under review, and you should check the latest position with an Irish embassy or consulate.

QUALIFICATIONS

An essential qualification in the Irish job market is a good level of spoken and written English. All employers expect their staff to have 'adequate' English, the definition of which depends on the type of job you're after – the more skilled the position the better your English must be.

Theoretically, qualifications recognised by professional and trade bodies in any EU country should be recognised in Ireland. However, recognition varies from country to country, and in some cases foreign qualifications aren't recognised by Irish employers or professional and trade associations. All academic qualifications should also be recognised, although they may be given less prominence than equivalent Irish

qualifications, depending on the country and the educational establishment.

A ruling by the European Court declared that when examinations are of a similar standard with just certain areas of difference, then individuals should only be required to take exams in those particular subjects. In general, degrees from universities in most Western countries are considered equivalent to degrees from Irish universities and most school qualifications are considered equivalent to Irish school qualifications, at least so far as employers and university admissions staff are concerned.

With regard to industry-specific qualifications, these vary greatly from one sector to another. In each area there may be reciprocal agreements with certain other countries or acknowledged similarities in courses and work experience. Although the national training and employment agency, FÁS, helps Irish companies to recruit abroad, it's left to individual employers to check whether foreign qualifications are acceptable. In the case of professions such as teaching and nursing, the relevant government department will issue guidelines as to qualifications and experience required to work in Ireland.

For certain jobs you must be registered with the appropriate Irish professional organisation. The registration process includes an assessment of your professional or trade qualifications and leads to membership of the appropriate body, thus allowing you to work in Ireland.

If your trade or profession is one where registration is required, you should contact the relevant body well in advance as you may need to take an examination or undergo a period of retraining, for which you must pay. In some cases, examinations can be taken in other countries, although they may be held on one or two days a year only. You should check with the relevant trade or professional association (see below).

Under EU rules, certain professions are regulated, which means that those qualified in one member state may apply for (and normally obtain) recognition of their qualification(s) in another member state. A list of regulated professions in Ireland and information on where and how to apply for recognition can be found on the Irish Department of Education & Science website (⌨ www.education.ie and click on 'Mutual Recognition of Professional Qualifications').

If your profession isn't regulated either in your home country or in Ireland, you don't need recognition to practise in Ireland. If it's regulated in Ireland but not in your home country, you may need to obtain a 'certificate of experience' before being able to practise in Ireland; details can be found on the above website. Further information about unregulated professions and about the recognition of foreign academic qualifications in Ireland can be found on the website of National Qualifications Authority of Ireland (formerly NARIC, ⌨ www. qualificationsrecognition.ie).

JOB HUNTING

According to the IDS Media Group, which markets mailing lists, there are 190,000 businesses in Ireland, 65 per cent of them employing fewer than five people, 22 per cent between five and nine people and only 1.25 per cent (around 2,375 companies) with more than 100 staff. When looking for a job with a company, it's best to use every route available (see below); the more applications you make, the better your chance of finding something suitable. Contact as many prospective employers as possible, in writing, by telephone or by calling on them in person. Naturally it's easier to find a job after you've arrived in Ireland, although you should start preparing the ground before you get there by doing research into potential employers and contacts.

Irish Newspapers

Obtain copies of as many Irish newspapers as possible, all of which contain 'positions vacant' sections. To save money, it's worth checking libraries abroad, as they sometimes have Irish newspapers. If you live near an Irish Consulate or High Commission or an Irish Immigration Service information office, you may find they have a reading room containing recent copies of Irish newspapers. Otherwise most Irish newspaper publishers will send you a free copy or you can take out a subscription.

Situations vacant are usually advertised on specific days, e.g. *The Irish Times* on Fridays, the *Irish Independent* on Thursdays, the *Sunday Independent*, the *Sunday Business Post* and *Sunday Tribune* and the weekly *Job News*). Most newspapers carry a 'Situations Wanted' column, although unless you're exceptionally well qualified or have a skill that's in short supply, you cannot expect much of a response when placing an advertisement of this kind. Most also have websites (see below).

Foreign Newspapers

If you're seeking an executive or professional position, you will find that vacancies are sometimes advertised in the national newspapers of other countries. For example, the UK's *Times Higher Education Supplement* occasionally carries vacancies for jobs in Ireland. However, local employers usually go to the trouble of advertising jobs abroad only when vacancies are proving hard to fill locally, or when they require unusual or exceptional skills and qualifications.

Internet

Most of the leading Irish newspapers have websites aimed at jobseekers. These include ⌨ www.ireland.com (*The Irish Times*), ⌨ www.loadza.com (*Irish Independent*), www.sbpost.ie (*Sunday Business Post*) and www.tribune.ie (*Sunday Tribune*). You can also look at the websites of the leading Irish job agencies, such as CPL Computer Placement (www.cpl.ie), Grafton Recruitment (www.grafton-group.com), Hays www.hays.ie), Marlborough (www.marlborough.ie), Premier Recruitment (www.premier.ie) and Richmond Recruitment (www.richmond.ie). Other specialist sites include www.irishjobs.ie, www.stepstone.ie (both of which claim to be Ireland's number one job site), www.monster.ie, www.recruitireland.com, www.topjobs.ie, www.exp.ie, and www.jobfinder.ie, which lists more than 3,000 vacancies, mainly in the IT sector, and also has useful information about working in Ireland. The FÁS website is www.fas.ie.

A list of the 800 or so Irish companies currently recruiting can be found on www.jobsnews.ie/2008/03/03/employers-recruiting-in-ireland-irish-jobs

An increasing number of Irish companies, particularly in the IT sector, are recruiting online; visit the sites of the companies you're interested in for details of making an online application.

Trade Journals

Some trades and professions have their own magazines, journals or newsletters, published independently or by the trade association, in which jobs are advertised. Contact the relevant association(s) listed below or look under *Associations & Institutions* in the *Golden Pages*. Professional and executive opportunities in Ireland are sometimes also advertised in trade journals in other English-speaking countries, e.g. the UK and the US.

Government Employment Service

Visit your local FÁS office in Ireland (see **Government Employment Service** on page 30). Jobs on offer are mainly non-professional, skilled, semi-skilled and unskilled.

Recruitment Agencies

If you're looking for an executive or professional position, you can apply to recruitment consultancies in Ireland and abroad, specialising in the kind of position you're seeking. (They will usually be pleased to help and advise you, whether or not you've applied for permission to live in Ireland.) Unlike their UK counterparts, Irish employment agencies and recruitment specialists (listed separately in the *Golden Pages*) are essentially the same, although some specialise in certain areas of employment. Executive search companies, on the other hand, operate in a different way, being retained by particular clients to recruit staff on their behalf.

Professional Organisations

If you're a professional, it may be worthwhile contacting relevant professional organisations in Ireland (listed in the *Golden Pages* under *Associations and Institutes*). Although they cannot find you a job, they can often help with advice and provide the names of prospective employers.

Government Departments

If you're considering a position or career with a government department or another public body, you will need to contact the Public Appointments service (☎ 01-858 7400 or ☎ 1890-449999, www.publicjobs.ie), which deals with all government recruitment, including administrative and technical staff of Health Boards and local authorities. All appointments are made by a process of open competition, although current legislation restricts applications to EU citizens.

> There are three entry levels to the civil service: clerical officer, administrative officer and executive officer.

For clerical officer positions no qualifications are required but candidates must take an aptitude test. For administrative officer jobs, you must have at least five honours passes at Leaving Certificate (or the equivalent in other EU countries). Only first class graduates are considered for executive positions. A fourth type of position, that of third secretary in the Diplomatic Service (part of the Department of Foreign Affairs), is equivalent to an executive officer but, since only around a dozen of these posts become available each year, competition is extremely strong.

In addition, the civil service recruits a number of professional and technical staff (e.g. prison and welfare officers, meteorological staff, accountants and legal staff, agricultural, veterinary and engineering inspectors, architects and librarians). When applying for any position, you will be asked to state your preference of government department, but may be allocated to a different department by the Commission.

Unsolicited Job Applications

Apply to companies directly in Ireland, whether or not they're advertising vacancies. Needless to say, it's a hit-and-miss affair, but the big advantage is that you aren't competing directly with hundreds of other applicants as with an advertised job vacancy. This approach can be particularly successful if you have skills, experience and qualifications which are in short supply in Ireland. When writing from abroad, enclosing an international reply coupon may help elicit a response.

A list of the 30 largest companies in Ireland at the end of 1999 can be found in the *Local Ireland Almanac* (Local Ireland). Useful addresses can also be obtained from trade directories (such as *Kompass Ireland*), which are available at major libraries, and from Irish Chambers of Commerce abroad or Chambers of Commerce in Ireland (☎ 01-661 2888, 🖥 www.chambers.ie).

☑ SURVIVAL TIP

Only around a quarter of Irish businesses now accept CVs by post, the great majority insiting that they're submitted by email.

Networking

Networking (which, like so many simple but effective ideas, originated in the US) is basically making and using business and professional contacts. You should make use of contacts both in Ireland and with any Irish people you come into contact with abroad, including friends, relatives, colleagues, customers, clients and suppliers. If you're already in Ireland, you can contact or join local expatriate social clubs, churches, societies and professional organisations (see **Appendix A**).

GOVERNMENT EMPLOYMENT SERVICE

The Irish national training and employment authority is known as FÁS (which stands for Foras Áiseanna Saothair and is pronounced 'foss') and is funded by the Irish Government, the European Social Fund and the European Regional Development Fund. It was established in 1988 to provide training and retraining, employment schemes, placement and guidance services, assistance to community groups and workers' co-operatives towards the creation of jobs, assistance to people seeking employment elsewhere in the EU, and consultancy and human resource related services (on a commercial basis) outside Ireland.

FÁS is divided into ten regions comprising 56 Employment Offices (generally in main towns and cities), 20 Training Centres and 45 Community Training Workshops. In towns where there's no FÁS office, there may be a weekly clinic run by a FÁS representative in a hotel, for example. FÁS also runs Community Employment programmes for jobless people, and operates Local Employment Services targeted mainly at the long-term unemployed.

You must register with FÁS and provide details of the type of job you're looking for. These details will then be matched with vacancies notified to FÁS by employers. FÁS staff will also help you to prepare your CV and practise interview techniques. All FÁS offices offer a self-help scheme called Career Directions, which involves answering a series of questions on a computer programme to access relevant information and guidance. FÁS registered vacancies are listed on Teletext pages 580–584.

FÁS handles around 130,000 registrations annually and is notified of almost 70,000 vacancies. Nearly 100,000 people, both employed and unemployed, complete FÁS programmes, more than 30,000 are provided with training and financial support, and over

7,000 apprentices are recruited. It also runs more than 3,000 Community Employment programmes, employing some 40,000 people.

In January 2006, FÁS launched the 'Jobs Ireland' programme, an 'online marketplace' where jobseekers and employers can exchange information and match their requirements. FÁS Jobs Ireland can be accessed via the internet (💻 www.fas.ie), on WAP-enabled mobile phones, at touch screen (WATIS) kiosks in FÁS offices and via a freephone service (☎ 1800-611116).

Under its 'National Employment Action Plan', FÁS further seeks to help disadvantaged groups (including older people and women) to find employment.

FÁS can help if you're looking for a job, if you're already in a job but want further training, if you're thinking of starting a business and need advice or training or are looking to recruit staff. Job-finding services are available not only to those who are unemployed, but also to school and college leavers, to those wanting to return to work after a break, and to job-changers. All FÁS services are available to all EU citizens.

FÁS International and FÁS International Consulting, which have clients in over 35 countries, provide technical assistance and consultancy and training services to government ministries, state organisations, international agencies and private companies throughout the world. Employers wanting vacancies to be advertised in other EU and EEA states can make use of the   EURES (European

Placement System) which electronically links FÁS to the other public employment services in the EEA.

Those considering working in Europe can obtain information on jobs, as well as on living and working conditions through EURES, or by speaking to one of FÁS's Euroadvisers. As part of the government's plan to attract foreigners to work in Ireland, FÁS has recently launched a glossy quarterly magazine called *Jobs Ireland*, which is distributed at job fairs and through Irish embassies as well as by Irish companies recruiting overseas. A CD-ROM version of *Jobs Ireland* is available free to employers (☎ 01-607 0506). Further information is available from the FÁS, 27/33 Upper Baggot Street, Dublin 4 (☎ 01-607 0500, 💻 www.fas.ie).

RECRUITMENT AGENCIES

There are many organisations in Ireland that can find you a job (or at least try to). These are listed under *Employment Agencies and Recruitment Specialists* in the *Golden Pages*. There's little or no difference between the two, which are referred to here as recruitment agencies. Some immigration consultants can arrange an introduction to recruitment agencies. Usually an agency cannot help you unless you're in Ireland, although they're normally willing to provide general information about local job prospects over the phone.

Recruitment   agencies are engaged by   employers to

fill vacancies, and therefore don't charge you for finding you a job (they normally charge employers a percentage of the successful applicant's first year's salary). Signing on with a recruitment agency, whether for a permanent or for a temporary position, normally involves being tested on various skills such as typing speed and familiarity with computer software packages. You will need to take a current CV with you, and will be interviewed by the agency before they register you. They will then endeavour to get you interviews for positions they feel are suitable.

☑ SURVIVAL TIP

Other services such as compiling CVs and counselling may be offered, for which you may be charged, so check in advance.

If you're taking up temporary work through an employment agency, you may find that you're in fact employed by the agency.

Some recruitment agencies have offices abroad and, if you plan to use them, it pays to make a few simple checks before doing so. For example, the law of your home country may permit them to make a charge for finding you a job or even for simply registering your details. Also check exactly what they will do for you. A recruitment consultant who merely sends your CV to prospective employers is unlikely to find you a job, whereas a consultant with employers on his books in the industry in which you want to work (ask for evidence) could prove to be a useful contact.

The leading Irish job agencies include CPL Computer Placement, Grafton Recruitment, Hays, Marlborough, Premier Recruitment and Richmond Recruitment (see **Internet** on page 28). One of Ireland's largest recruitment agencies is Manpower (💻 www.manpower. ie), which has offices in seven cities and offers training courses as well as a job-finding service, including over 1,000 free online courses. A comprehensive list of recruitment agencies can be found on 💻 www.niceone. com (click on 'Careers & Jobs').

Major management recruitment agencies include Deloitte, Hay Group, KPMG, MERC Partners, PE International and PricewaterhouseCoopers, all of which are members of the Executive Selection Consultancies Association (ESCA, 💻 www. esca-ireland.com), which enforces a code of professional practice aimed at assuring clients of a certain standard of service. Contact details of all members can be found on the ESCA website.

Executive Search Companies

If you're looking for a managerial position, it might be worth registering with one or more executive search companies. These are 'retained' by firms looking to expand their existing operations or set up new businesses, rather like an 'out-house' personnel or HR department. If the company thinks your credentials are suitable, you will be put forward for a job.

CONTRACT JOBS

Contract jobs are available through many employment agencies in Ireland which specialise in providing workers for a limited period to companies that employ freelance workers for certain jobs, rather than hire full-time employees. The contract market has grown enormously over the past five years or so, particularly in the IT and finance sectors, but also in pharmaceuticals, construction and catering. With skills shortages in a number of areas in Ireland, an increasing number of foreigners are being attracted to work in Ireland on short and long-term contracts. In the IT sector, for example, up to a third of contract workers are non-Irish (a large number coming from India), and in the construction industry, British and German contractors are in turn sub-contracting to labourers from countries such as Poland.

Contract rates vary considerably, from €10 per hour for catering staff to €1,250 or more per day for senior IT consultants. Software developers, for example, can earn between €200 and €300 per day. Most contract workers are based at the company's offices, but remote or tele-working (i.e. working from home) is becoming increasingly common.

irrespective of the number of hours worked) are available in most industries and professions and are common in offices, pubs, shops, factories, cafes and restaurants. Many young foreigners combine part-time work and study, for example improving their English or studying for a trade or professional qualification, although many educational institutions specifically forbid part-time working, and study visas aren't valid for employment. Most part-time workers are poorly paid, although you should now be assured of at least receiving the national minimum wage (see page 25).

As a part-time employee, you're also entitled to the same bonuses, holidays, etc. as full-time employees, on a pro rata basis. You may, however, have little protection from exploitation by your employer, although some employers give part-time employees the same rights as full-time employees. Some companies operate a job share scheme, where two or more people share the same job. See also **Temporary, Casual & Seasonal Jobs** below and **Recruitment Agencies** on page 31.

TEMPORARY, CASUAL & SEASONAL JOBS

Temporary, casual and seasonal jobs that last for a few days, weeks or months are available throughout the year. The tourist industry in particular is busy during the summer, and farms are in need of labourers in spring for sowing and in autumn for harvesting, as well as throughout the year in certain sectors. If you aren't an Irish citizen or resident, it's important to make sure that you're eligible to work in Ireland before you arrive (see **Chapter 3**).

In common with other countries, pay and conditions for casual and temporary jobs are usually poor, although you shouldn't be paid less than the national minimum wage (see page 25) and you should qualify for holiday pay, even if you're on a short-term contract. Those with basic skills (e.g. secretarial or call centre staff) can expect to earn at least €10 per hour, those with more advanced skills (e.g. computing or accountancy) €15 or more. Temporary workers are liable for income tax at the normal rates (see page 287), which will automatically be deducted if you've been found work by an agency.

Apart from specialist agencies such as Computer Placement, the best source of contract jobs is the internet (sites such as www.stepstone.ie), which has displaced magazines such as *Freelance Informer* and *Irish Computer* from a job-seeker's point of view. Agencies will assist with visa or work authorisation applications and provide training where necessary.

Contract workers from EEA countries may either be employed by the company they're working for on a pay-as-you-earn (PAYE) basis or establish their own limited companies. Non-EEA nationals must obtain a work permit or work authorisation in the normal way (see page 75) and can either set up their own business, provided that they've obtained business permission, or become an employee. In the case of employees, their employer, or the agency which recruited them on the employer's behalf, acts as a guarantor (also referred to as a 'sponsor' or 'owner') that they won't abuse the system by claiming Social Welfare benefits or otherwise becoming a burden on the state.

PART-TIME JOBS

Part-time jobs (officially defined as jobs in which you work fewer than five days a week,

Areas in which temporary, casual and seasonal work can be found include those listed below. There are many books for those seeking holiday jobs, including *Summer Jobs Abroad* by David Woodworth and *Work Your Way Around The World* by Susan Griffith (both published by Vacation Work).

Business

Employment agencies specialise in temporary and casual job vacancies in offices and shops in most parts of the country. It's obviously an advantage if you have some experience; if you have a qualification in a profession such as banking, finance, insurance, accountancy or law, you might even walk into a well-paid job.

Construction

The continuing building boom in Ireland and the resultant shortage of construction workers mean that temporary work on building sites is relatively easy to find. The largest agency specialising in construction jobs, temporary and permanent, is MCR Building Services (☎ 01-887 3900), which covers all types of building work, from labouring to project management.

Farming

There are thousands of farms in Ireland which usually need help, particularly during busy periods such as at sowing and harvesting times. Work is likely to be hard and the hours long, but in addition to wages you may receive free accommodation and food. Most farms recruit casual labour locally, but placements of three months or more (including permanent positions) are also dealt with by Farm Relief Services (☎ 0505-22100, 🖥 www.frsnetwork. com), which has 22 regional offices acting as a recruitment service for local farmers – call or visit the website for a list.

Farming vacancies are also advertised in the weekly *Irish Farmers' Journal*, available in some European countries or direct from 🖥 www.farmersjournal.ie. An organisation called Macra na Feirme (Sons of the Land) arranges exchange programmes with similar organisations throughout Europe for young people (mostly in their early '20s) already in farming, under its Seasonal & Horticultural Workers' Scheme (SHAWS). Exchanges

are for a minimum of three months, and participants are paid 'pocket money' and provided with board and lodging.

> To join a programme, you need to register with the relevant organisation in your home country. Contact Macra na Feirme for details (☎ 01-426 8900, 🖥 www.macra.ie).

Hotels & Catering

Hotels, restaurants and bars normally have a demand for waiters/waitresses, bar staff, chambermaids, receptionists and handymen throughout the year. Many employment agencies deal with this type of vacancy. If you want to go it alone, there's nothing to stop you approaching hotels and restaurants directly, although it's advisable to telephone and ask about vacancies before travelling to the 'back of beyond' looking for work.

Industry

As in most countries, there are often casual jobs available in factories and warehouses such as cleaning, labouring, portering or security. Particularly numerous are casual, temporary and seasonal jobs in some of the many food processing plants. This kind of work is notoriously unreliable: plants that may be working flat out one week stand idle the next, e.g. when there's a slump in the market or the season is over. Jobs of this kind can be found through employment agencies, in local newspapers or simply by turning up at the factory gate (very early!).

Nursing

Another area in which Ireland is acutely short-staffed is nursing and, provided you have relevant qualifications and experience, you may be able to find short-term work (see **Nursing & Healthcare** on page 21).

Tourism

Ireland attracts tourists year-round, but particularly during the summer (April to October, peaking during the school holidays from late July to early September), when some

140,000 people are taken on to help manage the flood of tourists, although an increasing number of visitors are taking short breaks in Dublin and elsewhere all year round. Jobs are available in shops, at tourist attractions, and on boats and beaches throughout the country.

Other

Other types of temporary or casual job include exhibition work (setting up and manning stands), sorting mail during the pre-Christmas period, gardening, market research, modelling (art colleges hire models of all shapes and sizes), security work, newspaper and magazine distribution, driving and courier work.

VOLUNTARY WORK

It's essential that, before coming to Ireland for any kind of voluntary work, you check whether you're eligible and whether you will be permitted to enter Ireland under the immigration and employment regulations. You may be required to obtain a visa or other entry clearance (see **Chapter 3**). The usual visa regulations apply to voluntary workers and your passport must be valid for at least one year.

There are dozens of organisations offering voluntary work in Ireland, at national, regional and local level, listed under *Charities & Caring Groups* in the *Golden Pages*. The minimum age for voluntary work in Ireland is 16 years and most organisations require good or fluent spoken English. No other qualifications are usually required and the minimum length of service varies from around one month to one year (often there's no maximum length of service). Disabled volunteers are also welcomed by many organisations.

Voluntary work is normally unpaid, although meals and accommodation are usually provided and sometimes also 'pocket money'. This may be insufficient for non-essential expenses such as entertainment and alcoholic drinks, so you should ensure that you bring money with you.

The following organisations operate voluntary schemes in Ireland:

♦ Conservation Volunteers Ireland (☎ 01-495 2878, ⌨ www.cvi.ie) – aims to provide practical opportunities for individuals and groups to work on cultural and heritage projects; to access the full list of its projects you need to pay a membership fee (€18 for an unemployed individual, €25 for an employed individual and €35 for a family);

♦ i-to-i (UK ☎ 0800-011 1156, ⌨ www.i-to-i. com) – a UK-based organisation, enabling people to teach English and undertake other voluntary work in 25 countries, including Ireland;

♦ Voluntary Service International (VSI, ☎ 01-855 1011, ⌨ www.vsiireland.org) – places up to 450 volunteers annually on various projects in Ireland;

♦ Volunteering Ireland (☎ 01-636 9446, ⌨ www.volunteeringireland.com) – formerly the Volunteer Resource Centre – recruits over 100 volunteers each year for projects lasting between a day and a year, and publishes a free guide to its services, downloadable from the website.

Details of these and other voluntary organisations can be found in the *International Directory of Voluntary Work* (Vacation Work), a guide to 400 agencies and sources of information on short to long-term voluntary work in Ireland and worldwide.

Work Camps

Work camps are intensive projects, usually lasting two or three weeks (mostly during the summer) and generally aimed at environmental conservation or the preservation of an historical site or monument for which there is insufficient state funding. Camps consist of 10 to 30 participants, mostly aged between aged 18 and 30. They may come from many countries and the lingua franca is usually English.

No special skills are necessary, but participants are expected to work a 30-hour week and the work can be physically demanding, occasionally in difficult terrain and bad weather. There may be a small charge for accommodation, which is shared with your fellow workers and can be fairly basic (it's normally in schools, hostels or tents). Meals are usually prepared by the participants themselves.

You will need to make your own travel arrangements to and from the work camp and apply for any necessary visa or permit./

Groundwork (☎ 01-860 2839, 🖥 www. groundwork.ie), a section of the Irish Wildlife Trust concerned with conserving Ireland's oak woods, organises rhododendron clearance work camps in the Killarney and Glenveagh National Parks, and bog clearance in central Ireland between June and September each year, for people aged 17-65. Camps are subsidised by the National Parks and Wildlife Services, so the cost of accommodation and meals is only €30 per person for one week or €45 for two weeks. The work takes place on weekdays, while weekends and evenings are spent exploring the National Parks and enjoying the local hospitality. Details of other organisations can be found in the *International Directory of Voluntary Work* (Vacation Work).

SELF-EMPLOYMENT & STARTING A BUSINESS

The idea of becoming self-employed or starting a business in Ireland is appealing, and often considered by those planning to live there. Irish people aren't traditionally entrepreneurial and there isn't an ingrained enterprise culture. Most people work nine to five for a large company – going-it-alone, which often involves

working up to 18 hours a day, isn't seen as an attractive proposition. Nevertheless, since the mid-'90s, a more entrepreneurial attitude has spread throughout the country, and a wide range of small businesses has been started, Ireland now being ranked second in the EU and seventh among OECD countries for entrepreneurial activity.

It's estimated that there are over 200,000 small and medium-size businesses (called SMEs) in Ireland and that the number is increasing by 10 per cent a year. Some 7.7 per cent of the adult population (almost 200,000 people) are currently planning to establish or are in the process of establishing a business.

Of course, starting a business and making a success of it are two quite different things, and the new business failure rate is as high in Ireland as in any other country. Generally speaking, it isn't wise to start or buy a business in which you don't have previous experience. Setting up a restaurant or a B&B may seem like a good idea at the time, particularly if your only experience of Ireland is a holiday, but it's rarely as simple as it appears. That said, there's still room in Ireland's booming economy for specialist service businesses and many of them do very well.

As a self-employed person you don't have the protection of a limited company should your business fail, although there are certain tax advantages.

 Caution

Always obtain professional advice before deciding whether to operate as a sole trader or form a company in Ireland, as it has far-reaching social security, tax and other consequences.

All self-employed people must register for income tax and Pay-related Social Insurance (PRSI – see page 248), and in certain cases pay government levies for health, training, employment and apprenticeship training.

There's considerable (though fragmented) state support for enterprise in Ireland).

Professional Advice

Before embarking on a business project in Ireland, ensure that you take legal and financial advice from a good lawyer and accountant. As an employer you might also consider joining the Irish Business & Employers' Confederation (IBEC, ☎ 01-605 1500, 💻 www.ibec.ie), which represents businesses in Ireland and provides various services including training courses and advice on employee relations and employment law, as well as lobbying the government on behalf of Irish industry generally. Small and medium-size businesses may benefit from the services of the Irish Small and Medium Enterprises Association (ISME, ☎ 01-662 2755, 💻 www.isme.ie).

Finance

You should usually reckon on having at least 50 per cent of the cost of a business purchase or start-up. Loans (properly called debt) are of course available from Irish banks, but they will look more favourably upon an application for a loan if you have a substantial lump sum of your own to invest, not to mention good business experience and a well-thought-out business

plan. As with banks elsewhere, they will also expect security for your loan, preferably in the form of property in Ireland.

Most major banks have start-up schemes. When it comes to obtaining grants, Irish financiers tend to operate on a 'matching funds' basis, so you will only be loaned as much as you've raised yourself. The Revenue Commissioners (💻 www.revenue.ie) produce an information pack called *Guides for Small Business*, covering financial matters such as tax and social security.

If you're an EU national or a permanent resident with a residence permit, you can work as a self-employed person or as a sole trader in Ireland. If you wish to be self-employed in a profession or trade in Ireland, you must meet certain legal requirements and register with the appropriate organisation, e.g. a professional must become a member of the relevant college. Members of some professions and trades must possess certain qualifications and certificates recognised in Ireland, and are usually required to sit a written examination.

You're subject to any professional codes and limitations in force, e.g. a medical practitioner must have his qualifications accepted by the medical college of the county where he intends to practise and by any controlling bodies. You must also show that you're in good standing with the professional authorities in your home country. In certain professions, such as law, it's unusual to be permitted to practise in Ireland without Irish qualifications.

Quality Certification

If you're thinking of setting up your own business, whether as a sole trader or a limited company, you should seriously consider obtaining quality certification. Certification is becoming increasingly important in Ireland. In fact, in some areas of business, it's essential and the IS standards are now a minimum requirement if you want to supply many foreign-owned multinationals. These are awarded by the National Standards Authority (☎ 01-807 3800, 💻 www.nsai.ie).

Other recognised Irish standards are the Hygiene Mark and the W Mark, awarded by Excellence Ireland (EIQA), formerly the Irish Quality Association (☎ 01-660 4100, 💻 www.eiqa.com), which is important in certain areas.

Note that both the Small Firms Association and the Irish Small and Medium Enterprises Association operate group ISO schemes to alleviate the cost of certification.

Social Insurance

You won't need to pay any tax until after your first year of trading. Anyone with an income in Ireland requires a PPSN (Personal Public Service Number) – previously called a Revenue and Social Insurance (RSI) number – and must register with the Department of Social and Family Affairs using form SE3, available from local Social Welfare Offices or from the Self-employment Section of the Social Welfare Services Office (☎ 01-874 8444 or ☎ 051-874177).

There's a specific social insurance scheme for self-employed workers, most of whom are liable for what are called PRSI Class S contributions. In addition to covering social insurance, these include a health contribution and an employment and training levy when your income reaches a certain level. In general, PRSI contributions for the self-employed are lower than for salaried employees, but you receive fewer benefits. Unlike an employee, who's entitled to dental and optical treatment, plus sickness and unemployment benefit, you will receive little more than an old age pension.

Self-employed women are also entitled to maternity benefits, but the wives or partners of self-employed men aren't. Note that if a relative such as your husband, wife, mother, father, brother, sister, son or daughter helps with the business without being an official partner, they're exempt from PRSI contributions. On the other hand, if they're paid a salary they should contact the Scope Section of the Department of Social and Family Affairs for a decision as to their insurability.

Tax Registration

You must register for income tax and value added tax (VAT – see below) with the Revenue Commissioners for Income (💻 www.revenue. ie) using form TR1 if you're a sole trader or TR2 if you're a company, plus a PREM Reg – Employer (PAYE/PRSI) Tax Registration Form if you intend to employ staff. Soon after registration, you may receive a visit (in fact, you can request one) from a Revenue official, who will advise you on matters relating to business tax.

> You won't need to pay any tax until after your first year of trading, and two months before the year ends you will be sent a preliminary tax notice informing you of when your first tax payment is due.

Value Added Tax

You must register for VAT if your taxable supplies are likely to exceed €55,000 (in the case of goods) or €27,500 (in the case of services). You aren't obliged to register if your turnover will be below those limits, although you may register voluntarily. It's worth taking advice, however, before doing so. Registration for VAT is done on form TR1 or TR2 (see **Tax Registration** above) and it must be declared and paid every two months, and an annual return of sales and purchases submitted (which can be for any 12-month period you choose). You must keep a record of all sales and purchases for six years.

You can pay VAT by direct debit or, in certain cases, annually. The Revenue Commissioners publish a *Guide to VAT for Small Businesses* (IT49), available from the Revenue's Forms and Leaflets Service (☎ 1890-306706) or downloadable from the Revenue's website (💻 www.revenue.ie – you can find the guide easily by using the search facility at the top).

Buying a Business

As in other countries, it's much easier to buy a going concern in Ireland than to start a business from scratch. The bureaucracy is reduced considerably, as is the risk. It isn't entirely risk-free, however, and every precaution must be taken to ensure that you don't buy a going-nowhere concern. You can find businesses for sale through local estate and commercial agents and through advertisements in local and regional newspapers. There are also a few websites listing businesses for sale, such as 💻 www.irishbusinessesforsale.com, although most of the opportunities listed here are fairly small-scale.

It's vital to inspect a business personally (never rely solely on the glowing description you're given by an agent) before agreeing to buy it, to shop around and compare it with similar businesses, and to gain independent advice regarding its market value and prospects.

One of the most important aspects to consider when buying a business in Ireland is its location, particularly if what appears to be a thriving concern is offered for quick sale at a temptingly low price. One thing to look out for is a situation where a town centre has been left as a ghost town (or shortly will be) by the opening of a bypass or an out-of-town shopping mall, or the building of a new road which will take passing trade right past your new business – at 100kph! Plans for new roads or shopping developments are usually available from the local town planning department.

Starting a Business

Most people are over-optimistic about the prospects for a new business, whether in their home country or abroad. Be realistic or even pessimistic when estimating your income, overestimate the costs and underestimate the revenue (then reduce it by up to 50 per cent!). While hoping for the best, you should plan for the worst and make sure that you have enough money not only to set up a business, but also to keep it going until it's established.

Bear in mind that while Ireland is an expanding market with many new business opportunities yet to be exploited, it's also a small and relatively conservative market. In the good times, fortunes have been made by shrewd entrepreneurs, but if the economy takes a nose-dive they can be lost just as easily.

While there's always room for the entrepreneur in Ireland, it makes sense to play it safe, hedge your bets and not choose anything too risky. Newcomers tend to have an idealistic view of starting a business, which is all very well, but try to be practical and also look at the downside of your proposed 'dream' business. For example, riding instruction, agri-holidays and genealogy may be great business ideas, but they're all hard work and largely seasonal.

Restrictions

EU Citizens: There are few restrictions on the kinds of business that can be started (or purchased) by EU citizens. The main point to bear in mind is that you're unlikely to obtain state support if your business competes or conflicts with an indigenous business, or employs only non-Irish people or is exclusively export-orientated. Note also that if your business involves practising a trade or profession that must be registered in Ireland, you will need to register before you can start (see **Qualifications** on page 27). There are no accounting, auditing or reporting requirements except that you should inform your local tax office and register for income tax and Pay-related Social Insurance (PRSI).

Non-EU Nationals: Non-EU nationals wishing to start a business in Ireland need to obtain 'business permission' from the Department of Justice, Equality & Law Reform. This involves demonstrating that the proposed business will:

♦ result in the transfer to Ireland of a minimum capital sum of €300,000;

♦ add to Ireland's commercial activity;

♦ at least maintain existing employment in the relevant business area;

♦ allow the substitution of Irish goods for imported goods;

♦ be a viable enterprise, and provide the applicant with sufficient income to support himself without resorting to state welfare or other employment.

Applications for business permission must be accompanied by a passport or national identity papers, a registration certificate if you're already living in Ireland, a statement of character from the police authorities of every country in which you've resided for more than six months during the ten years preceding your application, and a business plan, preferably endorsed by a firm of accountants. A decision is normally made within a month and permission is usually granted for an initial period of a year.

You may start trading immediately on receipt of permission, but must apply for renewal at least one month before it expires, supplying audited accounts and evidence that you've paid all the appropriate taxes. If your business has met the above criteria, your business permission should be extended for a further five years. Further information on business permission can be obtained from the Department of Justice, Equality & Law Reform, 72 St Stephen's Green, Dublin 2 (☎ 01-602 8202, 🖳 www. justice.ie).

Non-EU nationals moving to Ireland with the intention of becoming self-employed or of starting a business may be permitted to bring some tools and business equipment with them free of customs duty (i.e. Common Customs Tariff) and, in certain cases, VAT. These exemptions apply only to professional people (e.g. doctors, lawyers) and those engaged in non-profit activities, who have ceased business activity in their home country within the last 12 months, and intend to set up a similar business in Ireland.

Imported vehicles will be exempt only if they're 'used in the production process'. Anything imported free of duty may not be sold, hired or lent for 12 months after import. Note that you can bring any household effects (which can include those with a combined work and household use) to Ireland free of VAT and duty when you first settle there, but the same restriction applies to selling, hiring or lending. For further information contact Customs &

Excise (☎ 01-877 6200) or refer to 🖳 www. revenue.ie.

Location

Choosing the location for a business is even more important than choosing the location for a home.

☑ **SURVIVAL TIP**

Depending on the kind of business, you may need to be near a housing development, have access to main roads or be close to a tourist resort. Don't forget that development plans can affect the desirability of the location.

Plans for new roads or shopping developments are usually available from the local town planning department.

Support

There's considerable, although fragmented, state support for industry in Ireland, principally for manufacturing and internationally traded services. Other kinds of service industries, with the notable exception of tourism, don't benefit from state support, although this situation may change. Nevertheless, there are many organisations to help people start and develop businesses, some of which are state or state-aided bodies, while others operate on a commercial basis.

The following is a summary of the various organisations and their areas of responsibility. Links to the websites of these and other organisations can be found on the 'Business Access to State Information' (BASIS) website (🖳 www.basis.ie):

♦ **Business Innovation Centres** – in Cork, Dublin, Galway and Waterford, offering EU-funded support to nurture new businesses during their first three to five years; details can be found on the Enterprise Ireland website (🖳 www.enterprise-ireland.com);

♦ **Chambers of Commerce of Ireland** (☎ 01-661 2888, 🖳 www.chambers.ie) – represent the interests of a broad range of businesses, with a particular emphasis on overseas promotion and foreign investment in Ireland;

♦ **City and County Enterprise Boards** – There are 35 boards responsible for developing projects that aren't covered by the state industrial development agencies and can provide information about opportunities, business expansion, improving productivity, R&D development and collaborative projects; a list of contact details can be found on the Enterprise Ireland website (⌨ www.enterprise-ireland.com).

♦ **Department of Enterprise, Trade and Employment** (DETE, ☎ 01-631 2121, ⌨ www.entemp.ie) – has overall responsibility for Irish enterprise. Its provisions are carried out regionally through Shannon Development and Údarás na Gaeltachta, and locally through the City and County Enterprise Boards and Area Partnership Companies. Information on starting a business can be obtained from the DETE's website (⌨ www.entemp.ie – click on 'Start Your Own Business/BASIS'). The Department also publishes a free leaflet called *Look Before You Leap*, available from the County Enterprise Boards (see below).

♦ **FÁS** – (☎ 01-607 0500, ⌨ www.fas.ie) – the national Training and Employment Authority, offering training and employment programmes and a recruitment service. FÁS runs 'start your own business courses' during which you can receive the equivalent of unemployment benefit and any other benefits you're entitled to.

♦ **Forfás** (☎ 01-607 3000, ⌨ www.forfas.ie) – Ireland's national policy-making and advisory board for enterprise, trade, technology and innovation, operating under the auspices of the DETE;

♦ **IDA Ireland** (☎ 01-603 4000, ⌨ www.idaireland.com) – a subsidiary of the DETE which deals with incoming industry;

♦ **Irish Business and Employers' Confederation** (IBEC – see **Professional Advice** on page 37) – operates a graduate training scheme called the European Orientation Programme to encourage Irish exporting. Grants of up to 50 per cent are available from various state organisations.

♦ **Liffey Trust** (⌨ www.liffey-trust.com) – a voluntary, non-profit organisation devoted to job creation with private sector funding. To date, the Trust has helped over 200 businesses in various ways.

♦ **Shannon Development** (⌨ www.shannon-dev.ie) – officially the Shannon Free Airport Development Company, the Regional Development Agency for the Shannon region (Counties Limerick, Clare, north Tipperary, south-west Offaly and north Kerry), which provides grants and assistance within these areas, such as the START Programme and Entrepreneurs' Programme;

♦ **Small Firms Association** (SFA, ☎ 01-605 1602 ⌨ www.sfa.ie) – represents the interests of small businesses, and provides various member discount schemes including insurance, standards, health insurance and debt collection. The Irish Small and Medium Enterprises Association (☎ 01-662 2755, ⌨ www.isme.ie) does the same for owner-managed businesses.

♦ Small-business training and support materials are published by Oak Tree Press and can be ordered from the

publisher's website (💻 www.oaktreepress.com) or its associated site (💻 www.startingabusinessinireland.com). Additional information and advice can be obtained from the local County Development Officers (see above) and the Central Statistics Office (☎ 021-453 5000 or ☎ 1890-313414, 💻 www.cso.ie). The Revenue Commissioners (💻 www.revenue.ie) produce an information pack called *Guides for Small Business*, covering financial matters such as tax.

♦ **Údarás na Gaeltachta** (💻 www.udaras.ie) – provides incentives and support schemes for new businesses in the *Gaeltacht* (Gaelic-speaking) regions of Donegal, Mayo, Galway, Kerry, Cork, Waterford and Meath.

In addition to the above, there are various organisations dealing with specific industry sectors, including the following:

♦ **Bord Bia** (💻 www.bordbia.ie) – provides assistance to businesses in the food sector.

♦ **Bord Iascaigh Mhara** (💻 www.bim.ie) – a state agency responsible for the development of the fishing industry, and which provides grants and training;

♦ **Enterprise Ireland** (☎ 01-808 2000, 💻 www.enterprise-ireland.com) – a government agency whose aim is to 'transform Irish industry' by fostering the development of world-class Irish companies – specifically through improving productivity and sales and investing in R&D. Through its network of 13 Irish offices and 33 international offices, Enterprise Ireland also offers a business start-up service (especially in the food sector) and assistance to foreign companies looking for Irish suppliers.

♦ **Fáilte Ireland** (💻 www.failteireland.ie) – the Irish tourist board, which promotes tourism-related businesses;

♦ **Food Product Development Centre** (☎ 01-814 6080. 💻 www.fpdc.dit.ie) – assists with innovative food concepts;

♦ **National Food Centre** – a division of TEAGASC (the Agriculture and Food Development Authority, 💻 www.teagasc.ie), the centre provides help with research, consultancy, training and product and process development for businesses in the food industry (except milk products, which are the responsibility of the National Dairy Products Centre). TEAGASC also provides services and training programmes.

♦ **National Microelectronics Application Centre, Limerick** – (owned by Shannon Development) is concerned with developing electronic, software and IT products for Irish industry, and can help if you have a worthwhile idea.

♦ **Tyndall National Institute, Cork** (💻 www.tyndall.ie) – formerly the National Microelectronics Research Centre, the Institute provides technological assistance to all kinds of industrial businesses.

The City of Dublin Vocational Educational Committee (CDVEC, 💻 www.cdvec.ie) runs a 'Start Your Own Business' course, and publishes a *Guide to Courses*.

Finance

Various grants and other types of funding are available for the set-up of new businesses in Ireland. Bear in mind, however, that the authorities are looking for innovative ideas that will fill new market niches and create economic growth for Ireland. They will foster indigenous business which leads to 'import substitution', not projects which are likely to infringe on existing domestic businesses or in sectors already suffering over-capacity.

Your project must have the potential for providing long-term jobs and demonstrate likely success. Most new businesses don't receive grant-aid for this reason, but the application process can be beneficial in itself, as it will force you to assess the viability of your business plan and also give you access to valuable information, expertise and advice. Note also that most Irish financiers operate on a 'matching funds' basis, so it's important to raise as much as possible yourself.

If you set up as a limited company, you can invite individuals and other business entities to invest in the company by buying shares.

Another way of raising capital is to establish a partnership with another business, which can have the added benefit of providing you with a ready-made market for your products or services.

Grants for new business feasibility studies (i.e. market research, financial projections, assessments of manufacturing processes, plant and equipment, raw materials, negotiation of joint-ventures or manufacturing licences) are offered by Shannon Development (see above) and Enterprise Ireland (see 🖥 www. enterprise-ireland.com/Grow/Finance/OrdinaryFeasibilityStudyGrants.htm).

The City and County Enterprise Boards (see above) offer four types of financial incentive:

♦ **Feasibility study grants** – Border, Midland and Western (BMW) region, maximum €6,350; South and East regions, maximum €5,100;

♦ **Capital grants** – up to €75,000;

♦ **Employment grants** – up to €7,500 per new employee, up to ten employees. An employment grant may also apply to a person starting a business.

♦ **Equity finance** – up to €75,000; can be invested in qualifying limited companies.

Sources of venture capital are listed on the Enterprise Ireland website (🖥 www. enterprise-ireland.com – click on 'Start a business' and then 'Finance') and on the website of the Irish Venture Capital Association (🖥 www.ivca.ie). Business Innovation Centres will match businesses seeking funds with individuals or companies looking for investment opportunities. The Financial Services Sector of the *Kompass Directory* is also a useful reference for sources of venture-capital.

Seed capital: Seed capital is available from Enterprise Ireland (see 🖥 www.enterprise-ireland.com/Grow/Finance/Seed_Capital_Scheme.htm), Shannon Development (see above), Business Innovation Centres (see above) and the Revenue Commissioners, who will repay income tax up to a certain limit to people leaving employment to start their own business (their booklet, *The Seed Capital Scheme: Tax Refunds for New*

Enterprises, is available from the Revenue's Forms and Leaflets Service, ☎ 1890-306706 or downloadable from the Revenue's website, 🖥 www.revenue.ie).

Loans: Loans (properly called debt) are of course available from banks. Most major banks have business start-up schemes. For example, the Bank of Ireland (🖥 www.boi.ie) offers *Business Start-up Guides* as well as a 'business start-up package' including a loan of up to €200,000; and AIB Bank (🖥 www.aib.ie), Permanent TSB (🖥 www.permanenttsb.ie) and Ulster Bank (🖥 www.ulsterbank.ie) also offer business loans.

Low-interest loans are also available for certain types of business start-up from First Step Ltd (☎ 01-260 0988, 🖥 www.first-step.ie) and The Society of St Vincent de Paul (🖥 www.svp.ie).

If your business is structured as a co-operative, you may be entitled to a Credit Union loan; if you're a member of a Credit Union, you may be eligible for a personal loan to start a business.

Business Entities

The simplest way to operate a business in Ireland is as a sole trader, which involves unlimited liability, i.e. you have no protection if your business fails! To limit your liability, you must set up a limited company. There are four types of Irish limited company:

- **Private company limited by shares** – The members' liability, if the company is wound up, is limited to the amount, if any, unpaid on the shares they hold. The maximum number of members is 50.

- **Company-limited by guarantee not having a share capital** – As this is a public company, there must be a minimum of seven members. The members' liability is limited to the amount they've undertaken to contribute to the assets of the company if it's wound up. If a guarantee company doesn't have a share capital, its members aren't required to buy shares in it. Many charitable and professional bodies prefer this form of company, as they wish to secure the benefits of having a separate legal entity and of limited liability, but don't need to raise funds from members.

- **Company limited by guarantee having a share capital** – The members (maximum 50) have liability for the amount, if any, that is unpaid on the shares they hold, and for the amount they've undertaken to contribute to the assets of the company if it's wound up.

- **Public limited company** – This company type must have a minimum of seven members. Their liability is limited to the amount, if any, unpaid on shares held by them. The nominal value of the company's allotted share capital must not be less than €38,092.14, at least 25 per cent of which must be fully paid up before the company commences trading or exercises any borrowing powers.

Other types of business entity include the following:

- **Single member company** – A single member company is a private company limited by shares or a guarantee company having a share capital, which is incorporated with one member, or whose membership is reduced to one person. However, the company must have at least two directors and a secretary. The sole member can dispense with the holding of General Meetings, including Annual General Meetings (AGMs). However, certain modifications laid down in the European Communities (Single-Member Private Limited Companies) Regulations 1994, must be made. Also the accounts and reports that would normally be laid before the AGM of a company must be prepared and forwarded to the member.

- **Limited partnership** – A partnership consists of a minimum of two people and there's normally a maximum of 20. Certain

financial partnerships may, however, have up to 50 members. A partnership isn't a separate legal entity, i.e. it has no legal identity other than those of its partners.

> Note that a partnership that adopts a name other than the names of its partners must register the name as a business name (see below).

The partners contribute a stated amount of capital, and aren't liable for the debts of the partnership beyond the amount contributed.

♦ **Unlimited company** – In an unlimited company, there's no limit on the liability of the members. Recourse may be had by creditors to the shareholders in respect of any liabilities owed by the company which the company has failed to discharge. Such a company must have a minimum of two shareholders.

♦ **Co-operatives** – Co-operatives (or industrial and provident societies) are registered under the Industrial and Provident Societies Acts 1893–1978, which provide for a society to be registered to engage in certain industries, businesses or trades with limited liability. The largest and best-known are in the agriculture and food areas. A co-operative must consist of at least seven people, who must draw up a set of rules governing the operation of the society. These rules must be submitted to the Registrar for approval.

♦ There are a number of representative groups for co-operatives with which the Registrar has agreed forms of Model Rules. The Irish Co-operative Organisation Society (ICOS) has agreed Model Rules for straightforward co-operatives, as well as co-operatives involved in horticulture, fishing, sheep breeding and group water schemes. ICOS can also assist in the establishment and registration of a co-operative (a service for which it will charge a fee). Other representative groups are the National Association of Building Co-operatives and the Co-operative Development Society.

♦ **Friendly societies** – Friendly societies are registered under the Friendly Societies Acts 1896–1977. They're established for various purposes, mostly to provide small life assurance benefits, sick benefits and death benefits to members, to provide benefits to non-members or to promote particular activities or interests. Friendly societies include benevolent societies and workingmen's clubs.

Registering a Business Name

If you want to operate a business under a name other than your own, you must register it with the Companies Registration Office (CRO), which can now be done online at its website (🖳 www.cro.ie).

To register a business name, you must submit one of the following forms, along with the registration fee (€40 for paper filing/€20 for electronic filing), to the CRO within one month of adopting the business name: Form RBN1 for an individual; Form RBN1A for a partnership; Form RBN1B for a company.

Registering a business name doesn't protect you against duplication of the name, nor guarantee that the name will prove acceptable as a company name, as its use could be prohibited for other reasons (e.g. trade mark rights might exist in the name).

The CRO doesn't check proposed business names against names on the registers of companies or business names. It's therefore advisable to check that others don't have rights in the name before spending money on business stationery, etc. You can check the register of companies and register of business names free of charge using the CRO's search facility, or undertake a search of the trade mark register at the Patents Office.

Certificate of registration: The registrar issues a certificate of registration for each business name registered. A copy of the certificate of registration must be exhibited in a conspicuous position in every branch, office or other place where the business is normally carried on.

Business stationery: The name(s) of the proprietor(s) must be shown on all business stationery. In the case of a company, stationery should also show the names of the directors and their nationality if not Irish, the place of registration (e.g. registered in Dublin, Ireland), the registered number (i.e. the number of the certificate of incorporation), the address of the registered office (where this is already shown on the document, the fact that it is the registered office must be indicated). Where the company share capital is mentioned on business letters and order forms, the reference must be to the paid-up share capital.

Forming a Company

To form a company, you must submit the following documents, along with the appropriate registration fee (which varies according to the type of company being formed and the processing scheme chosen – see below), to the CRO:

♦ memorandum of association;

♦ articles of association;

♦ Form A1.

Applications to incorporate companies can be submitted under any of three processing schemes:

♦ **Ordinary** – no guaranteed service level but usually takes 15 working days;

♦ **Fé Phrainn** – a streamlined process taking not more than ten working days;

♦ **CRODisk** – an electronic processing scheme taking not more than five working days.

To form a limited partnership, you must submit Form LP1 (application for registration of a limited partnership) and Form LP3 (statement of the capital contributed by the limited partners).

Applications to form a co-operative or friendly society must be submitted to the Registrar of Friendly Societies.

Charging

Your hourly, daily or weekly rate needs to take into account your overheads (e.g. office equipment, staff) and expenses (e.g. travel), as well as the fact that at least 20 per cent of what you earn will be taken from you by the tax man (see **Chapter 14**). You should charge what you're worth, which is governed by market forces. In the IT sector, for example, demand for skilled technicians is such that you can earn more as a freelance contractor than as a salaried employee

– from €300 per day as a programmer to €1,500 or more as a project manager.

Employees

If you're starting a new kind of business or one which requires specialist skills, you should check that these skills are available in the local workforce. The Irish workforce is well educated and trained, but certain sectors have grown so fast in recent years that it's difficult to find skilled and qualified staff. When you do find staff, you may discover that they demand sky-high salaries. Make enquiries with FÁS regarding unskilled and skilled staff, as well as with employment agencies if you're going to need executives and specialist staff.

You will also need to investigate the regulations governing the employment of staff (see **Chapter 2**) and the cost of doing so (e.g. national insurance contributions).

Insurance

Anyone contemplating setting up a business in Ireland should be aware that business insurance is very expensive (many jobs have been lost in recent years as a result of huge increases in insurance premiums), as claims can take a long time to settle and therefore incur exorbitant legal fees.

Taxation

Your business must be registered for tax (see **Tax Registration** on page 38). In addition, if you're employing staff, you must register for 'pay-as-you-earn' (PAYE) tax and pay-related social insurance (PRSI) and, if you're running a limited company, you must register for corporation tax. A *Moving to Ireland Tax Guide* is available on the Revenue Commissioners' website.

PAYE/PRSI: You must register for PAYE and PRSI if you pay more than €8 per week (or €36 per month) to an employee (or €2/€9 if the employee has more than one job). To register, you must complete Form PREM Reg, Form TR1 (if registering as an individual or partnership) or TR2 (if registering a company). These forms, which can also be used to register for VAT, can be obtained from the Revenue Commissioners' Forms & Leaflets Service (☎ 1890-306706) or from any district Revenue office; TR forms can be downloaded from the Revenue website (🖳 www.revenue.ie). The Revenue service publishes guides to registration, including *Paying PAYE/PRSI* and *PAYE/PRSI & Small Employers*.

> If you hire employees, you must obtain their P45 or tax-free allowance certificate and notify the tax office that you've employed them.

If neither a P45 nor a current year's tax-free allowance certificate is available (e.g. with first-time employees), you will need to operate PAYE/PRSI on an 'emergency' basis until a tax-free allowance certificate is received (first-time employees should complete form 12A). At the end of each tax year, you're required to complete tax declarations for each employee.

If you're a director of a limited company, you must submit a declaration to the tax office yourself. As an owner-director you will make lower PRSI contributions than other employees, but will incur the same rate of PAYE. You will also need to make a self-assessment of your income.

Corporation Tax: Limited companies must register for corporation tax (on form TR2), which is levied at 12.5 per cent on profits from trading income and 25 per cent on profits from non-trading income. In your first year of operation, you must pay preliminary tax and make a tax return (CT1) within nine months of the end of your accounting period. You're also required to supply certain trading details to the Revenue Commissioners within 30 days of starting trading.

TRAINING & WORK EXPERIENCE

EU citizens are free to come to Ireland and enrol on training schemes run by the national training and employment service, FÁS. Ireland is a participant in the international Training and Work Experience Scheme (TWES), which is designed to give young people the opportunity for further education and occupational training, and to enlarge their professional experience and knowledge of other countries. The other participating countries include Austria, Belgium, Canada, Denmark, France, Finland, Germany, Luxembourg, Netherlands, Norway, Spain, Sweden, Switzerland, the UK and the US.

Applications for training are considered even if the training is available in the applicant's home country. Training usually applies to professions or occupations in which the training leads to the acquisition of occupational skills or professional qualifications. Trainees should have relevant qualifications where necessary and must not replace any existing staff. TWES permits are issued by employers (recruitment agencies cannot issue permits) and aren't normally issued for training for a qualification which can be obtained on a full-time study basis. In these cases, you should seek permission from the Home Office to come to Ireland as a student. Permits aren't usually issued for training or work experience in the sports and entertainment sectors.

Trainees must be aged between 18 and 54 and work experience applicants, who must also be at the start of their careers, between 18 and

35. The training or work experience must be for a minimum of 30 hours per week and for a fixed period. Positions are usually granted for one year and can sometimes be extended for a further six months, although in exceptional circumstances they can be extended to two years. Trainees occupy full-time positions with a normal salary, and conditions of employment similar to those for on-the-job training in the area.

> Around two-thirds of Irish companies offer work experience – paid in 95 per cent of cases.

Work experience differs from training in that it doesn't usually result in a formal qualification, the worker doesn't fill a full-time position, and wages are paid in the form of pocket money or a maintenance allowance and are much less than would be paid to an ordinary employee (unless a statutory minimum wage is applicable). Applications are considered even when applicants have no relevant experience, provided that they have relevant qualifications and that the work experience is closely related to their future career.

Although the training and work experience scheme is intended to develop applicants' industrial and commercial experience, a secondary objective is to improve their knowledge of the English language (where applicable), although applicants must have an adequate knowledge of English before they're accepted. Applicants may not transfer from training or work experience to full employment in Ireland, and aren't permitted to work under the main work permit scheme for at least two years after the completion of their training or work experience. Trainees must sign an undertaking to return to their home countries once they've completed their training or work experience.

Selected schemes are outlined below. Further Information about the TWES can be obtained from the Department of Employment/Labour (or similar) in participating countries.

♦ **AIESEC** – AIESEC, which claims to be the world's largest student organisation, arranges exchanges for students at more than 800 universities in over 85 countries, placing them for up to 18 months in private and public sector employment. Further information is available on the AIESEC website, 🖥 www.aiesec.org.

♦ **BUNAC** – The British Universities North America Club (BUNAC, 🖥 www.bunac.org) runs an Irish government-approved 'Work in Ireland' programme that allows US students to travel and work in Ireland for up to four months.

♦ **Careers Europe** – Careers Europe (🖥 www.careerseurope.co.uk) is an independent organisation, based in Bradford, UK, that produces information about working, training, studying and living in EU and EEA countries.

♦ **Farm Apprenticeship Board** – The Farm Apprenticeship Board (☎ 01-450 1980, 🖥 http://homepage.eircom.net/~wjbr), which is largely financed by TEAGASC, places agricultural students on farms for between one and three years to train in farm management. Virtually all their apprentices are Irish nationals, but if you have experience in areas where there are skill shortages in Ireland (e.g. pig farming), you may be able to get on an FAB programme. The FAB also runs a job placement service, matching employers with job seekers.

♦ **IAESTE** – Science and engineering students who wish to gain experience by working in industry and commerce in Ireland during their holidays can apply to the International Association for the Exchange of Students for Technical Experience (IAESTE, 🖥 www.iaeste.org.uk), which has more than 60 member countries. A good knowledge of English is essential, and applicants must be enrolled at a college or university and be studying engineering, science, agriculture, architecture or a related subject.

♦ **Leonardo** – On 1st January 2000, the EU launched a seven-year vocational training programme called Leonardo da Vinci. Details of Leonardo projects can be found on 🖥 www.leonardo.org.uk. At the same time, the EU introduced the Europass (now called National Europass) system, whereby trainees moving from one member state to another can register and record the training they've undertaken.

- ◆ **SWAP** – This organisation arranges work visas, and provides 'support' for Canadian students and non-students wishing to work for up to a year in Ireland, but it doesn't find them a job; the minimum age is 18, and there's a registration fee of $395. Further details can be found on 🖥 www.swap.ca.

- ◆ **USIT** – The Union of Students International Travel (USIT, ☎ 01-602 1906, 🖥 www.usit.ie) is Ireland's student, youth and independent travel specialist, and offers cheap flights, accommodation, car hire and insurance as well as working abroad programmes; and it also arranges working visas.

AU PAIRS

Single EU citizens aged between 18 and 28 (these are European guidelines rather than regulations) are eligible for a job as an au pair in Ireland. Note that male au pairs are also permitted under EU regulations and many families now prefer them. It isn't possible for non-EU citizens to obtain visas for au pair work. Au pairs normally register with an agency; or with a school specialising in teaching English, which may have links with several agencies. To do so, you need to write a letter about yourself, enclosing photographs of yourself with children, and two references. You will also need to have medical insurance and should bring a medical certificate with you.

Some understanding of English is generally required, but the schools often accept applicants whose English is poor. You will initially join a family for a trial period of two weeks, during which you will be given advice and help by the school. On successful completion of the trial period, you're required to keep in touch with the school by attending lessons twice a week throughout your stay in Ireland. The school will endeavour to move any au pair who is unhappy with a family as quickly as possible.

Au pairs are usually contracted to work for a minimum of six months and a maximum of two years.

It's also possible to work for two or three months during the summer holidays. Au pairs staying for longer than three months must

register with the *Gardai* within seven days (see page 78).

As an au pair, you receive free meals and accommodation and have your own room. You're required to pay your own fare to and from Ireland, although some families contribute towards the fare home for au pairs staying six months or longer. Holidays tend to be flexible rather than set for any particular period relating to months worked. Quite often, families will take you on holiday with them or ask you to work over the Christmas/Easter periods, giving you days off in lieu.

Working hours are officially limited to five hours per day (morning or afternoon), five days per week (a total of 25 hours). You should have at least two days a week free of household responsibilities and should be free to attend religious services if you wish. If you work more than five days, you should be paid extra. Au pairs are paid the princely sum of around €75 a week (possibly more in Dublin), which means you stand little chance of getting rich.

A useful book for prospective au pairs planning to work in Ireland or abroad is the *Au Pair and Nanny's Guide to Working Abroad* by Susan Griffith & Sharon Legg (Vacation Work).

Further information can be obtained from the Swan Training Institute, 9/11 Grafton Street, Dublin 2 (☎ 01-677 5252, ⌨ www.sti.ie). Note that it's possible for responsible English-speaking young women (without experience or formal training) to obtain employment as a 'nanny'. Duties are essentially the same as for an au pair, except that a position as a nanny is a real job with a proper salary!

LANGUAGE

According to the 1937 Constitution, Irish (or Gaelic – from the Irish word *Gaelige*) is still 'the first official language' of Ireland, yet only 1 per cent of the population claims to speak Irish daily (although 30 per cent can speak it). Ireland's second official language, English, on the other hand, is spoken by almost everyone, and in most situations it isn't necessary to know a word of Gaelic, whereas proficiency in English is virtually essential; particularly if you have a job which requires a lot of contact with others, or involves speaking on the telephone or dealing with other foreigners, who may speak their own 'dialect' of English.

Whether you speak British or American English (or some other form) is usually irrelevant, although some Irish people will have difficulty understanding strong non-Irish accents, and you may find that Irish pronunciation takes some getting used to. There are also one or two other words and phrases deriving from Gaelic with which you will need to be familiar. Most important perhaps is the word *garda* (pronounced 'gorda'), which is what a policeman is called (the police are collectively called the *Garda Síochána*, although this is often abbreviated to *Garda;* and policemen are *gardaí*, pronounced 'gordee').

Then there are words such as *ben* for mountain, *glen* for valley, *knock* (or *cnoc*) for hill, *lough* for lake or inlet and *strand* for beach. *Mór* (or *more*) means big, *wee* is little and a *wean* (pronounced 'wain') is a child. If your car won't go, it's said to be *banjaxed* and if it's *mizzlin* (as it often is in Ireland) it's raining gently.

Other words that sound familiar are used in strange contexts: *messages* are groceries and *minerals* soft drinks; if something is *clever* it fits well; a *chick* isn't a young woman but a child, who, if he is naughty, is said to be *bold*; if someone is *brave* he is a worthy sort, but if he is a *caution* he is a devil-may-care fellow; to be *cut* is to be insulted, to be *destroyed* is to be exhausted, and to be *scalded* is to be vexed; if you're feeling unwell, you might be said to look *well shook*; *fairly* means excellently; *fierce* and *terrible* mean extremely; a *skiff* is a shower of rain; and if it's *soft* – you've guessed it – it's raining! If you're a homeowner, you will be known as a *blow-in*, if you're in *fiddler's green*, you're in a mess, and if an Irishman says to you, "I'm after meeting your wife," he doesn't mean he would like to meet her – he already has!

If you wish to improve your English in Ireland before starting work or a course of study there, you can attend one of the many English-language schools throughout the country (see page 181).

stone circle, Drombeg, Co. Cork

2.
EMPLOYMENT CONDITIONS

Employees in Ireland generally enjoy good employment conditions, although there's often a huge disparity between the employment conditions of hourly paid workers and salaried (i.e. monthly paid) employees, even between those employed by the same company. As in most countries, managerial and executive staff generally enjoy a much higher level of benefits than lower-paid employees. Employees hired to work in Ireland by a foreign (non-Irish) company may receive a higher salary (including fringe benefits and allowances) than those offered by Irish employers.

Until the end of the 20th century, industrial relations in Ireland were good. A series of three-year national wage agreements or 'pacts', initiated in 1987, resulted in a period of harmonious relations – employees, unions, employers and government would meet and try to sort out problems, so strikes were few. Even the 1,200 or more overseas companies that had recently set up in Ireland generally experienced few disputes.

In 1999 and 2000, however, Ireland was hit by a spate of strikes as workers in various industries tried to cash in on the booming economy by submitting exorbitant wage increase claims. Since then, there have been fewer and fewer major disputes – down from 24 in 2001 to just six in 2007. *Industrial Relations News* is a weekly newssheet covering Irish industrial relations issues, available online (at ☐ www.irn.ie) or by post (phone ☎ 01-497 2711 with your details).

The Irish trade union system is a British legacy, but since independence Irish unions have moved away from the traditional British confrontational ethos and are now more like those in Germany, where there's little of the 'them and us' attitude and senior managers are themselves often union members. Similarly, staff make up 30 per cent or more of the boards of public companies such as An Post and Aer Lingus.

Some aspects of employment conditions are prescribed by law, while others are dependent on an employee's contract of employment and an employer's general terms. Employment legislation in Ireland governs only a few crucial and basic areas such as minimum wages and maximum hours. These are detailed in a series of booklets and leaflets (principally *Guide to Labour Law*) published by the Department of Enterprise, Trade and Employment (DETE, ☎ 01-631 3131) and information is available on the DETE's website (☐ www.entemp.ie).

A few industry sectors, including agriculture, catering, construction, contract cleaning, electrical services, hairdressing, printing, security, tailoring and certain retail sectors, are governed by Employment Regulation Orders and Registered Employment Agreements, details of which can be found on the website of The Labour Court (☐ www.labourcourt.ie).

Otherwise, employment law is much less onerous from the employer's point of view than in other European countries, which means that employers enjoy considerable 'flexibility' in dealing with staff. This is of course not ideal from an employee's viewpoint, but fortunately Ireland also has a labour court and conciliation service as well as extensive equal rights legislation (see below).

Employers normally publish a set of general terms and conditions which apply to all employees, unless otherwise stated in individual contracts of employment. General terms are usually referred to in employment contracts, and employees usually receive a copy on starting employment (or in some cases, beforehand).

EQUAL RIGHTS

Ireland is a signatory to the Social Chapter in the Maastricht Treaty, which gives employees the right of consultation, and equality legislation derives essentially from European Union (EU) directives on equality at work. Citizens of EU member states working in Ireland have the same rights as Irish nationals; for example with regard to pay, employment conditions, vocational training and trade union membership.

> The employment conditions of non-EU nationals are generally the same, although their employment is usually subject to the granting of a work permit and its renewal, and many non-EU workers are subject to discrimination (see **EU & Non-EU Citizens** on page 26).

A succession of laws, including the Anti-discrimination Pay Act, 1974, the Employment Equality Act, 1977, the Employment Equality Act, 1998 and the Equality Act, 2004, have outlawed direct and indirect discrimination at work and in employment conditions on nine distinct grounds: gender; marital and family status; sexual orientation; religion; age (doesn't apply to those under 16); ability (i.e. whether or not you're disabled); race; and membership of the Traveller community (Ireland's 'gypsies'). The law applies to both the public and private sectors, including people employed through

agencies, and even covers applicants for employment and training.

The Equal Status Acts of 1997 and 2000-04 provide similar protection to European Economic Area (EEA) citizens against discrimination in non-employment areas including education, provision of goods, accommodation and disposal of property, and services (including access to public places, banking and insurance services, entertainment, catering and transport).

Equality legislation refers specifically to equality between the sexes and between people of different marital status, but allows exceptions in cases where, for example, physical strength is needed or a job requires one sex or the other (e.g. modelling or acting). The Acts also cover sexual harassment at work.

The Equality Authority (☎ 01-417 3333 or ☎ 1890-245545, ✉ info@equality.ie), established in 1999, is the body responsible for eliminating discrimination and promoting equality of opportunity. The Director of Equality Investigations deals with equality cases other than those involving dismissal, which are referred to the Labour Relations Commission.

CONTRACTS

Technically, anyone who works for an employer for a regular wage or salary automatically has a 'contract' of employment, whether this is written or not, although the Terms of Employment (Information) Acts, 1994 and 2001, oblige an employer to provide certain particulars in writing. Of course, it's much safer to have a written contract, to which you're entitled within two months of starting work (unless you work less than eight hours per week or are on a contract of less than a month). If you're employed through an agency, the agency counts as your employer and should provide you with a contract. An employment contract should set out the terms and conditions of your employment and must include:

◆ your job title or a description of the nature of your work;

◆ the address of your normal place of work or a statement that you're required to work at various places;

the Unfair Dismissal Acts; and the Protection of Employees (Fixed-term Work) Act, 2003 requires an employer to justify the non-issue of an indefinite-term contract when renewing a fixed-term contract. In general, an employer may not employ you for more than four years on fixed-term contracts, and must advise you of permanent vacancies and opportunities within the company.

PLACE OF WORK

Unless there's a clause in your contract stating otherwise, your employer cannot change your place of work without your agreement. Note that the place of work refers to a town or area of a large city, rather than a different office or a new building across the street. Some contracts state that you may occasionally be required to work at other company locations.

SALARY & BENEFITS

Your salary is stated in your contract of employment, where salary reviews, overtime rates, piece and bonus rates, planned increases and cost of living rises may also be included. Only general points such as the payment of your salary into a bank account and the date of salary payments are usually included in an employer's general terms. You're entitled to an itemised pay statement (or wage slip) showing your gross wages and all deductions (e.g. tax, PRSI and any agreed contributions towards pensions, etc.), either with your salary if it's paid weekly, or separately when your salary is paid monthly. Regular employees are normally paid by direct transfer into their bank account, but you're entitled to request payment in cash, by postal or money order, or by cheque or bank draft.

Salaries in Ireland are generally reviewed once a year, although the salaries of professional employees or all employees in certain 'highly competitive' businesses (where employees are in high demand and short supply) may be reviewed every six months. The salaries of new employees may also be reviewed after six months.

Annual increases may be negotiated by individual employees, by an independent pay

♦ the date you start work;

♦ an explanation of how your remuneration is to be calculated and when you're to be paid;

♦ your normal hours of work and any requirement to work overtime;

♦ your holiday and paid leave entitlements;

♦ your entitlement to sick pay and an occupational pension, if applicable;

♦ specification of probation and notice periods.

An employer is obliged to notify you in writing of any changes to your terms of employment within a month of those changes taking effect.

Fixed-term Contracts

If you're employed for a fixed-term project (or are employed by the *Garda* or civil service), you must sign a special contract (which is excluded from certain provisions of the Unfair Dismissal Acts – see page 64) specifying the term of the contract and the nature of the work involved. Note that employers aren't allowed to issue a series of short-term contracts to permanent employees in order to get round review board or by a union (or unions) when the majority of a company's employees are members (called collective bargaining). Generally, you're better off if you can negotiate your own salary increases. A percentage of your annual salary increase is usually to compensate for a rise in the cost of living (currently around 5 per cent), although some employees (particularly in the public sector) may receive pay rises below the annual rate of inflation.

When you take up employment in Ireland, you must provide a P45 or tax-free allowance certificate or you will be subject to 'emergency tax', which is unlikely to be to your benefit. In any case, if you start work part way through the tax year intending to stay only a few months, you may be restricted to a temporary or emergency tax allowance. Note that if you lose your P45, a copy may not be made and the necessary information must be sent by your employer in a letter to the Revenue Commissioners (www.revenue.ie).

Commission & Bonuses

Your salary may include commission or bonus payments – calculated on your individual performance (e.g. based on sales) or the company's performance (profit) as a whole – which may be paid regularly (e.g. monthly or annually) or irregularly, and may apply to all employees or only to senior managers. Some employers pay all employees an annual bonus (usually in December), although this isn't normal practice in Ireland. In industry, particularly in small firms, production workers are often paid on 'piece-work' rates based on their productivity. When a bonus is paid it may be stated in your contract of employment, in which case it's obligatory. In your first and last year of employment, an annual bonus is usually paid pro rata if you don't work a full calendar year.

Company Car

Some Irish employers provide company cars to senior employees such as directors, senior managers and professionals, as well as to sales reps and others who need to travel regularly on business. If you're provided with a company car, you will usually receive details about its use and your obligations on starting employment.

> ### ⚠ Caution
>
> If you lose your licence (e.g. through drunken driving) and are unable to fulfil the requirements of your job, your employment will usually be terminated (i.e. you will be fired) and you may not be entitled to any compensation.

If a company car is provided, check what sort of car it is, whether you will be permitted to use it privately, and if so, who will pay for the petrol for private mileage. The employer normally pays for tax, insurance (which usually covers the employee's spouse as well), repairs, servicing and all fuel, though in some cases the amount of fuel paid for is limited.

Most company cars are leased by the employer (as opposed to being hired or purchased outright) and are replaced after three years' use, when the user is often given the option of purchasing the car at an advantageous price.

Whereas a company car used to be regarded as a perk (as well as a status symbol), it can now be something of a liability from a tax point of view, thanks to a series of tax increases on benefits in kind over the last 10 to 15 years. For this reason, many employees opt for a car allowance rather than a company car.

If you need to use your own car on company business, you're normally entitled to claim mileage, but check with your insurer that you're covered for business use.

Expenses

Expenses paid by your employer are usually listed in its general terms. These may include the reimbursement of travel costs from your home to your place of work (although these are normally 'included' in your basic salary) and for travel on company business, and a lunch allowance or luncheon vouchers.

Relocation

Relocation expenses depend on what you've agreed with your employer, and are usually included in your employment contract or conditions. They should normally include 'reasonable' expenses (e.g. legal fees, stamp duty, removal costs and subsistence during your move). If these expenses are taxable (which they won't be if they're 'reasonable' expenses), you should ask who is going to pay the tax – you or your employer. If you're hired from outside Ireland, your air ticket and other travel costs are usually booked and paid for by your employer or his representative.

In addition, you can usually claim any incidental travel costs, for example the cost of transport to and from airports and hotel expenses en route. Most employers pay your relocation costs to Ireland up to a specified amount, although you may be required to sign a contract stipulating that if you leave the employer before a certain period (e.g. five years), you must repay a percentage of your relocation costs.

An employer may pay a fixed relocation allowance based on your salary, position and size of family, or he may pay the total cost of the move. An allowance should be sufficient to move the contents of an average house, and you must usually pay any excess costs (such as insurance for valuable items) yourself. If you don't want to bring your furniture to Ireland or have just a few belongings to ship, it may be possible to use your allowance to buy furniture locally; check with your employer.

When they're liable for the total cost, companies may ask you to obtain two or three estimates. Depending on the employer, you may be expected to settle the shipper's bill and then claim reimbursement, or you may be able to instruct an Irish shipper with an agent in your home country to handle the move and bill your employer directly.

If you change jobs within Ireland, your new employer may pay your relocation expenses when it's necessary for you to move house. If you're moving from the country to Dublin, you will need a pay rise to cover the extra cost of buying or renting a home! See also **Relocation Agents** on page 89.

Working Hours & Overtime

The Irish generally aren't workaholics; they value their social life too highly for that. They won't work weekends if something can wait until Monday, nor work long hours or take an evening job unless they have to. The standard Irish office day is from 9am until 5.30pm with an hour for lunch, taken between 12 and 2pm. Many offices, including government departments, are closed between 12.30 and 2pm. The average Irish working week is 39 hours and the legal maximum 48 hours (note that this is averaged over 4, 6 or 12 months, depending on your circumstances, so your actual working hours could fluctuate considerably).

Working hours are governed by EU directives, which stipulate that you're entitled to a minimum of 11 hours' continuous rest in every 24 hours, and at least one rest period in a working day of more than six hours. You're also entitled to at least 24 hours' continuous rest every week, and to a 15-minute break for every four-and-a-half hours worked, or 30 minutes for every six hours. Employers are required to compensate staff for Sunday working (i.e. pay them more than their normal daily wage), and night workers are entitled to a free health assessment before starting night work, and at regular intervals thereafter.

Flexi-time

Some Irish employers operate 'flexi-time' working hours, the conditions and rules of which vary from employer to employer. A flexi-time system usually requires all employees to be present between certain hours, known as the core or block time. For example, from 9 until 11.30am and from 1.30 to 4pm. Employees may make up their required working hours by starting earlier than the required core time, reducing their lunch break or by working later.

Many business premises are open from around 7am until 6pm or later, and smaller companies may allow employees to work as late as they wish, provided they don't exceed the maximum permitted daily working hours. The government has recently tried to persuade more large companies to introduce flexi-time in order to ease congestion on the roads and on public transport, but this seems to have had little effect, and flexi-time working is less common than in some other countries.

HOLIDAYS & LEAVE

Annual Holiday

Your annual holiday entitlement usually depends on your profession, position, employer and individual contract of employment. Holiday pay and entitlements are decided by individual or collective bargaining (e.g. by unions). According to the Organisation of Working Time Act, 1997, you must take your holiday entitlement within six months of the end of the holiday year. You should be paid in advance for each holiday period and, if your normal pay varies with the amount of work you do, your holiday pay should equate to your average pay over the 13 weeks prior to the start of the holiday.

According to the Organisation of Working Time Act, 1997, employees are allowed 20 days' (i.e. four weeks') paid holiday per year, and the average Irish worker has between four and five weeks' holiday. Some employers give employees over a certain age, e.g. 50, an extra week's holiday, and offer additional holidays for length of service and for senior positions (but no time to take them!).

A company's holiday year may not correspond to a calendar year, and your

holiday entitlement is calculated on a pro rata basis (per completed calendar month of service) if you don't work a full 'holiday year'. Part-time staff may be entitled to paid holidays on a proportional basis. Usually, all holidays must be taken within the holiday year in which they're earned (although they may be carried forward for up to six months with an employer's consent).

Before starting a new job, check that any planned holidays will be approved by your new employer. This is particularly important if they fall within your probationary period (usually the first three months), when holidays aren't generally permitted. Holidays may normally be taken only with the permission of your manager or boss, and in many companies must be booked a year or more in advance.

Most companies allow unpaid leave in exceptional circumstances only, such as when all your holiday entitlement has been exhausted. If you fall ill while on holiday, your holiday entitlement may be credited to you, provided you obtain a doctor's certificate. If you resign your position or are given notice, most employers will pay you in lieu of any outstanding holidays, although this isn't an entitlement and you may be obliged to take the holiday at your employer's convenience.

Regular part-time workers (i.e. those who normally work at least six hours per week) are entitled to six hours' paid holiday for every 100 hours worked (or pro rata for shorter periods worked). In the case of public holidays, if you would normally have worked on that day, you're entitled to a normal day's pay; if you wouldn't normally have worked, you're entitled to a pro rata payment calculated as the number of hours you normally work in a week divided by five (i.e. the number of days in a normal working week).

Public Holidays

Ireland has nine public or national holidays, on which schools, businesses and many shops are closed. These are:

Irish Public Holidays	
Date	**Holiday**
January 1st	New Year's Day
March 17th	St Patrick's Day
March/April	Easter Monday (the date changes each year)
May (first Monday)	Labour Day
June (first Monday)	simply referred to as the 'June Holiday'
August (first Monday)	'August Holiday'
October (last Monday)	'October Holiday' (also referred to as the Halloween Holiday)
December 25th	Christmas Day
December 26th	St Stephen's Day

If St Patrick's Day, Christmas Day or St Stephen's Day falls on a Saturday or Sunday, the following Monday is taken as a public holiday. Good Friday (the Friday before Easter Monday), although not officially a public holiday, is generally taken as one. An increasing number of Irish companies close during Christmas and New Year, i.e. from 24th December (usually around midday) until 2nd January. To compensate for this 'shutdown',

employees may be required to work extra hours throughout the year, or they may be required to count it as part of their annual holiday entitlement.

You aren't required to work on public holidays unless this is stated in your contract of employment, in which case appropriate remuneration is normally incorporated into your basic salary or in a shift allowance. Otherwise, if you're asked to work on a public holiday, you're entitled to either a paid day off within a month following the holiday or an extra day's pay (your employer decides which); this applies even when you wouldn't normally work a full day on the public holiday.

Sick Leave

There's no legal requirement in Ireland for employers to pay staff if they're off sick, but most salaried employees (i.e. monthly paid staff) continue to receive normal pay when they're sick for a short time. Usually, you must have been employed for a minimum period before you're entitled to sick pay, e.g. 13 weeks, which may coincide with your probationary period. If you're off sick for more than three days, you may receive social welfare illness benefit (or, after four days, injury benefit if you're off work as a result of an injury).

Notification

There's no legislation governing requirements to notify your employer if you're unable to work; these vary from employer to employer, and are normally covered by your employment contract or general terms of employment. You're usually required to notify your employer as soon as possible of sickness or an accident that prevents you from working, i.e. within a few hours of your normal starting time. Failure to do so may result in your not being paid for that day's absence. You're usually required to keep your boss or manager informed about your illness and when you expect to return to work. If you need to consult a doctor, you should obtain a certificate confirming that you've been advised to stay off work for a certain period. A doctor will normally issue you with a certificate as part of his standard consultation fee.

Special & Compassionate Leave

The only statutory requirements for employers to allow special leave are when employees are called for jury service, are looking for a job after being made redundant, or need to look after a relative or other person in need of full-time care (in accordance with the Carer's Leave Act, 2001). Whether or not you're paid for time off work or time lost through unavoidable circumstances (e.g. public transport strikes or 'acts of God') depends on your employer and often varies according to your status; executives and managers tend to have more leeway regarding time off than, say, manual workers. There's no legal requirement for employers to pay staff for time spent attending union meetings or engaging in other union activities.

Employees are, however, entitled to paid compassionate leave (known as *force majeure* leave) in the event of the injury or illness of a child (including adopted children) or person to whom they're *in loco parentis*, spouse or partner, brother or sister, parent or grandparent. *Force majeure* leave is limited to three days per year and five days in three years. Absence for part of a day counts as a day's leave.

Many Irish companies provide paid leave on certain other occasions, which may include your own or a family marriage, the birth of a child and the death of a family member or close relative. The grounds for special and compassionate leave may be listed in an employer's general terms.

Maternity, Parental & Adoptive Leave

The Maternity Protection (Amendment) Act, 2004, which amended the Maternity Protection of Employees Act, 1994, entitles women to 26 weeks' paid maternity leave, at least two weeks of which must be taken before the birth and at least four after (these rules are adjusted in the case of early and late births); the remaining time may be taken whenever you wish, although most mothers take the full 20 weeks immediately after the birth.

During this period, women who meet the PRSI contribution requirements receive social welfare maternity benefit of 80 per cent of their normal weekly earnings (up to a maximum of €280 with a guaranteed minimum of €221.80 per week). In some cases, employers will 'top up' this amount so that women continue to receive their full salary during maternity leave.

In addition to this period, expectant mothers are entitled to time off for routine ante-natal and post-natal check-ups, as well as at other times during pregnancy if their health or safety is at risk, without loss of earnings, and mothers are entitled to a further eight weeks' unpaid leave (i.e. they receive no social welfare payments), which must follow immediately on the paid leave period.

All women under a contract of employment are entitled to maternity leave, including apprentices and those on probation, whether employed directly or through an agency; although those on fixed-term contracts, whose contract ends during their maternity leave, may not be entitled to the full 22-week period.

The Maternity Protection Act also forbids employers to dismiss women for any pregnancy-related reason, and entitles women to return to their job after the specified leave period.

The Parental Leave (Amendment) Act, 2006, which amended the Parental Leave Act, 1998,

entitles both men and women to 16 weeks' unpaid leave (in addition to maternity leave), which can be taken at any time during their child's first eight years and may be broken into shorter periods by agreement with their employers. This also applies to adopted children. Fathers are entitled to paid leave only if the mother dies within 24 weeks of giving birth.

The Adoptive Leave Act, 1995 entitles a woman or man adopting a child to between 10 and 14 consecutive weeks' leave from the date of the child's 'placement'. Social welfare benefits are normally payable for ten weeks.

All these entitlements are dependent upon adequate notice being given to employers. Further information about maternity and parental leave is available from the Equality Authority (☎ 01-417 3333, ✉ info@equality.ie), to which applications for leave should be made.

HEALTH & INSURANCE

Social welfare

State social welfare consists of a health contribution that entitles you to a pension and unemployment and other benefits.

> Health contributions are compulsory for most residents of Ireland, and are deducted at source from your gross salary by your employer or must be included with your annual income tax payment.

Medical Examination

Some Irish companies require prospective employees to have a pre-employment medical examination, performed by a doctor nominated by them and covering basic factors such as sight and blood pressure. This may be required for employees over a certain age only (e.g. 40) or for employees in particular jobs, e.g. where good health is of paramount importance for safety reasons.

Drugs & Alcohol

Although there's currently no legislation governing drug or alcohol testing, an Irish employer can be prosecuted under health and safety legislation for an accident arising due to a worker being under the influence of alcohol or drugs, and an increasing number of employers are instigating tests. Aer Rianta was the first company to drug test all recruits (in 1999), and other airline pilots are routinely tested. Drug and alcohol testing is also common in 'safety-sensitive' sectors such as manufacturing and transport. Your contract of employment may also stipulate restrictions on alcohol consumption while you're at work or on company business.

Smoking

Since 29th March 2004, it has been an offence to smoke in any enclosed public place, including workplaces. Employers may designate an outdoor area as a smoking area, but they aren't obliged to allow employees time off (other than their statutory allowance for breaks – see page 57) for a smoke. Anyone breaking the no-smoking rule is liable to a fine of €3,000. Further information is available from the Office of Tobacco Control (☎ 045-892015 or ☎ 1890-333100, 💻 www.otc.ie).

Safety

Employers in Ireland are obliged to provide a safe place for their employees to work (including safe means of access to and exit from the workplace), safe systems of work (including safe machinery and equipment), appropriate training and supervision, and protective clothing if necessary. All staff must be made aware of safety procedures by way of a written Safety Statement. Employees must, in turn, take reasonable care in the exercise of their duties to ensure their own and others' safety and, if necessary, may appoint a safety representative.

The Health and Safety Authority (☎ 01-614 7000, 💻 www.hsa.ie) is responsible for promoting safety at work and can provide advice to employees and employers.

Health Insurance

Income protection in the event of sickness or an accident varies according to your employer, your contract of employment, your length of employment and whether you're paid weekly or monthly. Although Irish employers aren't legally required to pay staff if they're off sick, most salaried employees (i.e. monthly paid) continue to receive normal pay when sick for a short time (see **Sick Leave** on page 59). If you're off sick for more than three days, you may receive Social welfare injury benefit. Otherwise, you can take out private health and/or accident insurance to cover both the cost of treatment and loss of income resulting from your being incapacitated by an accident or illness.

Almost 70 per cent of Irish companies offer employees some level of private medical insurance. Some have their own group health insurance schemes that pay for medical expenses such as doctors' consultation fees, prescription charges, and hospital outpatient charges. Some even provide exclusive private medical treatment.

These schemes may be contributory or non-contributory. In cases where they're non-contributory, they should be considered as part of your salary rather than a 'freebie' from your employer, and the value of the benefits (on which you will be taxed) will depend on the scheme. If a scheme is contributory, you aren't obliged to contribute, although as schemes usually take advantage of bulk insurance rates, it's unlikely that you would be able to purchase similar cover for less, independently.

Accident Insurance

As there's no legal requirement for employers to have accident insurance, you should check whether your employer has it and, if so, what it covers you for (e.g. accidents that occur when you're travelling to and from work or on company business). It may be advisable to take out a personal accident insurance policy (see page 259). Alternatively, in the event of an accident at work, you can answer one of the many solicitors' advertisements (e.g. in the *Golden Pages*) for personal injury litigation on a 'no-win-no-fee' basis – you might get rich!

Other Insurance

Most employers provide short-term disability benefit (e.g. for up to six months), but companies tend to provide critical illness cover rather than long-term disability benefit. Many Irish employers now also offer employees some kind of life assurance, although this may

only apply in the case of accidental death at work.

JOINING & LEAVING A COMPANY

References

An Irish employer isn't legally obliged to provide an employee with a written reference but, if you leave an employer on good terms, he will normally provide a reference on request (bear in mind that an agency or prospective employer will be looking at what **isn't** mentioned in a reference, rather than what is!).

> Prospective employers might ask you to produce a *Garda* statement confirming that you don't have a criminal record. It isn't illegal for them to do so, but you aren't obliged to comply – although, if you don't, you won't exactly fill them with confidence in you!

Probationary & Notice Periods

For most jobs there's a probationary period, which applies equally to employers and employees, during which you and your employer decide whether or not you're suitable for the job and if the job suits you. This may be two weeks for hourly-paid employees and three or six months for salaried (monthly-paid) employees; the maximum length of a probationary period is one year.

Unless otherwise stated in your contract of employment, there's a legal minimum notice period for employees who work more than eight hours per week and who have completed at least 13 weeks' service. This is one week for up to two years' service, two weeks for between two and five years' service, four weeks for five to ten years' service, six weeks for 10-15 years and eight weeks for 15 or more years. As an employee you're required to give your employer at least one week's notice, unless your contract states otherwise. Your contract may also allow you to take pay in lieu of notice.

Retirement

There's no fixed or statutory retirement age in Ireland (except in the civil service, police force and armed services), but most employment contracts specify a retirement age, which is usually 65. Most contracts also make provision for early retirement, whether voluntary or for health reasons. However, you don't become eligible for a state retirement pension, known as a State Pension – Contributory, until you're 66.

Note also that after the age of 66 you're no longer protected by the Unfair Dismissal Acts (see below). If you wish to continue working after you've reached retirement age, you may need to negotiate a new contract of employment. You should also check the terms of your occupational or personal pension scheme. This also applies if you opt to retire early or accept an offer of early retirement from your employer.

You should be eligible to claim unemployment benefit for up to 15 months and thereafter receive social insurance credits, but you may not be able to claim any pension payments until you reach the age of 65 or 66.

Many companies present employees with a gift on reaching retirement age (e.g. the key to their ball and chain), the value of which usually depends on your number of years' service.

Redundancy

If you're dismissed under particular circumstances (see below) or laid off or asked to work part-time (i.e. earn less than half your normal wage) for at least four consecutive weeks or any six out of 13 consecutive weeks, you're said to have been made redundant and are entitled to certain compensation. The relevant circumstances are that your employer is ceasing trading, moving the business to another area (at least 25km/15mi away), changing the nature of the business, reducing the workforce or allocating your duties to other employees; or that the skills required for your duties have changed to such an extent that you're no longer capable of doing the job.

Your employer must give you written notice of redundancy in accordance with your contract of employment, subject to a minimum notice period of two weeks. The redundancy notice (which must be copied to the Minister for Labour!) should be accompanied by a completed form RP1 and, on the day you leave, you should be given your redundancy payment, together with a redundancy certificate (form RP2), which you sign to acknowledge receipt of the money.

The Redundancy Payments Acts (the latest of which was passed in 2003) state that any employee aged 16 to 66 who has worked continuously for two years or more is entitled to a redundancy lump sum payment. The minimum payment, which is due unless your employment contract specifies a higher sum, is two weeks' pay for each year of continuous service between the ages of 16 and 41 and a week's pay for each year of service plus one week's normal pay, subject to an overall limit of €600 per week.

Apprentices who are made redundant are entitled to redundancy pay, but those who are dismissed during the month following the completion of their apprenticeship aren't.

No redundancy money is payable if you're engaged by another employer immediately after the end of your notice period.

Irish companies are increasingly making use of 'outplacement' consultants to assist employees who are made redundant (or employees can contact such companies individually – they're listed in the *Golden*

Pages under *Outplacement Services*). Services include advice and counselling on job prospects, job hunting, state benefits, retirement, retraining and setting up in business, and financial advice for employees who receive large redundancy payments.

Executives, managers and key personnel may have a clause in their contract whereby they receive a generous 'golden handshake' if they're made redundant, e.g. after a takeover. The receipt of a redundancy payment, irrespective of the amount, doesn't affect your eligibility to claim unemployment benefit.

For further information about redundancy payments contact the Department of Enterprise, Trade and Employment (☎ 01-661 4444).

Dismissal & Disputes

Most large and medium-size companies have comprehensive grievance and disciplinary procedures, which must usually be followed before an employee can be suspended or dismissed. If you've been employed continuously for less than a year or normally work less than eight hours per week for an employer, you can be dismissed without notice or compensation.

Otherwise, you're protected by the Unfair Dismissals Acts (the latest having been passed in 2001) – unless you work for the *Garda* or Defence

Forces, the civil service, Health Boards, local authorities or Vocational Education Committees (VEC – see page 174), or are a trainee or apprentice or have reached retirement age. If you're dismissed because of trade union activity or for reasons related to pregnancy or maternity, even within your first year of work, you're also protected by the Unfair Dismissals Acts.

A disciplinary procedure must include counselling followed by a verbal warning and at least two written warnings. Instant or summary dismissal without any right to notice, or salary in lieu of notice, is permissible only in exceptional circumstances, such as acts of gross misconduct. These may include refusing to work (without a good reason); cheating or stealing from your employer; competing with your employer; insulting your employer or colleagues; assaulting your employer or a colleague; or drunkenness during working hours on your employer's premises (office parties excepted).

If you're given notice, you're required to work through it unless your employer's behaviour is such that you're unable to do so. In this case (known as 'constructive dismissal') you may be entitled to leave before the end of your notice period, but note that the dividing line between constructive dismissal and voluntary resignation is a fine one!

You can claim unfair dismissal if you're fired because of trade union membership or activity, religious or political beliefs, race or colour, age, pregnancy or matters relating to it. In fact, under Irish law, all dismissals are presumed to be unfair, and it's up to the employer to prove otherwise! Fair reasons for dismissal, apart from those listed above, include incompetence, inadequate qualifications or health for the job, and redundancy (see above). In these cases, employees are entitled to an explanation of the reason(s) for their dismissal, and have the right of reply and the right to an impartial hearing.

If you believe you've been unfairly dismissed, you can take your case to a Rights Commissioner or the Employment Appeals Tribunal (EAT) within six months of your dismissal (and must inform your employer that you've done so). The EAT (☎ 01-631 3006 or ☎ 1890-220222, 💻 www.eatribunal.ie) deals with disputes over redundancy, notice periods, maternity leave, employment terms, etc. If the case goes to court, you will be liable for any costs, whether or not you're successful – a law which is currently under review.

An employee found to be unfairly dismissed will be either reinstated (or 're-engaged' by the same employer in a different job) or compensated – the decision is made by the Rights Commissioner or by the tribunal or court. The maximum compensation for unfair dismissal is two years' pay.

Further information about unfair dismissal can be obtained from the Department of Enterprise, Trade & Employment's Employment Rights Information Unit (☎ 01-631 3131 or ☎ 1890-201615, ✉ erinfo@entemp.ie) and from the Labour Relations Commission (☎ 01-613 6700 or ☎ 1890-220227, 🖥 http://lrc.ie).

Grievances & Strikes

Your contract of employment or company handbook will normally set out procedures for handling disputes or grievances. Equal pay claims should be addressed initially to the employer; if that is unsuccessful, you should refer to an Equality Officer and if necessary to the Labour Court. The Rights Commissioner Service – part of the Labour Relations Commission (☎ 01-613 6700 or ☎ 1890-220227, ✉ rightscomm@lrc.ie) – deals with disputes resulting from individual grievances.

The Industrial Relations Act, 1990 allows unions to organise strikes in disputes between employees and employers, but unions are obliged to hold a secret ballot before initiating strike action. The Act also legalises peaceful picketing.

OTHER CONDITIONS

Occupational Pension

Over 95 per cent of companies in Ireland have occupational pension schemes, the average cost of which is between 10 and 20 per cent of employees' salaries, depending on whether the scheme is funded entirely by the employer or whether employees make a

contribution. Employees' contributions can be either compulsory or voluntary – around three quarters of company pension schemes involve compulsory contributions.

Your employer should provide you with details of the scheme and you may decide to opt out and arrange a private pension scheme instead, although most company pension funds offer much better terms than you can obtain privately. For more information on occupational and personal pension schemes, see pages 255 and 257.

Employee Assistance Programmes

An increasing number of Irish employers are offering staff some sort of employee assistance programme (EAP), which is an independent and confidential advice and counselling service to help deal with work-related problems such as stress. This may be free or employees may have to pay to use it.

Confidentiality & Changing Jobs

Your contract will normally include some kind of confidentiality clause, particularly if your work involves dealing with data. Otherwise, you're generally bound by common law, which requires you to behave in an honest and ethical manner, e.g. not to disclose any confidential company information (particularly to competitors) and not to steal any secrets or confidential information, e.g. customer mailing lists. If you change jobs, you may, however, use any skills, know-how, knowledge and contacts acquired during your previous job, although your contract may contain a restraint against competing with your previous employer. Your contract may also contain a clause defining the sort of information that the employer considers to be confidential, such as customer and supplier relationships and details of business plans.

If you're a key employee, your contract may prevent you from joining a competitor or starting a company in the same line of business as your employer and, in particular, enticing former colleagues to join your company. However, such a clause is usually valid for a limited period only. If there's a confidentiality or restraint clause in your contract which is unfair, e.g. it inhibits you from changing jobs, it will probably be invalid in law and therefore unenforceable. If you're in doubt, consult a solicitor who's an expert in employment law about your rights.

Education & Training

Education and training provided by your employer may be stated in your employment conditions. This may include training abroad, provided that it's essential for your job (although you may need to convince your employer). It's in your own interest to investigate courses of study, seminars and lectures that you feel will be of direct benefit to you and your employer.

Most employers give reasonable consideration to a request to attend a course during working time, provided you don't make it a full-time occupation! In addition to relevant education and training, employers must also provide the essential tools and equipment for a job (although this is open to interpretation). It's also compulsory for companies to provide appropriate and adequate health and safety training for all employees.

If you need to improve your English ability, language classes may be paid for by your employer. If it's necessary to learn a foreign language in order to perform your job, the cost of language study should be paid by your employer. An allowance may be paid for personal education or hobbies which aren't work related or of direct benefit to your employer – it's always worth asking.

Moonlighting

Restrictions on part-time work for anyone other than your regular employer (commonly known as moonlighting) may be included in your employment conditions. Many Irish companies don't allow full-time employees to work part-time for another employer, particularly one in the same line of business. You may, however, be permitted to take a part-time teaching job or similar part-time employment (or you could write a book!).

Acceptance of Gifts

If your work involves purchasing or placing contracts with suppliers, you should check with your employer what, if anything, you're permitted to accept as a gift. This may be limited to bottles of wine or spirits or other small gifts at Christmas. If your contract doesn't refer to gifts, common law applies, which means that you shouldn't accept anything which might be construed as 'corrupting'. If in doubt, you should declare any gifts received to your immediate superior, who will decide what should be done with them – most bosses pool them and divide them among all employees. (If you accept a bribe, make sure it's a big one and that you have a secret bank account!)

Union Membership

The Irish Constitution enshrines the right of individuals to 'associate', which is understood to include the right to subscribe to trade unions. However, it also incorporates the right to 'dis-associate', which employers have taken to mean that they aren't obliged to recognise unions. This apparently contradictory state of affairs has given rise to copious legislation regarding the extent to which employees may be 'represented' by unions – the latest being the Industrial Relations Acts, 2001–2004, which authorise unions to represent employees in court where there's a dispute.

Under existing law, you cannot be dismissed for belonging to a trade union or for any lawful union activity, including striking and peaceful picketing. Theoretically, you cannot be obliged to join a union either, yet in many sectors this is in effect a condition of employment (prospective employees are required to obtain 'clearance' from the relevant union). In some cases, there's a choice of unions; in others a single union will run what is in effect a 'closed shop'. This is neither legal nor illegal; it's a situation the Irish simply accept.

In still other cases, an employer will refuse to recognise any unions, making it difficult for employees to unionise (as with Ryanair). There's no legislation regarding the holding of ballots or stipulating minimum numbers of employees for union recognition, as in the UK.

Despite a recent decline in union membership, there are still over 500,000 union members (in percentage terms ten times as many as in the UK) and Irish unions have considerable influence. There are 57 trade unions affiliated to the Irish Congress of Trade Unions (ICTU). The two largest, the Services, Industrial, Professional & Technical Union (SIPTU) and the Amalgamated Transport & General Workers' Union (ATGWU), account for around 40 per cent of union members.

Information about trade unions can be obtained from the ICTU (☎ 01-889 7777, 🖥 www.ictu.ie).

3.
PERMITS & VISAS

Ireland is one of the least bureaucratic countries in Europe when it comes to the red tape of immigration. There's little of the 'fill-it-out-in-triplicate' system found in countries such as France, Italy and Spain. In fact, Irish immigration laws have traditionally been so lax (more people have always wanted to leave Ireland than go there!) that during the '90s, many African and East European *émigrés*, attracted by Ireland's new-found prosperity and generous welfare handouts, started knocking at her door and requesting asylum (see Population on page 371). The number of what the Immigration Office calls 'registered aliens' (i.e. immigrants from non-European Economic Area – EEA – countries) also increased dramatically, the largest numbers coming from the US and China, with substantial numbers from Australia, India, Malaysia and Pakistan.

This policy led to what the government – and many members of the public – perceived as an unacceptably high number of non-nationals (especially asylum seekers) giving birth to children in Ireland, and subsequently applying for permission to stay. Up to January 2003, around 11,000 families with Irish-born children had lawfully applied for residence. To address this issue, the Supreme Court ruled in January 2003 that non-national parents of children born in Ireland no longer had an automatic right to residence. Instead, residence would be decided on a case-by-case basis; the factors to be taken into account include the length of stay of families in Ireland, their circumstances, and the 'general requirements of the common good'.

In early 2004, the government took a more drastic step, proposing a referendum to remove the constitutional guarantee of citizenship for children born to non-national parents in Ireland. (This was partly in response to a few, well-publicised cases of non-nationals arriving heavily pregnant in Ireland, and giving birth a short time after their arrival.) The citizenship referendum, held on June 11, 2004, was overwhelmingly accepted, with 79 per cent of votes in favour of the change. Legislation necessary to implement the referendum

followed in autumn 2004 (see **Citizenship** on page 357).

According to the latest national census, carried out in 2006, there are at least 400,000 non-Irish nationals resident in the Republic, representing 9.4 per cent of the total population. Around 20,000 of these are reckoned to be asylum seekers. Almost 85 per cent of foreign workers are from the EU, some 30 per cent of the total being from the countries that joined the EU in 2004.

With regard to labour immigration, Ireland has maintained policies that are among the most liberal in Europe. In the absence of quotas, the number of employment permits issued to non-Irish migrant workers exploded from fewer than 6,000 in 1999 to over 47,000 in 2003, the great majority of them employed in low-skilled occupations. This is in contrast to many other European countries' labour immigration programs, which are regulated by quotas and often exclude low-skilled workers.

Ireland further granted citizens of the ten countries that joined the European Union (EU) in May 2004 immediate free access to the Irish labour market (only the UK and Sweden shared this policy; all other countries of the pre-enlarged EU decided to continue employment restrictions for accession state nationals), though the number of employment permits issued in 2005 was down to just over 27,000. Workers from Bulgaria and Romania, which joined the EU in January 2007, are, however, required to obtain an employment permit.

While it remains to be seen how policies will develop in the next few years, the government appears to favour a 'skills-based' immigration policy that increases the restrictions on the employment of workers from outside the enlarged EU, especially in low-skilled occupations.

Before making any plans to live or work in Ireland, you must therefore ensure that you have the appropriate entry permits (e.g. visa or employment permit – see below), as without the correct documentation you will be refused 'leave to land'. If you're in any doubt as to whether you require clearance to enter Ireland, enquire at an Irish Embassy or High Commission in your home country before making plans to travel to Ireland. Note that in some countries, entry clearance can take some time to be granted.

In recent years, the Irish government has passed a number of laws aimed at combating illegal immigration and has increased the number of deportations. The latest of these, in January 2008, gave the *Gardaí* increased powers to arrest failed asylum seekers, and the government voted not to 'opt into' an EU directive, issued in June 2008, encouraging the 'voluntary' return of illegal immigrants.

⚠ Caution

Penalties for breaches of regulations range from a fine or six months' imprisonment (for failure to register) to deportation for flagrant abuses.

Immigration is a complex subject and the rules are constantly changing. You shouldn't base any decisions or actions on the information contained in this (or any other) book without confirming it with an official source. The latest information about immigration, permits and visas can be obtained from the Department of Justice, Equality & Law Reform (☎ 01-602 8202, 🖳 www.justice.ie).

ENTRY REQUIREMENTS

The citizens of certain non-Irish countries (known officially as 'aliens') require a visa to enter Ireland (see **Visas** below). If you're a non-EU national and arrive in Ireland from outside the EU, you must go through immigration for non-EU citizens. Non-EU citizens are required to complete immigration registration cards, which are provided on aircraft and ferries (e.g. from France) in order to be granted leave to land. If you're a non-EU national coming to Ireland to work, study or live, you may be asked to show documentary evidence (see below). Immigration officials may also ask non-EU visitors to produce a return ticket, proof of accommodation, a health insurance certificate and evidence of sufficient financial resources, e.g. cash, travellers' cheques and credit cards.

The onus is on visitors to show that they're genuine and that they don't intend to breach Irish immigration laws. Immigration officials aren't required to prove that you will break the law and can refuse you entry on the grounds of suspicion only. You may wish to get a stamp in your passport as confirmation of your date of entry.

Since June 2006, the Irish government has made a charge of €100 to all non-EEA citizens (including students) coming to live or work in Ireland for more than three months. The fee is payable to the Immigration authorities on arrival in Ireland. Those staying less than three months must show evidence that they plan to leave the country within this period in order to avoid having to pay the fee.

Nationals of EEA countries may enter the country without a visa but are nevertheless subject to certain formalities. If you arrive in Ireland from the UK, you're exempt from immigration control at the port of entry into Ireland, but you may not stay longer than one month without obtaining permission to remain (see page 73). The Irish Republic and Great Britain are part of a 'Common Travel Area', which means that foreigners travelling to Ireland via the UK must meet British immigration requirements and will then be free to enter Ireland.

US, Uruguay, Vatican City, Vanuatu and Venezuela.

All other nationalities require at least a 'short-visit' visa (valid for a maximum of 90 days) to visit Ireland. Most visitors require a full passport, although EEA and Swiss nationals can enter Ireland with a national identity card only.

If you require a visa, you should apply to the Irish embassy or consulate in your country of permanent residence and you may be required to attend an interview. If there's no Irish embassy or consulate in your country of residence, you may apply to the designated Irish embassy or consulate for your country. You can download a visa application form from the website of the Irish Nationalisation and Immigration Service (INIS, 🖥 www.inis. gov.ie), which also provides instructions on how to complete it in English, Arabic, Chinese, French, Russian, Turkish and Urdu. Nationals of some countries can apply online (this facility should be available to all Irish embassies by the end of 2008). In either case, you should apply at least eight weeks before you plan to come to Ireland.

If you're a British citizen arriving in Ireland from the UK, you don't require a passport, although it's advisable to take some form of identity with you. All other nationals require a valid passport (or national identity card) and in some cases a visa (see below). If you're taking your car with you, ensure that you have its registration document, an insurance certificate valid for Ireland and your driving licence, and that the car has a nationality sticker on the back.

VISAS

Visitors from EEA countries (including British dependent territories) don't need a visa to visit Ireland. Neither do visitors from Andorra, Antigua and Barbuda, Argentina, Australia, Bahamas, Barbados, Belize, Bolivia, Botswana, Brazil, Brunei, Canada, Chile, Costa Rica, Croatia, Dominica, El Salvador, Fiji, Grenada, Guatemala, Guyana, Honduras, Hong Kong, Israel, Japan, Kiribati, Lesotho, Macao, Malawi, Malaysia, Maldives, Mauritius, Mexico, Monaco, Nauru, New Zealand, Nicaragua, Panama, Paraguay, Saint Kitts and Nevis, Saint Lucia, Saint Vincent and the Grenadines, Samoa, San Marino, Seychelles, Singapore, Solomon Islands, South Africa, South Korea, Swaziland, Switzerland, Tonga, Trinidad and Tobago, Tuvalu, the

The INIS has offices in the following countries:

China	www.embassyofireland.cn
Egypt	www.embassyofireland.org.eg
India	www.irelandinindia.com
Nigeria	www.embassyofireland.org.ng
Russia	www.embassyofireland.ru
UK	www.embassyofireland.co.uk

You will need to submit your passport, which must be valid for at least six months after the intended date of departure from Ireland. You will also need to send three passport-size photographs, and documents relevant to your intended visit; e.g. an invitation from an Irish company or conference organiser if you're visiting on business; a letter of registration from a school or college if visiting for educational purposes; or confirmation of a hotel booking or a letter of reference from an Irish resident who will accommodate you if you're planning a holiday. Children under 16 who are accompanying a parent or guardian don't require a visa to enter Ireland, provided that they have their own passports or are named on those of a parent or guardian.

If you need a visa to enter Ireland and attempt to enter without one, you will be refused entry. However, the granting of a visa doesn't necessarily give you permission to enter the country either; Irish immigration officials have the authority to deny you admission. You should therefore ensure that you take with you the originals or copies of all documents submitted with your visa application. You will also need a visa each time you enter Ireland, even if you travel to the UK. This also applies if you have permission to reside in Ireland, when you may apply for a re-entry visa at the Visa Office of the INIS, 13-14 Burgh Quay, Dublin 2 (☎ 01-616 7700 or ☎ 1890 551500), which is open only on Mondays, Wednesdays and Fridays between 10am and 12.30pm (nice work if you can get it).

If you apply for a **single-journey** (also called single-entry) **visa,** this is valid for only one entry into Ireland within 90 days from the date of issue. If you wish to leave Ireland for a short period (even to visit Northern Ireland), you must apply for a re-entry visa, which requires you to register with the Garda (see **Registration** on page 78). Before making any travel arrangements, you must complete a re-entry visa application form and submit it to the Visa Office of the INIS. In particular, you should check the photographic requirements for re-entry visas. Your application should be processed and returned to you by registered post within four working days.

If you apply for a multi-entry (multiple-entry or multiple-journey) visa, you must also register with the Garda and the visa is valid from the date of issue until the expiry date on your registration certificate, or the expiry date of your passport, whichever is earlier. This will allow you to leave and re-enter Ireland any number of times while your visa is valid.

The 'visa application processing fee' is €60 for a single-journey visa or €100 for a multi-entry visa. Citizens of certain countries and spouses of EEA citizens are exempt, though the list of countries and the criteria for exemption change from time to time, and you should check with your local embassy or consulate or with the Visa Office.

There's an appeals process for those whose visa applications are refused, which is handled by the Department of Justice, Equality and Law Reform (☎ 01-602 8202, 🖳 www.justice.ie).

There are three types of visa, detailed below. An employment permit (see below) **doesn't** function as a visa, and you need the appropriate entry visa.

Tourist Visa

A tourist visa is valid for only three months, but you may be allowed to stay longer on application to the INIS via the Garda.

Business Visa

Non-EEA nationals travelling to Ireland on business (e.g. for a meeting or to attend a conference or course, but not to take up employment, for which an employment permit is required) need a business visa. To obtain a business visa, you must supply a letter from the company or business person you're meeting, outlining the purpose of your visit; or confirmation from the conference or course organiser that you're enrolled, confirmation of where you will be staying in Ireland, and confirmation of who will be responsible for your expenses (e.g. your employer).

Student Visa

Non-EEA nationals coming to Ireland to study must apply for a student visa, and should

ensure that their passports are valid for at least six months **after** the end of their course. Copies of previous passports should also be supplied. The course provider (e.g. college or university) should provide a letter confirming that the student has been accepted on a privately funded course entailing at least 15 hours' study; and should specify the subject to be studied, and provide evidence that the course fees (including accommodation costs) have been paid in full, or that a payment of €7,000 has been made, if the fees exceed this amount.

> Students must give details of their accommodation, and provide evidence that they have sufficient funds to support themselves and to cover any emergencies that might arise, without recourse to state assistance.

You must have private medical cover as well as being insured by the course provider, but are entitled to public health services in Ireland if the course lasts more than a year. Students are also required to disclose details of any relatives (including first cousins, aunts, uncles, nieces, nephews and grandparents) already residing in Ireland or another EU country.

Full-time students are permitted to work up to 20 hours per week. If you plan to stay in Ireland longer than three months, you must register with the Garda (see **Registration** on page 78). If you need to leave Ireland during your period of study, you must obtain a re-entry visa.

Since April 2007, non-EEA students who graduated on or after 1st January 2007 with a primary, master's or doctorate degree may remain in Ireland for six months in order to follow the Third Level Graduate Scheme, which enables them to find employment and apply for an employment permit. During this six-month period, you may work full time. You should apply for an extension to your student visa at your local immigration registration office.

Permission to Remain

An Irish visa doesn't grant permission to stay in Ireland for any set period. The date of validity shown on the visa indicates only the date by which it must be presented to immigration. The length of stay is decided by immigration officers at the port of entry, who grant 'permission to remain' (also called permission to reside) for up to three months by way of a stamp in your passport, sometimes accompanied by a Certificate of Registration (inserted in your passport). This can be obtained either from an Immigration Officer at the port of entry or from the Registration Officer for the area where you're staying. A list of Registration Officers is available from the Department of Justice, Equality & Law Reform (see above).

You will need to produce a valid passport and evidence that you have sufficient funds to support yourself and any dependants. Students additionally need confirmation of registration with a school or college, evidence that the necessary fees have been paid, and proof of private medical insurance. Employees and the self-employed must present an employment permit of one kind or another (see below).

Employment Permits

Employment permits aren't required by EEA nationals, although they must register with Garda if they plan to stay longer than three months (see **Registration** on page 78). Non-EEA nationals and nationals of Bulgaria and Romania require a permit to work in Ireland unless they:

♦ are dependent relatives of EEA nationals residing in Ireland;

♦ are spouses or parents of Irish nationals;

♦ have been posted to Ireland for a maximum of four years by a company or group of companies which has operations in more than one EU state;

♦ have been posted to Ireland for a maximum of three years for company training;

♦ have been granted refugee status in Ireland or temporary permission to remain while an asylum application is being processed.

Non-EEA full-time students can legally work for 20 hours per week during terms and full time during holiday periods, while young

Australians, Canadians, and New Zealanders can be employed under Ireland's working holidaymaker scheme.

Employment permits are issued to employers rather than to individual workers and aren't transferable; they're normally valid for one year, but may be renewed annually. In general, all of Ireland's labour immigration programmes for non-EEA nationals involve the issue of temporary permission to work and reside in the country. As a result, naturalisation, which is possible after five years of residence, is currently the only way for non-EEA workers to secure permanent residence in Ireland.

Although in theory it's the Department of Enterprise, Trade & Employment (DETE) that grants or refuses employment permits, it's the Department of Justice, Equality & Law Reform that decides who may work in Ireland. Employment permit approval will depend on your skills. The basic criterion is that no suitable EU candidate can be found for the job, and the onus is on the employer to 'prove' that all reasonable steps have been taken to recruit a suitably qualified EU national, and that you were better qualified for the job than any of them.

You must therefore provide the prospective employer with proof of your previous employment, training qualifications and other skills that you have. You should also submit letters of recommendation from your previous employers. The issue of an employment permit to a non-EU national is considered to be a privilege rather than a right, and doesn't in itself authorise entry to or residence in Ireland, which are both subject to the control of the immigration authorities.

Until April 2003, Ireland's employment permit policies were almost entirely 'employer-led': provided they were prepared to go through the applications procedure, which required proof that 'every effort' had been made to recruit an EEA national before the application was made, Irish employers were entitled to recruit as many non-EEA workers as they wished, from whatever countries they wanted, and to employ them in any job, irrespective of the skill level required.

As a result, the number of employment permits issued to non-EEA nationals increased by more than 700 per cent – from 5,750 to

47,700 – between 1999 and 2003, though by 2005 it was down to just over 27,000 and by 2008 there were fewer than 15,000 workers with permits in Ireland. Moreover, around three-quarters of permits issued during this period were for employment in relatively low-skilled and/or low-wage occupations, especially in the service sector. For example, around a quarter of all employment permits issued were for employment in the catering sector.

The Employment Permits Bill, enacted in April 2003, marked the beginning of a more interventionist employment permit system. This bill simultaneously granted workers from the ten EU accession countries free access to the Irish labour market upon EU enlargement on 1st May 2004 and regulated the number and selection of other migrant workers – partly on the assumption that employers would be able to fill most of their vacancies by recruiting workers from within the enlarged EU, and partly on account of the uncertainty as to how many accession state workers would migrate and take up employment in Ireland. First, the DETE and the state training authority (FÁS) published a list of occupational categories that were ineligible for work permit applications, most of them involving low-skilled work (see **Work Permits** below).

Second, in November 2003, the DETE started to return employment permit applications for workers from outside the enlarged EU, whenever workers from the EU accession countries could be available to fill the vacancy. Third, in 2006, it decided to require workers from Bulgaria and Romania, which joined the EU in January 2007, to obtain permits.

An employment permit application can be made by either the employer or the employee (and not by an agency) but is granted to the employee, along with a statement of his rights and entitlements. The employer is prohibited from deducting recruitment expenses from the employee's pay or retaining the employee's personal documents.

All employment permit applications except those in the 'spousal/dependant' category (see below) must pass a 'labour market needs test', which means that the vacancy must have been advertised with the FÁS/EURES employment network and in local and national newspapers for at least three days. This is to ensure that an EEA or Swiss national or, failing those, a Bulgarian or Romanian national cannot be found to fill the vacancy.

⚠ Caution

Employees working on employment permits are protected by employment legislation (see **Chapter 2**) in exactly the same way as other employees.

Recently, trade unions, non-government organisations and the media have persistently reported stories of violations of migrant workers' rights, especially those pertaining to the wages and employment conditions of those employed on employment permits, and it has been suggested that such abuses result from 'tying' migrant workers to the employer who obtained the employment permit on their behalf. Consequently, there have been calls for a change in policy to allow permits to be issued to migrant workers themselves rather than to their employers, thus giving them the freedom to change jobs.

The government has so far rejected these calls, pointing out that it takes a flexible approach to applications and renewals (the DETE has approved an annual 2,000 to 3,000 applications for migrant workers who are changing employers). Further information about employment permits is available from the Economic Migration Policy Unit of the DETE (🖳 www.entemp.ie) and from an independent website, 🖳 www.workpermit.com.

Since the enactment of the Employment Permits Act, 2006, there have been four types of employment permit, detailed below.

WORK PERMIT

Work permits are issued mainly for occupations with an annual salary of at least €30,000; a small number of permits are available for lower-paid jobs. Nevertheless, certain types of worker are ineligible for work permits; the list of excluded occupations currently includes clerical and administrative staff, general operatives, production staff and labourers, retail staff, sales representatives and supervisory or specialist sales staff, drivers (excluding HGV drivers), nursery/crèche workers, child minders/nannies, hotel, tourism and catering staff except chefs, and various types of craft worker and apprentice/trainee craft worker.

Work permits are granted initially for two years but can be renewed for a further three. You should wait until shortly before your permit expires before applying to renew it. Either you or your employer can make the application, and a labour market needs test (see above) isn't required. However, if you wish to change employers (you're expected to remain with your initial employer for at least a year), a new application for a work permit must be made and (unless the job is similar) a needs test carried out.

After five years, an unlimited work permit can be applied for, or long-term residence (see **Residence** on page 79), which exempts you from the need for a work permit.

Note also the following allowances and restrictions relating to work permits:

♦ A work permit application for a domestic staff position will be entertained only where it has been established that the person has been in employment with a family abroad for at least a year prior to the date of applying for a work permit. Permits, where issued, are subject to strict conditions.

♦ A person on a working holiday visa can no longer transfer to a work permit.

♦ There are no special regulations for au pairs, who must obtain a work permit in the normal way.

♦ There are special arrangements for work permit applications for sports professionals (players only), nurses and doctors (see below), which aren't subject to a labour market needs test, for example.

Applications for work permits must be made to the Employment Permits Section of the DETE, Davitt House, 65a Adelaide Road, Dublin 2 (☎ 01-417 5333, 🖳 www.entemp.ie), which is open from 9.30am to 1pm and from 2 to 5pm on weekdays. Applications can be made by the prospective employer or employee, who must use the new employment permit application form, accompanied by:

♦ evidence that a labour market needs test has been undertaken;

♦ evidence of your qualifications;

♦ two recently taken passport-size photographs;

♦ the appropriate fee (see below).

If the proposed employee is resident in Ireland, copies of all visas, residence stamps and the Garda registration certificate (see **Registration** on page 78) must also be supplied; if the proposed employee isn't resident in Ireland, he should apply for a visa (see above).

The fee for a work permit depends on its duration: up to six months, €500; from six months to two years, €1,000.

Either the employer or the employee can apply for a renewal using the renewal application form. The fee is €1,500 for a three-year renewal. There's no fee for an unlimited permit.

Nurses & Doctors

Nurses undergoing adaptation may apply for a work permit for up to two years (including the adaptation period). You must supply a copy of the employment contract and specify where the adaptation will take place. The type of permit issued will depend on the duration of the job offer and on the starting salary after adaptation, which must be specified in the employment contract. Further information can be obtained from *An Bord Altranais* (The Nursing Board, ☎ 01-639 8500, 🖳 www. nursingboard.ie).

Interns and doctors fully registered with the Irish Medical Council can apply for a work permit; temporarily registered doctors don't require a work permit but must obtain a stamp from the Department of Justice, Equality and Law Reform (see above).

Green Card Permit

The Green Card permit, which replaces the 'working visa' and 'work authorisation', is for those taking up jobs with a salary of over €60,000 or, in certain sectors where there are skill shortages, of over €30,000. Sectors include information technology, healthcare, industry, education, financial and services. There's no requirement for a labour market needs test (see above), but a permit won't be granted if your employment would mean that more than half of the company's employees were non-EEA nationals. Green Card permits are initially issued for two years but can normally be renewed for an indefinite period. The spouses of Green Card holders can join them immediately.

To be eligible for a Green Card permit, as well as meeting the abovementioned requirements, you must have a job offer from a company or employer trading in Ireland and registered with the Revenue Commissioners and the Companies Registration Office; offers made by recruitment agencies and other intermediaries aren't acceptable.

As for a work permit, applications should be submitted to the Employment Permits Section of the DETE (see above). They can be made by the prospective employer or employee, who must use the new employment permit application form, accompanied by:

♦ a job offer for at least two years, on company headed paper, dated within the previous 60 days; including a description of the employment, the starting date, annual salary and information on the employee's qualifications, skills or experience required for the job;

♦ evidence of your qualifications;

♦ a copy of your passport, which must be valid for at least three months after the proposed expiry date of the Green Card permit;

♦ copies of visas, residence stamps and the employee's Garda registration certificate, where applicable;

♦ the fee (€1,000).

If you're a medical professional, you must also supply a copy of the registration with the appropriate medical body, or a validation of qualifications from the Department of Health and Children. A list of registration and validation bodies for medical professionals is included in the Guide to Green Card Permits, available from the DETE or on its website.

If you're already working in Ireland on a work permit, you may apply for a Green Card permit, provided you meet the criteria.

If this is your first employment in Ireland, you're expected to remain with your employer for at least a year, after which you may change employers, but you must make a new Green Card permit application.

To renew a Green Card permit, which costs €1,500, you must submit the same documentation as for your initial application (your passport must be valid for at least a further year), plus copies of your P60s for each year of employment on a Green Card permit, and copies of three recent pay slips (dated within the previous three months).

Intra-company Transfer Permit

An intra-company transfer permit (also written 'intra company transfer permit', even in DETE information), introduced in 2006, is designed to facilitate the transfer of foreign senior managers, trainees and 'key' personnel from an overseas branch of a multinational corporation to its Irish branch. You must be earning at least €40,000 and have been working for the company for at least a year. Permits are initially granted for a maximum of two years but can be extended for a further three. Needless to say, the permit holder cannot change employers during this period. The number of intra-company transfer permits issued to a company cannot normally exceed 5 per cent of its workforce. No labour market needs test is required.

Applications must be made by the company, not the employee, and the fee is

Derryclare Lake, Co. Galway

€500 for up to six months or €1,000 for up to two years, the renewal fee being €1,500.

SPOUSAL/DEPENDANT WORK PERMIT

Since February 2007, spouses and dependants of employment permit holders are allowed to apply for a work permit for any occupation, without the requirement for a labour market needs test. In fact, they **must** have a permit if they wish to work in Ireland. In the case of spouses, they must have a legally recognised marriage certificate, and the employment permit holder must have a work permit for at least 12 months, a Green Card permit, or an intra-company transfer permit for at least 12 months.

Dependants' permits are normally available only to dependent unmarried children under 18 who are resident in Ireland with the employment permit holder, although exceptions are sometimes made for those over 18 who became legally resident in Ireland before their 18th birthday. Permits are normally issued for the same duration as the employment permit holder's permit, and those granted a spousal/dependant permit must remain with their first employer for at least a year.

Either the employer or the employee can apply, to the Employment Permits Section of the DETE (see above), submitting a copy of the employment holder's passport, employment permit and Garda registration certificate, a letter from the employer of the employment permit holder confirming his employment, and the spouses' marriage certificate or the dependant's birth certificate. There's no fee for either a first application or a renewal.

REGISTRATION

If they intend to remain in Ireland for longer than three months, non-EEA nationals (except those under 16 years of age, those born in Ireland or the UK, and women married or widowed to an Irish national) must register with the Garda National Immigration Bureau (GNIB) at 13-14 Burgh Quay, Dublin 2 (if living in Dublin) or the local Garda District Headquarters (if living outside Dublin) – preferably within a few days. (Note that if you're arriving from the UK to take up employment or set up a business, you must report to the Registration Officer with seven days of your arrival.)

To register, you will need your passport (with an appropriate visa if required – see page 71), four recent passport-size photographs, and documentation relating to your entry into Ireland (e.g. a work permit or business permission, evidence of funds, or confirmation of enrolment on a recognised course). Most applicants must pay a €100 fee (a few categories of person are exempt). You will then be granted permission to remain for up to 12 months, and issued with a registration certificate (sometimes referred to as a 'GNIB card', as it's issued by the Garda National Immigration Bureau), which must be kept up to date. Certificates are the size of a credit card and are not identity documents, merely proof that you're legally resident in Ireland.

Your permission to remain mustn't be allowed to lapse, but can be renewed for additional 12-month periods. You will be required to produce current documentation at each renewal. If you're employed in Ireland, the permit must be completed by your employer, who must also submit a letter detailing the nature and period of your employment. There's no fee for registration.

Once you've registered, you must inform your Registration Officer of any change in your circumstances (including any absence of more than a month) within seven days of the change. If you move to a different registration area, you must notify your original Registration Officer within 48 hours of your move. You aren't allowed to engage in any activity for which you don't have permission to remain, e.g. students mustn't work unless it is a recognised part of their course. If you require a visa for entry into Ireland, you should therefore make sure that you state the exact reason for your stay; permission to remain and residence permits are granted only on the basis of the reasons stated on your visa application form.

RESIDENCE

In accordance with the European Communities (Free Movement of Persons) Regulations, which came into effect in April 2006 (incorporating into Irish law European Directive 2004/38/EC), EEA nationals need not apply for permission to reside (i.e. remain for more than three months) in Ireland, provided they meet at least one of the following criteria:

♦ are engaged in economic activity (employed or self-employed);

♦ have sufficient resources and health insurance to ensure that they don't become a burden on the social services of Ireland;

♦ are enrolled as a student or vocational trainee;

♦ are a family member of an EEA citizen who meets one of the above criteria.

After five years' uninterrupted legal residence (also referred to as 'residency') in Ireland, you're entitled to apply for permanent residence (using Form EU 1). This takes the form of a permanent residence certificate. Non-EEA family members of a permanent residence certificate holder (including children under 16, who previously required no residence document) may apply for a permanent residence card after three months' legal residence in Ireland (using Form EU 2; Form 3 should be used by those resident for over five years); a separate application form must be used for each dependant. Spouses must have been married to the certificate holder for at least two years.

Completed application forms should be sent by registered post to EU Treaty Rights Section, Irish Naturalisation and Immigration Service, Department of Justice, Equality and Law Reform, 13-14 Burgh Quay, Dublin 2. Enquiries should be addressed to the same office or via email to ✉ immigration_mail@justice.ie.

Permanent residence status is forfeited if you spend more than two successive years outside Ireland, but non-EEA dependants of a certificate holder may remain in Ireland if the certificate holder dies or divorces.

Non-EEA citizens who aren't married to or dependants of an EEA citizen may apply for a five-year 'residency extension' (also known as 'long-term residence') after five years' continuous residence, on the basis of an employment permit and, if they wish, for exemption from the requirement for an employment permit. Their dependants may also apply for long-term residence, but they must continue to renew employment permits where applicable.

Applications for long-term residence should be addressed to The Long-Term Residence Section, General Immigration Division, 3rd Floor, INIS, 13-14 Burgh Quay, Dublin 2, and accompanied by copies of employment permits, registration certificates and passports. **Applications for long-term residence normally take 18 months to be 'processed'.**

If you're refused a residence certificate or card, you will be notified of the reason(s) and have the right of appeal (which must be made in writing to the Visa Appeals Officer at the above address), unless you're considered a danger to the security of the Irish State, in which case you will be 'asked' to leave on the next plane! See also **Citizenship** on page 357.

4.

ARRIVAL

On arrival in Ireland, your first task will be to negotiate immigration and customs. Like the UK, Ireland isn't a signatory to the Schengen agreement (named after a Luxembourg village on the Moselle River where it was signed), which came into effect on 26th March 1995 and introduced an open-border policy between many continental European Union (EU) countries. This means that all visitors and immigrants are subject to customs and immigration checks on arrival in Ireland, irrespective of their country of departure – with one exception. The Irish Republic and the UK are part of a 'Common Travel Area', which means that foreigners travelling to Ireland via the UK must meet British immigration requirements and will then be free to enter Ireland. If you arrive in Ireland from the UK, there are therefore usually no immigration checks or passport controls at the port of entry into Ireland. Non-EU nationals may require a visa (see page 26).

In addition to information about immigration and customs, this chapter contains checklists of tasks to be completed before or soon after arrival in Ireland, plus suggestions for finding local help and information.

IMMIGRATION

In recent years, Ireland has found itself facing an immigration 'problem' and has tightened its immigration policies, particularly with regard to foreign workers and asylum seekers. Those arriving from European Economic Area (EEA) countries are free to enter Ireland, although there are certain formalities that must be observed, such as presenting a valid identity document. If you're a British citizen arriving in Ireland from the UK, you don't require a passport, although it's advisable to take some form of identity with you. All other nationals require a valid passport (or national identity card) and in some cases a visa. However, citizens of many non-EU countries, including Australia, Canada, New Zealand, South Africa and the US, don't require visas (see page 26).

If you need a visa to enter Ireland and attempt to enter without one, you will be refused entry. If you're arriving by car, ensure that you have its registration document, an insurance certificate valid for Ireland and your driving licence, and that the car has a nationality sticker on the back.

Non-EU citizens are required to complete immigration registration cards, which are provided on aircraft and ferries, e.g. from France. If you're a non-EU national coming to Ireland to work, study or live, you may be asked to show documentary evidence. Immigration officials may also ask non-EU visitors to produce a return ticket, proof of accommodation, a health insurance certificate and evidence of sufficient financial resources, e.g. cash, travellers' cheques and credit cards.

You may wish to get a stamp in your passport as confirmation of your date of entry.

The onus is on visitors to show that they're genuine and that they don't intend to breach Irish immigration laws. Immigration officials aren't required to prove that you will breach those laws and can refuse you entry on the grounds of suspicion only.

CUSTOMS

If you import goods valued at more than €10,000, you must complete a 'declaration of value' for Irish Customs. Excise duty is payable on the import of products containing alcohol (including perfume), hydrocarbon oil (including petrol) and tobacco. For further information on Customs requirements for the importation of personal effects into Ireland, contact the Customs Tariffs & Reliefs section of the Revenue Commissioners (☎ 01-676 3440). Copies of the forms mentioned below can be obtained from the Revenue Commissioners' website (💻 www.revenue.ie – click on 'Forms', then 'Customs & Excise Forms' under 'Forms for Individuals') or from any Irish Customs & Excise or Vehicle Registration office.

Prohibited & Restricted Goods

There are restrictions on the quantities of certain goods you're permitted to import into Ireland and certain others may require a licence or be prohibited. For example, if you're planning to import sporting guns into Ireland, you must obtain a certificate from an Irish Consulate in your home country (you will be required to produce a valid firearms certificate) and present it to Customs on arrival. The import of certain ozone depleting substances (ODS) and products which contain them (e.g. certain fridges and aerosols) is either prohibited or requires the authority of an import licence issued by the European Commission.

Further details are available from the European Commission website (💻 www.europa.eu.int/comm/environment/ods/home/home.cfm). If you're unsure whether particular goods are prohibited or restricted, you should check with Irish Customs before your departure.

Animals & Plants

Rabies-susceptible animals require an Irish import licence. Certain pets may be imported without the need to undergo quarantine if they comply with the conditions of the Pet Passport Scheme (see page 368). Endangered species and their products, e.g. parrots, tortoises, birds of prey, monkeys, caviar, ivory and coral, need specified permits or other documentation. The furs of certain animal species may be brought into Ireland only if accompanied by evidence of their legal origin.

All plants intended for growing and certain fruits, vegetables, nuts and other plant products must have an import licence. In most cases, this must be accompanied by a Phytosanitary (plant health) Certificate. At least 48 hours' notice of importation must be given and an inspector will inspect your goods on arrival. Note that you may not be allowed to import hay or straw, so these shouldn't be used to pack personal effects. To find out whether a licence is required and how to obtain one, contact the Department of Agriculture & Food (☎ 01-607 2000 or ☎ 1890-200510, 💻 www.agriculture.gov.ie). Licences are issued free of charge.

Certain types of timber and forestry products must also be covered by a Phytosanitary Certificate. Details are available from the Forestry Service department of the Department of Agriculture & Food (💻 www.agriculture.gov.ie/forestservice).

Food

Certain kinds of food may not be taken into Ireland, e.g. pet food must be tinned and pre-cooked and have been manufactured in the EU (even then only a limited amount may be imported). Products containing meat, milk, animal bones or blood, eggs, sausage skins and fishery products are required to undergo veterinary health checks at a Border Inspection Post (BIP). You must complete a Common Veterinary Entry Document (CVED) and submit it at least 24 hours in advance of importation.

Drugs

Visitors arriving in Ireland from 'exotic' regions, e.g. Africa, South America, and the Middle and Far East, may find themselves under close scrutiny from customs and security officials looking for illegal drugs. Information about legal and illegal drugs in Ireland can be found on the website of the National Drugs Strategy and Drugs Awareness Campaign (🖳 www.drugsinfo.ie).

Visitors

Certain goods may be imported for up to two years (officially known as 'temporary' importation) without payment of excise duty or VAT. This applies to private cars, camping vehicles (including trailers or caravans), motorcycles, aircraft and personal effects, for which no import formalities apply. Other goods may be temporarily imported on completion of Form C&E 1047. In this case, security for the duties and taxes normally payable will be required. Customs officials can stop anyone for a spot check, e.g. for drugs or illegal immigrants.

Students & Trainees

Everyone except UK nationals must obtain permission to stay in Ireland as a student or trainee. Initial permission is granted by immigration officials at the port or airport of entry. You must then go to the Aliens' Office of the Department of Justice, Harcourt Square, Harcourt Street, Dublin 2 (☎ 01-475 5555) if you're intending to stay in Dublin or to the relevant Aliens' Office – usually the local Garda (police) station – elsewhere. The Dublin office is open from 9.30am to 12.30pm and from 2 till 4pm Mondays to Fridays; opening times of provincial offices vary.

Permission is normally granted for a year at a time. You must present your passport, confirmation of your place on a course of study or traineeship and evidence that you can support yourself financially for at least a year.

If you're intending to stay more than three months, you must complete a lengthy document with personal details and submit four passport-size photographs. Registration can take several weeks to be processed.

Permanent Residence

EU Nationals

The shipment of personal effects from another EU member state when taking up permanent residence in Ireland isn't subject to customs formalities on the basis that excise duty and VAT will already have been paid in the country of origin. If you're importing a vehicle from another EU country as part of your transfer of residence, however, you must complete form C&E 1077 in order to claim exemption from vehicle registration tax (VRT – see page 198).

In order to qualify for VRT relief, you must be able to prove that you've owned and used the vehicle outside Ireland for at least six months before the date of your transfer of residence; you will therefore need to produce appropriate documentation such as the vehicle's registration document and insurance certificate. In addition, you may not dispose of, hire or lend the vehicle to anyone during the 12 months following its registration in Ireland.

Non-EU Nationals

Non-EU nationals intending to stay in Ireland for more than three months must register their presence at the District Headquarters of the Garda Síochána (national police); in Dublin, this is the Garda National Immigration Bureau, 13–14 Burgh Quay, Dublin 2, which is open from 8 to 10am Mondays to Thursdays and 8.30am to 4pm on Fridays. You must present your passport or other national identity document and a photograph of yourself; you may also be required to give fingerprints. There's a charge of €100, which is waived if you're under 18 or married to an Irish citizen. Payment must normally be made by bank giro, although some offices accept debit and credit cards.

You will be issued with an Immigration Certificate of Registration (also known as a registration certificate and a GNIB card), which is the size of a credit card and includes your name, address and photograph. A registration certificate isn't an identity card but must be produced along with your passport or identity card on request.

⚠ **Caution**

Any change to the length of your stay or intended move to a different *Garda* district must be notified to the same office.

Non-EU nationals planning to take up permanent residence in Ireland are permitted, under certain conditions, to import household and personal effects free of excise duty and taxes. This excludes property intended for commercial use, with the exception of portable 'tools of the trade' of people such as artists, doctors and solicitors. Other self-employed people transferring their business activities to Ireland may be eligible for relief from duty and tax.

You must have owned all such goods for at least six months and had your usual place of residence outside the EU for a continuous period of at least 12 months prior to your move (relief may also be granted if you can prove that it was your intention to reside outside the EU continuously for 12 months). Note that 'normal residence' is considered to be the place where you live for at least 185 days of a year. You will therefore need to produce documentary evidence such as sales invoices or receipts, proof of residence abroad and transfer of residence to Ireland, of disposal of your home in your previous country of residence and of any employment in Ireland.

All non-EU nationals must declare all property at the place of importation on form C&E 1076, which should include an inventory of all items imported, except used clothes, toiletries and accessories. If you use a shipping company to transport your belongings to Ireland, it will usually provide all the necessary forms and take care of the paperwork. Always keep a copy of all forms and communications with customs officials (both in Ireland and in your previous country of residence).

If the paperwork isn't in order, your belongings may end up incarcerated in an Irish customs storage depot. If you personally import your belongings, you may need to employ a customs agent at the point of entry to clear them. You should also have an official record of the export of valuables from any country, in case you wish to re-import them later.

You may import personal effects (excluding vehicles) up to six months in advance of, or one year after, your arrival, and you may not sell or otherwise dispose of them during the year following their importation unless you pay the import charges.

If you're importing a vehicle on transfer of residence from outside the EU, you may qualify for relief from VAT and VRT. The vehicle must be registered on its arrival in Ireland and have been owned and used by you for at least six months prior to your transfer of residence. You must include the vehicle on form C&E 1076 and present a completed copy of form VRT4 (used cars) or VRT5 (new or used motorcycles). You must also produce documentary evidence of ownership, usage and taxes paid in your country of origin, e.g. the vehicle registration document, insurance certificate and invoice. You may not dispose of, hire or lend the vehicle to anyone during the 12 months following its registration in Ireland, and you must import the vehicle within 12 months of your transfer of residence.

Secondary Residence

The same criteria (as outlined above) regarding duty and tax relief on the importation from non-EU countries of household effects (i.e. furniture, furnishings and equipment) apply to a secondary residence. However, you're required to have owned or rented your secondary residence for not less than two years and to undertake not to let it to any third parties. In practice, this means that most non-EU nationals will be unlikely to be able to furnish a second home in Ireland with duty-free imported goods and may as well buy new furnishings locally. There's no VAT relief on goods imported to furnish a secondary residence.

Value Added Tax

Value Added Tax (VAT) is levied on goods imported from outside the EU, in addition to

Dunmore East, Co. Waterford

any customs and excise duties that may be payable. In general, goods are liable to VAT at the same rate as applies to the sale of similar goods within Ireland (e.g. vehicles are subject to VAT at 20 per cent). VAT is also payable on excise duty and on the transportation, handling and insurance costs of goods as they're conveyed to their final destination (i.e. your home). VAT is usually due at the same time as excise duty, but payment may be deferred subject to the approval of the Revenue Commissioners.

The criteria for relief from VAT aren't the same as those for relief from excise duty. For example, relief from VAT cannot be obtained for personal effects imported for a secondary residence. A listing of the rates of VAT applicable to a wide range of goods and services can be found on the Revenue website (💻 www.revenue.ie/services/tax_info/vatrate/vatrate.htm).

FINDING HELP

One of the major problems facing new arrivals in Ireland is how and where to obtain help with day-to-day problems such as finding accommodation, enrolling children in school and obtaining insurance. In addition to the comprehensive information provided in this book, you will need detailed local information. How successful you are at finding local help depends on your employer, the town or area where you live (e.g. residents of Dublin and large towns are better

served than those living in rural areas), your nationality and your English (or Irish) language proficiency. An additional problem is that much of the available information isn't intended for foreigners and their particular needs.

You may find that acquaintances and work colleagues offer advice based on their own experiences, but this may not apply to your particular situation.

Your local town hall may be a good source of information and help when applying for an Irish driving licence and other official documents.

One of the best places to obtain expert and impartial advice is at a Citizens [sic] Information Centre (CIC), which provide free, confidential information on virtually any subject. There are CICs in most Irish towns (a CIC 'locator' can be found on 💻 www.citizensinformationboard.ie), but opening times vary (many are open only in the morning). In the major cities and towns, foreigners are served by embassies and consulates. These usually provide their nationals with local information, including details of solicitors, doctors, schools, and social and expatriate organisations. Contacts can also be made through many expatriate magazines and newspapers (see **Appendix A**).

CHECKLISTS

The checklists below include tasks which you may need to complete before and after arrival in Ireland.

Before Arrival

◆ Check that your family's passports are valid!

◆ Obtain a visa, if necessary, for all your family members. Obviously this must be done before arrival in Ireland.

◆ Obtain an international driving permit if necessary.

◆ Arrange travel insurance for yourself and your family if you aren't covered by an international health insurance policy, and won't be covered by Irish social security.

◆ If you don't already have one, obtain an international credit or charge card, which will prove invaluable during your first few months.

◆ Open a bank account in Ireland and transfer funds. You can open an account with many Irish banks while abroad, although it's best done in person in Ireland.

◆ Obtain some euros before arrival, as this will save you having to change money at a port or airport, where you will probably be given a poor exchange rate.

◆ If you plan to become a permanent resident, you may also need to do the following:

  – Arrange schooling for your children.

  – Organise the shipment of your personal and household effects.

  – Obtain as many credit references as possible, for example from banks, mortgage companies, credit card companies, credit agencies, companies with which you've had accounts, and professionals such as solicitors and accountants. These will help you when opening bank accounts, setting up a business in Ireland and obtaining credit.

  – Don't forget to take all your family's official documents with you. These may include birth certificates; driving licences; marriage certificate, divorce papers or death certificate (if a widow or widower); educational diplomas and professional certificates; employment references and curricula vitae; school records and student identity cards; medical and dental records; bank account and credit card details; insurance policies (plus records of no-claims bonuses); and receipts for any valuables. You will also need the documents necessary to obtain a residence permit, plus certified copies, and numerous passport-size photographs (students should take at least a dozen).

After Arrival

The following checklist contains a summary of the tasks to be completed after arrival in Ireland (if not done before):

◆ On arrival at an Irish airport or port, have your visa cancelled and your passport stamped, as applicable.

◆ If you aren't taking a car with you, rent or buy one locally if applicable.

◆ Open an account at a local bank and give the details to your employer (if applicable) and any companies that you plan to pay by direct debit or standing order (such as utility companies).

☑ **SURVIVAL TIP**

Arrange whatever insurance is necessary, such as health, car, household and third-party liability.

◆ Contact offices and organisations to obtain local information.

◆ Make courtesy calls on your neighbours and local businesses within a few weeks of your arrival. This is particularly important in small villages and rural areas if you want to be accepted and integrate into the local community.

◆ If you plan to become a permanent resident in Ireland, you will need to do the following within a few weeks of your arrival (if not done before):

  – Apply for a residence permit.

  – Register with the Garda National Immigration Bureau.

  – If necessary, apply for an Irish driving licence.

  – Find a local doctor and dentist.

5.
ACCOMMODATION

Accommodation, whether to rent or to buy, isn't difficult to find in most areas of Ireland, depending, of course, on what you're looking for. There are, however, a few exceptions, e.g. Dublin, where property at an affordable price is in high demand and short supply, and where rents (in relation to average salaries) can be astronomical. Between 1995 and 2006, property price increases were greater in Ireland than in any other Organisation for Economic Co-operation & Development (OECD) country: average prices tripled in real terms (i.e. allowing for overall cost of living inflation). In 2007, however, house prices declined nationally by 7.3 per cent, and the average price paid for a new home by February 2008 was around €320,000, the average resale home costing around €375,000 – similar to figures recorded in March 2006.

Nevertheless, the rate of home ownership in Ireland is over 80 per cent – the highest in Europe (compared with some 65 per cent in the UK and just 35 per cent in Germany) and one of the highest in the world. The country boasts a million homeowners out of a population of 3.6m and the growth in property investment (by both nationals and foreigners) in recent years has been phenomenal, although it's predicted that the property market will 'cool' over the coming years. The market has been partly fuelled by a recent influx of foreigners, who in some areas (particularly in and around Dublin) are buying as much as 30 per cent of available housing. A detailed survey of the current Irish property market can be found on the website of the Irish Auctioneers' & Valuers' Institute (IAVI – ☎ 01-661 1794, 💻 www.iavi.ie).

This chapter includes information on temporary accommodation, relocation agents, buying and renting property, estate agents, moving house, home security, utilities and heating.

TEMPORARY ACCOMMODATION

On arrival in Ireland you may find it necessary to stay in temporary accommodation for a few weeks or months, e.g. before moving into permanent accommodation or while waiting for your furniture to arrive. Some employers provide rooms, self-contained apartments or hostels for employees and their families, although this is rare and usually only for a short period. Many hotels and bed and breakfast (B&B) establishments cater for long-term guests and offer reduced weekly or monthly rates.

In most areas, particularly in Dublin, serviced and holiday apartments are available. These are self-contained, furnished apartments with their own bathrooms and kitchens, which are cheaper and more convenient than a hotel, particularly for families. Serviced apartments are usually rented on a weekly basis. In most regions, self-catering holiday accommodation is available, although this is prohibitively expensive during the main holiday season (July/August). For further information, see **Renting** on page 91.

RELOCATION AGENTS

If you're fortunate enough to have your move to Ireland paid for by your employers, it's likely that they will arrange for a relocation agent to handle the details. If you want to engage a relocation agent privately, however, you may find this difficult and costly. Relocation agents in Ireland are listed on the website of the European Relocation Association (💻 www. eura-relocation.com).

> It's possible to engage a relocation agent as an individual, but they usually deal exclusively with corporate clients with lots of money to pay their fees.

Home-search companies are becoming more common in many countries, although there are relatively few in Ireland. One is The Property Finders (💻 www.thepropertyfinders. com), who operate only in the southern counties. Home-search companies normally arrange short-term rentals (e.g. six months) initially and can then help clients find a suitable property to purchase, although you can of course switch to an estate agent at this stage (see page 91). To find a rental property, a company normally charges a month's rent, e.g. around €1,000 for a family house). For a property to buy, a fee of between 1 and 2.5 per cent of the purchase price (the lower the price, the higher the percentage!) is normal, with a minimum charge of around €4,000; there is, of course, no estate agent's fee (see page 114) on top.

Finding accommodation for single people or couples without children can usually be accomplished in a week or two, depending on the area, while homes for families usually take a bit longer. You should generally allow at least two months between your initial visit and moving into a purchased property. Rental properties (see page 91) can usually be found in two to four weeks, depending on the location and your requirements.

A relocation agent may provide some or all of the following services:

- ♦ **House hunting** – This is usually the main service provided by relocation agents and includes both rented and purchased properties. Services usually include locating a number of properties matching your requirements and specifications, and arranging a visit (or visits) to Ireland to view them.

- ♦ **Negotiations** – Agents will usually help and advise with all aspects of house rental or purchase and may conduct negotiations on your behalf, organise finance (including bridging loans), arrange surveys and insurance, organise your removal to Ireland and even arrange quarantine for your pets (see page 368).

- ♦ **Local information** – Most agents provide a comprehensive information package for a chosen area, including information about employment prospects, state and private health services, local schools (state and private), shopping facilities, public transport, amenities and services, sports and social facilities, and communications. They may even arrange an 'orientation tour' to familiarise you with the area.

- ♦ **Other services** – Some agents provide advice and support (particularly for non-working spouses) before and after a move, counselling for domestic and personal problems, help in finding jobs for spouses and even marriage counselling (moving to another country puts a lot of strain on relationships).

Although you may consider a relocation agent's services expensive, particularly if you're footing the bill yourself, most people consider them money well spent, as they can save you considerable time, trouble and money, particularly if you have unusual requirements. Indeed, using an agency with experience and knowledge of the relevant area may be the only way of finding a suitable home, as many properties never 'come onto the market' but are sold through word of mouth. On the other hand, beware of agents who are trying to sell you a property; **you should never deal with anyone who is acting for both the seller and the buyer**.

If you just wish to look at properties for rent or sale in a particular area, you can make appointments to view properties through estate agents in the area where you plan to live and arrange your own trip to Ireland. However, you must make **absolutely certain** that agents know **exactly** what you're looking for, obtain property lists in advance and **check (and**

Valuers in the *Golden Pages*) deal in short and long-term rentals. Some agencies charge a registration fee, while others take a percentage of the rental fee from the landlord so that their service is effectively free (although you may find yourself paying a higher rent as a result).

In general, you should try to obtain a reference before signing up with an agency and, particularly if you're being asked to pay a registration fee, find out how likely the agency is to find you suitable accommodation; i.e. what sort of accommodation it has to offer and how frequently its lists are updated. You should also ask whether the agency is licensed (see **Estate Agents** on page 114), what services are provided and whether you're entitled to a refund if the agency fails to find you accommodation within a reasonable period. Also ensure that you receive a receipt for any money paid.

Standards of rented accommodation in Ireland are generally good. The Housing (Standards for Rented Houses) Regulations, 1993 specify certain minimum requirements regarding structural condition, the provision of sinks, toilets, baths/showers, cooking and food storage facilities, the safety of electrical and gas installations, the adequacy of heating, lighting and ventilation, and the maintenance of communal areas, so you shouldn't be offered anything less than habitable. Most rental properties, whether long or short-term, are let furnished; long-term unfurnished properties are particularly difficult to find.

A rental contract is necessary when renting any property in Ireland, whether long or short term (except for holiday lettings), and must contain certain information, including the address of the accommodation, the names and addresses of the landlord and letting agent, the tenant's name, the length of the tenancy, the rent and when and how it's to be paid, details of other charges that aren't included in the rental fee (e.g. telephone, electricity), the deposit to be paid and the conditions under which it may be returned, the basic rights of the tenant and the landlord, and an inventory of items included with the accommodation.

double-check) that any properties you're interested in are still available before travelling to Ireland to view them.

RENTING

Rented accommodation is the answer for people who don't want the trouble, expense and commitment involved in buying a house, or who are staying in Ireland less than around three years (when buying isn't usually practical or economical). Unlike most European countries, Ireland doesn't have a strong rental market, as families have traditionally preferred to buy rather than rent (over 80 per cent of Irish householders own their homes).

From the late 1990s to the summer of 2002, rents were constantly increasing, even in real terms, but they then suddenly started to fall and continued falling well into 2005. The tide is now starting to turn again, helped by the influx of migrants to Ireland. Demand for rental property in Dublin and other cities and large towns is high, so that properties aren't remaining on the market very long.

If you're looking for a long-term rental, e.g. three to six months, it's best not to rent unseen, but to rent a holiday apartment for a week or two to allow yourself time to look around for a longer term rental. Properties for rent are advertised in local newspapers and can also be found through property publications in many countries (see **Appendix A**).

Many estate agents in Ireland offer a long-term rental service, and a number of agencies (listed under *Auctioneers, Estate Agents &*

In accordance with the Housing (Rent Books) Regulations 1993, your landlord must provide you with a rent book or written lease that specifies the above, and all rental and other payments must be recorded in the rent book or provided in writing.

With all rental agreements it's important to establish under what circumstances your landlord may have access to the accommodation, and what maintenance or repair costs you're liable for. Also ensure that you have an emergency contact number for your landlord. If you require additional information about rented accommodation in Ireland or experience a problem with a landlord, you should contact a Threshold Advice Centre in Cork (☎ 021-427 8848), Dublin (☎ 01-678 6096) or Galway (☎ 091-563080, 🖥 www.threshold.ie). Threshold, a voluntary body funded by the Department of the Environment and local government, also publishes various information leaflets to help you find suitable accommodation and avoid the less reputable accommodation agencies.

Rent is usually payable monthly in advance, and an initial deposit of one or two months' rent (one or two weeks' rent for a weekly tenancy) is required as security. Whereas Irish landlords could until recently legally raise the rent by as much and as often as they liked, The Residential Tenancies Act, 2004 limits them to an annual rent review and prohibits them from charging rent that's above the 'market' rate. The Act also provides for a six-month 'probationary' period, at the end of which a landlord may terminate a rental agreement (given adequate grounds and subject to suitable notice); after this period, a tenant has the right to remain in the property for at least a further three-and-a-half years.

Nevertheless, if you sign a lease, you're committing yourself to renting for that period, so don't sign one unless you're happy with all the terms and conditions. If you want to leave before the lease expires, you will usually be liable for the rent for the remaining period. However, if you can arrange for someone else to take over the lease, the landlord may waive any charges.

The establishment of the Private Rented Tenancies Board (PRTB) in September 2004 has reduced the number of unresolved disputes between tenants and landlords.

> ## ☑ SURVIVAL TIP
> You may be eligible for tax relief on rent and should check with the Revenue Commissioners (see Chapter 14).

The maximum amount of tax relief is currently €400 per person if you're under 55 and €600 per person if you're over 55.

Long-term Rentals

The usual minimum 'long-term' rental period in Ireland is six months, although three-month lets can be found, and the maximum three years. Most rental contracts, however, are for 9 or 12 months.

Rental costs vary considerably according to the size (number of bedrooms) and quality of a property, its age and the facilities provided. However, the most significant factors influencing rents are the region, city and neighbourhood.

Not surprisingly, Dublin commands the highest rent, apartment prices starting at around €650 per month for a studio and rising to around €1,500 for a four-bedroom flat. For houses, prices start at around €600 per month, for a room within a house or a small house, rising to €4,000 per month for a large detached property. The cheapest places to rent near the capital are in western Co. Dublin, e.g. in Lucan and Blanchardstown. The price range in Cork is similar, whereas in Galway, Limerick and Waterford you can expect to pay at least €600 per month for a one-bedroom apartment or €800 for a two-bedroom apartment, and away from the major cities €800 per month can secure you a three-bedroom house.

Agencies that deal mostly in long-term rentals include Home Locators (☎ 01-679 5233, 🖥 www.homelocators.ie) in Dublin and Rose Property Services (☎ 021-429 3333, 🖥 www.rose-property.com) in Cork.

Short-term Rentals

For information about hotels, B&B, hostels and self-catering accommodation, see **Chapter 15**.

BUYING PROPERTY

Since the start of Ireland's economic boom, buying a house or apartment has been an excellent long-term investment, and in recent years even short-term gains have been astronomical – although, of course, you cannot realise these gains unless you move to a country where prices are lower. If you're staying for less than two or three years, you may be better off renting (see page 91) – by avoiding the costs involved in buying and selling a home. For those staying longer than three years, buying is normally the better option, particularly as paying a mortgage on a property (see **Mortgages** on page 278) is generally no more expensive than paying rent and you could make a healthy profit.

Most property in Ireland is sold by 'private treaty', which means that the sale is a private agreement between the vendor and the purchaser, although the vast majority of private treaty sales are handled by an estate agent (see page 114), who acts as an intermediary (and takes a healthy commission for bringing seller and buyer together and 'handling' the transaction).

If several people are interested in buying a property, the seller (or his agent) may suggest a closed or private tender, whereby written or oral bids must be submitted by a set time on a 'best and final offer' basis. In a private treaty sale, you must bear in mind that the purchase isn't secure until all the formal documentation has been signed and exchanged between buyer and seller; up to that point, the seller may still accept a higher offer, i.e. 'gazump' the buyer – a highly unethical practice 'imported' by the Irish from England and unfortunately becoming increasingly common.

Even some (less than scrupulous) estate agents continue to invite bids on a property after the vendor has verbally accepted an offer – and there's nothing you can do about it (at least, legally!). Members of the Irish Auctioneers' & Valuers' Institute (see **Estate Agents** on page 114) are obliged to cease marketing a property when a deposit has been paid, although this doesn't prevent you from being gazumped, as the vendor can still 'accept' a higher offer.

A few property sales (around 5 per cent and generally of the most expensive properties) are conducted at auction, the province of Galway enjoying the country's liveliest auction market. If you choose this method of buying, it's essential to take expert legal advice, as once your bid is accepted you're committed to a purchase!

Types of Property

New Homes

According to the Irish Homebuilders Association, Ireland has the greatest housing demand and consequently the highest rate of house building in Europe. But while demand has remained fairly constant since the late '90s, the supply of new homes has greatly increased since 2001. There were over 80,000 homes built in 2005 and a staggering 93,419 in 2007, though the prediction for 2008 was less than half that figure. Despite this high rate of construction, many people are purchasing plots and having their own homes built to order (see **Building a Home** below).

Most new properties in the main cities are apartments, whereas in rural areas the majority are detached bungalows, which are springing up almost everywhere you look. Prices of new properties vary considerably according to their type (new apartments are increasing in price much more slowly than houses – a 'mere' 7.5

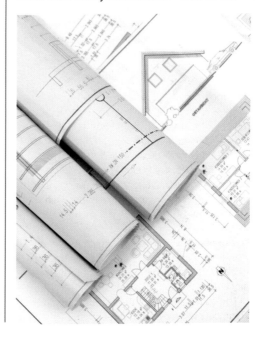

per cent compared with almost double that rate in the house market), location and quality, but it's often cheaper to buy a new home than an old property requiring modernisation, as the price is fixed; whereas the cost of renovation can soar way beyond original estimates (as many people have discovered to their cost). If required, a new property can usually be let immediately and modern homes have good resale potential. On the other hand, new homes may be smaller than older properties and have less land.

A major advantage of buying new is that you don't have to pay stamp duty if the property has a floor area of less than 125m^2 and you pay a reduced rate of stamp duty on a property over 125m^2, although first-time buyers pay no stamp duty, whether they buy new or old and buyers of new property incur connection charges for electricity, water and sometimes gas.

In certain cases, it's even be possible to obtain a grant from the Department of the Environment towards the cost of a new house, although grants are generally available only to older or disabled people, those on low incomes and those who want to buy or build in the Gaeltacht (the Irish-speaking area of Ireland, in the extreme west and north) – details of grants can be found on the government's 'Citizens Information Online' website (💻 www.citizensinformation.ie/categories). Most new properties are also covered by a ten-year warranty called a 'Homebond', which is transferable to a new owner if a property is sold within the warranty period.

The quality of new property in Ireland is variable, although all builders must conform to certain standards. The quality of a building and the materials used will be reflected in the price, so when comparing prices ensure that you're comparing similar quality. Cheaper properties aren't usually the best built, although there are exceptions. Most builders include in the basic price a standard bathroom suite and kitchen sink unit, a back boiler and radiators, twin sockets in each room, and floor and wall insulation. Some also include fitted wardrobes, an electric shower, ventilation units for bathroom and kitchen, and a fire alarm. Optional extras may include double glazing, oil or gas central heating and exterior paving. Items such as carpets, kitchen units and light fittings need to be installed separately by specialist contractors.

Resale 'New' Homes: Buying 'new' doesn't necessarily mean buying a brand new home of which you're the first occupant. There are many advantages to buying a modern resale home, which may include: an established development with a range of local services and facilities in place, individual design and style, fixtures and fittings and other extras included in the price, a mature garden, and possibly a larger plot. With a resale property, you can see exactly what you're getting

for your money, most 'teething troubles' will have been resolved, and the previous owners may have made improvements or added extras, such as a loft conversion or conservatory, which may not be fully reflected in the asking price.

Building a Home: If you want to be far from the madd(en)ing crowd, you can buy a plot and have a house built to your own design and specifications or to a standard design provided by a builder. Note, however, that building permission is quite difficult to obtain, particularly in the south-west, where it's strictly controlled by the local authorities. In general, building a home in Ireland, or anywhere else for that matter, isn't recommended for the timid. However, there are many excellent builders in Ireland who will build an individually designed house on your plot or sell you a plot and build a house chosen from a range of standard designs.

Some builders offer 'package deals' which include the land and the cost of building a home. However, it isn't always wise to buy a plot from the builder who's going to build your home, and you should shop around and compare separate land and building costs. If you do decide to buy a package deal from a builder, you should insist on separate contracts for the land and the building, and obtain the title deed for the land before signing a building contract. **You must take the same care when buying land as you would when buying a home.** It's particularly important to obtain a land registry map to certify that the plot has been properly registered and to ensure that the land has been approved for building and that the plot is large enough and suitable for the house you plan to build. You should also check whether there are restrictions on the type of building that may be constructed. In scenic areas, for example, there may be limits on a building's height.

Some plots are unsuitable for building as they're too steep or require prohibitively expensive foundations. Also check that there aren't any obstructions such as high-tension electricity lines, water pipes or rights of way that may restrict building. Note that the cost of providing services to a property in a remote rural area can be prohibitive and it must have a reliable water supply.

⚠ Caution

If applicable, always ensure that the purchase contract is dependent on obtaining the necessary planning permission and check for yourself that the correct planning permission is obtained (don't simply leave it to the builder). If planning permission is flawed, you may have to pay extra to improve the local infrastructure; the property may even need to be demolished!

When looking for an architect and builder it's best to obtain recommendations from local people you can trust, e.g. neighbours or friends. Note that estate agents and other professionals aren't always the best people to ask, as they may receive a commission. You're advised to use an architect who's a member of the Royal Institute of the Architects of Ireland (RIAI, ☎ 01-676 1703, 💻 www.riai.ie), which requires a high standard of qualification and competence. A comprehensive list of Irish architects and builders can be found on the Irish Building Industry website (💻 www.irishbuildingindustry.ie).

A good architect should be able to recommend a number of reliable builders, but you should also do your own research. There are few large building companies in Ireland, where most builders are more or less 'one-man bands'. When choosing a builder, make sure that he's registered with Homebond, the scheme set up by the Construction Industry Federation and operated by the National House Building Council (UK ☎ 0844 6331000, 💻 www.nhbc.co.uk – the NHBC is administered from England). If a builder is a member of the Irish Home Builders' Association (IHBA – part of the Irish Construction Industry Federation, ☎ 01-406-6000, 💻 www.cif.ie), he will automatically be Homebond registered.

Homebond provides three types of guarantee: against the loss of a deposit in the event of the builder going bust; against water and smoke damage for two years after completion; and against major structural defects for ten years after completion. Note that banks and building societies require Homebond registration on new houses.

If you want a house built exactly to your specifications, you will need to personally supervise it every step of the way or employ an architect to do so for you.

A building contract should include a detailed description of the proposed construction and a list of the materials to be used (with references to the architect's plans), the exact location of the building on the plot, the building and payment schedule, which must be made in stages according to building progress, a penalty clause for late completion, the retention of a percentage (typically 10 per cent for domestic work) of the building costs for up to

12 months as a guarantee against defects, and explanation of how any disputes will be settled.

Ensure that the contract includes all costs, including the architect's fees (unless contracted separately), landscaping (if applicable), all permits and licences, and the connection of utilities (electricity, gas, etc.) to the house, not just to the building site. VAT should be included; the only extra is usually the cost of the mains water connection. It's vital to have a contract checked by a solicitor, as they're often heavily biased in the builder's favour.

On completion of the work, your architect must complete an 'opinion on compliance' with Planning and Building Regulations. This document is required to sell a property, and banks and building societies also usually insist on it before providing a mortgage.

Resale Homes

Resale (or second-hand) properties represent good value and are often more attractive and interesting than new buildings. Another advantage of buying a resale property is that you can see exactly what you're getting for your money and will save on the cost of installing such things as telephone lines and connections to services. When buying a resale property in a development, you should ask the neighbours about any problems, planned developments and anything else that may affect your enjoyment of the property. Most residents are usually happy to tell you (unless of course they're trying to sell you their own property!)

Old Properties: If you want a property with abundant charm and character, a building for renovation or conversion, outbuildings or a large plot, you must usually buy an old property (i.e. at least 50 years old). However, old country homes such as farmhouses may be hard to find and you will need to go to small local estate agents rather than large national companies.

Occasionally, owners advertise their properties directly in a local paper or by simply putting a 'for sale' sign in the window. But, although you can save money by buying directly from an owner, particularly when he's forced to sell, you should always employ a solicitor to carry out the necessary checks; this is especially important with an old property. If

you're unsure of the true value of a property, you should obtain a professional valuation; before buying an old property, you should also have a full survey carried out.

Some old homes lack basic services such as electricity, a reliable water supply and sanitation. Because purchase prices are often low, many foreign buyers are deceived into believing that they're getting a wonderful bargain, without fully investigating renovation and modernisation costs (see **Renovation & Restoration** below).

Renovation & Restoration: Some old country or village homes are in need of restoration, renovation or modernisation. Before buying a property requiring restoration or modernisation, you should consider the alternatives. An extra few thousand euros spent on a purchase may represent much better value than spending the money on building work. It's often cheaper to buy a restored or partly restored property than a ruin in need of total restoration, unless you're going to do most of the work yourself – but many people who have restored a 'ruin' would never do it again and advise others against it.

Even if you intend to do most of the work yourself, you will still need to hire specialists for certain jobs. If you aren't into do-it-yourself in a big way, you may be better off buying a new or recently built property, as the cost of restoration can be double or even treble the price of the original property.

If you're planning to buy a property that needs restoration or renovation and aren't planning to do the work yourself, make sure you obtain a realistic estimate of the costs **before** signing a contract. Don't believe a vendor or agent who tells you that a roof or anything else can be repaired or patched up, but obtain expert advice from a local builder. Old buildings often need a damp-proof course, timber treatment, new windows and doors, a new roof or extensive roof repairs, a modern kitchen and bathroom, rewiring and central heating.

Electricity and mains water should preferably already be connected, as they can be expensive to extend to a property in a remote area. If a house doesn't have electricity or mains water, it's important to check the cost of extending these services to it. **Bear in mind**

only to run out of money before it's completed and be forced to sell at a loss.

Be sure to obtain evidence of your expenditure (i.e. quotations, invoices and receipts) so that you can offset some or all of the costs against tax.

Leasehold Properties

In Ireland, as in the UK, properties with common elements (whether buildings, amenities or land) shared with other properties are usually sold on a leasehold rather

that, when you come to sell a property you've restored (or had restored), its value may not reflect the cost and amount of work that went into it.

If modernisation of an old building involves making external alterations, such as building an extension or installing larger windows or new doorways, you may need permission from your local planning authority, and you should ensure that a conditional clause is included in the contract stating that the purchase is dependent on obtaining permission.

If you aren't on the spot and able to supervise work, you should hire a 'clerk of works' such as an architect to oversee a large job, or it could drag on for months or be left half-finished. This will add around 10 per cent to the total bill, but it's usually worth every penny. Be extremely careful whom you employ if you have work done in your absence, and ensure that your instructions are accurate in every detail. It isn't unusual for foreign owners to receive huge bills for work done in their absence that shouldn't have been done at all!

As a rough guide, you should expect the cost of totally renovating an old 'habitable' building to be at least equal to its purchase price and possibly much more. Always keep an eye on your budget (which will inevitably be at least 50 per cent below what you actually spend) and don't be in too much of a hurry. Some people take many years to restore a home, particularly when they're doing most of the work themselves. It isn't unknown for buyers to embark on a grandiose renovation scheme,

than freehold basis. Leasehold property owners also own a share of the common elements of a building or development, including foyers, hallways, passages, lifts, patios, gardens, roads, and leisure and sports facilities (such as a gymnasium or tennis court). This means that you will become part of a management company responsible for the insurance and upkeep of the common elements of the property. Note that being part of a management company is usually to your advantage, in that you have some control over expenditure on the property, rather than it being determined ad hoc by an absentee landlord.

When buying a leasehold property, however, you should check whether the company has a healthy reserve or 'sink fund' and whether any major expenditure (e.g. a new roof) is imminent. Otherwise, you could find yourself being asked for several thousand euros shortly after moving in. When you sell a leasehold property, you transfer your membership of the management company to the buyer.

When considering buying a leasehold property, the first thing you should do is ascertain the length of the lease, i.e. how many years it has left to run. If it's a new apartment, this may be as many as 9,999 years, in which case you needn't worry too much about outliving your lease! However, if there are only, say, 80 years left, you should take into account that, if you resell the property in 10 or 20 years, it may be difficult to find a buyer (note that a lease cannot be extended).

On the other hand, once the lease expires, the lessee acquires the right to purchase the freehold, in which case a short lease may be attractive (although this right applies only to owner-occupiers, not to investors). The Landlord and Tenant Act makes it illegal to purchase a freehold property and resell part of it on a leasehold basis.

The advantages of owning a leasehold property may include increased security (all new apartments must be fitted with full fire alarm systems and most have individual intercom-controlled access), a range of communal facilities, community living with frequent social contacts and the companionship of close neighbours, no garden maintenance, and fewer of the responsibilities of home ownership.

The disadvantages of leasehold properties can include excessively high management fees, restrictive rules and regulations, a confining living and social environment and possible lack of privacy, noisy neighbours (particularly if neighbouring properties are rented to holidaymakers), limited living and storage space, expensive parking (or insufficient off-road parking), and acrimonious management meetings. Before buying a leasehold property, you should talk to current owners to ascertain whether any or all of these disadvantages will apply!

Management fees are usually billed annually and are calculated according to each owner's share of the development or apartment building (i.e. the size of each apartment or unit), rather than whether they're temporary or permanent residents. Fees vary enormously according to the quality of the development, the extent of the grounds, the facilities provided, and the age and condition of the property. You may pay as little as €300 per year, but the average annual management fee is around twice as much. If the fee is very low, you should check whether you will be liable for extra charges for any major repairs that need to be done.

☑ SURVIVAL TIP

If you're buying an apartment from a previous owner, always ask to see a copy of the management fees for previous years.

Finding a Property

There are many ways of finding homes for sale; the main methods are listed below:

◆ Newspapers and magazines, including the Thursday edition of the *Irish Times* and Friday's *Independent*, the *Irish Property Buyer* magazine, national newspapers in your home country (if you're looking for an expensive property), local magazines, papers and news sheets (which may have private property advertisements), property magazines published by Irish estate agents, and general retail publications (e.g. *Daltons Weekly* and *Exchange & Mart* in the UK);

◆ Property exhibitions (see **Appendix A**).

◆ The internet, where there are many sites devoted to Irish property, including those run by Irish and foreign property agents (see **Appendix C**).

◆ Visiting an area. Many properties are sold privately and the only way to find out about them is to tour the area you're interested in, looking for 'FOR SALE' signs and asking local residents or officials if they know of properties for sale.

◆ Developers, some of whom sell direct, others via agents in Ireland or abroad.

◆ Estate agents (see page-114).

Make sure you avoid national holidays when visiting Ireland on a house hunting trip. When you are house hunting remember to take a calculator (to work out how few euros you will get for your money), a mobile phone that works in Ireland (and a charger and plug adapter), a camera and/or video camera, and instructions for remotely accessing your home answer phone, as well as a notepad, maps and contact numbers.

Property Prices

Despite the current popularity of Ireland as a place to live and work and the recent rise in property prices, a slice of the quiet life still needn't cost the earth, although the idyllic dream of a traditional thatched cottage on a bit of land overlooking the sea for €25,000 is very much a thing of the (distant) past and you must add a nought and then some to bring yourself up to date. Small two-bedroom rural properties start at around €200,000 and detached three-bedroom houses at around €260,000. However, if you're after a property in one of the fashionable regions (such as the south-west) or in Dublin, where there's strong demand from foreign buyers, you can expect to pay a premium of between 50 and 500 per cent.

Until 2007, Irish property prices had risen every year for 38 years except in 1986-87. Ireland, of course, has not been the only country to experience a fall in property prices in 2007-08 – a worldwide phenomenon sparked by the US 'sub-prime' mortgage lending crisis. So far (to mid-2008) prices have fallen by around 7.5 per cent, i.e. back to early 2006 levels. According to the Economic & Social Research Institute (ESRI), property was overvalued by some 12.5 per cent at the end of 2007 and prices should fall by around 6.3 per cent in 2008 and a further 1.5 per cent in 2009.

From the mid-'90s there was a marked swing towards the European practice of apartment living, but the popularity of apartments has waned in recent years – so much so that prices fell annually between 2000 and 2003 and only in 2004 began to rise again – which means that apartments are one of the few 'bargains' left in Ireland. Nevertheless, in prime areas new apartments are much in demand; there have been reports of developments being snapped up within half an hour of 'release'!

Apart from obvious factors such as size, quality and   land area, the most

important consideration influencing the price of a house is its location. Properties in the cities, particularly in and around Dublin and in Galway and Cork, can cost up to five times as much as equivalent properties in rural parts. There's also a considerable price variation between sought-after west coast areas such as County Kerry and less popular inland counties.

Average property prices aren't, of course, necessarily an accurate indication of the relative values of specific properties or even property types in different areas (there may be a greater number of cheaper or more expensive houses in one area than another, which skew the overall statistics), but they give some idea of the variation in values across the country.

For details of prices in different regions of Ireland, see **Regions** on page 102.

The quality of properties obviously varies considerably in respect of materials, fixtures and fittings, and workmanship. You should therefore compare at least half a dozen properties in order to get a good idea of their relative values.

When property is advertised in Ireland, the number of rooms is usually stated, but the floor area isn't, although the size of the plot or garden is generally specified. The dimensions of individual rooms are given only in the agent's details. If you're in any doubt about the size of rooms you should measure them yourself, rather than rely on the measurements provided by the vendor or agent, who may 'cheat' by measuring into bay windows, alcoves and doorways.

Fees

Various fees are payable when buying a property in Ireland, which usually add a minimum of 5 per cent to the purchase price. The fees payable when buying a property in Ireland include some or all of the following. Always ensure you know exactly what the total fees will be before signing a contract.

Selling Agent's Fees

These are normally 'included' in the property price (see page 98).

Stamp Duty

Stamp duty is a tax on the purchase deed payable by the buyer when the sale is closed and traditionally a fee for 'stamping' the deed – now a government method of raising lots of money without doing anything at all! Stamp duty, when applicable, is the main fee involved when buying a home in Ireland, but first-time buyers who are owner-occupiers pay no stamp duty (and there are partial exemptions for certain transfers between family members). The full rates of stamp duty, which applies equally to 'investors' (i.e. non-owner-occupiers) and owner-occupiers, were revised in December 2007 (changes described by Ernst & Young as 'tinkering with an antiquated tax') and are now as follows:

Stamp Duty Rates (2008)	
Value of Property	**Rate**
Up to €125,000	0%
€125,000 to €1m	7%
Over €1m	9%

This means that on an 'average' property costing €350,000, you will pay a massive €14,000 in stamp duty – unless you're a first-time buyer.

Note that the cost of any fixtures and fittings (e.g. carpets and curtains) included in a purchase is taken into account when calculating the stamp duty due. There's also a mortgage deed stamp duty of €1 per €1,000 on mortgages above €254,000 – e.g. €246 for a €500,000 mortgage.

Legal Fees

Solicitors' fees for conveyance aren't subject to a fixed scale of charges and you must agree them in writing in advance. According to the Incorporated Law Society of Ireland you should expect to pay between 1 and 1.5 per cent of the property price (a percentage which hasn't changed over the years despite soaring property prices – Irish solicitors must be rubbing their hands in glee!). Legal fees are exclusive of 'disbursements' (expenses in plain English) and are subject to VAT at 20 per cent.

Although engaging a solicitor and paying legal fees is optional, it's highly recommended.

Deed Registration Fee

Your solicitor will pass on to you the charges relating to registration of the title deed to a property. There are two kinds of land in Ireland – registered and unregistered – and roughly equal amounts of each, although rural land is more likely to be registered. Registered land is recorded at the land registry, whose register provides proof of ownership. In the case of unregistered land, title documents are lodged with the registry of deeds.

The cost of registering a deed of purchase with the registry of deeds is €44 (if you have a mortgage, this must also be registered, which doubles the cost). The land registry charges from €380 (for a property valued at less than €254,000) to €634 (for a property costing over €381,000), plus a 'folio opening fee' of €66 if the property is new. A number of additional registration-related fees will be added to your bill, for which you should allow at least €300; details can be found on the land registry website (💻 www.landregistry.ie).

Survey or Valuation Fee

A 'valuation report' is usually a minimum requirement of mortgage lenders and involves a cursory appraisal of a property's value (sometimes disconcertingly referred to as a 'drive-by' valuation), usually costing between around €100 and €150, depending on the lender and the property's value, although it may be free for mortgages below a certain percentage of a property's value.

Some lenders insist on a 'full valuation' (which presumably requires the valuer to stop his car and actually inspect the property) where the mortgage requested is over a certain percentage of the property's value (e.g. 75 per cent); this costs between €125 and €200. The valuer's travelling expenses are sometimes added to the bill. If the mortgage is refused, the valuation fee is refunded.

If you employ a surveyor to inspect a building or plot before you offer to buy it (which is strongly advised), the fee will depend on the kind of survey, any special requirements (e.g. checking the foundations of an old building) and the value of the property. The cost of a full structural survey is generally around €250 in addition to the valuation report fee, but if you use the same firm for both, you may be able to negotiate a reduced rate. A mortgage lender may insist on a structural report if a property is over 100 years old.

Utility Connection Fees

These apply only to new or possibly very old properties.

Mortgage Costs

These may include an application fee, mortgage indemnity fee (on loans above a certain percentage of the purchase price), and life assurance or a mortgage protection policy (see page 281).

Other Costs

In addition to the above, you budget for annual 'running' costs, such as rent or mortgage payments, utilities, building and contents insurance, maintenance, ground rent (leasehold properties only and usually a nominal sum such as €10 per year or even zero) and a management fee (apartments only – normally around €750 per year). If you're letting a property, you should also allow for property management fees, income tax on rental income and possibly a tax consultant's fees. There are no local authority charges, 'rates' or 'poll taxes' for residential property in Ireland.

Location

Apart from obvious considerations such as work, schools, health services, shops, leisure, public transport, parking and crime, you may want to consider the likelihood of a property being affected by radon.

Radon

Radon is a naturally occurring radioactive gas formed underground by the radioactive decay of uranium, which is present in small quantities in rocks and soils and is particularly prevalent in Ireland. It's estimated that more than half of the radiation dose received by the average person in Ireland is due to radon. For the majority of people, the radiation received from radon isn't high enough to be a cause for concern. Radon surfacing in the open air

is quickly diluted to harmless concentrations. However, when it enters an enclosed space, such as a house, it can sometimes build up to dangerous concentrations. The acceptable limit for radon concentration (known as the 'reference level') is 200 becquerels per m^3 of air ($200Bq/m^3$).

It has been shown that prolonged exposure to concentrations of radon above this level increases the chance of contracting lung cancer; in a minority of homes and other buildings in Ireland with very high radon levels, there's a significant health risk for occupants. To put this risk into perspective: whereas the average person in Ireland has a 3 per cent risk of contracting fatal lung cancer, someone living in a building which is above the reference level may have a 4 or 5 per cent risk of the same fate. Building regulations require all new houses to have a radon 'sump' and those in high risk areas a radon 'barrier'.

Recognising the possible danger of radon, the government has undertaken a survey of the whole country, which identifies the areas of greatest risk. There are high risk areas in most parts of the country, but Counties Carlow and Sligo have more such areas than other parts of the country. A copy of the survey and a leaflet entitled *Radon Radiation in Homes* can be obtained free of charge from the Radiological Protection Institute of Ireland (RPII, ☎ 01-269 7766; ⌨ www.rpii.ie).

There are three important points to bear in mind when considering the possible effects of radon gas on your choice of property:

♦ The health danger of high radon levels is small, particularly if you're only spending short periods in your Irish home.

- Radon cannot be seen or smelt, but it can easily be detected by special equipment. The necessary equipment can be hired from the RPII for €50. However, readings should be spread over at least three months, so it may not be possible to obtain a reliable measurement before you buy a property.

- Even if a property is found to contain a high level of radon gas, there are ways of reducing it to a safer level. Various measures that can be taken are outlined in two guides: *Understanding Radon Remediation – A Householders* [sic] *Guide*, published by the RPII, and *Radon in Buildings – Corrective Options*, available from Government Publications (☎ 01-679 3515).

REGIONS

Ireland comprises 26 counties divided between four provinces (or regions), Connacht, Leinster, Munster and Ulster, each of which has particular geographical features and a distinct identity forged in history and enshrined in local laws and customs. The provinces and counties are described below. See also **Appendix E**.

Connacht

In the north-west of Ireland is the province of Connacht (or Connaught), encompassing 21 per cent of the Republic and comprising Counties Galway, Leitrim, Mayo, Roscommon and Sligo. Once regarded as a wilderness and the scene of the worst suffering during the potato famine of the 1840s, the west of Connacht is a get-away-from-it-all area of rugged mountains, craggy cliffs, lakes and valleys, where little seems to have changed in centuries and many of the people habitually speak Irish Gaelic. The inland part of the province, bounded by the ubiquitous Shannon river, is less striking, consisting of tidy fields and stone walls.

Galway

County Galway, the second-largest county in Ireland, is full of contrasts – flat in the south, alternately mountainous and boggy in the north. Traditionally referred to as the 'real Ireland',  because its population is the least anglicised (half of its inhabitants still speak Gaelic as their first language), Galway is the centre of the *Gaeltacht* (Irish-speaking area), where people are encouraged by government grants to go and live. The Industrial Development Authority (IDA) has even managed to attract industrial businesses to the area.

Efforts to preserve the language are supported by Galway-based Raidió na Gaeltachta and the new national Irish-language newspaper, *Foinse*, as well as by summer colleges where students from all parts of Ireland (and abroad) study Gaelic and learn traditional *céilí* dancing.

Galway city: Connacht's capital, Galway city, is Ireland's fourth-largest city, with a population of some 57,000 – a busy place that has benefited from tourism and European Union (EU) subsidies to such an extent that it's now one of Europe's fastest growing cities. Galway has its origins in the 13th century, when it had strong commercial ties with Spain (the so-called Spanish Arch remains to this day) and tradition has it that Christopher Columbus said a prayer at St Nicholas's Collegiate Church in Galway before setting out to 'discover America'. In the 16th and 17th centuries, the city's 'fat cats' traded skins for Spanish wine.

Today its young population, combined with 10,000 or more students from University College and Galway's many other educational establishments, make the city a lively, cosmopolitan place. It's famous for its festivals, notably the Galway Races and Oyster Festival, and manages to retain a friendly, intimate atmosphere. Galway city is also the business capital of the west, offering some of the best conference facilities in Ireland.

Connemara & the Aran Islands: The city is the gateway to the strikingly beautiful Connemara, a wonderland of lakes and mountains and now a national park. Ferries provide a year-round link to the Aran (*Árainn*) islands, as does the world's shortest scheduled air service, Aer Arann's daily six-minute flights from Galway airport. Surprisingly, there are airfields on all three main islands, the smallest of which, Inisheer (*Inis Oírr* in Gaelic, meaning South Island), measures just 3km by 4km (2 by 3mi).

Irish Gaelic is the first language on the islands, where ancient traditions co-exist with a more modern lifestyle. The largest island, Inishmore (*Inis Mór*, Big Island) is 12km (7mi) long and has a population of 900, while the middle island of Inishmaan (*Inis Meáin*, Middle Island) is said to be one of the most unspoilt places in the world: apart from one of Europe's most important pre-historic monuments (the cliff fort at Dun Aengus), you will find only one pub and no bank – except once a month, when the bank pays the island a flying visit!

Leitrim

Leitrim (pronounced 'lee-trim') is a quiet county, which seems to have been forgotten by the rest of Ireland. It stretches from the sea to the island's centre, with all the varied landscapes that implies. Carrick-on-Shannon in the south-west of the county claims to be the loveliest town on the Shannon and is the principal base for cruising Ireland's most famous river. It's

also a picturesque and lively place with plenty of visitor attractions.

Lough Allen is the first great lake on the Shannon and has recently been linked to the Shannon Navigation by the restoration of the Lough Allen Canal. Along with neighbouring County Mayo and County Cavan (in Ulster), Leitrim is an angler's paradise with literally hundreds of lakes offering unrestricted access.

Mayo

Even wilder than Galway, although no longer remote since the opening of Knock (or Horan) International Airport in 1986, is the neighbouring county of Mayo, where towering cliffs alternate with sandy inlets and the countryside is littered with ancient monuments. It's one of Ireland's loveliest counties and today earns most of its income from tourism, although foreign companies have been encouraged to set up factories here. The so-called Barony of Erris (Mayo's *Gaeltacht* area) incorporates Europe's largest area of bog, barely inhabited, but teeming with wildlife. Mayo also boasts the earliest known land enclosure in the world, known as Ceide Fields.

The county is an angler's paradise, with some of the best salmon, brown trout and sea fishing in Europe, and it boasts excellent facilities for climbing, hill walking and golf. Ten of Mayo's beaches have been awarded EU Blue Flags for cleanliness, four of which can be found on the island of Achill (Ireland's largest), joined to the Corraun Peninsula by a bridge. Achill is 22km (14mi) long and 19km (12mi) wide with a population of 3,000, while Clare Island (just to the south) is home to just 150 people and can be reached only by ferry.

The people of Mayo are considered by some to be the 'purest' Irish and the county lays claim to some celebrated inhabitants, such as Michael Davitt (founder of the Land League in 1879, the biggest mass movement in modern Irish history), Mary Robinson (the first female President of Ireland) and Captain Charles Boycott, whose name has passed into the English language. Mayo's administrative capital is Castlebar, a market town of 6,000 people, which is in every way the centre of the county. Its second-largest town is Ballina in the north, with just 7,000 inhabitants.

The coastal town of Westport, one of Ireland's most popular resorts, is unusual in that it's a 'planned' town. The nearby Croagh Patrick mountain (known locally as The Reek) isn't just a famous landmark but a place of pilgrimage; Saint Patrick is reputed to have spent 44 days and nights praying and fasting on its slopes in 441AD and every July some 20,000 faithful spend two or more hours climbing the 760m/2,500ft high mountain, many in bare feet and some on their knees, to atone for their sins and earn a place in heaven.

The Marian Shrine in the village of Knock, where in 1879 20 villagers claimed to have seen the Virgin Mary, St Joseph and St John, attracts more than 1.5m pilgrims from throughout the world each year and has been visited by the late Mother Teresa and Pope John Paul. Ireland's largest church, the Basilica of Our Lady, Queen of Ireland, was built in 1976 to accommodate 12,000 people; and in 1986, Knock International Airport was opened to handle the vast influx of visitors (there are daily scheduled flights to and from the UK, as well as charter flights from Switzerland and Germany during the summer). In contrast, the resident population is sparse – little over 100,000 in the whole county.

Roscommon

Inland is County Roscommon, the only county in Connacht without a coastline. Rich farmland in the centre gives way to bog at its edges, while lakes and rivers abound. Lough Key Forest Park near Carrick-on-Shannon is Ireland's largest public forest, where herds of deer are among the abundant wildlife. The population of just 50,000 is almost entirely rural, and the small town of Roscommon – which recently experienced a 'boost' thanks to the opening of a Dunnes department store – is the largest in the county.

Sligo

The gentle, civilised landscape of County Sligo (pronounced 'sly-go'), to the north-west, is broken spectacularly by the Ben Bulben and Knocknarea mountains. Sligo is noted for its archaeological remains and its music, traditionally played on the violin or 'fiddle'. It's also W. B. Yeats' county, and most of the places that inspired his poetry remain unspoilt. Colourful Sligo town, the largest town in north-west Ireland and its unofficial capital, is a busy and prosperous place famous for its Yeats Summer School.

Leinster

The province of Leinster covers east and south-east Ireland. Although it includes the greatest number of counties (Carlow, Dublin, Kildare, Kilkenny, Laois, Longford, Louth, Meath, Offaly, Westmeath, Wexford and Wicklow), it's only the third-largest province, covering around 23 per cent of the Republic. With slightly more sunshine and less rain than the rest of Ireland, although just as green, Leinster is a pleasant place to live. It's an area of tranquil rivers and soft hills contrasting with bogs and mountains. Outside County Dublin (with its 1m inhabitants) the province is largely rural and has many attractions. The coastline boasts long, sandy beaches and picturesque towns such as Wexford and Kilkenny.

Leinster also has more than its fair share of castles, monasteries, mansions and ancient monuments, and has always enjoyed a reputation for wealth thanks to its fertile soil.

Carlow

Carlow is the second-smallest county in Ireland and is mostly flat, although it borders mountains to the south-east and north-east. It's particularly unspoilt, being far enough from Dublin to escape the notice of commuters, and having also managed to avoid the indiscriminate construction of bungalows ('bungalow blight'), which are so often a blot on the landscape of the western counties. The rivers Barrow and Slaney are excellent angling waters, and the county is a good place for pony-trekking and golf.

Carlow is known as the Celtic Centre of Ireland, but contains many Druid and early Christian as well as Celtic relics. Most of its few inhabitants are farmers or workers at the sugar-beet factory in historic Carlow town, although multinationals including Braun have established factories nearby, and the town's new Fairgreen Shopping Centre is attracting big-name retailers such as Argos, Next and River Island.

Dublin

County Dublin is dominated by the city of Dublin (*Baile Átha Cliath* in Irish, meaning 'the town at the ford of the hurdles'), whose rapid growth over the last 25 years has affected the whole county. The county is divided into four regions: Finghal to the north of the city, Dun Laoghaire Rathdown to the south-east, South Dublin to the south-west and Dublin city itself.

Covering an area of 448km² (173mi²), Finghal is the fastest growing region in County Dublin, and includes several burgeoning city suburbs as well as Dublin airport and the industrial area of Balbriggan. On the other hand, Finghal boasts some magnificent coastline, with picturesque seaside villages such as Loughshinny, Rush and Skerries, Finghal's 'jewel'. Inland there are tranquil river valleys and unspoilt villages such as Ballyboughal, Garristown, Naul and Oldtown, as well as some 30 golf courses.

The Howth peninsula (just a few minutes from the capital) is a popular centre for sailing and other watersports, and provides spectacular views of Dublin Bay. Just to the north are the two-mile long 'Velvet Strand' of Portmarnock and the heritage town of Malahide with its marina and 14th-century castle. One of the newest and largest shopping centres in the Dublin region is at Blanchardstown, just west of the city.

On the opposite side of Dublin city, Dun Laoghaire Rathdown also has a beautiful

stretch of coastline and some attractive seaside resorts. One of these is Dun Laoghaire itself (pronounced 'dun leary'), one of the main ports for ferries from Britain and the site of a vast new shopping centre. Nearby Blackrock is known for its traditional weekend market.

Dalkey and Killiney, just south of Dun Laoghaire, have become favourite locations for the rich and famous, reputedly including such luminaries as Chris de Burgh, Nigel Mansell, Damon Hill, Lisa Stansfield, Gloria Hunniford, Neil Jordan and Enya – so much so that the area has recently earned the nickname 'Bel Eire'.

Inland among the foothills of the Wicklow Mountains (also referred to as the Dublin Mountains) are several scenic areas such as Marlay Park, the starting point for walks along the Wicklow Way. Ireland's highest pub, Johnnie Fox's, renowned for its seafood and unique atmosphere, is here (if you can find it!).

South Dublin boasts 1,400 hectares (3,360 acres) of fine parks, where there are facilities for golf, riding, angling and watersports. King John's Bridge in Lucan's Griffeen Valley Park is claimed to be Ireland's oldest. The Griffeen River is a tributary of the better known Liffey, which holds a special place in the hearts of Dubliners. The

Liffey Valley, which separates South Dublin from Finghal, has recently been developed into an 'amenity' offering a variety of recreational facilities.

South Dublin also has a vast, modern shopping centre (The Square in Tallaght), as well as a wealth of more traditional shops in villages such as Clondalkin, Lucan, Newcastle, Rathcoole, Rathfarnham, Saggart and Tallaght itself. South Dublin's position, on the main road and rail routes westward out of the capital and equidistant from Dublin airport and the seaports of Dun Laoghaire and the city, has made it an important centre for conferences and business meetings. The number of hotels in the area, particularly at the cheaper end of the market, is constantly increasing.

Dublin city: Ireland's capital, Dublin city is more than five times the size of any other city in the country and is generally regarded as a separate province in itself. Sometimes referred to as 'dear dirty Dublin' by the Irish themselves, the city is certainly no Paris or Prague and suffered particularly in the '70s from careless town planning.

Its Millennium Celebrations (not to be confused with those for the year 2000) in 1988 prompted a good deal of renovation, as did its selection as European City of Culture three years later. Unfortunately, there are still thoughtless developments such as the recent construction of a 'virtual' motorway through the city centre. However, Dublin isn't about architecture, but atmosphere and there's no shortage of that, although the relaxed reputation of the many bars is somewhat tempered by the conspicuous presence of bouncers at almost every door.

Kildare

County Kildare is one of Ireland's most densely populated counties (relatively speaking), being within easy commuting distance of Dublin. Towns such as Kildare, Naas and Newbridge (all lying near the M7 motorway) have recently experienced growth of up to 600 new homes

a year, and their population is growing annually at almost 10 per cent (half of Newbridge's property sales are to Dubliners), while villages like Celbridge and Leixlip have been all but swallowed by the rapidly expanding capital. In fact, Collinstown Industrial Park near Leixlip, where just 15 years ago there were stud farms and potato fields, is now Ireland's 'silicon valley', home to Intel Ireland (the European subsidiary of one of America's largest microchip producers), Hewlett Packard and IBM, among other giant corporations.

Millions of euros have recently been spent on improvements to the county's roads – bypasses around Kildare and Monasterevin have opened, and there's a new motorway (the M7) linking Naas and Portlaoise – and Iarnrod Eireann is spending €350m on improving commuter rail links between Kildare town and Dublin. Newbridge's new Whitewater shopping centre is complete, and two retail parks are currently under construction in Naas, whose long-planned €45m shopping centre has finally been given the go-ahead.

None the less, there's still plenty of countryside to be enjoyed in County Kildare. The river Barrow, for example, provides good fishing and attractive cruising, and there are lovely drives and walks (and even barge trips) along the Grand and Royal Canals, which meet near Robertstown on their way to Dublin and the sea. Even the rather unattractive town of Kildare lies on the edge of the famous Curragh, a 2,000-hectare (5,000-acre) plain where some of the world's best racehorses are bred and trained. The National Stud and Horse Museum is at Tully, adjacent to the famous Japanese Gardens.

Kilkenny

To the west of Carlow is Kilkenny, one of the most 'English' counties of Ireland, with its neat villages and fields. It's a prosperous agricultural area noted for its craftsmen, particularly in Kilkenny city, Ireland's mediaeval capital and one of its architecturally most interesting towns. If Carlow is the Celtic Centre of Ireland, Kilkenny claims to be its 'hospitable heart': an abundance of hotels, restaurants, pubs, festivals and warm-hearted people make Kilkenny an excellent place for relaxation and enjoyment (but then the same could be said for most of Ireland!). Kilkenny town is currently witnessing a €100m development of shops, car parks, offices, restaurants, bars, a hotel and residential accommodation.

Laois

The furthest south of this group of counties is Laois, a rural area divided by the N7 Dublin/Limerick road. Laois is the latest county to become a commuter area for Dublin, its (so far) affordable homes attracting buyers from the capital. Its only proper town, Portlaoise, has been bypassed by one of the few stretches of motorway outside the capital. The major employer in this part of Ireland is the Irish turf development authority, Bord na Mona, which provides work for some 5,000 people.

Longford

The counties of Longford, Westmeath, Offaly, and Laois, in the centre of Ireland, are flat and wet, being covered with lakes and bogs. They tend to be ignored by visitors passing through on their way from Dublin to the south and west, and as a result are generally quiet, though not without interest. Longford is a peaceful and picturesque county bordering Lough Ree, one of the great lakes on the Shannon. It has many pretty villages including Ardagh, Lanesborough and Newtowncashel. Nevertheless, as every square metre of the county is subject to the Rural Renewal Scheme, development – both residential and commercial – is proceeding apace. The presence in Longford town of Abbott Laboratories has fuelled the local property market.

Louth & Meath

Louth and Meath, the most northerly counties in Leinster, are predominantly farmland, but Louth, Ireland's smallest county, has a wild side and the Cooley Peninsula near the Northern Ireland is one

Louth

of the most beautiful and unspoilt places in the whole country. The coastal town of Dundalk is the county capital and contains a number of fine 15th-century buildings, while nearby Carlingford has even earlier remains including a castle and mint. Ancient relics are concealed in the rich pastures of Meath (the seat of the ancient kings of Ireland is said to be on Tara Hill, from where you can see seven counties), but the county also boasts the popular seaside resorts of Bettystown, Clogherhead and Laytown, all part of a 'coastal resort' scheme.

Meath's principal town,Drogheda, is a colourful place with medieval origins, while Dundalk in County Louth is a site of industrial development, where Rank Xerox employs over 2,000 people.

Meath

Both towns are currently undergoing transformations, with the construction of huge new shopping centres to meet the demand from the growing population.

Both counties have experienced a huge increase in population in recent years, as people with jobs in Dublin have settled there and commute to the capital. Particularly high growth has been experienced by Ashbourne, Dunboyne, Dunshaughlin and Navan, as well as Drogheda and Dundalk, where 'idyllic country cottages' are now virtually impossible to find.

Offaly

Offaly to the south, boasts the internationally famous monastic site at Clonmacnoise (one of Ireland's holiest places), the Slieve Bloom mountains with their cascading streams and waterfalls, the restored 18th-century town of Birr (with the world's tallest box hedges!), and one of the Shannon's main boating centres at Banagher. The principal town of Tullamore is another cruising base, but on the Grand Canal rather than the River Shannon (it's also home to a famous Irish whiskey).

Westmeath

Westmeath is similarly tranquil, although watersports enthusiasts are attracted to its chain of small lakes (Derravaragh, Ennel, Lene and Owel) and the county is starting to attract Dublin commuters unable to afford homes nearer to the capital – resulting in both residential and retail development. Westmeath is particularly rich in places of interest such as Edgeworthstown House, 17th-century Fore Abbey and Tullynally Castle (one of the 'Seven Wonders of Fore'), Delvin Castle and Castlepollard, the largest castellated house in Ireland.

The historic town of Athlone, once one of the few crossing points on the Shannon, is now the largest town on the river, a busy and prosperous place – whose town centre has recently undergone a €150m redevelopment, making it one of the largest retail centres in the Midlands – and a popular base for pleasure cruisers.

The county town of Mullingar ('capital of the lakes'), a thriving business and industrial centre on the Royal Canal, is also undergoing development, costing €100m, which will see the construction of two underground car parks, a 150-bed hotel and two major department stores.

Glasson, known as the village of the roses, is in the heart of 'Goldsmith Country', where Oliver Goldsmith, one of Ireland's most famous poets, lived in the 18th century. Kinnegad, in the extreme east of the county, lies at the junction of the main roads from Galway and Sligo to Dublin, and is the centre of *An Boreen Bradach*, a walker's paradise.

Wexford

At the south-eastern tip of Ireland is County Wexford, the warmest and driest place in the country. In fact many Irish families spend their summer holidays there in preference to Spain! Wexford has some 200km (124mi) of coastline and numerous unspoiled sandy beaches, including the magnificent Curracloe Beach (which doubled as the scene of the Normandy landings in Steven Spielberg's film *Saving Private Ryan*). Wexford is one of the world's most important wild bird sanctuaries, visited by flocks migrating to and from the Arctic. Known as the 'model county', Wexford also offers heritage parks and museums, golf courses and race tracks (greyhounds as well as horses), while the Blackstairs Mountains in the north-west of the county are a popular hiking area.

Wexford is the closest point to Wales and in the past has been the landing place of many a foreign invasion, while Rosslare Harbour is a major ferry port for modern 'invaders' from the UK and France. Nearby Wexford town is among the most atmospheric and historically interesting places in Ireland and is internationally famous for its annual Opera Festival in October.

Although distant from the capital, the county is proving particularly attractive to Dubliners, who are finding that they can sell a relatively modest property in the capital and buy a similar one in Wexford for half as much, and to those who simply cannot afford (or even find) suitable properties nearer the city. Gorey, in particular, has in recent years become a favourite commuter 'dormitory', and construction of the Arklow/Gorey bypass, which was finished in September 2007 (ahead of schedule!), has reduced traffic in the town considerably.

Wicklow

County Wicklow, to the north, is another quintessentially Irish county, yet it's within half an hour's drive of Dublin. City dwellers call it the 'garden of Ireland', although it may be more accurately described as the 'playground of Dublin'. Many of the growing population of 100,000 work in the capital and commute from towns such as Greystones and Blessington, where the Liffey Valley was flooded in 1940 to create the Blessington Lakes. Further south, on the other hand, farming is widespread and the Wicklow Mountains are among the most impressive in Ireland (the film *Braveheart*, supposedly set in Scotland, was filmed here).

The sixth-century monastic complex at Glendalough, one of Ireland's greatest national monuments (although far from being one of its most attractive or interesting sites), nestles in the heart of the mountains at the spectacular Wicklow Gap, and there are other fascinating places nearby such as the Devil's Glen Forest Park, wild and beautiful Glenmalure, the 'meeting of the waters' at Avoca (location for the popular British TV series *Ballykissangel*), Baltinglass Abbey and Roundwood (Ireland's highest village).

The county town of Wicklow is situated on the slopes of Ballyguile Hill, overlooking a wide curve of coastline. On the coast, the fishing port of Arklow is renowned for its pottery, Brittas Bay boasts 5km (3mi) of safe sandy beach and Bray, on the border with County Dublin, is one of Ireland's principal resorts, with an elegant, hotel-lined 'front'.

Wicklow contains no fewer than five of Ireland's finest Heritage Gardens and also claims to be one of the best golfing counties in Ireland, with more than 20 courses including the country's oldest at Woodenbridge.

Just 30 miles south of Dublin, Wicklow town is also becoming a popular commuter base – with correspondingly rising property prices (see **Property Market** below).

Munster

Munster is Ireland's largest province, covering almost 30 per cent of the country and including the counties of Clare, Cork, Kerry, Limerick, Tipperary and Waterford. It's Ireland's most southerly region and the most popular with both holidaymakers and foreign homebuyers. The counties of Cork, Kerry and Waterford are particularly sought-after – Bantry Bay in west Cork has become something of a magnet for the international jet-set (e.g. American and British film and pop stars) and a few once parochial fishing villages now have a cosmopolitan feel.

Geographically, Munster has everything that's considered typically Irish: brooding mountains, a craggy coastline with sandy bays between rocky cliffs, and alternately fertile and barren plains. Cut off from the rest of Ireland by mountains, bogs and the River Shannon, Munster has become a land of myth and legend with strong musical and poetic traditions. Its people are also traditionalists:

warm and relaxed, but with an argumentative streak – or so the popular stereotype goes.

Clare

County Clare is one of the most barren parts of Ireland and is almost untouched by tourism despite the nearby presence of Shannon Airport. Covering an area of 160km² (62mi²), the area known as the Burren is particularly desolate and has a unique landscape (with no bogs and few pastures) strewn with limestone slabs and boulders.

Legend has it that one of Oliver Cromwell's soldiers described it as 'a savage land, yielding neither water enough to drown a man, nor tree to hang him, nor soil enough to bury him'.

Nevertheless, the Burren is also famous for its variety of plant and animal life, including the rarely seen pine marten and 26 of the country's 33 species of butterfly, one of which, the Burren Green, is particular to the area.

With three-quarters of its border on the sea, County Clare is one of Ireland's premier holiday centres. Traditional seaside resorts such as Kilkee, Lahinch and Spanish Point, and the spectacular Cliffs of Moher plunging more than 200 metres into the Atlantic, make it popular with both foreign and Irish holidaymakers. Clare also has a fair share of historical interest, like the ancient town of Ennis and the Poulnabrone Dolmen (or Portal Tomb), one of Ireland's most photographed monuments.

Ennis is of interest for another reason: in a national competition sponsored by Telecom Éireann in 1997, it was selected as Ireland's 'Information Age' town, where the government invested millions in cutting-edge IT development for both businesses and the local community.

Nearby Shannon is Ireland's only new town to have been built for centuries, having developed as recently as the '60s to accommodate workers at the Shannon Industrial Tax Free Zone, created by an act of parliament in 1947. Today it's a thriving small town of 10,000 inhabitants. Ireland's largest hydro-electric plant, the Shannon Scheme, is also in County Clare.

Cork

Munster's principal town is Cork city, the second-largest city in Ireland and capital of its biggest and most southerly county of the same name. The 2005 City of Culture, Cork is the unofficial capital of the south of Ireland; its citizens, whom Dubliners dismiss as culchies or 'country folk', think it should be the capital of the country. Sophisticated and cosmopolitan, with its own university, Cork is much smaller than Dublin (its population is just 180,000) and has managed to retain a friendly, small-town atmosphere.

It's nevertheless a lively place full of young people and bustling with traffic. Ringaskiddy and Little Island near Cork city are among the few industrial areas in Ireland (the largest being at Leixlip near Dublin), where a number of large pharmaceutical companies have established major concerns.

Cork county has some of the richest farming land in Ireland, as well as some of the most spectacular coastal and mountain scenery, combined with gentle bays and hills and numerous marshes (the name Cork comes from the Gaelic *Corcaigh*, meaning 'marshy place'). Nearby is the port of Cobh (pronounced 'cove'), from where some 2.5m people have emigrated to America since 1848.

County Cork is also home to the famous Blarney Stone, which is supposed to bestow the 'gift of the gab' upon whoever kisses it – unless you're Irish, in which case you're born with it! Unreasonably located at the top of Blarney Castle tower, the stone requires you to hang upside down over a sheer drop in order to put your lips to it – you have been warned!

Blarney is to see a €750m investment over eight years (from 2006) in 2,500 new homes in a development called 'Stoneview', a redesigned and enlarged town centre, new shops, a hospital and two schools –

scheduled to coincide with the reopening of Blarney railway station and making the town a major commuter centre.

The eastern part of the county, and especially towns like Midleton which are within commuting distance of Cork city, has witnessed something of a housing explosion since the opening of the Lee Tunnel, and major infrastructure improvements in and around the city (including the Ballincollig bypass and the upgrading of the Dunkettle Interchange).

Kerry

The archetypal Ireland is to be found in County Kerry, which contains three of the country's most visited places: the rather commercialised town of Killarney with its magnificent lake, the Iveragh Peninsula  (better known as the Ring of Kerry) and the Dingle Peninsula – not to mention its grandest and highest range of mountains, MacGillycuddy's Reeks. Ballybunion is one of Ireland's premier seaside resorts and Kinsale is popular for yachting, as well as laying claim to be Ireland's gourmet capital (it has hosted the International Gourmet Festival in October since 1987).

Tralee is home to the internationally famous Festival of Kerry and Rose of Tralee Festival, which was established in 1939 in an attempt to attract visitors away from Killarney, as well as to Ireland's biggest selection of all-weather visitor attractions. Both Tralee and Killarney are popular among retirees, particularly from Dublin.

Kerry is said to be where you will find Ireland's friendliest, most flamboyant and humorous people; it's certainly where you will encounter its wettest weather, although the Gulf Stream keeps the climate fairly mild, and snow and frost are rare.

The recent property boom has centred on Kerry, which boasts easy access (direct flights to Dublin as well as Luton and Manchester in the UK), some of the cleanest water and air in Europe, and 10,000 hectares (25,000 acres) of national park for golf, fishing and walking.

Limerick

Limerick was a county long before it became a 'nonsense' verse; the tradition of inventing rhyming five-line stanzas is said to have originated in the 18th century in the drinking games of a group of would-be poets from  the town of Croom. County Limerick is a peaceful farming area with some of the

Ruin, Co. Tipperary

country's finest dairy cattle (it's also famous for its horses). The fertile pastures are dotted with the ruins of hundreds of castles and surrounded by hills and mountains. To the north is the River Shannon, which unofficially divides the south-west from the west of Ireland.

Where the Shannon meets the Atlantic lies the ancient city of Limerick, the country's third-largest city (after Dublin and Cork). Once rather drab, the city has recently had a substantial facelift and boasts smart clothes shops as well as a thriving arts centre and lively nightlife. Limerick is also the home of one of the most important collections of mediaeval artefacts in the world, the Hunt Collection; and has lately won worldwide renown as the setting of Frank McCourt's autobiographical novel *Angela's Ashes*. There's still high unemployment, but new industries have been established in and around the city; Dell computers, for example, recently built a €30m plant at Raheen. A new dual-carriageway road linking the Annacotty, Castletroy, Dooradoyle and Raheen areas has spawned residential and commercial development.

Colourful market towns are scattered throughout the county, notably Castleconnell, Kilfinane, Kilmallock and Newcastle West. Adare, with its old-world, thatched cottages and mediaeval churches, recalls a bygone way of life and claims to be Ireland's prettiest village.

Tipperary

'It's a long way to Tipperary' goes the song, but that rather depends on where you set out from. Tipperary is the most southerly of the inland counties of Ireland (Carlow, Cavan, Kildare, Kilkenny, Longford, Laois, Monaghan, Offaly, Roscommon and Westmeath also lack a coastline) and one of the most beautiful. Tipperary is rich in contrast with flat, fertile farmland (known as the Golden Vale) interspersed with low but spectacular mountains: the Silvermines and Devil's Bit in the north and the Galtee in the south.

The River Suir is noted for its trout, and Lough Derg on the river Shannon is Ireland's largest lake, while hunting is a popular pastime in other parts of Tipperary. Clonmel (in the south) means 'honeyed meadows' and has a prosperous air deriving from the abundance of food produced in the county.

Significant public and private investment is being made in County Tipperary, which has long attracted large pharmaceutical companies and is also a major tourist centre. Business and enterprise parks are springing up around the county, as it experiences a feeling of change.

Waterford

Waterford is a fertile county watered by three rivers, which come together at Waterford city, and is noted for its mountains, tiny lakes and pine forests, as well as an abundance of ruins. West Waterford's mountain passes are among the most beautiful scenery in Ireland, while the south-east coast is one of the sunniest parts of the country, offering miles of safe, sandy beaches.

The capital, Waterford city, is most famous for its glass factory, which has been producing Waterford crystal for over 200 years. It's also a bustling maritime centre with regular visits from cruise ships, yachts and other vessels, not to mention its own sizeable fishing fleet.

A new outer ring road has improved traffic flow in the city and spawned a number of residential and commercial developments, particularly to the north (where planning permission has been granted for up to 2,000 houses in the Belmont/Ferrybank area), south and south-east. Developers are generally showing a keen interest in the city, where holiday homes are popular.

Ulster

Ulster is Ireland's most northerly province, most of which is part of the United Kingdom. The counties of Antrim, Armagh, Down, Fermanagh, Londonderry and Tyrone form the region known as Northern Ireland, which remained part of the UK when the Irish state was established in 1921, but Counties Cavan, Donegal and Monaghan are within the Republic.

Cavan

With a population of just 4,000, landlocked Cavan is a peaceful, unspoilt county (it's said to be Ireland's 'Garden of Eden'), although the recent reopening of the Ballinamore-Ballyconnell Canal (constructed in 1860, but only operational for nine years before the railway superseded it) between the Shannon and Erne waterways is attracting a good deal of tourist traffic and the county is starting to attract Dublin commuters unable to afford homes nearer to the capital – resulting in both residential and retail development.

Cavan is a favourite of anglers because of the abundance of fish in its many beautiful lakes and rivers, winding between wooded hills.

Ireland's longest river, the Shannon, has its source here, on the slopes of Cuilcagh in a pool known as the Shannon Pot.

Donegal

The most northerly county in Ireland and one of its largest, Donegal is virtually cut off from the rest of the country by the Northern Irish county of Fermanagh. It changed less during the 20th century than almost anywhere else in Ireland and has the largest Gaelic-speaking population of any county, although the Ulster dialect has more in common with Scottish Gaelic than 'official' Leinster Irish and the county retains strong links with Scotland: the buses even go to Glasgow (via ferry)!

Donegal has something of everything found in the rest of the country: cliffs, mountains, heather-clad moors, bogs and fertile pastures. The coastal town of Killybegs, where the *Gaeltacht* begins, is untypical of the area, having developed into one of Europe's principal fishing ports, complete with fishmeal factory whose smell pervades one end of the town. (It's said that the best fish and chips in Ireland are to be had at Melly's, opposite the harbour – which rather depends on how hungry you are!)

Monaghan

Neighbouring Monaghan is an undulating county where lakes alternate with gentle hills. Market towns, farms and quiet waterways make up the quintessentially Irish landscape, which is dotted with ancient monuments and ruined castles. Renowned as an angling centre, Monaghan also offers watersports, golf, riding and other outdoor pursuits, although it has no coastline. It's a peaceful place, yet just an hour's drive from Dublin in one direction and Belfast (in Northern Ireland) in the other, thus offering the best of several worlds. The recent opening of the Carrickmacross bypass has further shortened Dublin journey times, resulting in a surge in demand from commuters unable to afford property less distant from the capital.

ESTATE AGENTS

The vast majority of property sales in Ireland, particularly those where overseas buyers are involved, are handled by estate agents, who are – somewhat confusingly – usually referred to as auctioneers. Some Irish agents advertise abroad, particularly in the publications listed in **Appendix B**, and in expatriate magazines and newspapers in Ireland. If you want to find an agent in a particular town or area, you can look under *Auctioneers* in any of the seven regional Irish *Golden Pages* (available at main libraries in many countries).

Irish estate agents are regulated by law and must be professionally qualified and licensed. However, until now they haven't been required to have 'proficiency' in the job; a recent report by the Irish Auctioneers' and Valuers' Institute (IAVI) has recommended that licence applicants prove proficiency and show evidence of 'continuing life-long learning', as well as having professional indemnity cover – recommendations which are likely to become law before long.

Indeed, in late 2005, the Justice Minister announced his intention to set up a regulatory agency to monitor estate agents, but as yet nothing has come of it. As in any field of human activity involving money, there are unlicensed practitioners, some of whom have been found guilty of illicit and immoral practices and who should of course be avoided like the proverbial plague.

You should first ensure that an agent has a current auctioneer's licence and preferably choose one who's a member of a professional association such as the IAVI (www.realestate.ie), which is by far the largest professional body in Ireland, or the Institute of Professional Auctioneers and Valuers (IPAV, www.ipav.ie). IAVI members, for example, are obliged to display their licence prominently in their offices, are 'bonded' (i.e. provide security against claims) to the sum of €75,000 in the high court, are subject to a disciplinary code, and must have professional indemnity insurance.

When you pay a deposit to an agent, it must (by law) be deposited in a separate client or current account, so that the agent derives no interest from the money. Note that the rules for Irish estate agents also apply to foreigners, who cannot sell property in Ireland without an Irish auctioneer's licence.

Agents' Fees

There are no government controls on agents' fees in Ireland, but the commission charged by most Irish agents is between 1 and 3.5 per cent (depending on the value of the property – the higher the value the lower the commission), although it's usually around 2.5 per cent and is subject to VAT (at 20 per cent).

Estate agents' fees are usually paid by the vendor. They are, however, normally included in the asking price, so in effect they're paid by the buyer. Foreign agents may work with Irish agents and share the standard commission, so vendors usually pay no more by using them. When buying, check whether you need to pay commission or any extras in addition to the sale price, apart from the normal fees and taxes associated with buying a property. Normally, you would be responsible for a separate fee only if you retained an agent to purchase a property on your behalf, in which case you should agree a fee in advance and confirm it in writing.

Most agents offer after-sales services and will help you to arrange legal advice, insurance, utility connections, interior decorators and builders; many also offer a full management and letting service on behalf of non-resident owners. Note, however, that agents may receive commissions for referrals, so you may not always receive independent advice.

PURCHASE PROCEDURE

As in most other countries, buying a home in Ireland involves a complicated process of checks and registrations (known as conveyance, but usually, improperly, referred to as conveyancing), which is normally carried out by a solicitor. It's possible to do your own conveyance, but it isn't recommended! Essentially, the procedure is as follows.

Once the selling price has been agreed between the vendor and the buyer (you), the vendor's solicitor prepares a contract and sends it to your solicitor, who checks the 'title' (i.e. that the property in fact belongs to the vendor and that he has the right to sell it) and asks you to sign the contract and pay a deposit to secure the property. If you're obtaining a loan (mortgage), the contract will be subject to the loan being granted, which in turn will be subject to a satisfactory valuation report or survey.

Some selling agents insist that the valuation is carried out before negotiations are concluded (and provisional loan approval can be secured within 72 hours), in which case the vendor's solicitor will generally refuse a contract that's subject to loan approval. Your solicitor will then draft the purchase deed and raise his queries (requisitions) on title before sending the deposit, draft deed and any objections with regard to title back to the vendor's solicitor.

Note that at this stage you've committed yourself to buying (subject to satisfactory title), whereas the vendor isn't yet committed to selling and may therefore still 'gazump' you by accepting a higher offer. Your solicitor will also need to check whether capital gains tax (CGT) has been paid by the vendor (if applicable).

When he has received satisfactory replies to his queries, your solicitor will draw up the definitive deed transferring title in the property to you and give the lending institution a certificate of title. If the vendor is happy with the contract, he will also sign it – at which point he is committed to sell to you. The draft deed is then approved by the vendor's solicitor and returned for 'typing up' (engrossment) by your solicitor before being returned again to the vendor's solicitor for signing by the vendor (no wonder solicitors' fees are so high!).

 Caution

You shouldn't even think about buying (or selling) property in Ireland without taking expert, independent legal advice. You should certainly never sign anything or pay any money before doing so.

Before hiring a solicitor, compare the fees charged by a number of practices and obtain quotations in writing. Always check what's included in the fee and whether it's 'full and binding' or just an estimate (a low basic rate may be supplemented by more expensive 'extras'). Note that you shouldn't use the vendor's solicitor, even if this would save you money, as he's primarily concerned with protecting the interests of the vendor and not the buyer.

Contract

Your solicitor should draw up the purchase contract and ensure that it includes everything required, particularly any necessary conditional clauses. The basis of all house purchase contracts in Ireland is the 'Standard Incorporated Law Society' contract (copies are obtainable from the Law Society of Ireland), which is revised from time to time. If you're buying a new property from a builder, there are appropriate standard contracts that can be used, and there may be separate contracts for the purchase of the site and for the construction of the building.

Most contracts contain a number of conditional clauses that must be met to ensure the validity of the contract. Conditions usually apply to events beyond the control of either the vendor or buyer, although almost anything the buyer agrees with the vendor can be included in a contract. If any of the conditions aren't met, the contract can be suspended or declared null and void, and the deposit returned. However, if you decide to withdraw from purchase and aren't covered by a clause in the contract, you will forfeit your deposit and could be compelled to go through with the purchase.

If you're buying any ancillary items from the vendor, such as carpets, curtains or furniture, which are included in the purchase price, you should have them listed and attached as an addendum to the contract.

Deposit

When you sign the contract for a new or resale property or a plot, you must pay a deposit. If you're buying a resale or a new finished property (i.e. not off plan) you usually pay a deposit of 10 per cent when signing the contract (the amount may be negotiable), the balance being paid on completion when the deed of sale is signed.

Inheritance & Capital Gains Tax

Before registering the title deed, carefully consider the tax and inheritance consequences for those in whose name the deed will be registered. Property can be registered in a single name, both names of a couple or joint buyers, the name or names of children, giving the parents sole use during their lifetime, or in the name of an Irish or foreign company. However you decide to register a property, it should be done at the time of purchase, as it will be more expensive (or even impossible) to change it later.

Completion

Completion (or closing) is the name given to the signing of the final deed of sale (strangely, the vendor must sign the deed before completion, but you have a further month to do so), the date of which is usually five to eight weeks after signing the purchase contract. The exact date will be set by your solicitor once your mortgage has been approved. Before completion, your solicitor will carry out final checks on title.

Before signing the deed of sale, it's important to check that the property hasn't fallen down or been damaged in any way, e.g. by a storm or vandals (or the previous owner!). Property is sold subject to the condition that it's accepted in the state it's in at the time of completion; you should therefore be aware of anything that occurs between signing the purchase contract and completion, and make a final inventory immediately prior to completion (the previous owner should have already vacated the property) to ensure that the vendor hasn't absconded with anything that was included in the price.

If you've employed a solicitor or are buying through an agent, he should accompany you on this visit. This is particularly important if furniture and furnishings (and major appliances) were included in the price. You should also ensure that expensive items (such as kitchen appliances) haven't been substituted by inferior (possibly second-hand) items. You should refuse to go through with the purchase if you aren't completely satisfied, as it will be difficult or impossible to obtain redress later. If it isn't possible to complete the sale, you should consult your solicitor concerning your rights and the return of your deposit and any other fees already paid.

At completion, you must pay the balance of the purchase price (less the deposit and, if

applicable, the amount of a mortgage), plus other payments such as solicitor's fees, taxes and duties, by banker's draft or bank transfer. A banker's draft is usually more convenient, as you have the payment in your possession (a bank cannot lose it!) and the solicitor can confirm it immediately. It also allows you to withhold payment if there's a last minute problem that cannot be resolved.

Non-resident buyers no longer need a certificate from an Irish bank stating that the amount to be paid has been exchanged or converted from a foreign currency, although it must be reported to the Bank of Ireland in accordance with legislation relating to money laundering (see **Importing & Exporting Money** on page 273). Non-residents may also be required to confirm their tax situation (i.e. whether or not they're liable for income tax in Ireland). After you've paid, your solicitor should give you a receipt and an unsigned copy of the purchase deed showing that you're the new owner of the property. You will also receive the keys!

MOVING HOUSE

It usually only takes a few weeks to have your belongings shipped from within continental Europe. From anywhere else the time varies considerably, e.g. around four weeks from the east coast of the US, six weeks from the US west coast or the Far East, and around eight weeks from Australasia. Customs clearance is no longer necessary when shipping your household effects between European Union (EU) countries.

However, when shipping your effects from a non-EU country, you should enquire about customs formalities in advance. If you fail to follow the correct procedure, you can encounter problems and delays and may even be erroneously charged duty or fined (see **Customs** on page 82). Shipping companies usually take care of the paperwork and ensure that the correct documents are provided and properly completed.

It's wise to use a major shipping company with a good reputation. For international moves it's best to use a company that's a member of the International Federation of Furniture Removers (FIDI) or the Overseas Moving Network International (OMNI), with experience in Ireland. Members of FIDI and OMNI usually subscribe to an advance payment scheme providing a guarantee, whereby if a member fails to fulfil its commitments to a client, the job is completed at the agreed cost by another company or your money is refunded. Some shipping companies have subsidiaries or affiliates in Ireland, which may be more convenient if you encounter problems or need to make an insurance claim.

You should obtain at least three written quotations before choosing a shipping company, as rates vary considerably.

Shipping companies should send a representative to provide a detailed quotation. Most companies will pack your belongings and provide packing cases and special containers, although this is naturally more expensive than packing them yourself. Ask a company how they pack fragile and valuable items, and whether the cost of packing cases, materials and insurance (see below) are included in a quotation. If you're doing your own packing, most shipping companies will provide packing crates and boxes. Shipments are charged by volume, e.g. the square metre in Europe and the square foot in the US.

You should expect to pay between €4,000 and €7,500 to move the contents of a three or four-bedroom house within western Europe, e.g. from continental Europe to Dublin. If you're flexible about the delivery date, shipping companies will usually quote a lower fee based on a 'part load', where the cost is shared with other deliveries. This can result in savings of 50 per cent or more compared with a 'dedicated' delivery. However, whether you have an individual or shared delivery, always obtain the maximum transit period in writing, or you may have to wait months for delivery!

Make sure that you fully insure your belongings during shipping with a well established insurance company. Don't insure with a shipping company that has its own insurance, as they will usually fight every penny of a claim. Insurance premiums are usually between 1 and 2 per cent of the declared value of the goods, depending on the type of cover chosen. It's wise to make a photographic or video record of valuables for insurance purposes.

Most insurance policies cover for 'all risks' on a replacement value basis. Note, however, that china, glass and other breakables can usually only be included in an all-risks policy when they're packed by the shipping company. Insurance usually covers total loss or loss of a particular crate only, rather than individual items (unless they were packed by the shipping company). If there are any broken or damaged items, they must be noted and listed before you sign the delivery bill (although it's obviously impractical to check everything on delivery).

If you need to make a claim, be sure to read the small print, as some companies require clients to make a claim within a few days of delivery, although a week is usual. Send a claim by registered post. Some insurance companies apply an excess of around 1 per cent of the total shipment value when assessing claims. This means that, if your shipment is valued at €50,000, there's no point in making a claim for less than €500.

If you're unable to ship your belongings directly to Ireland, most companies will put them into storage, and some offer a limited free storage period prior to shipment, e.g. 14 days.

⚠ **Caution**

If you need to put your household effects into storage, it's imperative to have them fully insured, as warehouses have been known to burn down!

Make a complete list of everything to be moved and give a copy to the shipping company. Don't include anything illegal (e.g. guns, bombs, drugs or pornography) with your belongings, as customs checks can be rigorous and penalties severe. Provide the shipping company with detailed instructions regarding how to find your Irish address and a telephone number where you can be contacted. If your

Irish home has poor or impossible access for a large truck, you must inform the shipping company (the ground must also be firm enough to support a heavy vehicle). Note also that if large items of furniture need to be taken in through an upstairs window, you may need to pay extra.

After considering the shipping costs, you may decide to ship only high-value items of furniture and personal effects, and to buy new furniture and appliances in Ireland. If you're importing household goods from another European country, it's possible to rent a self-drive van or truck. Note, however, that if you rent a vehicle outside Ireland you will usually need to return it to the country where it was hired, which is prohibitively expensive.

If you plan to transport your belongings to Ireland personally, check the customs requirements in the countries you will pass through. Most people find that it isn't wise to do their own move unless it's a simple job, e.g. a few items of furniture and personal effects only. It's no fun heaving beds and wardrobes up stairs and squeezing them into impossible spaces!

If you're taking pets with you, you may need to ask your vet to tranquillise them, as many pets are frightened (even more than people) by the chaos and stress of moving house. They may also need several weeks or even months to become accustomed to their new surroundings, if they aren't required to go into quarantine.

Bear in mind when moving home that everything that can go wrong often does, so you should allow plenty of time and try not to arrange your move to your new home on the same day as the previous owner is moving out. That's just asking for 'Murphy' to intervene!

Inventory

One of the most important tasks to perform after moving into a new home is to check the fixtures and fittings and, if applicable, the furniture and furnishings, to ensure that the previous owner hasn't absconded with anything that was included in the price (see **Completion** on page 116).

When moving into a long-term rental property it's necessary to complete an inventory of its contents and a report on its condition. This includes the condition of the fixtures and fittings, the state of furniture and furnishings, the cleanliness and state of the decoration, and anything that's damaged, missing or in need of repair. An inventory should be provided by your landlord or agent and may include every single item in a furnished property (down to the number of teaspoons). If an inventory isn't provided, you should insist on one being prepared and annexed to the lease. If you find a serious fault after signing the inventory, send a registered letter to your landlord and ask for it to be attached to the inventory.

The inventory check should be carried out in your presence, both when taking over and when terminating a rental agreement. If the two inventories don't correspond, you must make good any damages or deficiencies or the landlord can do so and deduct the cost from your deposit. Although Irish landlords are generally no worse than those in most other countries, some will do almost anything to avoid repaying a deposit. Note the reading on your utility meters (e.g. electricity, gas and water) and check that you aren't overcharged on your first bill. The meters should be read by utility companies before you move in, although you may need to arrange it yourself.

It's a good idea to obtain written instructions from the previous owner regarding the operation of appliances and heating systems, maintenance of grounds, gardens and lawns, care of special surfaces such as wooden or tiled floors, and the names of reliable local maintenance people who know the property and are familiar with its quirks. Check with your local town hall regarding regulations for such things as rubbish collection, recycling and on-street parking.

HOME SECURITY

When moving into a new home it's often wise to replace the locks (or lock barrels) as soon as possible,

as you have no idea how many keys are in circulation for the existing locks. This is true even for new homes, as builders often give keys to sub-contractors. In any case it's a good idea to change the external lock barrels regularly, particularly if you let a home. If they aren't already fitted, high security locks (e.g. five-lever mortise deadlocks) are recommended. Patio doors should be fitted with key-operated locks and a stop should be fitted in the top of the door frame to prevent the doors from being lifted out.

All ground floor windows should be fitted with key-operated locks or bolts. Extra keys for high-security locks cannot usually be cut at a local hardware shop and, if they're already fitted, you will need to obtain details from the previous owner or your landlord. In areas with a higher risk of theft (e.g. central Dublin), your insurance company may insist on extra security measures.

You may wish to have a security system fitted, which is usually the best way to deter thieves and may also reduce your household insurance (see page 264). It should be fitted to Irish Standard 199 (1987), covering all external doors and windows and incorporating infra-red security beams. It may also include a coded entry keypad (which can be frequently changed and is useful for clients if you're letting the property) and 24-hour monitoring (with some systems it's possible to monitor properties remotely from another country). With a monitored system, when a sensor (e.g. smoke or forced entry) detects an emergency or a panic button is pushed, a signal is sent automatically to a 24-hour monitoring station. The person on duty will telephone to check whether it's a genuine alarm and, if he cannot contact anyone or the wrong password is given, someone will be sent to investigate. Some developments and estates have security gates and are patrolled by security guards.

You can deter thieves by ensuring that your house is well lit at night and not conspicuously unoccupied. External 'passive infra-red' (PIR) lights (which switch on automatically when someone approaches), random timed switches for internal lights, radios and televisions (TV), dummy security cameras, and tapes that play barking dogs (etc.) triggered by a light or heat detector may all help deter burglars. You can also fit UPVC (toughened plastic) security windows and doors, which can survive an attack with a sledge-hammer, and external steel security blinds (which can be electrically operated), although these are relatively expensive.

A dog can be useful to deter intruders, although it should be kept inside where it cannot be given poisoned food. Irrespective of whether or not you actually have a dog, a warning sign showing the image of a fierce dog may act as a deterrent. Bear in mind that prevention is better than cure, as stolen property is rarely recovered.

If you leave your home unoccupied for any length of time, cancel deliveries of milk, etc. and advise your local police (*Garda*) station, leaving a contact name and number in case anything should happen while you're away. Ask

neighbours to park their car in the drive and to pop in from time to time. If they're very friendly, they may even be persuaded to cut the lawn for you! If you have a holiday home in Ireland, it's wise not to leave anything of great value (monetary or sentimental) there and to have comprehensive insurance for your belongings (see page 264).

One of the best ways to protect a home when you're away is to engage a house-sitter to look after it. This can be done for short periods or longer if you have a holiday home in Ireland. It isn't usually necessary to pay for house-sitting, as you can usually find someone to do it in return for free accommodation. However, you must take care whom you engage and obtain references.

An important aspect of home security is ensuring that you have early warning of a fire, which is easily achieved by installing smoke detectors.

Battery-operated smoke detectors can be purchased for around €10 and should conform to Irish Standard 409 (1988). They should be tested periodically to ensure that they're working properly and the batteries should be replaced twice a year. Fire extinguishers and fire blankets are also recommended. A 2.5kg dry powder or multi-purpose chemical extinguisher (which should conform to Irish Standard 290 of 1986) is ideal for the average house. Fire blankets should comply with Irish Standard 415 (1988). You can also fit an electric gas-detector that activates an alarm when a gas leak is detected.

When closing a property for an extended period, e.g. over the winter, you should ensure that everything is switched off and that it's secure. If you vacate your home for a long period, you may also be obliged to notify a caretaker or landlord or your insurance company, and leave a key with a caretaker or landlord in case of emergencies. If you have a robbery, you should report it immediately to your local police station, where you must make a statement. You will receive a copy, which will be required by your insurance company if you make a claim.

ELECTRICITY

Mains electricity is available in virtually all parts of the country, and the network is currently undergoing a €3bn overhaul, involving the refurbishment or conversion of the medium voltage supply. There are no nuclear power stations in Ireland, where most electricity is generated by conventional coal, gas and oil burning stations. Ireland's seven hydroelectric stations and five peat stations produce around 5 and 15 per cent of the total supply respectively.

Ireland's exposure to the full force of Atlantic winds, especially along its western coast, means that it's the ideal place for 'wind farms', of which there are an ever-increasing number. Although wind energy presently accounts for only around 5 per cent of Ireland's total electricity output, the government is committed to reducing carbon dioxide emissions and it's predicted that in the next five to ten years as much as 20 per cent of electrical power could be generated by wind. The major provider is Airtricity (formerly Eirtricity, which was a much better name!) – see **Suppliers** on page 122.

Electricity services in the Republic of Ireland have traditionally been provided by the Electricity Supply Board (ESB, 🖳 www.esb.ie), a state-owned and controlled body. But in accordance with EU rules the Irish electricity market was opened to competition in 2005 and ESB is now only one of several electricity suppliers (see **Suppliers** on page 122).

Nevertheless, the electricity generation and transmission system continues to be state-operated: the former by the recently formed EirGrid plc (🖳 www.eirgrid.com), which operates 19 major power stations and a number of smaller stations throughout the country, the latter by ESB Networks (🖳 www.esb.ie/esbnetworks).

Even if you choose a supplier other than ESB, you must still apply to ESB Networks for connection to the electricity network. This can be done by calling ☎ 1850-372-757 or emailing ✉ esbnetworks@esb.ie rather than by visiting an ESB shop. ESB Networks is also responsible for reading electricity meters and dealing with supply problems, such as power cuts, but payment must be made to the relevant supplier (ESB Networks should help you to change suppliers if you wish).

Most modern properties (i.e. less than around 20 years old) in Ireland have good electrical installations. However, if you buy a property to which the electricity supply has been disconnected for more than six months, you will be required to have the wiring checked by a registered electrician (see **Connection** below).

☑ **SURVIVAL TIP**

You should ensure that the electricity installation is in good condition before buying a house (e.g. through a survey), as rewiring can be very expensive.

Connection

The following procedures apply according to your situation.

Brand New Home

If you're buying a new home from a builder or developer, an electricity connection should already have been made and you need only contact ESB Networks (see above) to advise them when you intend to move in, quoting the Meter Point Reference Number (MPRN) given to you by the builder. You will, however, need to sign up with an electricity supplier (see below).

If you're building your own home, you should contact ESB Networks early in your planning to obtain a Networks Application Form (NC2), which can be downloaded from the ESB Networks website. The completed form must be accompanied by detailed maps and site plans.

If the site is within 500m of the medium voltage network, you should receive a quotation for connection within seven days; if it's more than 500m from the network, a 'designer' will visit the site and you should receive a quotation within 15 days. The cost of connection depends on a number of factors, the **minimum** charge being €1,744 for a 12kVA supply (adequate for most domestic installations) or €2,364 for a 16kVA supply (which may be needed if, for example, you have lots of high-power appliances or electric central heating).

Unless major work is required, the connection should be made within 12 weeks of your payment being received (of course, you must pay in advance!).

Home with an Existing Supply

If you're taking over a property where there's already an electricity supply, the procedure depends on whether the supply has been disconnected and, if so, for how long.

Connected: If the supply hasn't been disconnected, it's simply a matter of asking for the account to be transferred to your name. Take a meter reading when you move in (and before making a celebratory cup of tea), if possible getting the vendor to agree it, and complete a Supply Agreement form (downloadable from the ESB website, ⌨ www. esb.ie).

Disconnected for less than six months: Contact an electricity supplier (see below), who will arrange reconnection.

Disconnected for between six months and two years: Before contacting an electricity supplier, you must have the property's wiring checked by a registered electrical contractor and obtain a Certificate of Completion from him.

Disconnected for over two years: In addition to the above, you must apply to ESB Networks for an Application Pack (containing form NC2); an additional fee will be payable.

Suppliers

There are currently six electricity suppliers, as follows:

♦ Airtricity (☎ 1850-404070, ⌨ www.airtricity. com);

♦ Bord Gáis Energy Supply (☎ 1850-632632, ⌨ www.bordgais.ie);

♦ CH Power (☎ 1850-247835, ⌨ www. chpower.ie);

♦ Energia (☎ 028-9068 5900, ⌨ www. energia.ie);

♦ ESB (☎ 1850-372372, ⌨ www.esb.ie);

♦ ESBIE (☎ 1800-200513, ⌨ www.esbie.ie).

Charges

Electricity charges depend on your supplier (see above). The information given below is for ESB and is intended only as a guide to electricity prices. The following tariffs apply to both 12kVA and 16kVA supplies (see above).

Standing Charges

There are four ESB standing charges (i.e. fixed fees you must pay irrespective of your consumption), which depend on whether you're in an urban or rural area and whether your installation allows you to take advantage of lower night-time tariffs (known as a 'Nightsaver' system), in which case you will have two meters – although you can have a second meter installed for night-storage heaters even if you aren't on the Nightsaver system (the cost of which is shown as 'optional' in the table)! The 'Public Service Obligation' (PSO) levy of €9.72 per year, which related to ESB's investment in renewable energy sources, was stopped in 2007.

For more information on standing charges contact ESB Customer Supply on ☎ 01-852 9534.

ESB Standing Charges	
Urban	
Annual standing charge	€65.04
Annual night storage heating standing charge (optional)	€6.48
Urban Nightsaver	
Annual standing charge	€114.12
Rural	
Annual standing charge	€101.04
Annual night storage heating standing charge (optional)	€6.48
Rural Nightsaver	
Annual standing charge	€159.06

Consumption Charges

Consumption is calculated in 'units', one unit being equal to 1,000 watts of electricity used for one hour (written as 1KWh) or, for example, a 100W bulb left on for ten hours or roughly eight hours' television viewing or cooking for one person for a day. The night-time consumption charges (per unit/KWh) is around half of the standard consumption charge.

Plugs, Fuses & Bulbs

Depending on the country you've come from, you may need new plugs or a lot of adapters. Plug adapters for most foreign electrical apparatus can be purchased in Ireland, although it's wise to bring some with you, as well as extension leads and multi-plug extensions that can be fitted with Irish plugs. Most modern properties have at least two sockets in each room, although there may be a shortage of electric points in older Irish homes. Most Irish plugs are of the three-pin IS411 (BS 1363) type (as in the UK), apart from shaving sockets, which are of the standard international two-pin kind.

A transformer (see below) is needed to convert American appliances (unless they're dual-voltage) and some items, like clocks, won't work even with a transformer. Cordless telephones may not work either, and even TVs that do work are of limited use because of the different broadcasting standards in Ireland. As in the rest of Europe, most videos are in PAL format, so American video recorders won't be of any use.

Small, low-wattage electrical appliances such as table lamps, small TVs and computers, don't require an earth. However, plugs with an earth must always be used for high-wattage appliances such as fires, kettles, washing machines and refrigerators. Electrical appliances that are earthed have a three-core wire and must never be used with a two-pin plug. **Always make sure that a plug is correctly and securely wired, as bad wiring can be fatal.**

In modern properties, fuses are of the earth-trip type. When there's a short circuit or the system is overloaded, a circuit breaker is tripped and the power supply is cut. If your electricity fails, you should suspect a fuse of tripping, particularly if you've just switched on an electrical appliance.

Before reconnecting the power, switch off any high-power appliances such as a hob, oven, washing machine or dishwasher. Make sure you know where the trip switches are located and keep a torch handy so that you can find them in the dark (see **Power Supply** below).

Electric light bulbs in Ireland are generally of the bayonet kind, but screw fitting (Edison) bulbs are also widely available. Bulbs for non-standard electrical appliances (i.e. appliances that aren't made for the Irish market), such as refrigerators and sewing machines, may not be available in Ireland, so you should bring some spares with you.

Power Supply

The standard domestic electrical supply in Ireland is 230 volts AC with a frequency of 50 Hertz (cycles). Most shaving sockets also support 110 volts. Power cuts are rare in Ireland. Nevertheless, if you use a computer it's a good idea to fit an uninterrupted power supply (UPS) with a battery backup, which not only allows you time to shut down your computer and save your work after a power failure (the battery should continue to supply power for around 15 to 20 minutes), but also protects it from power surges.

If the power keeps tripping off or fuses blow when you attempt to use a number of high-power appliances simultaneously, e.g. an electric kettle and a heater, it could mean that the power supply is inadequate (i.e. you need a 16kVA supply instead of a 12kVA supply) or the wiring is inappropriate.

You should never simply put in heavier fuses, as inadequate wiring can cause a fire,

but get an electrician to check the wiring and if necessary 'uprate' it to your requirements.

If you have a problem with your power supply (e.g. interruptions or surges), you should contact ESB Networks on ☎ 1850-372999 (open 24 hours).

Converters & Transformers

Assuming that you have a 230-volt power supply, if you have electrical equipment rated at 110 volts AC (for example, from the US) you will require a converter or a step-down transformer to convert it to 110 volts. Converters can be used for heating appliances, but transformers are required for motorised appliances. However, some electrical appliances are fitted with a 110/220-volt switch. Check whether there is one (it may be inside the casing) and make sure that it's switched to 220 volts before connecting to the power supply. Add the wattage of all the devices you plan to connect to a transformer and make sure that its power rating exceeds this sum.

Generally all small, high-wattage electrical appliances – such as kettles, toasters, heaters and irons – need large transformers. Motors in large appliances, such as cookers, refrigerators, washing machines, dryers and dishwashers, will need replacing or fitting with a large transformer. In most cases, it's simpler to buy new appliances in Ireland, which are of good quality and reasonably priced (see page 353). Note also that the dimensions of cookers, microwave ovens, refrigerators, washing machines, dryers and dishwashers purchased abroad may differ from those in Ireland, so they may not fit into a standard Irish kitchen.

An additional problem with some electrical equipment is the frequency rating, which in some countries, e.g. the US, is designed to run at 60 hertz (Hz) and not Ireland's 50Hz. Electrical equipment without a motor is generally unaffected by the drop in frequency (except TVs). Equipment with a motor may run with a 20 per cent drop in speed; however, automatic washing machines, cookers, electric clocks,

record players and tape recorders must be converted to 50Hz.

If the label on the back of the equipment says 50/60Hz, it should be all right; if the label says 60Hz, you can try it, but first ensure that the voltage is correct as outlined above. Bear in mind that the transformers and motors of electrical devices designed to run at 60Hz will run hotter at 50Hz, so make sure that the apparatus has sufficient space around it to allow for cooling.

Bills

Electricity bills are sent out every two months, usually after meters have been read. If ESB Networks is unable to read your meter, you will be charged for an estimated consumption. If the estimate is wildly inaccurate, you can submit a corrected reading (make sure that you know how to read your electricity meter!) and you will be sent a revised bill. Normally only one estimated reading per year is permitted. Once you've received an accurate bill, you have 14 days in which to pay. If you fail to do so, your supply can be cut off without warning, although in practice no action is usually taken for up to six months. If your electricity supply is cut off, you must pay to have it reconnected (see **Connection** on page 121).

It's best to pay all your electricity (and other utility) bills by direct debit from an Irish bank account. If you own a holiday home in Ireland, you can have your bills sent to an address abroad. Bills should then be paid automatically on presentation to your bank, although some banks cannot be relied on 100 per cent. Both the electricity company and your bank should notify you when they've sent or paid a bill. Alternatively, you can pay bills at any

authorised bank or at one of your supplier's 'shops'.

GAS

Most people in Ireland use gas for hot water and central heating (see below) and many for cooking as well. Mains gas is available in all but eight counties of Ireland (Donegal, Kerry, Leitrim, Longford, Mayo, Roscommon, Sligo and Wexford), but not in all areas of all the other counties; it's supplied by the state-owned company Bord Gáis Éireann (which calls itself simply Bord Gáis, ☎ 1850-632632, 💻 www. bordgais.ie), whose website includes a map and lists of where gas is available.

Like the electricity supply system, gas supply has recently been 'liberalised', which means that while Bord Gáis continues to manage the network, consumers have a choice of 'supplier' – and therefore of services and tariffs – although there are currently only two 'licensed' suppliers (see **Suppliers** below).

Where mains gas isn't available, bottled gas can be used for cooking and heating (see below).

Suppliers

Bord Gáis Energy Supply (☎ 1850-632632, 💻 www.bordgaisenergysupply.ie) is the supplier of natural gas in all gas supply areas (see above), with the exception of Athlone, Ballinasloe, Clara, Galway, Mullingar, Oranmore, and Tullamore, where Flogas Natural Gas (☎ 041-987 4874, 💻 www. flogasnaturalgas.ie) is the licensed supplier.

Connection

When buying a brand new property, first find out whether mains gas is available (see above) and then contact a registered installer (also listed on the Bord Gáis website), who must submit a Certificate of Conformance to Bord Gáis for approval before you can be connected. Then register with a supply company (see above), which will arrange connection for you.

When moving into a property with mains gas, contact your supplier (see above) to register the account in your name. You must supply your previous address and the meter reading when you moved out (if possible, verified by

the buyer), if applicable, and the meter reading of the new property when you moved in (if possible, verified by the vendor).

> Connection to a new property should take around a week, but reconnection to a property that was previously supplied with gas can be done in a day.

As with electricity, you're billed every two months and bills include VAT at 13.5 per cent. Like all utility bills, gas bills can be paid by direct debit from an Irish bank account. In fact, if you're a non-resident property owner or are renting a property and want to obtain a gas supply, you will have to set up a direct debit and pay a deposit of €290 or ask someone who has been a customer of Bord Gáis for at least 14 months to act as 'guarantor' and sign the form for you.

Tariffs

Flogas's tariffs are simple – a standing charge of €0.155 per day (€56.75 per year) plus a usage charge of €0.05018 per KWh – although they offer an 'equaliser tariff' for those who want to spread their bills more evenly through the year (instead of having high bills in winter and low in summer). Bord Gáis Energy Supply's tariffs are complicated: the Standard Tariff costs €56.75 per year plus €0.05118 per KWh, but there are other options, as follows:

♦ **No standing charge** – you pay €0.0686 per KW up to 3,490KW and thereafter €0.05118;

♦ **Winter saver tariff** – you pay a standing charge of €227 plus €0.05118 per KW and you receive a credit of €175.04 for the period 1st December to 31st March.

Higher charges apply to households using over 73,000KW per year (known as the 'Large Residential User Tariff').

Bottled Gas

In most areas of Ireland, liquefied petroleum gas (LPG) bottles can be delivered by Calor Gas (☎ 01-450 5000, 💻 www.calor.ie), which supplies more than one in four homes. A few developments, such as the Eagle Valley housing estate in Enniskerry and apartment projects in Letterkenny and Wexford, are entirely Calor run.

If you want to use bottled gas, you must first have your property inspected and decide whether to use bottles (also known as cylinders) or have a tank installed; if you're planning to run central heating with gas, you will almost certainly need a tank. A 1,250 litre tank costs €250 to deliver and install and €110 per year to rent thereafter. The gas itself currently costs around €0.60 per litre (i.e. around €750 to fill a tank), which works out at around €0.0723 per KWh.

There are two main types of gas cylinder: butane and propane. Butane, which comes in 11.34kg/24lb bottles (usually yellow), should be used only when it's to be stored indoors, as butane won't vaporise at less than -2°C. Propane, which is the gas used in tanks, comes in 11.34kg (grey) bottles, 34kg/75lb (red) bottles and 47kg/103lb (green) bottles. Small bottles costs around €25 to refill, medium-size bottles €65 and large bottles €90.

You must also pay a non-returnable deposit (€27.50 for a small bottle, €60 for a large 34kg bottle). On average, bottled gas works out at around €0.12 per KWh. You should keep a spare bottle handy and make sure that you know how to change them (get the previous owner or a neighbour to show you).

A bottle used just for cooking will last an average family around six to eight weeks. Bottles can be connected into 'banks' and a four-bottle bank is enough to run a complete central heating system. Calor Gas also install boilers (their 'Combi' boiler provides central heating and instant hot water). If you opt for a 'condensing boiler', you may be able to reduce your annual fuel bills by up to 30 per cent.

You must have your gas appliances serviced and inspected at least every five years. If you have a contract with Calor Gas, they will do this for you or it will be done by your local authorised distributor. Calor's headquarters are in Dublin and they also have depots in Cork, Claremorris (County Mayo), New Ross (County Wexford) and Sligo.

HEATING

Heating is essential in winter (and sometimes in summer!) in Ireland. Central heating systems

may be powered by gas, electricity, oil or solid fuel (usually wood or peat but sometimes coal).

- ◆ **Gas** – Gas central heating is by far the most common in Ireland. But, even if you have no mains gas, it's possible to install a central heating system operating from a gas tank or bottles (see above). Stand-alone gas heaters using standard gas bottles cost around €150 and are an economical way of providing heating in all but the depths of winter. Note that gas heaters must be used only in rooms with adequate ventilation and that it can be dangerous to have too large a difference between indoor and outdoor temperatures.

- ◆ **Electricity** – Electric central heating is rare in Ireland, as it's relatively expensive and requires good insulation. Stand-alone electric heaters are also expensive to run and are best suited to holiday homes. However, a system of night-storage heaters operating on the night tariff can be economical. If you rely on electricity for all your power and use the night tariff, you should expect to pay around €50-75 per month.

- ◆ **Oil** – A 1,000 litre tank for domestic heating oil costs around €300 to buy (installation is normally done by the plumber who's putting in the central heating system) and around twice as much to fill. The price of oil and kerosene, which has lower emissions, has rocketed in the last few years to around €0.90 per litre, so that oil heating works out at around €0.078 per KWh – around the same as bottled gas. A tank will need refilling around twice a year depending on the amount you use. Further information about oil heating can be obtained from Emo (🖥 057-867 4700, 🖥 www.emo.ie).

♦ **Solid fuel** – Many people still have open fires in Ireland, particularly in rural areas, where many houses have open coal, wood or peat-burning fires and stoves that are often combined with a central heating system. Coal costs around €250 per tonne, which works out at around €0.03 per KWh and peat (sold in 'briquettes' bundled into 'bales') around €3 per bale, which equates to around €0.045 per KWh.

WATER & WASTE

The provision of water and waste services in Ireland is the responsibility of the 88 Sanitary Authorities (corresponding to the local authorities), which must follow policies laid down by the Department of the Environment, Heritage and Local Government (🖥 www.environ.ie). The recent growth in the economy and tourism has led to a significant increase in demand for water and waste services. The government has responded by committing €3.7bn to a National Development Plan comprising some 870 improvement schemes (details of the programme can be found on the above website).

Mains water is free unless you run a business from home, but it's widely feared that charges, which were abolished in 1999, will be reintroduced in the not-too-distant future.

Supply

One of the most important tasks before renting or buying a home in Ireland is to check the reliability of the local water supply (over a number of years). Ask your prospective neighbours and other local residents for information. It's essential to have the water supply checked and if necessary you should install your own water purification system. Domestic water in Ireland is currently free, so you won't need to worry about paying bills (or being cut off for failing to do so!),

but there has recently been pressure from the OECD to fit water meters to all new houses in line with its policy of 'eco-taxation'.

Over 80 per cent of Irish homes are connected to a public water supply, which is generally good; tap water can safely be drunk in most areas.

The peaty nature of Irish soil causes occasional discolouring of the water as well as slight alkalinity, but water everywhere is pleasantly 'soft' (which no doubt accounts for those rosy Irish complexions!).

Of the remaining 20 per cent, mainly in rural areas, three-quarters have small private supplies (i.e. wells), while a quarter have so-called group water schemes, where a number of households manage their own supply. In some of these, water isn't purified or disinfected in any way, so there's a risk of contamination from sources such as septic tanks or animal slurry pits.

A 2004 study by the Food Safety Authority of Ireland found that 40 per cent of schemes didn't comply with current water quality standards and almost a quarter of schemes were seriously contaminated.

Grants are available for the installation or improvement of individual supplies in houses over seven years old which aren't connected to either a public or group scheme water supply. The maximum household grant is around €2,030 and may not exceed 75 per cent of the cost. Application forms and explanatory notes are available from the Rural Water Programme Liaison Officer at your local County Council.

Hot Water

Water heating in apartments may beprovided by a central heating source for the whole building, or apartments may have their own water heaters. If you install your own water heater, it should have a capacity of at least 75 litres. If you need to install a water heater (or fit a larger one), you should consider the merits of both electric and gas heaters. An electric water boiler with a capacity of 75 litres (sufficient for two people) costs between €150 and €300 and usually takes between 60 and 90 minutes to heat water to 40C (104F) in winter.

A gas flow-through water heater is more expensive to purchase and install than an electric boiler, but you get unlimited hot water immediately whenever you want it. Make sure that a gas heater has a capacity of 10 to 16 litres per minute if you want it for a shower. A gas heater costs between €100 and €300 (although there's little difference in quality between the cheaper and more expensive heaters), plus installation costs.

Note that a gas water heater with a permanent flame may use up to 50 per cent more gas than one without. A resident family with a constant consumption is better off with an electric heater operating on the night tariff, while non-residents using a property for short periods will find a self-igniting gas heater more economical.

Connection

The connection of water supplies to new properties is a local matter in Ireland and is controlled by the county or urban district council (or in some cases the borough corporation). Connection charges vary considerably from county to county and even from village to village, as private local schemes proliferate; they can be as low as €150 or as high as €1,000 and may be even higher if major work is necessary, e.g. roads need to be dug up.

The good news is that, since there are no standing or consumption charges for domestic water anywhere in Ireland, if you move into a property that already has a water supply you won't have to pay a penny. However, if you run a business from home (or, for example, offer bed and breakfast), you may be liable for commercial water rates.

Sewerage

There's no direct charge for sewerage services in Ireland. Some 85 per cent of properties, including the vast majority in urban areas, are connected to the mains sewerage system. The remainder, mostly in rural areas, has septic tanks, which are emptied regularly by the local council.

REFUSE COLLECTION & RECYCLING

The Irish government is committed to reducing the amount of household waste that ends up in landfill centres; in fact the number of landfill centres is to be reduced to just 20, while recycling facilities are developed.

Refuse collection is managed locally and charges vary from county to county. In some places (e.g. parts of Dublin City) there's no charge at all, while in others charges range from as little as €40 per year (in Kilkenny, for example) to €450 or more in County Limerick. The average charge per household in County Dublin is around €220. Note, however, that you may claim tax relief on refuse collection charges – up to a limit of around €400. In many areas, the service has been privatised and costs are falling as a result. In some areas, there's no annual charge but a charge per bag or per bin (see below). In some remote parts no refuse collection service is provided, and residents must make their own arrangements (often with a local farmer) to dispose of household waste.

Most areas use wheelie bins for household waste. These are supplied free of charge by the local council, but collection may be charged for on a per-bin basis, in which case you must buy a tag (usually costing around €5) from a local shop or garage and attach it to your bin; bins without tags won't be emptied.

Some local authority and private waste collectors operate a system of waste separation, whereby different types of waste must be put in colour-coded bins, e.g., brown for compost, green for recycling and black or grey for waste that will go to a landfill.

When you move to Ireland (or to a new area of the country), you must register with the appropriate refuse disposal authority; a list of authorities and contacts can be found on the government's environmental information website (💻 www.enfo.ie). You may have a choice between the local authority's service and private operators.

If you have a large volume of waste, you can hire a skip or take it to a local civic amenity centre or landfill site. To save money on refuse collection you can buy a composter; these are sometimes sold by the local authority and cost around €25.

Recycling

Another way to save money on refuse collection (and to protect the environment) is to recycle waste. Some local authorities collect recyclable waste on certain days from outside houses, but there may be a charge (e.g. €1.50 per bag); in other areas you must take recyclable waste to a civic amenity centre (CAC) or 'bring centre'. The latter are simply an assortment of 'banks' for different types of material (glass, paper, cans, etc.), whereas CACs are usually staffed and may have composting facilities for 'green waste' (e.g. leaves and cuttings). There's no charge for local residents to use a CAC.

Items that can be recycled include the following:

♦ glass bottles and jars (some bring centres also recycle plate glass or windows);

♦ paper (e.g. newspapers, magazines, telephone books, office paper, junk mail, comics, light cardboard, paper cups and drink cartons);

♦ aluminium and other metals (e.g. cans, foil and bottle tops);

♦ plastic (e.g. drink and detergent bottles and tops, carrier bags, clingfilm, bubblewrap, yogurt and butter cartons);

♦ batteries (including lead acid, nickel cadmium, nickel metal hydride, lithium/lithium ion and all household primary, powerpack and mobile phone batteries);

♦ green waste (see items that can be composted below);

♦ textiles (e.g. clean-clothes, bed linen, towels);

♦ tyres;

♦ oil (e.g. mineral, vegetable and engine oil);

♦ white goods (e.g. washing machines, cookers, dryers, dishwashers and fridges);

♦ other household electrical appliances (e.g. kettles, toasters and computers);

♦ wood (without nails).

Note that waste electrical and electronic equipment (known to the EU as 'WEEE') **must** be recycled.

Waste electrical and electronic equipment can be taken to an amenity site or a registered recycling company (listed in the phone book and on 🖥 www.weeeregister.ie) and disposed of free of charge; if this isn't possible, contact your local authority to arrange collection, which will be charged for.

Items that can be composted include the following:

♦ teabags & coffee grounds;

♦ egg cartons;

♦ grass cuttings;

♦ hedge clippings;

♦ weeds and old plants;

♦ fruit and vegetable waste;

♦ leaves;

♦ egg shells;

♦ newspapers;

♦ light cardboard.

The following items cannot be recycled and should not be left at bring centres or CACs:

♦ crystal glass, Pyrex, television tubes, opal glass (i.e. alcohol bottles where a large amount of foil is glued to the bottle) and car windscreens;

♦ porcelain, pottery, stones and ceramic tiles;

♦ lead foil (used on certain brandy bottles);

♦ carpets, rugs, cushions and mattresses.

Various symbols on products and packaging indicate whether or not they're recyclable. The most common is the mobius loop (three arrows in a circle), which means that a product is either recyclable or has some recycled content. Unless the percentage of recycled content is stated, the symbol usually means that the product can be recycled. Another common symbol is a green dot, which means that the supplier of the packaging is 'committed to protecting the environment', but doesn't necessarily mean that it's recyclable.

6.
POSTAL SERVICES

The Irish postal service, like that of most other European Union (EU) countries, is in the process of 'liberalisation', under the aegis of the national Commission for Communications Regulation (ComReg). International postal services were opened to competition in January 2004 and the handling of domestic post over 50g in January 2006; domestic post under 50g, which remains the monopoly of Ireland's state-controlled postal service provider, An Post, is to be liberalised in January 2009.

In practice, however, it's unlikely that any other company will be able to compete with An Post in the day-to-day handling of bulk post, and most 'alternative providers' concentrate on express post and parcel services. A list of alternative providers can be found on ComReg's website (💻 www.comreg.ie). In any case, An Post's service is as efficient, reliable and inexpensive as any in Europe; only its services and rates are detailed here. The three divisions of An Post – Letter Post, Special Delivery Services and Post Offices – have been amalgamated.

There's a post office in almost every city, town and village in Ireland, as well as at main railway stations, airports and ports, but only 84 of them are main post offices (known as branch offices), run by An Post staff; the remaining 1,280 are known as contract offices and are operated on an agency basis.

As in many other European countries, post offices are being closed at an alarming rate; over a quarter of Irish post offices have disappeared since 2000. All main offices and 902 contract offices offer the full range of An Post services. In addition, around 170 retail outlets are designated postal agencies, known as 'PostPoints', where you can pay bills, top up your mobile phone, and buy international calling cards as well as stamps.

It's estimated that almost 50 per cent of Irish people do business in their local post office every week, which makes An Post the country's largest network of retailers, as well as of financial services, communications and distribution (the mail delivery service alone uses almost 3,000 vehicles and employs around 3,600 staff, handling 750m items of mail per year – over 200 for every Irish person).

To save queuing for stamps at a post office counter, books of stamps can also be bought from shops. These, as well as sheets and rolls of stamps, can be ordered from the An Post website (💻 www.anpost.ie). Stamp collectors should visit 💻 www.irishstamps.ie.

An Post produces a number of free brochures about postal rates and services, most of which are available from any post office. If you have any complaints about any post office service, you should contact the Customer Services Department (Ground Floor, GPO Freepost, Dublin 1, ☎ 01-705 7600 or ☎ 1850-575859, ✉ customer.services @anpost.ie). Further information can be found on the An Post website (💻 www.anpost.ie) or using the following contact numbers/email addresses:

- ◆ **Financial services** – ☎ 01-705 7200 or ☎ 1850-305060, ✉ savings@anpost.ie;

- ◆ **Philatelic services** – ☎ 01-705 8600 or ☎ 1850-262362, ✉ stamps.direct@anpost.ie;

- ◆ **Postal services** – ☎ 01-705 7600 or ☎ 1850-575859, ✉ customer.services @anpost.ie;

- ◆ **Television licences** – ✉ tv.licence @anpost.ie.

BUSINESS HOURS

Business hours at main post offices are usually from 9am until 1pm and from 2pm until 5.30pm Mondays to Fridays, and from 9am to 1pm on Saturdays. Offices in major towns don't close for lunch and may also provide limited services outside normal business hours. The General Post Office in O'Connell Street, Dublin, is open from 8am to 8pm Mondays to Saturdays and 10am to 6.30pm on Sundays and public holidays (on Sundays and holidays only stamps and foreign exchange are available).

Sub-post offices in small towns and villages usually close one day a week at 1pm. Post offices at airports are generally open during normal hours.

DELIVERY & COLLECTION

There are no postcodes in Ireland (except that Dublin is divided into 22 areas for postal purposes; these are numbered 1, 2, 3, 4, 5, 6, 6W, 7, 8, 9, 10, 11, 12, 13, 14, 15, 16, 17, 18, 20, 22, and 24) so the name or number of the house or business, the street, town and county are all that's required on envelopes (An Post recommends also putting your own address in the top left corner of the front of the envelope in case the letter has to be returned). The first line of the address should be at least 40mm from the top of the envelope and no part of the address should be within 18mm of the bottom or either side. Punctuation marks and underlining should be avoided and addresses should be typed if possible.

Post boxes are green and are usually free-standing, but may be set into (or attached to) a wall. Main and sub-post offices have post boxes outside; main post offices also usually have them inside. Collection times are shown on post boxes. There are usually at least three collections on weekdays, one or two on Saturdays and in some places one also on Sundays. Provided you post a letter before the latest time shown, it should arrive the next day, but if you post a letter on a Friday or a Saturday, it won't arrive until the following Monday, as there are no deliveries on Saturdays or Sundays. Post is delivered once a day only, in the morning, from Monday to Friday. Leaflets are available at Christmas time giving the last posting times for Ireland, Europe and the rest of the world.

Items sent abroad must have the appropriate customs declaration label: CN22 for items worth up to €300 and weighing up to 2kg; CP72 for items worth over €300 and over 2kg.

If the postman calls when you're not in with post requiring a signature or payment (e.g. a registered letter, a surcharged or cash on delivery item) or one that is too bulky to fit your letter box, he will leave a collection form. You can choose to collect the item from the address shown on the collection form or you can instruct the post office to allow it to be collected on your behalf by someone else (who will need a letter of authorisation from you), redeliver it on a date of your choosing or deliver it to another address, e.g. your workplace or a neighbour (this isn't an option for registered post).

If you decide to collect the item yourself, you should take the collection form with you. Collection offices are normally open from 7am until 5.30pm Mondays to Fridays. Identification may be required, e.g. a driving licence or passport, preferably with your address on it (which should be the same as that on the item to be collected). Post is retained for up to three weeks, with the exception of registered post, which is retained for three days only.

If you're likely to receive a lot of undeliverable mail, you can have it stored in a private box at the nearest post office for collection (see page 134). Private courier companies must obtain a signature for all deliveries so, if you aren't at home, they will leave a form asking you to contact them to arrange collection or re-delivery.

RATES & SERVICES

Letters

Domestic post (i.e. within the Republic of Ireland, which is termed 'Zone 1') is known as standard post (there's no 'first' and 'second' class mail in Ireland) and more than 90 per cent of it is delivered the next day (claimed to be one of the highest percentages in Europe), provided it's posted before the specified latest posting time, which varies from area to area. Postcards and letters weighing up to 100g cost €0.55. Large envelopes (up to C4) weighing up to 100g cost €0.95, up to 250g €1.35, up to 500g €1.90 and up to 1kg €3.00. Items over C4 size or over 1kg must be sent as packets or parcels (see **Packets & Parcels** below).

Small letters or postcards (being sent to Europe or the rest of the world) that eigh up to 100g cost €0.82. Large letters up to 100g cost

€1.50, up to 250g cost €3.00 and up to 500g €4.25. Letters to the UK usually take two or three working days and to other EU countries three or four days. You should allow five to seven days for airmail letters to eastern Europe, the US, Australia, New Zealand and Japan, and up to nine days for other destinations.

If a letter has been sent with insufficient postage, the addressee must pay the excess due plus a handling charge.

Packets & Parcels

Items larger than a 'large envelope' (see above), but measuring no more than 100mm x 70mm x 25mm and/or weighing up to 2kg are classed as 'packets', and items exceeding any of these dimensions and/or weighing more than 2kg (up to a maximum of 20kg) are called 'parcels'. Sample rates for domestic deliveries are shown in the table below.

Domestic Rates		
Weight	**Packet**	**Parcel**
100g	€2.20	€6.50
250g	€2.70	€6.50
500g	€3.85	€6.50
1kg	€6.00	€6.50
2kg	€7.50	€7.50
5kg	n/a	€14

International deliveries are priced according to destination: Zone 2 = UK, Zone 3 = rest of Europe and Zone 4 = rest of world. Sample rates are shown in the table below.

International Rates						
Weight	Zone 2		Zone 3		Zone 4	
	Packet	Parcel	Packet	Parcel	Packet	Parcel
100g	€2.70	€18.25	€2.70	€22	€2.70	€22
250g	€3.50	€18.25	€3.50	€22	€3.50	€22
500g	€4.85	€18.25	€4.85	€22	€4.85	€22
1kg	€7.50	€18.25	€7.50	€22	€10.40	€22
2kg	€10.75	€25	€10.75	€30	€16.60	€30
5kg	n/a	€40	n/a	€55	n/a	€55

Express Post Services

An Post offers various express services, described below:

Express Post

Express Post is a guaranteed next-day domestic delivery service. The same four size/weight categories apply as to ordinary post and rates start at €5.25 for a letter/postcard, large envelope or packet up to 100g and €10 for a parcel up to 100g. Items can be tracked online (if you have nothing better to do!) and, for an additional €2, can be insured for up to €350 and require a signature on delivery. Items must have an 'Express Post' label.

Courier Post

Courier Post is a guaranteed service, by noon the next day throughout Ireland and within specified time limits internationally (e.g. the next working day to the UK). Courier Post items must be at least A4 size and must be taken unsealed to a post office, where a 'Courier Post' label must be attached. Within Ireland, the service costs €15.95 for any item up to 100g and €22.95 for anything between 250g and 1kg. To the UK items up to 100g cost €20.50, to other EU countries €28, to non-EU European countries €23.14 and to other countries €26.

REGISTERED POST

If you're sending valuables or important documents, within Ireland or abroad, you can have them registered.

Registered post is tracked (so that, if it doesn't arrive, it can at least be found – theoretically!); if you've nothing better to do, you can even follow its progress on the internet!

Most items (except those that are fragile) are insured: for €320 within Ireland and the UK; for up to €150 to the rest of Europe (cover varies from country to country); for up to €100 (parcels) or €35 (other items) outside Europe. You will be given a receipt when you pay for postage and the item must be signed for on delivery.

Charges start at €5.25 for letters, large envelopes and packets up to 100g within Ireland. To all other destinations, letters up to 100g cost €5.17, large envelopes up to 100g €5.85 and packets up to 100g €7.05. Parcels start at €10.50 for Ireland, €23 for the UK, €27 for the rest of the world.

OTHER POSTAL SERVICES

An Post provides numerous other services, including the following for personal customers:

- ◆ **Poste restante** – Non-residents' post can be held for up to three months free of charge.

- ◆ **Private PO Box** – Your mail can be addressed to a Private PO Box and held until collected. There's an annual charge of €250.

- ◆ **Redirection** – If you've recently moved, you can have any mail addressed to your old home redirected to your new one. This service costs €50 for three months, €70 for six months or €100 for a year if you've moved within Ireland, or €70, €105 or €140 if you've moved abroad.

If you receive post for the previous occupants of your home or post that has been delivered to the wrong address, there are three things you can do with it: you can send it on to the addressee by crossing out the address, writing the new or correct address and dropping it in a post box, without a stamp; if you don't know the addressee's new address, you can cross out the address and write 'Gone Away' or 'Not at this Address' and drop it in a post box; or you can throw it away – but note that it's illegal to tamper with someone else's mail!

Business services include bulk and direct mail handling, business response services, with an optional Freepost address, dedicated collection, discounted rates for publications, and online ordering of stamps and stationery. For details, refer to the Business Customers section of the An Post website (💻 www.anpost.ie) or contact

☎ 01-705 8600 or ☎ 1850-262362 or ✉ business.desk@anpost.ie.

NON-POSTAL SERVICES

In addition to handling mail, An Post acts as an agent for a number of government departments, local authorities and private companies, offering a wide range of facilities to both businesses and individuals. These are listed alphabetically below. An Post has recently discontinued many of its services, including airline ticket purchase, bureau de change, 'eCards' and cassette post, discount cards and film development.

♦ **Bill payment** – BillPay is a service offered at all post offices, which accept payments for electricity, gas, cable and telephone bills, as well as on behalf of various local authorities and a number of charities and private companies (listed on 💻 www.anpost.ie). No charge or handling fee is involved. Bills can even be paid via the internet (💻 www.billpay.ie).

♦ **Dog licence** – Buy your dog licence at the post office.

♦ **Finance & insurance** – An Post offers a range of insurance and financial services, including car insurance, life insurance and loans, through One Direct, a direct sales operation based in Athlone, Co. Westmeath. Payments to One Direct can be made at most post offices. For details call ☎ 1890-222222 or visit 💻 www.onedirect.ie.

♦ **Gift vouchers** – An Post gift vouchers are accepted by some 500 retailers nationwide. For details go to 💻 www.giftvouchershop.ie.

♦ **Money transfer** – An Post provides a number of methods of sending and transferring money:

– postal money orders, which can be used only within Ireland. Postal orders are available in fixed denominations from €0.60 to €650 and charges range from €0.80 to €3.70;

– Eurogiro is an electronic money transfer system (normally taking four working days), which allows the recipient to cash or bank up to €1,904.61 (don't ask why this amount) in his own currency without incurring any redemption fee (the sender is charged €5.08). Eurogiros are currently accepted in Belgium, France, Germany, Italy, Luxembourg, the Netherlands, Spain, Switzerland and the UK.

– Sterling drafts of up to €2,000, which can be sent anywhere in the world, but may only be paid into a bank account and can be purchased only at main post offices. There's a fixed charge of €4.

– Some post offices also handle Western Union transfers, which are accepted in around 190 countries and take around ten minutes to complete, although the charges are high (Western Union will accept Visa or MasterCard, but not American Express; Amex card holders can use Amex's Moneygram service to transmit money to the nearest American Express office in just 15 minutes).

♦ **National lottery** – In 1987, An Post established the An Post National Lottery Company to operate Ireland's first national lottery. Lottery tickets, which cost a minimum of €3, are available from all post offices as well as other retailers. Most post offices also sell scratch cards. For details go to 💻 www.lotto.ie (see also **Gambling** on page 321).

- ◆ **Passport applications** – Guarantees customers a new passport within ten days, for a charge of €7.50 in addition to normal passport fees.

- ◆ **Phone cards** – An Post offers a wide range of phone cards and mobile telephone top-ups, including international call cards.

- ◆ **Prize bonds** – Prize bonds offer a 'flexible, state-guaranteed, risk-free investment' and the chance to win up to €150,000 each month (the risk being that you don't win anything!). The minimum 'investment' is €25. For further information go to 🖳 www.prizebonds.ie. See also **Gambling** on page 321.

- ◆ **Savings & investments** – An Post offers a range of savings and investment products, many tax-free and all state-guaranteed.

Social Welfare Payments

An Post acts as an agent for the Department of Social Welfare so that you can receive state pensions, unemployment benefit and many other social welfare payments at your local post office.

- ◆ **TV licences** – Television licences (see page 214) are sold at all post offices. You can also buy Television Licence Savings Stamps (through the BillPay service – see above) to help you save for renewal day.

Salthill, Co. Galway

7.

TELEPHONE

The Irish are renowned for their loquacity, and they live up to their reputation in their use of the telephone. The Irish government is committed to keeping Ireland's communications network at the forefront of technology and the recent explosion of competition in the telecommunications sector has made calls among the cheapest in Europe.

TELEPHONE COMPANIES

Like postal services, telephone services are regulated by the national Commission for Communications Regulation (ComReg, 🖥 www.comreg.ie), whose consumer website (🖥 www.askcomreg.ie) provides a wealth of useful information and advice regarding telecommunications in Ireland, including a 'cost calculator' that enables you to compare the charges of all authorised operators for similar services.

As in most European Union (EU) countries, the telecommunications market has been opened to competition and consumers have a wide choice of service providers, although fixed line connections are still controlled by the national telephone company, Eircom (🖥 www.eircom.ie), whose service isn't always as efficient as it might be. The official 'standard time frame' for the connection of a new line is 28 days, although in many cases connection is made within a few days. On the other hand, in remote areas you might have to wait up to three months! (See **Mobile Phones** on page 146). Eircom used to boast that 97 per cent of faults were remedied within two working days, but no such figure is currently available!

Authorised telephone service providers arelisted in the table overleaf.

Unless otherwise stated, the information in this chapter relates to Eircom services.

INSTALLATION & REGISTRATION

When moving into a new home with a telephone line, you must have the account transferred to your name. If you're planning to move into a property without a telephone line, you will need to contact Eircom if you want one installed – unless you have access to cable services (see page 154) and wish to use the telephone system offered by your cable company.

You can have a telephone installed or reconnected without even visiting your local Eircom office (the 18 regional Eircom sales centres are listed on the website). Simply dial 1901 and give your name and address and the existing telephone number of the property (if there is one). If you're renting, you will need to pay a deposit or find someone with an Eircom account to act as a guarantor. If you're taking over a property from the previous occupants, you should arrange for the telephone account to be transferred to your name from the day you take possession. Before buying a property, check that the previous bills have been paid, or you may find yourself liable for them.

It can take up to five weeks to get a telephone line installed, although it usually takes just a week (five working days) or two in most areas. The cost of having a private line installed is €119.99 (including VAT at 21 per cent) for a 'hi-speed' line or €121.93 for a standard line, even

Telephone Companies

Company	Telephone Number	Website
All Communications Network	01-247 7772	www.acneuro.com
ATS Voice	01-207 9500	www.ats.ie
Blue Face	01-524 2000	www.blueface.ie
BT Ireland	1800-923-924	www.btireland.ie
Chorus	1890-940624	www.chorus.ie
Clarity Telecom	1800-855111	www.claritytele.com
Colt Telecom	1800-943 111	www.colt-telecom.ie
Direct Dial Telecom	1800-930338	www.directdialtele.com
Dome Telecom	1890-927001	www.dometelecom.com
Euphony	01-676 0033	www.euphony.ie
Gaelic Telecom	1890-929422	www.gaelictelecom.ie
Greencom Telecommunications	1890-946246	www.greencom.ie
IFA Telecom	1890-924851	www.ifatelecom.ie
Imagine	01-437 5000	www.imagine.ie
Magnet	1890-625638	www.magnet.ie
Newtel	1800-639835	www.newtel.ie
NTL	1890-940624	www.ntl.ie
Perlico Communications	1890-252148	www.perlico.com
Pure Telecom	01-289 5555	www.puretelecom.ie
Skytel	1890-886005	www.skytel.ie
Swiftcall	1800-929803	www.swiftcall.ie
TalkTalk	1800-944861	www.talktalk.ie
UTV	1890-926000	www.utv.ie
Worldlink	01-855 2560	www.worldlink.ie
Zefone	0818-272727	www.zefone.ie

if the network has to be extended to do so, although if the cost of extending the network exceeds €7,000 (e.g. for a remote property) the customer must pay the cost above this amount.

To find out whether connecting a property is likely to incur additional charges, call Eircom's installation team on ☎ 1800-211445.

A deposit of 50 per cent of the installation fee is required, the balance being added to your first telephone bill. The charge for taking over an existing line (which takes up to a week) is €50.

Telephones (and fax machines) can be bought from Eircom shops or a number of retail outlets.

Call-outs & Complaints

Service and repairs to Eircom installations are free, but Eircom charges for attending to faults with or caused by non-Eircom equipment. Charges start at around €50 and rise to around €130 for an out-of-hours call-out, plus around €25 per hour after the first half hour.

If you're dissatisfied with Eircom's service, you should address your complaint to the Customer Care Department (5th Floor, Telephone House, Marlborough Street, Dublin 1, ☎ 1901 (free) or ☎ 1800-200481), giving your account number.

USING THE TELEPHONE

Tones

The following standard tones are used in Ireland:

♦ **Dial tone** – A continuous high pitched hum when you lift the receiver indicates that the phone is connected to the network and you can start dialling.

♦ **Ringing tones** – A repeated burr indicates that the dialled number is ringing.

♦ **Engaged** – A single beep at short intervals means that the dialled number is busy (engaged). Sometimes you will hear a recorded message telling you that 'All lines are busy, please try later' or even 'The number you are ringing is busy' – in case you didn't already know!

♦ **Unobtainable** – A continuous steady tone means that you've dialled a number which isn't in use or is temporarily out of service or out of order. Check the code and number and dial again. If unsuccessful, check the number with directory enquiries (see page 142) or that it's in service by calling the operator (see page 142). In some cases you will hear a recorded announcement, for example when an area code or number has been changed.

Codes

Main towns and their surrounding areas have dialling codes consisting of two to four digits, as shown below. When making a call to a number with the same area code as the number you're calling from, you don't dial the code.

Numbers beginning with 01 relate to the Dublin area, those beginning 02 areas in Cork City and County, those beginning with 04 eastern areas, 05 the south-east, 06 the south-west and mid-west, 07 and 09 the west and north-west.

Mobile phone numbers are prefixed 083, 085, 086 or 087. The international code for Ireland is 353; when calling from abroad, omit the initial 0 of the area code, e.g. 353 1 for Dublin numbers. When making an international call from Ireland, dial 00 before the country code.

Emergency & Service Numbers

As in the UK, the standard emergency number is 999, which is a freephone number. You may also dial 112. In both cases, you are connected to an operator, who will ask which service(s) you require: fire, police (Garda), ambulance, coastguard, or mountain and cave rescue. Note that you can be fined a **very** large sum and/or imprisoned for up to five years for making hoax calls to the emergency services!

Area Codes								
Arklow	0402	Enniscorthy	054	Roscommon	0903
Athlone	0902	Galway	091	Rosslare	053
Ballina	096	Kilkenny	056	Shannon	061
Bandon	023	Killarney	064	Sligo	071
Bundoran	072	Letterkenny	074	Thuries	0504
Carlow	0503	Limerick	061	Tipperary	062
Castlebar	094	Longford	043	Tralee	066
Cavan	049	Mallow	022	Tuam	093
Clonmel	052	Monaghan	047	Tullamore	0506
Cork	021	Mullingar	044	Waterford	051
Donegal	073	Naas	045	Westport	098
Drogheda	041	Navan	046	Wexford	053
Dublin	01	Nenagh	067	Wicklow	0404
Dundalk	042	Portlaoise	0502	Youghal	024
Ennis	065	Rathluire	063		

Service numbers include the following:

♦ **10** – Operator assistance;

♦ **11811** – Directory enquiries for residential numbers within Ireland, for which you will be charged €0.84 for each 30-second call, with a supplement for longer calls. You may ask for up to three numbers per call.

♦ **11818** – Directory enquiries for residential numbers outside Ireland, including Northern Ireland, for which the charge is €1.58 for each 30-second call, with a supplement for longer calls. You may ask for up to three numbers per call.

♦ **1901** – To order Eircom services, pay your bill, report a fault or order a phone book or change your phone book entry.

Other emergency, information and helpline numbers are listed at the front of the phone book.

OPERATOR SERVICES

Eircom provides a range of operator and other services, including the following:

♦ **1471** – If you don't have an answerphone but you want to know who was the last person to call you (e.g. while you were out), you can dial 1471 to be told the last caller's number and the time of the call. This facility is also useful if you're receiving suspicious calls where the caller hangs up as soon as you answer. However, foreign and ex-directory numbers aren't recorded, and it's possible for callers to withhold their number. You're charged each time you use this service.

♦ **Advice of Duration & Charge** – Enables you to find out how long a call you've made lasted and how much it cost. You're charged each time you use this service.

♦ **Alarm Call** – Also referred to as an alarm clock call and a reminder call, this programmes your telephone to ring at a set time, for example to wake you or to remind you to do something. Calls cost less if you set it up yourself instead of asking the operator (dial *55*, then the time you want the phone to ring, e.g. 0730 for 7.30am, then #) – but an alarm clock may work out cheaper still.

♦ **Call Forwarding** – Allows you to divert calls to another telephone number automatically, e.g. from home to office (or vice versa) or to a mobile telephone, without callers knowing that the call is being diverted. You need to register for call forwarding, for which there's a minimal one-off charge.

♦ **Call Tracking** – Allows you to keep a record of the calls made by up to eight people – useful for a shared house. Each caller must enter a code before dialling a number. There's a small monthly charge for this service.

♦ **Call Waiting** – Lets you know when another caller is trying to contact you (by interrupting your conversation with beeps) when you're already making a call and allows you to speak to the new caller without terminating your current call. Call waiting is a free service, but you need to request it.

⚠ **Caution**

If using the line for internet access, don't forget to de-activate the call waiting service, or your internet connection will be broken; it's possible to divert calls to the messaging service instead (see below).

♦ **Caller Display** – Allows you to check who's calling before you answer the phone, when the caller's number is shown on an LCD display. If your phone isn't fitted with a display, you can buy a separate 'caller display' unit (which will store up to 20 numbers). The service itself is free, but you must request it.

♦ **Caller Line Restriction** – Prevents your number being displayed on the phone of the person you're calling (see **Caller Display** above). The service is free but, if your number is ex-directory, it won't be displayed anyway.

♦ **Messaging** – An answerphone service that allows you to pick up messages 'remotely', records messages while you're using the line for internet access, converts text messages to speech and provides up to four 'mailboxes' on a single line. There is a small monthly charge for this service.

♦ **Personal Call** – Equivalent to an American person-to-person call. You're charged each time you use this service.

♦ **Reverse Charge Call** – You can ask the operator to reverse the charge of a call, in which case the person you're calling will be asked if he is willing to accept the charges, which will be considerably higher than the normal call rate – and you will also incur a small fee for the service.

♦ **RingBack** – Automatically redials an engaged number for up to 45 minutes. To activate the service, dial *37# when you hear an engaged tone. You're charged each time you use this service.

♦ **Telemessage** – Allows you to send a message to someone by phone without actually speaking to him. You're charged per word each time you use this service.

♦ **Three-way Calling** – Allows you to talk to two people at once. Dial a number, then press R, which puts that person on hold while you dial another number, then press R3 to speak to both people at once or R2 to alternate between them (e.g. for a game of Chinese Whispers). The service is free.

Home Country Direct

Ireland subscribes to a Home Country Direct service that allows you to call a number giving you direct and free access to an operator in the country you're calling, e.g. for the UK you dial ☎ 1800-550144. The operator will connect you to the number required and will also accept credit card calls. Countries with a Home Direct service include Australia, Belgium, Brazil, Canada, Chile, Denmark, Finland, France, Germany, Guatemala, Hong Kong, Indonesia, Japan, South Korea, Norway, the Netherlands, Portugal, Spain, Sweden, the UK, Uruguay and the US.

CHARGES

It isn't possible to list here all the call charges made by every service provider; the charges

shown below are examples of Eircom's charges, which are competitive with most other providers. For a list of alternative service providers, see page 144. You can compare the charges made by all providers on ⌨ www.callcosts.ie, a service set up by the Irish telecommunications regulator, ComReg.

For calls within Ireland there are three different 'time bands': daytime (between 8am and 6pm Mondays to Fridays); evening (6pm to 8am Mondays to Fridays); weekends (all day Saturdays and Sundays and on public holidays). These bands also apply to calls to certain other countries. Within Ireland, there's also a distinction between local calls (i.e. calls to numbers with the same area code) and national calls (i.e. calls to numbers with a different code). The table overleaf gives examples of Eircom call charges to different destinations; these don't take into account any discounts that may be available by booking a call 'package'. Charges are shown in cents (i.e. hundredths of a euro) and to the nearest whole cent.

Charge per Minute (cents)			
Call Type/Destination	Daytime	Evening	Weekend
Local call	5	1	1
National calls	8	5	1
Calls to mobiles within Ireland	21-26	15-18	10-14*
Calls to the UK	15	14	12
Calls to mobiles in the UK	35	28	28
Calls to Near Europe	24	24	24
Calls to Mid Europe	39	39	39
Calls to Far Europe	92	80	80
Calls to the US & Canada	19	15	15
Calls to Australia & New Zealand	85	68	44

* The cost of calls from a fixed line phone to a mobile varies with the mobile operator.

Operator-connected calls (local and national) are charged differently according to the time: between 6pm on Friday and 8pm on Sunday (cheaper) and between 8pm on Sunday and 6pm on Friday (more expensive).

Calls to numbers beginning 18 and 15 are the same at any time (see **Free & Fixed Rate Numbers** below).

Call Plans

All telephone service providers offer a bewildering array of 'call plans', ostensibly designed to simplify your life and reduce your phone bill to a minimum, but actually disguising the cost of calls so that you never know whether you're paying the lowest possible rate or not. It's impossible to list all the plans offered by all the operators and in any case these are changed so frequently that any such information would soon be out of date. The following is a sample of the call plans offered by Eircom in July 2008.

◆ **Talktime 15c** – for 'long talkers', who use the phone infrequently but make the most of it when they do, costing €27 per month;

◆ **Talktime Weekender** – for 'weekend chatters', costing €27 per month.

◆ **Talktime After Hours** – for 'busy bees', i.e. those who use the phone mostly in the evenings, costing €31 per month;

◆ **Talktime 200** – for 'light diallers' (presumably not referring to their weight), costing €34 per month;

◆ **Talktime UK** – for 'UK talkers', costing €36 per month.

◆ **Talktime International** – for 'global talkers', costing €36 per month.

◆ **Talktime Anytime** – for 'big talkers' (no doubt popular among the Irish!), costing €41 per month;

◆ **Talktime Mobile** – for those whose friends are always out and about, costing €41 per month.

Free & Fixed Rate Numbers

Calls to any number beginning 1800 are free, no matter how long you're on the line. Calls to 1890 numbers (sometimes advertised as 'lo-call' numbers) are charged at normal local call rates (see above).

Premium Rate Numbers

Premium rate numbers begin 15 and generally apply to weather forecasts, horoscopes, gambling, flight information, and chat and sex lines. Premium rate call charges vary according to the prefix and, in the case of 1512 calls, to the time of day (evenings and weekends are cheaper) as follows (charges are rounded to the nearest cent):

Premium Rate Call Charges			
Prefix	Charge per Minute	Prefix	Charge per Minute
1512	€0.25 to €3.61	1530	€0.33
1513	€0.60	1540	€0.60
1514	€0.75	1550	€0.95
1515	€1	1559	€0.89
1516	€1.50	1560	€1.25
1517	€2	1570	€1.75
1518	€3	1580	€2.40
1520	€0.15	1590	€2.90

International Calling Cards

You can obtain an international telephone calling card from telephone companies in many countries that allows you to make calls from abroad and charge them to your telephone bill in your home country. American long distance telephone companies (e.g. AT&T, MCI and Sprint) compete vigorously for overseas customers, and all offer calling cards allowing foreign customers to bill international calls to a credit card.

The benefits of international calling cards are that they're fee-free; calls can be made to/ from most countries; calls can usually be made from any telephone, including hotel telephones; and calls are made via an English-speaking operator in the US (foreign-language operators are also available). Most important of all, call charges are often based on the 'callback' system and are charged at American rates (based on the cost between the US and the country you're calling from and to), which is usually much cheaper than calls made via local telephone companies.

Some companies offer conference calling facilities that allow you to talk to a number of people in different countries at the same time. Other features may include a 'world office' facility that allows you to retrieve voice and fax messages at any time, from anywhere in the

world. Note that if you do a lot of international travelling, it's advisable to have a number of phone cards, as the cheapest card often depends on the countries you're calling from and to.

Eircom offers its customers a Global Telecard, which can be used in a similar way in over 40 countries; to apply for a card, call ☎ 1800-404700. The charge for a Telecard depends on the type of account you have with Eircom. Prepaid calling cards, confusingly called Eircom Global cards, are also available for phoning Ireland from abroad as well as for making calls within Ireland and from Ireland to around 20 countries.

BILLS

You're normally billed every two months by Eircom for your line rental and, if applicable, phone rental and calls, but you can request a monthly bill. If you're a new customer, your connection fee is included in your first bill. Eircom provide itemised bills on request. These are free if you're on one of Eircom's call plans. Bills can be paid by direct debit, by cheque or credit card (online payments only). If you aren't on direct debit, you can make payments:

♦ by post (using the envelope provided);

♦ at any bank, by bank giro – if you're with the Bank of Ireland, you can use an ATM;

♦ at a post office;

♦ at an Eircom telecentre;

♦ online (at 🖥 www.billpay.ie), where it's possible to set up a direct debit;

♦ by electronic funds transfer (EFT) from abroad.

There are no savings or discounts for using any of these payment methods. If you don't pay your phone bill within two months (i.e. by the time you receive the next one) you will be sent a reminder and must pay within the next two weeks. If you don't pay your bill within this period, your phone will be disconnected, usually without any further notification, and you will be charged a reconnection fee (see

Installation & Registration on page 139). If you have a query about your account, dial 1901.

PUBLIC TELEPHONES

Owing to the rapid increase in the use of mobile phones, the number of public telephones in Ireland fell from around 8,000 in 2001 to just a few thousand in 2008, mainly in rural areas. Public phone boxes can still be found on streets, in post offices and at railway and bus stations. Phones, which are operated by Eircom and the ITG Group, almost all require a phone card (known as a callcard), which can be bought in post offices and from most newsagents and many shops and petrol stations.

Coin phones have virtually been phased out and only a small number of credit card phones are available, generally in hotels, although these may also accept callcards. Calls from public telephones made with a callcard are a lot cheaper than calls made with a credit card.

Be wary of using public phones in pubs, restaurants, hotels, shopping centres and petrol stations. The charge rate for these phones is set by the owners and can be extortionate. The call charge should be displayed, although it often isn't (would you advertise to your customers that you're ripping them off?). You should also avoid using hotel room phones, where fees can be astronomical. Some hotels even charge a fee to connect guests to free (e.g. 1800) numbers!

Unlike public phones in some countries, which are often vandalised or simply not working, Irish payphones usually work (Eircom claims that some 95 per cent of its payphones are working at any given time).

Eircom offers its customers a charge card (called a Global Telecard – see **International Calling Cards** on page 145), which can be used in payphones instead of a callcard or credit card; the cost of the call is simply added to your home phone bill – but you will pay a premium for the convenience!

International 'phone credit' cards are available from a number of companies, including Dome Telecom (www. dometelecom.com) and Swiftcall (www. swiftcall-phonecard.co.uk), and can be bought at post offices and other retail outlets.

If you use the directory enquiries service from a payphone, you're charged an initial amount (usually £1) for an enquiry lasting up to 80 seconds, thereafter a supplement; and an additional amount (around €0.50) if you choose to be connected directly to the number requested instead of dialling it yourself (in Ireland, even idleness has its price!).

MOBILE TELEPHONES

The Irish mobile (cell) phone system runs on the digital network and initial problems with coverage, caused by mountainous terrain, appear to have been eliminated. Analogue phones won't work in Ireland. Americans wanting to make mobile phone calls in Ireland need an unlocked dual-band or tri-band GSM phone and a SIM card. Unlocked phones allow the use of any SIM card, provided the frequency capabilities are correct. These are 900/1800 Mhz for dual band, 900/1800/1900 Mhz for tri-band. Other Europeans can tap into one the local networks (see below). Alternatively, buy a mobile phone locally.

Before buying a phone, compare battery life, memory capacity, weight, size and features. Don't rely on getting good or impartial advice from retail staff and always deal with an independent company that sells a wide range of phones and can connect you to any network. The Carphone Warehouse (☎ 1850-943800, 🖥 www.carphonewarehouse.ie) publishes an independent guide to choosing your mobile phone, available free from any of its outlets.

In recent years there has been widespread publicity regarding a possible health risk to users from the microwave radiation emitted by mobile phones.

Mobile Networks

You can choose from the following mobile networks, all of which cover virtually the whole country (there remain only a few valleys and mountaintops where a mobile is a worthless accessory):

♦ **3** (🖥 www.3ireland.ie) – dialling code 083;

♦ **Meteor** (☎ 01-430 7085 or ☎ 1905, 🖥 wwwmeteor.ie) – dialling code 085;

♦ **O2** (🖥 www.o2online.ie) – dialling code 086;

♦ **Vodafone** (🖥 www.vodafone.ie) – dialling code 087.

All four companies offer a choice between a pre-pay (or pay-as-you-go or top-up) service, where you pay for a certain value of calls in advance, and a post-pay (or contract) service, where you're billed monthly in arrears. Post-pay services usually include a 'discounted' or 'free' phone, but of course the cost is hidden in the call charges you commit to for a minimum period and you may have to pay a monthly 'rental' fee.

On the other hand, pre-pay charges are often higher on a per-call basis than post-pay tariffs. Bear in mind that the web of tariffs is designed primarily to confuse customers! Don't be seduced by a cheap phone when the real costs lie in high call and line rental charges. Generally, the higher the connection and line rental charges, the lower the cost of calls. Once you sign a contract you're usually stuck with the same phone for at least 12 months.

As with fixed-line phones, there's a plethora of 'call plans' to choose from and these are constantly changing, so it's impossible to provide even a summary of what's on offer here. For a package allowing you to make 400 minutes of calls per month within Ireland at any time you can expect to pay between around €40 and €70 per month; for 600 minutes between around €60 and €100 per month.

Top-up cards start at €5 (Meteor and O2) or €10 (Vodaphone) and can be bought at post offices or numerous retail outlets.

You can compare the charges made by the four networks, as well as other features of their respective services (e.g. whether and where they offer 3G coverage), on 🖥 www.callcosts.ie, a service set up by the Irish telecommunications regulator, ComReg. Enter your calling pattern (i.e. how many calls you make to what destinations at what times) to be given a comparison between relevant call plans offered by the various operators. When choosing between the four networks, take into account also their coverage, contract termination terms and charges, disconnection and reconnection charges and, if applicable, international 'roaming' charges. If you change networks, you can retain your number – or at least all of it except one digit, as the dialling code changes (see above).

☑ SURVIVAL TIP

When buying a mobile phone for car use you should choose one which provides hands-free use, as you can be prosecuted for using a hand-held phone while driving.

DIRECTORIES

Irish telephone subscribers, both business and private, are listed in directories, commonly known as phone books, one for each of the six phone code areas of Ireland: Dublin (numbers beginning 01), Cork (02), the north-east (04), south-east (05), west (06) and north-west (07 and 09). All phone books except the Dublin directory incorporate 'white pages', listing private and business numbers alphabetically, and *Golden Pages*, a classified directory of business numbers including advertisements. For the Dublin area, the white pages and *Golden Pages* are in separate volumes, and private and business numbers are listed separately in the white pages.

All subscribers receive a free phone book (both books in the Dublin area), which are usually updated annually. If you don't have the latest local phone book when you move into a new home, you can get one free from your local Eircom shop or from any post office or Citizens' Information Centre. Additional copies of your local directory can be ordered from Eircom by completing the form at the front of any white pages directory or by calling ☎ 1800-202020.

To obtain more than one entry in your local phone book, e.g. when a husband and a wife both retain their family names or when two or more people share a telephone, you can complete the form in the back of the phone book or simply call ☎ 1800-488588, which is also the number to call if you wish your number to be 'ex-directory' (i.e. not to be listed either in the phone book or with directory enquiries).

Useful local telephone numbers are also listed in local monthly guides published by councils and chambers of commerce. For those who can never find anything in the phone book or *Golden Pages*, there's *Golden Pages* Talking (☎ 11811). Fax numbers are also listed in *Golden Pages* directories, while business and residential telephone and fax numbers, as well as email and website addresses, are available online (⌨ www.goldenpages.ie). Business numbers can also be found in the *Europages Online Directory* and the *Kompass Directory*.

INTERNET

Needless to say, internet service provision in Ireland is state-of-the-art, but broadband (ADSL) connection isn't available in all parts of the country (and Eircom has no plans to extend availability to remote parts), although in some rural areas you can obtain a connection via satellite or wireless telephony. There's no 'coverage map' and to find out whether a particular area is covered you must either go to ⌨ www.eircom.ie and enter a local telephone number or call Eircom Residential Sales on ☎ 1800-242633. As with telephone and mobile services, there's a choice of internet service providers (ISPs) – see below.

Internet Service Providers

Irish ISPs include the following:

♦ BT Ireland (⌨ www.esat.net);

♦ Chorus (⌨ www.cablenet.ie);

♦ Digiweb (⌨ www.digiweb.ie);

♦ Eircom (⌨ www.eircom.ie);

♦ IFA Telecom (⌨ www.ifatelecom.ie);

♦ Irish Broadband (⌨ www.irishbroadband.ie);

♦ Magnet Entertainment (⌨ www.magnetnetworks.com);

♦ NTL (⌨ www.ntl.ie);

♦ Perlico (⌨ www.perlico.com);

♦ Smart Telecom (⌨ www.smarttelecom.ie);

♦ UTV (⌨ www.utvlive.com);

Some of the above provide broadband only via fixed lines, others via satellite or wireless connections. Alternatively, you can sign up with a global provider such as AOL.

There are two types of internet connection – dial-up and broadband – and four types of payment arrangement: pay-as-you-go, partial flat rate, full flat rate and 'always online'.

A partial flat rate normally includes all connection between set times (e.g. during off-peak hours), while at other times you must pay per minute; a full flat rate usually allows you a set number of hours' connection at any time.

A dial-up connection uses a standard telephone line and charges are similar to those for telephone usag; 'always online' isn't an option for a dial-up connection. Most broadband connections are permanent, i.e. you're always online, but some providers offer pay-as-you-go and flat rate options. As with fixed-line and mobile telephone services, there's a welter of options on offer from the various ISPs and it's impossible to give a breakdown of all costs here, but only a general indication.

Costs for broadband connection vary not only according to whether you want an 'always online' or flat rate arrangement (see above), but also with the speed of connection (from 1MB to 8MB). Flat rates start at around €10 per month plus the cost of calls, while 'always on' connections start at around €20 per month for 1MB, rising to around €80 for 8MB. To further confuse matters, many providers offer combined telephone and internet (and sometimes also mobile phone) packages. You can compare the charges made by the various ISPs, as well as other features of their respective services, on ⌨ www.callcosts.ie

or 🖳 www.askcomreg.com, a service set up by the Irish telecommunications regulator, ComReg.

When choosing an ISP, don't only compare prices, but check the minimum contract period and its terms and conditions (especially regarding termination, e.g. whether there's a required notice period or compulsory penalty), whether any connection charges or usage limits apply, whether you can switch between connection types and payment options, what security features (e.g. firewall or anti-virus software) are included or offered, and what technical support is provided.

Installing a standard broadband connection to an existing telephone line, which must be carried out by an Eircom 'technician' (often in fact a sub-contractor), costs around €100. Note also that a telephone line may not be required to connect to the internet; you may be able to access the internet via cable or satellite (see page 157) or even using an aerial, via wireless technology, although these types of connection may not also support telephone communication.

MOVING HOUSE OR LEAVING IRELAND

When moving house or leaving Ireland you must notify your telephone company, preferably well in advance (particularly if you want to get a deposit repaid), although it's possible to call Eircom up to a day before you move. You can either have

your line disconnected, in which case anyone who wants to take over the line will have to pay a reconnection fee, or it can be transferred to the new user free of charge. In either case, your final bill will be sent to you around two to three weeks after you move. (Don't forget to do one or the other, or the new owners or tenants will be able to make calls at your expense!)

Similarly, if you're moving to another house in the same area code area (e.g. 01 for the Dublin area) with an existing phone line, it may be possible to take over the previous owners' number (free) or take your number with you (for a fee), although the latter may be possible only if you remain within the same exchange area (there are several exchange areas within each code area).

MALICIOUS CALLS

It's an offence to make malicious or nuisance calls in Ireland (telephone salespersons please note). If you receive malicious or obscene phone calls, Eircom gives the following advice:

♦ Don't enter into any conversation.

♦ Don't give any details (e.g. your name or number).

♦ Simply place the handset beside the telephone and ignore it; don't hang up immediately.

♦ Contact Eircom on the number given in your local phone book.

♦ If the caller phones repeatedly, don't say anything when you pick up the handset; a genuine caller will speak first.

If you receive persistent malicious calls, you can call Eircom's Malicious Calls Bureau on ☎ 1800-689689 (between 9am and 5pm Mondays to Fridays) or the 24-hour helpline ☎ 1800-475475. Another possibility is to subscribe to Eircom's Caller Display service (see page 142) which allows you to identify callers before answering the phone. As a last resort you can arrange for the operator to block all your calls for a period or obtain a new number and ask for it to be ex-directory.

8.

TELEVISION & RADIO

As in most other countries, watching television (TV) and, to a lesser extent, listening to the radio are among the most popular national pastimes (or a national epidemic, depending on your point of view) and it's common to find TVs blaring in pubs and radios blaring in people's homes from morning to night. Fortunately they've yet to completely replace sociable activities such as talking and singing, for which Ireland is renowned, and the Irish do at least show some discrimination in their choice of programmes, generally preferring homemade to imported entertainment, be it American or British. Nevertheless, limited funding for RTÉ, which relies in equal measure on advertising and licence fees, means that the TV schedules are filled with the inevitable quota of cheap American programmes.

Irish TV and radio services are operated by Radio Telefís Éireann (RTÉ), the public broadcasting company, and all Irish terrestrial TV and radio stations are regulated by the Broadcasting Commission of Ireland (🖳 www.bci.ie).

TELEVISION

Television programmes (terrestrial, satellite and cable) are listed in daily newspapers and weekly guides such as the *RTE Guide* (Ireland's best-selling publication), as well as in daily newspapers and on RTÉ's website (🖳 www.rte.ie), where you can find detailed programme information (and not just RTÉ programmes). Programme listings can also be displayed via Aertel Teletext.

Many satellite stations also provide Teletext information, and Sky programmes are listed in a number of publications such as *What Satellite*, *Satellite Times* and *Satellite TV* (the best), which are available on subscription. The annual *World Radio and TV Handbook* (Billboard) contains over 600 pages of information, and the frequencies of all radio and TV stations worldwide.

Standards & Equipment

The standards for TV reception in Ireland aren't the same as in some other countries. Ireland, like the UK, uses the PAL I standard, so TVs and video recorders (VCRs) operating on the French (SECAM) or North American (NTSC) systems won't work. Machines operating on the European PAL B/G system can be converted for around €100 to €150. It's also possible to buy a multi-standard European TV (and VCR) containing automatic circuitry that switches between different systems. Some multi-standard TVs also include the North American NTSC standard, and have an NTSC-in jack plug connection allowing you to play back American videos, although prices are high – almost twice as much as standard TVs/VCRs. Some immigrants opt for two TVs, one to receive Irish TV programmes and another (e.g. SECAM or NTSC) to play back their favourite videos.

The cost of TVs and other electrical equipment in Ireland can be ascertained from the DID Electrical website (🖳 www.didstore. com). The prices quoted in this section are intended only as a guide.

Televisions

A small portable colour TV can be purchased for as little as €30. A 55cm (21in) TV costs from around €100 depending on the make and features (around €300 for one with Nicam stereo), LCD (flat screen) TVs start at around €350 and a wide-screen 'home cinema' system at around €800, while the latest high-definition 'virtual reality' model will set you back up to

€2,000 – but you save on holidays, sporting activities and other dangerous pastimes. Interest-free credit for up to 12 months can be obtained on some makes of TV and VCR.

Teletext

If you decide to buy a TV in Ireland, you will find it advantageous to buy one with Aertel Teletext, which, apart from allowing you to display programme schedules, also provides a wealth of useful and interesting information. In fact most new TVs (apart from very basic ones) come with Aertel Teletext, which is also available via the RTÉ website (💻 www.rte.ie) – complete with Courier typeface!

Digital TV

Digital television is now widely available in Ireland – via satellite, cable and even aerial. It offers not only a superior picture, better (CD) quality sound and the option of widescreen cinema format, but also a wider choice of programmes, as a number of channels broadcast only digitally.

> Note that you don't need a digital TV to receive digital satellite transmissions.

Satellite Dishes & Receivers

The dish diameter required varies from 35cm to 2m according to location; check with a local installer, as online 'link budgets' aren't always reliable. The principal satellites are Astra 1 (which transmits the UK's BBC and ITV channels, for example), for which a 'mini-dish' is adequate, and Hotbird, for which an 80cm dish is recommended. For Sky TV (see page 155) and the BBC channels, a 60cm dish is sufficient. Different channels are transmitted by different satellites, so you must choose which satellite you wish to direct your dish at, or have a dish with a double feed (dual LNBs) antenna, several dishes, each pointed at a different satellite, or a motorised dish (at least 1.2m in diameter), which re-orientates itself automatically according to which channel you choose to watch, and enables you to receive hundreds of stations in a multitude of languages from around the world and turn yourself into a vegetable.

To receive programmes from any satellite, there must be no obstacles between the satellite and your dish, i.e. no trees, buildings or mountains must obstruct the signal, so check before renting or buying a home. Before buying or erecting a satellite dish, check whether you need permission from your landlord or the local authorities. In general, dishes of up to 1m in diameter don't require planning permission, provided that they aren't positioned on the front wall or roof and don't protrude above the top of a roof, and that there's only one per house.

Dishes can usually be mounted in a variety of unobtrusive positions and can be painted or patterned to blend in with the background. Satellite dishes should not be mounted on chimneys, as they can damage them in high winds and even bring them crashing to the ground.

There are numerous satellite sales and installation companies in Ireland (listed under *Television* in the *Golden Pages*). Alternatively you can buy (or import) a satellite dish and receiver and install them yourself. Free-to-air and free-to-view systems (see **Satellite TV** on page 155) cost from around €250, including installation, motorised satellite kits around €350, receivers around €150 and dishes around €50 (for a 60cm dish) and €60 (80cm). Further details of prices can be found on 💻 www.satellite.ie.

New blocks of flats or apartments are generally fitted with at least one communal satellite dish. Less expensive blocks may have only CATV, which provides seven or eight popular satellite channels to each apartment, whereas the more expensive ones will often have SMATV, which allows each apartment to have its own control unit ('flave').

Video & DVD Players

Video players (VCRs) are more or less obsolete, but can still be bought from some outlets. DVD players start at around €100, but a good machine linked to a 'home cinema' system can cost as much as €500. Needless to say, prices are coming down all the time.

Terrestrial TV

Terrestrial TV in Ireland is limited to three stations, detailed below – unless you live in Dublin, in which case you also have access to

the British channels BBC1 and BBC2, and UTV (💻 www.utvplc.com), which is part of the ITV network and popular in Northern Ireland. In addition, parts of the south-east of Ireland can receive Welsh TV channels (BBC1 Wales, BBC2 Wales, ITV1 Wales, S4C and Five); and the UK's digital terrestrial television (DTT) system, Freeview, which offers BBC1, BBC2, UTV, Channel 4 and Five, can be received in most areas bordering Northern Ireland, as well as in parts of Counties Roscommon, Sligo, Westmeath, Wexford and Wicklow. There's no DTT system in Ireland, although one is currently being trialled by RTÉ and the Department of Communications, Marine & Natural Resources.

RTÉ

When RTÉ was created, in 1961, its brief was to produce recognisably Irish programmes, and these are still among the most popular programmes in Ireland, tending to be more informal than their British equivalents, for example. RTÉ transmits nationally on three channels, detailed below. If you have a complaint about an RTÉ programme, you should address it initially to the Freedom of Information Office, Radio Telefís Éireann, Donnybrook, Dublin 4 (✉ complaints.review@rte.ie) or the Broadcasting Commission of Ireland (💻 www.bci.ie).

RTÉ 1

RTÉ 1 provides news and talk shows, drama series, documentaries and 'information

entertainment' such as interior design and crime-busting programmes, but the bulk of its schedule is taken up with Irish and foreign 'soap operas', including EastEnders (from the UK), Home & Away (Australia) and Shortland Street (New Zealand).

RTÉ 2

Formerly called 'Network 2', RTÉ 2 shows children's programmes from 6am until 5.30pm (including a news programme aimed at kids), and then lapses into a diet of soaps, including Australia's Home & Away and Neighbours and The Simpsons from the US, imported drama series, chat shows, dating games and 'candid camera' comedy, although there's also news and late films.

TG4

RTÉ's 'Gaelic-language station' (in fact, half of TG4's output is in English, although it attracts less than 4 per cent of TV viewers) also devotes a considerable part of its schedule to children's programmes (from 7.30 to 9am and from 2 to 4.30pm), and subjects viewers to American sitcoms and 'reality' shows, as well as discussion programmes, news and drama.

TV3

The country's first (and only) independent national terrestrial TV station, launched in late 1998, TV3 (💻 www.tv3.ie) offers a similar mix of news, documentaries, drama, soaps (including the UK's Coronation Street, which is shown no fewer than three times a day – so that viewers have a chance of understanding it), US talk shows (including Oprah Winfrey), sitcoms and sport.

TV Licence

Although RTÉ is a partly commercial station (i.e. programmes are interspersed with advertising), it's a public service broadcaster and approximately half its revenue derives from licensing. As in the UK, every household in which there's one or more TVs – whether purchased or rented – must be covered by an annual TV licence (only one licence is required irrespective of the number of TVs in the house). A TV licence currently costs €160. Certain people (e.g. those over 70 or on low incomes) qualify for a free TV licence; for details, contact the

Department of Social and Family Affairs (⌨ www.welfare.ie).

Licences can be purchased at post offices and can be paid for in cash, by cheque, by direct debit or using a credit card by phone (☎ 1890-228528); alternatively, you can spread the payments by buying licence stamps whenever you have spare money.

There are no refunds available to those who leave Ireland before the end of their TV licence period!

There's no 'period of grace' when it comes to getting a TV licence; as soon as you obtain a TV (whether purchased or rented), you must license it. An Post has a database of addresses where they suspect that TVs lurk, and teams of inspectors tracking down unlicensed TV owners.

▲ Caution

It is a prosecutable offence to be found in possession of an unlicensed television set, for which the fine can be up to €635 for a first offence.

Cable TV

Ireland is Europe's most 'cabled' country, and more homes receive TV programmes via cable than via satellite. The term 'cable' includes multi-channel (or microwave) multipoint distribution service (MMDS) transmission, which works on a digital wireless system and forms a national 'grid' covering virtually the whole country, whereas actual cables are laid only in the main towns. The disadvantage of MMDS is that the signal can be interrupted by obstacles such as buildings and mountains. In areas not covered by cable or MMDS (particularly in the south and west), many people use the services of 'deflectors', which pick up British terrestrial channels and retransmit them on local UHF signals, although these are officially illegal (the law legalising them expired in 2001, but nothing has since been done to prosecute anyone).

Both analogue and digital services are currently available. Most analogue programmes are unencrypted, although decoders may be required for 'premium' services and are needed if you have a TV set that cannot receive VHF signals (e.g. many British TVs). Digital services use the European standard transmission system and programmes are usually encrypted, although EuroNews and Channel 6 are unencrypted on NTL. Analogue services – particularly those carried via overhead cables, which are common in pre-1985 developments – are subject to signal degradation and are gradually being phased out. All cable TV providers must provide the terrestrial channels (see above).

There's a choice of cable operators in most areas, the main company being UPC Ireland (⌨ www.upc.ie – Chorus and NTL recently joined forces to become one company and have called themselves UPC). They offer a variety of packages, from 'basic' analogue or digital packs of around 20 TV channels and several FM radio stations, for around €20 per month, to movies-and-sports packages that will keep you 'entertained' from dawn till dusk for around €35, as well as integrated services combining TV with telephone and internet connection.

Programmes on offer include the usual international offerings as well as Irish channels such as the following.

Channel 6

Channel 6 (⌨ www.channel6.ie) claims to be Ireland's first 'dedicated entertainment channel' (as if other channels were dedicated to boring their viewers) and is aimed at 'adults' from 15 (Irish children mature early) to 34 by providing an 'exciting mix of movies, drama series, music and comedy, and airing both acquired programming and domestic produced content'. Channel 6 is available only via NTL.

City Channel

The City Channel (⌨ www.city.ie) is a cable TV station, launched in October 2005 in Dublin, and has since spread to Waterford and Galway. Provided by NTL, the City Channel provides mainly local programming in the early evening.

Setanta

Setanta (⌨ www.setanta.ie) is a dedicated sports channel available via Chorus and NTL, as well as via Sky (see below) which claims a bigger audience than Sky Sports.

Other Cable Channels

Other cable channels include Cabletext Waterford, available only in that town; Province5, available only in the town of Navan via Chorus; and Sky News Ireland, a one-hour daily news broadcast available via most cable companies.

Satellite TV

Some 25 geostationary satellites are positioned over Europe, carrying more than 200 TV stations broadcasting in a variety of languages. All these can be received throughout Ireland; the Astra and Hotbird satellites provide a particularly strong signal which requires only a small dish (see **Satellite Dishes** on page 152).

Satellite broadcasts can be free-to-air (FTA), which means they can be viewed free by anyone with a suitable satellite dish and receiver, free-to-view (FTV), i.e. free but requiring a decoder, or requiring payment, either on a 'per view' basis or via an annual or monthly subscription.

Oddly, the Irish terrestrial channels aren't free via satellite, but must be available only as part of a subscription service. There are many satellite subscription services, one of the most popular being Sky (see below).

Sky Television

Sky TV is available (legally!) in Ireland via the Astra 2 satellite, but only digital services are now offered. To receive Sky you need a Sky 'digibox', of which there are three types: a standard digibox, which is supplied free along with installation to new customers; a Sky Plus box, which allows you to record programmes digitally, even while you're watching a different programme (a standard box allows you only to record to a video cassette recorder), costs €150; an HD box, costing a whopping €450 but offering you **even more** channels, is required if you have a high-density TV and want to receive a high-density picture.

Various channel packages are available, costing from around €20 to around €65 depending on the extent of the vegetative state you wish to achieve: partial or persistent. When you sign your contract (for a minimum

of a year), you will be sent a satellite viewing card (similar to a credit card), which must be inserted in the digibox to switch it on (cards are frequently updated to thwart counterfeiters). A Sky subscription also entitles you to obtain a British Freesat card (costing an additional €65), which enables you to receive Channel 4 and Channel 5 programmes.

Further information can be obtained and registration made on ☎ 0818-719819 or via the Sky website (🖳 www.sky.com).

BBC

The BBC has stopped encrypting (scrambling) its channels coming from the Astra satellite that it shares with Sky, which means that you don't need a Sky digibox to receive the BBC channels, including BBC interactive services; any digital satellite receiver will work.

The BBC's commercial subsidiary, BBC World Television (formerly called BBC Worldwide Television) broadcasts two 24-hour channels: BBC World (24-hour news and information) and BBC Prime (general entertainment). BBC World is free-to-view, while BBC Prime is encrypted. BBC World is normally included as part of the 'international' packages offered by cable and digital satellite service providers, whereas BBC Prime costs around GB£90, and there's a one-time charge of around GB£15 for a smart card.

For more information and a programme guide contact BBC World Television (☎ 020-

8433 2221). A programme guide is also listed on the internet (💻 www.bbc.co.uk/worldservice/programmes) and both BBC World and BBC Prime have their own websites (💻 www.bbcworld.com and 💻 www.bbcprime.com). When accessing them, you need to enter the name of the country so that schedules appear in local time.

VIDEO & DVD

Video cassettes and DVDs can be hired from libraries and video rental shops throughout Ireland, although cassettes are gradually being phased out. Library rental is free, but the choice of films is limited and recent releases are unlikely to be available. Video shops are generally open seven days a week from between 9am and noon until as late as midnight (11pm on Sundays).

To hire a film, you need to become a member, for which you must produce two forms of identity and a passport-size photograph. Most shops restrict membership to over 18s (children must use a parent or guardian as a guarantor), but some have no age limits.

You will be issued with a membership card, which can be used to hire up to four films

(sometimes more) at a time. Prices range from €1.50 per night to €6 for recent releases. There are sometimes special offers on children's videos. If tapes aren't returned by a certain time the following day, a further day's hire is charged. Damaged cassettes and discs must be paid for.

Ex-rental cassettes and DVDs can sometimes be bought at knock-down prices from video shops, secondhand shops and markets. New pre-recorded videos cost between around €10 and €20 and blank tapes for home recording €2 to €5 each, usually in packs of three or five (but note that recordings of television programmes may only be made for private use and it's illegal to copy pre-recorded tapes). New DVDs now cost around the same as videos, which are becoming obsolete.

RADIO

Ireland has a variety of official radio services, detailed below, as well as a number of unofficial and mostly illegal broadcasters! Timetables of radio programmes can be found in the *RTE Guide* and on Aertel Teletext.

National Radio

RTÉ transmits on four channels: Radio 1 (on 88–89FM – round-the-clock news, current affairs, chat and 'middle-of-the-road' music), 2fm (90–92FM – popular music), Lyric fm (96–99FM – jazz, classical and 'world' music and arts programmes), and *Raidió na Gaeltachta* (93FM – RTÉ's Irish language channel).

All RTÉ stations are broadcast on FM; Radio 1 is also broadcast on VHF, but this is intended mainly for reception outside Ireland. Radio 1 and *Raidió na Gaeltachta* are also available via the Astra satellite, and a number of RTÉ programmes are available live, and as audio files, via its website (💻 www.rte.ie).

Today FM (💻 www.todayfm.com) is the only other national broadcaster, offering the usual mix of news, talk and popular music.

RTÉ Radio 1 is Ireland's most popular radio station, attracting 31 per cent of radio listeners, followed by 2fm (28 per cent) and Today FM (13 per cent). Independent stations in general attract over 50 per cent of listeners, and between 55 and 75 per cent of listeners tune to their local station (see below).

Regional & Local Radio

There are around 25 commercial local stations (known collectively as independent local radio or ILR), some covering several counties. Several local stations, including Dublin's Q102, Cork's 96FM and 103FM, Limerick's Live 95FM, LMFM and U105 (see below) are operated by UTV (💻 www.utvinternet.ie).

Dublin and Cork cities each have several services, including 98FM and FM104 (general stations), Dublin's Country Mix 106.8, Dublin's Q102 (aimed at older listeners), Newstalk (news, discussion and information), Phantom FM (rock music) and Spin 1038 (for youngsters) in the capital; and 96FM and 103FM (general stations) and Red FM (for young people) in Cork.

Connacht and Ulster are served by Galway Bay FM, Highland Radio (Donegal – reputedly Ireland's most popular local radio station), Mid-West Radio (Mayo), Northern Sound Radio (Cavan and Monaghan), Ocean FM (Sligo and parts of Donegal and Leitrim) and Shannonside RM (Longford and Roscommon and parts of Galway and Leitrim).

In Leinster there's East Coast Radio (Wicklow), KCLR 96FM (Carlow and Kilkenny), Kfm (Kildare), LMFM (Louth and Meath), Midlands 103 and Midlands Gold (Laois, Offaly and Westmeath) and South-East Radio (Wexford).

Stations in Munster include Clare FM, Live 95FM (Limerick), Radio Kerry, WLR FM (Waterford) and Tipp FM (Tipperary).

A station that covers several counties in several provinces is Beat 102-103, launched in July 2003, which can be received in Carlow, Kilkenny, southern Tipperary, Waterford and Wexford. It offers a mix of contemporary popular music, news and programmes relevant to young adults.

Ireland also has a number of community radio stations, which are becoming increasingly popular. These are represented by the Community Radio Forum of Ireland (CRAOL), on whose website (💻 www.craol.ie) you can find details of all stations. In addition, there are six licensed institutional services (Beaumont Hospital Radio, Mater Hospital Radio and St Ita's Hospital Radio in Dublin, CUH FM Hospital Radio in Cork, Regional Hospital Radio in Limerick and South Tipperary General Hospital Radio) and one licensed 'special interest' service, called Dublin City Anna Livia or DCAL FM (💻 www.dublincityannaliviafm.com), which offers 12 hours of programmes per week for and by people from Russia, Africa, China, Korea, Pakistan and Poland, as well as standard programming.

BBC World Service

The BBC World Service is broadcast on short wave on several frequencies (e.g. 12095, 9410, 7325, 6195, 3955, 648 and 198 khz) simultaneously, and you can usually receive a good signal on one of them. The signal strength varies depending on where you live, the time of day and year, the power and positioning of your receiver, and atmospheric conditions. All BBC radio stations, including the World Service, are available on the Astra satellite.

Cable & Satellite Radio

If you have cable or satellite TV, you can also receive many radio stations via your cable or satellite link. For example, BBC Radio 1, 2, 3, 4 and 5, BBC World Service, Sky Radio, Virgin 1215, plus many foreign-language stations, are broadcast via the Astra satellites. For details of receiving the four RTÉ channels, see **Digital Radio** below. Satellite radio stations are listed in British satellite TV magazines such as the *Satellite Times*.

If you're interested in receiving radio stations from further afield, you should obtain a copy of the *World Radio TV Handbook* by Nicholas Hardyman (WRTH Publications).

Digital Radio

Like digital TV, digital radio provides clearer reception, although this isn't necessarily of CD quality and if the signal is weak you may receive only silence! Digital audio broadcasting (DAB) also provides visual data, such as information about the music being broadcast, sports results and stock prices. For in-car listening, DAB offers the considerable advantage of a 'single frequency network', which means that you don't have to keep re-tuning as you move from place to place (although there are often 'jumps' in reception as you move between receivers). There are currently four methods of transmitting digital radio signals, all of which require special equipment.

♦ **Internet live audio streaming** – Provided your computer has a suitable sound card and Real Player or similar software, you can listen to many radio stations, including all four of RTÉ's channels, via the internet.

♦ **Internet 'podcasting'** – You can download radio programmes in MP3 format and listen to them whenever you want on your computer (e.g. via Windows Media Player) or MP3 player. A broadband connection is required for most programmes, as the files are large.

♦ **Satellite** – The four RTÉ channels can be received in digital form via the Sky Astra Digital satellite, 24 hours a day. Radio 1 is also available via the Eurobird 1 and Hotbird satellites. In addition to a satellite dish, you need a digital TV receiver. Details can be found on ⌨ www.rte.ie/radio/worldwide.html.

♦ **Digital audio broadcasting (DAB)** – If you have a digital radio receiver, you can receive transmissions directly via an aerial, although DAB is currently available only in Dublin and the north-east. It's expected that the service will spread to other parts of the country in the near future.

Ha'penny bridge, Dublin

9.

EDUCATION

According to the independent 2007 IMD World Competitiveness Report (IMD Business School, Switzerland, 🖳 www.imd.ch), Ireland's education system is the best in the world, ahead of those of Belgium, the Netherlands, the US, France, Germany, the UK and Spain. The Irish generally have always been hungry for education – perhaps because for centuries they saw it as their only hope of escape from a life of poverty.

Whatever the reason, a high percentage of Irish children remain in school after the statutory leaving age; 37 per cent of the population has undergone tertiary education – the highest proportion in the world (equal with that of France and ahead of Denmark, the UK, Switzerland, the Netherlands, Germany and Hungary) – and over a quarter of those aged 25 to 65 have a third-level qualification. There's a considerable disproportion between the number of males and females in full-time education in Ireland: over 60 per cent of females compared with just 45 per cent of males.

The Irish government is due to spend some €9bn on education in 2008, but that spending is biased towards the tertiary sector, and facilities in most Irish schools leave something to be desired. Ireland's student:teacher ratios have been steadily improving in recent years and are currently around 20:1 in primary (first level) education and 13.4:1 in secondary (second level – 14:1 in secondary schools and 12.8:1 in other second-level establishments).

Until recently, the Irish education system was essentially based on a private letter written in 1831 by Edward Stanley, Chief Secretary for Ireland to the British government, to the Duke of Leinster, the first chairman of the then new Education Board (known as the Stanley letter) and on three articles of the 1937 Constitution. These documents had established the basic right of parents to choose the best education for their children and the duty of the state to provide free, non-denominational schooling for young children.

> By 1970, however, the Irish education system had become largely controlled by the Catholic Church, which owned and managed the great majority of schools – so much so that a campaign for the separation of Church and State was set up and groups of dissatisfied parents even began to found their own multi-denominational schools.

Government attempts at reform were haphazard, and various types of schools – vocational and community schools, community colleges, comprehensives – were created during the '60s and '70s, each with a different management structure and funding mechanism, resulting in one of the most complex education systems in the world.

The Education Act, 2000 was the first piece of formal legislation relating to the Irish education system. It aimed to rationalise that system and make it more 'accountable' by setting out the roles, responsibilities and rights of everyone involved in education. It didn't, however, enact one of the Education Bill's original proposals, to devolve responsibility for the coordination of first and second-level education to regional Education Boards.

This responsibility still lies with the Department of Education and Science (DoES) in Dublin, although the Minister for Education is entitled to set up Executive Agencies; and certain administrative functions (e.g. setting examinations) are being hived off to separate, albeit centralised, organisations. These include the National Educational Psychological Service and the National Council for Special Education (created in 2005 following the Education for Persons of Special Needs Act, 2004, which sought to make greater provision for 'special' education).

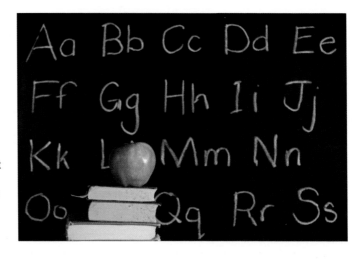

Nevertheless, the Education Act introduced a number of other long-overdue reforms:

◆ The Education Boards are obliged to promote the right of parents to send their children to a school of their choice.

◆ School patrons are obliged to appoint boards of management.

◆ The boards of management are obliged to produce a detailed school plan setting out its key aims and objectives for the guidance of staff, for the information of the community and as a basis for evaluation of its performance by the Inspectorate. The plan must be circulated among parents, as must an annual report on the performance of the school.

◆ The boards are also required to promote the establishment of parents' associations, which are now a statutory parental right.

◆ National associations of parents have, for the first time, been given statutory recognition with particular reference to the National Parents Council.

◆ Parents also have statutory rights of representation on all boards of management and on the Education Boards themselves.

◆ For the first time, parents have the right of access to their children's assessment records.

◆ Parents and students over 18 may now appeal to the board of management against decisions made by members of staff.

◆ In secondary schools, students are encouraged to establish student councils.

In addition, more rigorous control procedures were introduced for private commercial colleges, to ensure the quality of education that they provide.

Since then, in a questionable attempt to 'give children a stronger voice on issues that affect them', the government has set up the Office of the Minister for Children within the Department of Health and Children and Youth Affairs, Hawkins House, Dublin 2 (☎ 01-635 4000, 💻 www.omc.gov.ie), and given it responsibility for implementing a National Children's Strategy and the National Childcare Investment Programme (see **Pre-primary** below).

Generally, the Education Act reinforces the principal aims of the Irish education system as being to promote pluralism, equality, partnership, quality and accountability, together with the protection of fundamental civil and human rights, and the promotion of social and economic well-being. The DoES sets out its mission as 'to ensure the provision of a comprehensive, cost-effective and accessible education system of the highest quality, as measured by international standards, which will enable individuals to develop to their full potential as persons and to participate fully as citizens in society'.

Nevertheless, Irish education has been criticised for its lack of support for underachievers, too many of whom leave school without any qualification. In general, Irish 15-year-olds have good literary, but poor numeric and scientific skills. Critics also point to the underfunding of universities and the lack of part-time further education courses and retraining opportunities for older people (only 38 per cent of those over 55 have an upper-secondary level qualification compared with three-quarters of 25–35-year-olds.

THE EDUCATION SYSTEM

The Irish education system consists of four levels. Although children aren't obliged to attend school until the age of six, as in most other European Union (EU) countries, many do (although probably not voluntarily!) and are said to be at pre-primary level. Primary or first-level education is for children aged 6 to 12, second-level (sometimes called post-primary) for pupils aged 12 to 18 and third-level or tertiary education consists of universities and colleges (see page 176). Second-level education is divided into two cycles, junior (12 to 16) and senior (16 to 18). The minimum school leaving age is 16.

There are almost three times as many women teachers as men and, unlike their British counterparts, school principals don't teach.

Information booklets and leaflets on the Irish education system are available free of charge from the Department of Education and Science, Marlborough Street, Dublin 1 (☎ 01-889 6714) and similar information can be found on its website (🖥 www.education.ie). Further information about the Irish Education system can be found on the websites of the Teaching Council (🖥 www.teachingcouncil.ie), the National Children's Office (🖥 www.nco.ie), and the National Quality Framework for Early Childhood (🖥 www.siolta.ie).

Pre-primary

Although children in Ireland aren't obliged to attend school until the age of six, over half of four-year-olds and virtually all five-year-olds do so, and classes are provided in state primary schools for children aged four and over. However, there are no separate public nursery schools – a consequence, no doubt, of the traditional Irish belief that children should be looked after at home – and the pre-

school services that exist have, until recently, developed mainly on a voluntary or private basis and parents must pay for them.

> Childcare in Ireland is reported to be more expensive than almost anywhere else in Europe: over half of parents spend more than €150 per week on childcare, and 10 per cent over €300.

An annual childcare supplement of up to €1,100 (received in four payments) for families with children aged six and under, is available to those on low incomes. This supplement is automatically received by those in receipt of Child Benefit.

Until recently, state pre-school provision was directed mainly at the disadvantaged. For example, regional health authorities provided grants to voluntary bodies to provide pre-schooling for children with disabilities and for disadvantaged groups. This takes place mainly in nurseries and community playgroups run by voluntary agencies (a list of voluntary organisations is available from the Citizens [sic] Information Phone Service (☎ 1890-777121) or Database (formerly the National Social Service Board, 🖥 www.citizensinformation.ie).

In response to an increasing (and acute) shortage of childcare facilities, in 2006 the government launched the National Childcare Strategy, incorporating the National Childcare Investment Programme (2006–2010), whose key objective was to develop the childcare infrastructure to meet the changing needs of children and their parents – i.e. to provide more, and affordable, childcare places so that couples can work full time and bring up a family. Some €575m has been allocated, and it is anticipated that the programme will create up to 50,000 new childcare places.

The new Office of the Minister for Children, which is responsible for the regulation and inspection of pre-school centres, coordinates a network of 33 City and County Childcare Committees, which provide information about local childcare facilities. A list of these, with telephone numbers and website addresses, can be found on the Department of Justice, Equality & Law Reform's website (🖥 www.

justice.ie). Details of local childcare facilities can also be obtained from the Health Service Executive (☎ 1850-241850, 🖳 www.hse.ie), which is divided into four administrative areas. Further information about pre-primary education can be found on the website of the National Play Resource Centre (🖳 www.playinireland.ie).

There are essentially four types of pre-school service, described below. Other options include a live-in nanny or au pair.

Sessional Services

These include playschools, playgroups, crèches and Montessori groups. Sessions of up to three-and-a-half hours (normally two-and-a-half to three hours), usually in the mornings, for children aged two to six take place in schools, community halls and, mostly, private houses which have been converted for use as pre-school centres. Some are open five days a week, many only four. The average weekly cost for sessions is around €25 per child. All sessional services must have a child:adult ratio of no more than ten.

Almost 2,000 'childcare service providers', as they're officially known, are registered with the Irish Preschool Playgroup Association (IPPA, ☎ 01-463 0010, 🖳 www.ippa.ie). For details of Irish language playgroups, called naíonraí, contact the Naíonraí association (Forbairt Naíonraí Teoranta) (☎ 01-477 3151, 🖳 www.naionrai.ie).

Day Care

All-day care for children from as young as three months to six years is provided by crèches and nurseries, which are normally open from 8am until 6pm. Some are privately owned and charge up to €250 per child per week, including meals. Not surprisingly, charges are highest in Dublin, and the national average for full-time day care is around €180 per week. Others are run by volunteers (known as community crèches) and may charge as little as €40 per week, although even a community crèche in Dublin can cost €130 per week. Some centres offer a discount for two or more children.

Around 450 centres are members of the National Children's Nurseries Association (NCNA, ☎ 01-460 1138, 🖳 www.ncna.net), which monitors standards in day care facilities. A list of members and a useful free booklet entitled 7 Steps to Choosing a Nursery are available from the NCNA. All day care centres must comply with statutory minimum adult:child ratios – 1:3 for children up to one year old, 1:6 for one to three-year-olds, and 1:8 for children aged three to six.

Childminders

Childminders (also known as home carers) provide some 70 per cent of pre-school care in Ireland. Childminders look after your children in their home and are limited to six children, including their own. Hours, rates and duties are subject to negotiation, but you should expect to pay around €75 to €150 per week for full-time care. Childminders should adhere to the National Guidelines for Childminders, published by the Department of Health and Children (DOHC) in 2006.

Drop-in Centres

These are often provided in leisure and shopping centres and are usually free, although you can only leave children for a short period. Similar adult:child ratios apply as for day care centres (see above).

First Level

There are almost 3,300 first-level or primary schools (which used to be, and often still are, called national schools) and 127 'special' schools (for children with learning difficulties). Despite the closure of almost 1,000 one and two-teacher primary schools in recent decades, the average number of teachers per school is just six, and over 50 per cent of primary schools still have four or fewer teachers (there are 17 schools with a single teacher and just over 500 with ten or more) – the government claims that it considers educational quality first and economics second when it decides whether small schools should continue to receive funding.

Class sizes vary; around 15 per cent of classes have fewer than 20 pupils while 25 per cent have over 30; the largest class has 41 pupils. The majority of primary schools are mixed, and the number of single-sex schools is declining (originally there were no mixed schools at all); although there are still over 400 single-sex schools – around 65 per cent of them all-boys'. Over 80 per cent of primary school teachers are women.

As well as paying teachers' wages, the government makes a grant called a capitation grant. This is calculated according to the number of pupils at a school and is supposed to cover four-fifths of a school's running costs (i.e. maintenance, heating, lighting, cleaning, insurance and teaching materials), the remaining fifth to be raised by the school's management board – and the capitation grant is only made when this supplementary amount has been paid into the school account!

In practice, however, schools often find that they need to raise far more than this required minimum, because the average school running costs work out considerably higher than what's allowed for by the government. Part of this extra money comes from other types of grant available to schools, but most of it has to come from parents, either directly or though parish contributions. Inevitably, schools in wealthy areas are able to afford better maintenance and teaching materials than those in poorer areas, although the latter benefit from additional grants.

There are also some 80 private primary schools in Ireland. These receive no state funding and are independent of the rules governing state schools.

Multi-denominational Schools

In 1974, a group of parents who were dissatisfied with primary education provision in Dalkey, a suburb of Dublin, met to discuss a plan to set up their own multi-denominational school. After four years of wrangling with the DoES, and despite a slander campaign from a group calling itself COSC, the Dalkey School Project National School finally opened. Since then, a further 40 such primary schools have been founded, almost half of them in the Dublin area (all listed on the website below).

These schools, which are co-educational, child-centred and democratic, as well as multi-denominational, are now an established part of the Irish education system. In fact, many have become so popular that there are long waiting lists for places. Multi-denominational primary schools have their own coordinating organisation, Educate Together (☎ 01-429 2500, 🖥 www.educatetogether.ie), which is a limited company and a charity comprising delegates from each school, who meet every six weeks to discuss matters affecting the schools.

Gaelscoileanna

Some 175 schools (136 primary and 43 secondary) are 'Irish-medium' schools (properly called *Gaelscoileanna*), in which all teaching is conducted in Gaelic – pupils are even forbidden to speak English in the playground! These originated in the *Gaeltacht* (designated Irish-speaking areas of Ireland), where most schools are all-Irish but have spread to all parts of the country. A list of schools in each county, and other details, can be obtained from Gaelscoileanna (☎ 01-477 3155, 🖥 www.gaelscoileanna.ie). Four new Irish-medium primary schools (*gaelscoileanna*) have received temporary recognition, and are planned to open in September 2008.

Second Level

At second (oddly termed 'post-primary') level (age 12 to 18) there's a bewildering variety of schools: there are some 750 state schools (i.e. schools that are recognised by the DoES), comprising over 400 secondary schools, 250 vocational schools and community colleges, and almost 100 community and comprehensive schools (the last two types of school are classified together by the DoES). Of these, the majority are owned by religious orders (mostly Catholic, but 20 or so are Protestant owned and there's one Jewish owned school, Stratford College in Dublin 6), but over 300 are multi-denominational.

Some of the 400 secondary schools cater for boarders and day pupils, some for boarders only. Boarders are always required to pay fees, but only around 20 secondary schools charge day pupils fees and are consequently not state funded (even though they're DoES recognised!). Among the other types of state school, only a handful – including St John Bosco Community College in Kildysart (Co. Clare), Ashton School in Cork, and the Royal and Prior School in Raphoe (Co. Donegal) – admit boarders, who must pay for accommodation.

Over half of secondary schools are single-sex (around 60 per cent of them all-girls'), though the number is gradually declining. Some have an imbalance between the sexes (at the Presentation Secondary School in Galway, there was recently one boy among 321 girls, and at the Mount St Michael Convent in Claremorris, one among 464; it isn't known how much the boys' parents pay for their schooling!).

Of the 250 vocational schools and community colleges, only two are single-sex (one of each), but ten have mostly girls and 25 mostly boys. Of the 85 community schools and comprehensives, five are single-sex (three boys' and two girls'), four have mostly boys and one has mostly girls.

> The average size of second-level schools has greatly increased in recent decades and 65 per cent of them now have more than 500 pupils.

Secondary Schools

Roughly 55 per cent of second-level pupils attend secondary schools, which are the oldest type of second-level school in Ireland and originally all fee-paying, although enrolment is falling by around 2 per cent per year in favour of other types of second-level school. Today only some 50 secondary schools charge fees to day pupils (others charge for boarders).

Secondary schools are privately owned and managed, but receive funding from the state, which pays over 95 per cent of teachers' salaries and makes further allowances and capitation grants to the 95 per cent of secondary schools that are DoES recognised. The school owners pay teachers a nominal fee in recognition of the fact that the teachers are employees of the school, but even this can be claimed back from the DoES if the school participates in the free education scheme! Parents are then asked to make a contribution to the school's running costs, and it's estimated that as much as 20 per cent of secondary school funding comes from donations and fundraising.

Vocational Schools & Community Colleges

Almost 30 per cent of second-level children are educated at vocational schools. These began to appear in the '30s following the Vocational Education Act, 1930, which aimed to establish a network of schools providing both general education and practical courses preparing children for employment in principal trades. These new schools were to be administered by 38 Vocational Education Committees (VECs) – one in each county plus one in each of the major towns.

Until the mid-'60s, vocational schools were regarded as inferior to secondary schools, offering only two-year compared with five-year courses. But from 1966 vocational schools began to offer the full range of secondary subjects to pupils aged 12–19. Then, in the early '70s, the VECs, which had been invited to participate in the management boards of the new community schools (see below) and saw these as a threat to vocational schools, established their own alternative community colleges.

These and the vocational schools are now collectively known as the Vocational Sector, which also includes a number of third-level institutions. Unlike secondary schools, they must take in children from their own catchment areas.

Vocational Sector schools are on average smaller than secondary schools; half have

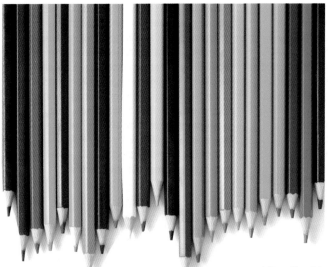

vocational and secondary schools. Despite opposition from prominent clergymen of all denominations, the plan was carried out and the first community school opened in Tallaght, near Dublin in 1972. Since then 80 more have been established, mainly in urban areas, but ironically they're now considered as part of the Vocational Sector, and run by the Vocational Education Committees, alongside the vocational schools and community colleges they were intended to supersede.

Like other Vocational Sector schools, community schools take in all children in their area and, although supposedly multi-denominational, are also Catholic orientated with state-paid chaplains. Some 5 per cent of the initial building costs of community schools is supposed to be contributed by the local Vocational Education Committee (which actually comes out of government funds) and 5 per cent by the Church, though in some cases the Church is lax about making its contribution. Otherwise, community schools are 100 per cent state funded.

Private Schools

In addition to these 750 schools, there's a small number of private, fee-paying schools which aren't recognised by the DoES, either because they have specialised curricula or because they're regarded as money-making enterprises (i.e. their fees don't just cover pupils' subsistence). For details of private schools see page 173.

Gaelscoileanna

There are 43 'Irish-medium' second-level schools (see page 165).

Curriculum & Examinations

The Irish school curriculum is formulated by the Minister for Education and Science, on the advice of the National Council for Curriculum and Assessment (NCCA), and implemented by the DoES through its Inspectorate. Details

fewer than 300 pupils. Vocational Sector schools are more than 90 per cent state funded, the balance being provided by funds generated by the VECs. In theory, Vocational Sector schools are multi-denominational, but most have Roman Catholic chapels or oratories, and are extensively decorated with Catholic symbols (teachers of religion must also be approved by the local bishop!).

Comprehensives

Between 1963 and 1974, the DoES built 16 comprehensive schools to provide second-level education in parts of the country not covered by secondary and vocational schools. These average 500 pupils and offer technical as well as academic education: all pupils must take at least one practical subject. As in their British counterparts, streaming (the segregation of the more gifted and less able pupils) is avoided in the early years.

All comprehensives are denominational (12 Catholic, 4 Protestant), but may not exclude children on grounds of religion. They're 100 per cent state funded.

Community Schools

Not content with the existing second-level school structure, in 1970 the DoES drew up a plan for the 'school of the future', an all-purpose multi-denominational school. Its ultimate purpose was to amalgamate of the current curriculum at all levels can be found on the NCCA website (💻 www.ncca.ie) and the entire curriculum is available on a CD-ROM from Government Publications, Molesworth Street, Dublin 2 (☎ 01-647 6000). The curriculum can, however, be adapted to suit the character of each school and should be set out in the school plan.

Presently, all schools are required to operate the certificate courses laid down by the DoES and enter their pupils for the same national examinations. Examination papers are produced by the DoES, but the actual marking of papers is done by teachers, under the supervision of Assisting Advisory Examiners, who are in turn directed by Chief Examiners, who are always Departmental Inspectors. However, reforms of both junior and senior cycle curricula are currently under way, involving a fundamental shift of emphasis towards school-based assessment methods in the junior cycle and a wider range of assessment methods in the senior cycle.

These reforms are also aimed at making Irish education more vocationally orientated, with a shift away from purely academic subjects towards technical and technological subjects. The school IT 2000 Initiative, launched in November 1997, was the first project and one of the most ambitious of its type in the world, achieving the installation of 60,000 computers in Irish schools and connecting every school to the internet by the end of the year 2000. Other schemes include the piloting of new school software and the establishment of a special schools intranet, called 'Scoilet', which will link to other similar networks abroad.

First Level

The current first-level curriculum focuses on literacy and numeracy, the arts, the Irish language and science, as well as introducing European awareness programmes and promoting health and wellbeing, including teaching about sexuality and relationships. The government is continuing to expand the Discover Science and Engineering programme and has set out to further increase the numbers of students studying the physical sciences by promoting a positive attitude to careers in science, engineering and technology and by

fostering a better understanding of the value of science to society.

The average amount of time per week spent on each subject at first level is as follows: Irish 5hs 30mins, mathematics 5hrs, English 3hrs, religion 2hrs 30mins, reading 2hrs, arts and crafts 1hrs 30mins, history 1hr, geography 1hr, music 1hr, PE 45mins, social and environmental studies 40mins, science 30mins, and speech & drama 15mins. Primary school pupils are also expected to do approximately one hour's homework each evening.

In 2003, a review of the English, mathematics and visual arts curricula was initiated, and a 300-page report of the first phase was published in 2005; however, it could be some time before any changes are implemented.

The Irish are reputed to be even worse at learning foreign languages than the British (which is saying something!) and until 1997 no foreign languages were taught at primary level. Then a pilot project was launched in 200 schools, where fifth and sixth year pupils were subjected to an hour and 30 minutes' tuition a week in French, German, Italian or Spanish. The current focus is on Irish and English only, and even then there is debate as to whether Irish should be a compulsory subject.

There's no formal examination at the end of the first-level education cycle. However, primary school teachers usually carry out an assessment of pupils' performance using either their own or standard tests.

Second Level

Second-level education in Ireland tends to be academic but less specialised than in the UK, for example. It consists of a three-year junior cycle, culminating in the Junior Certificate examination, followed by a two or three-year senior cycle. In the senior cycle, there's an optional Transition Year Programme followed by a choice of three two-year programmes leading to the Leaving Certificate examination, which is normally taken at the age of 17 or 18.

All schools at second level must include one-and-a-half hours per week of religious instruction, which became an examination subject at Junior Certificate level in 2003, as well as civics and PE (physical education), neither of which is an exam subject. Most schools prescribe certain 'core' subjects, students being allowed to choose others.

For the Junior Certificate, core subjects include English, Irish, mathematics, social and political education, and civic studies. In addition to these, pupils must choose two subjects from a list of optional subjects including languages, science, business studies, art and music. Secondary school pupils must also study history and geography. In order to allow for differences in children's needs, abilities and aptitudes, mathematics, Irish and English are offered at three levels for Junior Certificate: Foundation, Ordinary and Higher; other subjects are offered at Ordinary and Higher levels. In 1996, the Junior Certificate Schools Programme was introduced to cater for pupils 'whose learning needs aren't adequately met by the Junior Certificate'.

An optional Transition Year Programme was introduced in 1987 and was designed to cater for pupils who had completed their junior cycle and wanted to study for the Leaving Certificate exam, but who weren't considered mature enough to begin the programme. It also caters for pupils who don't wish to continue with second-level education, but want to take advantage of one more year of study (approximately 5,500 pupils take this option each year). The Transition Year Programme is interdisciplinary and doesn't involve any kind of assessment. The programme can include cultural and social studies, environmental studies, technology, languages, field trips, work experience and learning how to run a business.

Pupils are encouraged to take responsibility for their own learning, so programmes vary from pupil to pupil, some being highly imaginative and including work experience with local companies.

Pupils following the established Leaving Certificate Programme must take between five and seven subjects, which makes it more like the French baccalauréat than British A-Levels. Compulsory subjects are mathematics, history, Irish and a foreign language, but Irish isn't part of the Leaving Certificate exam and most pupils find it an irrelevant chore (it's only required 'nominally' for entrance to universities and colleges). As well as the usual European languages, 'exotic' languages such as Arabic are sometimes available. As with the Junior Certificate, most subjects can be taken at either ordinary or higher level; Irish and mathematics can also be taken at foundation level.

There are two 'variations' on the established Leaving Certificate Programme: the Leaving Certificate Vocational Programme (LCVP) and the Leaving Certificate Applied Programme (LCAP). Pupils taking the LCVP, which was introduced in 1989, take five subjects including two from a broad selection of vocational subjects. They must also follow a recognised course in a modern European language and take three Link Modules (short courses): Enterprise Education, Preparation for Work and Work Experience.

The framework of the LCAP consists of a number of modules grouped under three general headings: General Education (at least 30 per cent of the syllabus), Vocational Education (at least 30 per

'points' which must match the minimum entry requirement of the university or college they wish to enter and the course they wish to study. Competition for some courses, e.g. medicine and law, is intense, and candidates usually need at least 500 points – the maximum possible being 600!

CHOOSING A SCHOOL

At primary level, you have a choice of whether to send your child to an ordinary state (national) school, a multi-denominational school, an all-Irish school or a private school. Then you may have a choice between different schools in your chosen category. You aren't obliged, for example, to send your child to the nearest national school, but can apply to the school of your choice. In some cases you will have to settle for your second or third choice, but most children are accepted at their parents' preferred school (preference is generally given to parents who already have one or more children at the school).

It's a similar situation at second level, where there's a choice between secondary, vocational and community schools. Despite the freedom of choice which the Irish system allows, most parents find it necessary to send their children to the nearest school for the sake of convenience; in any case, in some areas there's only one primary or second-level school.

Finding the 'best' school is something that you need to do largely unaided and (thankfully) there's no 'league table' of schools as there is in the UK. In fact, in May 2004, the Irish education authorities banned the publication of information that could allow such tables to be compiled! The DoES publishes lists of state schools (including state recognised fee-paying and boarding schools), which are available from Government Publications (☎ 01-647 6000).

The *List of Post-Primary Schools in Ireland* is updated annually and costs around €3, while the *List of National Schools* is updated only every five years or so (the current list dates from 2005/06) and costs €7. There's also a list of schools in each region in the *Golden Pages* under *Schools & Colleges*.

Enrolment

Enrolments are made simply by contacting the principal of the relevant school. If your children

cent) and Vocational Preparation (at least 25 per cent). Students are required to complete nine 'tasks' during the course.

A Curriculum Development Centre in the mid-west of the country has prepared a series of courses which a number of schools in the region offer as an alternative to the normal Leaving Certificate Programme. Students who successfully complete the programme are awarded a qualification called the Senior Certificate.

Pupils who have completed the senior cycle can go on to take post-Leaving Certificate courses, which are aimed at providing young people with the vocational and technological skills necessary for employment and progression to further education and training, as well as encouraging innovation and adaptability. There are currently some 20,000 students on post-Leaving Certificate courses, which can lead to an NCVA (National Council for Vocational Awards) Level 2 award.

Access to third-level education is very competitive in Ireland, particularly to the professional faculties. In the January preceding their Leaving Certificate exams, students complete application forms ranking their course and institution preferences. They're then graded on their six best subject scores, at least two of which must be at higher level, and given have attended another school, it's a good idea to take their last school report and examples of their work (if it's in English) to help the principal assess their ability.

Language

To get the most out of the Irish educational system, students of all ages must be able to communicate in English (or Gaelic if they attend an Irish-medium school). There's no government requirement for this and each case is assessed by the school principal. In some cases, children will be allocated extra resources to help them with their English (or Irish) and, in English-speaking schools, may be exempted from Irish language classes. Nevertheless, the amount of tuition provided may be insufficient for some children and you may need to pay for private language classes.

Complaints

If you're unhappy with any aspect of the school your children are attending, you should take the matter up initially with the principal and management board. You can also contact the National Parents' Council (☎ 01-887 4034, 🖳 www.npc.ie).

State or Private?

If you're able to choose between state and private education, the following checklist will help you make your decision:

♦ How long are you planning to stay in Ireland? If you're uncertain, it's probably better to assume a long stay.

> ### ☑ SURVIVAL TIP
>
> Due to language and other integration problems, enrolling a child in an Irish state school is advisable only for a minimum of one or two years, particularly for children who aren't native English speakers.

♦ The area where you choose to live will affect your choice of school(s). For example, it's usually more convenient to send a child to a state school near your home; if you choose a private day school, you must take into account the distance from your home to the school.

♦ What educational level are your children at now and how will they fit into a private school or the Irish state school system? The younger they are, the easier it will be to place them in a suitable school.

♦ Will a private school provide a more broad-based education, with a wider choice of subjects and a more varied approach to sport, music, drama, art, etc?

♦ Will a private school have smaller classes, allowing more individually tailored lessons?

♦ If your child has special needs, will a private school be able to cater for them better than a state school?

Obtain the opinions and advice of others who have been faced with the same decisions and problems as yourself, and collect as much information from as many different sources as possible before making a decision. Before making a choice, it's important to visit the schools on your shortlist during term time and talk to teachers and students (if possible, also speak to former students and their parents). Where possible, check out the answers to the above questions in person, and don't rely on a school's prospectus or principal to provide the information. If you're unhappy with the answers, look elsewhere.

Most parents also find it pays to discuss alternatives with their children before making a decision. Finally, having made your choice, keep a check on your child's progress and listen to his complaints. Compare notes with other parents. If something doesn't seem right, try to establish whether the complaint is founded or not, and if it is, take action to have the problem resolved. Never forget that you, or your employer, are paying a lot of money for your child's education, and you should ensure that you receive good value.

STATE SCHOOLS

Hours & Holidays

The minimum number of teaching days per year is prescribed by law: primary schools must operate at least 183 days per year; second-level schools must operate at least 179 days, including 12 days for exams. The minimum length of the primary school day is 5 hours 40 minutes for children aged six and over (to include a minimum of 4 hours 10 minutes of secular instruction, 30 minutes of religious instruction and 30 minutes of recreation) and 4 hours 40 minutes for children under six; the second-level school day must be at least six hours long.

Primary schools are required to close throughout July and August, but otherwise it's left to the management boards of individual schools to fix school holidays, as well as to decide on the times classes start and finish, lunch period, etc. The vast majority of schools operate five days a week, although a number of secondary schools are open six days a week. The school day normally starts at 9.30am and incorporates a 15 minute, mid-morning break and a 45 minute lunch break. Schools don't normally have canteens and pupils eat a packed lunch in their classroom. Most lessons last 40 minutes.

Uniforms

Most Irish schools require pupils to wear a uniform, but these vary considerably from school to school. A basic uniform consisting of trousers, shirt and jumper for a boy or dress and cardigan for a girl might cost around €50. If a school has an official sports kit, this might cost an extra €30 or €40 or more if it includes a track suit. If your child is growing fast, a uniform might last less than one school year. Parents on a limited budget can buy second-hand uniforms from local shops.

Costs

Educating children can be an expensive business in any country and Ireland is no exception. Even in state schools, parents are asked to make a contribution towards school funds and are expected to pay at least €75 a year. In some cases, they're also required to make parish contributions, part of which go towards local schools.

As well as these 'voluntary' contributions, there are books and stationery (which can cost €100 or more per year at primary level and considerably more at second level), uniforms (see above) and exam fees (the lowest fees apply to first-time entrants), as well as transport to and from school (see below). There's an additional fee payable for a copy of your Leaving Certificate results.

If you want your child to take part in extra-curricular activities, such as specialist sports coaching or music tuition (schools provide only a basic education in these areas), you need to allow for the cost of this. In addition, there are school trips, in which most parents wish their children to participate. Many schools organise residential trips, where the entire class spends a week together; for example, studying the environment or participating in adventure sports, sometimes abroad, and these can be expensive.

Free Transport

Ireland operates a free school transport scheme, whereby children who live more than a certain distance from school are entitled either to the use of a free school bus or to a grant (known as a remote area grant) towards the cost of travelling to and from school. In the case of primary schools, the required distance is 2 miles (3.2km); in the case of second-level schools 3mi (4.8km).

If there's a sufficient number of qualifying children (normally seven), a bus is provided; otherwise the children's parents are paid up to €46 per term for junior certificate students and €71 per term for leaving certificate students. The actual amount given depends on how much they earn and how far from the school they live, and in most cases the grant is less than the actual cost of transport.

These entitlements only apply if a child is attending the nearest suitable school (i.e. the nearest Catholic school if he is a Catholic, the nearest Irish-medium school if you want him to be educated in Irish, the nearest special school if he has special needs, etc.). In the case of second-level schools, if there are several suitable schools in your area, one will be designated as the school to which the free transport scheme applies.

⚠ Caution

If you decide to send your children to another school, they won't be eligible for free transport or a remote area grant, even if you live more than 4.8km from the designated school (though your children may be able to travel on the school bus for a small fee).

Class Grading

Children below the statutory minimum school age of six who attend pre-primary classes are normally classified as infants (four to five years) and high infants (five to six years). These classes correspond to Pre-Primary level in the International Standard Classification of Education. First-level education normally consists of six classes: pupils start in the first class and end in the sixth, after which they transfer to second-level education.

The three years of junior cycle are usually referred to as first, second and third year, the transition year as fourth year and the two years of senior cycle as fifth and sixth year. Pupils who don't take the optional transition year would take the Leaving Certificate exam in their fifth year, those that do in their sixth.

Students usually progress from one grade to another at the end of each academic year, irrespective of their level of attainment. Students who are absent for a large part of a school year or have failed to make sufficient progress in one year may repeat the previous year's study by agreement between their parents and the school principal, although this is rare. In this case, pupils would probably forego the optional transitional year if they intended to progress to senior cycle.

PRIVATE SCHOOLS

The DoES recognises around 80 fee-paying primary schools and 50 fee-paying secondary schools, which cater for some 20,000 pupils. Unlike the recognised primary schools, some private secondary schools receive state funding, which goes towards teachers' wages; these must be 'approved' by the DoES as regards the curriculum taught and other criteria, including the level of fees, which must be principally to cover subsistence.

There are a small number of private second-level schools that aren't recognised by the DoES. These are entirely self-funding and self-regulating, and may charge whatever they like (or whatever parents are prepared to pay). There's no published list of non-recognised schools, which publicise themselves by word of mouth and advertisements.

Tuition fees vary considerably according to a variety of factors, including the age of students, the reputation and quality of the school, and its location (schools in major cities are usually the most expensive). Average fees are between around €2,500 and €4,000 per year.

Some private schools are boarding schools, although few schools accept boarders only. Children who board usually do so because they live too far from school to travel every day or because their parents are working overseas. The average fee for boarders (excluding tuition fees) is around €2,500 per year. This normally includes accommodation and meals and 24-hour supervision for five days a week (children are expected to spend weekends at home). Around two-thirds of Irish private schools are single-sex.

State-recognised private schools provide a similar curriculum to state schools and set the same examinations; non-recognised schools may offer completely different curricula. If you intend to remain in Ireland for a short period only, it may be a good idea to find a school which offers the International Baccalaureate (IB) examination, an internationally recognised university entrance qualification.

In general, private schools have better academic records than state schools. Don't, however, send your child to a school with high academic standards unless you're sure that he will be able to handle the pressure. Neither should you assume that all private schools are excellent or that they necessarily offer a better education than state schools.

In addition there are a few private international schools in Ireland, including The Muslim National School and (Jewish) Zion Parish School, both in Dublin (the others being for French, German, Japanese and Spanish speakers). There are also two international colleges affiliated to the European Council of International Schools, where pupils can sit the International Baccalaureate exams: St Andrew's College (💻 www.sac.ie) and Sutton Park School (💻 www.suttonpark.ie) – both in Dublin.

Make applications to private schools as far in advance as possible (before conception for the best schools). The best and most popular schools have a demanding selection procedure, so you shouldn't rely on enrolling your child in a particular school and neglect the alternatives, particularly if your preferred school has a rigorous entrance examination. When applying, you're usually asked to send previous school reports, exam results and records. Before enrolling your child in a private school, make sure that you understand the withdrawal conditions in the school contract; a term's notice is usual.

VOCATIONAL TRAINING & APPRENTICESHIPS

In Ireland, vocational training courses are offered by the national training and employment authority, FÁS, as well as by numerous private colleges. FÁS also operates a programme in conjunction with local education and training authorities, principally Vocational Education Committees, which provides young people who leave school without any formal educational qualification with education, training and work experience in a number of trades (e.g. the engineering, construction, motor, electrical, printing and furniture trades).

A recent expansion programme increased the number of education and training places to around 4,000, and the government has stated its intention to increase the list of designated trades on a phased basis. FÁS also provides training to meet the needs of the international telemarketing industry. Integral to the course is an extensive overseas placement of up to six months to give on-the-job training and immersion in the chosen foreign language and culture.

Further information is available from FÁS, 27/33 Upper Baggot Street, Dublin 4 (☎ 01-607 0500, 💻 www.fas.ie).

An apprenticeship lasts four years and, while traditionally young people were apprenticed on completion of compulsory schooling, an increasing percentage of apprentices have now already achieved Leaving Certificate standard. Standards to be achieved in each trade are measured through on-the-job competence testing and modular assessment, as well as formal examinations for off-the-job elements.

The normal pattern is to spend the first year off-the-job in training centres run by FÁS, and in Colleges of Technology, learning the practice and theory of the trade. At the end of this time, the apprentice sits the national Junior Trades Examination. The remainder of the apprenticeship is spent in employment, with further release to a technical college for theoretical instruction before the Senior Trade Examination is taken. A National Craft Certificate is jointly awarded by FÁS and the DoES on satisfactory completion of the apprenticeship.

Note that FÁS won't find an employer for you if you want to become an apprentice.

HIGHER EDUCATION

Over a third of the Irish population undergoes tertiary education; approximately 60 per cent of these go to university and around half take degree-level programmes. This impressive statistic disguises the fact that Ireland is producing too many graduates for the number of jobs available and many are forced to seek work abroad; it's correspondingly difficult for foreign graduates to find work in Ireland.

There are currently four universities (see **Universities** below), 14 institutes of technology and seven colleges of education (teacher training colleges) substantially funded by the state and, although they're theoretically autonomous and self governing, the government has a considerable amount of influence over the courses they offer, and can 'adjust' them periodically according to the country's needs. This state 'intrusion' into higher education is a cause of concern in some quarters, as is the government's inadequate funding of research in universities.

Despite the huge increase in the number of young people in higher education, there's concern too at the persistent socio-economic imbalance, particularly among university students, although the government is now addressing the situation.

In addition to these institutions, a number of independent private colleges have been established in recent years, offering a range of mainly business-related courses leading to professional qualifications and, in some instances, recognised diplomas and degrees. There are currently 22 of these institutions, as well as nine colleges of theology and divinity. Some 60 per cent of students at Higher Education Authority (HEA) institutions are female, compared with only 46 per cent at institutes and colleges of technology.

Two bodies oversee third-level education on behalf of the DoES: the HEA (💻 www.hea.ie), which is responsible for the funding and running of the Royal College of Surgeons of Ireland, the National College of Art and Design, and the Royal Irish Academy, as well as the universities and colleges of education; and the Higher Education and Training Awards Council (HETAC, 💻 www.hetac.ie), formerly the National Council for Educational Awards (NCEA), the statutory award-giving authority for non-university higher education qualifications, which include degrees.

HETAC also sets and monitors standards in colleges, validates courses offered in certain private colleges, and operates a transfer network whereby students can move from certificate to diploma to degree level, depending on their examination performance. Qualifications awarded by HETAC are internationally recognised by academic, professional, trade and craft bodies. Most colleges also have courses leading directly to the examinations of the many professional institutes.

Higher education in Ireland is still predominantly academic, although recently universities have been establishing closer links with industry. Both the government and the HEA are encouraging greater course modularisation, with credit transfer arrangements between institutions.

Applications for almost all full-time undergraduate courses are made through the Central Applications Office (CAO, Tower House, Eglington Street, Galway, ☎ 091-509800, 💻 www.cao.ie), which provides an applications pack with a handbook listing all the courses on offer and information on how to apply (downloadable free from the website). Students should obtain further information direct from universities an d colleges. They can list up to 20 choices (ten degree and ten diploma/certificate courses).

Applications can be submitted up to 1st May, but should, if possible, be made by 1st February. The fee for an application submitted before 1st February is €45 (paper) or €35 (online), which rises to €90/€70 for applications made between 1st February and 1st May. There's no charge for making an amendment to your choice of courses, which must be done using a 'Change of Mind' form and submitted by 1st July. Note, however, that the CAO recommends submitting applications at least a week before these closing dates. Offers of places are made in August, approximately one week after the Leaving Certificate results are published.

It's especially important for students to have a high standard of English, as they must be able to follow lectures and take part in discussions in the course of their studies. This may also require a much wider and more technical or specialised vocabulary. For this reason, most universities and colleges won't accept students who aren't fluent in English, and many require a formal qualification, e.g. a pass at GCSE or the Cambridge proficiency examination. Prospective students can assess their English fluency by taking the English Language Testing Service (ELTS) test at British Council offices in over 80 countries.

Universities

Ireland's universities range from the ultra-traditional Trinity College Dublin, founded in 1592 and modelled on Oxford and Cambridge, to the ultra-modern, go-ahead Limerick University, founded in 1972 and based on the American model. Apart from Limerick and Dublin City, Ireland's newest university, Irish universities are very like those in Britain, with a strong emphasis on extra-curricular activities.

Although all universities are theoretically non-denominational, the four colleges that make up the National University of Ireland have a Catholic 'ethos'. Irish universities also have an increasingly international outlook. Some of them include a foreign language in their entrance exams, and in 1987 the EU introduced the Erasmus exchange scheme, whereby selected students spend between 3 and 12 months in a foreign university. Some 10,000 Irish students have already benefited from the scheme, although more foreign students go to Ireland to study than the reverse.

The Irish university system offers programmes leading to a bachelor's degree, usually after four years, but sometimes after three or five, depending on the course followed (courses in veterinary medicine and architecture, for example, last five years).

In certain cases, this may constitute a professional qualification.

In recent years, some universities have introduced semesterisation and modularisation of courses, which allow students greater flexibility and mean that they don't have to repeat a whole year if they fail one part of the course.

A bachelor's degree may be awarded as a general degree, an honours degree or a special degree. Masters degrees are usually taken by coursework, research work or a combination of both, and require at least a further year's study. Doctoral degrees (or doctorates) are awarded on the basis of research after two more years of study.

Trinity College Dublin

For more than 200 years there was only one university in Ireland, Trinity College Dublin, which is still widely regarded as the country's 'top' university. TCD, as it's known, was for a long time a peculiarly British establishment: a ban on Catholic attendance imposed in 1875 wasn't lifted until 1970, and as late as the '60s more than 40 per cent of its students were British. Now, 90 per cent of students are Catholic, and fewer than 5 per cent are British (although one or two British traditions survive, such as the playing of cricket!). Unusually, only 650 of TCD's 10,000 students live in, the remainder having to find their own accommodation in and around Dublin.

Maynooth

The year 1795 saw the founding ofSt Patrick's College, Maynooth, by Act of Parliament, as a seminary for the Catholic priesthood. In 1899, Maynooth obtained approval to award degrees of the Pontifical University in Rome in philosophy, theology and canon law. Although primarily dedicated to the preparation of students for the priesthood, Maynooth now also admits lay students.

University College Dublin, Galway & Cork

In 1845, two more universities were founded, University College Dublin and University

College Galway. UCD, originally in the city centre but now in Dublin 4, is a rather traditional establishment, Catholic and middle-class. Galway, not very attractive architecturally, but lively and close to the town centre, is more liberal and favours the Arts. In particular, it has become a centre for Gaelic studies. Cork University, which was established nine years later, is comparatively small and especially popular with European students.

Trinity College, Dublin

National University of Ireland

The Irish Universities Act of 1908 established a new National University of Ireland (NUI), originally comprising UCD, Cork and Galway. Two years later these were joined by Maynooth. The NUI is organised on a federal basis, but the constituent universities enjoy a large measure of autonomy. The Royal College of Surgeons and the National College of Art and Design are also recognised colleges of the NUI.

Limerick & Dublin City

Although founded in 1972 and 1980 respectively, Limerick and Dublin City weren't established as independent universities until 1989. Reputed to be the country's most 'go-ahead' university, Limerick specialises in technology and hi-tech research and is situated in the suburbs of Limerick city. Dublin City University concentrates largely on business, as well as technology.

Institutes of Technology

The institutes of technology (ITs), which were introduced from 1969 to provide further education in technical subjects, are now an integral part of the Irish third-level system. They offer both full and part-time courses over a broad range of occupations including business studies, engineering and medicine.

There are regional ITs in Athlone, Carlow, Cork, Dundalk, Galway, Letterkenny, Limerick, Sligo, Tallaght, Tralee and Waterford and a number of specialised ITs: the Cork School of Music, the Crawford College of Art & Design, the Dun Laoghaire Institute of Art, Design & Technology and the National College of Art & Design.

The largest Institute of Technology, the DIT (Dublin Institute of Technology) is the biggest third-level institution in Ireland, with 22,000 students, and awards its own degrees. It has six constituent colleges, two Colleges of Technology, a College of Catering, a College of Marketing & Design, a College of Commerce and a College of Music.

Courses at ITs lead to certificates, diplomas, and in a limited number of areas, to degree qualifications awarded by HETAC. A certificate is a technical qualification normally requiring two years' study, a diploma a more advanced technical qualification usually requiring a three-year course (in some cases a certificate can be 'upgraded' to a diploma after an extra year's study). If you obtain a distinction in a diploma course, you may be able to transfer to a degree course, requiring a further two years' study. Regional ITs also offer apprenticeships and other training courses.

Colleges of Education & Home Economics

The system of teacher training differs between first and second-level school teachers. Typically, second-level teachers complete a primary degree at university and then follow up with the Higher Diploma in Education, again at university. Primary school teachers complete a three-year programme leading to a Bachelor of Education (BEd) degree, at one of the five Colleges of Education. Four of these, St Patrick's College, Church of Ireland College, St Mary Marino and Froebel College are in Dublin. Mary Immaculate College is in Limerick.

Teachers of Home Economics are trained in one of two Colleges of Home Economics: St Angela's in Sligo and St Catherine's in Dublin. These provide a full-time, four-year course leading to a Bachelor of Education (BEd) degree.

Teachers of art are trained in the National College of Art & Design in Dublin; and a specialist college for teachers of physical education and crafts, Thomond College in Limerick, was incorporated into the University of Limerick in 1991. All graduates of these colleges are awarded a university degree.

One of the entry criteria for primary school teacher training in Ireland (for overseas as well as Irish students) is proficiency in the Irish language. The Higher Education Authority is currently undertaking a comprehensive review of pre-service education for newly qualified teachers. All graduates will be required to complete an induction year before being registered as teachers.

Fees & Finances

Higher education institutions in Ireland receive income by way of state grants, tuition, registration and capitation fees and, in the case of the universities and technological colleges, income earned from research and development and other activities.

In 1997, tuition fees were abolished for first-time undergraduates who are EU nationals and have been ordinarily resident in an EU country for at least three of the five years preceding the start of their course, and who are attending an approved full-time course lasting at least two years. Nevertheless, these students are still liable for a 'student services fee' of around €800 and a 'student centre levy' of around €80 – which are nonsensically known as 'free fees'!

EU students who don't qualify for free tuition could pay anything between €500 and €8,500 per year, depending on the course. Those whose parents earn less than a certain amount (see **Maintenance** below) may qualify

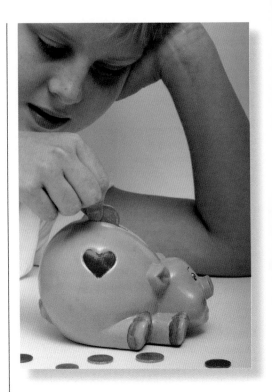

for Higher Education Grants or Vocational Education Committee Scholarships covering all, or part, of their tuition fees.

Those over 24 who are unemployed, single parents or disabled and wish to return to full-time education may be eligible for a 'Back to Education' grant. Details of all these grants and scholarships are available from the DoES.

Non-EU students must pay two-and-a-half or three times the standard tuition fee (e.g. over €27,000 per year for veterinary science!). There's a Support Scheme for students from developing countries, whereby a small number of students (e.g. ten per course per university) are allowed to pay the standard EU fee; otherwise, non-EU students should apply to their own education departments regarding grants and support. However, legislation introduced in 2005 means that non-EU students may not work even part-time to help pay for their studies unless they're attending a full-time course lasting at least a year.

Maintenance Grants

Apart from these fees, of course, there's the cost of living, while a student, to be taken into account. Again there are grants available (known as maintenance grants) but, as they're means tested, only around a third of students receive them. To qualify for a full maintenance grant, you must have been resident in the area covered by your local authority for at least a year, and your parents' total annual income must be less than €37,365 (2007/08 figures); for a part grant it must be under €44,365.

Applications for maintenance grants must be made to your local county council from May or June onwards for courses starting in September. There are also maintenance grants for trainees on one, two and three-year courses, details of which are available from the Vocational Education Committees.

The majority of students who don't qualify for a maintenance grant, like students everywhere, are reduced to begging, borrowing and working to get by – although many colleges expressly forbid students to take part-time work! – unless they're fortunate enough to have parents who can afford to pay their expenses. Many students obtain a loan to bridge the gap between their or their parents' contribution and their living expenses.

Most banks offer 'student accounts' with generous overdraft facilities and favourable interest rates (it can take a long time to pay off a €10,000 debt!), but some limit loans to students of the major universities (i.e. TCD and the NUI). Non-EU students can open a student account if they can provide evidence of solvency during the last six months!

Tax relief at the standard rate on tuition fees paid is available to part-time undergraduates on approved courses at publicly funded colleges lasting at least two years, students on approved courses at private colleges, full-time students on approved courses in other EU countries, and postgraduate students on courses in Ireland and other EU countries. You must present to the Revenue Commissioners a 'statement of fees' from the Fees Office of your university or college.

One of the rewards for suffering years of financial deprivation as a student is of course that, when you eventually start work, you can earn a higher salary than you would without a degree – at least in theory. Irish graduates with a primary degree (approximately 17 per cent of students) can expect starting salaries of between €25,000 and €30,000; the 20 per cent who obtain higher degrees can expect to start at up to €35,000.

> Further information on eligibility for grants is included in a booklet entitled *Financial Support for Further and Higher Education*, available from the DoES (☎ 01-873 4700).

Postgraduate Courses

All Irish universities offer facilities for postgraduate study and, as with undergraduate courses (see Fees & Finances above), there are three sets of fees: those eligible for free tuition pay only around €900 (to cover administration costs, student services and a 'student levy'); EU students pay between around €1,000 and €6,000 depending on the course; and non-EU students between around €10,000 and €25,000. All students must pay a 'facilities levy' of around €100 before registering for a course.

Similar grants are available as for undergraduate study (see above), provided you're over 23 (24 in the case of Back to Education grants) – at which age you're considered to be 'mature'! There's also financial support for mature students, mainly on technical courses, in the form of European Social Fund grants; details and application forms are available from your local Irish Vocational Educational Association (listed on 💻 www.ivea.ie). Graduates wishing to start their own business should contact Enterprise Ireland (☎ 01-808 2000, 💻 www.enterprise-ireland.com), which offers start-up funding to post-graduates with good ideas.

FURTHER EDUCATION

There has been a dramatic increase in recent years in the number of people taking further education (also referred to as continuing education or adult education) in Ireland. More than 130,000 people (almost 75 per cent of them women) are currently enrolled in further education. The Vocational Education Act, 1930, which established the Vocational Education Committees (VECs), gave responsibility to those committees for the provision of what was described in the Act as 'continuation education', and the VECs have traditionally been the main providers of further education in Ireland.

Initially, this was done through the vocational schools, but in recent years community and comprehensive schools have also provided an extensive educational service for adults in their areas. Most third-level colleges are also actively involved in the provision of further education through evening courses, extra-mural courses, distance-learning facilities, etc.

In 1984, a Commission on Adult Education appointed by the Minister for Education recommended the establishment of County and Borough Adult Education Boards, whose function is to draw up and administer a programme of further education for their areas. Many adult education organisations are affiliated to the National Association of Adult Education, which is known as AONTAS (☎ 01-406 8220/1, 🖥 www.aontas.com) and which receives financial assistance from the DoES.

In addition, grants are made available by the DoES to appropriate voluntary organisations and institutions, such as the National Adult Literacy Association (☎ 01-855 4332, 🖥 www.nala. ie), which provides help to people with 'literacy difficulties'. An annually updated list of courses is the *National Guide to Nightcourses*, published by Learning Ireland (🖥 www.nightcourses.com).

An increasing number of Irish people want to go on courses which are accredited, i.e. lead to a recognised qualification. Generally, diplomas and certificates are more valuable if they form part of a recognised university or HETAC programme (some institutions offer 'extra-mural' courses which aren't recognised in this way, so it's a good idea to check the standing of the course before you enrol).

☑ SURVIVAL TIP

Unfortunately, there's no consumer choice guide to the 'value' of further education courses in Ireland – expensive ones aren't necessarily better than inexpensive ones; as when buying any product, it pays to shop around.

If you're contemplating taking further education, you should bear the following points in mind:

◆ Read all the literature thoroughly.

◆ Talk to the course provider and to people already on the course to find out more about it.

◆ Check what support you're likely to receive from your employer, family and friends.

◆ Check the 'value' of the course in terms of its accreditation and transferability.

◆ Apply in good time (generally spring for courses starting in the autumn).

◆ Get yourself back into the habit of studying – build up gradually and work at a sensible pace (don't try to cram too much into too short a time).

◆ Discuss any aspect of the course you aren't happy with, or find difficult, with your tutor or the course provider – remember, you're the customer!

If you want advice or guidance on choosing a course, contact the Adult Education Officer for your area through your local VEC or through AONTAS (see above), which provides a free information pack to those wishing to take up further education. Useful publications are listed on the AONTAS website.

Distance Education

Distance education (or distance learning) is the name given to learning via books, tapes, CDs, TV, radio, email, computer software and interactive video, usually supplemented by occasional tutorial sessions at nearby centres or by telephone. The National Distance Education Centre (NDEC, or *Oscail* in Irish) was set up in 1982 within Dublin City University (although separately funded by the HEA) to take responsibility for providing all adults in Ireland with access to third-level education. The first distance education degrees were awarded in 1991, in science and technology.

Since then undergraduate courses in the arts, humanities, IT and nursing have been added, as well as postgraduate courses (in IT and in operations management). For further information contact the NDEC (☎ 01-700

5924, 🖳 www.oscail.ie). A *Directory* of distance education courses in Ireland is published by AONTAS (see above).

The NDEC is linked to the European Programme for Advanced Continuing Education (Euro-PACE) and, in 1990, signed an agreement with the UK-based Open University (OU) to allow Irish people to take Open University courses. The OU offers a choice of over 150 modules leading to BA and BSc degrees, as well as MA and MSc courses and diplomas in subjects including criminology and health & social welfare, MBAs, etc. Further details can be obtained from the Open University in Ireland (☎ 01-678 5399) or from the main Open University website (🖳 www.open.ac.uk).

Distance education students are able to design their own diploma or degree from a wide range of modular courses. A degree programme, for example, could consist of six modules, only two of which are set, and on each of which the student must complete a certain number of hours' study. All colleges affiliated to HETAC operate this scheme, so that students can build up 'credits' at different centres until they have enough for a degree or diploma. The NDEC and OU run similar schemes.

Students must begin by taking one of five foundation courses, which counts as one credit. Then they can take another foundation course or move on to a BA or BA Honours degree (six and eight credits   respectively).

A full credit course involves 12 to 15 hours a week, a half credit course six to eight hours. These credits can also be 'transferred' to centres in other countries. Some institutions will also grant credits in terms of 'exemptions' if a student has practical experience or has done non-accredited study in the subject

Fees & Grants

Usually, you must pay most, if not all, your course fees in advance, although you may be able to pay in instalments. You should therefore check the conditions under which you can claim a refund if you aren't happy with the course.

No state grants are available to part-time students in further education, although the DoES' 'Back to Education' programme offers support to unemployed and disabled people and single parents (see **Fees & Finances** on page 178).

Tax relief is available at the standard rate on fees for part-time further education and distance learning courses. If you're employed, your employer (particularly if it happens to be a financial institution) might look favourably on your educational aspirations – but not if you ask for time off to study! Many employers are even willing to pay employees to take further education: the *Garda*, armed forces, banks and civil service all offer such opportunities.

LANGUAGE SCHOOLS

Proficiency in the English language is, of course, essential if you're going to enjoy your stay in Ireland, however short or long, and make it beneficial. Fluency in English is also a prerequisite for most jobs and educational courses. Note that it's usually necessary to have a recognised qualification in English to be accepted at a college of higher or further education in Ireland.

Most people can learn a great deal through the use of language teaching books, tapes, CDs and videos. However, even the best students require some help. Teaching English is a thriving business in Ireland, with classes offered by language schools, colleges and universities, private and international schools, foreign and international organisations, local associations and clubs, and private teachers.

Tuition ranges from language courses for complete beginners through specialised business or cultural courses to university-level courses leading to recognised diplomas (there are even courses which combine English lessons with studies in holistic therapy or with golf lessons!).

A variety of classes and courses are offered by language schools to suit your current ability, the number of hours you wish to study each week, the amount of money you have to spend and the speed at which you want to learn. Full-time, part-time and evening courses are offered by most schools, and many also offer residential courses. Around 80 per cent of students choose 'homestay' courses, which involve staying with an Irish family, which is a good way of accelerating learning. Bear in mind that if you need to find your own accommodation, particularly in Dublin, it can be difficult and expensive.

Language classes generally fall into the following categories: general (10 to 20 hours per week), intensive (20 to 30 hours) and immersion (30+ hours). The most popular courses are general courses, which usually involve classes between 9am and 1pm. Intensive courses generally include afternoon classes, either in English or in aspects of Irish culture. Most schools offer general and intensive courses, as well as providing special courses for businessmen and professionals (among others). Courses may lead to examinations, most of which are recognised internationally.

Course fees are usually calculated on a weekly basis and vary considerably depending on the number of hours' tuition per week, the type of course, and the location and reputation of the school. Expect to pay between €85 and €150 per week for a general course and €250 for an intensive course. Immersion courses are provided by some schools, and are generally aimed at business people, although some also offer courses for young people in the summer.

Private tuition is also usually available for €25 to €50 per hour. Many schools offer discounts (e.g. 15 to 25 per cent) at certain times of year.

If you're starting more or less from scratch, don't expect to become fluent in a short period unless you have a particular flair for languages. Unless you desperately need to learn a language quickly, it's better to spread your lessons over a long period. Don't commit yourself to a long course of study (particularly an expensive one) before ensuring that it's the correct one.

It's important to choose the right course, particularly if you're studying English in order to continue with full-time education in Ireland and need to reach a minimum standard or gain a particular qualification. Some schools offer a free introductory lesson and a free test to gauge your ability. If you already speak English but need conversational practice, you may prefer to enrol in a course at a local institute or club.

For information about language schools in Ireland, visit an Irish embassy or tourist office or contact MEI-RELSA (💻 www.mei.ie), which is an organisation of 56 language schools throughout Ireland. A list of English language schools in Ireland can be found on the Learn English in Ireland website (💻 www.europa-pages.com/ireland).

⚠ Caution

Not everyone is suited to learning at such a fast rate (or has the financial resources – fees can run to €1,500 per week without accommodation and €5,000 per week for an all-in, live-in course!).

Kilkenny Castle, Co. Kilkenny

10.
PUBLIC TRANSPORT

Public transport throughout Ireland is the responsibility of the Department of Transport (🖳 www.transport.ie), whose 'Transport 21' scheme for the period 2006–2010 aims to 'increase accessibility, expand capacity, increase use and enhance quality'. Public transport services are provided by Coras Iompair Éireann (CIÉ, 🖳 www.cie.ie), the state-subsidised national transport company, and various private operators.

CIÉ has three subsidiaries, Irish Rail (Iarnród Éireann), Irish Bus (Bus Éireann), and Dublin Bus (Bus Átha Cliath), which together facilitate over 275m passenger journeys a year. As part of the government's commitment to ease the increasing urban grid-lock caused by cars and commercial vehicles, CIÉ invests some €35m a year in the bus network (over half of which is swallowed by Dublin Bus), and injected a massive €1bn into the railway system between 1999 and 2007.

Public transport is generally good in Ireland, although rail services are sparse or non-existent in many areas and buses are sometimes infrequent. Irish railways provide an efficient and reasonably fast service, particularly between cities served by *AVE* (which oddly stands for the Spanish *alta velocidad española*) high-speed trains. Ireland has comprehensive intercity bus and domestic airline services, and is also well served by international coach, train and air services. Taxis are common in main towns and cities, although they aren't a cheap form of transport.

Otherwise, public transport in major cities, particularly Dublin, is inexpensive and efficient, and includes comprehensive bus and suburban rail networks. Around Dublin, systems are integrated so that the same ticket can be used for all services, and a range of commuter and visitor tickets is also available. There are travel agencies in all major cities and large towns, and specialist agencies for young travellers such as USIT. An increasing number of buses are being adapted for people with disabilities.

STUDENT, SENIOR & TOURIST TICKETS

Students and certain other young travellers are entitled to reduced rates on many public transport services. On production of an International Student Identity Card (ISIC), which costs €12, you can save up to 60 per cent on single and return rail fares, as well as bus journeys and the return boat fare to the Aran Islands. An ISIC is available only to full-time students.

If you aren't a full-time student, but are under 26, you're entitled to a European Youth Card (EYC), which costs between €7 and €20, depending on where you buy it, and entitles you to low cost air fares, special travel insurance rates, reduced price maps and guidebooks, and discounts from certain retailers, restaurants and other outlets, and is valid in 29 European countries. Details can be found via the internet (🖳 www.euro26.org).

There are no reductions on public transport for senior citizens, but all residents over the age of 65 (and some below that age, e.g. blind and other disabled people) qualify for a free travel pass, covering all public transport and some private transport services (i.e. those operated by companies that have opted into the Free Travel scheme). If your spouse or partner has a free travel pass, you're entitled to free travel also, irrespective of your age.

If you're receiving a state pension or disability allowance, you should automatically receive a travel pass. Otherwise, you should obtain an application form from the Department of Social and Family Affairs (🖥 www.welfare.ie – forms can be downloaded from the website) or a post office.

> If you live in Cork, Dublin, Galway, Limerick or Waterford, you must exchange your pass for a 'photo pass' at a CIE office.

Those intent on 'doing' Dublin can save money with a Dublin Pass, which entitles you to travel anywhere in the city and includes admission to some 30 visitor attractions for around €15 per day. Details can be obtained by phone or via the internet (☎ 01-836 6111/6222, 🖥 www.dublinpass.com). Other discounted tickets are referred to under the relevant headings below.

TRAINS

As elsewhere in the world, the Irish rail network has suffered at the expense of roads: today there are 2,800km (1,739mi) of railway line compared with more than twice as much 50 years ago. The present network is operated by the Irish Rail (Iarnród Éireann, 🖥 www.irishrail.ie) arm of CIÉ, which handles an increasing number of passengers. Most railway lines radiate from Dublin, so the network (see map opposite) isn't much good for travelling up and down the west coast, for example, and there are no lines at all north of Sligo.

A map of the rail network can be found on 🖥 www.irishrail.ie/home/company_ information.asp (click on 'Routes and Maps' under 'Your Journey'). Details of new development projects can also be displayed from the same page (click on 'Projects').

Intercity (i.e. fast) services operate between Dublin and Ballina, Cork, Ennis, Galway, Limerick, Rosslare harbour,

Waterford, Wexford, Sligo, Tralee and Westport, the last three routes being the object of Irish Rail's latest investment programme. The only other intercity services are between Cork and Tralee, Cork and Limerick, and Limerick and Rosslare. Trains run frequently between the major airports and nearby city centres; services are reliable and efficient and fares reasonable (see below).

Apart from a suburban service between Cork city and Cobh, commuter rail services are limited to Dublin (see below).

Dublin Commuter Services

The Dublin area is served by the DART (Dublin Area Rapid Transit) suburban rail system which connects 24 stations around the capital, from Howth in the north to Bray in the south – soon to be increased with extensions to Malahide and Greystones. Daily, weekly, monthly and annual tickets are available as well as a Dublin four-day Explorer. The system is currently being upgraded, with new track and renovated stations.

LUAS – meaning 'speed' in Irish – is Dublin's new 'light rail tram' system, opened in June 2004, which currently operates on two lines: Green with 13 stops, from St Stephen's Green and extending south-east of the city as far as Sandyford; and Red with 23 stops, from Connolly to Tallact to the west. Trams operate from 5.30 to 0.30am on weekdays and from 6.30 or 7 to 0.30am at weekends, from every 20 minutes at night to every four or five minutes at peak times. There are six fare zones. Details can be found on a dedicated website (🖥 www.luas.ie).

The capital also plans to construct a 'Metro' system, combining underground and overground lines, to add to its commuter transport services. This will initially consist of two lines. Metro North, a 17km line connecting the Fingal County town of Swords to Dublin city centre and serving Dublin Airport, is forecast to handle 30m passengers per year, with trains up to every four minutes, and will link with both LUAS lines as well as the DART network. Metro West will link the towns of Tallaght, Clondalkin, Blanchardstown and Porterstown, interchanging with the LUAS Red line, the Kildare and Maynooth suburban rail

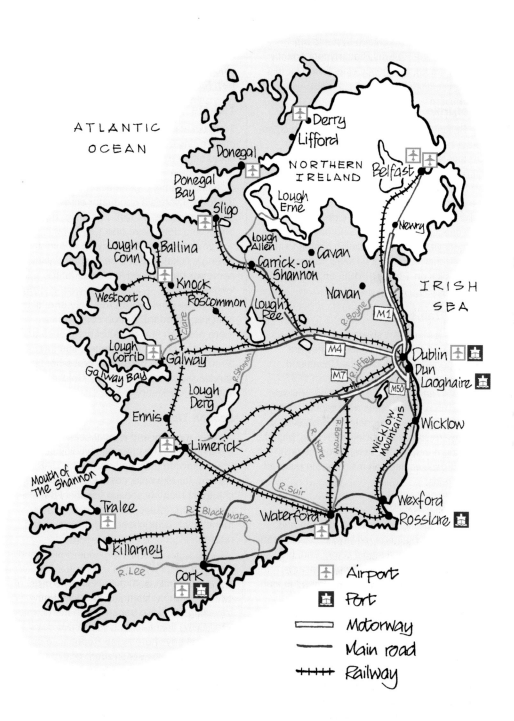

ATLANTIC OCEAN

Derry
Lifford
Donegal
NORTHERN IRELAND
Belfast
Donegal Bay
Lough Erne
Newry
Sligo
Lough Allen
Cavan
IRISH SEA
Lough Conn
Ballina
Carrick-on Shannon
Knock
Navan
Westport
Roscommon
Lough Ree
R. Boyne
M1
Lough Corrib
Galway
R. Clare
R. Shannon
M4
R. Liffey
Dublin
Dun Laoghaire
Galway Bay
Lough Derg
M7
M50
Ennis
Wicklow
Wicklow Mountains
Limerick
R. Nore
R. Barrow
Mouth of The Shannon
R. Suir
Wexford
Tralee
R. Blackwater
Waterford
Rosslare
Killarney
R. Lee
Cork

Airport
Port
Motorway
Main road
Railway

lines and Metro North. However, the route for the Metro West line has yet to be agreed and it could be several years before either service is operational.

Both the LUAS and Metro systems are operated by the Railway Procurement Agency (💻 www.rpa.ie), an agency established for this purpose in 2001.

Enterprise

The Belfast-Dublin Enterprise service is a cross-border rail link inaugurated in 1997 by Irish Rail and Northern Ireland Railways. Its 90mph trains can do the 182km (113mi) trip in under two hours (depending on the number of stops) at a cost of around €35 single or €50 return (valid for a month). There are eight trains in each direction, Mondays to Saturdays, and five on Sundays. Further information can be found on the Translink website (💻 www.translink.co.uk – click on 'ENTERPRISE' on the right of the page).

Steam Trains

Ireland is a Mecca for steam train enthusiasts as more and more narrow gauge lines are being opened up, including the Cavan and Leitrim Railway, which operated from 1887 until 1959, and the Tralee and Dingle Railway (1881–1953), which offers a 20 minute nostalgic ride (during the summer only). There's even a Railway Preservation Society of Ireland, based in Northern Ireland (💻 www.rpsi-online.org), which organises rides on main lines in restored steam trains.

Trains & Stations

Irish trains are fairly modern and clean and, although in some parts railwaymen still operate the signals from little signal boxes and even open the gates by hand at level crossings, computerisation is inexorably bringing the Irish rail system 'up to date'. It isn't permitted to smoke in station waiting rooms or on trains.

Bicycles

Bicycles may be carried on most trains, either in the guard's van or a special compartment at the back of a train. They aren't permitted on DART trains or on suburban trains arriving in Dublin between 7am and 10.30am and leaving Dublin between 4pm and 7.30pm. There's a charge of around €4 to €10 for each journey depending on the distance travelled.

Information

Rail information and timetables can be obtained from travel agents and Irish Rail offices or by phone (☎ 01-836 3333) or via the Irish Rail website (💻 www.irishrail.ie).

Tickets

Train tickets can be purchased at stations or on trains – the latter only if there was no ticket office (or the ticket office was closed) at the station where you boarded, or if you didn't have time to get a ticket before boarding the train. There's a conductor on every train checking tickets, as well as selling them to those who don't have one.

If you're thought to be trying to avoid buying a ticket, you can be fined and your name will be recorded in case of future infringements.

On most services, there's only one 'class' of ticket, standard, but on some trains there are also first class tickets. These are sometimes given fancy names, such as 'Premium' on the Enterprise cross-border service (see above) and 'City Gold' on suburban Cork services.

Season Tickets

Weekly, monthly and annual season tickets are available. The cheapest weekly season ticket allowing unlimited use of the DART service, for example, costs €22.50 and the cheapest monthly season ticket is €84. On less popular routes, it's possible to save money by buying cheap day and weekend returns.

Touring Tickets

A number of rail and rail/bus passes are offered for those planning to do a lot of travelling by public transport. An Irish Explorer (Rail Only) ticket entitles you to five days' rail travel anywhere in the Republic in any 15-day period for €145 (adult) or €73 (child) or anywhere in Northern Ireland as well for €180/90.

If you want to use buses as well as trains, an Explorer Rail & Bus ticket lets you travel within the Republic on up to eight days in any 15 for €210/133 and an Emerald Card throughout Northern Ireland as well for €248/124. If you're a frequent rail traveller (or a train spotter), you can even buy a season ticket valid for the whole of Ireland.

European Rail Passes

Ireland is part of the network covered by the Eurail pass, which allows any non-European unlimited travel for a fixed fee depending on how many days travel you require (up to a maximum of two months). A Eurail pass, which must be purchased outside Europe, also entitles you to free ferry travel to Ireland from France, provided you don't pass through the UK, which isn't part of the network. Details can be found on the Eurail website (💻 www.alleuroperail.com/eurail).

Interrail passes can be purchased by European Union (EU) citizens or people who have lived in an EU country for at least six months. An Interrail pass entitles you to 22 consecutive days' or one calendar month's travel throughout Europe. The cost depends on the number of countries you wish to travel through. Details can be found on the Interrail website (💻 www.interrail.com).

BUSES & COACHES

The efficient national bus service in Ireland is operated by Irish Bus (Bus Éireann, 💻 www.buseireann.ie), which is part of CIÉ. Buses are generally cheaper than trains and reach even the most remote corners of the country. Irish Bus offers a wide range of services including:

◆ **'Expressway'** – inter-city coach services;

◆ **Eurolines** – coach services to the UK and Europe;

◆ **City bus** – services in Cork, Galway, Limerick and Waterford;

◆ **Commuter bus** – services radiating from Dublin and other cities;

◆ **Local bus** – services throughout the country;

◆ **School bus** – services on behalf of the Department of Education;

◆ **'Breakaway'** – short holiday travel and accommodation packages in Ireland;

◆ **Guided day tours** – from Cork, Donegal, Dublin, Galway, Limerick and Sligo;

◆ **Ancillary services** – such as coach and bus hire, vehicle testing, contract maintenance, parcels delivery, etc.

Irish Bus also operates links between Cork airport and Cork city, and between Shannon airport and Limerick town. Alternative services are offered by Nestor Bus (which operates a Galway-Dublin service) and Suirway Bus Service (💻 www.suirway.com) in Waterford, among others. You can obtain timetables for certain provincial services from the CIÉ or from tourist offices and some newsagents.

Note that destinations shown on the front of buses are often in Irish. Dublin, for example, may be shown as *Átha Cliath*, so a timetable comes in handy for translation purposes. But don't try to find a place called *An Lár* – it means town centre!

Dublin Bus

Dublin Bus (Bus Átha Cliath, 💻 www. dublinbus.ie), another branch of CIÉ, is a

virtual monopoly operating all public bus services in the greater Dublin area (which includes parts of the counties of Wicklow, Kildare and Meath). Dublin Bus operates a fleet of over 1,000 vehicles on around 140 routes, carrying almost 150m customers annually.

Its services include an express rush hour service for commuters called Xpresso, a school bus service called School Link, a service linking the city and its main bus and rail stations with the airport called Airlink, a service linking the main rail stations with the financial centre called Railink, and a Thursday to Saturday night service operating hourly between 0.30 and 4.30am on 15 routes called – you've guessed it – Nitelink. Dedicated bus lanes have reduced journey times dramatically on some routes.

Fares

Bus fares are considerably cheaper than the corresponding rail fares. A return fare from Dublin to Cork or Limerick, for example, costs €18, from Dublin to Galway €16.70, and Dublin to Waterford €13.50. There are no group tickets, but up to two adults and three children can travel on a family ticket and there are other reduced rate tickets such as mid-week returns, ten-journey tickets and weekly season tickets. People over 65 with a Social Welfare travel card travel free.

Bus fares depend on the number of 'stages' (i.e. stops) travelled, and tickets are priced for 1-3 stages, 4-7, 8-13, 14-23 and over 23. An 'autofare' system operates on the majority of Dublin Bus's routes, which means that you must have the exact fare, as drivers don't handle cash. (If you don't have the right change, you will get a receipt for the overpayment which can be redeemed only at Dublin Bus headquarters!) Alternatively, you can buy '2 EASY' cards, which are prepaid for two journeys at a certain fare (i.e. double the above amounts) and must be used within a month.

There's a wide range of other discounted pre-paid tickets, including weekly, monthly and annual season tickets, Rambler tickets (see below), One Day and Short Hop tickets (unlimited travel for a day on various services), and a Travel 90 Handy Pack containing ten tickets entitling you to unlimited travel on certain services for 90 minutes. A monthly season ticket for unlimited travel, for example, costs €85.

Sightseers can buy an Irish Rambler ticket entitling them to unlimited travel on one day, three days, five days or seven days. Prices start at €6 for an individual (€10 for a family).

> Tickets can be purchased at any of the 200 plus bus ticket agencies located throughout the city and its suburbs, at the CIÉ Desk at Dublin Airport and the head office of Dublin Bus (see **Booking & Information** below).

Buses & Bus Stops

Shelters with seats are provided at most bus stops, where routes and destinations are displayed on yellow or illuminated signs. All buses should display their route number and destination (or an 'out of service' sign). Smoking on buses is illegal.

Booking & Information

Bus and coach tickets can be purchased at Bus Éireann offices in main towns or on the bus if you're joining outside a main town. Multi-journey and touring tickets can be bought online (at 🖳 www.buseireann. ie). Booking isn't usually necessary, except on Bus Éireann/Eurolines coach and ferry services to Britain and Europe. Information about these services can be obtained from Eurolines offices in most European countries or via the internet (🖳 www.eurolines.co.uk). Bus timetables are changed every May and September and, in the Dublin area, relevant bus timetables and route information are delivered to all residential premises at least once per year.

Both Bus Éireann and Dublin Bus head offices are at 59 Upper O'Connell Street, Dublin 1 (☎ 01-873 4222 for Bus Éireann or ☎ 01-872 0000 for Dublin Bus). Phone lines are open between 9am and 5.30pm Mondays to Fridays and from 9am to 1pm on Saturdays; outside these hours, information can be obtained from your local bus depot (normally until 11.30pm daily).

FERRIES

Ireland is linked to both the UK and France, its nearest neighbours, by regular ferry services. The British routes carry a staggering 4.5m passengers annually – more than the population of Ireland.

From various parts of Wales there's a choice of four routes and two main operators: Fishguard to Rosslare (Stena Line, 🖥 www.stenaline.co.uk), Pembroke to Rosslare (Irish Ferries, 🖥 www.irishferries.com), and Holyhead to Dublin (Irish Ferries or Stena Line) or Dun Laoghaire (pronounced 'leary') near Dublin (Stena Line). There's also a service from Liverpool to Dublin via the Isle of Man, operated by the Isle of Man Steam Packet Company (🖥 www.steam-packet. com).

If you're travelling from Scotland or northern England, it may be more convenient to cross to Northern Ireland and travel to the Republic by road. Stena offers a Stranraer-Belfast and a Fleetwood-Larne service.

Irish Ferries' services from France operate from Cherbourg and Roscoff to Rosslare, while Brittany Ferries (🖥 www.brittanyferries. com) sails from Roscoff to Cork.

Irish Islands

There are 18 inhabited islands off Ireland's coast; only the Aran Islands are accessible by air. To reach the others, you must take a ferry (or swim!). Most of the islands off the west coast can be reached by boat, although some in the summer months only; the type of vessel varies from a modern hydrofoil to a converted Second World War landing craft. You can take the ferry to the Aran Islands, which takes one and a half hours from Galway or 40 minutes from Rossaveal and costs around €25 return. Inishbofin (the 'island of the white cow') can be reached from the village of Cleggan near Galway, and the return fare is around €15.

Off Donegal is Aranmore Island and off County Mayo is Clare Island, which is accessible by ferry from Roonagh Quay (around 20km from Westport) for around €15

return. Further south, there's Cape Clear Island, which welcomes some 20,000 visitors each year. It can be reached in around 45 minutes from the village of Baltimore at a cost of around €12 return. The Irish Tourist Board publishes details of the various services, which can be obtained from local tourist offices.

Facilities

All ferries, including catamarans, carry cars and there are between one and six crossings daily in each direction, depending on the route and the time of year. There's little to choose between the different operators for comfort and standard of service, but fares vary considerably depending on the time of year and the amount of time you want to spend on the Irish Sea.

Times

Crossing times from the Welsh ports start at '99 minutes' (according to the adverts), on Stena Line's 'High-speed Sea Service' (HSS) from Holyhead to Dun Laoghaire and its Lynx service from Fishguard to Rosslare (near Wexford). Irish Ferries' Pembroke-Rosslare crossing takes three and three-quarter hours, while the Holyhead-Dublin route is half an hour quicker. Stena's HSS from Stranraer to Belfast takes 105 minutes.

Irish Ferries' services to France run approximately every other day throughout the year on the Cherbourg route and between April and November on the Roscoff route, while Brittany Ferries operates a weekly service from Roscoff to Cork. Crossings take around 15 hours from Roscoff and around 17 hours from Cherbourg.

Fares

As with all air and ferry fares, it's almost impossible to obtain general information and fares are calculated 'individually' on the basis of your dates and times of travel, number of passengers, type of vehicle and other criteria.

⚠ Caution

Some fares are more than double in mid-summer and you pay a premium for the faster services. Stena's HSS, for example, costs more than twice as much as its standard ferry crossing at peak times.

Where previously the standard fare was for a car, driver and up to four passengers, the ferry companies have introduced lower fares for car plus driver. For example, Stena's fares start at around GB£75 (low season) and rise to around GB£130 (high season) for a five-day return with a standard vehicle and one passenger on the Holyhead-Dublin Port ferry. For a longer trip with a full car, however, you will pay GB£120 and GB£150 or more respectively.

Rail & Coach Links

Those who prefer to leave their car at home can let the train take the strain. All ferry services from the UK are scheduled to link with InterCity trains serving Fishguard, Holyhead, Swansea and Stranraer, and at the Irish end some train services connect with incoming ferries. Inclusive train/ferry tickets are available from as little as €60 return from Manchester or Liverpool to Dublin and just €80 from London. As well as being a good deal cheaper than taking the car, the rail route can save you time. For example,

London (Euston) to Dublin via Holyhead-Dun Laoghaire takes around 11 hours and London (Paddington) to Wexford via Fishguard-Rosslare around 12 hours 30 minutes.

Irish Ferries also offer a coach/ferry service via Holyhead or Pembroke which is even cheaper, London-Dublin fares starting at just €35 return per person. Eurolines, a National Express company, operate daily coach/ship services from major UK cities to Cork, Dublin, Limerick, Tralee, Waterford and other main towns, with onward connections to over 100 destinations throughout Ireland. There's a choice of single, return (valid for six months) and open-dated return tickets. Prices for the London-Dublin route are similar to those of Irish Ferries.

Other bus services are provided by Irish Bus and numerous small companies which can be found on the back pages of Irish newspapers (available in the UK). The disadvantages of coach travel (slowness and relative discomfort) are offset by the advantage of being able to get to parts of Ireland other services cannot reach.

TAXIS

There are two types of private hire car in Ireland: taxis and hackneys. A taxi can stand for hire and ply for hire on the street, must display a 'TAXI' sign on its roof and is allowed to use bus lanes. Taxis have fixed fares (see below). A hackney must be hired by phone, email or direct contact at a hackney office and cannot be hailed in the street. Hackneys aren't permitted to use bus lanes, and fares should be agreed between the hirer and the hackney in advance of the journey.

Taxis are plentiful in most cities and towns in Ireland, although there's a shortage in Dublin. They're ordinary saloon cars (or minibuses). Generally, Irish taxis wait at ranks and outside airports, stations and the larger hotels; they can be stopped in the street, but they don't normally cruise around in the hope of being hailed.

Telephone numbers of local taxi and hackney companies are listed under Taxis & Taxicabs in the Golden Pages. In small towns, there may be only one or two operators, usually family owned businesses where the sons and nephews do the driving, so you should be sure to book well in advance or you might find there isn't a taxi available.

In Dublin, Cork and Limerick, all taxis have meters. In Dublin, the minimum fare for a single passenger is around €3.60, which covers you for 1km or 2 minutes and 48 seconds (whichever comes up sooner). You usually pay slightly more outside 'normal' hours (e.g. late at night or early in the morning). The following additional charges may apply: €0.50 for each additional passenger, each item of luggage (only two are permitted) or each animal (other than a guide dog); €1.50 for a telephone booking; €1.50 for a hire from Dublin Airport; €75 if you dirty a taxi!

The number of taxis in Dublin has increased in recent years and waiting times have correspondingly reduced, although it can still be difficult to find one – and almost impossible on Friday and Saturday nights (especially when it's raining)!

Elsewhere, taxis aren't metered, so you must confirm the fare before setting off. Average rates are between around €1 and €1.50 per km, but most drivers charge extra for long journeys to compensate for the fact that they may have no customers for the return trip.

Taxi drivers usually expect a tip of around 10 per cent of the fare, but are probably unique in occasionally rounding the fare **down** to the nearest euro! Complaints regarding a vehicle, driver or fare charged and queries relating to lost property should be addressed, during normal working hours, to Garda Siochana, Carriage Office, Dublin Castle, Dublin 2 (☎ 01 666 9850/1), quoting the roof sign number of the taxi concerned.

Everything you could ever wish to know about Irish taxis can be found on the 'industry' website (🖳 www. taxi.ie).

AIRLINES

It's possible to fly between major towns in Ireland, although most internal flights are routed via Dublin. In any case, the distances involved are quite small: the longest possible flight, from Donegal in the north to Cork in the south (via Dublin), is only 400km (250mi). The majority of internal flights are now operated by Aer Árann (🖳 www.aerarran.ie), which offers services between Cork and Galway and from Dublin to Cork, Donegal, Kerry, Knock, Shannon and Sligo as well as flights to the Aran Islands from Galway Airport. Aer Lingus (🖳 www.aerlingus. com) offers only one domestic service, between Dublin and Shannon, as does Ryanair (🖳 www.ryanair.com), between Dublin and Cork. Private aeroplanes and helicopters can be rented from Dublin and Shannon airports.

Airports & Airfields

There are nine airports in the Republic of Ireland: Donegal in the north; Sligo, Knock (officially called Ireland West Knock but also referred to as Connaught or Connacht), Galway (or Connemara Airport), Shannon and Kerry in the west; Cork and Waterford in the south; and Dublin in the east. Dublin is the main international airport (see below), while Donegal and Sligo offer only domestic services.

There are 25 other licensed airfields in Ireland, some public and some privately owned; in theory, details can be obtained from the Irish Aviation Authority (☎ 01-671 8655, 🖳 www. iaa.ie), although the writer was unable to do so. Note that private aircraft heading for Dublin must land at Dublin Airport, as there are no private airfields near the capital.

International Flights

Not surprisingly, the majority of international services to Ireland are from the UK. Cork, Dublin, Knock and Shannon offer numerous

services from all parts of the UK (more than 4m passengers are carried by air between Dublin and London each year), other airports limited services, as follows: Galway from Edinburgh, Glasgow, the Isle of Man, London (City and Luton) and Manchester; Kerry from London Stansted; Knock from Liverpool, London (Gatwick and Stansted) and Manchester; Waterford from London Luton.

Galway offers just one other international service – to and from Lorient in France (Brittany) – and Kerry three: Frankfurt, Newark and Philadelphia. It's possible to fly to Cork from cities in the Czech Republic, France, Malta, the Netherlands, Portugal and Spain, and to Shannon from France, Germany, Italy, Portugal and Spain as well as from Atlanta, Boston, Chicago and New York (JFK) in the US, and from Toronto in Canada. There are a number of charter services from Europe to Knock.

By far the biggest choice of destinations is to be had at Dublin airport, which serves most European countries, and Atlanta, Boston, Chicago, Los Angeles, New York (JFK), Newark, Orlando and Philadelphia.

For the north-east of Ireland, it may be more convenient to fly to Derry or Belfast in Northern Ireland. Belfast City airport offers mainly flights from the UK, plus a couple of services from France (and winter charter flights to Austria and Switzerland for skiers); Derry is served by various European cities, as is Belfast International, which surprisingly offers flights from only one North American destination, Newark.

Booking

Airlines operating within and into and out of Ireland are listed in the *Golden Pages* under *Airlines*. Most also have their own websites, including BMI (⌨ www.flybmi.com) and Easyjet (⌨ www.easyjet.com), as well as Aer Lingus and Ryanair (see above), where you can make bookings. Many operate 'air miles' schemes and other incentives.

Fares

Most airlines provide a vast range of tickets depending on when you want to fly, how many nights you want to stay, how much notice you give, which 'class' of seat you want, and whether you fly on a fixed (pre-booked) flight or an open ticket. Most also offer discounts and 'promotional' fares (i.e. they're advertised and are theoretically available, but no one knows anyone who has actually got hold of one!).

Return flights between the UK and Ireland can be had for as little as €50, whereas you should expect to pay at least three times as much for a trip to Continental European destinations such as Amsterdam, Brussels, Dusseldorf, Madrid, Paris, Rome or Zurich, and it can be cheaper to fly via London. Transatlantic fares start at around €350, though a 'standard' fare is usually almost double this.

Children under 12 years of age usually travel at 33 to 50 per cent of the adult fare (although there are no discounts on some routes) and have the same baggage allowance as adults. Most airlines don't charge for babies or infants who don't occupy seats, e.g. aged up to two or three years old, or charge a nominal fare only. Emergency supplies of baby food and nappies (diapers) are available on intercontinental flights.

Whatever your destination, it pays to shop around for the best deal and to be wary of offers that seem too good to be true; they usually are!

It's best to book holiday flights with a company that has an International Air Transport Association (IATA) licence, as IATA pays compensation should a member be unable to meet its commitments.

Holidays booked through a member of the Irish Travel Agents' Association (ITAA) are also covered by a bond system (☎ 01-679 4179, ⌨ www.itaa.ie). Airport taxes have been abolished in Ireland.

Students & Young People

Students with an International Student Identity Card (ISIC) or anyone under 26 years of age with an International Youth Card (IYC) can obtain discounted air fares. An IYC costs €12 and is valid for a year. For information on ISICs, contact USIT (☎ 01-602-1906, ⌨ www.usit.ie).

Commuter & Intercity trains, Connolly Station, Dublin

11.

MOTORING

I reland is reckoned to have the highest density of roads in the world, i.e. there are more kilometres of road per person than anywhere else, which means, in effect, that Irish roads are less crowded than those of almost any other country. Certainly, motoring in most parts of Ireland contrasts strongly with that in most other European countries. To begin with, there are hardly any motorways and only short stretches of dual-carriageway so, whereas in France or Germany you might expect to cover 200km in under two hours, in Ireland you should allow three, four or even five hours for the same distance.

Outside the cities and towns, Irish roads are also often deserted and traffic jams rare. Because there are few ring roads or bypasses, however, most towns suffer from congestion, which is particularly bad in Cork and Dublin. Although statistics state that of the major European capitals, Dublin has one of the lowest car-to-population ratios, you're no better advised to take your car into the city centre than to drive into London, Paris or Rome.

Unfortunately for road users, the current growth in Ireland's population and economy has led to a massive increase in the number of cars on the roads in recent years, despite the government's efforts to persuade more people to use public transport.

As elsewhere in the world, driving in Ireland is a hazardous business: 336 people were killed in road accidents in 2007 (including 138 car drivers and 70 passengers, 82 pedestrians, 31 motorcyclists and 13 cyclists). This may not sound many (and it's certainly an improvement on the peak death toll of 640 in 1972 and represents a drop of 30 per cent since 1997), but in relation to Ireland's small population it equates to one death per 12,500 people, which makes Irish roads more dangerous than those in the UK, where the annual death toll of around 3,500 equates to one person in every 16,500. The number of people injured on Irish roads every year is almost 8,000.

Traffic information is available from the Automobile Association on a dedicated website

(💻 www.aaroadwatch.ie) or a premium rate number ☎ 1550-131811. A recorded traffic report is continually updated between 6.45am and 6.45pm from Mondays to Fridays. The Dublin City Council monitors traffic flow in the Dublin area via a network of cameras; you can find traffic information on its website (💻 www.dublincity.ie – click on 'Traffic Management' and then 'Traffic Disruptions page') or by calling the traffic control centre on freephone ☎ 1800-293949. There are also regular traffic bulletins on Radio 1.

IMPORTING A VEHICLE

If you plan to import a motor vehicle into Ireland, either temporarily or permanently, first make sure that you're aware of the latest regulations. You should check whether you will be able to register and license a particular vehicle in Ireland and whether it can, if necessary, be modified to comply with Irish standards of construction.

⚠ Caution

There's no legal restriction on the import of left-hand drive vehicles, though you will find it restricting (and sometimes dangerous) to be sitting on the 'wrong' side of the car.

Transfer of Residence

If you're still resident abroad (i.e. not in Ireland), you won't have to complete any paperwork or pay import duty on your car but, if you're importing a vehicle from another European Union (EU) member state as part of a transfer of residence, you may be liable for vehicle registration tax (VRT – see below) and must present form C&E 1077, as well as the appropriate VRT form, which must be completed at the Vehicle Registration Office of the county where you plan to live not later than the next working day following the vehicle's arrival in Ireland.

Vehicle Registration Tax

As a general rule, every vehicle kept permanently in Ireland must be registered with the Revenue Commissioners. All vehicles that are to be registered in Ireland are liable to vehicle registration tax (VRT). A completed declaration form and the vehicle itself should be presented at any vehicle registration office (VRO). Declaration forms are available from any VRO. The VRT will be calculated by the official at the VRO after inspection of the vehicle. However, exemption from VRT is granted in certain circumstances.

In order to qualify for exemption from VRT, you must be able to show that you've owned and used the vehicle outside Ireland for at least six months before the date of your transfer of residence; you must therefore produce appropriate documentation such as the vehicle's registration document and insurance certificate.

In addition, you may not dispose of, hire or lend the vehicle to anyone during the 12 months following its registration in Ireland. You must include the vehicle on form C&E 1076 and present a completed copy of form VRT4 (cars) or VRT5 (motorcycles). You must bring the vehicle into Ireland within 12 months of your transfer of residence. Exemption is also granted to certain people with disabilities.

If you don't qualify for exemption (e.g. if you're importing a car owned for less than six months or buying a car in Ireland), you must pay tax calculated as a percentage of the reckoned retail price, including all appropriate Irish taxes, known as the 'open market selling price' (OMSP). The percentage varies according to the age, type and condition of the vehicle as well as (since 1st July 2008) the carbon dioxide (CO_2) emission rate of its engine, as shown in the table below. Electric-petrol 'hybrid' vehicles are eligible for a reduction of up to €2,500 in VRT (which replaces the 50 per cent reduction previously applicable), depending on their age.

Vehicle Registration Tax Bands (for standard cars)		
Band	CO_2 Emission Rate	VRT Rate
A	Less than 120g per km	14% of OMSP (minimum €280)
B	121 to 140 g/km	16% of OMSP (minimum €320)
C	141 to 155 g/km	20% of OMSP (minimum €400)
D	156 to 170 g/km	24% of OMSP (minimum €480)
E	171 to 190 g/km	28% of OMSP (minimum €560)
F	191 to 225 g/km	32% of OMSP (minimum €640)
G	Over 225 g/km	36% of OMSP (minimum €720)

This means that the tax on a 'gas guzzler' costing €50,000 would be a whopping €18,000 – a strong incentive to travel by bus.

Further information about VRT can be obtained from the Central Repayments Office, Coolshannagh, Monaghan (☎ 047-82800), which published an information booklet on the subject (reference VRT 7).

Customs Duty & VAT

Customs duties and value added tax (VAT) may also be chargeable, although exemption can usually be claimed if VAT has been paid in another country and if the importation is part of a transfer of residence.

CAR HIRE

Hiring (renting) a car in Ireland is expensive by American and even some European standards. A small saloon car (group A), for example, costs from around €55 per day or €150 per week in low season and twice as much in high season. International companies such as Avis (💻 www.avis.ie), Budget (💻 www.budget.ie), Europcar (💻 www.europcar.ie) and Hertz (💻 www.hertz.ie) have offices at major airports and in main towns, as do local companies. Car hire companies are listed in the *Golden Pages* under *Car Hire*.

Prices vary considerably, so shop around. Most companies have low rates for weekend hire and for rentals of 14 days or longer. When comparing rates, check what's included in the price. Basic third-party insurance is usually included in the hire charge, but make sure that you check exactly what you're covered for. In some cases, you can be liable for the cost of damage to a car unless you pay an additional Collision Damage Waiver (CDW) premium of between €5 and €10 per day, although this is usually included.

Personal accident insurance can usually be taken out for a similar premium and a second driver can be added for around €6 or €8 per day. Some companies don't offer unlimited mileage and provide a certain number of 'free' kilometres (or miles), after which there's a charge per kilometre, which usually works out more expensive unless you plan to drive a relatively short distance only. Theft protection is usually included, but VAT at 12.5 per cent may or may not be.

While smaller companies may offer cheaper rates, they usually charge extra for leaving the car anywhere other than where you hired it (particularly if it's in the middle of nowhere), whereas the multinationals allow you to do so for free, at least on a week's hire or longer (you will need to pay extra for the same facility on a day's hire). You can sometimes save money by booking (which is advisable at peak times – but see below), particularly if you take a fly-drive or sail-drive package through an airline, ferry company or tour operator.

If you're coming from the US and have credit card insurance (though not with American Express), you can save a significant amount on a week's car hire. Cars can be hired in Ireland by booking through the American offices of major international hire companies such as Avis (☎ 001-800-331-1212), Budget (☎ 001-800-527-0700) and Hertz (☎ 001-800-654-3131) and paying by credit card. This is a legitimate practice, although it may save you only a few euros on local hire rates. Freephone (800) numbers of other US-based rental companies can be obtained from international directory enquiries, although you pay international rates when phoning from abroad.

Note that booking doesn't guarantee you the car you requested (you are generally offered what's available, although in many cases that will be a better car than you 'booked'). Nor does it mean that you will save time when you collect the car; you will usually have to queue behind people who haven't booked and wait while yards of paperwork are completed and your frustration mounts.

You need to be aged at least 21 to hire a car, but most companies have a minimum age limit of 23 or more – some as high as 27. Some companies charge extra for 21 to 24 year-olds and there's usually an upper age limit too, which varies between 65 and 75. You also usually need to have held a driving licence for at least 12 months without endorsements. Drivers must produce a valid licence (a copy isn't acceptable) and some drivers require an international driver's permit. If more than one person is driving, all the drivers' names must be entered on the rental agreement.

Unless you use a credit card, you usually need to pay a cash deposit equivalent to the excess and possibly the whole rental cost in advance. When paying by credit card, carefully check your bill and statement, as unauthorised charges aren't unknown. It may be possible to sign a credit card authorisation slip and pay cash when you return a car. However, if you do this, you must make sure that you obtain (and destroy) the credit card payment slip. When booking, you should specify an automatic model if you're unused to a manual (stick-shift) gearbox, as most rental cars are manual – but note that automatics are often more expensive (by as much as 25 per cent in some cases).

If required, check that you're permitted to take a car out of Ireland, e.g. to Northern Ireland, as you may need extra insurance, although there's usually no additional charge. For an extra fee you may be able to obtain extras such as baby seats and roof racks. Note also that there's usually an accident 'excess', which can be as high as €1,000 (i.e. you pay the first €1,000 of any damage you cause, even in an 'accident'!). Again you can pay a 'waiver' of around €8 per day to secure peace of mind. Always thoroughly check the contract **and** the car (e.g. for body damage and to ensure that everything works) before setting out.

Around 22 car hire companies are members of the Car Rental Council of Ireland (CRCI), which means that they've been approved by the Irish Tourist Board (a list is available from the CRCI, ☎ 01-676 1690, 💻 www.carrentalcouncil.ie).

BUYING A CAR

New Cars

Making comparisons between new car prices in different countries is often difficult on account of fluctuating exchange rates and differing levels of standard equipment, which may include electric windows and mirrors, central locking, electric sun roof, alloy wheels, stereo radio/cassette/CD, power steering, ABS, air bags, automatic transmission, leather or power seats, cruise control and air-conditioning.

Some manufacturers include many of these items as standard equipment, while others charge dearly for them as 'optional extras'. Paying for expensive optional extras on many cars is unlikely to increase the car's value when you sell it, although many cars are easier to sell with options such as power steering, central locking and electric windows. Note that capital depreciation is a greater threat than rust

to a new car owner, as the car's value can drop by as much as 60 per cent in the first three or four years.

Nevertheless, as no vehicles are manufactured in Ireland, all cars and motorcycles must be imported, which means they're expensive. To make matters worse, the Irish government, committed to getting people out of their cars and onto public transport, imposes 20 per cent VAT and an even higher rate of vehicle registration tax (VRT – see page 198). This means that almost half the cost of a new car goes to the Revenue Commissioners.

New car prices start at around €11,500, for a small car such as a Peugeot 107. Mid-size cars start at around €17,000 (Ireland's most popular model, the Toyota Corolla, starts at just under €19,500) and bigger family cars, such as the Mazda 6, cost from €25,000. The cheapest BMW (the 116i) will set you back almost €30,000!

It's possible to cross the border into Northern Ireland and buy a new car at UK prices, which are considerably lower, but any savings are wiped out by the Revenue Commissioners, who levy a corresponding import duty when you bring the car back into Ireland.

Despite the high prices of new cars, Ireland's continuing economic boom means that new car dealers are having little difficulty in finding buyers and are therefore offering little in the way of financial incentives. Interest free loans and 'cashback' deals, such as are common in other countries, are almost unheard of in Ireland and the best you can hope for is a reasonable rate of interest on a hire purchase.

You can often obtain a good bargain by buying a model that has been, or is due to be, discontinued. When new registration numbers are issued (i.e. at the beginning of the year), you may be able to save money by buying a car with the previous year's number, although this sort of discounting isn't as common as in the UK or US. One way of picking up a bargain vehicle almost new is to look out for ex-demonstration models that are around six or eight months old and have 6,000-8,000km on the clock.

The manufacturer's list price normally includes VAT, motor tax, number plates and a tank of petrol, as well as a delivery 'package' comprising de-waxing, a pre-delivery inspection and a 600-mile service, in addition to delivery to your door. When comparing prices, ask dealers for the on-the-road price, including delivery and the other charges listed above. Manufacturers usually allow up to €500 for delivery, so if you're able to collect the car yourself or live only a few hundred yards from the dealership, it's worth asking for a discount!

On 1st July 2008, in conjunction with the change to vehicle registration tax (see page 198), a labelling system for new cars was introduced, indicating their CO_2 emission rates according to the seven tax bands and the consequent VRT rate, as well as the annual motor tax payable, the amount of fuel required to travel 18,000km (reckoned to be the average annual distance driven by the Irish) and basic information about the vehicle, such as its engine capacity and fuel type.

Another important aspect to consider when buying a new car is the warranty period, during which major parts are insured against replacement. Most manufacturers provide three-year warranties covering all mechanical and electrical parts (but not items such as light bulbs and wiper blades). Tyres are normally covered by a separate warranty.

Note, however, that warranties usually contain a range of get-out clauses for manufacturers.

If you're unlucky enough to buy a 'lemon' (one that was built on a Friday afternoon), you can have it inspected by a motoring organisation (see page 221) or a member of the Society of the Irish Motor Industry (☎ 01-676 1690, 💻 www.simi.ie), which usually provides irrefutable, independent evidence in the event of a legal battle with the manufacturer.

Used Cars

Unlike some other countries (such as the UK and the US), Ireland is a fairly 'safe' place to buy secondhand cars. Most new car dealers also sell used cars and the vast majority of garage owners are trustworthy and unlikely to pass

you off with a heap of junk. Devious practices such as clocking (winding back the odometer), falsifying test certificates, welding together the undamaged halves of two accident-damaged vehicles (known as a 'cut and shut' operation) are mercifully rare. This doesn't mean, however, that you will be spared the persuasive patter of the used car salesman – especially if he has kissed the Blarney Stone!

Not surprisingly, Ireland isn't the place to find 'car supermarkets'. One of the largest secondhand car dealers in Dublin is Merlin Motor City (💻 www.merlinmotorcity.ie), where there are usually at least 400 cars for sale. As in a food supermarket, there's no haggling over the price!

Publications

The three main publications in Ireland for buying or selling used cars are *Auto Trader* (💻 www.autotrader.ie), *Buy and Sell* (💻 www.buyandsell.ie) and the *Car Buyer Guide* (💻 www.cbg.ie), all of which are issued weekly and have regularly updated websites, where you can see the latest lists of cars for sale. The 'North & Midlands' edition of the UK magazine *Exchange & Mart* is available in Ireland, but contains very few Irish registered cars.

Auctions

As an alternative to buying a car frm a dealer or privately, you can buy at a car auction, although these are generally for the experienced buyer. The main car auctions in Ireland are run by Wilsons Auctions in Dublin (☎ 01-464 2800, 💻 http://wilsonsauctions.ie) and Merlin

(formerly Windsor) Car Auctions in Ashbourne, County Meath (☎ 045-988700, 💻 www.merlin carauctions.ie).

Price

There's no official (or unofficial) guide to used car prices in Ireland, so you should always do your own research in your area by comparing prices at dealers', in local newspapers and car magazines and on internet sites. Many private sellers are willing to take a considerable drop and dealers may be open to a certain amount

of 'haggling'. The average annual mileage for a car in Ireland is around 12,000 (19,311km) per year and cars with high mileage (e.g. 20,000mi/32,186km a year) can usually be bought for substantially less than those which have been used only for going to and from the local shops.

VEHICLE LICENSING & MOTOR TAX

All vehicles registered in Ireland must, of course, be licensed and are required to display current insurance and motor tax discs in their windscreen. Failure to do so can incur an on-the-spot fine of €65; the penalties for having an untaxed vehicle on the road are higher.

Licensing

The licensing of new vehicles, including the supply of number plates (license plates), is normally carried out by the garage or dealer who sells you the vehicle. The same usually applies if you buy a car secondhand from a dealer, but if you buy privately and need to re-license a vehicle in your name, you must obtain a new vehicle licensing certificate. If the vehicle was first licensed before 1st January 1993, it will have a brown registration document (log book), which (if you're selling privately) you must send to your local Motor Tax Office with a completed form RF200 (for change of ownership); if you're selling the vehicle to a dealer, you send only form RF200 to the Motor Tax Office and give the log book to the dealer.

If the car was first licensed after 1st January 1993 or later and you're selling it privately, you must give a vehicle licensing certificate to the buyer, who must complete Part B and send it to the Vehicle Registration Department, Department of the Environment and Local Government, Shannon Town, County Clare (☎ 061-364901). They will send the buyer a new certificate containing their details. If you're selling to a dealer, you must complete form RF105, which the dealer will supply, and send it to the address above; you give the vehicle licensing certificate and registration document to the dealer.

When selling to a dealer (irrespective of the age of the car), you must obtain a valid 'garage code', which the dealer should have obtained from the Department of Environment; if he is unable to supply a code, the change of ownership will be rejected.

There's no charge for re-licensing a vehicle but, if you (or the previous owner) should lose your certificate, you must pay for a replacement; the same fee applies to the replacement of a registration document. You must complete form RF134, have it witnessed by a policeman and submit it to your local Motor Tax Office.

EU-style number plates, which were introduced in 1988, are mandatory on all Irish-registered cars. It isn't possible to 'personalise' your plates as in the US and the UK, although you can reserve a particular number which is due to be issued either through a dealer or direct with the Vehicle Registration Department; however, you won't be able to register the vehicle until the number actually becomes available!

Motor Tax

Most vehicles registered in Ireland are subject to motor tax; certain disabled vehicles and public utility vehicles are exempt. Tax must be paid at a Motor Tax Office (there's one in each county, listed in the green-edged pages at the front of the phone book) and is charged on a sliding scale according to a vehicle's engine capacity. In line with changes to vehicle registration tax (see page 198), motor tax rates now vary according to the carbon dioxide emission level of a vehicle, as shown in the table below.

Motor Tax Rates		
Band	CO$_2$ Emission Rate	Motor Tax Rate
A	Less than 120g per km	€100
B	121 to 140 g/km	€150
C	141 to 155 g/km	€290
D	156 to 170 g/km	€430
E	171 to 190 g/km	€600
F	191 to 225 g/km	€1,000
G	Over 225 g/km	€2,000

It's possible to pay motor tax half-yearly or even quarterly, but of course you pay more per year if you do. If you lose your tax disc, you must pay €6 for a replacement.

If the vehicle is new, you must obtain a First Motor Tax Application form (RF100), which is supplied by the dealer, and take this and the appropriate fee to the local Motor Tax Office. In all other cases, you must complete form RF100A or RF100B and take it with the vehicle's registration document or vehicle licensing certificate (see above), insurance certificate and National Car Test certificate (see below) to the Motor Tax Offices. These tend to close early (e.g. 3.30pm), so don't leave it until the last minute to tax your car! Renewals can be made by post, but you should allow three weeks for receipt of your new tax disc.

You're probably wondering what the difference is between forms RF100A and RF100B. In theory, you will receive a form

RF100B automatically just before your tax disc is due to expire, but in practice not everyone receives it; if you don't, you must ask for a form RF100A at the Motor Tax Office. The forms are the same.

If your vehicle is stolen, written off or scrapped or hasn't been used on a public road since its last tax renewal, you can claim a refund, which is calculated from the first of the month following your claim, provided that the disc is valid for at least three further months. To claim a refund, complete form RF120 and take or post it with your current tax disc and vehicle licensing certificate, as well as evidence that the vehicle has been unused (e.g. a doctor's certificate of disablement or police theft report) to your Motor Tax Office. It isn't possible to claim a motor tax refund if you sell a vehicle before the tax period has expired.

NATIONAL CAR TEST

The National Car Test (NCT), which was introduced in January 2000, is reckoned to be one of the most comprehensive testing programmes in the world – it's estimated to have put 200,000 Irish cars off the road in its first year of operation! All cars over four years old must be tested for roadworthiness every two years. The NCT is due exactly four years after a car's first registration (in the country of origin for imported cars) and is valid for two years from that date irrespective of when the test is actually taken (your car may be tested for the first time up to six months before the due date and subsequently up to three months early).

The only cars that don't need to be tested are three-wheelers, vintage cars and cars used exclusively on islands not connected to the mainland.

Tests are carried out at 43 test centres operated by the National Car Testing Service (NCTS), which is independent of garage service and repair departments. The NCT covers most aspects of a car's operation (e.g. brakes, steering, suspension and transmission), as well as electrical systems, horn and lights, wheels and tyres, chassis and

♦ empty the boot and remove all belongings from seats (including baby seats);

♦ remove hubcaps if wheel nuts aren't visible.

It's also a good idea to have your brakes tested, as around 15 per cent of cars fail because of defective brakes. When you take the car to the test centre, make sure you take the car's registration document or licensing certificate with you. Further advice can be found on the NCTS website (see above).

After the test you are given a report itemising the points tested and indicating any which were 'refused' or 'failed'. If any points have been refused, it means that the car has failed the test and the specified defects must be repaired and the car re-tested within four weeks. If nothing has been refused, but certain points have been 'failed', the car is normally deemed to have passed (unless any of the 'failures' is dangerous). The 'failed' items are listed as 'advisory' on the NCT report (see below) and it's up to you to correct the faults listed. If you're caught driving a car without a valid test certificate, you're liable to a hefty fine.

Once your car has passed the NCT, you're issued with a certificate, which you must produce when you renew your motor tax (see page 203), a disc, which you must display in your windscreen, and a report, which your insurance company may ask to see. If you lose your certificate or disc, you need to go to your local *Garda* station and obtain form RF134 (stamped and signed) and send it with a cheque for €12.70 (payable to NCTS Ltd) to the Test Certificate Administrator, NCTS, Lakedrive 3026, Citywest Business Campus, Naas Road, Dublin 24. For a replacement NCT report, simply send your car registration number, make, model and owner details (and a cheque for €12.70!) to the same address.

It's unwise to buy a vehicle with a test certificate that is due to expire in a few days or weeks, even at a bargain price (which should make you even more suspicious), as around 50 per cent of older cars (i.e. pre-1992) fail the test, and over 30 per cent require substantial repairs before they pass. Nor should a test certificate be taken as a guarantee of a car's reliability.

bodywork, windows and mirrors, fuel systems and exhaust emissions (the latter with regard to the car's age), registration plates and the condition of the car's interior (especially seats and seat belts). The test procedure is outlined in the National Car Test Manual, which is available from Government Publications (☎ 01-647 6000) and on the NCTS website (🖥 www.ncts.ie).

You should be contacted by the NCTS approximately two months in advance of the due date and offered a provisional appointment at a nearby test centre, as well as being given a booking number. You must then contact the NCTS (☎ 1890-200670) to accept or rearrange your appointment, which will be confirmed in writing.

The NCT costs €49. If your car fails the test, you will be charged €27.50 for a re-test, unless the re-test doesn't require the use of testing equipment (e.g. failure was due to a minor problem such as a faulty brake light or windscreen wiper), in which case the re-test is free. Re-tests must be done within 28 days of the original test. If you cancel a test less than five days before your appointment, you will be charged a cancellation fee. You can pay in cash or by cheque, credit or debit card.

Before taking your car for a test, you should:

♦ top up oil and water;

♦ check tyre pressures;

♦ check all light bulbs and windscreen wipers;

♦ check headlamp alignment;

DRIVING LICENCES

The minimum age for driving in Ireland is 17 for a car or motorcycle with an engine capacity above 125cc, and 16 for a motorcycle up to 125cc (note also that motorcyclists are restricted to machines of less than 350cc for two years after passing their test).

In March 2006, the European Commission approved the introduction of a single EU driving licence to replace those currently in use in the 25 member states, but the new licence isn't expected to come into effect until 2012 (good job all European legislation doesn't take that long to implement!) and the current driving licences issued by each member state will be phased out by 2032. The following information explains the current situation regarding applying for or renewing a full driving licence in Ireland. **You're required to carry your driving licence with you when driving in Ireland.**

Foreign Licences

If you already hold a driving licence issued by a European Economic Area (EEA) country (including all EU countries), Australia, Gibraltar, the Isle of Man, Japan, Jersey, South Africa, South Korea or Switzerland, you may drive in Ireland on that licence for the duration of its validity. However, if you wish, you may exchange it for an equivalent Irish licence. Application for an exchange must be made within a year of expiry of the licence. You must complete an Exchange of Driving Licence form (D.900) and an Application for Driving Licence form (D.401).

Holders of other foreign or international driving licences can use them in Ireland for up to 12 months, after which they must obtain an Irish driving licence by following the procedure outlined below.

⚠ Caution

Note that a foreign licence becomes invalid if you're convicted of a driving offence that attracts penalty points, when you must obtain an Irish licence so that the points can be duly applied.

Theory Test

If you've never had a driving licence or your licence expired more than ten years ago or you hold a licence from a country that isn't part of the Exchange scheme (see above), to obtain an Irish licence you must first take the Driver Theory Test. This tests not only your knowledge of the rules of the road, but your ability to recognise danger and evaluate risk and to drive in an environmentally-friendly as well as other-road-user-friendly way. The *Rules of the Road*, a booklet published by the Department of Transport, is available from bookshops and some post offices. Note, however, that the Department of Transport is currently reviewing the rules, so make sure you have up-to-date information.

There are different tests for riding motorcycles and mopeds (licence categories A and M – see below) and for driving cars (categories B and W). The test, which costs around €37 and is of the multiple-choice type, must be taken (in English or Irish) at one of 41 test centres operated by the Driver Theory Testing Service. Theory tests should be applied for by contacting Driver Theory Test Headquarters, PO Box 144, Drogheda, County Louth (☎ 1890-606106). You will be asked for your Personal Public Service (PPS) number when you apply, and for identification when you arrive to take the test. In theory, the theory test can be taken at any age, but confirmation of passing it must date from no more than two years before you become eligible for a licence.

Licence Categories

There are 14 driving licence categories, including the following:

◆ **M** – entitling you to ride a moped (minimum age 16);

◆ **A1** – entitling you to ride a motorcycle with an engine capacity of not more than 125cc (minimum age 16);

◆ **A** – entitling you to ride a motorcycle with an engine capacity of over 125cc (minimum age 18);

◆ **B** – entitling you to drive a car, minibus or van not exceeding 3.5 tonnes and with accommodation for no more than eight passengers (minimum age 17);

♦ **C** – entitling you to drive a vehicle exceeding 3.5 tonnes, but with accommodation for no more than eight passengers (minimum age 18);

♦ **D** – entitling you to drive a vehicle with accommodation for more than eight pasengers (minimum age 21).

Provisional Licence

On successful completion of the theory test, you can – indeed, if you want to obtain a full driving licence, you **must** – apply for a provisional licence of the category for which you intend to have a full licence, though a new driver can apply only for categories M, A1, A or B. A provisional licence costs around €16 and is normally valid for two years, although you may renew it twice. Apply to your local Motor Tax Office using form D.201, accompanied by the following:

♦ two identical passport-size photographs, signed on the back;

♦ your passport or birth certificate;

♦ an eyesight report form (D.502), obtainable from any registered optician or doctor;

♦ a medical report form (D.501) if you're over 70, suffer from certain disabilities or are applying for a non-standard licence (e.g. for heavy goods vehicles);

♦ your current or previous licence if applicable.

Once you have a provisional licence you can apply for a driving test; there's no minimum time during which you have to have held a provisional licence as there is in some countries, but obviously you need to acquire sufficient skill to have a chance of passing a test (almost half of driving test applicants fail!). On the other hand, a provisional licence is valid only for five years, after which you must retake the theory test.

Holders of a provisional car licence must be accompanied when driving by a person with a full driving licence, and all provisional licence holders must display L-plates at the front and rear of their vehicles. You aren't allowed to tow a trailer, drive on a motorway or operate a taxi service. Driving instructors are listed in the *Golden Pages* and should be registered with either the Driving Instructor Register (DIR) or Association of Certified Driving Schools (ACDI).

Driving Test

Driver testing in Ireland is carried out directly by the Department of Transport to a standard that complies with the EU Directive on Driving Licences. There are 54 test centres throughout the country, all of which use the same testing procedures; and where possible, your test will be arranged at the centre you nominate on your application form. Waiting times vary from county to county; so it is advisable to apply for a test at least ten months before your provisional licence is due to expire.

If you're taking a test for a category B (car) licence, you must explain three technical and safety checks (e.g. tyres, engine oil and lights) as part of your test. The test takes approximately half an hour and you're told immediately whether you've passed or not. If you have, you're given a 'Certificate of Competency', which is valid for two years. If you fail to apply for a full licence during this period, you have to take a driving test again. If you fail your driving test, you will be given a detailed list of your failings!

Applications should be made to the Driver Testing Section, Government Offices, Department of Transport, Ballina, County Mayo (☎ 096-78289 or ☎ 1890-406040), accompanied by the appropriate fee (see above). Ten days' notice must be given if you need to cancel your driving test; otherwise the fee is forfeited.

Further information about driving licences and tests can be obtained from the Driver Testing Section of the Department of Transport (☎ 01-670-7444, 🖥 www.transport.ie/roads/drivertesting), the Road Safety Authority (☎ 096-25000 or ☎ 1890-506080, 🖥 www.nsc.ie) and on 🖥 www.drivingschoolireland.com.

Licence Application

There's no maximum age for obtaining your first licence, but certain limitations apply if you're over 60. Those under 60 may apply for a ten-year licence. If you're over 60 but under 67, your licence expires when you're 70. If you're between 67 and 70, you're limited to a three-year licence. If you're over 70, you may be entitled to a three or one-year licence, subject to certification from a doctor that you're fit to drive.

An application for a driving licence should include the following:

◆ a completed application form (D.401);

◆ two photographs (signed on the back);

◆ your current or most recent driving licence and/or provisional licence;

◆ a Theory Test Certificate;

◆ a Certificate of Competency if you've recently passed a driving test (see above);

◆ a medical report if appropriate (see Provisional Licence above);

◆ the appropriate fee (see below).

The fee for a ten-year driving licence is €25, for a three-year licence €15, and for a one-year licence €5. If you're over 70 and declared fit to drive, a licence is free! The same fees apply to renewal of licences. Payment should be made to the City or County Council to which you're making the application e.g. to Dublin City Council if you're applying to the Dublin Motor Tax Office.

You can obtain a new licence free if you move (and need to change the address on your licence), if penalty points are removed (see **Driving Offences** on page 212) or if you've passed a test to drive an additional category of vehicle. In all cases you must send a completed application form, two photographs (signed on the back), and any supporting documentation, e.g. a Certificate of Competency or medical report, to your local Motor Tax Office.

If you lose (i.e. misplace) your licence or it's stolen, you can obtain a duplicate by completing form D.800 and taking it, along with two photographs and €5, to your local *Garda* station. Needless to say, driving without a valid licence in Ireland is a serious offence and penalties can be severe.

VEHICLE INSURANCE

Under Irish law, all motor vehicles plus trailers and semi-trailers must be insured when entering Ireland. However, it isn't mandatory for cars insured in most European countries to have an international insurance 'green card' (see below) in Ireland. Motorists insured in an EU country, the Czech Republic, Hungary, Liechtenstein, Norway, Slovakia and Switzerland are automatically covered for third-party liability in Ireland. In addition to the many Irish insurance companies, car insurance is also available from a number of foreign insurance companies registered in Ireland.

In general, the Irish car insurance market is quite stable and there are few 'cowboy' operators to be avoided. The minimum term for motor insurance is normally 12 months. Short-term policies are available at a small premium from a few companies in Ireland, but if you're only staying in Ireland for a few weeks or months, it's generally preferable to extend your existing policy in your home country.

There are essentially two categories of car insurance available in Ireland:

♦ **Third-party** – Third-party insurance is compulsory and is the minimum required by law. A third party is anyone apart from the driver, including your own passengers, and you must be insured against third-party claims for personal injury and damage to property. There's no limit to your liability if you have third-party insurance, although it won't usually cover you against natural hazards such as rocks falling on your car. Additional cover can be purchased to protect against personal accidents as well as fire, theft (of the car or your possessions inside it), windscreen damage, roadside assistance, etc. Personal accident cover, for example, costs an additional €15 to €30 per year.

♦ **Comprehensive** – Comprehensive insurance usually covers all risks listed above, and includes damage to your own vehicle, irrespective of how it's caused. It usually includes theft of factory-fitted stereo systems and may also cover legal expenses in the event of a court case. Comprehensive cover is usually available on all vehicles irrespective of age, but cars more than four years old may need to be inspected before insurance is granted. Note that comprehensive cover may be compulsory for lease and credit purchase contracts. Irish insurance doesn't always pay for a replacement car when yours is being repaired after an accident, although this is becoming more common.

Premiums

Insurance premiums in Ireland vary enormously, according to numerous factors including the kind of insurance; the type and make of car; your age and sex; accident record; and the area where you live. A policy which costs €300 for a middle-aged female with a good driving record living in the country may cost a young Dublin man with a poor record €3,000. Even when all other factors are the same, there's usually a difference of up to 15 per cent between premiums for women and premiums for men.

There are some 25 companies providing car insurance in Ireland, each offering different packages and rates. Some companies separate cars into insurance brackets or groups, although most vary their rates according to the value, age and engine size of a car. Some won't insure high performance vehicles, while others offer special low-cost policies for experienced older drivers, e.g. those aged over 50 or 55, with a good safety record. Your annual mileage, on the other hand, won't usually affect the price you pay. Most companies charge men and women different rates (women generally pay less). You should therefore shop around or, better still, use an insurance broker.

Irish insurance companies generally charge an excess of around €150 on any claim, and don't normally allow you to waive this by paying an extra premium. To protect yourself against legal costs in the event of an accident landing you in court, you can usually pay an additional premium of around €30 per year, which will cover you for up to €75,000 of costs. There's no VAT on insurance premiums, but there's a government levy of 2 per cent which goes towards a fund to pay for injuries caused by uninsured drivers. Some companies allow you to pay insurance premiums in instalments or by direct debit, but normally they're payable 'up front'.

If you cancel your policy before the end of the term, you will receive a refund of premiums paid less a cancellation fee, which varies from company to company; generally, if you cancel within three months of the end of the term, you will get little or nothing back.

No-claims Bonuses

If you've been driving for a year or more without an insurance claim, you may be entitled to a 'no-claims bonus', which is effectively a discount on your insurance premium of up to 55 per cent after five years without a claim. No claims bonuses are usually transferable from one insurance company to another (even from a foreign company), provided you furnish sufficient evidence of no claims.

Green Cards

All Irish insurance companies and most other insurance companies in western Europe provide an automatic 'green card', which extends your normal insurance cover (e.g. comprehensive) to most other European countries. This is available on request and is usually free.

The exception is the UK, where insurance companies usually provide only third-party cover in other EU countries, and charge for a green card which is only issued for limited periods (i.e. 30 to 45 days) and for a maximum number of days a year, e.g. 90. (This is to discourage the British from driving abroad, where they're a menace and a danger to all road users, as most don't know their left from their right – particularly the politicians!) If you're British and have comprehensive insurance, it's wise to have a green card when visiting Ireland.

If you drive a British-registered car and spend more than six months a year in other EU countries, you may need to take out a special (i.e. expensive) European insurance policy or obtain insurance with a European company. Another alternative is to insure your car with a British insurance company in Ireland.

Irish residents are obliged to display a valid insurance disc in their car windscreen, and failure to do so can result in an on-the-spot fine of €65. Needless to say, driving without insurance is a serious offence, which can be punished by imprisonment.

RULES OF THE ROAD

The following general road rules and tips may help you adjust to driving in Ireland and avoid an accident:

Among the many strange habits of the Irish (most of them inherited from the British) is that of driving on the left-hand side of the road. You may find this a bit strange if you come from a country which drives on the right, but it saves a lot of confusion if you do likewise! It's helpful to have a reminder (e.g. 'THINK LEFT!') on your car's

dashboard. Take extra care when pulling out of parking spaces (particularly first thing in the morning!) and junctions and when negotiating roundabouts.

Drivers of left-hand drive cars should fit beam adjusters to their headlights in order not to dazzle oncoming drivers when driving at night. As a pedestrian, remember to look first to the right when crossing the road (actually, it's better to look both ways, just in case!).

♦ There's no automatic priority to the right (or left) on any roads, as there is in many European countries. At all crossroads and junctions there's either an octagonal stop sign (solid white line on road) or a triangular give-way sign (dotted white line on road), where a secondary road meets a major road. Stop or give way may also be painted on the road surface. You must stop completely at a stop sign (all four wheels must come to rest) before pulling out onto a major road, even if you can see that no traffic is approaching. At a give-way sign, you aren't required to stop, but must give priority to traffic already on the major road.

♦ At roundabouts (traffic circles), vehicles on the roundabout (coming from your right) have priority. Some roundabouts have a filter lane which is reserved for traffic turning left. Traffic flows clockwise round roundabouts and not anti-clockwise as in countries where traffic drives on the right. You should signal in the usual way as you approach the roundabout and then signal left at the exit before the one you intend to take. In addition to large roundabouts, there are also mini-roundabouts, indicated by a

round blue sign, at which the same rules apply in theory, but in practice it's generally a case of 'who dares wins'.

◆ All motorists are advised to carry a warning triangle, although it isn't mandatory. If you have an accident or a breakdown, you should signal this by switching on your hazard warning lights. If you have a warning triangle it must be placed at the edge of the road, at least 50 metres behind the car on secondary roads and at least 150 metres on motorways.

◆ The wearing of seat belts is compulsory for all front and rear seat passengers. Children's seat belts or restraints must be appropriate to their age and weight. Special harnesses and belts are also available for the handicapped. Note that all belts, seats, harnesses and restraints must be correctly fitted and adjusted. In addition to the risk of death or injury, you can be fined for ignoring the seat belt laws. Note that it's the driver's responsibility to ensure that passengers are properly fastened. If you're exempt from wearing a seat belt for medical reasons, a safety belt exemption certificate is required from your doctor. Note also that the fact that your vehicle is fitted with air bags doesn't exempt you from wearing seat belts!

◆ Don't drive in lanes reserved for buses and taxis, unless necessary to avoid a stationary vehicle or obstruction, and give priority to authorised users. Bus lanes are indicated by road markings, and signs indicate the period of operation, which is usually during rush hours only (although some lanes are in use 24 hours a day), and which vehicles are permitted to use them. Bus drivers get irate if you illegally drive in their lane and you can be fined for doing so.

◆ Headlights must be used on all roads as soon as street lights are switched on. You must use your headlamps or front fog lamps at any time when visibility is generally reduced to less than 100m. Note that headlight flashing has a different meaning in different countries. In some countries it means 'after you', while in others it means 'get out of my way' (It can even mean 'I'm driving a new car and haven't yet worked out what all the switches are for'.) In Ireland, headlamp flashing has no legal status apart from warning another driver of your presence, although it's usually used to give priority to another vehicle, e.g. when a car is waiting to exit from a junction.

◆ Fog lamps should be used only when visibility is seriously reduced, i.e. to less than 100m, and shouldn't be used when it's just dark or raining.

☑ **SURVIVAL TIP**

Hazard warning lights should be used only to warn other drivers of an obstruction, e.g. an accident or traffic jam on a motorway. Using them when parking illegally won't prevent you from being penalised, unless you've broken down.

◆ The sequence of Irish traffic lights is red, green, amber and back to red. Amber means stop; you may continue only if the amber light appears after you've crossed the stop line or when stopping might cause an accident. A green filter light may be shown in addition to the full lamp signals, which means you may drive in the direction shown by the arrow, irrespective of other lights showing.

◆ Always approach pedestrian crossings with caution, and don't park or overtake another vehicle on the approach to a crossing. At crossings with traffic lights, a flashing amber light follows the red light, to warn you to give way to pedestrians before proceeding. Where a road crosses a public footpath, e.g. when entering or emerging from property or a car park bordering a road, you must give way to pedestrians.

◆ White lines mark the separation of traffic lanes. A solid single line or two solid lines means no overtaking in either direction. A solid line to the left of the centre line, i.e. on your side of the road, means that overtaking is prohibited in your direction. You may overtake only when there's a single broken line in the middle of the road or double lines with a broken line on your side of the road. If you drive a left-hand drive car, take extra care when over-taking (the most dangerous manoeuvre in motoring) and when turning right. It's wise to have a special 'overtaking mirror' fitted to your car.

♦ On dual-carriageways and motorways it's illegal to overtake on an inside lane unless traffic is slow moving or being channelled in a different direction. Motorists should indicate before overtaking and when moving back into an inside lane after overtaking. Learner drivers, pedestrians, cyclists and mopeds aren't permitted on motorways.

♦ There are two kinds of railway level crossings: automatic and manual. Always approach a railway level crossing slowly and STOP:

– as soon as the amber light is on and the audible alarm sounds, followed by flashing red warning lights (automatic crossings);

– as soon as the gates start to close (manual crossings);

– in any case when a train approaches.

♦ Be particularly wary of cyclists, moped riders and motorcyclists. It isn't always easy to see them, particularly when they're hidden by the blind spots of a car or when cyclists are riding at night without lights. When overtaking, ALWAYS give them a wide . . . WIDE berth. If you knock them off their bikes, you may have a difficult time convincing the police that it wasn't your fault; far better to avoid them (and the police). Drive slowly near schools and be wary of children getting on or off buses.

♦ Drivers of foreign registered cars in Ireland must have the appropriate nationality sticker affixed to the rear of their car (not an assortment) or EU licence plates. Note that yellow headlights aren't illegal in Ireland, but left-hand drive cars should have their headlamps adjusted (i.e. with appropriate stickers) so that they don't dazzle oncoming drivers.

♦ If you need spectacles or contact lenses to read a number plate at a distance of 20.5m (67ft) in good daylight, you must always wear them when driving. It's wise to carry a spare pair of glasses or contact lenses in your car.

♦ Using a mobile phone while driving is an offence, punishable by two penalty points and a fine of €60. For details of other fines and penalties see **Driving Offences** on page 212.

The *Rules of the Road*, a booklet published by the Department of Transport, is available from bookshops and some post offices (although few Irish drivers seem to have read it!). Note, however, that the Department of Transport is currently reviewing the rules, so make sure you have up-to-date information. Foreigners are advised to pick up a free leaflet entitled *Traffic Rules*, which explains (in English, French and German) the most common road signs (see below). The Road Safety Authority (☎ 01-496 3422, 💻 www.nsc.ie), formerly the National Safety Council, provides free leaflets on various aspects of driving, including the safe use of mobile phones, driving at night, etc. A wealth of information about driving in Ireland can be found on 💻 www.drivingschoolireland.com.

SPEED LIMITS

The speed limit on motorways is 120kph (75mph), on other main roads (known officially as 'national roads'), including dual-carriageways, it is 100kph (62mph). The only exception to this is the N2 Finglas to Ashbourne dual-carriageway has a limit of 120kph. On non-national roads the limit is 80kph (50mph), and in built-up areas 50kph (31mph), unless otherwise indicated; a limit of 30kph applies in many school zones, for example. 'Traffic calming' schemes have been introduced in many parts of the country in an attempt to slow traffic as it approaches built-up areas, and there is often an intermediate (e.g. 60kph/40mph) restriction before you reach a town or village itself. There are speed cameras nationwide.

DRIVING OFFENCES

Fines can be exacted for a wide range of motoring offences in Ireland, and around 350,000 on-the-spot fines are made each year. A penalty points system, which extends to 35 offences, including the following (M indicates a mandatory appearance in court, the figure in brackets indicating the number of penalty points incurred if you're convicted). Note that the number of penalty points listed is the **minimum** incurred for each offence.

Even if you're a law-abiding driver, you should ensure that you're in good shape before driving in Ireland, as you can be taken to court and fined and have three points on your licence for 'driving a vehicle when unfit'!

Fines are increased by 50 per cent if not paid within 28 days. Points remain on your licence for three years and, once you've accumulated 12 points, you're disqualified from driving for six months. Further details can be found on ⌨ www.penaltypoints.ie.

Drinking & Driving

As in the UK and around half of European countries, the legal limit of alcohol in the blood (known as blood alcohol concentration or BAC) is 0.08 per cent (equivalent to 0.107 per cent of alcohol in the urine). You can be stopped by the *Gardaí* at any time and asked to 'blow into a bag'. If you fail the breath test, you can be arrested without a warrant and taken to a station where you must provide samples of either urine or blood (or pay a hefty fine for refusing). You may insist on the presence of your doctor, but you will have to pay to call him out. If you also fail this test, you will be summoned to appear in a District Court, where you can be fined up to €3,000 and/or be disqualified from driving for a year or even given a jail sentence. The advice of The Road Safety Authority is, "If you drink, don't drive".

TRAFFIC POLICE

Police must have a reason to stop motorists in Ireland, e.g. erratic driving or defective lights. You aren't required by law to carry your car or motorcycle papers when motoring, but a *garda* may ask to see the following:

Penalties for Driving Offences

Offence	Penalty Points	Fine
Speeding	2	€80
Holding mobile phone while driving	2	€60
Driving without insurance	M (5)	Set by court
Not wearing a seat belt	2	€60
Careless driving	M (5)	Set by court
Dangerous overtaking	2	€80
Not stopping at a 'stop' line/sign or traffic light	2	€80
Not giving way at a 'yield' line/sign	2	€80
Crossing an unbroken white line	2	€80
Driving on the hard shoulder of a motorway	1	€80
Failure to drive on the left hand side of the road	1	€60
Driving too close to the car in front	2	€80
Driving without reasonable consideration	2	€80
Not obeying signs or road markings	1	€60

- ◆ driving licence (Irish if held);

- ◆ vehicle licensing certificate or registration document (log book);

- ◆ National Car Test certificate;

- ◆ insurance certificate (or an international motor insurance certificate, if you're driving a foreign registered car).

If you don't have your papers with you when you're stopped by the police, you must take them personally to a police station (named by you), usually within ten days.

IRISH ROADS

Irish roads have changed radically in recent years. In the year 2000 there was only some 60km (37mi) of motorway in the whole of Ireland (all of it near Dublin) and barely more than twice as much dual-carriageway.

By 2010 there will be almost 200km (124mi) of motorway, and dozens of single-carriageway roads will have become dual-carriageways. And where previously, main roads ploughed through the middle of even major towns, bypasses are now springing up all over the country.

The following motorways were in existence in mid-2008 (see map in **Appendix E**):

- ◆ **M1** – from the northern outskirts of Dublin City to north of Dundalk (part of the Dublin–Belfast road);

- ◆ **M4** – from Lucan to Kinnegad (Dublin–Sligo road);

- ◆ **M6** – a short section of the N6 Dublin–Galway road at Kinnegad is designated as motorway;

- ◆ **M7** – from north-east of Naas to west of Portlaoise (Dublin–Limerick road);

- ◆ **M8** – from Rathcormac to Fermoy (Dublin–Cork road);

- ◆ **M9** – from west of Newbridge to south of Kilcullen (Dublin–Waterford road), linking with the M7;

- ◆ **M11** – the Bray/Shankill bypass (Dublin–Wexford road);

- ◆ **M50** – Dublin's ring road and, not surprisingly, Ireland's busiest motorway.

The following motorways were either under construction or planned for the next few years.

- ◆ **M3** – from Clonee to north of Kells (Dublin–Ballyshannon road);

- ◆ **M6** – a further section of the N6, between Galway and Ballinasloe, is to be designated motorway;

- ◆ **M7** – motorway to be extended to Roscrea and a Nenagh–Limerick section to be added;

- ◆ **M8** – Portlaoise–Roscrea section to link with M7 and N8;

- ◆ **M17** – Galway–Tuam;

- ◆ **M25** – Waterford bypass.

The following Euro Routes include Irish sections:

- ◆ **E01** – from Larne (Northern Ireland) to Seville (Spain) via Dublin and Rosslare;

- ◆ **E20** – from Shannon to St Petersburg (Russia) via Limerick and Dublin;

- ◆ **E30** – from Cork to Omsk (Russia) via Waterford, Wexford and Rosslare;

- ◆ **E201** – from Cork to Portlaoise.

Next in the hierarchy of Irish roads are national primary roads, numbered upwards from N1 (to currently N33); those from N1 to N11 are the most important routes (i.e. between major towns and cities), while those from N12 to N33 are mostly cross-country routes. National secondary roads are numbered from N51 upwards, and regional roads from R1xx in the north-east of the country to R7xx in the south-west. These are mostly single-carriageway country roads; the main exception is the R113 (Belgard) road, which is a dual-carriageway linking the N7 and N81.

Speeds of up to 120kph(75mph) are permitted on certain N roads – notably the N1 from Dundalk to the Northern Ireland border, and the N2 from the M50 to Ashbourne – and The Roads Act, 2007 made provision for the redesignation of certain dual-carriageways as motorways, provisionally as follows: the N6 from Kinnegad (where it meets the M6) to Athlone; the N7 between Borris-in-Ossery and Annacotty; the N8 from Urlingford to Fermoy; the N9 from Kilcullen to Waterford (where it's to meet the proposed N25).

Local roads are officially designated by four-digit numbers prefixed by L, although these are only just starting to appear on road signs and maps. In some areas there are still signs showing the old road designations: T for a 'trunk' (i.e. main) road and L for a link road.

The great majority of Irish roads still have just a single lane in each direction (although there's sometimes an extra lane on long hills for slow vehicles). A peculiarity of these roads is their so-called hard shoulder, which is indicated by broken yellow lines – so-called because it's used in rather a different way from hard shoulders in most other countries. Instead of being reserved for breakdowns or other emergencies, it's also used for overtaking. That doesn't mean that the Irish overtake on the inside, but that when you see a vehicle approaching rapidly from behind with the intention of overtaking, it's expected that you pull over onto the hard shoulder to let it pass.

Even more disconcerting is when you find an oncoming vehicle heading straight towards you on your side of the road and your only option is to veer onto the hard shoulder to avoid a head-on collision. The Irish won't thank you for doing so – not because they're inconsiderate, but because to them it's a completely normal manoeuvre.

Another feature of Irish roads is their unevenness. Although much resurfacing work is being done, many roads are bumpy and you need to keep a weather eye out for pot holes; it's a great relief to come upon one of the strips of new or resurfaced road, which will reassure you that your suspension is still working properly (or confirm that it isn't, as the case may be!).

Most Irish roads are passable at all times of the year, although some may be closed in winter if there's heavy rain or snow. Irish roads rarely have special facilities such as services or rest areas, although they're well served by petrol stations, cafés, restaurants and hotels (most main roads pass through towns rather than bypassing them) where you can stop for fuel, food, accommodation, and servicing or breakdown services.

Major roads are shown on the map in **Appendix E**. A map showing all roads can be found on 🖥 www.itravel.co.uk/maps/ireland-large.php. Details of the road network, including maps and a description of schemes under construction and planned, can be found on the National Roads Authority website (🖥 www.nra.ie).

Tolls

There are currently only four places in Ireland where you are charged a toll for using a road (charges were current in mid-2008):

- ♦ **M1** – Drogheda bypass – €1.80 for cars/€0.90 for motorcycles;

- ♦ **M4** – between Kinnegad and Kilcock via Enfield – €2.70/€1.40;

- ♦ **N8** – Rathcormac/Fermoy bypass – €1.80/€0.90;

- ♦ **M50** – East Link and West Link bridges on the Dublin ring road – €1.65/free and €2/€0.90 respectively.

The introduction of other tolls has been discussed, e.g. the Nenagh/Limerick section of the N7, the Clonee/Kells section of the N3 and a Fermoy bypass, but local opposition has so far kept these ideas firmly on the drawing board.

ROAD SIGNS

It's easy to lose your way in Ireland. Although most main routes are well sign-posted, minor route sign-posts are less reliable. Irish road signs, like all signs, are generally in both English and Gaelic, although in some of the more remote western areas (where Irish is in everyday use) English may be dispensed with, so it's as well to make a note of the Gaelic names of places you intend to go to. Sometimes you will also find alternative (English) spellings of place names: a small town on the west coast which is a Mecca for surfers, for example, is variously called Inniscrone, Enniscrone, and Inishcrone, depending on which map or shop front you look at!

Further confusion can be caused by the use of both miles and kilometres on road signs to indicate distances (very Irish!). The newer green and white signs (blue and white on motorways) are in kilometres, whereas the traditional black-on-white signs (which are now seen only occasionally) are in miles. To make matters worse, Irish roads are in the process of being renumbered, and what used to be T (trunk) and L (link) roads are being converted to N (national) and R (regional) roads – you will encounter both old and new numbers on road signs, although again, the old system is gradually disappearing.

Drivers should also be aware of the popular Irish pastime of 'sign redirecting' – swivelling signs on their posts so that they point in a direction other than the one they're supposed to (often the opposite direction!). This can lead to some unscheduled (although often scenic) detours so, if you actually want to get to a particular place by a particular time, you're advised to check your route on a map rather than relying exclusively on road signs.

A particular feature of driving in Ireland is the number of warning signs you will encounter: whenever you come to a bend, you will be warned that it's sharp; whenever the road opens out before you, you will be warned not to overtake ('pass') or that there

ATTENTION / ACHTUNG

Drive on left
Conduire a gauche
Links fahren

are hidden dips; you will be told to 'think road safety' and you will be warned that you're entering an 'accident black spot', i.e. a place where there have been lots of accidents – you may even be informed how many people have been killed and injured there! And if all this isn't enough to make you drive carefully, you will regularly see beside the road memorials to people who have been so careless (or unlucky) that they've lost their lives there. You have been warned!

The different types of traffic signs in Ireland can usually be distinguished by their shape and colour as follows:

- Warning signs are mostly diamond-shaped with black symbols on a yellow background; some (e.g. 'Yield Right of Way') are triangular with a red border.

- Signs within circles with a red border are generally imperative (e.g. 'Ahead Only') or, if crossed through by a diagonal red line, prohibitive (e.g. 'No Entry'); speed limit signs are also circular with a red border.

- Signs within blue circles, but with no red border, give positive instructions.

♦ Direction signs are mostly rectangular and are distinguished by their background colour: blue for motorway signs, green for primary routes and white for secondary routes. Signs with brown backgrounds provide directions to major tourist attractions.

A free leaflet entitled *Traffic Rules* explains (in English, French and German) the most common road signs, which are similar to those in the UK with a few exceptions.

IRISH DRIVERS

Because of the relative scarcity of traffic in Ireland, motorists tend not to be as aggressive as those found in many other countries nowadays. However, that isn't to say that they're necessarily good or even patient drivers. In fact, Irish drivers tend to fall into two categories: fast or very slow. Nevertheless, outside the main cities you will rarely hear a horn sounded in anger, and if raised fingers are a common sight, they invariably indicate thanks rather than rudeness.

It's common also to encounter animals on the road, particularly sheep, which will happily graze at the roadside inches from passing traffic. Quite often you will find yourself following tractors or other farm machinery or one of those very slow drivers (who are usually wearing tweed caps), who may pull onto and off main roads without warning or signals, at that unhurried pace which is the norm in rural Ireland. If you accept the fact and don't aim to cover more than 50km (30mi) in an hour, you may find yourself beginning to enjoy driving again – just like in the old days!

ACCIDENTS

No matter how careful you and other road users are, there's a chance that you will be involved in a car accident in Ireland; if so, you should do as follows:

1. Stop immediately. Switch on your hazard warning lights. In bad visibility, at night, or in a blind spot, try to warn oncoming traffic of the danger by sending someone ahead to flag down oncoming cars.

2. In the case of minor accidents, try to move your car off the road immediately. Many serious accidents are caused by other drivers ploughing into stationary vehicles that have had a minor bump.

3. If anyone is injured, call an ambulance and/ or the fire service immediately by dialling 999. If there isn't a public phone and you don't have a mobile phone, just ask at the nearest house.

4. Don't move an injured person unless it's absolutely necessary to save him from further injury, and don't leave him alone except to call an ambulance. Cover him with a blanket or coat to keep him warm.

5. Except in extremely minor cases where there's no damage or injury, you must call *Gardaí* (police) to the scene or report the accident to the *Gardaí* as soon as possible (if they don't come, you're obliged to remain at the scene for a 'reasonable' time).

6. While waiting for the *Gardaí*, don't move your vehicle or allow other vehicles to

be moved unless it's necessary to clear the road, in which case you should mark their positions with chalk. Alternatively, take photographs of the accident scene or make a drawing showing the position of all vehicles involved before moving them.

7. Check whether there are any witnesses to the accident, and take their names and addresses (noting those who have the same recollection of what happened as you do). Write down the registration numbers of all vehicles involved and their drivers' names, addresses and insurance details (as well as those of the other vehicle(s)' owner(s) if they weren't driving). These details should be displayed in the windscreen of the other vehicle(s). If asked, give any other drivers involved your (and the vehicle owner's) name, address and insurance details. It's also worth noting the name and number of any *garda* who comes to the scene and the address of his station, as well as other relevant information such as the date, time and location of the accident; the weather and road conditions; the speed of the vehicles involved; any road signs or markings; and, if appropriate, details of any injuries sustained.

8. If you've caused material damage, you must inform the owner of the damaged property as soon as possible. If you cannot reach him, contact the nearest *Garda* station (this also applies to damage caused to stationary vehicles, e.g. when parking).

9. If you're detained by the police, ask someone to contact anyone who may be worried by your lateness. Don't sign a statement unless you're certain you understand and agree with every word.

10. Your insurance company must be notified (in writing) of the accident as soon as possible. The company will send you an accident report form to complete and return. If there's more than €1,500 worth of damage to your car, an assessor will usually be sent to inspect the vehicle. The insurance company will usually require you to have repairs carried out at a specific garage, with which they have a direct payment arrangement.

> **☑ SURVIVAL TIP**
>
> You should not apologise, even if you think an accident was your fault, nor admit liability or offer to pay for repairs; the insurance companies will decide who was at fault and how any repairs or compensation should be paid.

If you're injured as a result of an accident which is wholly or partly the fault of another driver, you may be entitled to compensation. A number of solicitors offer a no-win-no-fee service for personal injury claims (you will find full-page adverts in the *Golden Pages*).

PARKING

Parking in most Irish cities and towns is a problem, particularly on Saturdays, when everyone's shopping. On-street parking is particularly hard to find and most roads have restricted or prohibited parking. Detailed information about parking in Ireland can be found on the AA website (💻 www.aaireland.ie), while on 💻 www.dublintraffic.com/carparks.htm you can find the current availability of spaces in all Dublin's car parks; you can even register to receive this information on your mobile phone!

As parking regulations are set by local councils, charges and time limits vary across the country; the information below is therefore of a general nature.

On-street Parking

On-street parking (waiting) restrictions in Ireland are indicated by yellow lines at the edge of roads, usually accompanied by a sign indicating when parking is prohibited, e.g. 'Mon–Sat 8am–6.30pm' or 'At any time'. If no days are indicated on the sign, restrictions are in force every day, including public holidays and Sundays. Yellow lines act as a guide to the restrictions in force, but signs must always be consulted.

Parking meters – of the 'pay-and-display' variety – are rarely encountered outside County

Dublin, where you must pay for parking between 7am and 7pm Mondays to Saturdays and from 2 to 6pm on Sundays. The charge is around €2.50 per hour in the city centre, €2 on the outskirts and €1 or €1.50 in the suburbs, and the maximum parking time is three hours. In parts of Dublin City it's possible to pre-pay for parking online or via your mobile phone using the 'mPark' system (visit 💻 http://parkserver.itsmobileparking.com/mpark/dublin.jspx for details).

In most other major towns, a disc system is used to control parking. These are 'scratch cards' on which you must indicate the date and time of your arrival so that a *Garda* or traffic warden can see that you haven't exceeded the waiting limit. This is normally one or two hours, depending on which 'zone' you park in (nearer the town centre you will usually be limited to an hour).

> In most towns in County Cork, for example, you must display a disc between 8.30am and 6.30pm Mondays to Saturdays at a cost of up to €2.00 per hour (for town centre parking). In small towns, discs may cost only €0.50.

Discs can be bought singly or in books of ten at shops or garages near town centres (where you see a 'parking discs sold here' sign), but as each city or county council has its own parking regulations, you may not be able to use the same discs throughout Ireland. In small towns and rural areas, there's usually no charge for on-street parking, but you may be allowed to remain in one place for only a limited time, e.g. two hours. If you have a valid 'Disabled Persons Parking Permit', you can park free in designated parking areas.

In some areas, residents' parking permits are available from the Traffic division of the local authority, costing approximately €25. Each car owner may have only one permit and no more than four permits will be issued to a household. Residents of purpose-built apartment blocks aren't eligible for permits, as parking should be provided within the development.

Car Parks

In most towns, there are off-road car parks, indicated by a 'P' sign. These may be surface (on one level, usually on a piece of waste ground) or multi-storey. If you use a multi-storey car park, make a note of the level and space number where you park your car; otherwise you can spend many frustrating minutes trying to find your car when you return!

Charges depend on a number of factors, not least whether a car park is private or local government-funded. When it isn't free (which parking sometimes is, even in cities), parking in car parks usually costs between €1 and €2.50 per hour – the most expensive car parks naturally being in Dublin. In some towns, you can park for several hours for a similar fee.

The usual method of payment is either pay-and-display or pay as you leave. In a pay-and-display car park, you must decide in advance how many hours parking you require (it's always more than you think), buy a ticket from a machine for this period and then display it inside the windscreen of your parked car.

The other method involves taking a ticket as you enter the car park (you may need to press a button) and paying (either by handing money to a person in a kiosk or by putting it into a machine) just before you leave. Wherever you drive in Ireland, keep a plentiful supply of coins handy for meters and ticket machines.

Some councils produce car park maps showing all local parking areas, which are available free from council offices, libraries and tourist information centres.

Penalties & Fines

Parking infringements in cities and major towns are dealt with by traffic wardens, who are entitled only to issue penalty notices (their permission to control traffic flow was removed, following complaints about their lack of training). There are around 100 wardens in Dublin, but only one or two in other cities and towns. Elsewhere, illegal parking is dealt with by the *Garda*, who issue around 200,000 parking fines every year.

Since April 2006, a national system of fixed penalties has been in operation. Instead of the previous on-the-spot fine, you receive a parking ticket showing the date, time and place it was issued, the registration number of your car, the amount of the fine and a reference number. Fines for most offences are around €40, but for example, parking in a dangerous position, in a disabled parking bay, on or near a pedestrian crossing or on a 'clearway' (a principal route into a main town) during rush hours naturally attracts a fine of at least €80.

If you fail to pay a fine within 28 days, the amount increases. If you fail to pay within a further 28 days you are taken to court and, if convicted, incur five penalty points on your licence , as well as an even higher fine.

In some cities, you shouldn't even think about parking illegally, as your car may be

clamped or towed away in the blink of an eye by private companies which, unlike the *Garda*, are out to make money and are in a position to exercise a total lack of discretion. In Dublin, you're charged at least €80 to have your car released from a clamp (in addition to the normal parking fine) and considerably more to recover a vehicle from the pound to which it has been towed. As well as the cost, there's the inconvenience of having to find the pound or wait (sometimes hours) for your car to be unclamped. If your car is clamped, telephone the Parking Shop (☎ 01-602 2500) to arrange release.

Owners of private car parks or private land may also clamp a car parked without permission and charge exorbitant fees for removal. You can take them to court if they do so, but as a trespasser you won't have much of a claim under Irish law!

Whether parking restrictions exist or not, when parking on a road be careful where you park as you can be prosecuted for parking in a dangerous position and could also cause an accident. If your parked car contributes to an accident you may also have to pay damages. Take care in car parks, as accidents often occur there and may not be covered by your car insurance. Parking on footpaths is illegal everywhere.

CAR CRIME

All European countries have a problem with car crime, i.e. thefts of and from cars, but happily

Ireland's is less severe than most, except perhaps in Dublin, where quite a lot of cars are stolen (often by young joyriders). 'Carjacking' has made an appearance in Ireland in recent years, although it's thankfully still rare.

It goes without saying that you should always lock your car and never leave any valuables inside it. If you drive anything other than a worthless heap you should have theft insurance, which includes your car stereo and personal belongings. If you drive a new or valuable car, it's wise to have it fitted with an alarm, an engine immobiliser (the best system) or another anti-theft device (some or all of which may be required by your insurance company in any case), plus a visible deterrent such as a steering or gear stick lock. It's particularly important to protect your car if you own a model that's desirable to professional car thieves, e.g. most new sports and executive models, which are often stolen by crooks to order.

Few cars are fitted with deadlocks and most can be broken into in seconds by a competent thief. However, even the best security system won't prevent someone from breaking into your car (which usually takes expert thieves a matter of seconds) and may not stop your car being stolen, but it will at least make it more difficult and may persuade a thief to look for an easier target.

If you buy an expensive stereo system, you should choose one with a removable unit or with a removable (face-off) control panel that you can pop into a pocket or bag. However, never forget to remove it (and your mobile telephone), even when parking for a few minutes. Some manufacturers provide stereo systems that won't work when they're removed from their original vehicles or are inoperable without a security code.

Thieves often smash windows to steal from cars, even articles of little value such as sunglasses or cigarettes. When leaving your car unattended, store any valuables (including clothes) in the boot (trunk). Note, however, that storing valuables in the boot isn't foolproof, as a thief may be tempted to force open the boot with a crowbar. You should never leave your original car documents in your car (which will help a thief dispose of it).

When parking overnight or when it's dark, it's wise to park in a secure overnight car park or garage or at least in a well lit area. If possible, avoid parking in insecure, long-term car parks, as they're favourite hunting grounds for car thieves. Foreign-registered cars, particularly camper vans and mobile homes, are popular targets, particularly when parked in ferry ports.

If your car (or any of its contents) is stolen, report it to the police in the area where the theft occurred. You can report it by telephone, but must go to the station to complete a report.

Don't, however, expect the police to find it or even take any interest in your loss. You should also report a theft to your insurance company as soon as possible.

FUEL

Unleaded petrol (gas) and diesel fuel are available at all petrol stations. Lead replacement petrol (LRP) is still available for old cars designed to run on leaded petrol. Prices vary from place to place (they tend to be higher in remote parts and lower in big towns and cities where there's more competition and a higher turnover) and according to the state of the world oil market, as well as changes in taxation. In mid-2008, you could expect to pay around €1.30 per litre for unleaded petrol and around €1.43 for diesel. Prices at petrol

stations throughout Ireland can be checked on 🖥 www.pumps.ie.

Liquefied petroleum gas (LPG) is also available, and a list of outlets can be found on the website of the national supplier, Flogas (🖥 www.flogas.ie). These can be few and far between outside the Dublin area, however (e.g. there's only one in the whole of County Clare and one in County Donegal).

If you hire or borrow a car, make sure to check whether it runs on unleaded or diesel (putting the wrong fuel in it can have disastrous consequences!), as well as which side the filler cap is on and how to open it! If you're thinking of buying an old car, find out if it has been converted to unleaded petrol or, if not, whether it will run properly on LRP (which is claimed to damage some engines).

Irish petrol stations usually stay open until around 8pm and most of them are open on Sundays and public holidays (in villages they tend to open after Sunday Mass). If you've run out of petrol or are about to and you cannot find a station open, a knock on the door and a polite request will generally get the pumps going.

Most petrol stations also provide air (there may be a nominal charge, e.g. €0.20, or you may be given a token if you buy petrol), use of a vacuum cleaner (fee around €0.20) and a car wash (€3 to €10 depending on the extent to which you wish your vehicle to be pampered). Many also have toilet facilities (you may have to ask for a key) and a shop selling a wide range of motoring accessories and other goods.

In fact, the main business of many petrol stations isn't selling petrol, on which profit margins are minimal (except for the government!), but selling everything from food and drink (even beer, wine and spirits) to newspapers and magazines, household goods, clothing, CDs and cassettes... some even offer video rental and dry cleaning services!

GARAGES & SERVICING

When buying a car in Ireland, it's wise to take into account local service facilities. If you intend to have the car serviced by an authorised dealer, you should check where the nearest one is. Authorised dealers, of course, generally charge more for servicing than small garages, although they may have a fixed charge for a main service (around €150-250) and an interim service (€100-150).

Note that when a car is under warranty, it must usually be serviced regularly by a 'competent mechanic' and you must keep a record of all work carried out in order not to invalidate the warranty (under EU law, dealers are no longer able to insist on carrying out all your servicing themselves!).

Always obtain a number of estimates for major mechanical work or body repairs, as these can vary wildly and some garages include the replacement of unnecessary parts. Always instruct a garage what to do in writing, and for anything other than a standard service, obtain a written estimate that includes labour, parts and VAT. Ask the garage to contact you and obtain your approval before doing anything that isn't listed, or if the cost is likely to exceed the original estimate. Check how the bill is to be paid and obtain a receipt listing all work completed, any replacement parts and the number of hours' labour involved.

For servicing and repairs, Irish garages are normally open from 8.30am to 5.30pm Mondays to Fridays, but are usually closed all day Saturdays and Sundays. Main dealers usually provide a free 'loan car' while yours is being serviced or repaired, although they won't normally collect your car from your home or office or deliver it back again after a service.

If you have an accident and your car needs body repairs, it's usually best (and cheaper) to take it to a specialist body shop (listed under *Car Painters & Sprayers* in the *Golden Pages*).

MOTORING SERVICES & ORGANISATIONS

If your car breaks down, there's no need to worry or feel embarrassed, as you might at home. You're unlikely to be left standing at the side of the road for long, and the next vehicle will probably stop to find out what's wrong and help you to get to a garage, or at least seek out a mechanic to get you back on the road.

Breakdown services are available from local companies, but the only national scheme is operated by the Automobile Association (AA, ☎ 01-617 9977, 🖳 www.aaireland.ie), with which you must take out membership in order to qualify for breakdown assistance. The AA has over 400,000 members (the RAC doesn't tell us how many it has). Both organisations provide technical and legal advice, route planning, traffic information and a variety of maps and books on motoring, as well as an emergency breakdown service. They also offer travel insurance, ferry bookings, even home insurance and mobile phones!

The AA publishes a quarterly magazine called *AA Motoring*. Basic membership of the AA costs €132 per year, in return for which the organisation will send a mechanic to repair your broken-down car at the roadside. Additional services, such as towing a broken-down car to a garage, getting it started when it's outside your home and providing you with a replacement vehicle, are subject to higher fees (from €175 to €200). The Royal Automobile Club (RAC, ☎ 1800-805498, 🖳 www.rac.ie) no longer offers breakdown cover.

If you're a member of a foreign motoring organisation, you may be entitled to use some AA or RAC services.

DISABLED DRIVERS

Disabled drivers can obtain a government grant to help them buy or adapt a car, and in certain cases are exempt from motor tax and vehicle registration tax, plus VAT and duty on fuel. You can also obtain a 'Disabled Persons Parking

Permit', which applies to the person rather than the vehicle, and can therefore be used by any vehicle transporting a disabled passenger.

Permits are issued by the Disabled Drivers Association of Ireland (☎ 094-936 4054 or ☎ 094-9364266, 💻 www.ddai.ie) and cost €25.

MOPEDS & MOTORCYCLES

Although most Irish roads are well suited to motorcycling, it isn't especially popular in Ireland, which may have something to do with the predominantly wet weather. In general, laws that apply to cars also apply to motorcycles; however, there are a few regulations that apply to motorcyclists in particular:

◆ You may ride a moped or motorbike of up to 125cc at the age of 16. At 17 you're entitled to ride a bike of up to 250cc. Motorists with a full motor car licence (Irish or foreign) may ride a moped (up to 50cc) without passing a test or obtaining a special licence.

◆ 'L' (learner) plates should be displayed by anyone who hasn't passed a motorcycle test, although it isn't a legal requirement.

◆ All riders, including moped riders, must obtain a full driving licence – see **Driving Licences** on page 205 for details of the procedure. Additional requirements for riders include showing how to put a bike onto its stand and how to take it off, and to move it 4 to 5m without the aid of the engine.

◆ Irish standard (or equivalent) approved crash helmets are compulsory for both riders and passengers.

◆ You should use dipped headlights at all times, although it isn't compulsory.

◆ You must have valid insurance (at least third party).

It's possible to buy a wide range of bikes although, like cars, they aren't cheap. Mopeds cost around €3,000 and a mid-range motorbike

(e.g. 500cc) at least €7,500. It isn't possible to rent motorcycles in Ireland.

The Road Safety Authority (☎ 096-25000 or ☎ 1890-506080, 💻 www.nsc.ie) has a list of motorcycle trainers in Ireland and produces a leaflet entitled *This is Your Bike* (downloadable from the website). Another recommended publication for motorcyclists is *Motorcycle Roadcraft – the Police Rider's Handbook*. Both the AA and RAC provide breakdown services for motorcyclists.

CYCLISTS & PEDESTRIANS

Over a quarter of people killed on the roads in Ireland are pedestrians or cyclists, so you should be just as careful when walking or cycling as you are when driving – or even more so! Pedestrian crossings are generally controlled by traffic lights, but even when the green man appears, you should look both ways before crossing. Take extra care when with children: never let them play on a road, however quiet. Bear in mind also that young children are unable to judge traffic speeds accurately and should usually be escorted to and from school.

Take particular care in country areas where there are no footpaths. Always walk on the side of oncoming traffic (except on blind bends), wear light coloured clothing and carry a torch (flashlight) at night. Take care also when using pedestrianised streets, some of which allow access to vehicles at certain times or may be shared by delivery vehicles and buses (cyclists also use pedestrianised streets, although it's illegal). When using footpaths, keep an eye open for skateboarders and rollerbladers (as well as cyclists).

Cycling isn't popular in Ireland, which means that there are virtually no cycle lanes or other concessions to cyclists. In theory, Dublin has 320km (200mi) of 'cycle track' (which cyclists are obliged to use), although most 'tracks' are part of public roads and not dedicated cycle tracks, and inadequate or even dangerous.

12.

HEALTH

One of the most important considerations when travelling or moving to another country is maintaining good health. In general, the Irish are as healthy as most other Europeans, although their average life expectancy of 77.9 (women have a 7 per cent higher life expectancy than men) is below the European Union (EU) average (life expectancy figures at the age of 40 are particularly low) and only 28th in the world. On the other hand, the infant mortality rate of five deaths before the age of one and six before the age of five per 1,000 births is comparable with the rest of Europe.

Cardiovascular disease is the major cause of death in Ireland, which has the highest death rate for heart disease in the EU (almost double the EU average), although the rate has been steadily declining since the mid-'70s, as has the rate of other cerebrovascular diseases (e.g. strokes and thromboses). Deaths from cancer, the second most frequent cause of death, are also above the EU average among women, but below it among men, and the rate has remained constant for the past 30 years.

On the other hand, the next most common cause of death, traffic accidents, is well below the EU average and the rate is declining gradually. However, the suicide rate has steadily increased and is now higher than that for road accidents and above the EU average.

As in most other Western countries, one of the fastest-growing health problems in Ireland is obesity, caused by a combination of poor diet and inactivity, which is reckoned to account for at least 2,500 deaths each year. More than one in eight Irish people are obese – i.e. roughly 20 per cent above their 'ideal' body weight, or more precisely, having a body mass index (weight in kg divided by height in metres squared) of 30 or more. This figure represents an increase of some 30 per cent since 2000, and Ireland now has the fourth-highest prevalence of obesity in men and the seventh-highest in women among EU countries.

From a foreigner's point of view, such statistics are fairly irrelevant unless you're planning to raise children in Ireland; what counts is the effect an Irish lifestyle will have on your general health. Ireland's slow pace of life is certainly beneficial to those who are prone to stress (it's difficult to remain up-tight while gazing out over green fields listening to the bleating of sheep), although it takes many foreigners some time to adjust.

In terms of the environment, although there's little heavy industry to pollute the atmosphere, Ireland had its knuckles rapped in late 2000 by the Organisation for Economic Co-operation and Development (OECD), which reported that 'per capita, pollution emissions' are higher than the OECD average and pollution control expenditure, at 0.6 per cent of gross domestic product (GDP), is lower than in many other countries. The report called on the government to take 'urgent measures', especially in the area of waste management and recycling. No doubt the Irish, who aren't generally known for their tidiness, will respond as effectively as they have to other calls to upgrade the country's infrastructure in recent years.

Total health spending is around 7 per cent of GDP, well below the average for OECD countries, which is almost 9 per cent, and below that of all other European countries bar Poland and the Slovak Republic! In terms of government spending, however, Ireland is just above the OECD average, spending more than the UK and even Japan, and its spending rate is growing faster than in almost any other OECD country.

The quality of healthcare and healthcare facilities in Ireland is generally excellent, although facilities are limited in some rural areas. The number of people per doctor (approximately 357 on average) is higher than in the UK, but below the average for OECD countries; while the number of nurses, at 15 per 1,000 population, is high. The number of public hospitals, on the other hand, is limited and there are fewer than three 'acute care' beds per 1,000 population compared with the OECD average of over four, although Irish medical staff are highly trained and provided with the latest equipment.

As in many other Western countries, however, the government department responsible for healthcare, the Department of Health and Children (DOHC), is increasingly pre-occupied with 'accountability' and saving money rather than with improving healthcare provision, which has been criticised for its fragmentary nature, the majority of infrastructure being in the private sector.

The Health Acts, 2004 and 2006 were concerned only with setting up, respectively, a new governing body, the Health Service Executive (HSE), which superseded the Regional Health Boards, and a quality control agency, the Health Information and Quality Authority (HIQA), ostensibly to ensure that services were being delivered to patients, but essentially to check that money isn't being wasted. The recent Admissions and Discharge Guidelines for hospitals, for example, claims to 'ensure that patients do not have to remain in hospital any longer than necessary' – a policy that is 'at the heart of the principle of "people-centredness" approach [sic] set out in the National Health Strategy.' In other words, the aim is to kick patients out as soon as possible!

The inadequacies of the public health system are highlighted by the fact that some 15 per cent of Irish employers provide free private health insurance as a standard benefit for employees and some 70 per cent make a contribution towards it.

That said, there are no special health risks in Ireland and no immunisations are required. However, although you're unlikely to get sunburn, you can suffer badly from midge bites on warm summer evenings, particularly on the west coast, so it's as well to stock up with insect repellent. Wasps, hornets and horseflies can also be quite persistent in the summer months. Those with respiratory or articulation problems should also note that Ireland's damp climate is unlikely to improve their condition.

Water

The peaty nature of Irish soil causes occasional colouring of the water, as well as slight alkalinity, but water everywhere is pleasantly 'soft' (which no doubt accounts for those rosy Irish complexions!). Tap water can safely be drunk in most areas (although the stout tastes **much** better!), but around 5 per cent of households (around 5,500) belong to so-called group water schemes, which manage their own water supply, and in some of these the water isn't purified or disinfected in any way, so there's a risk of contamination from sources such as septic tanks or animal slurry pits. A 2004 study by the Food Safety Authority of Ireland found that almost a quarter of schemes were seriously contaminated, although the current Water Services Investment Programme aims to rectify this situation.

Donations

If you're over 18 and under 65 and in good health, you can make a positive contribution to the nation's health by going to a 'clinic' organised by the Blood Transfusion Service (☎ 01-432 2800 or ☎ 1850-731137, 💻 www.ibts.ie). The website includes details of clinics nationwide. If you have any body parts you can no longer use, e.g. after your death, you can carry a Donor Card, available from pharmacies, doctors' surgeries and hospitals. For further information, contact the Irish Kidney Association (☎ 01-620 5306 or ☎ 1890-543639, 💻 www.ika.ie), which is part of the Irish Donor Network.

Information

Health information can be obtained from the DOHC (☎ 01-635 4000, 💻 www.dohc.ie) and from the health insurance group, VHI Healthcare (☎ 1850-444444, 💻 www.vhi.

ie). A number of health and crisis helplines are listed in the front of the *Golden Pages*, including Alcoholics Anonymous, Aware (for those suffering from depression), Childline, Drugs Treatment Centre Board, Narcotics Anonymous, Parentline (for parents under stress), Poisons Information Centre, Rape Crisis Centre, Samaritans, Victim Support and Women's Aid.

The Department of Social, Community and Family Affairs publishes a *Guide to Social Welfare Services*, as well as a range of leaflets on its various services, which are available from Social Welfare Local Offices. The DOHC also publishes a variety of information leaflets, listed on its website under 'Publications'.

EMERGENCIES

In a life-threatening emergency, you should call an ambulance to take you to the nearest hospital emergency centre. There are three types of ambulance service in Ireland, as follows:

♦ **Public ambulances** – provided by Health Service Executive (HSE) areas. In Dublin, the Dublin Fire Brigade provides an emergency ambulance service for the greater Dublin area, which isn't integrated with the HSE Eastern area service. The public ambulance service is normally limited to day hospitals, workshops, learning disability centres, renal dialysis units and external hospital clinics. Some HSEs provide transport services to hospitals for outpatient appointments and to day centres, although this is often done under contract to private operators. Occasionally, an HSE may assist with transport costs for a person who has to travel a long distance to a hospital. The situation varies considerably from one HSE Area to another and, in many cases, is dependent on circumstances. To obtain a public ambulance, dial 999 or 112 and ask for an ambulance. If you don't have a medical card (see page 229), you may be charged; policy varies according to the HSE.

♦ **Private ambulances** – including air ambulances, listed in the *Golden Pages*. You call them and pay for their services as you would for a taxi. They're occasionally brought in by an HSE to help with emergencies, in which case their services are normally free.

♦ **Volunteer ambulances** – generally used to provide first aid at public events.

If you're able, you should make your own way to the accident and emergency (A&E –casualty) department of your nearest hospital. When you move to a new area it's wise to find out where your nearest A&E department is, as only 35 hospitals are equipped to handle emergencies. Unless you've been referred by your general practitioner (GP) or you hold a medical card you may be charged for treatment.

Patients are treated in order of medical need, so if you have a relatively minor problem you may have to wait up to 24 hours – in rare cases even longer. If you're admitted to hospital following a visit to an A&E department, normal charges for inpatient hospital services apply unless you hold a medical card.

If your condition isn't serious enough to warrant a hospital visit, you should consult your family doctor. There may be times set aside for house calls, if required. Out of hours, your doctor's answering machine should give a number to call for a duty doctor. In towns and cities, there are 'after-hours clinics' where you can see a doctor concerning minor ailments when your doctor's surgery is closed.

In some areas, doctors have formed co-operatives to deal with patients out of hours, although these may be limited to regular patients of the doctors concerned. According to the Ministry for Health, over 2.5m people (well over half the population) have access to out-of-hours

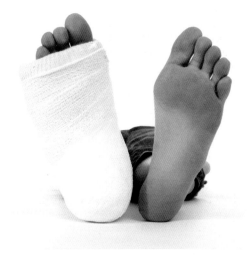

cooperatives. If you have a dental problem, phone your dentist or, if it's out of normal surgery hours, any dentist who provides an emergency service.

If you have a rare blood group or a medical problem which cannot easily be seen or recognised, e.g. a heart condition, diabetes, a severe allergy or epilepsy, you may be interested in the UK organisation, MedicAlert, which also covers Ireland. MedicAlert members wear an emblem on their wrists or around their necks that's internationally recognised. On the back of your emblem is engraved your medical problem, membership number and a telephone number. When you're unable to speak for yourself, doctors, police or anyone providing aid can immediately obtain vital medical information from anywhere in the world by phoning a 24-hour emergency number.

MedicAlert is a non-profit registered charity and life membership is included in the cost of the bracelet or necklace (from GB£30) plus an annual fee. For more information contact the MedicAlert Foundation, 1 Bridge Wharf, 156 Caledonian Road, London N1 9UU, UK (☎ 020-7833 3034 or ☎ 0800-581420, 🖥 www.medicalert.org.uk) or the MedicAlert Foundation International, 2323 Colorado Avenue, Turlock, CA 95382, US (☎ 209-668 3333 from outside the US or ☎ 888-633 4298 from within the US, 🖥 www.medicalert.org).

Visitors

Visitors to Ireland (i.e. those who aren't ordinarily resident there) from European Economic Area (EEA) countries and Switzerland are entitled to free urgent medical treatment, not including treatment by a general practitioner or private hospital. Unless you're a UK national, you need to produce a European Health Insurance Card (EHIC), obtainable from your home country. Australians are entitled to urgent medical treatment on the same basis as non-medical card holders, i.e. they must pay hospital charges; on presentation of suitable identification (i.e. a passport or evidence of residence in Australia) you're entitled to hospital services as a public patient, but will be invoiced for the relevant hospital charge.

Non-EU visitors are entitled to nothing free (not even a visit to an A&E department!) and therefore **must** take out private health insurance (see page 259).

PUBLIC HEALTHCARE

The structure of the Irish public health service was changed by the Health Act, 2004, which replaced the eight Regional Health Boards by a single, nationwide Health Service Executive (HSE), which operates via four administrative areas: Dublin Mid-Leinster, Dublin North East, West (which includes the north!) and South. As a whole, the HSE is now Ireland's largest employer – with over 65,000 employed directly and a further 35,000 indirectly – and has Ireland's biggest public sector budget, at €12bn.

There are three other national bodies responsible for providing health and social services: the National Hospitals Office (NHO), which provides public hospital and ambulance services; Primary, Community and Continuing Care, which provides ... community care services; and Population Health, which is responsible for ... the population's health (this is Ireland, after all), although their services are channelled through the four HSE administrative area organisations.

Ireland and the UK are the only EU countries where you can obtain public healthcare without having to make social

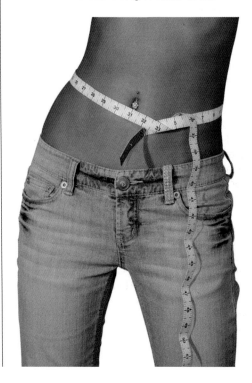

security contributions. EU citizens are entitled to healthcare irrespective of their situation. Non-EU citizens, on the other hand, must prove that they're 'ordinarily' or 'habitually resident' in Ireland, i.e. that they intend to remain in Ireland for a minimum of a year.

This means producing a Registration Certificate (see page 78) or residence/work permit, proof of property purchase or rental (including evidence that it's your principal residence), confirmation of registration with a school or college, or details of an Irish bank account. Note that if you establish ordinary residence, your dependants won't necessarily be eligible for public healthcare unless they are also ordinarily resident.

EEA citizens who are resident in Ireland but insured in another EEA country are automatically eligible for healthcare as are their dependants, although if you're self-employed you will receive few benefits. If you're ordinarily resident in Ireland and receiving a social security pension from another EEA country, you're entitled to public healthcare provided that you aren't earning **any** income from employment or self-employment in Ireland. (Note that this is a new condition; until recently, you could earn up to around €3,000 and still qualify for public healthcare.)

Unemployed people seeking work need form E119 and students form E109 to qualify for public healthcare. Temporary EEA visitors can obtain free emergency treatment on production of a European Health Insurance Card. Irish nationals returning to Ireland who aren't covered by EEA regulations are regarded as ordinarily resident if they're employed or self-employed in Ireland, or provide evidence that they intend to remain in Ireland for a minimum of one year. If they've been abroad for less than three years, they may be entitled to benefits in any case.

Anyone who doesn't meet any of the above criteria usually has to pay the 'commercial rate' for medical treatment and other benefits, although the Health Board may authorise urgent treatment at a reduced rate or even free in certain cases.

There are two categories of entitlement to public healthcare in Ireland: those who are eligible for a Medical Card, who are entitled to the full range of medical services without charge, and those who aren't eligible and who must pay for medicines and prescriptions, routine dental, optical or aural treatment, as well as for visits to a doctor (see below). Those on low incomes are entitled to a Medical Card under the General Medical Services (GMS) scheme, and those over 70 qualify, irrespective of income.

Many other people are entitled to a Medical Card, thanks to contributing to the Pay-Related Social Insurance scheme (see page 248). If you aren't entitled to a Medical Card, you're usually sent a letter by the Department of Health and Children confirming your entitlement to restricted benefits.

You have the same entitlement to public health services for mental illness as for any other illness, but must pay for accommodation and treatment in private psychiatric hospitals. Note, however, that health insurance companies sometimes treat psychiatric hospital costs differently from general hospital costs.

Medical Card

EEA citizens resident in Ireland but insured in another EEA country automatically receive a Medical Card, as do those over 70 and those seeking work in Ireland. Otherwise, eligibility for Medical Cards is means tested, i.e. assessed according to your income. The weekly income limits are shown in the table below, although those earning more than these limits may still get a Medical Card if they have 'exceptional medical needs'. Allowances are made for dependent children and other expenses.

Weekly Income Limits for Medical Card		
Category	Age	
	Under 66	66–69
Single person living alone	€184	€201.50
Single person living with family	€164	€173.50
Married couple	€266.50	€298

A Medical Card entitles you to free GP services; prescribed medicines; inpatient and outpatient services in a public hospital; dental, optical and aural services and appliances; and maternity and infant care during pregnancy and for up to six weeks after birth. Medical Card holders may also be able to get expenses involved in travelling to and from hospital refunded, although this scheme has been cut back in recent years.

In October 2005, a doctor-only medical card, known as a GP Visit Card, was introduced, which covers patients who are above the income threshold for a full medical card. Under this scheme GP consultations are free, but prescribed medicines must be paid for. Eligibility for the GP Visit Card is also means tested but under a different set of income guidelines.

Retirees & the Elderly

Many people are ill-prepared for old age and the possibility of health problems, although you're better provided for in Ireland than in many other countries. All retirees over 65, whether or not they have a Medical Card, are entitled to regular visits by a public health nurse and, if required, occupational therapy.

Meals on wheels and a home help service are provided by voluntary organisations on behalf of the HSE, usually for a small fee (a list of voluntary organisations is available from Comhairle (formerly the National Social Service Board) (☎ 1890-777121, 🖥 www.comhairle.ie).

There are also grants for security devices for elderly people living alone, although these aren't usually paid directly to individuals. Other schemes offer home improvement grants, free draught proofing and insulation (in some parts of the country), and house alterations for disabled people. The only supposedly universal benefit for elderly people is free travel for those over 66, but even that has various conditions attached.

PRIVATE HEALTHCARE

Private health treatment functions both within the Social Welfare system and independently of it. Even if you're entitled to free hospitalisation, you have the option to pay for private or semi-private treatment. Private hospitals will admit what are called 'self-payers', but costs are high and around half the Irish population takes out private health insurance (see **Health Insurance** on page 259). There are currently also 22 voluntary hospitals, which admit patients on a private and semi-private basis (see **Private Hospitals** on page 233).

Nursing Homes

The cost of private nursing homes is high in Ireland, as is the demand for places. However, if you're paying nursing home fees for your spouse (or, in certain cases, another relative), you may be entitled to tax relief, and those on lower incomes may qualify for assistance such as a Nursing Homes Subvention (a free leaflet explaining this scheme is available from Health Boards).

DOCTORS

There are excellent family doctors, generally referred to as general practitioners (GPs), in all areas of Ireland. Once you've received a Medical Card or notification of entitlement to benefits (see page 229), you are free to register with any doctor who can accommodate you. GPs are listed under *Doctors – General Practitioners* in the *Golden Pages,* or a list can be obtained from your local Health Board (Medical Card holders are sent a list of 'approved' doctors from which to choose).

The best way to choose a doctor is to ask your (healthy?) colleagues, friends or neighbours if they can recommend someone. Further information on Irish doctors is available from the Irish College of General Practitioners (ICGP, ☎ 01-676 3705, 🖳 www.icgp.ie).

Appointments & House Calls

Surgery hours vary, but are typically from 8.30am to 6pm, Mondays to Fridays. Emergency surgeries may be held on Saturday mornings, e.g. from 8.30 to 11.30am or noon. Note that most doctors operate an appointment system, where you must make an appointment in advance. You cannot just turn up during surgery hours and expect to be seen. If your problem is urgent (but not an emergency), your doctor will usually see you immediately, but you should still phone in advance. Most doctors' surgeries have answering machines outside surgery hours, when a recorded message informs you of the name of the doctor on call (or deputising service) and his telephone number. Some group practices operate their own 24-hour emergency service. There are also 24-hour deputising services in most areas, which arrange house calls for around €50 at any time of the day or night (e.g. 'Doctor on Duty' in Dublin, ☎ 01-453 9333). Most Irish doctors are happy to make house calls (for which they charge around €60).

Charges

Most GPs charge between €30 and €50 for a routine consultation. If a diagnosis involves a special procedure, you may be charged extra (e.g. €10 for a blood test). Visitors from other EU countries should be eligible for free consultations, provided they have the appropriate documentation (e.g. an EHIC). If you're taking up residence in Ireland, you may be entitled to free consultations during the 12 weeks following your move.

GP services which aren't reimbursed even if you have a Medical Card include the following:

♦ medical examinations or reports for legal purposes;

♦ examinations relating to insurance policies;

♦ examinations relating to fitness to drive including eye test;

♦ pre-employment examinations;

♦ school entry examinations;

♦ examinations in connection with fitness to take part in sports;

♦ some vaccinations;

♦ some family planning services;

♦ pregnancy tests;

♦ screening tests, including cervical smears and cholesterol testing.

Group Practices

Of the 2,500 or so GPs practising in Ireland, over 40 per cent are in single practice and around 30 per cent in practice with one other doctor. Only 30 per cent work in group practices of three or more doctors. Even fewer operate within a health centre, where other services, such as maternity care, cervical smears and breast screening, vaccinations, physiotherapy and chiropody, are available.

Bear in mind that, if your doctor is part of a partnership or group practice, when he's absent you will automatically be treated by a partner or another doctor (unless you wish to wait until your doctor returns); whereas in an individual practice, you may be required to see a locum (replacement doctor) when your doctor is absent.

Choosing a Doctor

It's a good idea to enquire in advance (e.g. by asking the receptionist) whether a doctor has the 'qualifications' you require, for example:

♦ Is the doctor male or female?

♦ Is he easily reached by public transport, if necessary?

♦ Is it a group practice?

♦ Does the practice run ante-natal, family planning, well woman (or well person), diabetic or other clinics?

- What are the normal surgery hours and are there weekend and evening surgeries?

- What is the procedure for home visits (most doctors are happy to make them)?

- Does the doctor practise preventative or complementary medicine?

- Does the doctor prescribe contraception?

- What are the doctor's charges?

It's normal practice in Ireland to meet a prospective doctor before deciding whether to register with him. Registration takes the form of a private contract between you and the doctor, and you may change doctors at any time or regularly see more than one doctor (see below).

Changing Doctors

You may switch to another doctor in the same area, depending on the availability of places, but be careful what reason you give for wanting to change doctors, as doctors tend to be wary of accepting a patient who has had a 'disagreement' with a colleague. One 'legitimate' reason for changing doctors is that you wish to be treated by a doctor of the opposite sex to your present one (it's hard luck if all doctors in your area are the same sex).

If you want a second opinion on any health matter, you may ask to see another doctor or a specialist, and most GPs are happy for you to do so. Note, however, that in many cases, a second doctor doesn't confirm the first doctor's diagnosis.

Complaints

If you have a complaint against your GP, you should address it to the Medical Council, Lynn House, Portobello Court, Lower Rathmines Road, Dublin 6 (☎ 01-498 3100, 🖳 www. medicalcouncil.ie).

HOSPITALS, CLINICS & HEALTH CENTRES

There are public, private and voluntary hospitals in Ireland. Public hospitals are located in all areas. Most major towns have a general hospital, which provides treatment and diagnosis for inpatients, day patients and outpatients, and offers the full range of hospital services including an A&E department. Areas without a major town are covered by a regional hospital, which offers services such as a maternity unit, but may not have an A&E department. In some rural areas, there are district hospitals, where a more limited range of services is provided.

In addition to general hospitals, there are hospitals that specialise in particular kinds of patients or types of treatment, most of them in the Dublin area. These include mental, remedial, psychiatric and orthopaedic hospitals, as well as hospitals for children and women (including the National Maternity Hospital). There's also an Eye & Ear Hospital and a Skin & Cancer Hospital. Specialist hospitals accept patients only on a doctor's referral.

A few hospitals are 'day hospitals', where services such as physiotherapy are available for a lower fee than at inpatient departments. A number of public hospitals have specialised geriatric departments, although these aren't intended for long-term care. For long-term geriatric care you need to be admitted to either a geriatric hospital or a welfare home.

In addition, there are a number of clinics (mostly in Dublin) that specialise in family planning,

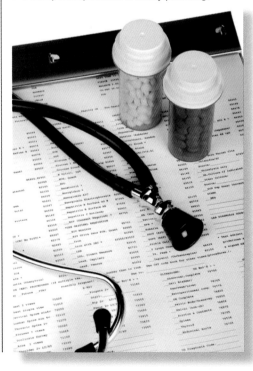

sexually transmitted diseases (see page 243), etc. You may visit a clinic without a referral. For routine treatment (e.g. inoculations) you can visit a health centre (listed under *Health Boards* in the *Golden Pages*), where nursing services are provided free of charge.

As in the UK, there are long waiting lists for treatment under the national health service (it isn't unknown for people to wait three years for a 'routine' operation such as a hip replacement), which is the main reason so many people take out private health insurance.

Private Hospitals

There are 19 private hospitals in Ireland (nine in Dublin, three in Cork, and one each in Galway, Kildare, Kilkenny, Mullingar, Sligo, Tralee and Wexford). These are used mainly by BUPA, Vivas and VHI but also admit 'self-paying' patients.

Voluntary Hospitals

As well as public and private hospitals, Ireland has 29 voluntary hospitals (a list can be found on the website of the Office of the Information Commissioner, 🖳 www.oic.gov.ie), which accept patients on a private and semi-private basis. In many cases their consultants also work in public hospitals. The voluntary hospitals were established before the establishment of the Health Boards, and until 2003 were independently run and self-financing (albeit with a subsidy from the Department of Health and Children); they're now managed by the HSE.

Choice of Hospital

Patients with private health insurance may be treated at the hospital of their choice, depending on their level of insurance cover. Non-private patients can ask to be treated at a particular hospital or to be referred to a particular consultant, but have no right to have their request met. In an emergency you will be treated at the nearest hospital. Children are usually admitted to a children's general ward or a children's hospital well stocked with games, toys, books and other children.

Accommodation

Public hospital accommodation is in wards of around six beds, some of which are mixed. Most public hospitals also have private and semi-private (i.e. four beds in a room) accommodation (see **Charges** below). However, there's some consolation to being in a general ward – just think how lonely and bored those poor private patients must be, ensconced in their luxury rooms with nobody to talk to all day!

Charges

Various charges apply to hospital accommodation, depending on your status and the type of hospital, as detailed below. Mental health inpatient and outpatient services are provided free of charge to children under 16 years. All charges include meals.

> Medicines given to outpatients or inpatients at a public hospital are free, but medicines prescribed to be taken at home must be paid for (in the same way as all prescriptions), unless you're entitled to free prescriptions.

Public Treatment

Accident and emergency & outpatients: If you go to the Accident & Emergency (A&E) department of a public hospital or register as an outpatient without being referred there by your doctor, you're normally charged €60. This charge is waived in the following cases:

♦ if you're referred to hospital by your doctor;

♦ if you hold a Medical Card;

♦ if you're admitted to hospital as a result of attending an A&E department (you will then be subject to inpatient charges – see below);

♦ if you're receiving treatment for certain infectious diseases;

♦ if you're unable to pay (in certain cases);

♦ children up to six weeks of age, suffering from certain diseases and disabilities or referred by child health clinics or school health examiners;

♦ women receiving ante or post-natal care.

If you have to return to hospital for further treatment in relation to the same illness or accident, you don't have to pay.

If you're referred by your doctor to the outpatients department of a public hospital for specialist treatment (e.g. X-rays, laboratory tests or physiotherapy) and you choose to be treated in a private capacity, you must pay the appropriate fee.

Inpatients: If you remain in a hospital overnight, you're considered to be an inpatient and must pay €66 per day up to a maximum of €660 per year, unless any of the following applies:

♦ you hold a Medical Card;

♦ you're receiving treatment for certain infectious diseases;

♦ you're unable to pay (in certain cases);

♦ you're a child up to six weeks of age, suffering from certain diseases and disabilities or referred by child health clinics or school health examiners;

♦ you're a woman receiving ante or post-natal care.

Private Treatment

Public hospital: If you're in a private bed in a public or voluntary hospital, you must pay for your accommodation at the daily rates shown in the table below, in addition to the public hospital inpatient charges (see above).

You must also pay for any appropriate specialists' fees.

Private hospital: The cost of private treatment in a private hospital is, needless to say, astronomical and most people undergoing such treatment have private health insurance (see page 259). If you don't have health insurance or are a visitor to Ireland, you will probably be asked to pay a deposit in advance, which may be the full cost of the treatment and accommodation (particularly if there's any doubt that you will survive the ordeal). Most private hospitals accept credit and charge cards. It's worth obtaining a number of quotes from different hospitals, as well as checking whether you can get the same treatment cheaper abroad, e.g. in the UK.

Long-term Treatment

Charges may be imposed on long-term patients in addition to normal inpatient charges. These vary according to the level of care provided, but the maximum charge in a public hospital is €120 per week (the charge is no longer based on your income). If you need to be admitted to a nursing home and there's no space at a state home (e.g. there are only eight in the Dublin area), the Health Board will pay a subvention (known as the Private Nursing Homes Subvention) of up to €300 towards the cost of accommodation in a private home (of which there are over 100 in Dublin), depending on your income and assets and the level of care you need. There's no state provision for long-term care in your home.

Visiting Hours

Visiting hours vary from one hospital to another, but are typically two hours during the afternoon (e.g. 2 to 4pm) and two hours in the evening (e.g. 6.30 to 8.30pm), unless the patient is receiving special treatment (e.g. in intensive care). The same hours normally apply to patients in public wards and private rooms, but there's usually a certain amount of

Private Bed Charges			
Type of Hospital		Type of Accommodation	
	Outpatient	Inpatient	
		Semi-private	Fully Private
Regional or voluntary teaching hospital	€546	€594	€758
County or voluntary non-teaching hospital	€362	€407	€506
District hospital	€161	€185	€217

'leeway'. In a private hospital or clinic, there may be no restrictions on visiting hours.

Complaints

Hospitals usually have an officer who deals with complaints. If you don't receive satisfaction, you should contact the Health Service Executive, Parkgate St Business Centre, Dublin 8 (☎ 1850-241850 or ☎ 01-635 2500) or the Customer Services Unit of the Dept of Health and Children, Hawkins House, Dublin 2 (☎ 1890-200311 or ☎ 01-635 3000).

DENTISTS

There are excellent dentists throughout Ireland, most of whom are in private practice, as the public health scheme doesn't extend to dentistry, except in the case of children. Medical Card holders and those who have made the required amount of Pay-related Social Insurance (PRSI) contributions (see page 248) are entitled to free routine dental treatment, and all children receive free annual dental check-ups. Routine treatment includes check-ups, X-rays, de-scaling, polishing, fillings, extractions, root treatment and removal, and partial and full dentures.

Owing to a shortage of practitioners, orthodontic treatment is allocated on the basis of need, those requiring immediate treatment (known as Category A patients), such as for a cleft palate, being given priority; and those needing only 'cosmetic' treatment (Category B) being put on a waiting list, although the HSE is reviewing this system.

To find a dentist, ask for recommendations from neighbours, colleagues and friends, or look under *Dental Surgeons* in the *Golden Pages*. It's a good idea to shop around, as fees can vary considerably, particularly for extensive repair work.

Typical dental fees are €30 to €50 for an initial check-up or cleaning/polishing, €40 to €75 for fillings or an extraction (up to €100 if an operation is required), €300 to €500 for a cap, and around €600 for a set of dentures. It's wise to obtain a quotation before having any 'expensive' treatment.

All dentists must be registered with the Dental Council of Ireland (☎ 01-676 2069, 🖥 www.dentalcouncil.ie), which also deals with complaints about individual dentists.

OPTICIANS

As with dentists, there's no need to register with an optician. You simply go to the one of your choice, although you may wish to ask your colleagues, friends or neighbours if they can recommend someone. Opticians are listed under *Opticians – Dispensing* and *Opticians – Ophthalmic* in the *Golden Pages,* and may advertise particular services such as contact lenses or an emergency repair service.

The optometrist business is competitive in Ireland and, unless someone is highly recommended, you should shop around for the best deal. Recent years have seen 'chain store' opticians such as Specsavers (🖥 www.specsavers.ie) and Vision Express (🖥 www.visionexpress.com) opening in high streets and shopping centres, although these are far less widespread than in some other countries.

Opticians (like spectacles) come in many shapes and sizes. Your sight can be tested only by a registered ophthalmic optician (or optometrist) or an ophthalmic medical practitioner. Most 'high street' opticians are both dispensing opticians (who make up spectacles) and ophthalmic opticians, who test eyesight, prescribe glasses and diagnose eye diseases.

An eye specialist may be an ophthalmic medical practitioner (a doctor who treats eye diseases and also tests eyesight and prescribes lenses), an ophthalmologist (a senior specialist or eye surgeon) or an orthoptist (an ophthalmologist who treats children's eye problems). If you need to see an eye specialist, you must usually be referred by your GP.

As with dental treatment, Medical Card holders and those who have made the required amount of PRSI contributions are entitled to free treatment by HSE-employed opticians and ophthalmic surgeons and designated private practitioners. All pre-school children and primary-school children referred by child health services or school health service examiners are entitled to free treatment, irrespective of whether their parents have a Medical Card. Tax relief can be claimed on the cost of some optical treatment.

Laser surgery to correct short-sightedness hasn't really 'caught on' as it has in some other countries, and there's a limited number of specialists offering this service. To find out if there's a specialist in your area, contact the HSE or a local hospital.

Further information about optical treatment can be obtained from the Association of Optometrists (☏ 01-453 8850), the Irish College of Ophthalmologists (☏ 01-230 2591) and the Irish Association of Dispensing Opticians (☏ 021-277655).

Spectacles

The price of spectacle frames varies considerably (e.g. from around €45 for a standard frame to hundreds of euros for 'designer' frames – the ones with an Italian-sounding name in large letters on both sides). The cost of lenses also varies widely, e.g. €60 for standard plastic lenses, €75 for lenses with an anti-scratch coating and €100 for anti-reflective lenses; charges for bifocal, varifocal tinted, polarising and other lenses being even higher. Special offers are common such as 'buy a new pair of glasses and get a second pair free', although the free pair may have only

standard lenses and frames (if you want the second pair to be prescription sunglasses, you usually have to pay a small charge, e.g. €20). Always carefully compare offer prices and consider whether you really need or want what's offered.

Ready-made reading glasses are available from pharmacies and other shops, without a sight test or prescription, for around €25. Some opticians also sell them, but only for 'emergencies', as they're usually reluctant to let you leave the shop without a prescription pair. Wherever you buy your spectacles, take advantage of any guarantee, after-sales service or insurance arrangements for repairs or replacements. Most spectacles come with at least a six-month warranty ('designer' glasses are usually guaranteed for a year). If you're sold defective glasses or contact lenses, you have rights under the law relating to the sale of goods.

Contact Lenses

Daily and monthly disposable and continuous-wear lenses (for up to 30 days) are widely available, as are tinted and coloured lenses. Obtain advice from a doctor or eye specialist before buying them. Daily disposable contact lenses cost around €90 for a month's supply (some opticians offer two months' supply for the price of one) and continuous-wear lenses for around €90 for three pairs, i.e. around three months' supply.

Sight Tests

Sight tests are valid for two years, although you should be aware that your eyesight can change considerably during this time. You don't need to buy your spectacles (lenses or frames) or contact lenses from the optician who tests your sight, irrespective of whether you're paying for the test, and you have the right to a copy of any prescription resulting from a sight test. Similarly, you may take a prescription to any optician and ask for glasses to be made up from it. The normal charge for a sight test is around €20; Medical Card holders and those with the prescribed level of PRSI contributions are entitled to a free test.

Complaints

If you have a complaint regarding an optician which you cannot resolve, contact the association to which the optician belongs. Most Irish-trained opticians are members of the Association of Optometrists (☎ 01-453 8850), but most opticians trained abroad (e.g. in the UK) belong to the relevant foreign association.

HEARING TESTS & TREATMENT

Hearing tests and hearing aids are provided free of charge in certain cases by HSE-employed professionals and some private practitioners. You will normally be referred by your doctor to an audiologist or an ear, nose and throat (ENT) specialist at your nearest health centre or hearing aid clinic. It may be possible to contact your hearing aid clinic or health centre directly and request a hearing test. There's no charge for a hearing test. Eligibility for free hearing aids is the same as for free dental treatment (see above). Further information is obtainable from the Irish Hard of Hearing Society (IHHA, ☎ 01-872 3800, 🖥 www.ihha.ie) and the Irish Deaf Society (☎ 01-860 1878, 🖥 www.irishdeafsociety.ie).

MEDICINES

Medicines are sold at chemists' (pharmacies), which are listed under *Chemists –*

Pharmaceutical in the *Golden Pages*. Chemists' sell prescription medicines (drugs), non-prescription medicines, and other products such as cosmetics and toiletries, but don't usually carry such an extensive range of goods as an American drugstore. Normal opening hours are 9am to 6pm Mondays to Saturdays (often later on Thursdays or Fridays) and sometimes on Sunday mornings or afternoons. Many chemists' are open until 9 or 10pm on weekdays and some open all day on Sundays and holidays. There are no 24-hour chemists' in Ireland; if you're in urgent need of medicines during the night, you must go to your nearest accident and emergency (hospital) department.

Unless you're a Medical Card holder, in which case you're entitled to free medicines, you must pay for prescribed medicines 'at cost' up to a maximum of €85. Under the Drugs Payment Scheme, if you or your family has a number of prescriptions to obtain, you can collect them all at once and gain the benefit of buying 'in bulk'; in this way you could get all the medicines required by your family for a month for €90. If you want to use this scheme, you need to register at a chemist's or with the HSE. In future, you may be issued with a swipe card, which you must present each time you take a prescription to a chemist.

Medicines purchased on a one-off basis can be expensive, e.g. €30 for a course of antibiotics. The cost of non-prescription items can vary considerably and non-drug items such as toiletries are considerably cheaper at supermarkets.

If you suffer from certain long-term conditions such as diabetes, epilepsy, multiple sclerosis or Parkinson's Disease, you can obtain a long-term illness book that entitles you to free medication.

☑ SURVIVAL TIP

Medical expenses can also be claimed against tax (you need to keep your receipts).

Most chemists' (pharmacists) provide general advice regarding the best medicines for particular conditions and many are trained to provide individual consultations and advice to customers. In some chemists', there may even be an area where you can have a more or less private consultation with a chemist. In the case of minor ailments, this service (which is always free!) can save you a great deal of money compared with visits to a doctor, as a chemist will also tell you which medicines can be purchased over the counter without the need for a prescription.

Always use, store and dispose of unwanted medicines and poisons safely, e.g. by returning them to a chemist or doctor, and never leave them where children can get their hands on them.

ALTERNATIVE & COMPLEMENTARY MEDICINE

A wide range of alternative and complementary medical treatments are available in Ireland (listed under *Alternative & Complementary Medicine-treatment* in the *Golden Pages*) including acupuncture, aromatherapy, reflexology, Reiki, Shen and Shiatsu, and there's an Irish Association of Holistic Medicine (☎ 01-830 4211, ☐ www.holistic-psychotherapy.org).

One of the world's leading 'spas' is the Delphi Mountain Resort and Spa in Leenane, County Galway (☐ www.delphiescape.com), which was refurbished in 2007. Ireland also

has a strong tradition of folk cures and herbal remedies (e.g. treating piles with boiled onions) and certain people are reputed to possess special healing powers (these aren't listed in the *Golden Pages*).

BIRTHS & DEATHS

Childbirth

The Maternity and Infant Care scheme provides for the care of expectant mothers ordinarily resident in Ireland, even if they don't have a Medical Card. Care is provided by GPs (virtually all of whom have an agreement with the HSE to provide maternity care) and hospital obstetricians. The GP makes an initial examination, if possible just before 12 weeks, and a further six examinations during the pregnancy, alternating with visits to a maternity unit or hospital. In addition, you're entitled to two post-natal visits to your GP – an examination of the baby at two weeks and an examination of both mother and baby at six weeks – and home visits by a public health nurse during the first six weeks.

When an expectant mother suffers from a significant illness, e.g. diabetes or hypertension, up to five additional visits to the GP may be provided. Treatment for illnesses which are co-incidental with but not related to a pregnancy isn't provided by the scheme, but must be undergone in the normal way.

Childbirth normally takes place in a hospital, where a stay of up to three days is usual. The Department of Health and Children strongly advises women to have children in hospital, in case there are complications and specialists and special facilities (e.g. incubators) are required. However, you're at liberty to have a child at home if you prefer; a mother and infant care service, including the services of a GP during pregnancy and for up to six weeks after the birth, is available free of charge to all women in Ireland. Your doctor will normally find you a midwife (a nurse specialising in delivering babies), but you may appoint your own (most midwives in Ireland are in private practice). Your doctor will also refer you to an obstetrician.

For hospital births, you can usually decide (with the help of your GP or midwife) the hospital where you wish to have your baby.

When the baby is due, you will automatically be allocated a bed. There's no charge for accommodation in a public ward (either as an outpatient or an inpatient), but semi-private accommodation costs around €1,500, and private accommodation, with the services of an obstetrician of your choice, can cost €3,000 or more. If you opt for a home birth, the HSE may provide a grant of up to €1,270 towards midwifery costs, although some HSE offices provide nothing.

If a baby is born in hospital, it's normally screened for metabolic disorders (using the Guthrie or heel prick test). If a baby is born at home, the test may be carried out by the GP or in the outpatients department of a hospital. This test requires parental consent.

Your GP should have the necessary forms for application for services under the Maternity and Infant Care Scheme. You should contact the public health nurse at your local health centre to enquire about the availability of ante-natal classes.

The National Maternity Hospital (☎ 01-637 3248) is in Dublin, where there are two other maternity hospitals: the Coombe Women's Hospital (☎ 01-453 8883) and the Rotunda Hospital (☎ 01-878 6070). Outside the capital, there are maternity wards in most general hospitals.

Find out as much as possible about local hospital methods and policies on childbirth, either directly or from friends or neighbours, before booking a bed. A number of hospitals are piloting the so-called Domino scheme, whereby the process of childbirth is made more relaxed and less institutionalised. Policy regarding the attendance of the father (or other person – known as the 'birthing partner') at a birth varies from hospital to hospital, but is normally permitted.

The Irish Childbirth Trust (*Cuidiu* in Gaelic) is an independent voluntary body, which publishes a *Consumer Guide to Maternity Services*, detailing both the services provided and the policy operated by every hospital in Ireland (☎ 01-872 4501, 💻 www.cuidiu-ict.ie).

Contraception & Abortion

Contraceptives were banned in Ireland until 1979, but are now widely available. There's nevertheless still some opposition to the use of contraceptives, and a few doctors refuse to prescribe the pill. Abortion is still illegal in Ireland, and it's estimated that 6,000 or more women travel to the UK each year for abortions (see also **Counselling** on page 241). Since the equal right to life of the mother and the unborn child (and therefore the right of a mother to an abortion if her life is threatened) was enshrined in the Constitution in the early '80s, no government has since dared to authorise a single abortion!

Information

Information about family planning and support in pregnancy and childbirth is available from Health Boards, GPs, family planning clinics, maternity hospitals and units, and pharmacies. A free leaflet on family planning and contraception is available from the Health Promotion Unit of the Department of Health & Children (☎ 01-671 4711). An information pack for unmarried parents is available from Treoir, the National Federation of Services for Unmarried Parents and their Children (☎ 01-670 0120 or ☎ 1890-252084, 💻 www.treoir.ie).

For information about benefits and other help during pregnancy and when your baby is born, see **Social Welfare** on page 250.

Registration

Births and deaths must be reported to your local Registrar of Births, Marriages and Deaths. Births and deaths of foreigners in Ireland may need to be reported to a consulate or embassy, for example to register a death in the deceased's country of birth. If you need to obtain a copy of a birth, marriage or death certificate, you can apply to the General Register Office in Roscommon (☎ 090-663 2900 or ☎ 1890-252076, 💻 www.groireland.ie) or to the registrar in the area where it was registered; a list of registrars and further details of how to register a birth or a death can be found on the website. An original certificate costs €10 and a copy €8.

Births

The hospital or, in the case of home births, your GP or midwife will advise you of the registrar's name, address and opening hours.

If the parents are unmarried, only the mother's name will be entered on a birth certificate. For both parents' details to be entered, both must attend the registrar's office or one parent must take a Statutory Declaration signed by the other and complete a Declaration Form. Stillbirths may also be registered and a certificate obtained from the General Register Office (see above).

Deaths

When someone dies in Ireland, a medical certificate of the cause of death must be completed and taken to the local registrar. If the person dies in hospital, the hospital normally does this automatically, and a relative of the deceased can collect the death certificate from the registrar's office. If the death occurs elsewhere, a doctor issues a cause of death certificate to a relative, who must take it to the registrar.

If someone dies suddenly, accidentally, during an operation, in unusual circumstances, or if the cause of death is unknown, the doctor notifies the police and/or a coroner, who decide whether a post-mortem is necessary to determine the cause of death. The registrar will need to know the personal details of the deceased, including his date and place of birth and death, and details of marriage (if applicable).

The death certificate should be given to a funeral director (or undertaker) to arrange the burial or cremation (or for the body to be shipped to another country for burial). You may wish to announce a death in a local or national newspaper, giving the date, time and place of the funeral, and your wishes regarding flowers or contributions to a charity or research.

Funerals

Funerals start at around €500 for a hearse, coffin and bearers to take the body from the place of death to a church (or wherever the funeral service is to take place) and on to a cemetery or crematorium. In addition, you need to pay at least €500 for a cremation, and between €300 and €1,000 for a burial, assuming that a grave has already been purchased (graves can cost anything from €300 to €3,000). Irish undertakers don't yet offer any 'pay-now-die-later' schemes, whereby you make regular payments into a funeral fund, which can be redeemed with an undertaker of your choice when the time comes. However, it's likely that such schemes will be available in the near future.

If you want to have a body buried abroad, or have someone who died abroad buried in Ireland, the body will probably need to be transported by air, which can be very expensive. In the event of the death of an Irish resident, all interested parties must be notified (see **Chapter 20**). You will need a number of copies of the death certificate, e.g. for the will, pension claims, insurance companies and financial institutions.

CHILDREN'S HEALTH

Children are entitled to free pre-school nursing, health examinations (including sight and hearing tests) and any necessary follow-up treatment, annual dental check-ups (and any necessary treatment) up to the age of 16, and immunisation against infectious diseases. The usual timetable for these is a BCG (against tuberculosis) at birth, doses of vaccine for diphtheria, whooping cough, tetanus, polio and Hib at two, four and six months, followed by an MMR against measles, mumps and rubella at 15 months, and boosters for diphtheria, tetanus and polio at four to five years.

All children aged less than six weeks and children under 16 years who suffer from any of a number of disabling diseases are entitled to free hospital treatment (both in and outpatient services).

The National Children's Hospital (☎ 01-414 2069 or ☎ 01-414 2072, 🖥 www.adelaide. ie) is incorporated in the Adelaide and Meath Hospital in Dublin, where there's also the Temple Street Children's University Hospital (☎ 01-878 4200, 🖥 www.childrenshospital.ie) and Our Lady's Hospital for Sick Children (☎ 01-409 6100, 🖥 www.olhsc.ie).

HELP FOR THE DISABLED

Ireland's provision for disabled people is improving as awareness of the need for such facilities increases (it's estimated that almost 10 per cent of Irish people suffer from some kind of disability). Building regulations introduced in 1991 require all public buildings to be wheelchair accessible, so that all modern hotels and restaurants, etc. have good access; and most tourist attractions have recently upgraded their facilities to facilitate wheelchair access.

The Irish Wheelchair Association, Áras Chúchulainn, Blackheath Drive, Clontarf, Dublin 3 (☎ 01-818 6400, 💻 www.iwa.ie) has a database of accessible buildings, and provides a list on request. The Disability Act, 2005 aimed to eliminate discrimination on the basis of (dis)ability; and the National Disability Authority (NDA) was set up to ensure that public bodies meet their obligations under the Act.

Various benefits are available to those with disabilities, although most are means tested. There's a disabled person's maintenance allowance for those aged 16 to 66 with a long-term (i.e. more than 12 months) disability, a mobility allowance, and a blind welfare allowance for those aged over 18.

The HSE and voluntary organisations provide a range of services to disabled people, including chiropody, physiotherapy, speech therapy, occupational therapy, 'meals on wheels', a laundry service and home help, as well as job training (a *Directory of National Voluntary Organisations* is available from Comhairle, formerly the National Social Service Board (☎ 01-605 9000 or ☎ 1890-777121, 💻 www.comhairle.ie). Hospital in and outpatient services are free to children under 16 who suffer from any of a number of disabling diseases.

COUNSELLING

Counselling and assistance for health and social problems is available within the Social Welfare system and from thousands of local community groups and volunteer organisations, ranging from national associations to small local groups (including self-help groups). If you need to find help locally, you can contact your local authority, local voluntary services or a Citizens' Information Centre for advice (listed on 💻 www.comhairle.ie).

Problems for which help is available on a national basis include drug rehabilitation, alcoholism (e.g. Alcoholics Anonymous), gambling, dieting (e.g. Weight Watchers), smoking, attempted suicide and psychiatric problems, homosexual and lesbian related problems, youth problems, battered children and women, marriage and relationship counselling (e.g. Relate), and rape. Relevant telephone numbers are listed at the front of the *Golden Pages*.

DRINKING, SMOKING & ILLEGAL DRUGS

The use (and abuse) of legal drugs (i.e. alcohol and tobacco) in Ireland is as high as elsewhere in the world, particularly among the young, despite stringent government measures to restrict it.

It's estimated that 750,000 Irish people are dependent on nicotine and 95,000 on alcohol, while another 22,000 are in danger of becoming tranquilliser-dependent.

Alcohol

The Irish (particularly men) have an unfortunate reputation for being heavy drinkers, and a 2002 survey by Eurostat, the EU statistical agency, indicated that Ireland had by far the highest proportion of regular drinkers in the European Union. The figures also showed a dramatic rise in alcohol consumption by young Irish women: 50 per cent of Irish women aged 15 to 24 were regular drinkers, compared with

the EU average of 19 per cent (in Italy the figure is just 5 per cent).

Some 53 per cent of Irish men were found to be regular drinkers, compared with the EU average of 33 per cent. This figure increased to 80 per cent for men in the 25 to 34 age group, compared with the EU average of 36 per cent and the next-highest rated country, the Netherlands, at 55 per cent. Overall, 51 per cent of Irish people were regular drinkers of alcohol, followed by 44 per cent of British people and 43 per cent of Danes, the EU average being 25 per cent. All these figures were significantly higher than those in the previous survey, in 1998. 'Binge' drinking is also on the increase in Ireland.

Between 4,500 and 6,500 Irish people are prosecuted each year for 'drunkenness simple and with aggravation' and some 4,000 for driving while over the limit; and more than 4,000 men and 1,000 women are admitted to psychiatric hospitals with alcoholic psychoses. Both the public health services and a number of voluntary organisations provide treatment for alcohol dependence. For Alcoholics Anonymous contact details, see **Counselling** above.

Smoking

As in other countries, there's a growing anti-smoking movement in Ireland, headed by pressure groups such as Action on Smoking and Health (ASH, ☎ 01-231 5021, 💻 www. ash.ie) and supported by the government. Tobacco advertising is illegal, all tobacco products carry strong health warnings and, since March 2004, smoking has been banned in any place where people work, which includes restaurants, pubs and bars, cinemas, theatres and other places of entertainment.

Nevertheless, an estimated 7,000 Irish people die from smoking-related diseases every year. The alarming fact is that, despite the government's (and others') anti-smoking campaigns, by the age of 14, around 20 per cent of children are already smoking regularly – a third of them by the age of 17. Those wanting to give up smoking should call the Smokers' Quit Line (☎ 1850-201203).

Illegal Drugs

As in many other countries, the use of illegal drugs is on the increase in Ireland, where there are 125 illegal (or 'controlled') drugs, including cannabis and cannabis resin, cocaine, mescaline, morphine, pethadine, opium and heroin. The problem is largely confined to the Dublin area, where 99 per cent of heroin offences are recorded, but there's also some drug abuse in Counties Cork, Kerry and Limerick, which between them account for 50 per cent of ecstasy offences. The smoking of cannabis is also fairly widespread, as is solvent abuse, although the use of other drugs such as LSD, amphetamines and cocaine is at quite low levels.

There's a strong anti-drugs campaign led by the government's Drugs Task Force, the Department of Education and the National Parents' Council. This has been partially successful in controlling the extent of drug abuse among children, although a recent Department of Health Survey indicated that almost 20 per cent of secondary-level school children have taken some kind of illegal drug or substance.

There's a plethora of drug awareness programmes and organisations, from government Drugs Task Forces and the Health Promotion Units of the HSE to the Gardai and community and voluntary groups including the Drugs Awareness Programme (DAP, ☎ 01-836 0911, ✉ info@drugawareness.ie, 💻 www.dap.ie – where a list of local help organisations can be found); the Social Care agency of the Dublin Diocese, the Irish Society for the Prevention of Cruelty to Children (ISPCC, ☎ 01-676 7960, 💻 www.ispcc.ie), which operates the AIB Schoolmate Programme and drugs awareness schemes in Clonmel, Dublin, Limerick, Monahan and Wexford; and Clubscene Ireland, which aims to raise awareness of drug use in the club scene in Ireland; also, Community Awareness of Drugs (CAD, ☎ 01-679 2681, 💻 www.aboutdrugs.ie).

Many schools have Social, Personal and Health Education programmes, which include substance abuse awareness instruction; Walk Tall is an awareness programme run in primary schools, and On My Own Two Feet, a programme aimed at post-primary schools.

Health Promotion (☎ 1850-241850, 💻 www.healthpromotion.ie) produces a number of leaflets about drugs awareness, including Drugs – Your Choice, Your Life and Understanding Drugs – A Parent's Guide, as well as a Directory of Alcohol, Drugs and elated Services in the Republic of Ireland.

SEXUALLY TRANSMITTED DISEASES

Sexually transmitted diseases (STDs – also known as sexually transmitted infections/STIs) prevalent in Ireland include ano-genital warts, chlamydia trachomatis, crab lice, gonorrhoea, HIV/AIDS, hepatitis B and C, herpes, syphilis, trichomonas and non-specific urethritis (NSU). Figures issued by the Health Protection Surveillance Centre (HPSC, 💻 www.ndsc.ie/hpsc) show that the rate of STD infection has increased annually in recent years, despite government awareness campaigns such as the recent 'Think Twice Every Time', the three most commonly notified diseases being warts, chlamydia and NSU.

Treatment for sexually transmitted diseases is provided at STD clinics in seven hospitals: the Mater and St James's in Dublin; the Victoria in Cork; the Regional Hospitals in Limerick and Waterford; University College Hospital in Galway; and Sligo General. Clinics also offer HIV testing, and counselling services for anyone concerned about being infected.

Health Insura
Insurance
Travel Insurance
Car Insurance
Life Insurance
Home Insurance

13.

INSURANCE

I t isn't necessary to spend half your income insuring yourself against every eventuality from the common cold to a day off work, but it's important to be covered against any event which could precipitate a financial disaster (like telling your boss what you think of him when you've had a few too many drinks). As with everything to do with finance, it's important to shop around when buying insurance. It bears repeating – always shop around when buying or renewing insurance! Simply picking up a few brochures from insurance brokers or making a few phone calls can save you a lot of money (enough to pay for this book many times over).

If you're coming to Ireland from abroad, you would be wise to ensure your family has full health insurance during the period between leaving your last country of residence until you arrive in Ireland. This is particularly important if you're covered by a company health insurance policy terminating on the day you leave your present employment. If possible, it's better to continue with your present health insurance policy, particularly if you have existing health problems which may not be covered by a new policy. If you aren't covered by the Irish social welfare system (see page 250), it's important to have private health insurance.

There are just two types of compulsory insurance for individuals in Ireland: buildings insurance if you have a mortgage (because your lender will insist on it) and third-party vehicle insurance, which is required by law.

Voluntary insurance includes personal accident, income protection, health (plus permanent health and long-term care), home contents, personal liability, legal expenses, dental, travel, and life assurance, all of which are covered in this chapter. Pensions are also discussed here. Vehicle insurance and vehicle breakdown insurance are covered in **Chapter 11**.

INSURANCE COMPANIES

There are numerous insurance companies to choose from in Ireland, many providing a wide range of insurance services while others specialise only in certain fields. You can buy insurance from many sources including traditional insurance companies selling through their own salesmen, through independent brokers or direct to the public; banks and other financial institutions, post offices and even motoring organisations.

The major insurance companies have offices or agents throughout Ireland, including most large towns, and should provide a free analysis of your family's insurance needs. Note also that you aren't obliged to use an Irish insurance company; under European Union (EU) rules, an insurance company registered in any EU member country can sell its policies in any other EU country.

Brokers

If you choose a broker, you should use one who's independent and sells policies from a wide range of insurance companies. Brokers may represent a large or a small number of insurance companies. The 500+ members of the Irish Brokers Association (IBA, ☎ 01-661 3067, 🖥 www.irishbrokers.ie or 🖥 www.iba.ie) are required to have at least five agencies and are all regulated by the Financial Regulator. Those with fewer agencies are regulated by the Central Bank, which keeps a register of insurance agents, including so-called tied agents.

Under Irish law, a company may not act as both an insurance company and a broker, so tied agents are effectively regulated by the insurance companies they represent, which in turn are regulated by the Irish Insurance Federation (IIF, ☎ 01-676 1820, 🖳 www.iif.ie).

A broker should research the whole market and take into account your individual requirements, why you're investing (if applicable), the various companies' performance, what you can afford and the type of policy that's best for you. He mustn't offer you a policy because it pays him the highest commission, which incidentally you should ask him about (particularly regarding life assurance) as he is obliged to tell you in accordance with the Insurance Act, 2000. It's also worth contacting internet brokers such as Screentrade (🖳 www.screentrade.co.uk), which usually provide competitive quotes. Most major insurance companies also have websites.

Direct Insurance

In recent years, direct marketing by insurance companies (bypassing brokers) has resulted in huge savings for consumers, particularly for car, buildings and home contents insurance. Most of the major insurance companies now have direct marketing operations and will provide quotations over the phone, and often you aren't even required to complete a proposal form.

Comparing Quotes

When buying insurance you should shop till you drop and then shop around some more! Premiums vary considerably, although you must ensure that you're comparing similar policies and that important benefits haven't been omitted. The less expensive companies may be stricter when it comes to claims and may also take longer to settle claims. The general wisdom is that it's better to pay for independent insurance advice than accept 'free' advice, which is often more expensive in the long run.

You should obtain a number of quotations for each insurance need and shouldn't assume that your existing insurance company is the best choice for a new insurance requirement. Buy only the insurance that you want and need and ensure that you can afford the payments (and that your cover is protected if you're sick or unemployed). Don't sign a contract until you've had time to think it over. In the case of life assurance, there's usually a 'cooling off' period of 14 days, during which you can cancel a contract without a penalty.

Complaints & Disputes

Regrettably, you cannot insure yourself against being uninsured or sue your insurance broker for giving you bad advice. If you have a complaint against an insurance company or broker, you should initially follow the company's own internal complaints procedure. If that gets you nowhere, you can refer the complaint to the body of which the company or agent is a member (e.g. the IBA, the IIF or Central Bank).

If you buy insurance through a registered insurance broker and discover that your insurance premiums haven't been paid or that you've been sold the wrong policy, you should be able to obtain compensation through the broker's compulsory professional indemnity insurance (insurance for insurance for insurance).

The 520 members of the IBA are bound by a code of conduct (they must meet a minimum standard of 'competence'), as well as being required to offer compensation of up to €100,000 should you suffer financial loss as a result of a member's negligence or bankruptcy. If all else fails, you can take the matter to the insurance ombudsman (☎ 01-662 0899 or ☎ 1890-882090, 🖳 www. financialombudsman.ie), whose job is to mediate between companies and individuals in dispute. If you decide to go to arbitration, the ombudsman's decision is usually binding on all parties.

The IIF also operates a free insurance information service (☎ 01-661 0274, ✉ iis@iif.ie).

INSURANCE CONTRACTS

When applying for insurance, you are normally required to complete what is called a proposal form, on which you must disclose all the facts relevant to the risk you're asking to be insured against. It's a fundamental principle of Irish insurance law that the utmost good faith (*uberrima fides*) be observed by both parties and, if you conceal any relevant fact (e.g. when applying for home contents insurance that your son is a pyromaniac), the company may 'void' or 'set aside' your insurance, i.e. refuse to pay out.

Although the person applying for insurance is protected to some degree by the *contra proferentum* rule (i.e. if there is a dispute over the meaning of a clause or provision in the insurance contract, a court will normally rule against the insurer), it's essential to read all the small print **before** you sign on the dotted line. Similarly, if an insurance contract is drawn up over the counter or over the phone, the onus is theoretically on the insurance company to ask you the right questions to elicit the information it needs; nevertheless, any dishonesty on your part could count against you if you make a claim.

Irish law doesn't specify the form that insurance contracts should take, but a contract is normally drawn up as a policy, which states the terms and conditions of the insurance. If you wish the insurance to take effect before the policy has been drawn up (i.e. while your proposal is being considered), you may be issued with a temporary cover note, which is effectively a separate contract with a short term of a week, a month or, exceptionally, a quarter. At the end of the cover note period, the insurance company may refuse to grant you long-term cover.

Note that Irish insurance companies can compel you to renew your insurance for a further year if you don't give adequate written notice (e.g. up to three months) of your intention to terminate it, although most companies allow policy holders to cancel on renewal. Check in advance.

Premiums

Insurance is a risk business (as well as a risky business!): the higher the risk, the higher the premium you have to pay. Theoretically, you can insure against it raining on your fête or cricket match, but in practice the premium would be so high (especially in Ireland!), that it would not be worth your while. There are, however, things that you can do to reduce the risk and consequently the insurance premium you pay, e.g. fitting an immobiliser to your car or window locks to your house, but you should consider the cost of these measures in relation to the saving you will make on premiums: it might be cheaper to pay for the insurance!

Most insurance policies have some sort of 'excess', i.e. an amount which is automatically deducted from any claim you make. This can vary from a nominal sum of around €100 to several hundred euros, so you should check your policy carefully and also find out if you can reduce the excess by paying an additional premium.

All insurance premiums in Ireland are subject to a government levy of 2 per cent.

Note that in the case of life assurance policies, insurance companies are required to reveal to customers how much of their premium goes towards administration and management fees and sales commission.

Claims

Although insurance companies are keen to take your money, most aren't nearly so happy to settle claims. Some insurance companies practically treat customers as criminals when they make a claim, and staff may be trained to automatically assume that claims are fraudulent. If you need to make a claim, you should provide as much documentary evidence as possible to support it, but don't send original bills or documents to your insurance company unless it's absolutely necessary (you can always send a certified copy). Keep a copy of all bills, documents and correspondence, and send letters by recorded or registered mail so that your insurance company cannot deny receipt.

You should always make a claim **irrespective** of any small print that appears to invalidate it, as this may be unreasonable and therefore legally unenforceable. You should also be persistent. Don't bank a cheque received in settlement of a claim if you think it's insufficient, as you may be deemed to have accepted it as full and final settlement. Don't accept the first offer made, as most insurance companies try to get away with making a low settlement (if an insurer pays what you claimed without a quibble, you probably claimed too little).

Insurers are increasingly refusing to pay up on the flimsiest of pretexts, as they know that many people won't pursue their cases, even when they have a valid claim. Don't give up on a claim if you're sure you have a good case, but persist until you've exhausted every avenue.

If you wish to make a claim, you must usually inform your insurance company in writing (by registered letter) within two to seven days of an incident or 24 hours in the case of theft. Thefts should also be reported to the local *Gardaí* (police) within 24 hours, as the police report, of which you receive a copy for your insurance company, constitutes irrefutable evidence of your claim.

Failure to report the loss or damage you've suffered may mean that your claim won't be considered. Check whether you're covered for damage or thefts that occur while you're away from your property and consequently unable to inform the insurance company immediately.

In the case of business insurance, it is essential that you keep proper accounts and produce regular stock records. If stock is destroyed or stolen, you will generally be required to prove that the stock was on the premises at the time of the loss.

> ### ☑ SURVIVAL TIP
>
> If you want to make a claim against a third party or if a third party is making a claim against you, you would be wise to seek legal advice (unless it's a minor claim).

Note that Irish law is likely to be different from that in your home country or your previous country of residence, and you should never assume that it operates in the same way.

SOCIAL INSURANCE CONTRIBUTIONS

Almost all working people in Ireland make Pay-related Social Insurance (PRSI) and health contributions, known collectively as social insurance contributions (and sometimes still referred to as 'stamps', although the system of paying for stamps and sticking them in a welfare book ceased in 1979!). Social insurance contributions are payable on income from all sources including benefits-in-kind. The only allowable deductions are contributions to an approved employee superannuation scheme. Social insurance contributions are made by employers on behalf of employees (i.e. deducted at source from your salary), whereas the self-employed must pay their own.

PRSI

If you're employed, your PRSI contributions depend on your job, each type of work being allocated a class or rate of contribution. If you work in a supermarket, for example, and earn more than €38 per week, you will make Class A contributions (as do most Irish employees), whereas a supermarket worker earning less than €38 per week will make Class

covered are contained in the Department of Social and Family Affairs Booklet *SW14*, available from social welfare offices. If there's any difficulty in deciding your class of contributions, contact the Scope Section of the Department of Social and Family Affairs (☎ 01-679 7777, 🖳 www.welfare.ie). Employees' social contributions are deducted at source, i.e. your pay is net of contributions. Your employer keeps a record of all your contributions.

If you're self-employed, you make Class S contributions, which are at the rate of 3 per cent on all income over €8,500 per year, and you're entitled to only a limited range of benefits, including widow's/widower's contributory pension, guardian's payment (contributory), state pension (contributory), maternity benefit, adoptive benefit and the standard bereavement grant.

If the Revenue Commissioners decide that you have no tax liability, you're exempt from social insurance contributions. Otherwise, you must register for Class S contributions with the Department of Social and Family Affairs using Form SE3 and pay your social insurance contributions directly to the Revenue Commissioners – usually at the same time as you submit your annual tax return. Contact your local tax office for information on methods of payment.

To check your social insurance contribution record, you must contact the Central Records Section, Gandon House, Amiens Street, Dublin 1 (☎ 01-704 3363), quoting your Personal Public Service (PPS) number (see below).

If you don't qualify for social insurance contributions, you can make voluntary contributions (e.g. to ensure that you get a state pension).

J contributions. In fact, most employees fall into Class A and are entitled to the full range of social welfare benefits. If you're in any other class (B, C, D, E, H, J, K, M, P and S), you aren't entitled to full benefits. Class J contributors, for example, qualify only for occupational injury benefit.

Employees insured under Class A pay the following social insurance contributions:

♦ If you earn less than €352 gross per week – none;

♦ If you earn between €352 and €500 per week – the first €127 of your earnings are ignored and you pay 4 per cent on earnings above that amount. (Officially, if you earn over €50,700 gross, you pay no social insurance on the income above this amount – though it is hard to see how you could earn €50,700 per year if your income is less than €500 per week ...).

♦ If you earn more than €500 per week – 2 per cent on the first €127 of your earnings, 6 per cent on earnings above that amount up to €50,700 per year and 2 per cent on any earnings above €50,700.

Details of the contribution classes, the occupations they apply to and the benefits

Health Contribution

The health contribution, which is also deducted at source, is currently 2 per cent of earnings up to €100,100 and 2.5 per cent of earnings above that amount. This is paid to the Department of Health and Children (DOHC) to pay for health services. If you earn less than €500 per week or hold a Medical Card or are receiving a one-parent family payment, deserted wives benefit/allowance or a widow's/widower's pension, you're exempt from the health contribution. You should inform your employer if you're receiving any of these benefits, as he may be unaware of the fact and be deducting health contributions from your pay. The self-employed must also pay a 2% health contribution unless they earn less than €26,000 per year.

PPS Number

All social insurance contributors are given a Personal Public Service (PPS) number (formerly the Revenue and Social Insurance/RSI number). You cannot apply for a PPS number before arrival in Ireland, but must go to your nearest Social Welfare office once you've established residence (you cannot obtain a PPS number by phone or post or online). You must produce evidence of your identity and residence in Ireland, the nature of which depends on your nationality (there are different requirements for UK, EU and non-EU nationals).

SOCIAL WELFARE

Social welfare isn't just for those who are receiving a pension or unemployed, and almost a million Irish residents receive some kind of social welfare payment. You may be entitled to welfare benefits for a number of reasons (e.g. simply because you have children) and it's worth finding out in advance the benefits for which you qualify. It's also important to keep records of any welfare

you receive in your country of residence. Many benefits cannot be backdated, so you should make a claim as early as possible.

The benefits available include jobseeker's (i.e. unemployment) benefit, illness-benefit, maternity benefit, children's allowance, one-parent family payment, adoptive benefit, health and safety benefit, invalidity pension, widow's/widower's contributory pension, guardian's payment (contributory), state pension (contributory), state pension (transition), bereavement grant, treatment benefit, occupational injuries benefit and carer's benefit – some of which are detailed below.

The pre-retirement allowance (PRETA), for people aged 55 and over who have ceased working, was terminated in July 2007.

Benefits fall into three categories: those dependent on social insurance payments (or the equivalent in the country from which you're moving), such as maternity benefit, jobseeker's benefit and contributory pensions; those that are made according to need (and subject to a means test), such as the one-parent family payment and non-contributory pensions; and universal benefits, such as child benefit and free travel, which are unrelated to social contributions or means. Even if you don't qualify for a contributory benefit, you may be entitled to a lesser, non-contributory, benefit.

If you're receiving certain types of social welfare payment (e.g. a pension or one-parent family payment), you may be entitled to secondary benefits. These include family income supplement, rent/mortgage interest supplement, fuel allowance (to help with heating costs during the winter months), smokeless fuel allowance (applicable in certain areas of Dublin and Cork where bituminous fuel is banned), butter vouchers, back to school clothing and footwear allowance, and even a Christmas bonus! Secondary benefits aren't paid immediately, and you may have to wait for a 'qualifying period' of up to 15 months.

In the case of contributory benefits, your entitlement depends on the following:

- the class/classes of social insurance you've paid (see **Social Insurance Contributions** above);

- your age when you started making contributions (this applies in the case of pensions);

- how many paid and/or credited contributions you've made since entering insurable employment;

- the number of contributions paid and/or credited in the tax year before the benefit year in which you make a claim (the relevant tax year is the second-last complete tax year before you make a claim);

- the annual average of the number of your contributions (in the case of some pensions).

Anyone claiming social welfare benefits in a European Economic Area (EEA) country or Switzerland is entitled, under EU regulations, to claim the same benefits in any other member country and to be treated exactly as a national of that country. If you're going to work in Ireland from another EEA country, you should take with you a record of your previous social welfare contributions on forms E301 and E304.

There are also bilateral welfare agreements between Ireland and Australia, Canada, New Zealand and the US. If you're moving from any non-EU country (including these four), you should contact the International Operations section of the Department of Social, Community and Family Affairs (DSCFA, ☏ 01-874 8444), which operates the Irish social welfare system.

Social welfare payments are usually made weekly and you can choose from four payment methods.

> Further information about social welfare benefits can be obtained from Social Welfare Information Services (☏ 01-704 3000).

Families & Children

Payments available to families and children include health and safety benefit (for pregnant and breastfeeding women whose work involves a risk to their or their baby's health), maternity benefit, adoptive benefit, child benefit, early childcare supplement, one-parent family payment, family income supplement, back to school clothing and footwear allowance, and deserted wife's social welfare payment.

Maternity Benefit

Maternity benefit is dependent on your social insurance contribution record (you must be in contribution class A, E, H or S) and must be applied for at least six weeks before you intend to take maternity leave (12 weeks if you're self-employed). You must complete Form MB10 (which can be downloaded from the Department of Social and Family Affairs website) and send it to Maternity Benefit Section, Department of Social and Family Affairs, Social Welfare Services Office, St Oliver Plunkett Road, Letterkenny.

The amount of benefit paid depends on your normal earnings and may be reduced if you're receiving other social welfare benefits. You will be disqualified from benefit if you undertake any paid work during your maternity leave period. Some employers continue to pay a salary to women on maternity leave, in which case her maternity benefit is paid to the employer. Women who meet the PRSI contribution requirements receive social welfare maternity benefit of 80 per cent of their normal weekly earnings (up to a maximum of €280 with a guaranteed minimum of €221.80 per week). Payments are tax free.

Further information can be obtained from the Maternity Benefit Section of the Department of Social and Family Affairs (☏ 01-704 3000, ✉ maternityben@welfare.ie).

Child Benefit

Child benefit (formerly known as the children's allowance) is payable to the parents or guardians of children under 16 (under 19 if they're still in full-time education or training or are disabled), irrespective of your means or social insurance contribution record. A claim form (CB1) and a copy of the child's birth certificate must be sent to the Child Benefit Section of the Department of Social and Family Affairs within six months of the child's birth or adoption or, in the case of immigrants, within six months of taking up residence in Ireland. (In the case of a birth, the Department of Social and Family Affairs normally 'applies' for you.)

Claim forms can be downloaded from the Department of Social and Family Affairs website and sent to the Child Benefit Section at the same address as for Maternity Benefit (see above). If you qualify for child benefit for a child under six, you will also be entitled to the early childcare supplement (irrespective of whether you use or need childcare!).

Child benefit is paid monthly at the following rates (2008): €166 for each of the first two children and €203 for each subsequent child.

Further information can be obtained from the Child Benefit Section of the Department of Social and Family Affairs (☎ 01-704 4480 or ☎ 1890-400400).

Sickness & Disability

Various payments are made to people who are sick or disabled, including occupational injury benefit, disablement benefit, disability allowance, illness benefit (formerly disability benefit), medical care payment, treatment benefit, invalidity pension, and blind pension.

Unemployment

If you're out of work, you may be entitled to jobseeker's benefit or jobseeker's allowance.

Jobseeker's Benefit

To qualify for jobseeker's benefit you must be under 66, be available for and seeking work, and have made a certain number of PRSI contributions, i.e. at least 52 weeks' since starting work or 39 weeks' in the tax year before last (e.g. 2006 for a 2008 claim) or 26 weeks' in the tax year before last and 26 weeks' in the year before that. Jobseeker's benefit is means tested and is paid at a maximum of €197.80 per week, normally for a maximum of 390 days (65 weeks) or, if you're under 18, 156 days (26 weeks).

Jobseeker's Allowance

If you don't qualify for jobseeker's benefit (or have 'used up' all your jobseeker's benefit), you may be eligible for jobseeker's allowance (for over 18s only), which is also means tested and is paid at the same rate.

Supplementary Welfare Allowance

Self-employed people don't qualify for jobseeker's benefit or jobseeker's allowance. They can, however, qualify for supplementary welfare allowance, provided they're resident in Ireland or satisfy the 'habitual residence condition' (automatic for EEA nationals but not for non-EEA citizens). The allowance, which is means tested, is paid at the same rate as jobseeker's benefit and jobseeker's allowance, i.e. a maximum of €197.80 per week.

Retirement & Old Age

Various payments are made to retired and elderly people, including various types of pension (see **Pensions** below), early retirement payments (see below) and, if you're fortunate enough to live to 100, a 'centenarian's bounty'! In addition, most people over 66 qualify for free travel on public transport, certain people over 66 are entitled to a living alone allowance, and certain people over 70 qualify for part or all of a household benefits package, consisting of allowances towards the cost of electricity, gas, and telephone line and equipment rental, and a free TV licence.

Early Retirement

Early retirement usually means ceasing work before the age of 65. This may be as a result of redundancy, voluntary retirement or a mandatory 'early retirement' age in your type of work, and your entitlement to social welfare payments will vary according to the reason for your early retirement.

If you've been made redundant, you may be entitled to a statutory redundancy lump sum. In any case, you may be entitled to jobseeker's benefit and subsequently to jobseeker's allowance. You may also be eligible for a range of back to work and back to education schemes.

☑ SURVIVAL TIP

If you retire early, for whatever reason, you should ensure that you maintain your PRSI contributions so that your entitlement to a state pension is maintained.

Death-related Benefits

Various benefits are payable in the event of the death of a close relative, including a widow's/widower's pension (see page 255), a bereavement grant, a widowed parent's grant, guardian's payments and a dependent parent's pension.

PENSIONS

Everyone who pays Pay-related Social Insurance (see page 248) is entitled to a state retirement pension, although for most people this barely provides sufficient income to pay for their basic needs, let alone maintain their pre-retirement standard of living (see **State Pensions** below). And, as in other Western countries, the inexorable 'greying' of the population means that the level of state pensions is likely to decrease further.

This means that, unless you have a large private income or pots of money, it's imperative to have a company or private pension to secure your future after retirement, particularly if you intend to retire early. Most people who have the opportunity join a company pension scheme or, if they can afford it, take out a personal pension plan (both of which are described below).

Various personal savings schemes are available, but only an approved pension plan allows you to claim tax relief at the highest available rate and to take part of your pension fund tax-free on retirement. You receive tax relief on all pension contributions at the highest rate paid on your earned income and can pay contributions into a personal pension fund net of income tax. The gains on investments from a pension are tax-free, but your pension on retirement is taxed as earned income (there are certain exemptions for non-resident pensioners). Occupational pensions are usually taxed at source, but all other pensions must be declared on your annual tax return.

The investment fund accrued by your pension may be invested in an annuity to pay your pension in your retirement years. When you retire, you have the right to shop around for the best annuity you can find from any insurance company. Many people fall into the trap of opting for an annuity recommended by their insurance company, which often costs them thousands or even tens of thousands of pounds. If you retire abroad, your Irish pension is paid gross, but you must obtain a declaration from the foreign country's taxation authorities that you're a resident there for tax purposes and are taxed on your worldwide income there.

If you've worked in more than one EEA country, you may qualify for a pension from each country. If you've made social insurance contributions in two or more member states, you should apply for a pension to the state in which you now live, or in which you had your last contribution, if you have made no contributions in the state where you now live. The authorities in the state in which you apply will then calculate with the other states what is due to you from each of them.

Before making any decisions regarding your pension, you should thoroughly investigate the various options available and take professional advice, e.g. from an independent broker or from the Pensions Board (☎ 01-613 1900 or ☎ 1890-656565, 💻 www.pensionsboard.ie),

which publishes a series of booklets on various pension-related topics.

State Pensions

There are various kinds of state pension available to retired or elderly people in Ireland, described below. Queries and requests for further information about state pensions should be addressed to the Pension Services Section of the Department of Social and Family Affairs (☎ 071-916 9800, ☎ 01-874 8444 or ☎ 1890-500000).

Transition Pension

A transition pension (previously known as a Retirement Pension) is payable to people aged 65 who have retired from work and who have made the required amount of social insurance contributions. It isn't means tested. In general, you must have been an employee and paying full-rate social insurance contributions, but a small number of self-employed people also qualify. Once you reach the age of 66, you will transfer to a contributory or non-contributory pension (see below).

If you're employed, you must be earning less than €38 per week and if self-employed less than €3,174 per year to qualify for a transition pension, whereas you may earn any amount when receiving a contributory pension. You should apply for a transition pension four months before reaching the age of 65 (six months if you've made social insurance contributions in more than one EU country).

Application forms (RP/CP1) are available from post offices and from Department of Social and Family Affairs offices, and should be sent to the Pension Services Office, Department of Social and Family Affairs, College Road, Sligo. There are currently delays in processing applications for state pensions, and you may not receive your first payment on time. However, you may qualify for supplementary welfare allowance while waiting.

The maximum State Pension (Transition) is around €210 per week, with additional payments for certain dependants.

Contributory Pension

The State Pension (Contributory) – formerly the Old Age Contributory Pension – is payable to people in Ireland from the age of 66 who have made the required amount of social insurance contributions. There are also a number of pro-rata pensions for those who have made different classes of contribution.

The Department of Social and Family Affairs publishes *Working it Out – A Guide to the Old Age Contributory Pension*, which will help you to work out whether you qualify for a State Pension (Contributory). However, as the qualifying conditions are complex, you should apply if you've made any contributions at any time – just in case you're eligible! A contributory pension isn't means tested, and you may have income from any other source while receiving it. A contributory pension is taxable.

The maximum State Pension (Contributory) is currently €210 per week if you're between 66 and 80, and around €220 if you're over 80. Additional payments are due in respect of certain dependent spouses or partners and children, and a Living Alone Increase may be payable – but only to those who live completely alone.

To apply for a contributory pension, complete an application form (obtainable from a post office, local office of the Department of Social and Family Affairs or the latter's website)

at least four months before you reach the age of 66 (six months if you've paid social insurance contributions in more than one country and send it to the Department of Social and Family Affairs, Pension Services Office, College Road, Sligo.

There are currently delays in processing applications for state pensions and you may not receive your first payment on time. However, you may qualify for supplementary welfare allowance while waiting.

Non-contributory Pension

If you're 66 or over and a 'habitual' resident of Ireland, but don't qualify for a State Pension (Contributory), you may be entitled to a State Pension (Non-contributory), although this is means tested (all your assets and income are taken into account).

The maximum non-contributory pension in 2008 is €212 per week if you're between 66 and 80 and €222 if you're over 80, with possible additional payments for a dependent spouse/partner and children. You should apply for a means test three months before you reach age 66 (application forms are available from post offices). You will then be visited by a social welfare officer, who will assess your means.

If you qualify for a pension, you should then complete an application form (downloadable from the Department of Social and Family Affairs website or obtainable from a Social Welfare Office) and send it to the Pension Services Office, Department of Social and Family Affairs, College Road, Sligo.

Widow's/Widower's Pensions

There are two types of widow's/widower's pension (formerly the survivor's pension and before that the widow's pension): contributory and non-contributory.

The contributory pension is automatically payable if the deceased person was receiving either a transition pension or a contributory state pension with a supplement for a dependent spouse. Otherwise, either the deceased person or the surviving spouse must have made sufficient contributions for the latter to qualify.

A contributory pension isn't means tested, but to qualify you mustn't be living with another person as 'husband and wife' and you cannot

claim a widow's/widower's contributory pension if you're already receiving a contributory state pension or a carer's allowance, but you may receive child dependant allowances and, if you're over 60, you may be eligible for free travel and electricity allowances. The maximum (2008) payments are €203.30 per week if you're under 66, €223.30 if you're between 66 and 79 and €233.30 if you're over 79.

A widow's/widower's non-contributory pension is a means-tested payment payable to a widow or widower who doesn't qualify for a contributory pension and has no dependent children. Those with dependent children should apply for the one-parent family payment. It's payable only until the age of 66, when you transfer to a non-contributory state pension. The maximum weekly payment is €197.80.

Occupational Pensions

More than 95 per cent of companies in Ireland offer occupational pension schemes as an employee benefit. Schemes vary from company to company, but all are regulated by the Finance Act, 1972 and the Pensions Act, 1990 and most are supervised by the Pensions Board (☎ 01-613 1900 or ☎ 1890-656565, 🖥 www.pensionsboard.ie), the ultimate arbiter being the Pensions Ombudsman (☎ 01-647 1650, 🖥 www.pensionsombudsman.ie).

The most common benefit, of course, is the payment of a regular income after retirement. This is normally between the ages of 60 and 70, except in special circumstances such as serious injury or illness. Some schemes allow for voluntary early retirement, with reduced payments, but in most cases employees must wait until the agreed pension age before being able to draw a pension. These are known as 'preserved benefits', which are transferable to another occupational pension scheme or to a personal pension.

☑ SURVIVAL TIP

You should check whether your scheme provides you with a different level of benefit if you're made redundant, choose to leave the company or have to retire through ill health.

Most schemes include provision for ill health and early (or late) retirement and also provide benefits to spouses and dependants, e.g. in the event of the death of the employee. Normally, this takes the form of a lump sum, which is tax-free (provided it doesn't exceed four times the employee's final pay, plus the value of his or her contributions, including interest); in some cases a pension can be paid instead. If the employee dies after retirement, a lump sum may be payable only if the employee's pension is guaranteed for a number of years after that time.

In some schemes, employees have the option to give up part of their pension to provide for dependants in the event of their death after retirement; the amount of pension you will have to forfeit depends on your age and sex, as well as that of the dependant (in general, the younger the dependants, the more expensive it is to provide for them).

The average cost of schemes is between 10 and 20 per cent of employees' salaries, depending on whether the scheme is funded entirely by the employer or whether employees make a contribution. The total pension payable is typically one-sixtieth of the final salary for each year of service, totalling two-thirds of final salary (the maximum private pension allowed by the Revenue Commissioners) after forty years' service.

The employer's contribution must be at least a sixth of the benefit cost. The employee's contribution can be either compulsory or voluntary (around three-quarters of company pension schemes involve compulsory employee contributions). Under a voluntary scheme, employees may make additional voluntary contributions (AVCs) of up to 15 per cent of their earnings, although the usual contribution is between 5 and 7.5 per cent. However, as you're entitled to tax deduction for all contributions, its worthwhile making as high a level of AVCs as you can afford. You should, however, take professional advice before making any AVCs.

Increasingly, occupational pension schemes are taking into account employees' state benefits. Euphemistically called 'integration' (or, in the public sector, 'co-ordination'), this actually means that state benefits are deducted in whole or part from the occupational pension. In other words, the employer's contributions are lower if employees are also receiving social welfare benefits (see below).

There are essentially two kinds of occupational pension scheme in Ireland: defined benefit (sometimes called a 'final salary' scheme), where the employee's pension is defined in advance; and defined contribution (also known as a 'money purchase' scheme), where the employer's contribution is defined in advance.

In defined contribution schemes, a percentage of your total base salary is contributed by the employer, whereas in defined benefit schemes your 'pensionable'

Killary Harbour, Co. Galway

salary means your salary after a portion has been offset in respect of your state pension. There are also differences in the extent to which, as a pension scheme member, you can influence the value of your eventual pension.

Investment decisions for defined benefit schemes are made by the pension trustees, whereas in defined contribution schemes members make a choice between cash and managed funds, and their pension operates like a pension bank account. Around three-quarters of company pension schemes are defined benefit, although smaller and more recently established companies have tended to prefer defined contribution schemes.

There are several tax advantages to making pension contributions. Not only do you qualify for income tax relief on your contributions (up to 15 per cent if you're aged under 30, up to 20 per cent if you're between 30 and 40, 25 per cent if aged between 40 and 50 and 30 per cent if you're over 50), but your employer's contributions are treated as a non-taxable benefit. You also won't have to pay tax on the growth of funds that you've invested in your pension.

Finally, on retirement you are able to take a cash lump sum from your pension fund (see below). Members of occupational pension schemes in Ireland pay a nominal annual fee (a few euros) to the Pensions Board.

When you retire, you're entitled to a tax-free lump sum of one and a half times your final salary (provided that you've been in service for a minimum of 20 years) or 25 per cent of your pension fund. You may then receive the remainder of the pension fund as income over a period of up to ten years or use it to purchase an annuity.

In many schemes, pensions are guaranteed for a minimum period, but this may be for five years only and you should check whether you have the option to extend the period of payment. If you opt for 'escalating' payments, the amount you earn is calculated to increase annually in line with inflation. Because it's income, your annual pension is liable to income tax. You may also be subject to PRSI and government levies, depending on your level of income (see below). If you die before you retire, the value of your pension fund at the time of your death is paid to your dependants, who may then be liable for capital acquisition tax (see page 294).

Personal Retirement Savings Accounts

Personal retirement savings accounts (PRSA), introduced in 2003, are designed to be used instead of occupational pension schemes by employers who don't wish to sponsor such schemes. They may also be used to supplement occupational scheme benefits, as additional voluntary contributions (AVCs) and as a substitute for personal pension schemes (see below). In fact, employers must offer access to at least one standard PRSA to any employee who isn't eligible to join an occupational pension scheme within six months of taking up employment, and must offer a PRSA for AVC purposes if there's no facility for AVCs within the scheme.

Further information about PRSA is available from the Pension Board's website (💻 www. pensionsboard.ie).

Personal Pensions

To be eligible for a private or personal pension (properly known as a retirement annuity contract/RAC) you must be resident in Ireland for tax purposes and your income must be 'earned', i.e. you cannot take out a personal pension with, for example, rental income or income from investments. If you're self-employed or aren't a member of a company pension scheme, you should contribute to your own pension fund (although it's estimated that 75 per cent of self-employed people in Ireland don't).

In fact, changes introduced by the 1999 and 2000 Finance Acts gave the self-employed greater flexibility in retirement planning: they may now take up to 25 per cent of the fund tax free and buy Approved Retirement Funds (ARF), which they will own outright in retirement. If you're the owner of a business, you may now transfer taxable business income from the company into a retirement plan.

A number of organisations, including the Irish Small and Medium Enterprises Association (ISME, ☎ 01-662 2755; 💻 www. isme.ie) and the Small Firms' Association (SFA, ☎ 01-605 1500; 💻 www.sfa.ie), offer schemes for the self-employed. It's also possible to contribute to a personal pension as well as an occupational pension, although not from the same employment and you may not qualify for all the tax advantages of both schemes.

The usual investment options for private pension schemes are equities (domestic and international), gilts, property and managed funds, which are a mixture of the other three types. You may also be able to invest in with-profit funds, which is a less volatile option particularly suitable for those nearing retirement. If you're a member of a large company pension scheme, you may have no choice in the matter, but if you run your own company or are self-employed you can influence the kind of investment or even set up a small self-administered scheme that allows specific stock selection.

Tax relief is available at the same rates as for an occupational pension scheme (see above). However, the Finance Act, 2006 introduced a limit on the value of an individual's pension fund which may attract tax relief. This is currently 15 per cent of earnings (gross in the case of employees, net in the case of the self-employed) for those under the age of 30, 20 per cent for those between 30 and 40, 25 per cent for those 40–50, 30 per cent for those 50–55, 35 per cent for those 55–60 and 40 per cent for those over 60. If the fund is greater than the limit, tax will be charged at 41 per cent on the excess when it's withdrawn from the fund.

As with an occupational pension, if you cancel your pension plan within the first year, you will derive no benefit from it, but if you cancel it after the first year it will remain 'paid up', which means that the amount you've contributed remains invested and you can use it to buy a pension on retirement.

⚠ Caution

There's no Pensions Board levy on personal pensions, but some pension companies make charges to manage private pension plans. These may be as high as 1.25 per cent, per annum plus a small monthly 'contract charge' (e.g. €5). Before taking out a personal pension, you should check the charges.

When choosing a personal pension scheme (or when choosing between employers offering different occupational schemes), you should ask the following questions:

♦ How is my pension likely to relate to my final pay?

♦ Will my pensionable service be long or short?

♦ Will I receive the maximum permitted lump sum on retirement?

♦ What pension will be left after I've taken my lump sum?

♦ Who will my dependants be when I retire, e.g. are my children likely to be still dependent?

♦ What provision is made for them if I die before or after retirement?

♦ Can I make extra provision for them?

♦ What increases can I expect to receive on my pension after retirement?

♦ What happens if I have to retire early?

♦ What happens if I'm made redundant?

♦ Is the pension 'integrated' or 'co-ordinated' with my social welfare benefits?

Under the Pensions Act you're entitled to:

♦ an annual report on the progress of your pension scheme;

♦ an explanation of your benefit expectations and, under a defined contribution scheme, the current value of the fund held in your name;

♦ a detailed statement of all the options available to you when you leave a scheme.

Further information on pensions in Ireland is available from the Pensions Board (☎ 01-613 1900 or ☎ 1890-656565, 🖥 www.pensionsboard.ie).

CRITICAL ILLNESS INSURANCE

You can insure against being disabled by critical illnesses such as heart disease, cancer and kidney failure. Policies specify the illnesses that apply (generally around 30) and usually include a 'hospital cash plan', i.e. an amount

serious illness insurance policy, it's available as a stand-alone product from a number of companies, often sold in 'units'. For example, a unit may 'buy' you (or your next-of-kin) a lump sum of €7,500 or a weekly payment of €50 to €75 in the event of death or serious injury and you may be able to purchase up to ten units, ensuring you a lump sum of €75,000 or a weekly payment of €500 to €750.

The cost of a unit normally depends on your occupation: the lowest premiums would be for clerical and other non-manual workers, the highest for mechanics, plumbers, electricians, etc. (stunt men need not apply!). Add-on units may be available to provide cover for spouses, and there may be an age limit (e.g. 75).

PERSONAL LIABILITY INSURANCE

Although common on the continent of Europe and in the US (where people sue each other for $millions at the drop of a hat), personal or legal liability insurance is unusual in Ireland. However, home buildings or contents policies (see below) usually include personal liability insurance up to €1m and it's usually also included in travel policies (see page 268).

Personal liability insurance provides insurance for individuals and members of their families against claims for compensation for accidental damage, injury or death caused to third parties or their property. It usually covers anything from spilling wine on your neighbour's Persian carpet to your dog or child biting someone. You can also insure yourself against legal costs in the event of your being sued by a third party.

PRIVATE HEALTH INSURANCE

If you're visiting, living or working in Ireland and aren't entitled to public health care (see page 228), it's extremely risky not to have private health insurance for your family, because if you're uninsured or under-insured you could be faced with some **very** high medical bills. When deciding on the kind and extent of health insurance, make sure that it covers **all** your family's present and future health requirements in Ireland.

A health insurance policy should cover you for **all** essential health care whatever the

per night spent in hospital or per treatment (e.g. €2,000 for an appendectomy and €20,000 for a heart bypass).

Unlike ordinary private medical insurance, premiums are age-related and increase sharply as you get older. They're also sex-related, which means that women pay up to 50 per cent less than men. A 65-year-old male smoker could pay €500 or more per month for €100,000 worth of cover. Critical illness insurance premiums cannot be offset against tax.

PERSONAL ACCIDENT INSURANCE

Personal accident insurance is becoming increasingly popular in Ireland, particularly among self-employed people who are keen to safeguard their weekly income in the event of a temporary or permanent disability resulting from an accident. Since there's no legal requirement for employers to have accident insurance, employees should check whether their employer has it and, if so, what it covers (e.g. accidents that occur when you're travelling to or from work or on company business).

Although personal accident insurance is normally an add-on to a life assurance or reason, including accidents (e.g. sports accidents) and injuries, whether they occur in your home, at your place of work or while travelling. Don't take anything for granted, but check in advance.

Even if you're eligible for public health care, it's advisable (if you can afford it) to have private health insurance, which provides a wider choice of medical practitioners and hospitals, and more importantly, frees you from public health waiting lists.

Under the state system you may need to wait six months for a routine (non-urgent) operation, whereas with private insurance you can expect to be treated immediately or within a few weeks.

Carefully kissing the Blarney Stone!

Some 40 per cent of Irish people have private health insurance, mainly to bypass waiting lists.

Proof of health insurance must usually be provided when applying for a visa or permission to set up a business in Ireland, so that the authorities can be sure you won't be a burden on the state if you require medical treatment. Visitors to Ireland should have holiday health insurance if they aren't covered by a reciprocal agreement.

Note that some foreign insurance companies don't provide sufficient cover to satisfy Irish regulations, and therefore you should check the minimum cover necessary with an Irish consulate in your country of residence. Long stay visitors should have travel or long stay health insurance or an international health policy. If your stay in Ireland is limited, you may be covered by a reciprocal agreement between your home country and Ireland.

Health insurance is governed by the Health Insurance Acts, 1994, 2001 and 2003, which stipulate three general principles: community rating (whereby everyone pays the same premium irrespective of age), open enrolment and lifetime cover. Health insurance companies are regulated by the Health Insurance Authority (☎ 01-406 0080, 🖥 www.hia.ie), whose website provides general information about health insurance.

When travelling in Ireland you should carry proof of your health insurance with you at all times.

Residents

The three main private health insurers in Ireland are Quinn-Healthcare (☎ 1890-891890, 🖥 www.quinn-healthcare.com), which bought the UK-based BUPA Ireland in April 2007, Vivas Health (☎ 818-200016 from outside Ireland or ☎ 1850-716666 from within Ireland, 🖥 www.vivashealth.ie) and the Voluntary Health Insurance Board (☎ 1850-444444, VHI, 🖥 www.vhi.ie), although BUPA has recently 'threatened' to withdraw from the Irish market on account of a government 'risk equalisation plan' that would compensate VHI for its older client base – at the expense of BUPA and Vivas.

If you're already covered by private health insurance abroad, you may be able to transfer directly (i.e. without a waiting period – see below) to Quinn-Healthcare, Vivas or VHI in Ireland (Quinn-Healthcare and VHI have reciprocal agreements with certain foreign insurance companies). EU legislation requires insurers to allow members to transfer to another provider without penalty.

Both VHI and Quinn-Healthcare premiums are calculated on the basis of 'community rating', which means that all members pay the same amount and premiums don't increase with age. This means that younger people generally pay more than they would under a purely risk-based system, although there are normally reductions for younger members (e.g. under 23 or under 18) who are part of a family policy.

There's no longer an age limit to joining. All three companies impose a 'waiting period' of 26 weeks if you're aged under 55 and 52 weeks if you're over 55, during which you're unable to make claims – unless you've had a policy with another recognised health insurance company within the previous 13 weeks. Additionally, VHI imposes a waiting period of 104 weeks if you're over 65. Vivas is the only company to insist on members being 'screened'(i.e. to have a health examination) before joining.

If you become pregnant within 52 weeks of joining, you won't be entitled to maternity benefit. If you have a 'pre-existing' medical condition, you will need to have been a member for at least five years (seven years if you're aged over 55 but under 60 and ten years if you're over 60) before being able to claim for treatment for that condition. These conditions are standard among all private health insurance companies in Ireland, but they're also 'transferable', i.e. if you've been a member of VHI for 26 weeks and transfer to Quinn-Healthcare or Vivas (or vice versa), you will be entitled to claim immediately.

VHI is a non-profit organisation established in 1957 and the largest health insurer in Ireland. Quinn-Healthcare, also a 'not-for-profit' organisation, was established in 1996.

Vivas Health is a recent entrant to the Irish market, whose arrival sparked something of a price war, as Vivas claims to offer lower premiums across the board. However, in mid-2008 its premiums started at €332 per year for a single adult (its oddly named Me plan) compared with BUPA's at €295 (for its Essential Starter plan) and VHI's at €463 (for its plan A), although of course each offers different benefits and stipulates different conditions. For example, whereas VHI offers

treatment in around 60 hospitals, Vivas claims to provide a choice of almost twice as many hospitals and clinics.

Vivas offers just three plans (Me, I and We, the last for families) whereas VHI offers nine (called simply A, B, C, D and E with variations – called 'options' – on each) and Quinn-healthcare no fewer than 11 (with names such as Essential Starter, Essential Plus, Essential Gold, HealthManager Starter, HealthManager Silver and HealthManager Gold). BUPA's and VHI's premium plans, offering comprehensive cover, cost €1,838 and €2,036 per year respectively for a single adult, compared with Vivas's €1,842. Both BUPA and VHI (but not Vivas) operate group schemes for companies and organisations, providing a 10 per cent reduction off individual rates.

Visitors

Visitors spending short periods in Ireland (e.g. up to a month) should have a travel health insurance policy (see page 268), particularly if they aren't covered by an international health policy. If you plan to spend up to six months in Ireland you should take out either a travel, long-stay or an international health policy (which should cover you in your home country and when travelling in other countries). Note that premiums vary considerably and it's important to shop around.

Most international health policies include repatriation or evacuation (although it may be optional), which may also include shipment (by air) of the body of a person who dies abroad to his home country for burial. An international policy also allows you to decide to have non-urgent medical treatment in the country of your choice.

Most international insurance companies offer health policies for different areas, e.g. Europe, worldwide excluding North America, and worldwide including North America. Most companies also offer different levels of cover, for example basic, standard, comprehensive and prestige. There's always a limit on the total annual medical costs, which should be at least €250,000 (although many provide cover of up to €1m) and some companies also limit the charges for specific treatment or care such as specialists' fees, operations and hospital accommodation. A medical examination isn't usually required for international health policies, although existing health problems are excluded for a period, e.g. one or two years.

Claims are usually settled in all major currencies and large claims are usually settled directly by insurance companies (although your choice of hospitals may be limited). Always check whether an insurance company will settle large medical bills directly, because if you're required to pay bills and claim reimbursement from an insurance company, it can take several months before you receive your money (some companies are slow to pay). Most international health insurance companies provide emergency telephone assistance.

The cost of international health insurance varies considerably depending on your age and the extent of cover.

Note that with most international insurance policies, you must enrol before you reach a certain age, e.g. between 60 and 80 depending on the company, in order to be guaranteed continuous cover in your old age.

Premiums can sometimes be paid monthly, quarterly or annually, although some companies insist on payment annually in advance. When comparing policies, carefully check the extent of cover and exactly what's included and excluded from a policy (often indicated only in the **very** small print), in addition to premiums and excess charges.

In some countries, premium increases are limited by law, although this may apply only to residents in the country where a company is registered and not to overseas policyholders. Although there may be significant differences in premiums, generally you get what you pay for and can tailor premiums to your requirements.

The most important questions to ask yourself are: does the policy provide the cover required and is it good value for money? If you're in good health and are able to pay for your own outpatient treatment, such as visits to a family doctor

and prescriptions, then the best value may be a policy covering specialist and hospital treatment only.

Choosing a Policy

Before choosing a private health insurance plan, it's essential to check exactly what's included and, more importantly, what isn't included in the policy. When comparing the level of cover provided by different schemes, the following points should be considered:

♦ Does the scheme have a wide range of premium levels and are discounts or special rates available for families or children?

♦ Is private hospital care or private rooms at local hospitals available? What are the costs? Is there a limit on the time you can spend in hospital?

♦ Is dental cover included? What exactly does it include? Can it be extended to include extra treatment? Dental insurance usually contains numerous limitations and doesn't cover cosmetic treatment.

♦ Are there restrictions regarding hospitalisation, either in Ireland or abroad?

♦ What is the qualification period for special benefits or services?

♦ What level of cover is provided outside Ireland and what are the limitations?

♦ What is the cover regarding pregnancy, hospital births and associated costs?

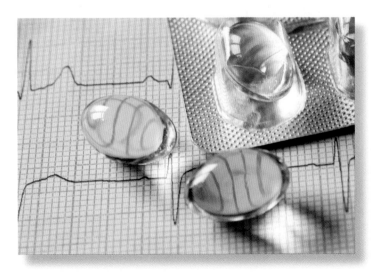

- What is the position if conception occurred before joining the insurance scheme?

- Are drugs and medicines included?

- Are convalescent homes or spa treatments covered when prescribed by a doctor?

- What are the restrictions on complementary medicine, e.g. chiropractic, osteopathy, naturopathy, massage and acupuncture? Are they covered? Must a referral be made by a doctor?

- Is life assurance or a disability pension included or an option?

- Are extra costs likely and, if so, what for?

- Are spectacles or contact lenses covered and, if so, how much can be claimed and how frequently?

- Is the provision and repair of artificial limbs and other health aids covered?

- What benefits will you lose if you change your health insurance company?

OTHER HEALTH INSURANCE

Permanent Health Insurance

Most employees are paid by their employer if they're sick for short periods and some are eligible for disability or injury benefit paid by the state.

> ☑ **SURVIVAL TIP**
>
> To ensure an adequate income when you're unable to work, particularly if you're self-employed, you should take out permanent health insurance (PHI), also called income replacement insurance, which guarantees you a fixed amount each week in the event of illness, injury or invalidity.

Standard private health insurance (see page 259) normally covers you only for a two-week convalescence period following a stay in hospital. A PHI policy pays you a fixed amount each month or a percentage of your salary if you're ill for a long period or permanently disabled in an accident. PHI policies typically pay up to 75 per cent of your gross annual earnings (up to a maximum salary of around €75,000), although you can insure a smaller proportion of your salary to reduce the premiums.

The longer you wait for income protection insurance to pay out, the lower your monthly premium. This is known as the 'deferred period', which is normally 13, 26 or 52 weeks. For example, if your company pays your salary for the first 26 weeks of your illness, you can choose to defer payments from your PHI policy for this period. Some policies pay benefits for a limited period only, e.g. up to a maximum of five years, while others continue payments until you return to work or retire. The longer the period for which you require cover, the higher your monthly premium will be.

Premiums also depend on your health record (including whether you smoke), age, salary, sex and occupation (i.e. high or low risk: occupations are divided into four categories as with personal accident insurance and certain occupations are specifically excluded from cover, including that of a taxi driver!). For example, a 30 year old male earning €40,000 a year might pay around €75 per month, whereas a 60 year old male with the same salary would probably be paying more than twice that amount.

Depending on your age and type of job, some insurance companies may require you to have a medical examination or will obtain a report from your family doctor. With any PHI policy, it's important to check exactly what is defined as a disability, and you should avoid a policy that defines it as the inability to do any job! PHI premiums are tax-deductible (at the higher rate of 44 per cent) up to 10 per cent of total income, but the income you receive from the insurer is taxable.

Serious Illness Insurance

Serious illness insurance (also known as critical illness insurance) is more like life assurance, in that it pays out a lump sum if you're diagnosed as having a serious illness or suffer a stroke or heart attack, even if you're subsequently fit to return to work. Specified illnesses vary from insurer to insurer, but normally include cancer, coronary artery disease (requiring surgery), kidney failure, benign brain tumours, multiple sclerosis, motor neurone disease, blindness, loss of limbs and severe burns.

Some policies provide cover also if you suffer any condition that causes you 'loss of independent existence', i.e. being confined to a wheelchair or being unable to carry out certain basic activities, such as washing, feeding and dressing.

Serious illness cover can also be used to protect mortgages, or you can take out a mortgage protection policy for around €6 per €100 monthly repayment. Note, however, that a minimum 'survival period' is normally quoted, usually 14 days. If you die within that period, the policy is invalidated and you (or your dependants) will have to rely on your having taken out life assurance as well. Most Irish life assurance companies offer serious illness policies.

To qualify for PHI or serious illness insurance, you may need to have a medical examination or provide a doctor's report.

If you already have a serious condition, such as heart trouble, there may be restrictions on the cover, but most people will be able to get either insurance at standard rates.

Permanent Disability Insurance

You can insure for an additional lump sum if you're permanently unable to work (before the age of 60) as a result of an accident or illness. This is known as permanent disability insurance and is usually an add-on to serious illness insurance (see above). For a lump sum of €75,000 in the event of death, serious illness or permanent disability, a 30-year-old male non-smoker might pay around €50 per month.

DENTAL INSURANCE

There are currently no companies offering dental insurance in Ireland, although limited dental insurance is included in some private health insurance plans (see page 259) and some foreign health insurance policies and worldwide health schemes. Treatment required as the result of an accident may, however, be covered by a standard personal accident policy. For details of dental treatment covered by social welfare.

HOUSEHOLD INSURANCE

Household insurance generally includes the building, its contents and third-party liability, all of which are contained in a multi-risk household insurance policy. Policies are offered by both Irish and foreign insurance companies, and premiums are similar, although foreign companies may provide more comprehensive cover.

Buildings

When buying a home, you're usually responsible for insuring it before you even move in. If you take out a mortgage to buy a property, your lender will generally insist that your home (including most permanent structures on your property) is insured from the time you exchange contracts and are legally the owner. Usually referred to as buildings insurance, it normally covers damage to a building caused by fire, smoke, lightning, water, explosion, storm, freezing, snow, theft, vandalism, acts of terrorism, impact, broken windows and natural catastrophes (such as falling trees), as well as the cost of renting temporary accommodation. Insurance should include glass, external buildings, aerials and satellite dishes, gardens and garden ornaments.

It's particularly important to have insurance for storm damage in Ireland, as this can be severe in some areas. If floods are one of your concerns, ensure that you're covered for water coming in from ground level, not just for water seeping in through the roof. Always read the small print of contracts. Note that if you own a home in an area that has been hit by a succession of natural disasters (such as floods), your household insurance may be cancelled.

If a claim is the result of a defect in building or design, e.g. the roof is too heavy and collapses, the insurance company won't pay up either (another reason why it's wise to have a survey done before buying a home). Note also that there may be an excess for some claims, which is intended to deter people from making small claims.

Buildings insurance should be renewed each year and insurance companies are continually updating their policies, so you must take care that a policy still provides the cover required when you receive a renewal notice.

Lenders fix the initial level of cover when you first apply for a mortgage and usually offer to arrange the insurance for you, but you're usually free to make your own arrangements. Note that if you change your building insurance from your lender to another insurer, you may be charged a small transfer or 'administration' fee (designed to discourage you from changing). If you arrange your own building insurance, your lender will insist that the level of cover is sufficient. Most people take the easy option and arrange insurance through their mortgage lender, which is generally the most expensive option.

Buildings insurance is based not on the current market value of the property (i.e. the price it would fetch if put up for sale), but on the cost of rebuilding it should it be totally destroyed, and consequently should be increased annually in line with inflation. It's commonly thought that these figures are similar, but in fact the market value of a property often bears little relationship to the cost of rebuilding, which varies depending on the type of property and the area. There's generally no deduction for wear and tear and the cost of redecoration is usually met in full.

The Society of Chartered Surveyors in Ireland (☎ 01-676 5500, 🖥 www.scs. ie) publishes a *Guide to House Rebuilding*

Insurance (downloadable from the website), according to which the rebuilding cost of properties in and around the main cities in July 2008 was between around €1,965 per square metre (for a bungalow) and €2,200 (for a terraced house) in the Dublin area and between around €1,500 and €1,700 per square metre in all other parts of the country. (Note that these costs don't include garages or other outbuildings, patios or boundary walls, built-in wardrobes, carpets, furnishings or expensive fittings or finishes). Building insurance policies in Ireland usually include third-party liability, e.g. up to €500,000.

Most lenders provide index-linked building insurance, where premiums are linked to inflation and building costs (premiums are usually added to your monthly mortgage payments). It is, however, your responsibility to ensure that your level of cover is adequate, particularly if you carry out improvements or extensions which substantially increase the rebuilding cost of your home. If your level of cover is too low, an insurance company is within its rights to reduce the amount it pays out when a claim is made, in which case you may find you cannot afford to have your house rebuilt or repaired should disaster strike.

The cost of buildings insurance varies depending on the insurer, the type of building and the area.

Premiums are usually calculated on the size of a property, its age and type of construction, but the amount you will pay may vary considerably according to a property's location and the measures you take to protect it from accidental damage and burglary. Smoke detectors, window locks and security alarms, for example, can reduce your insurance bill by as much as 15 per cent, and participation in a local Community Alert scheme by a further 5 per cent.

A typical three-bedroom house fitted with smoke detectors and security alarms in a Dublin suburb valued at €400,000 would cost around €200 a year to insure. For a similar property outside Dublin you may pay up to 30 per cent less. You may have to pay extra for accidental damage, e.g. when your son blasts a football through the kitchen window. On the other hand, you may be able to reduce your premiums by accepting a higher excess (deductible), e.g. a 10 per cent reduction for a €500 excess, instead of the standard €125, and a 15 per cent reduction for a €1,000 excess. Always ask your insurer what isn't covered and what it will cost to include it (if required). Premiums are normally paid annually, but can usually be paid monthly, although there may be an extra charge.

Most insurance companies provide emergency telephone assistance for policyholders requiring urgent advice. Should you need to make emergency repairs, e.g. to weather-proof a roof after a storm or other natural disaster, most insurance companies allow work up to a certain limit (e.g. €1,000) to be carried out without an estimate or approval, but check first. If you let your house (or part of it) or you intend leaving it unoccupied for a period of 30 days or longer, you must usually inform your insurance company.

Buildings insurance is often combined with home contents insurance (see below), when it may be termed household insurance, although it's often cheaper to buy buildings and home contents insurance separately.

Leasehold Properties

If you own a leasehold property, such as an apartment or flat, buildings insurance will be arranged by your landlord or the management company (it's worth checking that it's adequate), so you are responsible only for insuring the contents of a property.

Holiday Homes

Premiums are generally higher for holiday homes, because of their high vulnerability, particularly to burglaries. Most policies include restrictions if a property is unoccupied for more than 30 days at a time. Premiums are usually based on the number of days a year a property is inhabited and the interval between periods of occupancy. Cover for theft, storm, flood and malicious damage may be suspended when a property is left empty for an extended period. Note that you're generally required to turn off the water supply at the mains when vacating a building for more than 72 hours.

It's possible to negotiate cover for periods of absence for a hefty surcharge, although valuable items are usually excluded (unless you have a safe). If you're absent from your property for long periods, e.g. longer than 30 days a year, you may be required to pay an excess on a claim arising from an occurrence that takes place during your absence (and theft may be excluded).

Note that (where applicable) it's important to ensure that a policy specifies a holiday home and not a principal home. In areas with a high risk of theft (e.g. Dublin), an insurance company may insist on extra security measures. It's unwise to leave valuable or irreplaceable items in a holiday home or a property that will be vacant for long periods. Note that some insurance companies will do their utmost to find a loophole, making you negligent and relieving them of liability.

 Caution

You should ensure that the details listed on a policy are correct, otherwise your policy could be void.

Rented Property

Your landlord will usually insist that you have third-party liability insurance. A lease requires you to insure against 'tenants' risks', including damage you may make to the rental property and to other properties, e.g. due to flood, fire or explosion. You can choose your own insurance company, and aren't required to use one recommended by your landlord.

Contents

Because you're far more likely to incur damage to or loss of items contained in your home than damage to or destruction of the building itself, contents insurance is virtually essential (unless you live in a 'communal' environment without possessions). Contents are usually insured for the same risks as a building (see above) and are insured for their replacement value (new for old), with a reduction for wear and tear for clothes and linen. Valuable objects are covered for their actual declared (and authenticated) value. Most policies include automatic indexation of the insured sum in line with inflation.

Contents insurance may include accidental damage to sanitary installations, theft of money, credit cards, bicycles, garden furniture, satellite dishes, replacement of locks following damage or loss of keys, frozen food, alternative accommodation, and property belonging to third parties stored in your home. Some items are usually optional, e.g. contact lenses, caravan and camping equipment, musical instruments, emergency assistance (plumber, glazier, electrician, etc.), redecoration, garaged cars, replacement pipes, loss of rent, and the cost of emergency travel to Ireland for holiday homeowners.

Many policies include personal third-party liability, e.g. up to €500,000, although this may be an option. Items of high value (e.g. over €2,000) must usually be itemised and documentation (i.e. a valuation) provided. A photograph may be required for anything worth over €7,500. Some companies even recommend or insist on a video film of belongings.

Take care that you don't under-insure your house contents and that you periodically reassess their value and adjust your insurance premium accordingly. You can arrange to have your insurance cover automatically increased annually by a fixed percentage or amount by your insurance company. If you make a claim and the assessor discovers that you're under-insured, the amount due will be reduced by the percentage by which you're under-insured.

If you're aged over 50 or 55, you may qualify for an extra discount of 10 per cent. Some companies also offer 'no-claims' bonuses of up to 20 per cent. Several companies offer combined buildings and contents policies where the contents are automatically insured for 50 per cent of the value of the building. Some companies offer discounts (for alarms, community alert, etc.) only if you take out a combined policy, while others offer an extra 30 per cent discount on buildings and/or contents insurance if they also insure your car.

A typical three-bedroom house fitted with smoke detectors and security alarms in a Dublin suburb with €100,000 worth of contents would cost around €275 a year to insure. For a similar property outside Dublin you may pay up to 30 per cent less. Certain 'valuable' items (e.g. wedding and engagement rings) can be insured for 'all risks' both inside and outside the home for an additional premium. As with buildings insurance, you may be able to reduce your premiums by accepting a higher excess. All insurance premiums are subject to a government levy of 2 per cent.

As with buildings insurance, it's important to shop around for the lowest premiums, which vary considerably depending on the insurer. If you're already insured, you may find that you can save money by changing insurers, particularly if you're insured through a bank or building society, which are usually the most expensive. However, watch out for penalties when switching insurers.

When claiming for contents, you should produce the original bills if possible (always keep bills for expensive items) and bear in mind that replacing imported items in Ireland may be more expensive than buying them abroad. Contents policies always contain security clauses and if you don't adhere to them a claim won't be considered. If you're planning to let a property, you may be required to inform your insurer.

Note that a building must be secure with key operated locks on ground-floor windows and patio doors. Most companies offer a discount if properties have high security locks and alarms (particularly alarms connected to a monitoring

station), but only if they're installed to certain recognised standards. An insurance company may send someone to inspect your property and advise on security measures.

Policies pay out for theft only when there are signs of forced entry and you aren't covered for thefts by a tenant (but may be covered for thefts by domestic personnel). All-risks policies offering a worldwide extension to a household policy covering jewellery, cameras and other items aren't usually available from Irish insurance companies, but are provided by a number of foreign companies.

Combining your contents insurance with your building insurance (see above) can save you money, although it's often cheaper to buy separate insurance. However, it can be advantageous to have your buildings and contents insurance with the same insurer, as this avoids disputes over which company should pay for which item, as could arise if you have a fire or flood affecting both your home and its contents.

Insuring Abroad

It's possible and legal to take out buildings and contents insurance in another country for a property in Ireland (some foreign insurance companies offer special policies for holiday homeowners), although you must ensure that a policy is valid under Irish law. This may seem like a good option for a holiday home in Ireland, although it can be more expensive than insuring with an Irish company and can lead to conflicts if, for example, the building is insured with an Irish-registered company and the contents with a foreign based company.

> ☑ **SURVIVAL TIP**
>
> Most experts advise that you insure an Irish home and its contents with an Irish insurance company through a local agent.

HOLIDAY & TRAVEL INSURANCE

Holiday and travel insurance is recommended for all who don't wish to risk having their holiday or travel ruined by accident, illness or other unforeseen problems. As you probably know, anything can and often does go wrong with a holiday, sometimes before you even get started (particularly when you **don't** have insurance).

Travel insurance is available from many sources including travel agents, insurance companies and agents, banks, automobile clubs and transport companies (airline, rail and bus). Package holiday companies and tour operators also offer insurance policies, some of which are compulsory, too expensive and don't provide adequate cover. You can also buy 24-hour accident and flight insurance at major airports, although it's expensive and doesn't offer the best cover.

Before taking out travel insurance, carefully consider the range and level of cover you require and compare policies. Short-term holiday and travel insurance policies should include cover for holiday cancellation or interruption; missed flights; departure delay at both the start **and** end of a holiday (a common occurrence); delayed, lost or damaged baggage; personal effects and money; medical expenses and accidents (including evacuation home); flight insurance; personal liability and legal expenses; and default or bankruptcy insurance, e.g. against a tour operator or airline going bust.

Medical Cover

Medical expenses are an important aspect of travel insurance and you shouldn't rely on insurance provided by reciprocal health arrangements, charge and credit card companies, household policies or private medical insurance (unless it's an international policy), none of which usually provide adequate cover (although you should take advantage of what they offer). The minimum medical insurance recommended by experts is €500,000 in Ireland and most of the rest of Europe, and €1-2m for the rest of the world.

If applicable, check whether pregnancy-related claims are covered and whether there are any restrictions for those over a certain age, e.g. 65 or 70 (travel insurance is becoming increasingly expensive for those aged over 65, although they don't usually need to worry about pregnancy!).

Always check any exclusion clauses in contracts by obtaining a copy of the full policy document, as not all relevant information is included in an insurance leaflet. High risk sports and pursuits should be specifically covered and **listed** in a policy (there's usually an additional premium and 'dangerous' sports are excluded from most standard policies). Third-party liability cover should be at least €3m in North America and €1.5m in the rest of the world. Note that third-party liability cover isn't usually applicable when you're using a car or other mechanically propelled vehicle.

Cost

The cost of travel insurance varies considerably, depending on where you buy it, how long you intend to stay in Ireland, your age and the benefits provided (e.g. the amount of payments for hospitalisation). Generally, the longer the period covered, the cheaper the daily cost, although there's usually a maximum period, e.g. six months. With some policies, an excess must be paid for each claim; with others the excess applies only to certain items such as luggage, money and medical expenses.

As a rough guide, travel insurance for Ireland (and most other European countries) starts at around €40 for one week, €60 for two weeks and €80 for a month for an individual and around twice as much for a family, although some policies cost three times as much. Premiums may be higher for those aged over 65 or 70.

Annual Policies

For those who travel abroad frequently, whether on business or pleasure, an annual travel policy usually provides the best value, but check carefully exactly what it includes. Many insurance companies offer annual travel policies for a premium of around €200 to €300 for an individual (the equivalent of around three months' insurance with a standard travel insurance policy), which are excellent value for frequent travellers. Some insurance companies also offer an 'emergency travel policy' for holiday homeowners who need to travel abroad at short notice to inspect a property, e.g. after a severe storm.

The cost of an annual policy may depend on the area covered, e.g. Europe, worldwide excluding North America and worldwide including North America, although it doesn't usually cover travel within your country of residence. There's also a limit on the number of trips a year and the duration of each trip, e.g. 90 or 120 days. An annual policy is usually a good choice for owners of a holiday home in Ireland who travel there frequently for relatively short periods. Again, carefully check exactly what's covered (or omitted), as an annual policy may not provide adequate cover.

Claims

If you need to make a claim, you should provide as much documentary evidence as possible to support it. Travel insurance companies gladly take your money, but they aren't always so keen to pay claims and you may need to persevere before they pay up. Always be persistent and make a claim **irrespective** of any small print, as this may be unreasonable and therefore invalid in law. Insurance companies usually require you to obtain a written report and report a loss (or any incident for which you intend to make a claim) to the local police or carriers within 24 hours. Failure to do so may mean that a claim won't be considered.

14.
FINANCE

One of the most important aspects of living and working in Ireland (or anywhere else) is finance, which includes everything from transferring and changing money to mortgages and taxes. If you're planning to invest in property or a business in Ireland that's financed with money earned or held in a currency other than euros, it's important to consider both present and possible future exchange rates (don't be too optimistic!). If you wish to borrow money to buy property or for a business venture in Ireland, you should carefully consider where and in what currency it should be raised. Note that it's difficult for foreigners to obtain business loans in Ireland, particularly for new ventures, and you shouldn't rely on it.

On the other hand, if you earn your income in euros this may affect your financial commitments abroad, particularly if the currency is devalued. If your income is received in a foreign currency, it can be exposed to risks beyond your control when you live in Ireland, particularly regarding inflation and exchange rate fluctuations. List all your probable and possible expenses, and do your homework thoroughly before moving to Ireland – afterwards it may be too late!

They say there are only two disadvantages to living in Ireland: the weather and the taxes. Nothing can be done about the weather, but taxes – or at least some of them – can be avoided. The Irish have always believed that they're the most highly-taxed people in Europe. In fact, Irish taxes are slightly below the European Union (EU) average and there's neither property tax nor wealth tax in Ireland – but even the Irish have to have something to complain about! Belgians, Dutch people and Scandinavians will find Irish income tax low, while most other Europeans will pay around the same or less as in their home countries. Only those from Canada and the US will find Irish taxes particularly high.

Before deciding to settle in Ireland permanently, you should obtain expert advice regarding Irish taxes. This will (hopefully) ensure not only that you don't make any mistakes that you will regret later, but also that you take full advantage of your current tax status.

There are usually a number of things you can do in advance to reduce your tax liability, both in Ireland and abroad. Be sure to consult a tax adviser who is familiar with both the Irish tax system and that of your present country of residence. For example, you may be able to avoid paying tax on a business abroad if you establish both residence and domicile in Ireland before you sell. On the other hand, if you sell a foreign home after establishing your principal residence in Ireland, it becomes a second home and may then be liable to capital gains tax.

⚠ Caution

Tax evasion in Ireland is a criminal offence, for which offenders can be heavily fined or even receive a prison sentence.

On the other hand, tax avoidance, i.e. legally paying as little tax as possible (if necessary by finding and exploiting loopholes in the tax laws) isn't only legal, but highly recommended!

Although the Irish generally prefer to use cash rather than credit or charge cards, the use of credit cards is on the increase and personal debts are mounting. In any case, it's wise to have at least one credit card when visiting or living in Ireland (both Visa and MasterCard are widely accepted).

Even if you don't like credit cards and shun any form of credit, they have their advantages: for example, no-deposit car rentals; no pre-paying hotel bills (plus guaranteed bookings); obtaining cash 24-hours a day; simple telephone and mail-order payments; greater safety and security than cash; and above all, convenience. Note, however, that while 'plastic' is now widely accepted in the larger shops, hotels, and restaurants, not all Irish businesses accept credit cards.

When you arrive in Ireland to take up residence or employment, ensure that you have sufficient cash, travellers' cheques, credit cards, luncheon vouchers, coffee machine tokens, gold coins, diamonds, etc., to last at least until your first pay day, which may be some time after your arrival. During this period you will also find an international credit card (or two) useful.

If you plan to live in Ireland you must ensure that your income is (and will remain) sufficient to live on, bearing in mind possible devaluations (if your income is paid in a foreign currency), rises in the cost of living, and unforeseen expenses such as medical bills or anything else that may reduce your income – such as stock market crashes and recessions!

Foreigners, particularly retirees, shouldn't under-estimate the cost of living in Ireland, which has increased significantly in the last decade. If you're planning to live permanently in Ireland, it's important to seek expert financial advice, as it may offer the opportunity to (legally) reduce your taxes significantly.

This chapter includes information on Irish currency, importing and exporting money, banking, mortgages, taxes (income, capital gains, capital acquisition, etc.) and the cost of living. See **Chapter 13** for information about social security, pensions and life assurance.

FINANCIAL REPRESENTATION

If you're a non-resident with property in Ireland you should appoint someone locally to look after your financial affairs and declare and pay taxes on your behalf. This person would normally be an accountant or tax consultant, to whom all communications will automatically be sent by the Irish tax authorities. You can also have your representative check your bank statements, ensure that your bank is paying your regular bills by standing order (such as electricity, gas and telephone), and that you have sufficient funds in your account to pay them.

Note that if you're a non-resident and are collecting rent on a property in Ireland, you need to appoint a 'collecting agent' of some kind; otherwise your tenants are obliged to deduct tax at the standard rate from their rental payments. A collecting agent doesn't need to be an estate agent (auctioneer), accountant or tax consultant, but can be anyone who is resident (and therefore paying tax) in Ireland.

If you need someone to keep your tax affairs in order and to complete an annual return on your behalf, an Irish accountant or tax consultant will charge around €700 a year for this service, depending on the complexity of your finances.

IRISH CURRENCY

The euro (€) became Ireland's currency on 1st January 2002, replacing the Irish pound (*punt*), which was worth €1.2. The euro is divided into 100 cents and coins are minted in   1, 2, 5, 10, 20 and

50 cents, and 1 and 2 euro denominations. Coins all have a common European face with a map of the European Union and the stars of the European flag, while the obverse is different for each member country. Coins are minted by individual countries, although irrespective of where they're made, they can be used throughout the member countries of the euro zone.

Not surprisingly, the manufacturers of coin-operated machines are wary of this aspect of the single currency, as machines must be able to accept coins minted in all the euro zone countries.

Euro bank notes are printed in denominations of 5, 10, 20, 50, 100, 200 and 500 euros. The design of the notes was subject to considerable debate and contention, and the winning design depicts 'symbolic' representations of Europe's architectural heritage. None of the 'representations' on any of the notes are supposed to be actual buildings, bridges or arches, although there have been numerous claims in the press and elsewhere that the structures shown are actually landmarks in certain countries.

☑ SURVIVAL TIP

It's advisable to obtain some euro coins and notes (e.g. €50 to €200) before arriving in Ireland and to familiarise yourself and your family with them. This will save you having to change money on arrival at the port or airport, where exchange rates are usually poor and there may be a long queue.

It's best to avoid €200 and €500 notes (unless you receive them as a gift!) as they sometimes aren't accepted, particularly for small purchases or on public transport.

IMPORTING & EXPORTING MONEY

Exchange controls have been abolished in Ireland (as in other EU countries) and in principle there are no restrictions on the import or export of funds. However, when you open an account, a bank must routinely inform the Central Bank of Ireland of any large account

movements as required by the EU Directive to deter money laundering. Similarly, cash, notes and bearer-cheques in any currency (plus gold coins and bars) may be freely imported or exported by residents and non-residents without approval or declaration. However, if it's possible that you will re-export more than €10,000, you should declare it, as this will certify that the foreign currency was imported legally and will allow you to convert euros back into a foreign currency without suspicion. If you don't declare it, you may find the bank will contact you to enquire where the money came from.

International Bank Transfers

When transferring or sending money to (or from) Ireland you should be aware of the alternatives and shop around for the best deal. A bank-to-bank transaction can be made by a normal transfer or by a SWIFT electronic transfer.

A normal transfer is supposed to take three to seven days, but in reality it usually takes much longer (particularly when sent by mail), whereas a SWIFT telex transfer should be completed in as little as two hours.

Note that it's usually faster and cheaper to transfer funds between branches of the same bank or affiliated banks than between non-affiliated banks. If you intend sending a large amount of money to Ireland for a business transaction or for buying property, you should ensure that you receive the commercial rate of exchange rather than the tourist rate. Charges for transferring funds to Ireland vary, depending on the method of transfer. An electronic transfer, for example, may cost you around €20. If a cheque or bank draft is sent, normal bank charges apply (see below).

There's usually no difference in charges, whether a transfer is made in euros or foreign currency. However, in many cases the charge is incurred by the bank sending the funds. Always check charges and rates in advance and agree them with your bank (you may be able to negotiate a lower charge or a better exchange rate).

Bank Drafts & Personal Cheques

Another way to transfer money is by bank draft, which should be sent by registered mail. Note, however, that if it's lost or stolen, it's impossible to stop payment and you must wait around six months before a new draft can be issued. Bank drafts are treated as cash in Ireland, so they don't need to be cleared like personal cheques, but there's usually a small charge (around €5).

It's possible to pay personal cheques and cheques drawn on a foreign account into an Irish bank account; however the money can take a number of weeks to reach your account as cheques must be cleared with the paying bank. Note that personal cheques from foreign banks aren't accepted by retailers anywhere in Ireland unless they're Eurocheques supported by a Eurocheque card.

Eurogiros

A eurogiro, which is an electronic money transfer (normally taking four working days), allows the recipient to cash or bank up to €1,904.61 (don't ask why this amount) in his own currency without incurring any redemption fee. Eurogiros are currently issued in Belgium, France, Germany, Italy, Luxembourg, Spain, Switzerland and the UK.

Telegraphic Transfers

One of the fastest (it takes around ten minutes) and safest methods of transferring cash is by telegraphic transfer, e.g. Western Union, but it's also one of the most expensive with very high charges. Western Union will accept Visa or MasterCard, but not American Express. Amex card holders can use Amex's Moneygram service to transmit money to the nearest American Express office in Ireland in just 15 minutes.

Obtaining Cash

One of the simplest methods of obtaining (usually relatively small amounts) of cash is to draw on debit, credit or charge cards. Many foreigners living in Ireland (particularly retirees) keep the bulk of their money in a foreign account (perhaps in an offshore banking centre) and draw on it with a cash or credit card in Ireland. This is an ideal solution for holidaymakers and holiday homeowners (although homeowners still need an Irish bank account to pay their local bills).

Otherwise, most banks in major cities have foreign exchange windows where you can buy and sell foreign currencies and buy and cash travellers' cheques. Banks and building societies throughout Ireland have cash machines (automated teller machines or ATMs) and you can usually withdraw money directly from a foreign bank account using your usual debit or credit card.

Note that most banks charge around 1 per cent commission on foreign currency withdrawals with a minimum charge of €1 and a maximum of around €10. There are numerous private bureaux de change in Ireland (including most travel agents), but you should compare exchange rates and fees with banks before changing any money. Post offices, tourist information centres and some stores also provide a bureau de change service. Post offices tend to charge a slightly higher commission rate than banks, e.g. 1.5 per cent.

There are also exchange desks at Dublin, Shannon, Cork and Knock airports. Note that bureaux de change at airports and ports usually offer the worst exchange rates and charge the highest fees. The euro exchange rate for most European and major international currencies is listed in banks, post offices and daily newspapers, and announced on Irish radio and television. If you're changing a lot of money you may be able to negotiate a better exchange rate. Always shop around for the best rate and the lowest commission, as they can vary considerably.

There isn't a lot of difference in cost between buying Irish currency with cash, buying travellers' cheques (see below) or using a credit or debit card to obtain cash in Ireland. However, many people simply take cash when visiting Ireland, which is asking for trouble, particularly if you have no way of obtaining more money once you're there, e.g. with a credit card or travellers' cheques.

☑ **SURVIVAL TIP**

One thing to bear in mind when travelling anywhere, is not to rely on one source of funds only!

BANKS & BUILDING SOCIETIES

Financial services are regulated by the Central Bank of Ireland, the Department of Finance and the Department of Enterprise, Trade and

Employment. If you have a problem with a bank or building society that it cannot resolve to your satisfaction, you should contact the Financial Services Ombudsman's Bureau, 3rd Floor, Lincoln House, Lincoln Place, Dublin 2 (☎ 01-662 0899 or ☎ 1890-882090, 🖥 www.financialombudsman.ie) within 28 days of the date of your bank's final response.

When choosing a bank (or other institution) you should consider the convenience factor, e.g. how many branches it has, where you can use your ATM card and the international services provided. All banks and most building societies provide credit cards, most commonly Visa and MasterCard, but interest rates are steep (APRs usually start at 21 per cent). American Express and Diners' Club charge cards are also available, as is the US credit card MBNA, which provides more competitive rates, provided you keep the amount owed under control.

Irish Banks

All towns have at least one bank, which is generally housed in a town's most imposing building. There are seven Irish banks, as follows:

◆ **ACC Bank** – (🖥 www.accbank.ie) – around 40 branches;

◆ **Allied Irish Bank** – known as AIB (🖥 www.aib.ie) – around 300 branches;

◆ **Bank of Ireland** – (🖥 www.bankofireland.com) – around 300 branches;

◆ **First Active** – formerly the First National Building Society (🖥 www.firstactive.ie) – around 57 branches, including around 20 in Dublin;

◆ **National Irish Bank** – (🖥 www.nationalirishbank.ie) – 59 branches;

◆ **Permanent TSB Bank** – formerly Irish Permanent and TSB banks (🖥 www.permanenttsb.ie) – around 115 branches plus numerous agencies, where you can deposit or withdraw money, but cannot obtain other services;

◆ **Ulster Bank** – (🖥 www.ulsterbank.ie) – around 110 branches.

Allied Irish Bank, Bank of Ireland, the National Irish Bank and Ulster Bank are known as the Associated Banks, because they provide a clearing system for all other Irish banks. First Active and Ulster Bank are owned by the Royal Bank of Scotland, but operate independently.

Banking in Ireland is generally fairly non-bureaucratic, and branch managers have greater autonomy and authority than in many other countries (e.g. in granting or denying an overdraft facility or a loan). As elsewhere in the world, banking has become highly automated in recent years, and in terms of electronic services Irish banks are at least as sophisticated as those in other European countries.

Banks are usually open from 9.30 or 10am until 4pm (sometimes closing for an hour at lunchtime) on weekdays, with late opening until 5 or 5.30pm on one day (usually market day). In Dublin, for example, the banks close at 5pm on Thursdays, and the larger branches stay open during the lunch hour.

All the major banks now offer 24-hour telephone banking plus internet banking services (there are, as yet, no drive-in banks in Ireland!).

Bank Charges

Bank charges generally compare favourably with those in other European countries. As elsewhere, there's a trend towards increasing 'non-interest' income by levying charges against specific services while reducing net interest margins, i.e. the difference between the interest rate paid for deposits and the rate charged to borrowers. All the major banks make charges on personal as well as business accounts, although they vary from bank to bank (the charges listed below are based on those of AIB).

Government Charges: All banks are obliged to collect certain duties and fees from customers on behalf of the government. These include the following:

- **Cheques** – €0.30 per cheque;
- **ATM cards** – €5 per year per card;
- **Debit cards** – €5 per year per card if used either for withdrawing cash or for buying goods, €10 if used for both;
- **Credit cards** – €30 per year per account.

Account Fees: Certain types of account are 'fee free' and certain customers, including full-time students, graduates and those over 60 can apply for an exemption from account fees. In most cases, however, the following charges apply:

- **Maintenance** – €18 per year for the privilege of having an account;
- **Automated transactions** – €0.20 for each ATM withdrawal, standing order, direct debit, salary payment, internet or telephone transaction and debit card transaction;
- **Paper and 'staff-assisted' transactions** – €0.30 for each cheque processed and each over-the-counter withdrawal or deposit.
- **Bank service charges:** A variety of other charges apply for services above and beyond the call of duty, including the following:

  Duplicate statements – €2.54 per page
  Unpaid cheques, etc. – €7
  Bank drafts – €1.90 each
  Inter-bank transfers – €25.39 each
  Inter-branch transfers – €12.70 each

- **Non-euro ATM withdrawals** – currency conversion fee of up to 4 per cent plus a commission of 1 per cent (subject to a minimum of €1.27 and a maximum of €6.35);

- **Overdraft 'facility' fee** – €25.39 per year plus interest on the amount overdrawn; unauthorised overdrafts are penalised by high interest charges.

Foreign Banks

There are a number of foreign banks operating in Ireland, although fewer than in most other European countries, despite the fact that EU regulations now allow any bank trading in one EU country to trade in another. There are a dozen or so foreign banks in Dublin, although branches are rare in other cities. Most, however, offer corporate services only. Note also that foreign banks in Ireland operate in exactly the same way as Irish banks.

Building Societies

Ireland has only two building societies, which are mutual organisations supposedly run for the benefit of their members and not subject to the demands of shareholders.

- **Educational Building Society** – tautologically known as the EBS Building Society (💻 http://ww2.ebs.ie), with around 100 branches;

- **Irish Nationwide** (💻 www.irish-nationwide.com) – around 90 branches.

The ICS Building Society (part of the Bank of Ireland group) has become the Mortgage Store, offering only mortgage services, and there are rumours that the Irish Nationwide is to be sold and will no longer operate as a building society.

Building societies are open slightly longer hours than banks, generally from 9.30am to 5.30pm Mondays to Fridays (and in some cases also on Saturdays).

Increasingly, building societies are offering banking services and they generally don't make charges. However, you should check what kinds of account you can open.

Strictly speaking, building society accounts are savings accounts and not deposit accounts, although the Irish Nationwide calls two of its 'products' deposit accounts. This means that there may be a high minimum balance (e.g. €5,000 – which applies to all but one of the EBS's accounts) and you may not be issued with a cheque book. Interest earned on your account balance may be minimal (e.g. 0.5 per cent), unless you maintain a high balance.

Credit Unions

Another kind of financial institution is the credit union, a non-profit, community-based, co-operative organisation offering loans and savings facilities. Interest rates on loans tend to be quite low, while the rates on savings can be as high as those of a conventional bank. However, credit unions don't offer long-term loans or mortgages. Opening times vary, but all credit unions open on some evenings and some also open on Saturday mornings. There are over 500 credit unions and you should enquire locally for the names and addresses of your nearest branches. Further information on credit unions can be obtained from the Irish League of Credit Unions (☎ 01-614 6700, 🖳 www.creditunion.ie).

Post Office Banking

An Post, the Irish postal service, offers a more or less full banking service, including a range of savings and investment schemes, and their savings products have the advantage of being state-guaranteed. Also in their favour is the large number of 'branches' throughout the country. Further information about An Post's financial services can be obtained by phone or email (☎ 01-705 7200 or ☎ 1850-305060, ✉ savings@anpost.ie) or via the website (🖳 www.anpost.ie).

Opening an Account

You can open a bank account in Ireland whether you're a resident or a non-resident, and the procedure for doing so is the same; but residents are subject to tax on all interest earned whereas non-residents are entitled to earn interest on deposits free of Irish tax. It's best to open an Irish bank account in person, rather than by correspondence from abroad. In fact, most Irish banks will insist on seeing you in person before they will open an account for you.

Ask your friends, neighbours or colleagues for their recommendations and simply go along to the bank of your choice and introduce yourself. You must be aged at least 18 and provide two forms of identification (including one with a photograph, such as a passport), plus proof of residence in Ireland (e.g. a recent utility bill) if applicable. It's best to set up an account before moving to Ireland so that you can transfer funds in advance. It's also sensible to keep an account open in the country you're leaving, to deal with final bills and unexpected expenses.

If you need to open an account with an Irish bank from abroad, you must first obtain an application form, available from foreign branches of Irish banks or direct from banks in Ireland. You will want to select a branch near to where you will be living in Ireland. If you open an account by correspondence, you need to provide evidence of your place of residence and, if you're depositing a large sum of money, confirmation of where the funds originated.

Credit rating is calculated differently in Ireland from other countries, and you should supply as much information as possible about your financial status in your present country of residence.

If you're leaving a country where credit rating is important, such as the US, and to which you may return later, it's worth asking your bank or credit card company if you can maintain a credit card rating while resident abroad, as credit cards invoiced in Europe won't show in credit records in the US.

The Irish Credit Bureau (ICB, ☎ 01-260 0388, 🖥 www.icb.ie) is a private company operating a credit referencing system. For a small fee (€6) you can obtain a copy of your credit report, and challenge or request clarification of any details you believe to be incorrect or potentially misleading.

Non-residents

Since Ireland became a full member of the European Union (EU), banking regulations for both resident and non-resident EU citizens have been identical, so that even non-resident EU citizens may open a euro account. Although it's possible for non-resident homeowners to do most of their banking via a foreign account using debit and credit cards, you will still need an Irish bank account to pay your Irish utility and tax bills (which are best paid by direct debit). If you have a holiday home in Ireland, you can have all your correspondence (e.g. cheque books, statements, payment advices, etc.) sent to an address abroad.

Most banks offer non-resident savings accounts in which you can deposit money in virtually any major currency without incurring handling or administrative charges. To open a non-resident savings account, you need to provide proof of identity or a reference from your current bank. Non-residents can have interest paid gross in Ireland, provided that the relevant documentation has been completed. You may, however, have tax liabilities in your home country on income earned in Ireland.

Residents

You're considered to be a resident of Ireland if you have your main centre of interest there, i.e. if you live and work there more or less permanently. Even when you're resident, it isn't advisable to close your bank accounts abroad unless you're certain you won't need them in the future, and it's cheaper to keep money in local currency in an account in a country you visit regularly (such as the UK), rather than pay commission to convert euros. Many foreigners living in Ireland maintain at least two cheque (current) accounts: a foreign account for international and large transactions, and a local account with an Irish bank for day-to-day business.

MORTGAGES

Mortgages or home loans (for both residents and non-residents) are usually obtained from Irish banks and building societies. The Irish Mortgage Council (IMC), established in 2003, represents the 12 major mortgage lenders, who share over 95 per cent of the mortgage market and fund over 50,000 mortgages every year. Mortgages are also available from foreign banks in Ireland and offshore banks, some of which offer attractive packages. Bank of Scotland, for example, 'give' borrowers €1,000 towards legal fees and €150 towards valuation costs. However, if you raise a mortgage outside Ireland for an Irish property, you should be aware of any impact this may have on your foreign or Irish tax liabilities or allowances.

As a result of increased competition, lenders have tended to relax their criteria for borrowing, in recent years. Whereas previously you needed to be a long-term saver with a building society, you can now literally walk in off the street and, provided you have the required income, take out a mortgage with more or less any institution.

Mortgages are based on the lending institution's valuation, which is usually below the market value of the property. Until recently, the maximum mortgage in Ireland was 90 per cent of valuation, but with ever-increasing property prices lenders have started offering 95 and even 100 per cent mortgages (although there's usually a limit of 70 per cent for non-residents), subject to certain conditions – principally a clean credit history, a high income and evidence that you can repay the loan over the agreed term. (There are currently five lenders offering 100 per cent mortgages.) Note, however, that the amount you **may** borrow isn't necessarily the same as the amount you **can** borrow (i.e. can afford to repay)!

Most institutions will lend up to 250 per cent of annual income in the case of sole applicants or 250 per cent of the main income plus 100 per cent of the second income in the case of joint applicants (e.g. a husband and wife). For example, if one partner is earning €40,000 per year and the other €25,000, the maximum loan will be €125,000. The minimum cash deposit required on agreeing to buy a property is usually 10 per cent of the purchase price, although a 5 per cent deposit is often accepted. Repayments are usually made monthly, but can be made weekly, fortnightly, quarterly or even annually.

Mortgage Term

The normal mortgage term is 15 years, although mortgages can be repaid over as little as five years or up to 35 years.

▲ Caution

Bear in mind that, although a longer term may seem attractive because you pay less each year, you end up paying far more in total, owing to the increased interest charges.

In any case, some institutions impose a shorter maximum repayment period on non-residents.

Types of Mortgage

There's a variety of mortgages available in Ireland. The most straightforward is a repayment or 'annuity' mortgage, which is effectively a simple loan which you pay off monthly. In the early stages, a high proportion of your payments are taken up by the interest on the loan; as the amount you owe is reduced, you begin to pay off more of the capital. This type of mortgage is particularly attractive to first-time buyers because of the tax relief they can obtain on mortgage interest (see **Fees & Tax Relief** on page 281) – a benefit which is greatest during the first few years when buyers are most likely to be short of cash.

With a repayment mortgage, you usually have a choice between fixed rate repayments over a variable term and variable rate repayments over a fixed term. With the former method, the amount repaid each month remains constant regardless of fluctuations in interest rates, but the number of monthly payments varies (if interest rates go up, the term lengthens and vice versa). With the latter method, the reverse applies: the number of repayments is fixed, but the amount repaid each month varies with the prevailing interest rate. If interest rates are falling or stable, a variable mortgage is generally reckoned to be the better option. Around 70 per cent of Irish mortgages are currently variable.

There are advantages and disadvantages to each option and sometimes it's possible to have the best of both worlds. For example, you can fix the interest rate for a limited period only (usually up to ten years). Some banks offer split or combination interest rates, whereby part of the loan is repayable at a fixed rate and part at a variable rate. A type of variable mortgage is a 'tracker' mortgage, whose rate is linked to the European Central Bank base rate (known as 'euribor'), e.g. euribor plus 1 per cent.

Another option, which is becoming more common, is a capped rate mortgage, whereby you pay a premium to guarantee that your mortgage rate won't rise above the rate originally fixed. You can, of course, always increase the amount you repay each month or year, either as a fixed percentage or by lump sum payments. Needless to say, few people do! Note that, if you opt for a fixed rate mortgage or one where the rate of increase is limited, you may incur a redemption fee if you sell the property and redeem the loan (or part of it) before the end of the term. Similarly, if you

no repayments for the first one to three months of the term, is available only with repayment mortgages; a 'flexible month', whereby you don't make a repayment for one or two months of the year, but pay correspondingly more in the remaining months, is available with repayment and endowment mortgages, although the endowment element must be paid each month; a 'mortgage break' allows you to suspend your repayments for up to three months of a year (this can be done up to four times, making a total break of 12 months, but the mortgage must still be repaid within the original term).

Always shop around for the best offer (or engage a mortgage broker to do it for you) and ask for the effective interest rate, including all commissions and fees.

Rates

In 2008, the lowest annual percentage rate (APR) was around 4.67 per cent – for a 'tracker' mortgage – and the highest around 5.52 per cent – for a ten-year fixed-rate mortgage. A variable mortgage was at around 5.36 per cent.

Commercial Property

If you're purchasing commercial premises, the mortgage procedure is essentially the same as with a normal home loan, but the lending criteria are usually slightly different and it's generally less straightforward. Whereas you may be able to borrow 100 per cent of the value of a residential property, for example, you're usually limited to 75 per cent in the case of commercial property. If you're self-employed, you must usually provide a copy of your accounts or, in the case of a new business, a business plan in support of a mortgage application. If you're buying a residential property for letting, you must usually take out a commercial loan unless you opt for a fixed rate for ten years.

Mortgage Application

Mortgages are usually applied for locally. If you live abroad or in a different part of Ireland from where the property you're planning to buy is situated, you must submit written confirmation that you have employment in the area where

decide to switch from a fixed rate to a variable rate before the end of the fixed rate period, you may need to pay a 'funding fee'.

Another option is an endowment mortgage, which combines the mortgage repayment with savings through a life assurance policy; by the end of the mortgage term, the value of the endowment policy should have grown sufficiently to repay the mortgage and may leave you with a surplus. On the other hand, there's no guarantee that the proceeds of the policy will be sufficient to repay the mortgage loan and you risk being left with a substantial deficit (as many UK homeowners are discovering to their cost!). Endowment mortgages landed thousands of people in debt when interest rates plummeted in the late '90s, and they're now seldom offered.

Banks offer other schemes from time to time, as well as more sophisticated options such as pension mortgages, which are available only to those who are self-employed or work for a company that doesn't offer an occupational pension scheme. A pension mortgage operates in essentially the same way as an endowment mortgage: your monthly repayments cover only the interest on the loan, while separate payments are made into a personal pension plan. At the end of the mortgage term the proceeds of the pension plan pay off the capital, and the surplus provides you with a retirement income (you hope!).

Lenders offer variations on standard mortgages to attract customers (particularly first-time buyers), including the following: a 'deferred start' mortgage, whereby you make the property is located. If you're an employee on Pay As You Earn (PAYE), you will need to provide a copy of your most recent P60 or PAYE balancing statement, and a letter from your employer confirming your basic salary and your employment status. If you've been with your present employer for less than a year, you will need a reference from your previous employer. If you're self-employed, a copy of your audited accounts for the last three years will be required, with a letter from your accountant confirming that your tax affairs are in order.

If you're buying a house which is under construction, detailed plans, specifications and a site map need to be submitted. You will also need to produce the original National House Building Guarantee Scheme Certificate (HB47), which will be provided by the builder, or (if you're employing a builder directly) a letter from an architect confirming that he will supervise the construction, and certify compliance with planning permission and building regulations.

In all cases, you must also produce details of any outstanding loans, including your most recent annual bank statement showing all payments made to date, estimates for any proposed work to be done on the property (which should also be taken account of when making the valuation) and any documents relating to separation or divorce (if applicable).

Guarantor

If you don't meet the lender's criteria for a mortgage, you may be able to use a guarantor, which is usually a parent or close relative, who undertakes to make any payments you cannot. Some lenders insist that a guarantor guarantees the full loan amount, others only the difference between what is owed and what is paid.

⚠ Caution

Appointing a guarantor can lead to difficult family relationships if repayment problems arise!

Fees & Tax Relief

A number of fees can apply to a mortgage, including an application fee and an indemnity fee (if you borrow more than a certain percentage of the value of a property), although with increasing competition in the mortgage market, most lenders have waived fees and even offer 'cash' incentives to applicants.

Tax relief is available on mortgage interest payments (i.e. not on the loan itself) and is normally deducted at source by your lender. Tax relief is at 20 per cent, irrespective of your tax bracket, and is limited to annual interest payments of €10,000 per person (€20,000 for a widow or widower), i.e. €2,000 (or €4,000) of tax relief, for first-time buyers, and €3,000 per person (or €6,000 for a widow/widower) for other borrowers. There may also be a term limit (e.g. seven years for first-time buyers). Note, however, that the government plans to phase out all property-related tax relief and to cap total individual tax relief.

Mortgage Protection

You must normally obtain life assurance before your lender will agree to advance your mortgage; a mortgage protection policy is usually the minimum cover required. There are various plans available, costing between around €10 and €250 per month depending on your age, the mortgage term, the amount borrowed and other factors.

Buying Through a Broker

Between 30 and 40 per cent of all new mortgages in Ireland, plus an increasing proportion of re-mortgages and investment mortgages, are arranged through mortgage brokers (also known as 'advisers'), over 80 of whom (representing some 60 per cent of the mortgage broking market) belong to the Independent Mortgage Advisers' Federation (IMAF, ☎ 01-639 4064 or ☎ 1850-462323, www.imaf.ie). Whereas a broker may represent as few as two lenders, IMAF members must represent at least five, giving you a better choice of mortgages.

Using a broker saves you time and trouble shopping around, and some even provide a form-filling service, so that all you need to do is sign on the dotted line. If you're self-employed and derive your income from various sources, you may find it easier to obtain a mortgage through a broker rather than direct from a bank or building society. Note, however, that some brokers 'favour' certain lenders, as banks and building societies pay different commission rates (from nothing to one and a half per cent) for the business brokers introduce.

A few estate agents (such as Sherry FitzGerald) have their own brokerage service. Hooke & MacDonald owns 50 per cent of the Irish Mortgage Corporation, one of Ireland's bigger brokers, which also provides life and pensions advisory services, in addition to a tax consultancy. Such arrangements offer the advantage of a 'one-stop shop' for homebuyers and investors, and in some cases offer a better chance of obtaining mortgage approval before viewing properties, so that meaningful offers can be made on the spot, but they won't necessarily give you the best deal.

Mortgages for Second Homes

If you have spare equity in an existing property, either in Ireland or abroad, it may be more cost-effective to re-mortgage that property (or take out a second mortgage on it) than take out a new mortgage for a second home. It involves less paperwork and therefore lower legal fees, and a plan can be tailored to your requirements. Depending on the equity in your existing property and the cost of your Irish property, this may enable you to pay cash for a second home or take out an unsecured personal loan. The disadvantage of re-mortgaging or taking out a second mortgage is that you reduce the amount of equity available in a property.

> If you do take out a second mortgage, you will need to provide a recent statement from your existing mortgage lender. If you've paid off the mortgage on your existing property, you will be able to 'cross-secure' a loan on a second home.

If you let your second home, you may be able to offset the interest on your mortgage against letting income. For example, if you let an Irish property for three months of the year, the income will offset a quarter of your annual mortgage interest.

Foreign Currency Loans

It's possible to obtain a foreign (i.e. not Irish) currency mortgage, e.g. in pounds sterling, Swiss francs, US dollars or even 'exotic' currencies such as Japanese yen. This is an extremely risky way to borrow money, as interest rate gains can be wiped out overnight by currency swings. On the other hand, if the currency happens to be devalued, the rewards can be huge. Anyone who took out a yen loan a few years ago, for example, is now benefiting from its 20 per cent devaluation.

You may also pay lower interest rates, depending on the currency. Now that Ireland is a euro economy, however, foreign currency loans are generally less attractive, as only a few countries – such as Japan and Switzerland – may offer lower rates. If you do decide to take out a foreign currency loan, experts advise that it's in the currency in which you're paid. When choosing between an Irish currency loan and a foreign currency loan, make sure that you take into account all costs, fees, interest rates and possible currency fluctuations. Note that, if you have a foreign currency mortgage, you must usually pay commission charges each time you transfer foreign currency into euros and remit money to Ireland, and that most banks 'load' foreign currency loans (e.g. charge high fees). Irrespective of how you finance the purchase of a home in Ireland, you should always obtain professional advice.

Payment Problems & Changing Lenders

If you're unable to meet your mortgage payments, lenders are usually willing to re-schedule your mortgage so that it extends over a longer period, thus allowing you to make lower payments. Note that, if you simply stop paying your mortgage, your lender will embargo your property and could eventually repossess it and sell it at auction.

If you want to change lenders, you may be offered an incentive to do so by an institution that's keen to have your business, although this isn't common in Ireland. Also bear in mind that, if you make a change, you will usually incur solicitor's fees, and no lender will offer to pay those for you! Finally, note that when a mortgage is taken out on an Irish property, it's based on the property and not on the individual, so it isn't possible to take over (assume) an existing mortgage from a previous owner or pass your mortgage on when you sell a property.

INCOME TAX

Ireland is divided into four Revenue districts for tax purposes, as follows:

- **Border Midlands West** – Counties Cavan, Donegal, Galway, Leitrim, Longford, Louth, Mayo, Monaghan, Offaly, Roscommon, Sligo and Westmeath (☎ 1890-777425);

- **Dublin** – City and County (☎ 1890-333425);

- **East & South East** – Counties Carlow, Kildare, Kilkenny, Laois, Meath, Tipperary, Waterford, Wexford and Wicklow (☎ 1890-444425);

- **South West** – Counties Clare, Cork, Kerry and Limerick (☎ 1890-222425).

From outside Ireland, call ☎ +33 1-647 4444 for all offices. Other contact details can be found on the Revenue Commissioners website (🖥 www.revenue.ie). If you have a query regarding tax payment, tax relief or mortgage interest, you should contact the relevant office of the Collector General (also listed on the above site).

Liability

In general, liability for Irish taxes depends on your residence status.

You're considered resident in Ireland for tax purposes if you spend 183 or more days there in a tax year or 280 days in two consecutive tax years. (But if you're in Ireland for 30 days or less in either of those years, they won't count towards the 280 days.)

You become 'ordinarily resident' when you've been resident for three consecutive tax years. If Ireland is considered to be your permanent home, you're said to be 'domiciled' there (this is distinct from your legal

nationality and your residence status). You may choose to be treated as an Irish resident from the date of your arrival if you intend to remain in Ireland permanently and you think it will be to your tax advantage (you need to satisfy the Inspector of Taxes that you will be resident the following year). Note that the 183-day rule also applies to other EU countries and many countries (e.g. the UK) limit visits by non-residents to 182 days in any one year or an average of 90 days per tax year over a four-year period.

If you're returning to Ireland and you're both resident and domiciled in the year of your return, you will be liable to Irish income tax on all your income. However, if you've spent fewer than 183 days in Ireland during the previous year and therefore aren't resident, your employment income earned before your return will be exempt, although your non-employment income may be taxable.

Note that Irish residents are liable to tax on both Irish source income and foreign income (including foreign pension income) and that the latter is also liable for taxation in the foreign country. However, Ireland has double taxation agreements with 34 countries (see below), therefore you will obtain relief if your country of residence is among them.

If you take up employment on your return to Ireland, but haven't worked there since the start of the current tax year, you will need to complete Form 12A, which is available from a tax office or your employer. If you intend to reside in Ireland, you will probably receive

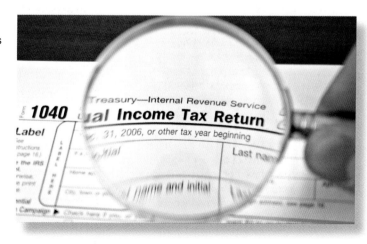

the full income tax allowance, but if you start work part way through the tax year intending only to stay a few months, you may be restricted to a temporary or emergency tax allowance (see above).

If you're a tax resident in two countries simultaneously, your 'tax home' may be determined by the rules applied under international treaties. Under such treaties you're considered to be resident in the country where you have a permanent home; if you have a permanent home in both countries, you're deemed to be resident in the country where your personal and economic ties are closer.

If your residence cannot be determined under this rule, you're deemed to be resident in the country where you have an habitual abode. If you have an habitual abode in both or neither country, you're deemed to be resident in the country of which you're a citizen. Finally, if you're a citizen of both or neither country, the authorities of the countries concerned will decide your tax residence between them!

If you intend to live permanently in Ireland, you should notify the tax authorities in your previous country of residence. You may be entitled to a tax refund if you depart during the tax year, which usually necessitates completing a tax return. The authorities may require evidence that you're leaving the country, e.g. evidence of a job in Ireland or of having bought or rented a property there. If you move to Ireland to take up a job or start a business, you must register with the local tax authorities soon after your arrival.

> ## ☑ SURVIVAL TIP
>
> If you're able to choose the country where you're taxed, you should obtain advice from an international tax expert. Paying Irish income tax can even be advantageous, as there are more allowances for some people than there are in many other countries.

Double Taxation

Irish residents are taxed on their worldwide income, subject to certain treaty exceptions (non-residents are taxed only on income arising in Ireland). Citizens of most countries are exempt from paying taxes in their home country when they spend a minimum period abroad, e.g. one year.

Double-taxation treaties are designed to ensure that income that has been taxed in one treaty country isn't taxed again in Ireland.

The treaty establishes a tax credit or exemption on certain kinds of income, either in the country of residence or the country where the income is earned. Ireland has double-taxation agreements with the following countries: Australia, Austria, Belgium, Bulgaria, Canada, China, Cyprus, the Czech Republic, Denmark, Estonia, Finland, France, Germany, Hungary, India, Israel, Italy, Japan, the Republic of Korea, Latvia, Lithuania, Luxembourg, Malaysia, Mexico, the Netherlands, New Zealand, Norway, Pakistan, Poland, Portugal, Romania, Russia, Slovakia, South Africa, Spain, Sweden, Switzerland, the UK, the US and Zambia.

Some of these agreements have recently been or are in the process of being re-negotiated (e.g. those with Canada and France), so you should check the current position before making any tax-related decisions. A number of new treaties are being negotiated, e.g. with Croatia, Egypt, Iceland, Singapore, Slovenia, Turkey and Ukraine. Copies of existing double-taxation agreements are available on the Revenue website (💻 www.revenue.ie – type in 'double-taxation agreements' in the search facility at the top of the home page).

Even when there's no double-taxation agreement between Ireland and your country of residence, you can still obtain relief from double taxation. In these cases, overseas tax may be deducted as an expense, but there are certain qualifying criteria. Note that if your tax liability in another country is lower than that in Ireland, you must pay the Irish Revenue Commissioners the difference. If you're in doubt about your tax liability in your home country, contact your nearest embassy or consulate in Ireland. The US is the only country that taxes its non-resident citizens on income earned abroad (US citizens can obtain a copy of a brochure, *Tax Guide for Americans Abroad*, from American consulates).

Leaving Ireland

When leaving Ireland, foreigners must pay any tax due for the previous year and the year of departure. A tax return can be filed before or

however, you could be paying tax at a mere 12.5 per cent or even at just 10 per cent (see **Corporation Tax** on page 291). This means that there can be a considerable tax advantage in operating a business through a company instead of as an individual.

Irish income tax is payable on both earned and unearned income. Taxable income includes salaries, pensions, capital gains, property and investment income (dividends and interest), and income from professional or business activities. It also includes employee perks such as overseas and cost of living allowances; contributions to profit sharing plans; bonuses (annual, performance, etc.); benefits in kind (such as a company car, preferential loan, health insurance, club subscriptions, free accommodation or meals); stock options; home leave or holidays (paid by your employer); children's private education; and storage and relocation allowances. Note that if you're returning to Ireland and your employer is paying your relocation expenses, you will need a tax exemption for these payments from the Inspector of Taxes.

Pension Income

Pension income is generally taxable in the same way as other income (there are certain exemptions for non-resident pensioners). Occupational pensions are usually taxed at source, but all other pensions must be declared on your annual tax return.

Property Income

Your liability to income tax on income earned from property investment or letting depends on your residence status, as follows:

♦ **Residents** – Property income earned by residents should be included in their annual income tax declaration, and tax is payable at their standard income tax rate. You're eligible for deductions such as repairs and maintenance, security, cleaning costs, management and letting expenses (e.g. advertising) and insurance, but can no longer claim a deduction for mortgage interest on a let property. You should seek professional advice to ensure that you're claiming everything to which you're entitled.

after departure and must include your income and deductions from the start of the tax year in the year of departure up to the date of departure. When departure is made before the start of the tax year, the previous year's taxes are applied. If this results in overpayment, a claim must be made for a refund. A tax clearance certificate isn't required before leaving Ireland.

Taxable Income

Employees' income tax is deducted at source by employers, and individuals aren't responsible for paying their own income tax, unless they have other sources of income. Self-employed people are liable to tax in the same way as employees, but it's collected differently and there are different rules regarding allowable expenses. If you're self-employed, you won't need to pay income tax until after your first year of trading. Two months before the year's end, you are sent a preliminary tax notice informing you when your first payment is due.

As a sole trader you pay income tax at the same rates as PAYE employees, but based on your net annual profit (i.e. after the deduction of legitimate expenses). If you're operating as a limited company,

- **Non-residents** – Non-resident property owners in Ireland are liable for income tax on income arising in Ireland, including income from letting a property (whether long-term or holiday letting). Because they aren't part of the self-assessment system, tax must be deducted at source. This means that where rent is paid directly to a non-resident, income tax at the standard rate (20 per cent) should be deducted by the tenant. You can reclaim tax if the amount deducted is greater than your Irish tax liability on the net profit from the rent. If you appoint an agent to collect rent on your behalf, the agent is responsible for paying the tax rather than the tenant.

Exemptions

There's no longer a tax exemption for people under 65, all of whose earnings are subject to income tax. Those over 65, however, are exempt from tax on the first €20,000 of their income.

Other exemptions include the following:

- **Maintenance payments** – If you're an unmarried parent and receive maintenance for your child, you don't have to pay tax on it.

- **Rent-a-room scheme** – If you let a room in your home, the first €10,000 rental income is exempt from tax.

- **Royalties** – In most cases, artists, writers and sports stars don't pay tax on their royalties.

- **Redundancy & retirement lump sums** – If your employment is terminated (e.g. by redundancy) and a payment is made to you, this may be exempt from tax. Statutory redundancy payments are exempt, as are ex-gratia payments on redundancy or retirement of up to €10,160 (plus €765 for each complete year of service) and immediate or deferred lump sums from a Revenue approved pension scheme. Ex-gratia payments made in connection with the death or injury of an employee are also tax exempt, as are certain compensation payments for salary reductions resulting from company restructuring schemes. However, the taxable element of ex-gratia payments is subject to PRSI at 2 per cent. Exemptions don't apply to retirement pension payments, which are taxed as income.

- **Businesses** – There are also various tax incentives and reliefs for companies, such as the Business Expansion Scheme (BES) relief, research and development incentives, and film investment relief.

 Caution

There are tax penalties for closely controlled family owned companies ('close' companies) if excess funds are allowed to build up.

If your business is expected to make a loss in its early stages, it may be better to operate initially as a sole trader, because losses can be offset against income from other sources (if you have any) and you can then establish a company without immediately incurring high taxes. In terms of individual income, there's a tax advantage in taking a dividend rather than a salary from the business, but the total tax paid by the individual and the company will be greater, as salary payments are tax deductible for corporation tax purposes.

Allowances

Before you become liable for income tax, you're entitled to certain allowances (also referred to as reliefs). For private individuals, these include the following:

- certain medical expenses, including certain dental and optical treatment;

- mortgage interest payments (see **Fees & Tax Relief** on page 281);

- payments to a permanent health or long-term care insurance scheme (up to 10 per cent of your income), the tax normally being deducted at source – life insurance premiums are no longer tax deductible;

- pension contributions;

- the cost of maintaining a guide dog;

- the cost of employing a carer for an incapacitated relative;

- rent of up to €4,000, if you're 55 or older.

For businesses, allowances include expenses incurred 'wholly and exclusively for the purposes of the trade' (e.g. capital expenditure, insurance, accountancy and staff entertainment). For employees and the self-employed, the amount of expenses you can claim depends on your job; a list is published by the Revenue Commissioners (the only example given on the Revenue's website is for airline cabin crew, who can claim an annual allowance of ... wait for it ... €64 – just about enough for dinner in Dubrovnik!).

Your total earnings less allowances is your 'taxable income', on which your social insurance (PRSI – see page 248) contributions and government levies are calculated. The tax due on this amount is called your 'gross tax' and from this you may then deduct tax credits (see below) to arrive at your net tax liability. (In order to equalise the value of tax reductions among all taxpayers, the government has reclassified many allowances as credits.)

Tax Rates

Taxable income (i.e. earnings above the exemption less allowances) is taxed at 20 per cent up to €35,400 for individuals (€39,400 for single parents) – known as the 'standard cut-off point' – and thereafter at 41 per cent. For married couples with a single income the cut-off point is €44,400; in the case of married couples with two incomes, this cut-off point is raised to €70,800 or the amount of the lower income, whichever is less. For example, if one spouse earns €50,000 and the other €20,000, the total income is taxed at 20 per cent; if one spouse earns €50,000 and the other €30,000, however, the 20 per cent tax rate applies only to €70,800, the remainder being taxed at 41 per cent.

If you take up employment in Ireland without a P45 or a PPS number (see page 250), you will be charged 'emergency tax', whereby you're entitled to minimal credits.

Note that if you lose your P45, a copy may not be made and the necessary information must be sent by your employer to the Revenue Commissioners. If you're a director of a limited company, you must submit a P45 or P46 to the tax office yourself.

Credits

You can deduct from your gross tax figure certain credits (confusingly also referred to as 'reliefs'), including the following:

♦ **Personal credits** – Everyone qualifies for a personal tax credit (formerly a personal allowance), which is €1,830 per person (i.e. €3,660 for a couple) except a widow(er) without dependent children, who is entitled to a credit of €2,430. If you're a single parent, you can claim double the normal personal credit (i.e. €3,660). There are additional credits for widowed parents and those with disabled children or other dependent relatives.

♦ **Disabled people** – Credits can be claimed by people with certain disabilities, e.g. those with restricted sight, who may claim €1,830.

♦ **Age credit** – If you or your spouse is 65 or over, you're entitled to a credit of €325 per person in addition to your personal credit. You may also reclaim any Deposit interest retention tax (DIRT) paid (see page 292); in fact, if you notify the relevant financial institution, your interest will be paid gross (i.e. no DIRT will be deducted at source).

♦ **Dependent relative** – If you're caring for an elderly or infirm relative, you can claim a credit of €80.

♦ **Nursing home fees** – Tax relief is available on the cost of a nursing home for a relative.

♦ **PAYE credit** – All employees in the PAYE system are entitled to a credit of €1,830. If

you're married and taxed according to joint assessment, both you and your spouse can claim a PAYE tax credit.

♦ **Trade union credit** – You can claim a credit of up to €70 in respect of trade union membership fees.

♦ **Employment benefits credits** – Most employment benefits (i.e. 'payments in kind', such as a company car) are taxable, but some can be claimed as a tax credit, including equipment supplied and expenses paid by an employer to enable you to work from home. If you're resident in Ireland, but commute to a place of work in another country, you can claim Trans-border Worker's Relief to compensate for tax paid in the other country.

♦ **Home improvements** – If you borrow money to repair or improve your home, you may be eligible for tax relief on the loan interest.

♦ **Service charges** – Tax relief is available if you pay charges for refuse collection, sewage disposal or domestic water supplies.

♦ **Higher education tuition fees** – Tax relief up to €5,000 is available on higher education tuition fees, provided the course is for at least two years and in an 'approved' institution.

Other credits include those due following separation or divorce or a death.

Any personal income taxes paid in another country can also be deducted from your tax base under double taxation agreements (see **Double Taxation** on page 284). Note, however, that if you pay higher tax abroad than would have been paid in Ireland, you won't receive a rebate from the Irish tax authorities!

Tax Returns & Payment

Tax returns must be submitted by both residents and non-residents with income in Ireland, unless they're on PAYE and have no other source of income The Irish tax year runs from 1st January to 31st December (it was changed from April/March in 2001). You must file a tax return and pay any tax due (known quaintly as the 'pay and file' system) by 31st October (known as the 'specified return date'). By this date you must pay your estimate of tax ('preliminary tax') for the current tax year, the balance of tax due for the previous year and any capital gains tax (see page 293) due for the period 1st January to 30th September of the current tax year. Note that this is the **latest date** for paying and filing.

Preliminary tax is an estimate of the income tax you will be charged in the current tax year and includes PRSI and the Health Contribution.

To avoid interest charges you must pay 90 per cent of your liability for the current year or 100 per cent of your previous year's tax bill or 105 per cent of your bill from the year before that (this last option is available only if you pay by direct debit), whichever is the lowest amount. If you don't pay preliminary tax on the due date, you are charged interest on the amount due at 1 per cent per month.

Companies liable to corporation tax must pay income tax and advance corporation tax (ACT), as well as preliminary tax on their profits, within six months of their accounting year end and make a final tax return within nine months. Close companies must account for distribution of profits within 18 months of their year end in order to avoid a close company surcharge. Claims for

excess capital allowances, trading and rental losses, and group or consortium relief must be submitted within two years of the end of the relevant accounting year. Final ACT adjustments must also be made by then.

Tax forms can be obtained only from tax offices in Ireland. If you're self-employed or a company director, you should use form 11; PAYE employees and pensioners should complete form 12 and first-time workers form 12A. Form 1 is for partnerships and Form CT1 for companies. A complete list of forms and their functions can be found on the Revenue website.

If you submit your return by 31st August, you will be sent a final tax assessment for the previous year before the 'pay and file' deadline of 31st October and can therefore be sure that you're paying the right amount; otherwise you must calculate it yourself (or pay an accountant to do so) and hope that you're right! Another option is to file your tax return online using the Revenue's 'ROS' system, which has the advantage that the amount of tax you owe is calculated for you instantly! You need to register for the system, however, which can take up to two weeks, as certain passwords must be sent to you through the post.

If you need help in completing your tax return, you can contact the central information office of the Revenue Commissioners (☎ 01-679 2777 or ☎ 1890-605090) or your tax office (there are 13 provincial tax offices, listed in the green pages of the phone book). Note, however, that this won't necessarily be the office in the area where you live. If you're an employee of a company whose headquarters is in another part of the country, for example, your tax office will be the one in that area.

If you wish to see an inspector, you should make an appointment, but general assistance is always available (staff will even help you complete your tax form!). When you go to the tax office, you should take along some form of identification (if you're a non-resident), your PPS number, your P45 (if appropriate) and any forms you've received from the Revenue Commissioners. It isn't necessary to take other documentation (such as rent books) unless requested to do so.

There are penalties for being late with either your tax return or your payments, and you can be fined up to €1,500 if you fail to produce the required documents or (either negligently or fraudulently) make a false declaration of your income. If you falsify your tax return in order to reduce your tax liability, you can be imprisoned for up to 12 months and will be fined up to twice the amount owing. If you fail to pay the fine, you can be imprisoned for up to eight years.

⚠ Caution

The Revenue Commissioners can publish a list of names of people who have been fined or imprisoned for tax evasion.

They also carry out regular checks (called 'revenue audits') to ensure that everyone is paying the correct amount of tax. A cross-section of returns is selected, as well as a certain number at random. From time to time, particular trades or professions are targeted for audit.

Before submitting your tax return, you should check that you've completed all the sections (where you have no income in a particular category, you should write 'none' rather than leave it blank). If you're claiming mortgage interest relief, you should enter the loan account number of your lender and attach your mortgage interest certificate stating the amount paid during the last tax year, as well as an estimate of the interest payable in the following year. Tax forms include customised pay slips showing your PPS number, tax type, etc., which must be returned with the tax form, even if you're making a nil return. You should also include copies of the following documents:

◆ form P60;

◆ form P45 if you've ceased employment;

◆ details of any benefit in kind (especially a company car);

◆ if you're receiving any social welfare income, a statement from the Department of Social and Family Affairs confirming the kind of income, the date payment began and the weekly amount;

◆ details of any rent paid (which should be entered on form 'Rent 1');

◆ if you're receiving rental income, a detailed account of gross rent and expenses such as furniture on which you may be entitled to a wear and tear allowance;

- details of any acquisitions and disposals of assets during the tax year which may be liable for capital gains tax;

- documentation relating to government stocks, rents and other income;

- the relevant claim form if you're claiming a dependent relative allowance for the first time;

- details of any allowable medical and dental expenses, which should be entered on forms 'Med 1' and 'Med 2' respectively;

- confirmation of any private health insurance subscriptions paid during the previous tax year;

- receipts for private tuition if appropriate;

- certificates of private pension contributions;

If you're a company or a sole trader, you also need to submit;

- a trading account showing details of sales and profit/loss for the tax year;

- a profit and loss account;

- a capital account;

- a balance sheet showing business assets and liabilities.

Finally, make sure that you sign the form!

There are a number of ways of paying your income tax in Ireland:

- **by cheque** – (payable to the Collector-General) posted to the Collector-General's Office using the pre-paid envelope provided with your tax form; note that a cheque is cashed on receipt;

- **by single debit authority** – (SDA) as above, the advantage being that an SDA isn't debited until the due date (i.e. 31st October);

- **in person** – at the Collector-General's Office, Apollo House, Tara Street, Dublin 2 or Sarsfield House, Francis Street, Limerick;

- **by bank giro** – (obligatory for payments of preliminary tax, VAT and employer's PAYE/PRSI);

- **online** – at the Revenue's website (💻 www.revenue.ie), either using a debit card or

setting up a debit instruction; if you have an account with AIB or Bank of Ireland, you can arrange payment directly from your account.

Further information about tax calculation and payment can be obtained from the Revenue website (💻 www.revenue.ie) and from leaflets I.T.10 (on the self-assessment system) and I.T.48 (on starting a business); the Revenue Commissioners also publish a *Guide to Completing Tax Returns*.

☑ SURVIVAL TIP

Unless your tax affairs are simple, it's prudent to employ an accountant or tax consultant to complete your tax return and ensure that you're correctly assessed.

Married Couples

If you're married, you should list your and your spouse's income separately. Income that arises in joint names should be split equally between you. In the year of marriage, a couple are taxed as two single people unless the tax paid as such is greater than the tax payable by a married couple, in which case a refund can be claimed, but only from the date of your marriage. In subsequent years, married couples have a choice of joint assessment, separate assessment or 'assessment as a single person' (i.e. assessment as single **people**!).

Unless you specify that you would like separate or single person assessment, you're automatically given joint assessment (also known as aggregation), which in any case is the only option when one partner isn't earning and is usually also the best arrangement in other cases.

Joint Assessment: Under joint assessment, you must decide which partner is the 'assessable spouse' (usually the higher earner), who's responsible for making the tax return and paying the tax. You both qualify for tax allowances as if you were single, but you're entitled to transfer allowances between you. If one partner is employed and the other self-employed, for example, there could be a cash flow advantage in transferring all the

allowances to the employed partner. As tax isn't payable under self-assessment until ten months after the end of the tax year, you would effectively be delaying payment of the bulk of your combined tax.

If one partner earns less than your combined total tax allowances, you can transfer 'unused allowances' to the other. Similarly, if one partner earns less than €32,000 (the maximum income taxed at the lower rate of 20 per cent), you can transfer the 'unused rate band' to the other partner. For example, if one partner earns €12,000 and the other €20,000, you can effectively both be taxed at 20 per cent on all your earnings.

Separate Assessment: Under separate assessment you're still entitled to transfer allowances between spouses, but each partner's tax affairs are treated separately, so that you must each submit a tax return and pay your share of tax. Separate assessment may be chosen by couples who prefer to be financially independent, yet don't want to lose out on the tax benefits available to married couples. The deadline for claiming separate assessment for the current tax year is 31st March.

Single Person Assessment: Single person assessment (or separate treatment) is similar to separate assessment in that each partner is treated separately for

tax purposes. The difference is that allowances aren't transferable between partners, so you can lose out on unused allowances and rate bands. This method of assessment is really only suited to couples who are both paying tax at the higher rate of 42 per cent.

Self-employed

If you're self-employed, you must first obtain a PPS number); then you must register for tax (not only income or corporation tax, but also VAT and, if appropriate, employer's PAYE/PRSI) by completing Form TR1 (for sole traders, partnerships and trusts) or TR2 (for companies). These forms can be downloaded from the Revenue website or obtained by post (☎ 1890-306706).

Like all other taxpayers, you must file a tax return and pay any tax due on 31st October (see **Tax Returns & Payment** on page 288). On this date you must also pay any capital gains tax (see page 293) due for the period 1st January to 30th September of the current tax year.

Your tax return should be for the previous year and include income/corporation tax and capital gains tax. VAT is paid separately (see below). All this can be done online via the Revenue website.

Corporation Tax

Most companies registered in Ireland and foreign companies operating a branch in Ireland must pay corporation tax. For most companies, this is at the rate of 12.5 per cent on trading income (i.e. income resulting from the sale of products or services) and 25 per cent on non-trading income (including discounts, interest, foreign income, patent royalties, and rental income from land and buildings). Certain companies qualify for a 10 per cent tax rate on trading income until 2010.

VALUE ADDED TAX

You're obliged to register for value added tax (VAT) if your taxable supplies are likely to exceed €55,000 (in the case of goods) or €27,500 (in the case of services) except in special cases, e.g. if you're operating a mail order business. You may register voluntarily before your turnover reaches those limits, e.g. if you're supplying goods or services to other VAT registered traders or if you're supplying zero-rated goods, but it's worth taking advice first.

There are four rates of VAT in Ireland, as shown in the table here.

Certain goods are exempt from VAT. (The difference between zero-rated and exempt supplies is that you can claim a VAT refund on your taxable business expenses if you make zero-rated supplies, but not if you make exempt supplies.) VAT is usually payable (or redeemable) every two months, but it's possible to set up a monthly direct debit and submit a VAT return once a year only. There's a new form BP1 (Business Profile) on which you can present simplified accounts for revenue inspection. All records relating to VAT calculation must be kept for a minimum of six years.

VAT Rates	
Rate	**Applicability**
21% (standard rate)	Most goods, including cars, fuel (other than for heating), telephone services, alcohol, computers and software;
13.5%	Heating fuel, electricity, hotel and restaurant bills, newspapers and most property transactions (see below);
4.8%	Livestock, greyhounds and hire of horses;
0% (zero-rated)	Exports, certain food and drink, medicines and medical services, insurance and banking services, books and children's clothing and footwear.

VAT on Property

The application of VAT to property in Ireland is complicated – in fact the former Minister for Finance, Charlie McCreevy, admitted that only a few people in the country could understand it! As a result, the Revenue Commissioners have vowed to review the current regulations, which are therefore subject to change, although according to Ernst & Young the changes are likely to complicate matters still further. For the time being, the following applies:

◆ Sales of property which haven't been developed since 1st November 1972 (the date VAT was introduced to Ireland) are exempt from VAT.

◆ Sales of properties which have been developed since 1st November 1972 attract VAT at 13.5 per cent.

◆ In the case of property letting, if a lease is for more than ten years, a landlord must charge VAT on the rent; if it's for less than ten years the rent is normally exempt from VAT, but a landlord can waive that exemption and charge VAT at 21 per cent, although the waiver can be cancelled in certain circumstances (we understand what Mr McCreevy means!).

Booklets entitled *Guide to Value-Added Tax*, *Property Transactions and VAT on Property*, *VAT on Property*, *Information Leaflet No.3* and *Information Leaflet No.4* are available from the Revenue Commissioners (☎ 01-679 2777 or ☎ 1890-605090).

DIRT

Deposit interest retention tax (DIRT) is deducted from the interest payable on savings in banks, building societies, etc. This happens whether or not you're liable for income tax. If you or your spouse is 65 or over or permanently incapacitated, however, you may reclaim the DIRT paid if you're exempt from income tax.

PROPERTY TAX

There's no longer a residential property tax, 'rates' or 'poll tax' in Ireland. The only charge you may incur is for refuse collection, which varies between nothing and over €500 per year, depending on the location of the property (see page 128).

When selling a property you may be required to provide evidence that any property tax due before its abolition has been paid, e.g. by obtaining a clearance certificate.

CAPITAL GAINS TAX

Capital gains tax (CGT) is levied on the profit realised on the sale of certain assets. If you're resident and domiciled in Ireland, you will be subject to CGT on the disposal of assets anywhere in the world. If you're a non-resident, your CGT liability is confined to certain Irish assets (mainly land and buildings). If you've been absent from Ireland for a period which includes three consecutive tax years, you may dispose of certain Irish assets free of CGT before your return, but you may incur tax in your present country of residence.

If you elect to be resident in the year of your entry into Ireland, you will be liable to CGT on gains in the whole tax year, even if you took up residence at the end of the year (although you will be eligible for relief on any foreign tax paid on disposals of assets). Note that the Finance Act, 2003 introduced an 'anti-avoidance' measure (i.e. a complication of the law), whereby the sale of any property during a temporary period of non-residence comes under suspicion of being subject to CGT.

The normal rate of CGT is 20 per cent, but a 40 per cent tax rate applies to the redemption of certain foreign investments, including life assurance policies. Gains made on the sale of your principal residence (and up to one acre of land) are exempt, as are gains of up to €2,450

made on the sale of other property, transfers of land (up to a value of €254,000) from a parent to a child for the purpose of building a child's principal residence, lottery and sweepstake winnings, and gains from the sale of certain types of security and life assurance policies.

In the case of a secondary residence, allowances are made for inflation and capital expenditure, so it's important to keep records of everything you spend on a property. Note that you may be entitled to only partial exemption from CGT if you vacate your principal residence for 'long periods'. If you let your family home in Ireland before leaving the country, you must reoccupy it on your return in order to preserve the 'principal private residence exemption' from CGT on the future sale of the property.

You're also entitled to a 'personal' CGT exemption of €1,270 per person, which you should take advantage of by, for example, selling any shares that have risen in value. It's no longer possible to transfer your CGT exemption to your spouse, and disposals between spouses or relatives (known as 'connected persons') are treated as if they were made at the open market value, with CGT payable in the usual way.

When calculating the gain that's subject to CGT, you may deduct the incidental costs of buying a property; any expenditure which enhances its value; costs incurred in establishing, preserving or defending title or rights to a property; and the incidental costs of disposing of a property, e.g. legal and professional costs, advertising and stamp duty. Note that all these expenses can be 'indexed' (i.e. increased to current values to compensate for inflation) except in the case of development land.

You cannot claim interest against CGT except where a company borrows money to build a property (but not to enhance an existing property) and capitalises the interest. In the case of leasehold property, rent from the grant of a lease is liable to income tax, but if you receive a lump sum on granting the lease this is liable to CGT (provided that the lease is for more than 50 years – if it's for

less than 50 years the lump sum is liable partly to income tax and partly to CGT).

If you sell a property for over €500,000, you must obtain a 'clearance' certificate from the Revenue Commissioners that CGT has been paid; otherwise the buyer is obliged to withhold 15 per cent of the purchase price against the possibility of CGT being unpaid.

Declarations should be made on the same forms as for income tax (see **Tax Returns & Payment** on page 288). Tax on gains made between 1st January and 30th September must be paid by 31st October of the same year; tax on gains made between 1st October and 31st December is due by 31st January of the following year. Late payment incurs a surcharge of 5 per cent or, if you fail to pay within a year, 10 per cent.

CAPITAL ACQUISITIONS TAX

Ireland imposes a tax on gifts and inheritances called capital acquisitions tax (CAT). In fact, it's three taxes: gift tax, inheritance tax and discretionary trust tax. (Probate tax was abolished in 2001.) CAT applies to Irish property whether the donor is resident or domiciled in Ireland or not. Foreign (i.e. non-Irish) property is subject to tax if either the donor or the beneficiary is resident in Ireland at the time of receipt.

Gift and inheritance tax are charged on the taxable value of a gift or inheritance (which is its market value less any relevant expenses incurred by the beneficiary) above certain thresholds (i.e. exemption limits), which depend on the relationship of the beneficiary to the donor (officially known as the 'disponer'!), as follows:

Capital Acquisitions Tax Exemptions (2008)	
Relationship	**Exemption**
Son or daughter (Group A)	€521,208
Parent, brother, sister, niece, nephew or grand-child (Group B)	€52,121
Other (Group C)	€26,060

Above these limits, the net value of gifts and inheritances is taxed at 20 per cent. Property inherited that is subject to a discretionary trust is taxed at 1 per cent per annum.

There are various exemptions and reliefs from CAT. Gifts between spouses, for example, are exempt, and reliefs apply to agricultural and business property, to charitable donations and to the disposal of items of cultural, scientific or artistic interest, provided that the recipient allows reasonable public access to them for at least six years after the transfer. The proceeds of certain life assurance policies may also be exempt from CAT if they're used to pay taxes due on the insured person's death. In addition, the first €3,000 worth of gifts received each year from a particular donor don't count towards your tax-free allowance.

A major exemption applies to principal residences (known to the Revenue Commissioners as 'dwelling-houses'!), which are exempt from CAT provided the following conditions are met:

♦ The beneficiary must have occupied the property continuously as his principal residence for at least three years before the date of the gift or inheritance.

♦ The beneficiary mustn't be entitled to inherit any other property.

♦ The beneficiary must continue to occupy the property for at least six years after, unless he is 55 years old – or, the wording of the law adds (somewhat superfluously), has died – at the time of the gift or inheritance.

If you want to spare your beneficiaries from CAT, there are certain measures you can take. For example, if your spouse is of pension age and you have no children, you should think about putting your property into a company, in which case no inheritance tax applies on your death. If you have children, you can set up a trust through which you and they jointly own the property (a trust is a concept of the common law system, which may be unfamiliar to mainland Europeans). There are certain charges involved in establishing and maintaining a trust, but these are negligible unless your net worth is extremely high.

Note that the same taxes apply to intestacy (i.e. if you have no will) as to disposition by will.

The rules of succession on intestacy state that, where there's no child or other descendant, the spouse takes all; where there's a spouse and descendants, the spouse takes two-thirds, the children one-third; where there's no spouse, the children take all.

Inheritance law is a complicated subject, and professional advice should be sought from an experienced solicitor who understands both Irish inheritance law and the law of any other countries involved. Your will is also a vital component in reducing Irish inheritance tax to the minimum, or deferring its payment.

Further information about CAT can be obtained from the Capital Taxes Division of the Taxpayer Information Service (☎ 1890-201104).

WILLS

It's an unfortunate fact of life, but you're unable to take your worldly goods with you when you take your final bow (even if you have plans to return!). Once you've accepted that you're mortal (the one statistic you can confidently rely on is that 100 per cent of human beings eventually die), it's a good idea to make a will, especially if you want your estate left to anyone other than those who would be entitled to it if you didn't make one.

Many people in Ireland die intestate, i.e. without making a will, in which case their property is subject to Irish intestacy law (i.e. the Succession Act), which divides your estate between your spouse and children in the proportion two-thirds:one-third. In fact all adults should make a will, irrespective of how much (or how little) they think they're 'worth'.

If you die in Ireland without making a will and aren't resident there, the intestacy laws of your home country will apply to the disposal of your estate. If you're a foreign national and don't want your estate to be subject to Irish law, you may be eligible to state in your will that it's to be interpreted under the law of another country. If you don't specify in your will that the law of another country applies to your estate, then Irish law will apply.

It isn't a legal requirement in Ireland to use a lawyer to prepare your will, although the relatively small fee (around €60) may save you considerable difficulties (the Irish

Probate Office has dormant files going back years relating to personal applicants who have been put off by the work involved). If you want to make your own will, you must sign it in the presence of two witnesses who aren't beneficiaries. If your circumstances change, you may amend your will or make a new one.

You should check your will every few years to make sure it still fulfils your wishes and circumstances (your assets may also increase dramatically in value). A will can be revoked simply by tearing it up. You and your spouse should make separate wills and, if you have children, set up a trust in case you both die at the same time. You should also make sure that you have a joint account, as in some cases the surviving spouse may be unable to gain access to the deceased's bank account.

You will need to appoint someone to act as the executor of your estate. This can be your solicitor or another professional. If you appoint a professional as executor of your estate, check the fees in advance (and whether they could increase in future).

It's best to make your beneficiaries the executors; they can then instruct a solicitor after your death if they need legal assistance.

If you don't appoint an executor, your estate will be 'administered' by your spouse, children, grandchildren, parents, or other relatives (in that order of priority), who will need to apply to the Probate Office for a 'grant of administration'. Note that when someone dies, his assets are 'frozen' until capital acquisition tax (see above) has been paid and probate (the official proving of a will) has been granted.

Keep a copy of your will in a safe place (e.g. a bank) and another copy with your solicitor or the executor of your estate.

It's useful to leave an updated list of your assets with your will, to assist the executor in distributing your estate. You should keep information regarding bank accounts and insurance policies with your will(s), but don't forget to tell someone where they are!

COST OF LIVING

No doubt you would like to try to estimate how far your euros will stretch and how much money (if any) you will have left after paying your bills. Unfortunately, the cost of living in Ireland is high, particularly when accommodation is taken into account (see **Chapter 5**). Cars, books, alcohol, tobacco and luxury items are also expensive. In fact, almost all Irish prices are higher than the EU average, except clothing and footwear. When calculating your likely cost of living, remember also to allow for income tax and social insurance contributions.

In the Mercer 2008 Cost of Living Survey (⌨ www.mercer.com/costofliving), Dublin was ranked the equal 16th (with Rome) most expensive city in the world. Selected other ranking were London (3rd, after Moscow and Tokyo), Copenhagen (6), Paris (12), Sydney (15), New York City (22 – the only US city in the top 50), Amsterdam (25), Madrid (28), Melbourne (36), Berlin (38), Brussels (39) and Hamburg (50).

The standard rate of VAT is high, at 21 per cent, although there are reduced rates for certain goods (see **Value Added Tax** on page 291). However, there's some compensation in the form of benefits to people aged over 66, which include free travel, healthcare, TV licences, telephone rental (plus a number of free calls), plus allowances for clothing, fuel, electricity and gas. This makes Ireland an attractive place for retirement, as an increasing number of foreigners have discovered.

> A somewhat biased look at the prices of various goods and services can be found on a website run by the Fine Gael political party (⌨ www. ripoff.ie) – the main party of opposition.

Inflation in March 2008 was 3.5 per cent (the highest rate for five years) and is expected to increase to as much as 5 per cent by the end of 2008.

15.

LEISURE

One of the spin-offs of Ireland's recent economic boom has been an increase in leisure spending (if not leisure time) and a proliferation of activities and entertainment on which to spend disposable income. The establishment of a national lottery in 1987 has helped to fund leisure facilities (almost 60 per cent of the €200m generated annually goes towards recreation and culture), which have also been extended to cope with the annual influx of almost 6m visitors to Ireland.

Fortunately, the inevitable invasion of Anglo-American culture, which threatened to swamp the country in the '70s and '80s, has at least partially been resisted by the recent revival of Irish dancing, music, sport and language. Other traditional Irish activities, such as pub-going, have suffered from the accessibility of new leisure pursuits, but there are still some that are unique to Ireland if you're prepared to seek them out. Where else in the world, for example, could you enjoy a relaxing seaweed bath except at an exclusive health club?

Ireland is a land of many faces, ranging from spectacular scenery to picturesque towns and villages to bustling modern cities. People are drawn to Ireland for many reasons, among which are its rich traditions, unique atmosphere and quality of live entertainment (particularly in Dublin). But don't make the mistake of visiting only Dublin and neglecting Ireland's attractive provincial cities and its magnificent countryside, where you will find a wealth of natural beauty and historic sights, including national parks, castles, country inns, charming villages, bleak and rugged mountains, farmlands, sandy beaches and imposing cliffs, rivers and lakes. Whether you're a country or city lover, there's something for you in Ireland. It's a small country and, no matter where you live, practically anywhere is within reach for a weekend trip.

In most towns, you will find entertainment guides – either in magazines and newspapers or in dedicated brochures and leaflets.

Weekly, fortnightly, monthly, bimonthly and quarterly entertainment and arts programmes and magazines are available from tourist information centres in all major cities and towns. Many councils also publish maps and brochures listing local places of interest and leisure facilities, arts and community centres, countryside and outdoor activities, useful contacts for the disabled, etc.

The main aim of this chapter (and indeed the purpose of the whole book) is to provide information that isn't found in standard guide books. General tourist information is available in literally hundreds of guide books, many encompassing the whole of Ireland, others concentrating on particular regions. Many of these are listed in **Appendix B**. Current entertainment and tourist information can also be obtained from the television teletext information service and from the internet. For information about sports facilities, see **Chapter 16**.

TOURIST INFORMATION

All Irish cities, towns and popular tourist spots have tourist information offices (henceforth referred to as tourist offices), of which there are 90 in Ireland, usually located in a prominent building and well signposted. They're designated by a white lower case letter 'i', either on a green background or in a red hexagon, with the words 'Tourist Information' beneath.

Tourist offices are run by the seven regional tourism centres and coordinated by the Irish tourist board (☎ 0800-039 7000, 🖳 www.ireland.ie), which is called Fáilte Ireland (meaning 'welcome Ireland', *fáilte* being pronounced like 'fault') in Ireland, but Tourism Ireland abroad.

Opening hours vary considerably; during the winter months (November to March) even main city offices are open only for limited hours, such as 10am to 4pm, and in small towns offices may be closed completely.

Tourist offices provide a wealth of information about local attractions, restaurants, accommodation, sporting events and facilities, package holidays, tours, public transport, car rental and much more. Offices can provide information on a wide range of leisure activities, so you should mention any special interests when making enquiries.

The Irish tourist board has offices in many countries, including Austria, Belgium, Canada, Denmark, Germany, Italy, Japan, Luxembourg, the Netherlands, Norway, South Africa, Spain, Sweden, Switzerland, the UK and the US, as well as agents in other parts of the world including South America. The addresses and telephone numbers of some of these offices are listed below:

♦ **Australia** – 36 Carrington Street, 5th Level, Sydney, NSW 2000 (☎ 02-9299 6177);

♦ **Canada** – 160 Bloor Street E., Suite 1150, Toronto, ON M4W 1B9 (☎ 416-929 2777 or freephone ☎ 800-223 6470);

♦ **New Zealand** – Dingwall Building, 2nd Floor, 87 Queen Street, Auckland (☎ 09-379 8720);

♦ **UK** – Nations House, 103 Wigmore Street, London, W1U 1QS (☎ 020-7518 0800 or freephone ☎ 0800-039 7000);

♦ **US** – 345 Park Avenue, New York, NY 10154 (☎ 800-223 6470 or ☎ 212-418-0800 or freephone ☎ 800-223 6470).

Its official 'corporate' website is 🖳 www.failteireland.ie and its international websites 🖳 www.discoverireland.com and 🖳 www.tourismireland.com (why it should have three sites is a mystery!). Other websites providing tourist information about Ireland include 🖳 www.goireland.com, 🖳 www.irelandforvisitors.com, 🖳 www.irelandseye.com and 🖳 www.irishtourism.com.

ACCOMMODATION

Ireland has an extensive selection of accommodation ranging from castles and stately homes to farmhouses, but also including hotels, hostels, guesthouses, bed and breakfasts and self-catering. In recent years, many of Ireland's castles and stately homes have opened their doors for both visits and accommodation. Some, like Bunratty Castle, offer a wide range of activities including mediaeval banquets, and many hotels have specialised accommodation packages such as gourmet weekends or stays which include adventure pursuits, golf or fishing.

Wherever you choose to stay, it's wise to book well in advance, particularly during the summer months, and bear in mind that quite a few establishments close between November and March.

Hotels

There are over 45,000 hotel rooms in Ireland, where hotels come in all shapes, sizes and standards, from elegant castles and stately homes or exclusive country clubs to simple family run establishments, where facilities may be basic, but the welcome is just as warm.

Star Rating

Most Irish hotels are graded by the tourist board using a star rating system. One-star establishments offer a certain minimum level of facilities, but in many cases include 'luxuries' such as a television (TV) and private shower or bathroom. Two-star hotels are usually family-run, all rooms having a telephone and most a private bathroom with a bath and/or shower, and offer full dining facilities. Three-star properties range from small, family-run premises to larger, modern hotels. All rooms have a private bathroom, and restaurants offer good quality cuisine with *table d'hôte* as well as *à la carte* menus.

Malahide Castle, Co. Dublin

Four stars indicate either high quality contemporary hotels or charming period houses renovated to high standards with all modern comforts. Half suites are usually available. Ireland's most luxurious hotels are awarded five stars and house some of the country's finest restaurants. Accommodation is luxurious and spacious, and suites are available.

Prices

Prices are invariably quoted on a per person basis and vary according to the time of year and the location of the establishment, as well as its star rating. Around 40 per cent of Irish hotels have a three-star rating (i.e. are mid-priced). Hotels and guesthouses in large towns and cities and popular coastal areas tend to be more expensive than comparable establishments in other parts of Ireland. In hotel terms, there are usually only two seasons: high (July/August) and low (the rest of the year). Average prices in 2008 were around €55 per person per night in an 'economy' (i.e. one- or two-star) hotel, €90 in a 'first class' (3- or 4-star) hotel and €155 in a 'luxury' (5-star) establishment.

Rates in Dublin tend to be 20 to 30 per cent higher than most other areas (except in parts of the south-west, where rates can be almost as high as in the capital) and low season rates are generally 30 to 40 per cent cheaper than high season prices. Reductions are usually available for children under 12, and those under four are often accommodated free if they share their parents' bedroom. If you're wanting to be extravagant, you could always stay at somewhere like Ashford Castle, on the shores of Lough Corrib (in County Galway), and pay anything up to €1,187 per person per night!

Different rates generally apply to full-board accommodation (including breakfast, lunch and evening meal) for a week or longer, and many hotels offer deals for weekend stays (two nights), three nights mid-week (one night free) and seven nights half or 'partial board', including evening meal and breakfast. Extra charges may be made under some circumstances, e.g. single occupancy of a double room, and services such as babysitting may also be charged for.

Note that accommodation vouchers, which are issued by some travel agents, aren't recommended, as they're often not accepted in Ireland, particularly at busy times. Be careful in particular not to clash with local festivals, international rugby matches, All-Ireland Hurling or Football Finals and avoid public holidays, when special (i.e. grossly inflated) prices can apply. All room rates quoted are inclusive of value added tax (VAT).

In most hotels, a 'full Irish breakfast' is included in the room rate. This is similar to an 'English breakfast' and consists of fruit juice or cereal, a hot main course of grilled bacon, eggs, sausages, black (or white) pudding, mushrooms, tomatoes and baked beans ('heart attack on a plate'), as well as toast and soda bread with marmalade or jam, and coffee or tea.

If you prefer to stay healthy (and slim), you can opt for a continental breakfast instead, but you will be charged the same price!

Most hotels with restaurants offer half or full board at advantageous rates.

Facilities

Although facilities vary considerably with the price and category of accommodation, you can usually expect en suite facilities (bath or shower) in hotels and guesthouses. Rooms are usually equipped with a telephone, radio or

TV, including selected satellite channels, plus tea and coffee-making facilities. Fridges and mini-bars are generally only found in the more expensive hotels, which also provide room service. Power points are usually provided and there's often a (two-pin) razor socket in the bathroom.

Most hotels have private parking; guesthouses often don't, although there's usually on-street parking or a secure off-road car park nearby. Most hotels also have photocopying and fax facilities for their guests' use, and more expensive hotels offer internet connection facilities; a few have swimming pools and gymnasiums.

Booking

A deposit (e.g. 10 per cent) may be required when booking a room. Most hotels and guesthouses will take a credit card number over the phone as security (and so that, if you don't turn up, they can take full payment!).

Agri-tourism

Agri-tourism offers a novel and unusual form of accommodation in rural areas for those who are tired of faceless and atmosphere-less hotels. A number of small farmers who are no longer able to make a living solely from the land have been forced to diversify and some have converted farm buildings

into accommodation. Working farms offering accommodation can be found on 🖳 www.irishfarmholidays.com.

Information

There are a number of directories of selected hotels, the most popular being *Ireland's Blue Book* (☎ 01-676 9914, 🖳 www.irelands-blue-book.ie), which focuses on luxury accommodation and restaurants, mostly in coastal areas. There's also a *Green Book*, whose listing includes castles (☎ 01-676 2555, 🖳 www.greenbook.ie). Further information can be obtained from the Irish tourist board (☎ 0800-039 7000, 🖳 www.ireland.ie), and from the Irish Hotels Federation (☎ 01-808 4419, 🖳 www.irelandhotels.com), which publishes a guide to hotels and guesthouses called *Be Our Guest* (also available from the Irish tourist board).

Bed & Breakfast Accommodation & Guesthouses

Bed and breakfast accommodation is widely available in Ireland; in fact in some areas it seems as if every other house is offering 'B&B'. Larger establishments, particularly in towns, may call themselves guesthouses, but these offer essentially the same type of accommodation as B&Bs – i.e. there are generally no communal areas such as lounges and bars, nor a restaurant other than some kind of breakfast room. The type of establishment varies from period homes to farms to modern bungalows. B&B or guesthouse accommodation is more informal than a hotel, and provides a friendly place to meet the Irish in their own homes; very often you will have breakfast with your hosts, for example. Evening meals are often available by arrangement.

Like hotel accommodation, B&B standards vary greatly from a basic single room sharing a bathroom to a luxury double room with en suite bathroom. Many B&Bs provide tea and coffee-making facilities in all rooms, as well as televisions, often with selected satellite or cable programmes. Most guesthouses and some B&Bs are star rated in the same way as hotels to reflect the facilities, quality and location of the accommodation. In two-star establishments at least half the rooms have a private bathroom with bath and/or shower, and other facilities should include a reading/writing room or lounge area. Three-star rooms all have a private bathroom and direct dial telephone. There should be a TV lounge and sometimes a restaurant. Basic room service should also be available.

Travellers' cheques may be exchanged and at least two major credit cards should be accepted. The highest classification for guesthouses is four- star, indicating that the accommodation includes half suites and all rooms have a private bathroom, direct dial telephone and a radio and colour TV with remote control. Room service should include full breakfast, and many establishments will offer dinner with *table d'hôte* and/or *à la carte* menus. Other facilities should include car parking, safety deposit boxes, fax, newspapers and babysitting.

Rates usually start at around €30 per person per night, the average being between around €45 and €50. At the top end of the scale there are exceptional properties offering B&B at over €100 per person (rates at Glin Castle in County Limerick **start** at €310!). Houses, Castles and Gardens of Ireland (☎ 01-288 9114, 💻 www.castlesireland. com) represents a number of exceptional properties offering B&B from €70 per person to over £400. B&B accommodation (as the name implies) includes a full Irish breakfast, and some offer evening meals, usually at reasonable prices, although these must be ordered in advance and you may have to take 'pot luck' as to what's on the menu!

☑ SURVIVAL TIP

It's generally wise to book well in advance, even out of season, particularly in B&Bs which are listed in accommodation guides.

If you're a smoker, you should check in advance whether smoking is permitted. When booking, confirm your arrival time to ensure that your hosts will be at home. If you're staying for more than one night, you may be expected to vacate your room for most of the day and to leave by 12 noon (or earlier) on your last day.

Tourist information centres have a wide range of brochures, guides and books containing information about B&B and guesthouse accommodation throughout Ireland. Further information can be obtained from the Town & Country Homes Association (☎ 071-982 2222, 💻 www.townandcountry. ie), which publishes a guide called *The Definitive Irish Bed & Breakfast & Self Catering Guide* (costing €10), and from the Irish Tourist Board (☎ 0800-039 4000, 💻 www. discoverireland.com), which markets a number of accommodation guides, although most of its own publications are now available only online. A useful book for those looking for unusual, but mostly inexpensive places to stay is *Special Places to Stay in Ireland* (Alastair Sawday Publishing).

Hostels

There are over 125 hostels in Ireland, mostly privately owned, varying in size from half a dozen to 250 or more beds, which offer cheap accommodation. The majority of beds are in dormitories (separate ones for males and females!), but most hostels also offer twin, double and family rooms and some also have camping facilities. Most hostels (over 100) are operated by Independent Holiday Hostels of Ireland (IHH). The IHH is an independent cooperative, but all its hostels are Irish tourist board-approved.

Hostels are open all year round and admit people of all ages. No membership fee is payable, and dormitory accommodation is available from €12 to €27 per person depending on the time of year and the location (hostels in Dublin not surprisingly being the most expensive). For an individual room, you will pay between €25 and €50 per person. If you're travelling around, you can book ahead from one hostel to another. Further information and a list of hostels can be obtained from the IHH (☎ 01-836 4700, 💻 www.hostels-ireland. com).

The Irish Youth Hostel Association (IYHA, *An Óige* in Irish, ☎ 01-830 4555, 💻 www.anoige. ie), a non-profit making organisation founded in 1931, represents a further 24 hostels. To stay at IYHA hostels you don't need to be a 'youth' or a member of the association, but if you aren't a member you will have to pay extra – charges vary from hostel to hostel, but start at around €15 per person per night (slightly less for under 18s) in an eight-bedded dormitory; individual rooms cost extra. There's a €2 reduction for members, and annual membership costs €10 for under 18s, €20 for adults or €40 for family membership and €100 for life membership.

Membership includes a biannual newsletter and entitles you to stay in any of 6,000 hostels worldwide and to discounts on clothing, entrance fees, travel, etc. in over 60 countries (including Ireland). If you're a member of a foreign association which is affiliated to the International Youth Hostel Federation, you won't need to join the IYHA, but can simply produce your own membership card. Unlike IHH hostels, IYHA hostels aren't open all year round, so you will need to check opening dates. Bookings can be made locally, at travel agents or via the internet. Further details and a copy of the Youth Hostel Accommodation Guide and Planner can be obtained via the website.

> ### ☑ SURVIVAL TIP
>
> If you're staying in a hostel, you should take your own sleeping bag or sheets, although sheets can be rented on arrival (private rooms usually include linen) and duvets or blankets are included in the price.

All hostels have fully equipped kitchens, dining rooms and common rooms, as well as shower facilities. Most also offer security lockers, bicycle hire, laundry and ironing facilities.

Hostelling is 'activity orientated' and many hostel owners organise workshops and music sessions, as well as horse-riding, canoeing, etc. The IYHA also offers membership of ancillary clubs such as a Hillwalkers' Club and Photographic Group.

Self-Catering

There's an abundance of properties for rent short-term in Ireland, including apartments, farmhouses, townhouses, bungalows, mansions, castles and even mobile homes. Self-catering accommodation ranges from modern purpose-built units to period houses and thatched cottages. Self-catering accommodation is often a good choice for a family or group of up to ten people, as it's much cheaper than a hotel room, provides more privacy and freedom, and allows you to prepare your own meals as and when you please.

Many agents let self-catering properties in holiday areas at a considerable reduction during the 'low season', which may extend from September to June. In some cases, the rental year is divided into as many as four seasons, e.g. November to March, April and October, June and September, and July/August, but there are usually three periods: July/August; May/June and September, and the rest of the year. Only a few owners charge the same rate all year round.

All self-catering accommodation registered with the Irish tourist board is classified on a star rating basis from one to four stars. One-star premises offer minimum facilities but comfortable accommodation and services. Two-star properties offer a good standard of furnishings and fittings and a well equipped kitchen. In three-star accommodation there should also be in-house laundry facilities (or close by) and the grounds should be attractively landscaped. Most four-star accommodation has a second bathroom or one bedroom en suite, and refreshments should be provided on arrival.

Prices vary greatly according to star rating, size, location and the time of year. For a three-star holiday cottage in a popular area such as Kerry, prices start at around €350 (per week), compared with at least double that in mid-summer; a two-bedroom apartment in Dublin would cost from around €400 to €1,000. In less popular areas, although the low season rate is similar, you usually pay 'only' €500 in July or August.

Before booking any self-catering accommodation you should check the changeover dates and times; what's included in the rent (fees usually include linen, but not electricity or gas, for example); whether cots or high chairs are available, and if pets are allowed; if a garden or parking is provided; and whether there's easy access to public transport (if necessary). Self-catering accommodation is usually let on a weekly basis from Saturday to Saturday.

The best source of short-term rental accommodation in Ireland is the tourist board. Short Term Solutions specialises in short-term rentals in Dublin, although mainly for business people (☎ 01-679 2222). If you're looking for somewhere different to stay, you could try one of the nine historic properties belonging to the Irish Landmark Trust (☎ 01-670 4733, 💻 www.irishlandmark.com), costing up to €1,000 per week in high season.

Many hotels also offer lower rates for long stays during the low season. Other useful websites include 💻 www.irishcottageholidays.com, 💻 www.irishholidayrentals.com and 💻 www.selfcatering-ireland.com.

Camping & Caravanning

There are around 135 camping and caravanning sites in Ireland, most of which are recommended by the Irish Caravan and Camping Council (ICCC, ☎ 98-28237, 💻 www.camping-ireland.ie) and listed on its website. All ICCC parks are registered with the Irish tourist board and graded according to a star system from one to four stars. Most sites are located in attractive areas by the sea or near lakes or forests, and many have entertainment facilities for children and adults either on site or nearby, as well as shops, laundries and cafés. Around 20 sites are open all year round.

Most sites admit tents, caravans and motor caravans and many have 'mobile homes' (which in most cases have remained rooted to the spot for years) for hire. These may have up to three bedrooms and are equipped with all modern conveniences. There's no published list of non-ICCC sites, which tend to have only basic facilities and may consist simply of a farmer's field.

Most ICCC campsites provide an electricity supply of between 5 and 10 amps (the blue Euro connection is standard). If you require gas, however, you're advised to take cylinders with you: they can be difficult to obtain, and Irish and British cylinders aren't compatible. Both gas and electricity are normally charged extra.

Pitch prices vary according to the location of the site, the facilities provided and the season, but are generally between around €20 and €30 per night for a 'family pitch' (i.e. space for up to two adults and two children). There's usually an extra charge, of between €3 and €10 per night, for a car, and a supplement of €3–5 for an electricity supply.

Some sites have mobile homes, for which the weekly rental is between €250 (low season) and €450 (high season) for a six-bed unit, and between €300 and €550 for an eight-bed. The cost of hiring a touring caravan for five people is around €500 per week in the low season. Motor homes are also available for hire.

There's no campers'/caravanners' association in Ireland, which is covered by the UK's Caravan Club (☎ 0800-328 6635 or ☎ 01342-326944, 💻 www.caravanclub.co.uk).

It's still legal to spend the night in a caravan or motor home at the side of the road, provided of course that it isn't on private property or causing an obstruction or hazard.

Other Accommodation

Accommodation is also provided by some public houses in Ireland, especially in the country, as well as by a few tourist attractions

and deserted! Ireland is proud of its beaches, no fewer than 77 of which have earned a European Union blue flag accolade for cleanliness. Outside the few seaside resorts, which are mainly in the south-east and south-west, there are few or no beachside facilities such as toilets, cafés, shops and amusements.

Ireland has less forest and woodland than almost any other European country (although the current rate of tree planting is higher than almost anywhere else), but what does exist is well worth exploring, e.g. there are deer to be seen in Lough Key Forest Park in County Leitrim.

A leaflet entitled *Discovering Ireland's Woodlands* is available from tourist information offices.

Most of Ireland's 5,000 or more *loughs* (lakes) are picturesque and accessible, although few have watersports facilities (see **Geography** on page 360 and **Boating** on page 331).

Ireland also has five National Parks: Killarney National Park in County Kerry is perhaps the best known, incorporating Lough Leane, with Muckross House and Gardens as its centrepiece; the Wicklow Mountains National Park near Dublin contains famous ruins at Glendalough; the Connemara National Park in County Galway is rather wilder with rugged mountains and lakes; bleaker still is the mountainous Glenveagh in County Donegal, with its own castle and gardens, and The Burren, County Clare, where barren hills are strewn with shattered limestone slabs like a gigantic rock garden.

Although there's usually no admission charge to lakes, parks and woodlands, several have Visitor Centres which you must pay to enter. Ireland's National Trust, *An Taisce* (☎ 01-454 1786, 🖳 www.antaisce.org), owns a few wildlife parks which you can visit free of charge.

such as mills and farms. These types of accommodation may not be advertised, so it's worth asking whether rooms are available.

Several of Ireland's universities offer low cost accommodation during the summer holiday period. Marketing University Summer Accommodation (MUS) arranges accommodation in the universities of Cork, Dublin, Galway, Limerick and Maynooth between June and September; for information contact University Summer Accommodation, Accommodation Office, University of Limerick, Limerick (☎ 061-202331, 🖳 www.ul.ie/campuslife/accommodation.htm).

USIT Accommodation Centres (☎ 01-602 1904 🖳 www.usit.ie) can provide details of accommodation at University College Dublin as well as at their Kinlay House hostels, which are registered with the IHH (see page 303). Alternatively, you can contact individual universities direct, e.g. Trinity College Dublin (☎ 01-896 1177, 🖳 www.tcd.ie/accommodation) or Plassey Campus Centre, University of Limerick (☎ 061-202433, 🖳 www.ul.ie/campuslife/accommodation.htm). The accommodation provided, while not up to hotel standard, is reasonable and competitively priced.

ATTRACTIONS

Beaches, Forests, Lakes & Parks

Although Ireland's climate is hardly conducive to sunbathing and swimming in the sea, beaches are among the country's principal attractions, many of them being long, sandy

Galleries & Museums

There are some 200 art galleries in Ireland, the majority of which feature Irish art, although major state galleries such as the National Gallery of Ireland and the Hugh Lane Municipal Gallery of Modern Art (both in Dublin) have permanent collections of international art.

Not surprisingly, the greatest concentration of art galleries is in Dublin, followed by Cork and Limerick. The Temple Bar area, Dublin's 'Left Bank', is where you will find the Graphic Studio Gallery (graphic arts), the Project Arts Centre (avant-garde painting and sculpture), the Gallery of Photography, the capital's only photographic gallery, and the Temple Bar Gallery and Studios itself, one of the largest studio/gallery complexes in Europe (which has its own website, 🖥 www.templebargallery.com).

Outside Dublin, the Crawford and Triskell galleries in Cork, the Belltable and City Gallery in Limerick, the Sligo Museum and Art Gallery, the Garter Lane in Waterford and the Butler Gallery in Kilkenny are among the principal regional art galleries. Limerick's Hunt Museum houses the Hunt Collection, one of the most important private collections of mediaeval art in the world, as well as works by famous artists up to the present time. Over the last 20 years, the Arts Council of Ireland has created a number of regional Arts Centres which incorporate art galleries.

Other important galleries in Dublin include the Kerlin and Taylor Galleries (mainly contemporary art), the Royal Hibernian Academy Gallery (traditional art), the Chester Beatty Library & Gallery of Oriental Art in Dublin Castle, the Douglas Hyde Gallery in Trinity College (young Irish and foreign artists) and the Irish Museum of Modern Art (IMMA), which opened in 1991 in the buildings of the former Royal Hospital, Kilmainham.

There's a wide variety of museums in Ireland, again mostly situated in Dublin, including the National and National Maritime Museums, the Natural History Museum, and the Ceol or Irish Traditional Music Museum, which provides an interactive insight into the evolution of Irish music. Others include the Civic Museum and the 'Dublinia Experience', which celebrate the capital's colourful history in traditional and hi-tec style; the Dublin Writers' Museum and the James Joyce Museum, the Irish Film Centre, including a film archive, library and display of cinema memorabilia, the Geological Museum and the Irish Jewish Museum.

Other interesting places to visit in the capital are the Old Jameson Distillery and the Guinness Hop Store, which display the history of two of Ireland's most famous products; the Hot Press Irish Music Hall of Fame (an interactive exhibition tracing the history of Irish rock and pop); the Genealogical Office and Heraldic Museum, Kilmainham Gaol, the National Library of Ireland, the Dublin Waterways Visitor Centre (which traces the history of Ireland's inland waterways); the Dublin Viking Adventure, and the Children's Cultural Centre. The most popular tourist attractions in and around Dublin are listed on the Dublin Tourism website (☎ 01-605 7700 or ☎ 1850-230330, 🖥 www.visitdublin.com).

Most museums and galleries are admission free, although some that are on the tourist track (such as Trinity College Library, which houses the famous Book of Kells) charge up to €10 admission.

Culture vultures can purchase an annual Heritage Card, which allows access to any site administered by the Office of Public Works (Dúchas) and the Department of the Environment, Heritage and Local Government (☎ 01-647 6000, 🖥 www.heritageireland.ie). Cards cost €21 for adults, €8 for children, €16 for the over-60s and €55 for a family.

Opening times vary, so check in advance, particularly when planning to visit smaller museums and galleries, some of which open only a few days a week.

Gardens, Houses, Castles & Abbeys

Unlike other countries, where palaces and stately homes have been preserved and restored for the enjoyment of tourists and other visitors, Ireland has very few grand old houses still intact – most have been converted into schools or hotels or are derelict. An Taisce, the Irish National Trust, cannot afford to buy them, so it's mostly left to private organisations such as the Irish Georgian Society to save them from rack and ruin, and grants towards restoration work are available from the National Heritage Council, formed in 1988. Belatedly realising that something needed to be done, the Irish government recently began surveying

some 50,000 properties nationwide with a view to 'listing' those most deserving of preservation.

Unlike the UK's National Trust, *An Taisce* (☎ 01-454 1786, 🖳 www.antaisce.org) is essentially a campaigning organisation, concerned with international environmental issues like global warming, as well as specifically Irish concerns such as the construction of 'interpretative centres' at Luggala and the Burren; it holds only a dozen properties 'in trust' (listed on the website) which you can visit free, but membership (which costs €45 for an individual, €55 for a family, €60 for a group, €10 for a student and €20 for those who are retired or unemployed) entitles you to discounted admission to a number of Irish gardens and properties.

There are numerous gardens that can be visited in Ireland, some of which are detailed in *Ireland for Garden Lovers* by Georgina Campbell (🖳 www.ireland-guide.com). Members of Houses, Castles and Gardens of Ireland can be found on 🖳 www.gardensireland.com. Other properties are listed on 🖳 www.heritageireland.ie.

Ireland is justly famous for its castles, among the best known being the Rock of Cashel in County Tipperary and Blarney Castle near Cork (where the famous Blarney Stone is to be found – but you will have to hang upside from the top of the tower to kiss it!). Two more of Ireland's most popular attractions are ruined abbeys, Clonmacnoise in County Offaly and Glendalough in County Wicklow. Of these, only Glendalough is free to visit.

All tourist offices provide details of local attractions, most of which are open throughout the year, although many have reduced opening hours from October to March.

Towns & Villages

Ireland may not have as many picture postcard towns and villages as the UK or France, for example, but there are many that are, as the Michelin Guide puts it, 'worth a detour'. A number of Irish towns and villages are unofficially designated 'Heritage Towns' (i.e. historically important and/or well preserved). Elsewhere, despite the Irish reputation for untidiness, there are numerous towns and villages that take part in Ireland's annual Best Kept Town and Tidy Town/Village competitions, which are now so hotly contested that they attract national prime-time TV coverage!

Zoos, Wildlife & Adventure Parks

Dublin Zoo in Phoenix Park (☎ 01-474 8900, 🖳 www.dublinzoo.ie), which opened in 1830 with animals supplied by London Zoo, is Ireland's only major zoo, housing large animals such as elephant, giraffe and hippopotamus. It's open all year round, but admission is a hefty €14.50 for adults and €10 for children between 3 and 16, with reductions for the unemployed, students and senior citizens, as well as family tickets **from** €42. There are a number of wildlife parks in other parts of the country, where smaller animals are kept or where wildlife is truly wild, such as the Fota Wildlife Park in Cork Harbour. These include the six National Parks – Ballycroy (County Mayo) the Burren (Clare), Connemara (Galway), Glenveagh (Donegal), Killarney (Kerry) and Wicklow (Wicklow) – details of which can be found on the National Parks & Wildlife Service website (🖳 www.npws.ie).

Ireland is mercifully free of 'theme parks', although there are other types of park, including the Bunratty Folk Park in County

Clare, and adventure parks offering activities such as canoeing, rock climbing, diving and even abseiling, bungee jumping and paintball, such as the Noreside Adventure Centre in Kilkenny (☎ 056-27273). More leisurely amusements can be found at the Tramore Amusement & Leisure Park in County Waterford. If you enjoy stomach-churning rides, you will need to look out for one of Ireland's several travelling funfairs.

THE ARTS

There isn't as much high-brow culture in Ireland as in most other European countries; the Arts tend to be more popular and traditional, which is no bad thing. In particular, Ireland hasn't much in the way of a tradition of visual arts, although the exemption from income tax on earnings from creative work, introduced in 1969, has attracted many artistic people to Ireland. The country's heritage is mostly literary and Ireland can boast more than its share of famous writers. For that reason, theatre has always been popular; Irish cinema is also booming and many foreign films are made in Ireland.

State support of the Arts in Ireland is poor. The Irish Arts Council (🖳 www.artscouncil. ie), a voluntary body appointed by the Minister for Arts, Sport and Tourism, is responsible for funding the arts (around half of its money coming from the National Lottery), but European Commission figures indicate that Ireland is bottom of the class when it comes to per capita spending. A huge 40 per cent of the little allocated goes to the Irish theatre and 20 per cent to music. Architecture gets a paltry 0.1 per cent. The Arts Council is also strongly criticised for being Dublin-biased.

The Irish National Ballet, established in Cork, had its subsidy terminated in the '80s and was forced to close; now there's no national ballet in Ireland. Cork's Opera House is also used for every type of entertainment (children's theatre, casino nights, pop concerts) in order to survive, although it does manage to stage the occasional opera as well (see page 313). Fortunately, business sponsorship of the arts has increased by a factor of ten since 1990, and there's an increasing amount of artistic activity throughout the country.

Details of what's on can be found in newspapers (The Irish Times has an entertainment supplement on Saturdays) and tourist office leaflets, as well as via the internet (e.g. 🖳 www. entertainment.ie).

Cinema

Ireland has always been a popular location for film-makers: David Lean shot his epic *Ryan's Daughter* in County Kerry in 1970, and John Huston (who made his home in Ireland) made several films in Ireland including his last, based on James Joyce's, *The Dead*, in 1987. Irish directors have also made their mark on the cinema world, Jim Sheridan and Neil Jordan winning Oscars for their films *The Crying Game* and *My Left Foot*; and Irish actors such as Liam Neeson and Pierce Brosnan have won international acclaim.

Today, directors come from all over the world to film in Ireland, and the Irish film industry, which has been growing by almost 20 per cent per annum for the last decade, employs over 4,300 people and contributes over €100m a year to gross domestic product. Recent productions have included Hollywood blockbusters such as *Braveheart* and *Saving Private Ryan*, as well as successful home-grown films such as *Angela's Ashes*, *Circle of Friends*, *Dancing at Lughnasa*, *The Field*, *The General* and *In the Name of the Father*.

When it comes to watching films, Ireland has the largest cinema-going audience relative to its population of any country in Europe, and Omniplexes, Multiplexes and Cineplexes have mushroomed in the suburbs of cities and towns in recent years (Dublin also boasts an IMAX cinema, showing 3D films on a giant screen). Sadly, though, many smaller cinemas have closed or now show only 'art' films.

The Irish Film Institute (☎ 01-679 3477, 🖳 www.irishfilm.ie), in Dublin's Temple Bar Area, houses two cinemas, the Irish Film Archive, a library, a film-themed bookshop and the offices of eight film-related organisations. Average cinema ticket prices are around €7.50; most cinemas offer cheaper seats before 5pm.

Films are classified as follows: 'General' rated films are suitable for all, 'PG' (parental guidance) films may be seen by children under 12 when accompanied by an adult, '12' films are restricted to those aged over 12, '15' films to those aged over 15 and '18' films to over-18s.

The Irish Times and Evening Herald, as well as local papers throughout Ireland, list films on show. For keen cinema-goers, the fortnightly magazine Hot Press (💻 www.hotpress.com) covers films, as well as pop music.

Dance

Although traditional Irish dancing is thriving, thanks in no small part to the *Riverdance* phenomenon, other forms of dance don't fare so well in Ireland, where there's only a small number of dedicated dance venues. In fact, there are no full-time professional dancers in Ireland, and limited teaching facilities for dance students, most of whom have to go abroad to study (and don't return).

What little dance there is, is confined mainly to Dublin – principally at the Irish Modern Dance Theatre (☎ 01-671 5113, 💻 www. irishmoderndancetheatre.com) – although Ireland's first dedicated dance centre, the Firkin Crane, was recently established in Cork, and the Arts Council proposes to develop dance in the coming years. The University Concert Hall in Limerick (☎ 061-331549, 💻 www.uch.ie) and the National Concert Hall in Dublin (☎ 01-417 0077, 💻 www.nch.ie) occasionally have dance shows, including ballet; tickets cost between €10 and €25.

Irish Dancing

Traditional Irish dancing dates from ancient times, and today's 'ring dances' can be traced back to the circular dances of the Druids. But foreign influences have also left their mark: the two words for 'dance' in Irish, *danse* and *rince*, come from the French *danse* and the English *rink*; Irish reels originated in Scotland, the hornpipe in England and the Irish set-dance derives from the French *quadrille*. The now popular *céilí* (literally a 'party with music') dates from the early 19th century, when dancing at the crossroads of the village was a popular pastime throughout Ireland.

Irish dancing was formalised with the establishment of the Gaelic League in 1893 and the Irish Dancing Commission (*Coimisiún le Rincí Gaelacha*, 💻 www.clrg.ie) in 1929. The Commission laid down rules governing Irish dancing, and published a handbook in 1939 detailing the required movements; it also organised dancing competitions (*feis*). After the War, solo dancing changed from being male-dominated to being female-dominated, and the rigid-arm style was introduced by the somewhat prurient League.

Paradoxically, it was a show which broke most of the rules that won Irish dancing a worldwide audience: Riverdance, first performed in 1994, and its successor Lord of the Dance made Irish dancing 'sexy' (a recent dance show called Dancing on Dangerous Ground has been described as the raunchiest yet!). Since then, Irish dance schools have been filled with youngsters hoping to emulate Michael Flatley and Jean Butler.

There are now some 500 Irish dance teachers in Ireland, and the annual All-Ireland Dancing Championships attract up to 200,000 competitors through regional qualifying events. Irish emigrants took traditional dancing to England, Scotland, the US, Canada, Australia and New Zealand, and dancers from these countries constitute over half of the 4,000+ competitors in the week-long World Dancing Championships, held in a different venue every April since 1970.

Details of dancing teachers and schools can be found on the Irish Dancing Commission's website (see above) and are contained in the monthly *Irish Dancing Magazine*, which you can order from bookshops or subscribe to via the internet (💻 www.irishdancing.com). One of the main Irish dancing schools is the Cunniffe Academy in Dublin. Dancing classes can cost very little if you enrol for a year's course; informal dance sessions are sometimes held in pubs. Various books are available from the Irish Dancing Commission (☎ 01-475 2220, 💻 www.clrg.ie), whose website contains information about dancing events, competitions and examinations.

Literature

Ireland has an ancient tradition of storytelling which is reflected in the richness of its literature. Beckett, Burke, Congreve, Goldsmith, Joyce, O'Casey, Shaw, Sheridan, Swift, Synge, Wilde,

In ancient times, the office of official poet (*file* in Gaelic) was second in importance only to that of the king. Today, the Irish buy more poetry books per capita than any other English-speaking people, and there are numerous poetry festivals and summer schools for budding poets. Even before he won the Nobel Prize for Literature, Seamus Heaney was a household name throughout Ireland, although he was actually born in Northern Ireland.

More than 100 books in the Irish language are published each year, books for children proving particularly popular.

Music

The English composer Arnold Bax declared that 'of all the antiquities in the world, Ireland possesses the most varied and beautiful music'. Ireland never developed a tradition of court music, which became classical music, but has a vibrant folk tradition which has enjoyed a huge revival in the last 20 years. Today, despite somewhat haphazard state support, music is one of Ireland's most dynamic art forms and is practised at local, as well as national, level.

The national music development organisation, Musicians' Network (☎ 01-671 9429, 💻 www.musicnetwork.ie), which is supported jointly by the Arts Council and the Electricity Supply Board, arranges tours by traditional, classical and jazz musicians to small venues in remote areas, and publishes the *Irish Music Handbook* (price €21.52 + P&P), a complete guide to classical, traditional and jazz music in Ireland (see also **Festivals** on page 315).

Irish Music

Irish music seemed to be dying out in the '50s in the face of the rock and pop invasion, but the formation in 1951 of Comhaltas Ceoltóirí Éireann (CCE), meaning 'Gathering of Irish Musicians', with the aim of promoting Irish music, was a turning point. Irish radio and TV also put their weight behind the revival, and by the early '60s there was an explosion of Irish folk music, with groups like the Chieftains and the Dubliners achieving international success, and others such as Altan, the Clancy Brothers, Clannad, Dé Danann, Planxty and Stocktons Wing, as well as individuals such as Christy Moore and Davy Spillane, national popularity.

CCE (☎ 01-280 0295, 💻 www.comhaltas.com) is now a huge organisation with more

Yeats... Considering its tiny population, Ireland has produced a remarkable number of world famous writers (Beckett, Shaw and Yeats all won Nobel Prizes for Literature); and continues to produce writers who could carry on that tradition, such as John Banville, Maeve Binchy, Elizabeth Bowen, Roddy Doyle (a Booker Prize winner), Patrick Kavanagh, Thomas Kinsella, Mary Lavin, Louis MacNeice, Patrick McCabe, Frank McCourt, John McGahern, Edna O'Brien, Flann O'Brien, Frank O'Connor and others.

Yeats and Joyce in particular are widely celebrated: on 16th June each year, Joyce's novel *Ulysses* is commemorated in Dublin, where it was set, by a tour of the city and suburbs, retracing the steps of the novel's characters. The international success of Frank McCourt's autobiographical novel *Angela's Ashes*, which was made into a film, has similarly prompted guided tours of Limerick.

The strict censorship of books introduced in the '20s was largely abolished in 1967; today, censorship is mainly directed at visual material, although the Censorship Board still has the authority to ban books (foreign books are occasionally banned).

Poetry is more highly regarded and less elitist than almost anywhere else in the world.

than 200 branches worldwide. Most small Irish music groups are affiliated to the CCE, which sponsors 45 annual music festivals (*fleadhanna*, the plural of *fleá* or *fleadh*, prounounced 'flah'). The most important of these is the annual All-Ireland Festival, which attracts some 20,000 entries and culminates in the finals every March.

Traditional Irish music has an aural tradition: melodies and lyrics are passed on from performer to performer, many of whom cannot read music. Its heartland is in counties Kerry and Clare, but it's performed throughout Ireland. Most music making is amateur, in the sense that it's done purely for fun (there are few full-time professional performers): a few musicians gather in a pub and put on an impromptu performance (known as a *seisun*), for which they receive no payment other than perhaps a few drinks.

Irish music can also be heard at local festivals, competitions and concerts (mainly in the summer months). The principal concert venues are the Geantraí Folle Theatre at the Cultúrlann na hÉireann in Monkstown, County Dublin and the Brú Ború Theatre in Cashel, County Tipperary. All concerts are listed on the CCE website, as well as in newspapers and event guides.

Most pieces are fast dances, and are played in the same few keys (usually one or two sharps) and within a restricted range (one or two octaves). Traditional instruments include the fiddle (violin), tin whistle, flute, uilleann pipes (rather like bagpipes), *bodhran* (small goatskin drum), accordion, melodeon and concertina, although the most ancient instrument, the harp (*cruit*) is seldom heard today; less 'authentic' instruments such as the banjo, mandolin, guitar, bouzouki (a Balkan instrument), dulcimer, and spoons or bones are often added.

Singing is normally unaccompanied, and unison duets are common, especially in *sean-nós* – a specific style of Irish language singing which tells of failed rebellions, unrequited love, tearful partings, homesickness and dead heroes. *Sean-nós*, which almost died out in the '40s, is now regarded by many as the purest form of Irish music.

If you play an instrument, you can join one of the 600 weekly informal gatherings organised by CCE (see above). If you want to learn an instrument, there are over 400 qualified teachers of traditional Irish music, and group

lessons can cost as little as €30 per term. There are also organised 'workshops' such as the *Lá na hAmhrán – Sean-Nós*, usually in the first week of March; and music schools, mostly in summer, such as The Flowing Tide, Maoin Cheoil an Chláir, the Lahinch Folklore School, the Joe Mooney Summer School, and Willie Clancy's in Miltown Malbay (County Clare), reputed to be Ireland's largest music summer school; details can be supplied by CCE.

Classical Music

Ireland's most famous classical composer was probably John Field (1782-1837), who 'invented' the Nocturne later popularised by Chopin. In more recent times, A. J. Potter (1918–1980) and Gerard Victory (1921–1995) have been influential figures on the contemporary classical music scene, as have Seoirse Bodley, Brian Boydell, Shaun Davey, Seán Ó Ríada and Michael O'Súilleabháin, whose works are strongly influenced by traditional Irish music.

As regards the performance of classical music, there are few public concerts compared with other European countries. Ireland has only one full-time professional orchestra, Radio Telefis Éireann (RTÉ)'s Concert Orchestra, and otherwise few employment prospects outside teaching for classically trained musicians. Even that is a poor option, as music is accorded a low priority in Irish (as in British) schools, so that Irish musicians, like dancers, often have to finish their studies abroad and find little to tempt them back again. Nor is there much state support for independent music schools.

Ireland's largest (and first) purpose-built concert hall is at Limerick University (☎ 061-331549, 🖥 www.uch.ie), where you can see everything from *La Bohème* to The Corrs for between €20 and €50 (with concessions for children and senior citizens). Tickets for the National Concert Hall in Dublin (☎ 01-417 0000, 🖥 www.nch.ie) can cost as little as €10, but as much as €100 for top international orchestras and soloists. RTÉ recently launched a national classical music radio station, Lyric fm (🖥 www.rte.ie/lyricfm), which offers a varied programme of music.

Opera

There are four main opera companies in Ireland: Opera Ireland and the Opera Theatre Company in Dublin, Wexford Festival Opera and the Cork Opera House. The Wexford Opera Festival (☎ 053-912-2144, 🖥 www.wexfordopera.com) is one of Ireland's major cultural successes: founded in 1951, it has become a highlight of the international opera season. During the 18-day festival there are three main opera productions, as well as numerous 'fringe' events.

Tickets for the main productions cost around €80–100, 'short' operas (i.e. those lasting less than half a day) cost around €20, and lunchtime operatic concerts as little as €12.50. Tickets for opera performances at the Cork Opera House (☎ 021-427 0022, 🖥 www.corkoperahouse.ie) cost between around €25 and €50. There's also the occasional opera at the University Concert Hall in Limerick (see **Classical Music** above).

Jazz

There are a number of jazz clubs in Cork, Dublin, Galway and Sligo (listed on 🖥 www.jazz-clubs-worldwide.com) and occasional jazz concerts at the University Concert Hall

in Limerick and the National Concert Hall in Dublin (see **Classical Music** above). There are also annual jazz festivals in Bray, near Dublin, and Cork. There's no dedicated jazz radio station, but there are jazz programmes on both Radio 1 and Lyric fm.

Pop

Ireland also has an international reputation for popular music, having produced numerous world-famous singers and groups, and won the Eurovision Song Contest no fewer than seven times, with consecutive victories in 1992, '93 and '94.

Irish pop began to blossom in the late '60s, when Van Morrison, Rory Gallagher and Gary Moore emerged, along with groups such as Thin Lizzy and Sweeney's Men; and its flowering continued into the '70s and '80s with the Boomtown Rats, Stiff Little Fingers, the Pogues and Moving Hearts, as the formerly separate musical worlds of traditional, folk, pop and rock began to overlap.

Ireland has produced a number of outstanding solo artists, such as Mary Black, Paul Brady, Enya, Bob Geldof, Glen Hansord, Brian Kennedy, Christy Moore, Daniel O'Donnell, Sinéad O'Connor, Davy Spillane and Andrew Strong; while recent Irish groups to achieve acclaim include Ash, Boyzone, B*witched, the Corrs, the Cranberries, Divine Comedy, Hothouse Flowers, The Sawdoctors, Therapy, U2 and Westlife.

Many other pop stars have moved to Ireland, e.g. Marianne Faithfull, Donovan Leach, Ronnie Wood (Rolling Stones), Elvis Costello, and Joe Elliot (Def Leppard); and several more have proudly claimed Irish descent, including John Lennon, Paul McCartney, Liam and Noel Gallagher, Morrissey and Johnny Marr.

Pop concerts are held in various venues, including the University Concert Hall in Limerick, the Point Depot, New Vicar Street and Hot Press music centres in Dublin; and occasionally at Dublin's National Stadium (a boxing venue) and the Royal Dublin Society (RDS), although planning restrictions limit the number of open air concerts. The fortnightly magazine *Hot Press* (⌨ www.hotpress.com) covers pop music, and gives details of forthcoming concerts.

Theatre

Theatre has traditionally been Ireland's strongest art form, and the list of Irish playwrights includes such luminaries as Samuel Beckett, Sean O'Casey, George Bernard Shaw, John Millington Synge, George Bernard Shaw, Oscar Wilde, and, more recently, Brian Friel, Declan Hughes, Tom Murphy, Joe O'Connor, Jim Sheridan and Gerry Stembridge. There are currently some 23 professional drama groups in Ireland, producing around 120 works each year, as well as numerous youth and amateur groups.

Dublin is, of course, famous for its theatres, principally the Abbey and the Gate. The Abbey was founded in 1904 by the poet W. B. Yeats, with the aim of presenting new Irish plays (the premiere of Synge's *Playboy of the Western World* in 1907 famously caused a riot), which is still its mission, although its productions tend to be rather conservative nowadays. The Gate was established in 1928 to present the work of foreign playwrights (initially Ibsen and Chekhov).

The long-standing rivalry between the two theatres was exacerbated when the Abbey was nominated as the official Irish National Theatre, and allocated a government grant five times the size of the Gate's, as well as full-time salaried actors. Other Dublin theatres include the Gaiety, the Olympia and the innovative Rough Magic Theatre Company at the Project Arts Centre in Temple Bar. Dublin's annual Theatre Festival, which takes place over two weeks in October, is a wonderful opportunity to see a range of Irish and visiting plays, in venues ranging from the National Theatre to smaller theatres around the city.

Outside the capital, it's the Druid Theatre Company in Galway, founded by two university students in 1975 and now Arts Council supported, which has taken over from the Abbey the role of fostering radical new Irish drama. Galway also has the Town Hall Theatre, which stages concerts as well as plays, and the *Taibhdhearc*, Ireland's only Irish language theatre (some of the plays are in English!). There are several theatres in Cork (principally the Everyman and the Triskel Arts Centre theatre), and one each in Waterford (the Red Kettle), Sligo (the Hawk's Well Theatre) and Limerick (the Belltable). Traditional Irish plays can also be seen at the National Folk Theatre in Tralee. Average ticket prices are between around €15 and €30.

Links to the websites of Dublin's major theatres can be found on (⌨ www.dublinuncovered.net/theatres.html) and a list of all Ireland's main theatres, with details of what's on, booking and how to get there, is on ⌨ www.theatresonline.com. Theatre details are listed in daily newspapers and on websites such as ⌨ www.entertainment.ie; seating plans are even shown at the front of the *Golden Pages*. Bookings can be made over the telephone or online.

> Tickets for shows in the capital are available from Dublin Tourism (by going to the Dublin Tourism Centre, Suffolk Street – ☎ 01-605 7700), or by visiting the Ticketmaster website (⌨ www.ticketmaster.ie) which is run by Dublin Tourism.

Theatres such as the Gaiety in Dublin hold professional drama coaching courses during the summer, and the Limerick Youth Theatre (which opened in 1997) provides training for aspiring young actors. Amateur dramatics are also popular throughout Ireland.

Comedy

Comedy shows are growing in popularity in Ireland, and a number of venues now provide at least one comedy night each week. The Tivoli Theatre in Dublin is one of the leading comedy theatres, featuring both Irish (e.g. Dylan Moran, Tommy Tiernan) and foreign acts, from established players to upcoming and innovative groups. Murphy's Laughter Lounge in Dublin has comedy shows every night of the week.

Visual Arts

It's estimated that there are 1,500 visual artists practising in Ireland, and they currently enjoy a higher profile, both at home and abroad, than ever before. Ireland's most famous painter is probably John Butler Yeats, brother of the poet W. B. Yeats, with other notable names including Robert Ballagh, Barrie Cooke, Patrick Collins, Michael Farrall, Nathaniel Hone, John Lavery, William Leech, Tony O'Malley, William Orpen, Walter Osborne, Patrick Scott and Camille Souter. Ireland's best known sculptors include John Behan, Michael Bulfin, Hilary Heron, Oisin Kelly, Brian King, Séamus Murphy, Ellis O'Connell and Michael Warran.

Apart from the major museums and galleries (see **Galleries & Museums** on page 306), Ireland boasts a number of smaller galleries devoted to the visual arts, principally the numerous arts centres that have been created since the late '60s to provide an opportunity for young artists to exhibit their work.

One of these, the Triskel Arts Centre in Cork, incorporates two artists' studios, as well as two art galleries; the Temple Bar Gallery & Studios in Dublin is Europe's largest studio complex, housing more than 30 working artists, whose studios can be visited by appointment.

Festivals

The Irish are great festival-goers, and every summer dozens of towns large and small

hold festivals (known as *féile*, singular *feis*, pronounced 'fesh'), the best known of which are listed above. Perhaps the most famous of all is the Rose of Tralee festival in the town of Tralee (which has been described as a 'sickly-sentimental, stage-Irish commercial, promoting an outmoded version of womanhood'!). As well as music, dancing, horse-racing and parades, there's the coveted Rose of Tralee title, which attracts young women of Irish descent from throughout the world.

Another festival that's famous throughout Europe, if not the world, is the six week long Lisdoonvarna festival: Lisdoonvarna in County Clare, which is Ireland's only working spa, hosts one of Europe's largest 'singles' festivals – thousands of Irish couples claim to have met at Lisdoonvarna!

The Dublin Music Festival (*Feis Cheoil*, pronounced 'fesh kol') has been running since 1897 and has been much imitated, e.g. the *Father Mathew Feis* in Cork, the *Sligo Feis Ceoil*, *Feis Shligigh* and *Féile Luimnighe* in Limerick, and others in Arklow, Ballina, Dundalk and Killaloe. At these festivals, vocal, choral and instrumental classes in classical music may be supplemented by competitions in traditional music, jazz and composition.

Some have specialised or adopted a theme and developed into international events, most notably the Wexford Opera Festival (see **Music** above), which was created to stage unfamiliar operas; the Cork Choral and Folk Dance Festival, which promotes Irish composers; the Dublin Organ Festival, the Waterford Festival of Light Opera, the GPA Music Festival, which takes place in stately homes throughout Ireland, the Dublin Festival of Early Music and, more recently, the Dublin Piano Competition, which started in 1988.

For jazz fans there's the annual Jazz Festival in Cork, on the October public holiday, featuring artists from all over the world; the Olympia Theatre Jazz Festival in Dublin, which runs throughout July, and a Jazz Week in September, also in Dublin. Other festivals have broadened their appeal by incorporating a wide variety of activities, such as the Adare Festival; and Kilkenny Arts Week, a ten-day extravaganza with an almost carnival-like atmosphere, whose primary purpose seems to be the retailing of the maximum quantity of booze – it's no accident that one of the event's major sponsors is the town's brewery, Smithwicks! The Baboro, which takes place in Galway in mid-October, is Ireland's only arts festival for children.

EATING & DRINKING

Ireland isn't noted for its cuisine, although the quality of Irish food has improved immeasurably in the last few years, and it's now among the biggest and most agreeable surprises you will encounter on your first visit (or if you haven't been for a while).

> As recently as 1993, the Irish commentator John Ardagh was writing that 'Ireland is still awash with soggy vegetables and frizzled chops', but now you can walk into almost any restaurant in any town and be served well cooked, interesting and attractively presented food at reasonable prices.

'Exotic' foods, which were almost unheard of in Irish shops and restaurants 25 years ago, are now commonplace. There are, of course, many traditional Irish dishes (see below), but they're mainly reserved for home cooking, although curiously staple dishes such as brawn (made from parts of a pig usually thrown away!) are reappearing on trendy restaurant menus! In a similar peculiar twist of culinary fashion, fish, which was traditionally regarded as 'penance food', to be eaten only on Fridays (Catholics being forbidden to eat meat on Fridays), is today Ireland's most popular restaurant food.

Among Irish people, the fashion for eating out began in the '70s and, whereas they would originally have eaten in a pub, they're now more inclined to go to a restaurant. Today, for Dubliners at least, dining out is an everyday occurrence rather than being reserved for special occasions.

Irish Food

For centuries, the potato was the staple food of millions of Irish people, being more or less the only crop that would grow in Ireland's peaty soil, and many traditional Irish dishes are based on the potato, the main meat ingredient being pig. Wherever you go in Ireland and whatever you eat, generous portions are the norm – it's a sign of inhospitality to provide a small meal.

Irish Breakfast

A 'traditional' Irish breakfast is similar to its English counterpart (from which it derives): a plateful of fried bacon, egg and sausage, sometimes with tomatoes, mushrooms, beans, hash browns and slices of black or white pudding, plus toast and soda bread (see below), often preceded by fruit juice or cereal (or porridge) and accompanied by a pot of tea. Unless you're anorexic or suffer from abnormally low cholesterol levels, it isn't recommended that you have a full Irish breakfast every day!

Irish Stew, Coddle & Colcannon

As the Hungarians have their goulash and the British their shepherd's pie, the Irish have their stew. Originally made with goat's meat (as no farmer would have sacrificed his lambs), today Irish stew usually consists of lamb, potatoes and onions. There are, of course, variations on this theme, and other vegetables, like carrots and swedes, are sometimes substituted (to the horror of purists!), but most agree that a good Irish stew should be thick and creamy. Irish stew's poor relation, coddle, which was once popular in Dublin, but is no longer in vogue, is a thick soup containing just about anything edible. An even poorer relation, but one suitable for vegetarians, is colcannon, a mixture of mashed potato, onion and cabbage boiled in butter and milk.

Boxty

Boxty (or potato brea) is a kind of pancake, usually eaten with bacon, eggs and sausage, which is enjoying something of a revival in popularity.

Soda Bread

Another Irish 'delicacy' is soda bread, made with sour milk and bicarbonate of soda, but without yeast. Almost more like cake than bread, soda bread is served at all times of the day, as an accompaniment to breakfast, lunch, tea and dinner, invariably with generous quantities of Irish butter – try not to eat too much of it or you will have no appetite left for your main meal!

Desserts

Another unhealthy habit the Irish inherited from the British is the eating of sickly puddings such as fruit pies and trifle (fruit, jelly and custard, sometimes laced with sherry). A more indigenous (and tasty) dessert is Irish jelly, traditionally made from carrageen moss – actually a kind of seaweed called *dulsk*, containing a natural jelling agent, that grows in shallow water around the Irish coast. The 'moss' is laid out to be washed by the rain and dried by the sun and then boiled with milk to make jelly. Like Guinness, it's something of an acquired taste! Barm Brack is a chewy, spiced teabread traditionally baked on Hallowe'en.

Cheese

Like the UK, Ireland produces a large number of excellent cheeses, most of them unknown to foreigners (and even to natives). Cheddar is, of course, well known and the Irish have their own versions of it, usually dyed orange. More interesting, though, are their goat's milk cheeses (e.g. Croghan from County Wexford) and sheep's milk cheeses (e.g. Knockalara from the south-west), soft cheeses (e.g. Gubbeen from County Cork), Emmenthal-style cheeses (e.g. Gabriel) and, especially blue cheeses (e.g. Cashel Blue from County Tipperary).

Restaurants & Cafés

In the mid-'70s, Ireland had few good restaurants, even in Dublin. Now there are as many as in any other major European country, including a wide choice of foreign cuisines. Dublin in particular has recently experienced a surge in the number of European, Eastern and Far Eastern eating establishments, and you can now choose from French, Italian and Mediterranean, Scandinavian, Moroccan, Russian, Japanese and Oriental, among others. Many of the cheaper, livelier restaurants are concentrated in the city centre, particularly in the Temple Bar and Dame Street area.

As in the UK, you will find a number of Chinese and Indian restaurants, as well as take-away fish and chip shops and, sad to say, McDonald's and KFCs. South Africa's most successful restaurant chain, Spur Steakhouse, recently opened its first outlet in Dublin, and aims to create the country's first steakhouse chain through a nationwide franchising operation. Vegetarians, on the other hand, are also fairly well catered for, and there's a growing number of exclusively vegetarian restaurants in Dublin, although elsewhere they're still rather thin on the ground. An internet search for 'vegetarian restaurants Ireland' brings up a number of sites listing establishments throughout the country.

Seafood is common in 'Irish' restaurants, thanks to the over 60 species of fish caught off Ireland's coast, which include cockles, mussels, scallops, oysters, sea urchins and, of course, the famous Dublin Bay prawns (which are neither prawns nor from Dublin Bay!); as well as lobster, crab and a wide range of fish, including wild salmon and strange deep sea creatures which appear on most menus. Even your average Irish fish and chips (known as a 'one on one' in Dublin) is, on the whole, more tasty than its British equivalent (the best fish and chips in Ireland is reputed to be had at Melly's in Killybegs in County Donegal).

In the main towns, particularly in Dublin, cafés are becoming increasingly popular. Bewley's Oriental Cafés are practically a Dublin institution, and US chain Starbucks has recently opened ten outlets, all in the capital. In out of the way places, even if there's no restaurant, you will usually find that the local pub

Soda bread

will have a reasonable selection of food on offer.

As in the UK, it isn't usual to dress up when you go out to eat, and only a few restaurants (mostly in hotels) insist on men wearing a jacket and tie.

 Caution

Smoking isn't permitted in any public places in Ireland, including bars, cafés and restaurants.

There are any number of guides to restaurants and cafés in Ireland, including online listings and portals taking you straight to the establishments' own sites. Restaurants are advertised in newspapers and magazines, and *The Irish Times* has a Saturday column devoted to eating out. The Irish tourist board publishes a booklet entitled *Dining in Ireland* and tourist information leaflets normally include details of local restaurants.

Opening Hours

Most restaurants are open seven days a week, although some close on Mondays; and in remote parts, they may open only at weekends during the winter months. Most restaurants offer lunch as well as evening meals, but a few do only Sunday lunches. Cafés and snack bars aren't usually open in the evenings. Restaurants are permitted to serve alcohol outside normal licensing hours (see below), provided that it's accompanying a meal. Bewley's in Dublin's Grafton Street stays open into the small hours during the weekend.

Prices

On the whole, restaurant prices are reasonable and portions are generous, so that eating out is good value. Main courses in reasonable restaurants start at around €10, and you may be able to get two courses for €15. In a smart establishment, you should expect to pay at least €30 per head, excluding wine ... and there's the rub. As in many other countries, restaurants make most of their profit on drinks, and wine is expensive: usually at least €15 a bottle for something ordinary, rising to €25 for

anything slightly up-market. However, you will generally be offered a comprehensive selection of wines, both 'old world' and 'new world'. Prices include value added tax (VAT).

A tip of 10 to 15 per cent is the norm in restaurants, unless a service charge has already been added to the bill – something that is becoming increasingly common, which means that you pay extra even for poor service (although, thankfully, service in Irish restaurants is generally excellent).

Pubs & Bars

Here's a riddle: How do you get from one side of Dublin to the other without passing a single pub? The answer: Go into them all! There are reckoned to be at least 400 pubs in Dublin and more than 10,500 nationwide – one for every 400 people. In some smaller towns and villages, there may be a pub for every 50 inhabitants and 'going for a quick one' is still a popular national pastime, although less so than it used to be. Pub-going, at least among Irish people, has been declining since the mid-'70s, and it's said that half of Irish pubs are now struggling to survive; like farmers, publicans are being forced to diversify, and many have other part-time jobs.

Nevertheless, the pub is still such a ubiquitous feature of Ireland that you will have little trouble finding one (except in some of the wildest parts of the north-west); in fact you're quite likely to be given directions with reference to pubs! However, quantity is one thing, quality quite another, and the traditional pub where young and old, rich and poor rub shoulders, and impromptu performances of Irish music (*seisuns*) create a unique atmosphere, is becoming something of a rarity. In its place is the 'pseudo-traditional' Irish pub (a meticulously designed but soulless replica of the real thing), continental style café/bars aimed at the young and trendy, and theme bars, which are particularly popular in Dublin.

Perhaps Dublin's most famous traditional pub is Mulligan's in Poolberg Street, dating from 1782. Others include the Brazen Head (Dublin's oldest, supposedly dating from 1198), Conway's, the Dawson Lounge (the city's smallest), Davy Byrne's, Doheny and Nesbitt's, Grogan's, Keating's, Kehoe's, McDavid's, Neary's, O'Donoghue's, Ryan's and Slattery's.

The Porter House has even revived the tradition of brewing its own beer.

Probably the most famous pseudo-Irish pub is Johnnie Fox's in the Wicklow mountains just outside Dublin (it claims to be Ireland's highest pub!), where people from all over the world flock for an organised Irish experience (if you want to eat there, you need to book several months in advance!).

An essential part of many people's visit to Ireland is a glass (or several) of Guinness, which is reputed to taste quite different in Ireland than abroad (this is a matter of opinion, and to some it tastes terrible wherever you drink it!). Guinness is, of course, only one of several brands of stout (or porter), which is still Ireland's favourite drink, although nowadays almost as much lager is drunk.

Most beer comes in draught form (note that, despite metrication, it's still sold in pints!) and one of the peculiar attractions of stout is that, like German beer, it takes time to settle – a pint of Guinness isn't supposed to be drunk until 119.5 seconds after it's poured. Those who find the stout undrinkable at any time might like to try a 'Black Velvet', a mixture of stout and Champagne (or the poor man's version, stout and cider), which is guaranteed to make you see leprechauns!

Cider on its own is becoming increasingly popular, Ireland's main producer being Bulmer (who claim that nothing is added to the apple juice except time). Wine consumption is also growing, but still accounts for a mere 6 per cent of alcohol consumption (Ireland has just one vineyard, near Mallow in County Cork, which produces a dry white wine that's as rare as Irish sunshine!).

Irish whiskeys are also popular, especially Jameson, and must under Irish law be stored in oak vats for at least three years (many are kept much longer, since the quality of a whiskey, like that of a good wine, is largely determined by its age). Whiskey has been drunk in Ireland for over 500 years (the word is supposed to come from the Gaelic *uisge beatha*, meaning 'water of life') and the Irish version is made from malted barley with a small amount of wheat, oats and sometimes rye.

If neat whiskey is too strong for your palate, try an Irish coffee – a glass of hot, sweet, whiskey-laced coffee with a 'head' of cold Irish cream – which is said to have been invented in Limerick in the early 1900s. More of an acquired taste is Bailey's Irish Cream, a mixture of Irish whiskey, other spirits and cream. But the most 'authentic' Irish drink of all is probably *poitín* (pronounced 'potcheen'), also known as 'the quare stuff', which is a fire-water distilled from potatoes. Banned by the British in 1831, it has never been legalised, and dozens of people are fined every year for distilling it, mostly in remote western parts!

Ireland also produces a number of sparkling waters, the best known being Ballygowan (from County Limerick).

As in the UK, most pubs offer food at lunchtime and in the evening (although it's more likely to be real food than the microwaved packet meals served up by most British establishments!), and a few put on entertainment – not just music, but fashion shows, Bridge tournaments, even plays.

Some pubs ban the use of mobile phones (hear, hear!) and cigarettes are generally sold from behind the bar rather than from machines.

Licensing Hours

There's an Irish saying: 'The only cure for drinking is to drink more'. Nevertheless, pubs and bars are permitted to open only at certain times – at least officially. The law states that Irish pubs and clubs may sell alcoholic drinks only between 10.30am and 11.30pm Mondays to Thursdays, between 10.30 and 12.30am on Fridays and Saturdays, and from 12.30 to 2pm and 4 to 11pm on Sundays (except on 23rd or 24th December if they fall on a Sunday, in which case weekday times apply). Pubs are closed on Christmas Day and Good Friday, and special times apply on St Patrick's Day.

However, pubs don't tend to fill up until after 9pm (if there's live music, it won't start until around 9.30pm) and many stay 'open' unofficially, well after the legal closing time (legally, you're allowed only half an hour's 'drinking-up time' after closing time). In Dublin, several pubs have late bars at the weekends, which are licensed until 1 or 2am. Licensed restaurants are allowed to sell alcoholic drinks to accompany 'substantial' meals between 12.30pm and 00.30am on weekdays and from 12.30 to 3pm and from 6pm to 00.30am on Sundays (1–3pm and 7–10pm on Christmas Day).

Age Limits

The legal drinking age in Ireland is 18 and, although many pubs and off-licences try to enforce over-21 or over-23 restrictions, these aren't in fact legal. However, under 18s are allowed in pubs and bars, although under 15s must be accompanied by a parent or guardian and may not be in a bar after 9pm. Those aged between 18 and 20 must carry an 'age document' if in a bar after 9pm; these can be obtained from any *Garda* station for a small fee; you will need to produce your passport or birth certificate and a photograph.

Smoking

Smoking isn't allowed in any enclosed area where people work, which includes pubs and bars, but not their gardens or terraces. Smokers must therefore go outside to indulge between rounds, although if outside is a public street they may not be allowed to take drinks with them, as drinking in the street is normally prohibited.

Prices

A pint of beer (bitter, stout or lager) or a measure of spirits (e.g. whiskey, brandy or vodka) in a pub or bar normally costs between €3.50 and €4, and a bottle of cider around €4 (more in Dublin). 'Happy' hours (when prices are reduced) are no longer allowed.

NIGHTLIFE

Irish nightlife varies considerably from one area to another; in small towns and villages you may be lucky to find a bar with music, whereas in Dublin you will be spoilt for choice of nightclubs and cabaret shows, catering for most musical tastes. The Temple Bar area in particular (sometimes dubbed Dublin's 'Left Bank') has recently become known as a 'happening' place, with trendy clubs (and pre-club bars) appearing (and disappearing) at an alarming rate. There's the Salsa Palace (Latin-American music), the Soul Stage (blues and jazz), Major Tom's ('70s–'90s music) and Break for the Border (country & western). Copper-Face Jack's and the Vatican are aimed at youngsters, while the Court attracts 'mature' people.

There are several clubs and late licence pubs in the Temple Bar area. The latest 'last orders' can be had in Leeson Street, where the basements of Georgian offices have

been converted to wine bars, serving until 3am. Some clubs have strict dress codes and restricted entry, e.g. POD (over 21s only) and Copper-Face Jack's (over 23s). Admission charges vary from nothing to €20, some clubs charging only after a certain time (e.g. 10.30pm) or only on certain nights of the week

Dublin doesn't have a monopoly on nightclubs, which can be found in most towns in Ireland. Perhaps the best known outside the capital is Reardan's in Cork, where there's also Club FX, Fast Eddie's, Havana Brown's, Sir Henry's and The Pavilion. In Galway, you can chose from Bogart's, The Cube, The Liquid Nightclub and The Warwick; while in Limerick there's The Globe and The Works, as well as the Royal George hotel, Schooners (a lively bar with music) and Dolan's, the biggest live music venue in Limerick.

Other forms of nightlife include party nights, 'supper clubs' and dinner cabarets. Traditional Irish cabaret shows, involving a mixture of singing, dancing and slapstick humour, can still be seen at a number of venues including Doyle's Irish Cabaret and Jury's Irish Cabaret in Dublin, the Abbey Tavern in Howth, and Clontarf Castle. Other venues, such as Dublin's Da Club, offer a more European-style cabaret show.

Ireland was one of the last European countries to accept homosexuality, which was a criminal offence until 1993; but there's now quite a lively gay scene in most cities and large towns – although not elsewhere – and intolerance is rare. Detailed information can be found on 🖥 www.dochara.com/info/gay-friendly.

Ireland also has plenty of social clubs, including clubs for single people, old people and ex-servicemen. These are listed under *Social Clubs* in the *Golden Pages*.

GAMBLING

The Irish are well known for their partiality to gambling, particularly when it comes to betting on horse (and greyhound) races. There are also two kinds of institutionalised gambling in the form of the national lottery and prize bonds.

National Lottery

The Irish lottery (🖥 www.lotto.ie) was established in 1987 to raise money for the health and welfare services, youth, sport,

the arts and culture, and the Irish language. It's operated on behalf of the government by An Post, the Irish post office, which has a nationwide network of on-line lottery terminals.

There's a guaranteed minimum weekly jackpot of €2m for those who guess all six numbers correctly, which may be shared between several winners (the odds of winning it outright are just over 5m to one), although on some occasions there's no outright winner, in which case the jackpot is 'rolled over' until the following week. Five correct numbers plus the bonus number wins you €25,000, lesser prizes being a percentage of the total prize fund.

As in the UK, draws take place every Wednesday and Saturday evening and are transmitted live on RTÉ television. Tickets, which can be purchased only by over 18s, start at €3 for two rows of numbers and are available from any of 3,500 outlets, including all post offices. Most of these also sell lottery scratch cards. Recently, the lottery has introduced a number of variations on the standard draw such as 'Lotto Plus' and 'Lotto 5-4-3-2-1', as well as a new game called TellyBingo, played on RTÉ 1 on a Tuesday night – all designed to separate ever more money from the ever-hopeful. Further information is available from the lottery website (🖥 www.lotto.ie).

Prize Bonds

An Post also operates a prize bond scheme that's similar to the British premium bond system. The minimum purchase is €25 and you can win up to €150,000 each month. All winnings are tax-free.

> You can purchase prize bonds online (at 🖥 www.prizebonds.ie) or from post offices, banks, and even stockbrokers!

Winning numbers are displayed on Teletext, and at around 1,000 post offices.

Bingo

Bingo is very popular in Ireland, where it's organised on a local community basis, and there are no large privately owned bingo halls.

Betting Shops

There are over 800 betting shops in Ireland, most of which are open 363 days a year (closed only on Christmas Day and Good Friday!), normally from 10.30am until 5pm in winter and 10.30am to 7pm in summer. These times may be extended if there's an evening event, e.g. a race meeting. Ireland doesn't have its own football pools operator, although betting shops take bets on the English leagues.

Casinos & Amusement Arcades

There are nine establishments calling themselves casinos in Ireland (eight of them in Dublin), but only two or three offer traditional table games such as roulette; details of all of them can be found on 🖥 www.worldcasinodirectory.com. There are many amusement arcades in Ireland, particularly in Dublin and in holiday resorts. Some have gaming machines from which you can win cash (the chances are you will lose it!); others aren't licensed for gambling, and offer only prizes such as teddy bears!

LIBRARIES

Library provision in Ireland is widely considered to be inadequate, and recent government spending cuts have hardly improved the situation. Nevertheless, there are over 350 libraries and 30 mobile libraries throughout the country. They're run by county and city councils, and controlled by the Library Council (☎ 01-676 1167, 🖥 www.librarycouncil.ie); a list of libraries and contact details such can be found on 🖥 www.library.ie.

Libraries are an excellent source of local information. Books, videos and most compact discs (CDs) can be borrowed free of charge, but there's normally a small fee for certain CDs. The usual borrowing period is two or three weeks, and a small fine is exacted if books are kept beyond this period without being renewed. This can usually be done by phone, provided that a book hasn't been reserved by another borrower. Larger libraries offer free internet access, although you may need to book a 'slot', which is normally an hour.

To register as a borrower, you need to produce two forms of identification, one of which must show your address. If you aren't resident in Ireland, you can still use libraries for reference. Main libraries are normally open five days a week, smaller libraries two or three days. Some stay open until 8pm on certain days. Remote areas are normally served by a mobile library; details of visiting times can be obtained from your nearest library.

Every university library in Ireland has legal deposit status, which means that they should have a copy of every book published in Ireland. However, only two libraries, the National Library and Trinity College Library, both in Dublin, acquire significant numbers of old books, although other historical libraries are gradually being opened to the public.

The National Library (☎ 01-603 0213, 🖥 www.nli.ie) can be used for reference purposes if your local library doesn't have the books you need. The National Council for the Blind (☎ 01-830 7033 or ☎ 1850-334353, 🖥 www.ncbi.ie) runs the NCBI Library and Media Centre, Unit 29, Finglas Business Centre, Jamestown Road, Finglas, Dublin 11 (☎ 01-864 2266), which also offers a 'talking book' service (i.e. spoken versions of books on tape) and provides cassette and CD players if required.

Achill Head, Achill Island, Co. Mayo

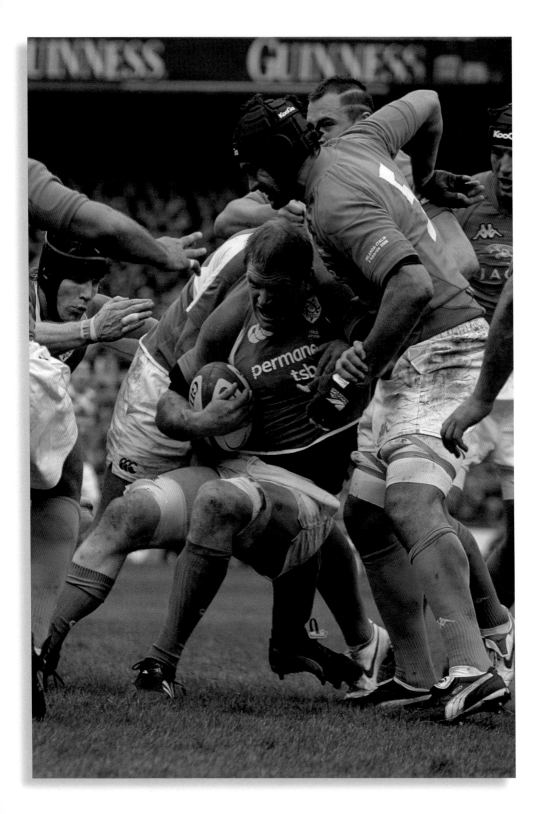

16.
SPORTS

Threat T he Irish are generally no more and no less physically active than other Europeans – which, of course, means that they're increasingly inactive. SLÁN, the national survey of lifestyle, attitudes and nutrition of people living in Ireland (☎ 1800-250172, 💻 www. slan06.ie), reported in 2008 that only around half of Ireland's adult population is 'physically active' (defined as taking part in exercise or sport for at least 20 minutes at least twice a week) and more than one in five are 'inactive' – though only 3 per cent of those surveyed attributed this to lack of access to suitable facilities.

As a result of similar findings in the previous report, published in 2004, the National Health Promotion strategy 2000-05 aimed to increase participation in regular, moderate physical activity, but since then there has been no further strategy. The Department of Health's Health Promotion Unit organised campaigns such as 'Get a Life, Get Active' (2001–02) and the less catchily phrased 'Let it Go, Just for 30 Minutes' and, for senior citizens, 'Let it Go through Dance' (2003), but again, there appears to be no current campaign.

The Irish Sports Council (💻 www.irish sportscouncil.ie), on the other hand, came up with a 'Building Sport for Life' three-year strategy in 2006 and also launched a Women in Sport initiative, comprising 41 projects and featuring its own website (💻 www.women insport.ie), which is designed to encourage greater participation among females.

Irish businesses too are increasingly encouraging fitness among staff by negotiating discounts at local health clubs. A few like Intel, Oracle and Hewlett-Packard, even have on-site gyms, and Waterford Crystal's swimming pool and sports facilities are available to all local residents. Events such as the annual Dublin City Marathon and Women's Mini-marathon attract ever greater numbers of participants, as do the many mini-marathons and fun runs held throughout Ireland.

As far as public sporting facilities are concerned, in 2004 the government announced its plan to build a 50,000-seat stadium at Landsdowne Road in Dublin for both (Gaelic) football and rugby, to develop a National Sports Campus at Abbotstown near Dublin and to redevelop the capital's Croke Park, now Ireland's largest sports stadium, accommodating over 82,000 people. In addition, the Sports Council annually funds over 700 projects to construct or improve sporting facilities throughout the country, and provides funding for the national governing bodies of sport in Ireland, 16 of which now have their headquarters at Sports HQ in Dublin's Park West, opened in May 2004.

A 2004 Sports Council survey, Sports Participation and Health among Adults in Ireland, revealed that the most common 'sporting activity' in Ireland is walking, which constitutes a form of exercise for around 60 per cent of the population (the remaining 40 per cent presumably only walking when the car won't start!). Next (among men) come golf, soccer, swimming and Gaelic sports; among women it's swimming and aerobics. In descending order of popularity are cycling, snooker/billiards, basketball, badminton, tennis, pitch and putt, running, bowls or bowling, angling, athletics, squash, weightlifting, table tennis, hockey, canoeing, riding, rock climbing, sailing, rowing, motor cycling, handball, volleyball, rugby and judo or karate.

An even smaller number go flying, orienteering, skiing, waterskiing and windsurfing or participate in archery, boxing, cricket, croquet, gymnastics, netball, sub-aqua or wrestling. Details of some of these sports are given in this chapter; a list of sports federations and links to their websites can be found on the site of the Federation of Irish Sport (💻 www.irishsports.ie).

Ireland has produced few world-beaters in sport: the list of Irish Olympic medallists since 1924 comprises a mere 16 names, and the most successful of all – the swimmer Michelle Smith, who won three gold and a bronze medal at the 1996 Atlanta Games – has since been disgraced for allegedly tampering with drug test samples; the list of Irish born sportsmen who won medals for **other** countries, on the other hand, is considerably longer! Perhaps it has something to do with the characteristic Irish lack of competitiveness; they engage in sport, as in business and other activities, largely for pleasure – and who's to say that's a bad philosophy?

> When it comes to watching sport, the Irish are as passionate and partisan as any other people, especially about their own sports: Gaelic (or Irish) football, hurling, handball and camogie.

Whether you want to watch or take part, the information in this chapter will help you to enjoy your sport in Ireland.

SPORTS CENTRES, GYMS & CLUBS

Unlike the UK and many other countries, Ireland doesn't have a 'network' of council-run leisure centres at which you can simply 'pay and play', although the government is currently funding the creation of more facilities. There are a few such facilities, known as recreation centres (e.g. Dundrum Family Recreation Centre in Dublin 16, which includes a 25m swimming pool, four tennis courts and two squash courts), where you can hire a squash

court for an hour for around €12 and a tennis court for around €8, although there's little in the way of non-sporting facilities such as bars and restaurants. Some offer membership schemes, whereby for a nominal annual fee (e.g. €30) you can benefit from discounts of 25 per cent or more on these fees.

Most sports facilities are privately owned and charge an inclusive annual membership fee, usually plus a hefty joining fee. There are just a few centres which admit anyone on a pay and play basis. One such is Spawell Golf Centre, Templeogue, Dublin 6W (☎ 01-490 7990, 💻 www.spawell.ie), where prices are rather higher than at council-run centres (i.e. €15 for squash, €12 for badminton and €10 for tennis), but facilities include a bar and restaurant and the centre incorporates a golf driving range, pitch and putt course, and children's mini-golf course, as well as snooker tables, and offers classes in aerobics, yoga and taekwondo (etc.). The centre is open from 9am until 10pm.

The majority of gyms (also known as fitness clubs and health centres), which are springing up in most towns and cities, charge membership fees that vary between high and astronomical. Despite this, many have long waiting lists of would-be members. Among the biggest and best-equipped gyms in Dublin are the three West Wood centres (💻 www.westwood.hosting365.ie), where monthly membership costs between around €55 and €75 (depending when and how much you want to use the facilities), plus a one-off joining fee of around €200.

Other gyms in the capital include Buzz Fit, Crunch Fitness UCD, David Lloyd Riverview Leisure, the Equinox Club, Iveagh Fitness Club, Phibsborough Gym and Slender Health Club. A list of gyms throughout Ireland can be found on 💻 www.fitnessireland.ie/gymlisting.php, according to which there are 79 in County Dublin, 13 in County Cork and no more than ten in any other county. Gyms are usually open between 6.30am and 10pm on weekdays, 8am–9pm on Saturdays and 9am–8pm on Sundays.

Before paying out several hundreds or thousands of pounds to join an exclusive club, ask yourself how often you will use it and whether you wouldn't be better off paying for occasional aerobics classes at your local village hall, swimming at the public baths or tennis in the park for around €5 per session!

Some activities are obviously more club-orientated than others: almost 80 per cent of those who play hurling or Gaelic football, for example, belong to a club, whereas only some 50 per cent of those who play squash are club members. To find out whether there's a club for your sport near you, contact the relevant sports association (see below).

Confusingly, recreation centres, sports centres and sports clubs, as well as the head offices of the various sports associations, are listed together under *Sports Clubs & Associations* in the *Golden Pages*.

GAELIC SPORTS

Ireland has at least four sports which are unique to the country (although some have been exported and exist in slightly different forms elsewhere): Irish (or Gaelic) football, hurling, camogie and handball. These sports are 'governed' by the Cumann Lúthchieas Gael or Gaelic Athletic Association (commonly known as the GAA, ☎ 01-836 3222, 🖳 www.gaa.ie), which was founded in 1884 in Thurles, County Tipperary (now regarded as the 'home' of Gaelic sport), in an attempt to revive the traditional sports that had been ousted by those 'imported from abroad' and to boost national identity in the face of British humiliation!

The GAA's impact was so great that every district now has its own division, and even small villages and schools have their own teams; in all there are 2,664 Gaelic sports clubs fielding 20,000 teams, which means that some 300,000 people (both men and women) play Irish sports – all of them amateurs.

The GAA itself, though still an amateur organisation (it's state funded), commands enormous influence. In fact, it's reputed to be the second most powerful organisation in Ireland – after the Catholic Church! (For an irreverent 'take' on the GAA and its activities, visit 🖳 www.anfearrua.com.) It has a quarter of a million members (1 in 16 of the Irish population!) and is staunchly nationalistic: it regards hurling and Gaelic football as an essential component of Irishness, and won't allow any 'foreign' games to be played at Croke Park stadium in Dublin, Gaelic games' holy of holies.

However, despite the strenuous efforts of the GAA, Irish football and hurling are currently being threatened in popularity by soccer, although that game isn't without its difficulties (see below); and the competition structure has recently been criticised for being unfairly biased towards the All-Ireland Championship (the equivalent of the British FA Cup) at the expense of county-level matches.

The major competitions in both hurling and football are: All-Ireland, Provincial (x 4), Inter-provincial, All-Ireland Minor, All-Ireland U21, All-Ireland Club Championships and the National League. Around 33 teams compete in the football Championship and 17 in the hurling Championship; each League consists of four divisions, but the Leagues are increasingly regarded as a warm-up for the All-Ireland; and provincial competitions such as the Dr McKenna Cup and O'Byrne Cup are now played on less popular Saturdays (instead of Sundays) in front of small audiences.

The successful Kerry football team (it won the All-Ireland ten times and the League eight times between 1969 and 1985) was responsible for introducing high levels of fitness to Gaelic games. Training for the Championships starts in October – nine months ahead of the start of competition. At club level, the focus is the summer county championships, for which training starts in January.

Hurling and football have a similar scoring system. The goal is like a cross between a soccer goal and rugby posts, the area below the crossbar having a net, and points can

be scored by getting the ball into the net (3 points) or over the crossbar between the posts (1 point). Unlike soccer and rugby, however, they're constantly fast-moving, fast-scoring games and there's no such thing as a goalless draw! Also, unlike soccer, rugby and hockey, they're essentially summer games, the national finals taking place in September.

Tickets for the All-Ireland finals are distributed through the clubs and cannot be purchased through any other channel.

For semi-final matches you can expect to pay up to €50, for quarter-finals €15-20 (less for regional games). There are discounts for senior citizens, etc. Although violence on the pitch is all part of the fun, hooliganism off it is thankfully rare.

Gaelic Football

Gaelic (or Irish) football is Ireland's most popular spectator sport. It's like a cross between rugby and soccer (although it claims to predate both) and allows the use of hands as well as feet. It is characterised by high, accurate passes, long kicks and extremely violent tackles. As in rugby union, there are 15 players per team, each with a goalkeeper, six defenders, two centre-field players and six attackers. The ball, which can be 'dribbled' with the hands or the feet, is round like a football (only slightly smaller). Matches consist of two 30-minute sessions.

Gaelic football was 'exported' to Australia in the 19th century and, although modern Australian Rules football has slightly different rules (or lack of them!), there is now an agreed 'conversion' which allows international matches between the two countries to be played.

Gaelic football is run by the GAA (see above). Ninety years after the formation of the GAA, the Ladies [sic] Gaelic Football Association (*Cumann Peíl Gael na mBan*, ☎ 01-836 3156, 🖳 www.ladiesgaelic.ie) was established (in 1974) and now boasts 600 clubs and 70,000 members – not all of them 'ladies'! Its All-Ireland final takes place in early October. For ticket information, see **Hurling & Camogie** below.

Hurling & Camogie

Hurling, Ireland's official national sport, is thought to date from the 9th century. The province of Munster claims to be its birthplace and County Tipperary is its heartland. The British once tried to ban it, but the game survived (in retaliation, the GAA forbade its members to play rugby and soccer in the 1920s, a sanction not lifted until 1971!).

Hurling, which is reputed to be the world's fastest ball game, is a distant cousin of hockey in that the ball is hit with a wide based stick or hurley (*camán* in Irish) made of ash and about three feet long. Unlike hockey, however, hurling allows the ball to be picked up on the hurley and either carried or hit into the air. The ball (*sliothár*) is similar in size and composition to a cricket ball, being made of cork covered with leather. It can travel at nearly 120km (74mph) per hour. Hurling has several points in common with Gaelic football: the number of players, the size of the pitch and the principle of goalscoring.

Camogie is a 'gentler' version of hurling, played by 13 women on a smaller pitch. Hurling comes under the auspices of the GAA (see Gaelic football above), but Camogie is run by the Gaelic Camogie Association

Irish Football

(*Cumann Camógaiochta na nGael*, ☎ 01-836 4619, 🖳 www.camogie.ie), which was founded in 1904 and has 500 clubs with some 78,000 members. The All-Ireland Camogie final takes place in early September.

Handball

Handball has similarities with fives, squash and pelota, being played in an alley or on a court. As in squash, there are two versions, softball and hardball, and each can be played singles or doubles. There are six teams in the National League.

The Irish Handball Council (*Comhairle Liathróid Láimhe na hÉireann*, ☎ 01-819 2385, 🖳 www.handball.ie) was founded in 1924 and has over 170 affiliated clubs with around 7,500 members. There's also an Irish Olympic Handball Association (🖳 www.olympichandball. org). Ireland is due to host the European One-Wall Championships in November 2008, and the World Championships (for the fifth time) in 2012.

ANGLING

Ireland is an angler's paradise, offering every kind of fishing – coarse, game, sea – and a great richness and variety of fish, most notably salmon, trout and pike. Salmon, trout and sea trout are native species and can be fished for in a variety of environments: rivers, lakes and coastal waters. Ireland has some of Europe's cleanest and least fished water, and there's somewhere to fish almost all year round, although the main season runs from May to October.

There are more than 26,000km (16,250mi) of river and canal bank and almost 5,000km (3,000mi) of coastline, as well as more than 1,500km² (578mi²) of lakes.

Inland fishing is centred on the counties of Roscommon, Leitrim, Cavan, Meath, Westmeath and Longford, as well as parts of Sligo, Galway and Clare. The river Moy in County Mayo is probably Ireland's most famous fishing area, where record salmon catches have regularly been made by wealthy fishermen – daily permits can cost over €200! Elsewhere, there are excellent fishing rivers like the Barrow (which flows through Counties Laois, Kildare, Carlow and Wexford), the Blackwater (Counties Cork and Waterford) and the Lee (County Cork).

Strict conservation rules apply to all angling in Ireland, particularly in relation to pike fishing.

Coarse Angling

The most common freshwater fish in Ireland is bream (the best months for catching it are May/June and September/October). One of the most distinctive of native Irish fish is the rudd, which is found especially in County Roscommon (best months May/June); and peculiar to Ireland is the rudd-bream hybrid, which can reach up to 3.4kg (7.5lb). Roach are now widespread and can be fished all year round (best months March–June), and there's also a roach-bream hybrid. Tench are found throughout the midlands in rivers and canals (best months June–August).

Perch and eel are widespread, too (good all year round, eel especially in July–October), as are carp (best April–October) and dace (best March–May). Irish pike are legendary, reaching 23kg (50lb) or more, and are found throughout Ireland (best months September–April).

There's no close season for coarse fishing, although most activity takes place between April and October, when there are festivals and competitions almost every week (some last a whole week!). Many Irish lakes and rivers have been especially developed to provide access for anglers, and there are tackle shops in all the main angling centres. Coarse fishing tends to be organised around towns and villages, where accommodation is provided with knowledgeable hosts who provide facilities for storing and even freezing fish (as well as for drying clothes). Some also have boats for loan or hire. A day's fishing can be had for around €25.

For local information you should contact the Fisheries Board in the area where you plan to go angling; the Central Fisheries Board (☎ 01-884 2600, 🖳 www.cfb.ie) will advise you of the nearest local Board. For details of coarse fishing clubs, contact the National Coarse Fishing Federation of Ireland (NCFFI,

☎ 049-433 2367, 🖥 www.ncffi.ie), with around 60 member clubs and 7,000 members. Another useful contact is the oddly named National Anglers Representative Association (NARA, ☎ 045-433068, 🖥 www.nara.ie), which has 110 affiliated clubs with 11,000 members.

Game Fishing

Salmon fishing in Ireland is accessible and inexpensive. Salmon can be caught from January until mid-June (the season runs from 1st January to 30th September) in rivers such as the Drowes, which flows into Donegal Bay, the Slaney in County Wexford, the Laune in Kerry and the Moy in Mayo; and lakes such as Lough Beltra near Newport and Lough Furnace in County Mayo, from March. Grilse (salmon that have spent a winter at sea) can be caught from mid-May until October at places like Delphi in County Mayo.

⚠ Caution

There are strict regulations governing the type of bait that can be used, so you should check with the local Fisheries Board (see above).

Trout can be fished almost everywhere in Ireland, which is one of the few places in Europe where wild brown trout can be fly fished (Irish fly patterns are famous). The river fishing season runs from 15th February to 30th September (in some areas as late as 12th October), but the best months are April–September. The rivers Suir in County Tipperary, Fergus (County Clare) and Boyne (County Meath) are among the best locations.

Lake fishing is also allowed between February and October (best in May) and is often done from boats. Prime spots include Loughs Carra and Corrib (County Galway), Lough Sheelin (County Cavan), Lough Owel (County Westmeath), where night fishing is traditional, Lough Ennell (County Westmeath) and Lough Conn (County Mayo), which is reckoned to contain more than a quarter of a million brown trout.

Licences are required for salmon and sea trout fishing. They can be bought from tackle shops and fishery offices. A fishing permit is usually also required and, in the Northern and Upper Shannon Fisheries Regions, a share certificate. Most towns have tackle shops, and angling centres provide facilities, including bait fridges and tackle/drying rooms. For further details contact the Trout Anglers' Federation of Ireland (☎ 094-954 1324).

Sea Angling

The warming effect of the Gulf Stream means that the sea fishing season extends into autumn, and unusual warm-water fish are sometimes caught, e.g. trigger fish, red mullet and bream, sunfish and amberjack. Conger, ling, cod, tope, skate and blue shark can all be caught off Ireland's south and west coasts. There are many charted wrecks off the Irish coast, where a wide range of fish can be found, including pollock, coalfish, turbot and megrim. In fact, Ireland boasts no fewer than 80 species of sea fish. Deep sea fishing boats can be chartered from many places for around €250–350 per day. Alternatively, smaller boats (14–18 ft) can be hired for inshore fishing.

Ireland also offers some of the best shore angling in Europe; mullet, pollock, wrave, bass, flounder, dogfish and tope can be caught (especially off the coasts of Clare, Galway and Mayo), as well as smoothound and ray (especially off Wexford) and codling (off Wicklow and Cork). There's good rack fishing from the Beara, Iveragh and Dingle peninsulas, and islands such as Valentia in the south-west. Other popular sea fishing locations are Rosslare and Dungarvan (County Waterford), Youghal, Ballycotton and Baltimore (County Cork), Cahirciveen (County Kerry), Westport, Newport, Belmullet and Achill Island (County Mayo), and Moville (County Donegal).

The sea fishing season officially runs from 1st January to 30th September, but not much can be caught before April, sometimes June. Most fish must be tagged and returned to the sea. Competitions are organised by the Federation of Irish Salmon and Sea Trout Anglers (FISSTA, ☎ 074-973 0300, 🖥 www.fissta.com), which has over 90,000 members in 91 clubs, and the Irish Federation of Sea Anglers (IFSA, ☎ 01-280 6873, 🖥 www.ifsa.ie), which has around 184 affiliated clubs with some 5,000 members. If the idea of catching sharks appeals to you, contact the Shark Angling Club of Ireland (☎ 086-822 8710, 🖳 http://homepage.tinet.ie/~sharkclubireland).

BOATING

Although Ireland is an island, the Irish aren't a maritime people. Public and media attention turns to the sea mainly at times of fishing boat tragedies, and boating and watersports facilities are generally under-developed. In fact, it's only now dawning on the Irish that their offshore territorial area, which is one of the largest in Europe and is ten times the size of Ireland, is one which could be 'exploited' in a number of ways – which means that, for the time being at least, those interested in boating can enjoy uncrowded water, if not blue skies and sunshine!

Responsibility for promoting offshore boating in Ireland lies with the Marine Leisure section of the Department of Communications, Marine and Natural Resources (☎ 01-678 2000 or ☎ 1890-449900, 🖳 www.dcmnr.gov.ie), which 'aims to progress the integration of marine and angling tourism and leisure, within the overall national tourism policy framework, by aligning its promotion and development within the national strategy for tourism development' (got that?).

Like the UK, Ireland has a free offshore and inshore lifeboat service, run by volunteers, which is linked to the Royal National Lifeboat Institution (RNLI) in the UK, founded in 1824 (UK ☎ 0845-122 6999, 🖳 www.rnli.ie). There are 30 lifeboat stations around the coast of Ireland. The RNLI receives a government grant, but is largely funded by contributions from members of the public.

The Irish Coastguard (formerly the Irish Marine Emergency Service) is wholly government funded (as part of the Department of Marine and Natural Resources) and has responsibility for coordinating sea rescues using its own two helicopters plus two operated by the Naval Service, the local Garda, and the lifeboat service (if necessary). In an emergency, you can call the Coastguard direct on ☎ 01-678 2000 or simply dial 999 or 112 and ask for the Coastguard.

For information about canoeing, rowing, waterskiing and windsurfing, see **Other Sports** on page 338)

Yachting & Dinghy Sailing

The main organisation for sailing in Ireland is the Irish Sailing Association (☎ 01-280 0239, 🖳 www.sailing.ie), founded in 1946 and now with some 22,000 members, which organises events and training and can put you in touch with local affiliated clubs (105 are listed on the site).

The main venues for yachting are Dublin Bay, Howth (near Dublin), Cork and Kinsale. Kilrush Creek Marina (in County Clare, ☎ 065-905 2072, 🖳 www.kilrushcreekmarina.ie) was Ireland's first integrated marina development, offering access to the sea at the Shannon estuary. There is a newly established marina (now complete and in full operation) at North Quay, Arklow in County Wicklow (🖳 www.arklowsc.ie).

Dun Laoghaire, just south of Dublin, is the largest sailing and watersports centre in Ireland, boasting four yacht clubs and an annual boating festival in July. Lough Ree Sailing Club (in County Westmeath) claims to be the second-oldest sailing club in the world, having been established in 1720, and is the home of the unique Shannon One-design sailing boat.

For those wishing to learn to sail there are plenty of schools, such as Glenans Irish Sailing School (🖳 www.gisc.ie), which claims to be the country's

largest, the Fíngal Sailing School near Dublin (☎ 01-845 1979, 🖥 www.fingalsailingschool.com), the Baltimore Sailing School (☎ 01-282 0141, 🖥 www.baltimoresailingschool.com) and the International Sailing Centre (☎ 021-481 1237, 🖥 www.sailcork.com) near Cork. A basic adult sailing course, which can be undertaken at weekends or in the evening, costs between around €220 and €300.

Inland Waterways

Ireland has over 5,000 lakes, 1,000km (621mi) of rivers and 250km (155mi) of canals, most virtually free of boats. These are found mainly on the Shannon and the lakes through which it flows. The biggest of these, Ireland's second-largest lake, is Lough Derg (between Counties Clare and Tipperary), which covers 117km2 (45mi2) and is termed 'Ireland's pleasure lake' in tourist brochures. Here you will find a variety of craft, from barges, motor cruisers and yachts to dinghies, sailboards and canoes.

Further upstream, in County Leitrim, is Carrick-on-Shannon, Ireland's motor cruising centre, where the river meets the Shannon-Erne Waterway running down from Belturbet in County Cavan. Other popular places for cruiser hire are

the Shannon-Erne link, the Grand Canal, the River Barrow and the River Erne.

Hire companies are located at Whitegate (in County Clare), Portmuna (County Galway), Tullamore (County Offaly), Athlone (County Westmeath) and Belturbet (County Cavan). Boats have from two to eight berths and are normally equipped with fridge, cooker, bed linen, and crockery, as well as charts and safety equipment. Some have central heating and hot showers. Radios and portable televisions (TV) can be hired and groceries ordered in advance. The weekly rate for hiring a four to six-berth barge or cruiser is between around €1,000 (in low season) to around €1,500 (high season). A deposit of around €400 is normally required against damage to the boat or its contents. Boat handling skills are an advantage but not essential, as instruction is provided for landlubbers.

If you're navigating the Shannon, where there are six locks, or any of the canals, you must pay a nominal fee each time you pass through a lock.

Details of waterways and hire companies can be obtained from the Inland Waterways Association of Ireland (☎ 1890-924991, 🖥 www.iwai.ie). A list of boat hire operators can be obtained from tourist offices or the Irish tourist board.

GOLF

Along with the UK, Spain and Portugal, Ireland is one of Europe's principal golfing countries. In fact, Ireland boasts more courses per head of population than anywhere in the world except Scotland. In recent years, the government invested millions of euros in golfing facilities as part of an eight-year programme culminating in Ireland's hosting of the Ryder Cup in 2006. New courses have sprung up throughout the country at a rate unequalled anywhere in Europe, and it's estimated that over half a million people a year visit the country specifically to play golf. The tourist board even has a website dedicated to golf in Ireland (☎ 1850-230330, 🖥 www.golf.ireland.ie).

Irish courses are renowned for being 'testing', but it's the beauty of the scenery and the lushness of the grass that make them unique. As in Scotland, the greatest courses are links (seaside courses), the most famous being Portmarnock (near Dublin), Mount Juliet (County Kilkenny) and Royal Portrush. Supposedly, the country's finest greens are to be found at County Louth Golf Club, known as Baltray (near Drogheda) and the smartest (i.e. most expensive) courses are at Adare Manor (in County Limerick), where a round will set you back €90, Dromoland Castle (County Clare – €60-110) and the K Club (County Kildare – €100-225), which hosted the 2006 Ryder Cup competition.

Legend has it that Scottish colonialists introduced golf to Ireland (in what's now Northern Ireland) at the beginning of the 17th century, but its spread was mainly a 20th century phenomenon. Today, there are 408 golf clubs, with a total of over a quarter of a million members, affiliated to the Golfing Union of Ireland (☎ 01-505 4000, 💻 www.gui.ie); and 384 clubs and 60,000 members affiliated to the Irish Ladies' Golf Union (☎ 01-269 6244, 💻 www.ilgu.ie), and which were founded in the 1890s and were the first golfing organisations of their type in the world. Lists of clubs and information about them can be found on 💻 www.uk-golf.com/ireland.

Some 175 of these clubs have 18-hole courses, and the major golfing areas are the Shannon region (32 courses and ten driving ranges, County Wicklow (30 courses), which promotes itself as the no.1 county in Ireland for golf, and County Mayo (15 courses). A small number of clubs offer tuition programmes and on-site accommodation. *The Golfer's Guide in the Republic* is available from most local tourist offices.

The main golfing events in the calendar are the Irish Open in July, the West of Ireland Golf Classic in August and the Donegal Irish Open in September.

Member Clubs

The established (i.e. old) golf courses are extremely popular and membership is difficult to obtain – you must generally join a long waiting list. Fortunately, new clubs are popping up all over Ireland where it's much easier to become a member. Fees range from around €500 for weekday membership of one of the less prestigious clubs to several thousand euros for full membership of one of the 'big name' clubs such as Mount

Juliet, Portmarnock, Royal Portrush and St Margaret's, plus a monstrous joining fee (around €10,000 at St Margaret's!). Some clubs have 'half memberships', which restrict the times you can play and the facilities you may use and are designed to make you feel inferior.

Non-members are usually welcome at certain times from Monday to Friday, but need to book at weekends and on public holidays.

Green fees (i.e. the cost of hitting a ball round 18 holes) vary between €25 and €200 or more, depending on whether you're accompanied by a member (in which case it's usually cheaper) and whether you're playing a little known course on a Monday afternoon in January or the K Club on a Saturday morning in August (in which case you will pay over €10 per hole!).

Club and trolley hire is usually available, and professional tuition can be arranged by appointment (for around €20 for half an hour). Most clubs forbid the wearing of jeans, trainers and collar-less shirts, and some insist on smart trousers and polo shirts (preferably with an expensive looking logo).

Public Courses

There are around 25 public golf courses in Ireland, which aren't affiliated to the Golf Union of Ireland. These have no members, and can be played by anyone, wearing almost any type of clothing! The cost of a full round varies between €15 on weekdays to €30 at weekends, when booking is recommended. Clubs can be hired for around €15 at some courses.

Driving Ranges

There are driving ranges in most parts of the country, and some clubs have their own ranges, especially the older clubs which have 'resident' professionals offering coaching (the newer courses generally don't have ranges or offer coaching). Ranges are usually open seven days a week, from around 9am to 9pm (9am to 6pm at weekends). The cost of a small basket (30-50 balls) is around €5, a large basket (100–120 balls) €7-10. Some ranges offer free club hire, while others make a charge of €2-4 for a half-set.

Pitch & Putt

Pitch and putt has become a popular alternative to golf for those who cannot afford the time or expense of going the full distance (or who spend more time off than on the fairway). Pitch and putt courses measure no more than 1,000m (3,280ft), no hole being longer than 75m (246ft). There are around 250 pitch and putt courses in Ireland, 119 of them affiliated to the Pitch and Putt Union of Ireland (💻 www.ppui.ie), which organises events and competitions; the remaining courses are independent operations. Affiliated courses, which must conform to certain regulations, charge between €3 and €10 per round, although at some it's possible to play all day for €10; whereas non-affiliated courses tend to be rather more expensive.

HORSE & GREYHOUND RACING

Greyhound and, especially, horse racing are big business in Ireland, although heavily government subsidised. In 2004, the government allocated a cool €550m to its Horse and Greyhound Racing Fund, which was created in 2001, to 'ensure that both the horse and greyhound racing industries have the necessary secure financial framework for the next four years, to enable them to bring about completion of their major development initiatives.' Around four fifths of this money goes to Horse Racing Ireland (see **Horse Racing** below), a fifth to the greyhound racing authority, the Irish Greyhound Board (see below).

Greyhound Racing

Reputed to be Ireland's fastest growing evening sport/entertainment, greyhound racing offers a cheap alternative to horse racing, and the 1,800 or more meetings each year are attended by some 750,000 people. There are 17 tracks throughout the country, nine of which are owned and operated by the Irish Greyhound Board, Bord na gCon (💻 www.igb.ie), which also controls betting at all courses, adding the profits to its generous government subsidy.

The main greyhound racing venues are Shelbourne Park in Dublin, the Kingdom Stadium in Tralee, and the tracks at Limerick and Thurles; other tracks are to be found at Clonmel, Cork, Dundalk, Enniscorthy, Galway, Kilkenny, Longford, Mullingar, Navan, Newbridge, Tipperary, Waterford and Youghal. Racing normally starts at 8pm on Mondays–Saturdays (a few meetings only take place on Sundays), and an evening consists of between eight and ten races, finishing at around 10pm. Admission is usually around €6 or €7, including a programme, and there are reductions for senior citizens and groups.

Horse Racing

Horse racing is one of Ireland's most significant sports, attendance at race meetings being a massive 1.4m (more than a third of the population!).

Horse racing is known to the Irish as 'the sport of Kings', and with good reason. In ancient times, it was strictly limited to princes and noblemen, and the horses themselves were held in high esteem.

Some say that the Irish worship the horse as passionately as they worship God (there are no fewer than ten places in Ireland call *Knocknagappul*, meaning 'hill of horses'), and Sundays are race days, as well as church-going days (Oliver Cromwell tried unsuccessfully to outlaw Sunday racing). The Irish certainly pride themselves on breeding some of the world's best thoroughbreds and on producing some of its finest jockeys (e.g. Richard Dunwoody, Charlie Swan and Michael Kinane) and trainers (e.g. Aidan O'Brien and Dermot Weld). The world's richest owners base horses in Ireland (the Aga Khan, John Magnier, Michael Tabor and the Maktoum family) and the National Stud at Tully in County Kildare is Ireland's (some would say the world's) horse breeding capital.

There's horse racing all year round in Ireland. There are some 250 race meetings at 25 different racetracks, the four most popular being just outside Dublin: Punchestown, 35km (22mi) south-west of the capital; Fairyhouse in

County Meath, 20km (13mi) to the north-west; Leopardstown, virtually in the town, 10km (6mi) from the centre; and probably the most famous horse racing venue in the world, The Curragh in County Kildare, 46km (29mi) south-west of Dublin.

From spring to autumn (mid-March to early November) is the 'flat racing' season, during which there are around 700 races; the 1,100 or so National Hunt races, in which horses must jump fences (hurdles), take place all year round. Flat racing attracts the bigger crowds (and prize money), the most popular races being the Irish Derby (at The Curragh), the Irish Oaks, the 2,000 and 1,000 Guineas (the original prize money, a guinea being a pound and a shilling – now around €0.90 – so you can be sure that today's prize money is a little higher!) and the St Leger. The biggest National Hunt races are the Irish Grand National (at Fairyhouse on Easter Monday), the Handicap Hurdle, the Kerry National Chase and the Galway Plate.

Almost as popular are Festival Meetings, which, as their name suggests, are part festival and part race meeting. There are about a dozen of these, the most highly regarded

being at Punchestown (the National Hunt Festival in late April), Killarney (mid-July), Galway (the famous Galway Races in late July/ early August), Listowel (late September), and Leopardstown (after Christmas). A peculiarity is the annual beach race in Laytown, the last of its kind in Europe. Show-jumping and Three Day Events (comprising show-jumping, cross-country and dressage) are also well-attended, and another essential part of the horse racing calendar is the annual Dublin Horse Show in mid-August, which has been staged since 1830.

Horse racing is controlled by Horse Racing Ireland (💻 www.horseracingireland.ie), a semi-state organisation which, like the Irish Greyhound Board, owns and operates the major tracks (Fairyhouse, Leopardstown, Navan and Tipperary Racecourses), although its subsidiary, Tote Ireland, controls all on- and off-course betting (a nice little earner!). In 2004, Horse Racing Ireland announced a €200m upgrade of facilities at The Curragh and Leopardstown, as well as at a number of other courses over the following five years.

Normal admission to the average race meeting is around €15 (students and senior citizens pay half price), although you can pay €50 or more for the best seats. Full-price admission to major events such as the Irish Derby and Grand National starts at €20. Children are welcome at race courses, and many have childcare centres (children under 14 are usually charged a nominal admission fee or nothing at all). A programme, known as a race card, costs €2 or €3.

If you're a racing addict, you can become a course member for between €150 and €250 (depending on the course and the membership 'level'), which entitles you to admission to all meetings and use of certain restricted areas – mostly bars! Race meetings generally start at between 12.45 and 1.30pm in winter, and between 2 and 2.30pm in summer, when there are also evening meetings.

Point-to-point

An increasingly popular form of horse racing is point-to-point (a sort of cross country race with horses running one at a time against the clock). There are 132 courses and over 150 race meetings between January and May, usually on Sundays, but also on Saturdays and mid-week. Admission is around €7.50 per person or €15 per car, plus €2 or so for a race card. Further details can be found on a dedicated website (💻 www.irish-point-to-point.com).

HORSE RIDING

Ireland has a higher horse:person ratio than any other European country, which means that there's ample opportunity to ride horses (or ponies), whatever your experience. Horse riding and pony-trekking are an ideal way to explore the countryside. There are 230 riding centres 'approved' by the Irish tourist board and the Association of Riding Establishments (AIRE, ☎ 045-`850800, 💻 www.aire.ie) – listed on the website.

The largest number of AIRE-approved centres are in Counties Cork (26) and Galway (21), followed by Kildare (18), Mayo and Wicklow (15 each), Clare, Donegal and Kerry (13), Dublin (12), Meath (11), Limerick, Sligo and Tipperary (9), Kilkenny and Wexford (8), Waterford (6), Louth and Westmeath (5), Monaghan and Roscommon (4); the remaining counties have three each, except County Longford, where there's only one. Information about stables can also be obtained from tourist offices, hotels and local people.

AIRE is one of 15 equestrian organisations affiliated to the Equestrian Federation of Ireland (☎ 045-850800, 💻 www.horsesport.ie). The others include the Irish Association of Riding Clubs (☎ 045-850850, ☎ 0818-270227, 💻 www.airc.ie), the Irish Pony Society (☎ 045-878987, 💻 www.irishponysociety.ie), the Irish Universities Riding Clubs Association (☎ 087-924 9674), and for disabled riders Para Equestrian Ireland (☎ 01-287 0989) and the Riding for the Disabled Association Ireland (☎ 01-287 6503, 💻 www.rdai.org).

A one-hour lesson for either a beginner or an experienced rider costs between €15 and €25. A two-and-a-half hour hack costs in the region of €30 and, if you're lucky, will include a gallop along a deserted beach! For the really adventurous (and saddle hardened), trail rides are available in some of the most beautiful areas of Ireland: Counties Donegal, Kerry, Wicklow and Sligo and the Connemara in County Galway.

On a trail ride, you spend up to six days and nights riding with a small party, accompanied by an experienced guide. Trails normally operate between April and September and prices vary between €500 and €1,200, depending on the type of accommodation and the number of days.

Further information about horse riding in Ireland can be found on 💻 www.equestrianvacations.com and 💻 www.trailriding-ireland.com.

RUGBY

Despite the popularity of Gaelic sports (see page 327), 'foreign' games such as rugby and soccer have gained a foothold in Ireland and now rival their traditional counterparts in popularity, particularly in schools.

> Dublin University was the first to establish a rugby club in Ireland in 1854 (students had learned the game at English public schools!), and other Dublin clubs soon appeared (NIFC in 1868, Queen's University and Wanderers in 1869, Lansdowne and Dungannon in 1873, UCC in 1874, and Ballinasloe in 1875).

It's Limerick which claims to be the capital of Irish rugby and has the five most famous clubs in the country: the Garryown and Shannon clubs, dating back to 1884, the Young Munster club, established in 1895, the Bohemians, in 1922, and the Old Crescent in 1947. The Irish Rugby Football Union (☎ 01-647 3800, 💻 www.irfu.ie) was founded in 1874 and today has 205 clubs (19 in Connacht, 71 in Leinster, 59 in Munster and 56 in Ulster), with some 50,000 male and 500 female members. Club membership costs around €150 for a year (€100 for juniors). There are also almost 250 rugby-playing schools in Ireland.

There are four divisions comprising 50 teams in the All-Ireland League (which includes Northern Ireland), and provincial teams participate in the European Cup. The Irish national team, which played its first game in 1875 (against England) is one of the strongest in the world and takes part in the

annual Six Nations competition, with England, France, Italy, Northern Ireland and Scotland. International matches are played at Lansdowne Road stadium in Dublin, which holds 50,000 spectators, 29,000 seated. Tickets cost between €20 and €50, but are all allocated to affiliated rugby clubs. To see an All-Ireland League game, you can expect to pay around €10, but as much as €60 for the final.

Further information about Irish rugby and a list of clubs can be found on 🖳 www.irishrugby.net.

SOCCER

Like rugby, soccer (what the British call football) was imported from the UK, although not until the 1920s. The Football Association of Ireland (FAI, 🖳 www.fai.ie) was founded in 1921. Soccer is one of Ireland's most popular sports (some schools in urban areas now struggle to get a hurling or Gaelic football team together). The national team has had little international success, however, and languishes at around 50th in the rankings.

Unlike Gaelic sports, soccer is played professionally in Ireland, where there are 22 teams in the national League (divided into two divisions, illogically named Premier and First). As in the

UK, there's an annual League Cup and the FA of Ireland Cup, in early May, played at the Dalymount Park stadium, which seats just 18,000.

But despite its popularity (there are around 5,750 FAI-affiliated clubs throughout Ireland), Irish soccer is in a far from healthy state. Every year at least one national League club finds itself in financial trouble, and over the last five years around half of the Premier League clubs have suffered some sort of financial crisis. Finn Harps, Longford Town, Cork City, Dundalk and Sligo Rovers are recent examples. Clubs' holding companies are frequently wound up, only to resurface under different names, and the FAI itself isn't in the best financial shape.

Tickets for ordinary matches cost between €10 and €20; for international matches expect to pay between €50 and €70. Tickets are available from the FAI, from Ticketmaster (☎ 0818-719300) or from the venue itself.

At amateur level, there are well-organised local leagues for all ages and abilities. For a weekly subscription of around €5, children aged 7–16 can join one of the 1,350 clubs under the aegis of the Schoolboys' Football Association of Ireland, which runs 34 leagues nationwide. Some clubs, like UCD in Dublin, offer free membership, but players must be of a certain standard. A list of leagues and contacts can be obtained from the FAI. The Women's Football Association of Ireland, which was set up in 1973 and is now part of the FAI, organises no fewer than 21 leagues, with 350 teams and 6,500 players.

Further details of soccer in Ireland can be found on 🖳 www.a2zsoccer.com.

SWIMMING

Ireland's most popular physical recreation after walking, swimming is enjoyed by around 650,000 Irish people. As a competitive sport, it had a surge in popularity after the 1996 Olympic Games, at which Michelle Smith won a bronze and three gold medals to become one of the most successful Olympic swimmers of all time (incredibly, ten years later she still held the Irish records for women at 50, 800 and 1500m freestyle, 100 and 200m backstroke, 100 and 200m butterfly, as well as 100, 200 and 400m individual medley!).

Despite this, Ireland still has no Olympic-size pool. There are around 220 swimming pools in

Ireland, the latest being Grove Island pool in Limerick, and a one-hour session costs around €5 for adults and €2 for children. Increasingly popular are 'aqua parks', such as the one at Kilkee (County Clare), which offer fun pools, wave machines, slides and flumes. The largest of these is the Aqua Dome in Tralee, County Kerry, which boasts a 90m (295ft) river and a 70m (229ft) flume.

Swim Ireland (☎ 01-625 1120, 🖳 www. swimireland.ie), which was founded (under another name) in 1893, is the governing body of the sport. It has 140 affiliated clubs with over 12,000 members.

WALKING & RAMBLING

The Irish have always been able to roam freely around their countryside, and even today, walkers enjoy few restrictions – a 'Keep Out' sign is a rare sight. Since 1978, when the Long Distance Walking Routes Committee (now the more impressively named National Waymarked Ways Advisory Committee, NWWAC, ☎ 01-860 8800, 🖳 www.walkireland.ie – part of the Irish Sports Council), was established, 31 designated 'ways' have been marked out, covering around 3,000km (1,864mi), and more are being developed.

These trails, which are signposted by a yellow arrow and a walking man symbol, are extremely varied, some following canal towpaths, some rocky peninsulas, some *boreens* (small paths formerly used for driving farm animals), 'butter' routes once taken by farmers carrying their wares to market, and even ancient 'coffin' routes, followed by funeral parties to the local graveyard.

⚠ Caution

Many of these routes cross bogs, which can be dangerous, so it is best not to go out alone and always keep to paths.

The first trail to be fully marked was the Wicklow Way, stretching 132km (82mi) from Dublin to the mountains and the scene of two annual walking festivals, in spring and autumn.

A brochure entitled *Walking Ireland – the Waymarked Ways* is available from the NWWAC and from the Irish tourist board.

Maps and guides to all the Ways are available from EastWest Mapping in Enniscorthy, County Wexford (☎ 053-937 7835, 🖳 http:// eastwestmapping.ie). Half a dozen shorter walks along marked ways are detailed in a tourist board brochure called *Walk a Different Path,* and the tourist board has its own walking website (🖳 www. walking.ireland.ie).

There are a number of companies specialising in walking holidays in Ireland, including Footfalls Walking Vacations (🖳 www.walkinghikingireland. com), Irishways (🖳 www.irishways.com), Joyce's Ireland (🖳 www.joycesireland.co.uk), South West Walks Ireland (🖳 www.southwestwalksireland. com) and Walking Cycling Ireland (🖳 www. irelandwalkingcycling.com).

In Dublin, you can follow the many walking routes indicated by the *Sh' na Sláinte* (Path to Health) signs, erected by the Irish Heart Foundation, or (for those less concerned with the state of their hearts) join one of the many organised literary or musical pub crawls!

OTHER SPORTS

The following is a selection of other sporting activities in Ireland, which are served either by private clubs or by public sports and leisure centres. For further information, you should contact the relevant association.

Athletics

There are 144 senior clubs and 135 junior clubs with around 18,000 members affiliated to the Athletics Association of Ireland (☎ 01-886 9933, 🖳 www.athleticsireland.ie). Ireland's main athletics stadium is the 10,000-seat Morton Stadium in Dublin.

Badminton

Badminton is played by over 40,000 people in Ireland. There are around 600 badminton clubs fielding 2,500 teams affiliated to Badminton Ireland (☎ 01-839 3028, 🖳 www.badminton.ie).

Basketball

Basketball is surprisingly popular in Ireland, which even has a 2,500-seat National Basketball Arena at Tymon Park in Dublin. Admission to major matches is from €5 to €30 for adults and from nothing to €10 for children. The 300 clubs affiliated to Basketball Ireland

(☎ 01-459 0211, 🖳 www.basketballireland. ie) – listed on the website – have over 10,000 registered adult players, as well as 80,000 registered basketball-playing schoolchildren! Basketball Ireland organises regional and national leagues.

Billiards, Snooker & Pool

Billiards and, especially, snooker are popular in Ireland. There are around 47 clubs affiliated to the Republic of Ireland Billiards & Snooker Association (☎ 01-625 1150, 🖳 www.ribsa. net), as well as numerous private clubs. The largest clubs are the Griffith Snooker Club in Dublin and the 147 Club in Wexford. Some clubs require a membership fee, which varies; at others you can simply 'pay and play' (for between around €8 and €10 per hour); if you join an associated club, part of your fee goes to the Association and this entitles you to enter snooker competitions around the country. Major competitions, including professional tournaments, are held at the Ivy Rooms in Carlow.

There are no recognised pool clubs, but pool is played in many pubs in Ireland, some of which organise competitions. Expect to pay at least €1 per game.

Bowling

In Ireland, bowling can mean either ten-pin bowling or green bowling (bowls). The latter game is regulated by the Bowling League of Ireland (for men – ☎ 01-831 3140), which has 27 clubs with around 2,000 members; and the Ladies' Bowling League of Ireland (☎ 01-493 1431) with 21 clubs. The two organisations share a website (🖳 www.irish lawnbowls.ie). There are a few indoor bowls centres in Ireland, including The Heritage Golf and Spa Resort in Killenard, County Laois (🖳 www.theheritage.com) and Cork Indoor Bowls (🖳 www.corkindoorbowls.4t. com).

There are around 30 public ten-pin bowling centres, mainly in towns and cities (listed on 🖳 www.irishtenpin.com), where a game costs around €5 for an adult. There are reduced rates for families/groups and for children, who pay around €3 per game. Charges include shoe hire. Around 20 centres are affiliated to the Irish Tenpin Bowling

Association (🖳 www.tenpinireland.com), which organises events and competitions.

Boxing

Ireland has a strong tradition of boxing, and there are currently around 165 clubs under the aegis of the Amateur Boxing Association (☎ 01-454 3525, 🖳 www.iaba. ie) – all listed on the website. Major fights are held at the 2,000-seat National Boxing Stadium in Dublin (☎ 01-453 3371, 🖳 www. nationalstadium.ie), where tickets cost between €25 and €50.

Canoeing

There are around 65 canoe clubs in Ireland, with some 4,500 members. Competitive canoeists might like to try the annual Liffey Descent in the autumn – which has its own website (🖳 www.liffeydescent.com). For further information, including a list of clubs, contact the Irish Canoe Union (☎ 01-625 1105, 🖳 www. canoe.ie).

Cricket

Another sport that has crossed the Irish sea from east to west is cricket, although it's hardly as popular as in the UK. The biggest crowd ever recorded at a cricket match was a mere 4,000 to watch Ireland v. Australia in 1993! Nevertheless, there are an estimated 9,000 male and 1,500 female cricketers in Ireland, and 34 teams compete in the annual Irish Cup. The Irish Cricket Union (☎ 01-845 0710 – staffed only between 10am and 12.30pm – 🖳 www.cricketeurope4.net/IRELAND/index.shtml) recognises around 45 men's and 17 women's clubs.

Croquet

There are just eight croquet clubs in Ireland – Carrickmines in South Dublin, Herbert Park and Trinity College in central Dublin, Kells in County Meath, Ardigeen Vale, Monkstown and Rushbrooke in County Cork, and Newcastle in County Wicklow. All but Ardigeen Vale are affiliated to the Croquet Association of Ireland (🖳 www.croquetireland.com).

Cycling

Although cycling isn't a popular method of transport in Ireland, there are around 2,500 people who cycle competitively as members of the 125 or so clubs affiliated to the Irish Cycling Federation (☎ 01-855 1522, 🖳 www.cyclingireland.ie).

For the less competitive there are guided cycling tours, such as Irish Cycling Safaris and Dublin Bike Tours, which take you along quiet streets and lanes at a relaxed pace, generally with frequent stops for 'refreshment'.

Tours generally run only between April and October and cost around €25 per person, which includes bike hire, the services of a guide, and insurance, but not refreshments. Alternatively, you can simply rent a bike for a day or a week and make your own itinerary (most hire companies provide suggested routes). Bike hire costs around €10-15 per day or €50-75 per week; helmets, panniers, baby seats, etc. are extra. Booking is recommended, especially at peak times.

Darts

As in the UK, darts is a popular pub game in Ireland. Each county has its own leagues (men's and women's teams are separated, to prevent hanky-panky!), matches being played mostly on weekday evenings. Each player must register with the County Darts Board, at a cost of around €3, and then normally pays a small fee for each match.

The Irish National Darts Organisation (☎ 01-451 2890), which has no website, includes 1,500 clubs fielding over 2,000 teams. There are county darts teams and even a national team. Clubs also hold open events, in which players from any county can take part. The biggest darts competitions are held at the Limerick Inn Hotel. Further information can be found on 🖳 www.dartsinireland.com.

Diving

Unlikely as it may seem, Ireland attracts divers from all over the world; there are 82 recognised diving locations, and Kilkee Bay in County Clare is reputed to be Europe's top diving location and one of the top five in the world. All divers must have at least the basic D1 diving qualification. For details, contact the Irish Underwater Council (☎ 01-284 4601, 🖳 www.cft.ie), which oversees Ireland's 47 diving clubs. Further information about diving in Ireland can be found on 🖳 www.diveinireland.com and 🖳 www.tempoweb.com/diveireland.

Hockey

Irish Hockey (☎ 01-260 0028, 🖳 www.hockey.ie) represents both men's and women's

hockey, the (men's) Irish Hockey Association and Irish Ladies' Hockey Union having amalgamated in 2000. There are around 200 affiliated clubs, with competitions at all levels, both junior and senior.

Hunting & Shooting

Unlike the UK, where firearms are banned and hunting with dogs is outlawed, Ireland still allows its citizens to keep guns (a licence must be obtained from the local *Garda* station) and tolerates hunting with hounds, a 'sport' which is overseen by the Hunting Association of Ireland (☎ 085-110 0645, ☐ www.hai.ie). There are 38 packs of dogs and an estimated 300,000 participants.

Almost every community has a gun club, and target shooting is governed by the National Rifle & Pistol Association of Ireland (☎ 087-900 7501, ☐ http://homepage.eircom.net/~ntsai/nrpa.html) and its affiliated organisations, the National Target Shooting Association of Ireland, the National Silhouette Association, the National Association of Sporting Rifle Clubs and the Pony Club Shooting Association.

Clay pigeon shooting is also popular; for information, contact the Irish Clay Pigeon Shooting Association (☎ 087-900 7501, ☐ www.icpsa.ie), which has over 500 members.

Motorsport

There's no Irish Grand Prix, but a number of major motor racing events are held at Mondello Park in Naas, County Kildare (☎ 045-860 0200, ☐ www.mondello.ie).

Motor cycle racing comes under the auspices of Motorcycling Ireland, incorporating the Motor Cycle Union of Ireland (☎ 01-841 5086, ☐ www.motorcycling-ireland.com), which has around 65 clubs with some 1,700 members; while rallying is overseen by Motorsport Ireland (☎ 01-677 5628, ☐ www.motorsportireland.com), whose 35 clubs have 3,600 members.

There are a number of outdoor and indoor karting tracks, including Abbeyspeedways near Limerick, Galway Kart Racing, Kart City and Kylemore in Dublin, and Sideways Motor Fun Park in Naas, County Kildare. Karting

events are organised by clubs affiliated to Motorsport Ireland (see above).

Orienteering

There are 21 orienteering clubs in Ireland, with around 1,100 members, affiliated to the Irish Orienteering Association (☎ 086-330 6931 or ☎ 066-712 6530, ☐ www.orienteering.ie), which organises events all year round.

Rowing

More than 8,000 people are members of the 70 clubs belonging to the Irish Amateur Rowing Union (☎ 01-625 1130, ☐ www.iaru.ie), which organises events. A National Rowing Centre at Inniscarra in County Cork was officially opened last year.

Squash & Racketball

There are over 100 squash clubs in Ireland, and many public leisure centres have courts; the latter include the Ballina Stephenites Sports Centre (in County Mayo), Fethard Racquetball Club (County Tipperary), Galway Handball & Racquetball Club in Galway City, Kells Racquetball Club (County Meath), Macroom Racquetball Club and Skibbereen Sports Centre (County Cork), St Marys Sports Centre in Sligo and Tralee Sports & Leisure Centre (County Kerry); and Dublin City University and University College Dublin. Contact Irish Squash (☎ 01-625 1145, ☐ www.irishsquash.com) for information.

Played on a squash court, racketball (or racquetball) has slightly different rules, and uses shorter rackets and a larger, bouncier ball. There are around 20 clubs affiliated to the Racquetball Association of Ireland (☐ www.racquetball-ireland.com), and the game is played at many sports and leisure centres (see above).

Surfing

Perhaps not surprisingly, Ireland is a popular destination for surfers, the Atlantic rollers having been uninterrupted for 3,000 miles before crashing onto beaches along the west coast.

Top surfing venues are Ballybunion, Bundoran, Lahinch, Portrush, Rossnowlagh, Strandhill, Tramore and Inniscrone (or Enniscrone or Inishcrone, depending on which map you're using!) – the last reputed to be something of a surfers' Mecca.

Officially, there are 18 surfing clubs with around 1,500 members. Contact the Irish Surfing Association (🖳 www.isasurf.ie) for further information.

Tennis

Around 25,000 men, 21,000 women and 46,000 children are members of Ireland's 220 tennis clubs, which are affiliated to Tennis Ireland (☎ 01-884 4010, 🖳 www.tennisireland. ie). The cost of club membership varies between around €200 per year for a small club and €1,500 or more for a prestigious club such as the David Lloyd Dublin; most clubs also charge a joining fee. Major tennis tournaments are held at the David Lloyd club, Fitzwilliam LTC and Donnybrook (home of the Irish Open) in Dublin. The main clubs outside the capital are Tennis Village and Sundays Well in Cork, and Galway LTC.

For occasional players, there are tarmac courts in almost every public park in Dublin, as well as in many of the other major cities' parks, where you can enjoy an hour's tennis for as little as €2 per person. Dublin's Parks Programme, which has been running since 1977, is a state-subsidised initiative to attract young people to tennis: children aged 6–17 can have up to three coaching sessions per week for eight weeks in the summer or spring for a nominal registration fee; for details contact the National Administrator (☎ 01-833 8711) or go to 🖳 www.parkstennis.com.

Tug of War

Believe it or not, there's an Irish Tug of War Association, which has 27 clubs and over 1,000 members (🖳 www.tugofwarireland.com).

Volleyball

Although beach volleyball has yet to catch on in Ireland (a bit more global warming might help its cause), conventional volleyball, played by people in loose-fitting clothing, is played in over 80 schools and at 15 clubs throughout the country. Contact the Volleyball Association of Ireland (☎ 01-670 7165, 🖳 www.volley ballireland.com) for details.

Cobh, Co. Cork

17.
SHOPPING

Shopping in Ireland is unusually pleasurable because you're never made to feel as if you need to buy something, so you can browse as much as you like. Shop assistants won't stand over you or watch your every move, but will politely ignore you until you're ready to buy or need help. You will invariably be warmly received in small shops where you're a regular customer and many shopkeepers will even allow you to pay another day if you don't have enough money with you.

Small family-run shops still constitute the bulk of Irish retailers, and the invasion of shopping centres and hypermarkets has, for the most part, been successfully resisted. They are, however, more common nowadays than they were a few years ago, particularly on the outskirts of the four major cities (Dublin, Cork, Limerick and Galway). Some of these, such as the new Jervis Centre in Dublin and those in the suburbs of Blanchardstown, Tallaght and Dun Laoghaire, are American-style 'malls' with a combination of major stores and smaller, specialist shops, providing a 'one-stop shop' (Nirvana or Gehenna depending on your shopping persuasion).

The major Irish-owned department stores, Arnotts, Dunnes, and Penney's, which have outlets in all the main towns, are being challenged by the recent influx of British and other foreign chains. Roche's Stores has recently been taken over by Debenhams. Marks & Spencer, for example, has opened three stores in Ireland. On the food front, Tesco is making rapid inroads, having recently taken over the Irish chain Quinsworth (see **Supermarkets** on page 347), while US stores such as Gymboree children's wear and German discount chains Aldi and Lidl have now opened outlets.

International specialist chains are also a familiar sight, although a wealth of specialist Irish food shops and boutiques have also sprung up in the last few years in areas such as Dublin's rejuvenated Temple Bar, and traditional Irish retailers such as Eason (newsagents') and Golden Discs (music) survive.

As in many other countries, there was a huge downturn in consumption during the recession in the early '90s. Since then the 'Celtic Tiger' phenomenon has caused a dramatic turnaround: retail sales have risen by an average of 7.5 per cent per annum since 1994. Major shopping areas are as busy as anywhere else in the world, and the big cities are up to date with the latest fashions.

Dublin's central shopping area, which runs from O'Connell Street to Grafton Street, is the best place in Ireland for concentrated shopping, at prices competitive with most other European cities. The pedestrianisation of Dublin's Grafton Street and Henry Street, and similar schemes in Cork and Galway (and other cities), has made shopping a more pleasurable experience (even for shopaphobics), accompanied as it so often is by the sounds of buskers and street entertainers.

Ireland is of course famous for its handicrafts – jewellery, lace, linen, tweed, knitwear, pottery, glass and silverware – and there's a plethora of shops offering these wares throughout the country. In most towns, you can pick up a free shopping guide or 'newsletter', giving details of local shops.

A Plastic Bag Environmental Levy was introduced in 2002 in order to reduce the number of plastic bags damaging the environment; an estimated 1.2bn bags were being provided free of charge to customers each year, and it's estimated that this figure has been reduced by an amazing 85 per cent since the introduction of the Levy.

All retailers are obliged to charge customers €0.15 per bag, although small bags used for dairy products, fruit and vegetables, sweets, ice and cooked food are exempt from the levy, as are 'bags for life' costing at least €0.70. Even these, of course, are made of plastic (and you may receive scornful looks if you use them), and most retailers sell canvas bags instead.

PRICES & PAYMENT

Generally, prices in Ireland are comparable with other European countries and similar to the UK, apart from a few items such as books, which are significantly more expensive. Nevertheless, the government has recently taken measures to increase competitiveness, which will inevitably lower prices, such as the abolition of the Groceries Order Bill of 1987, which set minimum prices for certain goods. Prices in Ireland are fairly consistent, but it's still worth shopping around and comparing them, as they can vary considerably, not only between small shops and supermarkets, but also among supermarkets in the same town.

Note, however, that price differences often reflect different quality, so ensure that you're comparing similar products. The best time to have a shopping spree is during the winter and summer sales in January/February and July/August respectively. You won't, however, find shops advertising sales all year round, as in the UK and US. The Irish value quality, and are far less 'discount mad' than most other Europeans. See also **Cost of Living** on page 296.

Credit cards are widely accepted in Ireland, even in out of the way places. Visa and MasterCard are preferred, but Diners Club and American Express cards are also accepted by many shops. Debit cards such as Laser and Maestro (European Debit Card) are usually accepted as an alternative to credit cards. On the other hand, some shops are reluctant to accept cheques, particularly if you don't have a guarantee card (which isn't usually issued until you've had an account for at least six months).

Value Added Tax

Value added tax (VAT) is levied on most goods and services in Ireland, and prices invariably include VAT. Most goods and services are taxed at the standard rate of 21 per cent, but heating fuel, electricity, hotel and restaurant bills, newspapers and most property transactions are taxed at 13.5 per cent; and basic foods and drinks, books and children's clothing and footwear are zero-rated. See also **VAT-free Shopping** on page 353).

Inflation

Inflation in March 2008 was 3.5 per cent (the highest rate for five years), and was expected to increase further to around 4.4 per cent by the end of the year. The highest rises (since March 2007) were in housing, water and electricity, gas and other fuels (+9.7 per cent). Other high risers included food and non-alcoholic drinks (+8.1 per cent), healthcare (+6.2 per cent) and education (+5.8 per cent). There were decreases in the cost of clothing and footwear (-2.8 per cent) and in furnishings, household equipment and routine household maintenance (-1 per cent).

The Consumer Price Index (CPI) is the official measure of inflation in Ireland, published monthly by the Central Statistics Office (CSO). It's calculated by valuing a 'basket', which currently contains some 1,000 items divided into ten 'commodity groups' (food, alcohol, tobacco, clothing and footwear, fuel and light, housing, household durables, other goods, transport and services). Each group is 'weighted' to reflect the proportion of the average person's expenditure in that group, e.g. food is given the most weight, household durables the least. The latest figures can be found on the CSO's website (💻 www.cso.ie)

SHOPPING HOURS

Irish shops are usually open from 9am to 5.30pm (6pm in Dublin), Monday to Saturday, although newsagents and convenience stores are often open for longer hours and even on Sundays. Craft shops generally also open on Sundays. Many towns have late night shopping (until 8 or 9pm) on Thursdays or Fridays or both days. In small towns and villages, there's usually an early closing day (usually Wednesday) when shops close at 1pm.

A number of supermarkets in the larger urban areas open on Sundays from 12 to 6pm, and large shopping centres (which have sprung up on the outskirts of bigger towns) usually open from 9am to 6pm (some as late as 11pm) daily. Opening hours are usually restricted on public holidays, when many shops close all day.

LOCAL SHOPS & MARKETS

Despite the proliferation of out-of-town shopping centres, there are still plenty of small local shops in most towns and city suburbs in Ireland. Shops tend to follow the British pattern, with a grocer (general provisions), butcher, baker, greengrocer (fruit and vegetables) and pharmacy (chemist). Increasingly common are 'convenience stores', mini-supermarkets which are often open long hours and sell a bit of everything, from alcoholic drinks to toiletries (e.g. Spar stores, of which there are almost 60 nationwide).

Convenience store chains include ADM Londis, Mace and SPAR (owned in Ireland by BWG) and SuperValu (see **Supermarkets** below). Smaller convenience store outlets include Costcutter, Vivo, and XL Stop and Shop. Prices in convenience stores are usually higher than in supermarkets, although they have the advantage of being focal points for the local community and an excellent source of help, information, advice and local gossip.

In common with other countries, petrol (gas) stations in Ireland usually carry a selection of basic grocery items, and are particularly handy in the evenings and on Saturday afternoons and Sundays when other shops are closed. Irish oil company Maxol has an alliance with Mace to provide convenience stores in its stations, while many TOP stations have Londis outlets (resulting from a former affiliation).

Esso Ireland, a subsidiary of Exxon Mobil, is expanding its 'On The Run' convenience store brand in the Dublin area, while Statoil Ireland offers the nonsensically named 'Fareplay' outlets, and Texaco Ireland (owned by Chevron Corporation) 'StarMarket' stores. Only Irish Shell (operated by Topaz Oil under a franchise agreement) currently has no convenience store brand; although most of its outlets have shops, which, as a result of Topaz's takeover of Statoil Ireland, are soon expected to become 'Fareplay' outlets.

Markets

Markets are cheap, colourful and interesting, and are often a good place for shrewd shoppers, although you sometimes have to be careful what you buy (beware of fakes, and goods that look as if they've 'fallen off a lorry'). Items for sale include food (particularly fruit and vegetables), clothes, handicrafts, household goods and second-hand goods (e.g. clothes, books, records, antiques and bric-a-brac).

Many Irish towns have small markets, usually one day a week, and larger markets are to be found in the cities, where you will also find street sellers offering everything from jewellery to flowers. Dublin has a daily open-air market, for example, and Limerick a permanent indoor market. Check with your local library, council or tourist office for details of nearby markets.

SUPERMARKETS

As elsewhere in the world, supermarket shopping is on the increase in Ireland and new outlets appear regularly, generally on the outskirts of towns, so you may need a car to get to them. Thankfully, Irish planning regulations currently limit the size of supermarkets to 3,500m² (37,500ft²) in the Dublin area and 3,000m^2 elsewhere, so you won't find the 'monster malls' that are common in most other countries; although the government is under increasing pressure from the big chains to raise the limits, and 'retail warehouses' may be up to 6,000m^2 (65,000ft^2).

The largest supermarket chain in Ireland is now SuperValu, with over 170 outlets, most of them run on a franchise basis. As the name suggests, these shops emphasise 'value' over quality. The other two main supermarket chains are Dunnes (see **Department Stores** below), some of whose 123 stores don't include a supermarket and others offer more of a 'convenience store'; and Tesco Ireland, which now has over 90 stores (including nine small outlets, branded as Tesco Ireland Local and Tesco Express stores, the smallest being known as 'superettes'); these differ little in terms of quality and price. In addition, there are 21 Superquinn stores (mainly in Leinster) and a few upmarket food stores run by Marks & Spencer.

Tesco supermarkets are normally open from 8am until 9 or 10pm seven days a week, although not all open on public holidays. Details of where to find stores can be found on the Tesco website (⌨ www.tesco.ie), which also lists the 'top ten buys' each week and offers an online shopping facility. Note that there's no home delivery service unless you buy online (see opposite).

DEPARTMENT & CHAIN STORES

Although foreign department stores such as Marks & Spencer are present in Ireland, a more authentic Irish shopping experience is to be found at the long-established Arnotts, Dunnes, and Penney's. In fact, Dunnes is Ireland's largest clothing retailer. For the uninitiated, a department store is a large shop, usually with several floors, which sells almost everything and may also include a food hall. In a large department store, each floor may be dedicated to a particular kind of goods, such as ladies' or men's fashions, or furniture and furnishings.

Chain stores are simply shops with a number of branches, usually in different towns and cities. International chains such as Benetton, The Body Shop, Debenhams,

Dixons, Next, River Island and Topshop have appeared on the scene in recent years to challenge indigenous chains such as Fields Jewellers, Tyler (Ireland) Shoes and Cripps, which sells clothing and shoes.

> Ireland's oldest and largest department store is Arnotts in Dublin. Dating from 1843 and covering some 30,000m^2, Arnotts is ranked in the top five stores in the UK and Ireland, along with London's Harrods and Selfridges.

Like Marks & Spencer, it offers its own 'store card' (actually a credit card) and offers regular customers perks such as 'preview buying' and even free advice on interior design. Arnotts is open between 9am and 6.30pm most days, with a late night (9pm) on Thursdays, and Sunday opening from 12 until 6pm. It has no fewer than four places to eat, and its own car park, although you will be charged around €3 per hour for the convenience of using it! Arnotts offers a delivery service and has its own website (⌨ www.arnotts.ie) where you can shop online. Another city centre department store is Clerys (⌨ www.clerys.com).

The most widespread department store in Ireland is Debenhams, with 12 stores. There are also 30 Argos stores, where low cost goods are ordered from a catalogue and fetched, while you wait, from an adjoining warehouse (it's also possible to order from home). There are two types of shop: 'regular' shops, which don't stock all 3,000 items, and 'extra' shops, which do. It has its own website (⌨ www.argos.ie), where there's a 'store locator'.

SHOPPING CENTRES & RETAIL PARKS

Out-of-town shopping centres, normally including a major supermarket, began to appear in Ireland in the '60s, Dunnes' Cornelscourt being one of the first. The first town-centre 'mall', in Stillorgan, was constructed in the late '60s, soon followed by the two major Dublin city centre shopping malls, the Ilac Centre and the Irish Life Shopping Mall. The capital's Jervis Centre dates from the '90s, when a new type of shopping centre was developed in the Dublin suburbs, not dominated by a supermarket, but with a number of 'high street' names, and usually a cinema. There are currently four of these: The Square, the Blanchardstown Centre, the Liffey Valley Shopping Centre, and Dundrum Town Centre.

Shopping centres have since emerged on the outskirts of other cities, such as Mahon Point in Cork, the Crescent Shopping Centre in Limerick and the City Square Shopping Centre in Waterford. In addition, there are smaller retail parks on the outskirts of some 20 towns, from Letterkenny to Limerick. These have no internal shopping malls, but usually consist of between five and ten outlets (e.g. Atlantic Homecare, Elverys sports shop and Woodies DIY, as well as British shops such as Argos and Homebase) surrounding a large free car park, and are located beside major roads for ease of access.

SECOND-HAND & CHARITY SHOPS

Second-hand goods, especially clothes, can be purchased from shops run by volunteers where the proceeds go to a charity such as Cerebral Palsy, Oxfam or the Irish Cancer Society. These are generally found in larger towns and cities and are sometimes referred to as 'used clothing shops'. There are dozens in the Dublin area.

Second-hand goods can also be bought at car boot sales, which are increasingly popular in Ireland, and by way of small advertisements

in local newspapers and newsagents' windows. Ireland also has plenty of second-hand book shops, particularly in university towns, as well as 'antique' shops (often a euphemism for junk shops), which are concentrated in Dublin's Temple Bar area (there are at least a dozen in Francis Street alone). Genuine antiques can be bought at auctions (Christie's have offices in Dublin). When looking for an auction, note that Irish estate agents are also referred to as auctioneers!

ONLINE & HOME SHOPPING

A number of Irish retailers offer online shopping, including the following:

♦ 💻 **www.argos.ie** – the popular 'everything in a box' retailer; have products delivered to your home or collect from your nearest shop;

♦ 💻 **www.arnotts.ie** – the site of Arnotts department store in Dublin;

♦ 💻 **www.buy4now.ie** – an online 'shopping mall', where you can buy anything from flowers and health food to cars – a good source of unusual gifts;

♦ 💻 **www.buyeire.com** – a general shopping site;

♦ 💻 **www.eason.ie** – Eason is Ireland's largest book shop chain, offering worldwide delivery on a wide range of books;

♦ 💻 **www.edirectory.ie** – another general shopping site;

♦ 💻 **www.louiscopeland.com** – the site of Louis Copeland & Sons' clothing shops);

♦ 💻 **www.superquinn.ie** – the site of the Irish supermarket chain, Superquinn;

♦ 💻 **www.tesco.ie** – Tesco Ireland's site, currently offering delivery only in and near major cities.

Needless to say, there are numerous other sites, including those of specialist retailers. There's usually a delivery charge on orders up to a certain value (e.g. €300).

Mail Order

A number of companies operate mail-order 'clubs' for books, CDs and DVDs and computer software, where new members are offered a number of items at a nominal introductory price (e.g. €1 each) or pay for one of five or seven items, in return for an agreement to purchase a further number of items (usually three to six) at full price during the following one or two years. There's no catch, although there may be a restricted choice and, if you want to resign before you've fulfilled your side of the bargain, you're usually required to repay the savings made on the introductory offer.

Virtually the only Irish mail order catalogue is Littlewoods Ireland (formerly known as Family Album, ☎ 01-811 2222, 🖥 www.littlewoodsireland. ie), although the major UK catalogues (e.g. Kays and Great Universal) are also available in Ireland.

Before committing yourself to buying anything by post, make sure you know what you're signing, and avoid paying for anything in advance.

It's foolish to send advance payment by post in response to an advertisement (or to anyone) unless you're sure that the company is reputable and offers a money back guarantee. If purchases aren't covered by a guarantee, you may find it extremely difficult to obtain redress, although when you purchase goods by post, you're usually protected by the Sale of Goods Act (see **Receipts & Guarantees** on page 355).

Buying Overseas

When buying goods overseas, ensure that you're dealing with a bona fide company and that the goods will work in Ireland (if applicable). If possible, always pay by credit card when buying by mail order or over the internet; when you buy goods costing over around €150, the credit card issuer is jointly liable with the supplier. When buying overseas, you should take into account shipping costs, import duty and VAT. Import duty is payable on all goods, at varying rates, and VAT at 21 per cent on anything purchased from outside the European Union (EU). Payments are collected by the post office or courier company on delivery (unless more than €750 is owed, in which case Customs & Excise collect payments directly).

FOOD

The range, quality and price of food in Ireland is similar to that in the UK. Fresh home-

grown and imported fruit and vegetables, Irish meat (particularly beef, lamb and pork), and locally caught fish and seafood are readily available in most parts of the country. The Irish also produce a number of cheeses, and specialities such as soda bread. Organic food is widely available in supermarkets and 'delicatessens' (where prices are higher), and there are a number of 'health food' shops for those wishing to follow special diets.

Those from the UK and US should note that all foodstuffs in Irish shops are sold in metric quantities, although you will probably be understood (especially by older staff) if you ask for half a pound of butter or five pounds of potatoes.

ALCOHOL & TOBACCO

In Ireland, you can buy alcoholic drinks from supermarkets and convenience stores or from specialist shops called off-licences (which means that they're licensed to sell alcohol, but you may not drink it on the premises). Pub licensing hours don't apply to retail outlets, which are open during normal shop hours, as well as up to 10pm. As in pubs, you must be over 18 to purchase alcohol. Many outlets display signs saying that they won't sell alcohol to anyone aged under 21, even though they cannot legally refuse to serve anyone over 18. This is to protect themselves against prosecution for accidentally serving someone who's under age so, if you **look** under 18 (lucky you!) you're advised to carry proof of your age with you to avoid embarrassing situations in off-licences and pubs.

Prices are similar in all outlets, i.e. high. Government taxes on wine and spirits are even more astronomical than in the UK, and are levied according to the number of units of alcohol rather than the price, so the higher the alcohol content, the more tax you pay. It's hard to find a bottle of wine, even paint-stripping plonk, for less than €5, and anything half decent will set you back at least twice as much.

A six-pack of the cheapest lager costs around €5 and a standard bottle of whiskey (or whisky if you prefer Scotch) around €20. You may save a few pence in a supermarket, but you will usually have a wider choice, particularly of wine, in an off-licence, and should be able to obtain expert help in choosing (although some off-licence staff barely know the difference between red and white wine).

As in many developed countries, smoking is fast becoming socially unacceptable in Ireland, and has been banned in all enclosed public spaces. It's also becoming prohibitively expensive. The government grabs an ever increasing proportion of the retail price of cigarettes and tobacco in duty, ostensibly to encourage people to give it up and promote good health (although, if everyone did, the government would lose a major source of revenue). The cheapest packet of 20 'fags' will set you back at least €7.

All major brands of cigarettes, cigars and tobacco are available in Ireland and are sold in almost every shop, supermarket, petrol station, pub, off-licence, hotel and convenience store. There are also a few that are peculiar to Ireland, e.g. John Player Blue and Fusion.

▲ Caution

The minimum legal age for purchasing tobacco products (and for smoking them) is 18.

NEWSPAPERS, MAGAZINES & BOOKS

There are four national daily newspapers, five national Sunday papers, around 50 regional and 12 local papers, as well as over 30 free papers, the last mainly confined to urban areas. The most popular daily is the *Irish Independent* (with a circulation of around 170,000), followed by *The Irish Times* (120,000), *The Star* (100,000) and the *Irish Examiner* (65,000). Both the *Independent* and *The Examiner* have evening supplements, the *Evening Herald* (105,000) and *The Evening Echo* (30,000) respectively.

By far the most popular Sunday papers are the *Sunday Independent* and the *Sunday World* (both over 300,000), followed by the *Sunday Tribune* (90,000), *Sunday Business Post* (55,000) and *Ireland on Sunday* (55,000). The three biggest-circulation regional papers are *Kerryman* (40,000), the *Connacht Tribune* (30,000) and the *Limerick Leader* (27,500).

Most Irish newspapers are politically conservative and aimed at a middle-class readership. *The Irish Times* is widely considered to be the 'best' (it's certainly the most 'serious') and is perhaps the most liberal, while the *Independent* is more gossipy and has more in the way of 'lifestyle' features and the *Irish Examiner* is somewhat provincial.

The only Irish tabloid newspapers are *Ireland on Sunday*, *Sunday World* and *The Star*, an Irish edition of the British *Daily Star*. This is probably due to the wide availability of British newspapers (especially the tabloids), which can be bought all over Ireland and are cheaper than Irish papers, as Ireland (unlike the UK) imposes VAT on the printing of newspapers. Approximately 25 per cent of daily and 33 per cent of Sunday newspapers sold in Ireland are British.

Newspapers can be bought from newsagents, supermarkets and convenience stores, but there's no home delivery service as in the UK and the US. *The Irish Times* and the *Independent* cost around €1.60. If your newsagent is unable to obtain British papers for you, it's possible to subscribe to them directly.

A wide range of magazines is available in Ireland, covering all major sports and hobbies, homes and gardens, and business affairs, the most popular being the *RTÉ* [television programme] *Guide*! There are numerous women's and men's magazines, which deal with topics such as health and sex. Many of these are specific to Ireland, but magazines published in Britain and other countries are also available.

Convenience stores have been gradually displacing the traditional newsagent's in Ireland, although they still exist. The Eason chain of high street newsagents and booksellers is the largest in the country.

The Irish are great book buyers, and there are numerous new and second-hand book shops in the major towns and cities, the best known new-book shop chain being Eason (🖳 www.eason.ie).

In Dublin, the two major local chains are Tuthill's and Bus Stop. Although there's no VAT on books, they tend to be expensive, and it may be cheaper to buy them via the internet from one of the many online 'book shops', the largest of which is the American company Amazon, which has a UK site (🖳 www.amazon.co.uk), but no Irish site, although 🖳 www.shopireland.ie operates 'in association' with Amazon UK.

CLOTHING

The biggest clothing retailer in Ireland is Dunnes, with over 100 stores. Penney's is another major clothing retailer, and Debenhams has a chain of department stores selling clothing (see also **Department & Chain Stores** on page 348). The high street chain River Island has 17 shops (three in Dublin).

For those who prefer to be a 'cut above' the rest, there's no shortage of good quality clothing outlets. One of the most up-market shops is Louis Copeland & Sons in Dublin, which claims to stock the largest range of men's clothing in Ireland, including over 5,000 suits in sizes ranging from 36 to 60!

Like Scotland, Ireland is famous for its knitwear. Aran sweaters in particular, originally worn by fishermen on the Aran islands off the coast of Co. Clare, and traditionally made from untreated wool, are widely available, either hand-knitted or machine made; although you should expect to pay around €100-150 for one. Tweed jackets and caps are also typically Irish garments, the best tweeds supposedly coming from County Donegal.

There are small specialist shoe shops in most towns, as well as chains such as Clarks and Cripps, a 100-year-old Irish family business. Shoe repairers' (known as heel bars) are also widespread, many of which also sell shoes (and not only those that customers have failed to collect!). Cripps also deal in sportswear, as do Athletic Sports, Elverys, McLaughlin Sports, O'Keefe Sport and Sportssmith.

Prices

Clothing prices are similar to those in the UK, i.e. approximately €120 for a woman's suit and €150 for a man's, €25 for a smart shirt or blouse, €50-70 for a pair of trousers, shoes or 'branded' jeans, €60-100 for 'name' trainers. If you aren't bothered about displaying someone else's name prominently on everything you wear, you can buy reasonable quality clothing at significantly lower prices.

FURNITURE & FURNISHINGS

A wide range of modern and traditional furniture is available in Ireland, although it tends to be of good quality and therefore isn't cheap. Do-it-yourself hypermarkets, such as those commonly found in other European countries, aren't easy to find in Ireland, where most things must be purchased in smaller, specialist shops. However, Swedish retailer IKEA obtained permission in October 2006 to build a store near Dublin, which is due to open in 2009. On the other hand, there are also a number of second-hand furniture dealers for those on a tight budget (look under *Furniture – Used* in the *Golden Pages*) and, if you're looking for antique or mock-antique

furniture, there's no shortage of genuine and reproduction antique furniture shops.

The best time to buy furniture and furnishings (and all expensive items) is during sales, when prices of certain items are reduced considerably. It's possible to pay for furniture (and large household appliances) over a period of up to 12 months. Payment over three months is usually interest-free, but you're charged interest on a 12-month payment period and may need to pay a 25 per cent deposit.

Prices

Examples of furniture prices are: single bed from €160; double bed from €190; king-size bed from €240; single divan bed from €160; sofa bed from €180; three-piece suite from €675; three-seat sofa from €300; armchair from €150; basic dining table plus four chairs from €160; solid wood dining table plus six chairs around €700; five-drawer chest in solid pine around €120; single wardrobe in solid pine around €250; triple wardrobe around €550.

HOUSEHOLD GOODS

Household goods in Ireland are generally of high quality, and the choice is as wide as in most other European countries. Bear in mind when importing household goods that aren't sold in Ireland that it may be difficult or impossible to get them repaired or serviced locally. If you import appliances, don't forget to bring a supply of spares and consumables, such as bulbs for a refrigerator or sewing machine, and spare bags for a vacuum cleaner.

Note that the standard size of kitchen appliances and cupboard units in Ireland may not be the same as in your home country, and it may be difficult to fit an imported dishwasher or washing machine into an Irish fitted kitchen. More importantly, foreign products may not meet Irish safety standards, and your household insurance may be invalidated if, for example, your British tumble dryer short-circuits and burns your house down.

With that caveat, if you already own small household appliances, it's worthwhile bringing them to Ireland, as usually all that's required is a change of plug. However, if you're coming from a country with a 110/115V electricity supply, such as the US, you will need a lot of expensive transformers, and it's usually better to buy new appliances in Ireland. Small appliances such as vacuum cleaners, grills, toasters and irons aren't expensive in Ireland, and are of good quality. Don't bring a television (TV) or video recorder without checking its compatibility first, as TVs made for other countries often don't work in Ireland without modification (see **Television** on page 151).

You won't usually be able to hire electrical goods in Ireland, with the exception of TVs and video recorders. Tools and do-it-yourself equipment can, however, be rented in most towns.

☑ SURVIVAL TIP

If you need kitchen measuring equipment and cannot cope with decimal measures, you will need to bring your own measuring scales, jugs, cups and thermometers, etc.

Eircom, Ireland's semi-state telecommunications provider, has its own chain of 19 shops, selling all types of electrical goods, including computers, plus phones and fax machines, etc., with free delivery within Ireland and Northern Ireland.

Prices

Kettles and irons start at around €15, rising to €100 for all-singing-all-dancing models. For a washing machine, you can expect to pay between €300 and €750 and for a tumble drier €400+, for a standard fridge around €200, a freezer €300 and a free-standing fridge-freezer from €350 and a dishwasher from €350. An electric cooker, including oven and hob, costs from around €700, a good microwave, food processor or vacuum cleaner €125, and a toaster from €25.

VAT-FREE & SHOPPING ABROAD

Non-European Union (EU) residents can reclaim VAT on goods purchased in Ireland, provided that they're taken out of the EU

although shopping excursions to mainland Britain and France are possible. A shopping trip across the border makes an interesting day out and can save you money, depending on what and where you buy and the exchange rate between euros and pounds. Most shops in towns near the border (such as Newry) will accept euros, although they're unlikely to give you a good exchange rate. Whatever you're looking for, always compare prices and quality before buying. Bear in mind that, if you buy goods that are faulty or need repairing, you may need to return them to the place of purchase.

Since 1st January 1993, there have been no cross-border shopping restrictions within the EU for goods purchased duty and tax paid, provided that all goods are for personal consumption or use and not for resale. Although there are no official restrictions, there are 'indicative levels' for items such as spirits, wine, beer and tobacco products, above which goods may be classified as commercial quantities. These indicative levels are:

♦ 10 litres of spirits (over 22° proof);

♦ 20 litres of fortified wine such as port or sherry (under 22° proof);

♦ 90 litres of wine (or 120 x 0.75 litre bottles/10 cases) of which a maximum of 60 litres may be sparkling wine;

♦ 110 litres of beer;

♦ 800 cigarettes, 400 cigarillos, 200 cigars and 1 kg of smoking tobacco.

If you're travelling to Ireland from a country outside the EU (including, for obscure reasons, the Canary Islands, Channel Islands and Gibraltar), you're allowed to bring the following, irrespective of whether duty and/or tax were paid in the country of purchase:

♦ 200 cigarettes or 100 cigarillos or 50 cigars or 250g of tobacco;

♦ 1 litre of spirits or 2 litres of still, sparkling or fortified wine;

♦ 60ml (50g) of perfume;

♦ 250ml of toilet water;

♦ other goods (including beer) up to a value of €175 (€90 if you're under 15 years old).

within three months of purchase. There's no longer a minimum value and you can claim a refund of any amount. You will need a Global Refund Tax Free Shopping Cheque (also known as a 'cashback' voucher), which needs to be stamped by the retailer and by customs before you leave Ireland. If you're planning to leave Ireland within two months of the date of purchase, you can have the VAT deducted on the spot and simply present the voucher at your point of departure.

Alternatively, you can pay the full amount including VAT, and then present your vouchers at the Global Refund desk at the airport or port for an instant refund (less a service charge of around 4 per cent), or send them to Customs & Excise on your return home (refunds will take a further six to eight weeks to reach you). For more information on VAT refunds, contact the Global Refund Head Office (💻 www.global refund.ie). With certain purchases, particularly large items, it's better to have them shipped directly abroad, when VAT won't be payable. Remember also that the prices of some items (e.g. children's clothes and books) don't contain any VAT.

Shopping 'abroad' (i.e. outside Ireland) is generally limited to day trips to Northern Ireland,

Travellers under 17 aren't entitled to alcohol or tobacco allowances.

RECEIPTS, GUARANTEES & RIGHTS

When shopping you should always insist on a receipt and keep it until you've left the shop or reached home. This isn't just in case you need to return or exchange goods, which may be impossible without the receipt, but also to verify that you've paid if an automatic alarm goes off as you're leaving the shop, or any other questions arise. You should check receipts immediately on paying (particularly in supermarkets), because if you're overcharged, it may be impossible to obtain redress later. You need your receipt to return an item for repair or replacement (usually to the place of purchase) during the guarantee or warranty period (see below).

It's advisable to keep receipts and records of all major purchases made while you're in Ireland, particularly if you're staying for only a short period. This may save you both time and money when you finally leave the country and are required to declare your belongings in your new country of residence.

When you buy or hire goods or pay for services in Ireland, you have a number of rights under the Sale of Goods and Supply of Services Act, 1980. In the case of goods, they must be of merchantable quality; they must be reasonably fit for their stated purpose; they must be the same as their description (including a picture on the box or an advertisement on TV) and they must conform to any sample you've been given or shown, e.g. in the case of carpets and wallpaper. If the goods don't meet these requirements, the retailer who sold them to you is obliged by law to rectify the situation: i.e. either to replace the goods or refund your money in full. You aren't obliged to accept a replacement, a credit note or an offer to repair the goods.

In the case of services, you're entitled to expect that the person supplying the service is suitably qualified to do so, that 'skill and diligence' will be used in providing the service, that any materials used will be fit for their purpose and that any items supplied as part of the service will be of merchantable quality, etc.

If the service fails to meet any of these criteria, you may be entitled to a full or partial refund or to have the situation rectified, depending on the circumstances. Exclusion clauses (such as 'all work is carried out at the owner's risk') are only valid if they're reasonable and you're made aware of them at the time you order the service (e.g. if a jeweller says he might not be able to repair a delicate item you've damaged).

> ## ☑ SURVIVAL TIP
>
> When you buy goods that are covered by a guarantee (there's no law in Ireland that says they must be guaranteed), you're usually required to complete and post a guarantee card at or soon after the time of purchase. If you fail to do this, the guarantee may not apply, although you may still have a case if the goods are faulty.

It's particularly important to return the guarantee card if you buy something as a present for someone else; as a third party, that person won't be entitled to a refund or replacement goods if they're unsatisfactory. Make sure also that you check the conditions of the guarantee and the guarantee period, e.g. you may be required to report a fault within a certain period after purchase.

Note that Irish law distinguishes between a guarantee and a warranty, which normally applies only to part of a product or service; if that part fails, you won't necessarily be entitled to claim a full refund or replacement of the whole product, but may have to return it for repair. Note also that, if you buy something that doesn't work and try to repair it yourself, this may invalidate any claim you might have had against the supplier or manufacturer.

If you have problems with goods or services which the supplier won't rectify, you should contact the Office of the Director of Consumer Affairs (ODCA), 4 Harcourt Road, Dublin 2 (☎ 01-402 5555); for further information visit the ODCA website (🖥 www.odca.ie).

BLARNEY CASTLE

ST. PATRICK'S DAY GREETINGS

18.
ODDS & ENDS

This chapter contains miscellaneous information. Although all topics aren't of vital importance, most are of general interest to anyone planning to live or work in Ireland, including everything you ever wanted to know (but were afraid to ask) about subjects as diverse as tipping, toilets and the Treaty of Limerick.

CITIZENSHIP

The Citizenship and Naturalisation Act, 2005 changed the law regarding Irish citizenship. Previously, any child born in Ireland was automatically eligible for citizenship. Now only children born in Ireland to Irish parents automatically become citizens. A child born to non-Irish national parents is entitled to Irish citizenship only if at least one parent has been legally resident in Ireland for a minimum of three out of the four years immediately preceding the child's birth, but citizenship isn't automatic and must be applied for.

If you were born outside Ireland and your parents or grandparents are Irish, you can apply for Irish citizenship by descent. An application must be made to have your birth entered in the Foreign Births Register at the Department of Foreign Affairs, or at the nearest embassy or consulate. Irish citizenship will be effective from the date of registration, not from the date of your birth; this is known as acquiring citizenship by descent.

For others, there are two ways to acquire citizenship:

◆ **By naturalisation** (known as acquired citizenship) – Once you've lived in Ireland for a certain length of time, you can apply for citizenship by completing Form 8A and sending it to the Immigration and Citizenship Division of the Department of Justice, Equality and Law Reform at 13/14 Burgh Quay, Dublin 2 (☎ 01-616

7700 or ☎ 1890-551500, 💻 www.justice.ie). Non-European Union (EU) nationals must have been resident for five years, with an undertaking to live in Ireland for at least 50 days in the two years following naturalisation.

Refugees can apply for citizenship after three years' residence. Applications can take two years or more to be processed, and the granting of citizenship is at the discretion of the Minister. If you're successful, you will receive a letter from the Department and will have to make a declaration of loyalty to the State at a district court and pay a fee (around €660). You will then receive a certificate of naturalisation and can apply for an Irish passport.

◆ **By marriage** – If you married an Irish national before 30th November 2002 (and are still married!), you may lodge a declaration accepting Irish citizenship with the Department of Justice, Equality and Law Reform (see above). You may only do this after you have been married for at least three years. If you married an Irish national after this date, you can become a citizen only by naturalisation (see above).

CLIMATE

Ireland's climate isn't an overwhelming attraction for most foreigners – although, who knows, with global warming it could soon become one. It's one of the wettest countries in Europe, with average annual rainfall in parts of the west coast (where it rains on at least half the days of the year) as high as 20cm (8in) a month, and nowhere is it much less than 5cm (2in) a month. The north-west tends to be more windy and overcast than the south-west, the driest regions being in the east and low-lying areas.

Influenced by the relatively warm waters of the Gulf Stream and the prevailing south-westerly winds from the Atlantic, Ireland enjoys generally mild temperatures and extremes of hot and cold are rare. July and August usually bring the highest temperatures, around 14°C to 24°C (57°F to 75°F), and most of the country enjoys an average of at least six hours of sunshine a day between May and August.

Statistically speaking, April is usually the driest month in Ireland, although June is driest in the southern part of the country. The reality, though, is that you're unlikely to encounter lengthy spells of dry, sunny weather.

The constant motion of air masses makes the weather extremely unpredictable. Bright intervals between showers are common, as are what the locals refer to as 'soft' days, when the rain is like a fine mist. The best advice is to expect constant rain and then you will be pleasantly surprised when the sun appears, as even the wettest days often have sunny intervals (perhaps this is why the Irish are habitually optimistic about the weather).

If summer is rarely hot, winter is seldom severe, with only occasional snow except on high ground. Spring tends to be relatively dry and autumn mild, until as late as the end of November. The coldest months are January and February, when average temperatures are usually between 4°C and 7°C (39°F to 45°F) and violent storms can batter Ireland's western shores. The reward for all that rain is, of course, the lush green vegetation for which Ireland is famous.

The Irish are almost as obsessed by the weather as the British, and frequent weather forecasts (generally predicting rain) are given on television (TV) and radio and in daily newspapers.

CRIME

Although Ireland is a safe country by today's standards, and official statistics claim an annual decrease in the number of 'headline offences' (a suitably vague term), as elsewhere in the world, crime is on the increase, though it's largely an urban phenomenon; the majority of indictable offences occur in the Dublin area (where less than 30 per cent of the population lives) and there has recently been an increase of 'rowdyism' and casual violence in provincial towns. In some parts of Dublin, robbery and vandalism have become so commonplace that many people don't bother to report minor crimes such as the theft of bicycles and garden furniture.

Drug-related 'turf wars' are on the increase, and the number of serious injuries and deaths is rising as gangs acquire more weapons. If not drug-related, much crime is alcohol-induced, particularly at nightclub closing time, when crowds of drunken (and sometimes also drugged) youths take to the streets with the intention of causing trouble. As in other western countries, the 'answer' to the increase in crime is to lock more and more offenders away (see **Prisons** opposite). The death penalty was abolished in 1990, although in fact only one person had been executed since the Second World War, in 1954.

Ireland's safest counties (based on reported crimes per 1,000 population) are Roscommon and eastern Galway (8.3 crimes per 1,000 per year), Clare and Donegal (8.4), Mayo (8.8), Cavan, western Cork and Monaghan (9). The most dangerous places, not surprisingly, are parts of Dublin, by far the worst being North Central (124 crimes per 1,000!) and South Central (97), followed by Eastern and Southern (24), Western (23) and Northern (20). Other relative 'trouble spots' are the Counties Cork (21), Kilkenny and Waterford (20), Carlow and Kildare (18) and Limerick (17).

Car theft (see page 219) is rife in parts of Dublin, and 'smash-and-grab' attacks on foreign and hired cars are increasing in all tourist areas, so don't leave valuables in your car at any time – even when paying for petrol. 'Car-jacking' is thankfully rare. However, in South Dublin particularly, the latest delinquent

compensation from the state; however, this will only cover expenses such as hospital costs and loss of earnings.

Since the '90s, the threat of terrorism by Republican or Loyalist extremists has greatly declined, and international terrorism has – so far – ignored Ireland. On the other hand, white collar fraud and corruption has increased in recent years, although 'scams' are relatively rare. Abortion is illegal and prostitution is an offence, as is picking up prostitutes (including kerb-crawling).

Since 1990, marital rape has been a recognised crime in Ireland, and boys under 14 can be convicted of rape. It's illegal for a man to have sex with a girl under 17, even with consent; and homosexual sex, which was legalised in 1993, comes under the law of buggery, which is forbidden between persons under 17. The maximum sentence for offenders is life imprisonment.

Lists of publications on crime in Ireland can be found on the website of the National Crime Council (💻 www.irlgov.ie/crimecouncil).

Prisons

The Irish prison system has changed little since 1922, when it was inherited from the British, the only significant change being the transfer of prison control from a Prison Board to the Department of Justice in 1928 (although in 1996 the government approved the setting up of an independent Prison Agency, which would effectively be equivalent to the old Prison Board!).

The 1980 MacBridge Report was the first serious enquiry into the Irish penal system for almost a century. Although standards of accommodation have improved, the system itself is criticised for being as much the cause of crime as the cure for it. The traditional view of prison as a place of isolation persists (until the 1850s, most criminals were transported – mainly to Australia!), and there's little attempt to rehabilitate criminals through counselling or psychiatric treatment.

There are currently 16 prisons in Ireland, housing some 3,200 prisoners – an increase of two prisons and almost 1,000 inmates since 2001! – and there are plans to increase prison places to 3,800, which presumably means that the prison population is expected

craze is stealing cars, playing dodgems (bumper cars) with them in the local park and then setting them on fire. At the end of a weekend's rampage there can be half a dozen or more burnt out wrecks strewn about the area. In any case it's a good idea to have an immobiliser and alarm system fitted to your car, although little notice may be taken of it when it's triggered.

That said, you can walk almost anywhere at any time of the day or night in most parts of the country without fear of being assaulted or robbed. However, it's important to take the same precautions as you would in any country, such as keeping a close eye on your belongings in shops, markets and other crowded places and when using public transport. Never tempt fate with an exposed wallet or purse or by flashing your money around. Avoid confrontation, as this often leads to violence.

If property is stolen from you or your car, you should make a claim to the *Gardai* (even if they don't recover it, you will need a police report for insurance purposes). If you suffer personal injury as a result of crime, you're entitled to to continue its rapid rise. The number of sex offenders has risen particularly rapidly, and these now comprise 1 in 8 of the total prison population.

Nevertheless, the number of prisoners (86 per 100,000 people – almost 10 per cent of whom are foreigners) is still one of the lowest in Europe. On the other hand, the percentage of male prisoners is higher than the EU average (98 per cent compared with 95 per cent) and the proportion of prisoners under 21 (more than one in four) is the highest in the EU. There are also six Special Schools for Young Offenders, housing some 125 children (over 90 per cent boys) and with a total of over 300 full-time staff.

Further information about Irish prisons can be found on the website of the Irish Prison Service (www.irishprisons.ie).

Drugs

Illegal drugs came to Ireland late, but then spread rapidly, particularly in the period 1979–83, when Dublin earned the dubious distinction of being the heroin capital of Europe. Since then, as in many other countries, drug abuse has continued to increase, particularly that of heroin and other opiates. Drug-related offences peaked in 1996/7 at nearly 8,000, since when numbers have fallen slightly, thanks mainly to a Garda drugs campaign known as Operation Dóchas.

The problem is largely confined to the Dublin area (half the offences relating to the use of cannabis and virtually all heroin-related offences are recorded in the Dublin area, where it's estimated that there are as many as 8,000 heroin addicts), but there's also some drug abuse in Cork and Limerick, as well as in Co. Kerry (these three areas accounted for 50 per cent of ecstasy offences in 1999 compared with 20 per cent in Dublin).

Marijuana (or cannabis) is widely available in its resinous form (hashish) thanks to gangs operating in Cork, Dublin and especially Limerick – and to the fact that fines and prison sentences for first offenders are fairly lenient. In late 2003, the United Nations Office on Drugs and Crime reported that young Irish people were the biggest users of amphetamines and ecstasy (a 'cocktail' of amphetamines and barbiturates) in Europe (and the fourth-highest

in the world). Cocaine was almost absent from Ireland until the early years of the 21st century, since when its use has gradually spread, but crack is almost unheard of and LSD use rare. The smoking of cannabis is fairly widespread, as is solvent abuse.

DEFENCE

Since the end of the civil war in 1923, the Republic of Ireland has managed to avoid armed conflict, remaining neutral during the Second World War (which the Irish refer to as 'the Emergency'). The present government of Ireland has pledged to retain Ireland's neutrality (Ireland isn't a member of the North Atlantic Treaty Organisation – NATO), while participating in 'genuine' peace-keeping missions (Ireland currently has 900 military personnel serving overseas), and defence spending is less than 1 per cent of Gross Domestic Product (GDP) at around €1.5bn.

There are currently some 21,000 defence personnel, but only half of them are permanent and salaried. The remainder are part-time volunteers known as reserves, who undergo training at the Civil Defence School in Dublin and engage in exercises for two hours one night a week. This Reserve Force is currently undergoing restructuring. Only 35 of the 1,300 officers and two of the 600 sergeants in the Irish defence services are women.

The Commander-in-Chief of the Irish defence forces, which are also required to assist the Gardaí and other civil powers, is the President, Mary McAleese. The headquarters of the defence forces are in Dublin, where the 2nd Eastern Brigade and the Air Corps are also based. The 1st Southern Brigade and the Naval Service are based in County Cork and the 4th Western Brigade in County Westmeath.

There's no compulsory military service in Ireland, where the minimum age for joining the forces is 17.

GEOGRAPHY

The Republic of Ireland (known in Irish as Poblacht na hÉireann or simply Éire, after a goddess of Irish mythology called Ériu) forms the greater part of the island of Ireland, which lies to the west of Britain between 51.5 and 55.5 degrees north (latitude) and between 5.5 and 10.5 degrees west (longitude). The island, which is one of the British Isles, also includes Northern Ireland, part of the United Kingdom.

The Republic is sometimes referred to as Southern Ireland, although that's a misnomer as the most northerly point on the island, Malin Head in County Donegal, is within the Republic. The island is separated from the British mainland by the Irish Sea and faces the Atlantic Ocean to the west. The Republic of Ireland covers an area of 70,282km2 (27,136mi2) and measures 486km (303mi) from north to south and 303km (189mi) from east to west.

Overall, Ireland resembles a shallow bowl with hills and mountains forming a rim around the coast, where often dramatic cliffs are interspersed with sandy beaches ('strands').

Ireland's highest mountain, Carrantuohill, rises to 1,041m (3,414ft) in a range called MacGillicuddy's Reeks in County Kerry in the extreme south-west.

Other mountain ranges are to be found higher up the west coast in the counties of Donegal and Galway. The most spectacular cliffs are also in the west, the highest plunging nearly 650m (2,000ft) into the sea at Slieve League in Co. Donegal.

The central part of Ireland consists of a flat or gently rolling limestone plain, occasionally interrupted by low hills (called *drumlins*) and

liberally scattered with lakes (*loughs*) and bogs where the land is below the water table. In fact over 15 per cent of Ireland consists of bogs and these contain Ireland's famous peat, which is a sort of natural compost of vegetation that has been decaying for the past 8,000 to 10,000 years. Ireland's equally famous lush grass grows on the higher ground, which is covered with rich, light soil.

The gently winding River Shannon is Ireland's longest river (358km/223mi), making it in fact the longest river in the British Isles) and almost divides the country in half. Other major rivers include the Barrow (190km/118mi), Sluir (182km/113mi), Blackwater (166km/103mi) and Slaney in the south, and the Erne in the north. There are literally thousands of lakes on the island (between 5,000 and 6,000, depending on how small an area of water counts as a lake, covering over 1,500km²/579mi² of the country).

The three largest (and among the most beautiful) lakes are Lough Corrib (170km²/65mi²), Lough Derg (117km²/45mi²) and Lough Ree (105km²/40mi²). Lough Corrib is in the west of Ireland, where the attractive Lough Mask and Lough Conn are also found. Loughs Derg and Ree are two of the three main lakes through which the River Shannon flows on its leisurely way down to Limerick and the sea, the other being Lough Allen.

There are also three major canals, the 130km (80mi) long Grand Canal linking Dublin with the mouth of the Shannon, the 35km (21mi) long Barrow Line, which runs off the Grand Canal, and the Royal Canal running from the capital towards Longford, only 90km (55mi) of which is currently navigable. The Shannon-Erne Waterway comprises 5km (3mi) of canal linking 57.5km (35mi) of rivers and lakes on its way from Loch Erne to Leitrim.

There are numerous tiny islands off the coast

of Ireland, most of them to the west, but only 18 are inhabited. The best known of these are the Aran Islands in Galway Bay (not to be confused with the Isle of Arran, off Scotland's west coast). More than 80 per cent of Ireland is pasture or arable land; woods and forests accounting for a mere 7 per cent.

Ireland is divided into four provinces of roughly equal size: Munster (south), Connacht (west), Ulster (north) and Leinster (east). These derive from pre-Christian times (roughly corresponding to the divisions made by the Fir Bolg invaders) and have no political significance. Part of Ulster, for example, is in Northern Ireland and part in the Republic. They are, however, socially and culturally important: Ulster is supposedly the land of battle, Munster the land of music, Leinster of prosperity, and Connacht of learning. How true this is today is open to question. The capital, Dublin (*Baile Átha Cliath*), lies on the east coast and is the only really large city in Ireland, with a population of just under 1m.

GOVERNMENT

Ireland is a parliamentary democracy modelled on the British system – not surprisingly, since Ireland was under British rule for 800 years. The basis of the Irish political system is set out in the Constitution of 1937, under which the head of state is the President (*tUachtarán*), currently Mary McAleese, elected by popular vote for a second seven-year term in November 2004 (the next one being in November 2011).

The President (who must be aged over 35) may not serve more than two terms and has no executive power, although she is supreme commander of the defence forces and has the authority to refer government bills to the Supreme Court if they violate the Constitution. The President also appoints the head of government or prime minister, the *Taoiseach* (pronounced 'teeshuck'), who is currently Bertie Ahern (and who has his own website at ⌨ www.taoiseach.gov.ie), on the advice of the *Dáil* (see below), and government ministers on the advice of the *Taoiseach*.

According to the Constitution there must be no fewer than 7 and no more than 15 ministers (there are currently 15) including the *Taoiseach*

and the *Tánaiste* (meaning 'second', i.e. deputy prime minister), currently Mary Harney, who is also Minister for Enterprise, Trade and Employment.

The other ministers are responsible for Finance; Foreign Affairs; Justice, Equality and Law Reform; Education and Science; Health and Children; Environment and Local Government; Social, Community and Family Affairs; Public Enterprise; Agriculture and Food; Defence; Marine and Natural Resources; Arts, Heritage, Gaeltacht and the Islands; Tourism, Sport and Recreation. These ministers comprise the Executive of government and are assisted by 17 ministers of state, who are also elected by the *Dáil* (see below).

The President is one part of the *Oireachtas* (parliament), which has the exclusive power to make laws. The other component of the *Oireachtas* is the Legislature, which (like its British counterpart) has two houses: the *Seanad Éireann* (Senate or Upper House) and the *Dáil Éireann* (House of Representatives). The *Dáil* has 166 members (known as TDs, short for *Teachtaí Dála*), who are elected by popular vote according to a system of proportional representation (see below). The *Seanad* has 60 members, 11 of whom are nominated by the *Taoiseach* and six elected

Former *Taoiseach* Bertie Ahern

by graduates of Trinity College Dublin and the National University of Ireland; the remaining 43 are elected by existing senators as well as TDs and County Councillors from among members of five vocational panels, onto which potential senators must get themselves nominated.

These panels represent the various sectors of the Irish economy, namely agriculture, culture and education, industry and commerce, labour, and public administration. Both *Seanad* and *Dáil* members, who must be over 20, serve five-year terms. Elections for the 30th *Dáil* took place in May 2007, when the *Fianna Fáil*/Progressive Democrats coalition was challenged by a 'rainbow' coalition between *Fine Gael* and the Labour and Green parties (see **Political Parties** below). *Fianna Fáil* on their own took 78 seats (three fewer than in 2002) and the coalition took 89, giving it an overall majority of 13. *Fine Gael* secured 51 seats (20 more than in 2002). Elections for the *Dáil* are every five years; the next is in 2012. The *Seanad* elections took place in August 2007.

There are 22 women TDs, which is 13 per cent of the total (compared with 18 per cent in the UK House of Commons, 37 per cent in the Scottish Parliament and 42 per cent in the Welsh Assembly); not surprisingly, the party with the highest percentage of women TDs (50) is the Progressive Democrats; lowest is *Fine Gael* with just 6 per cent.

Legislative Process

The government presents proposals for new laws or changes to existing laws to either the *Dáil* or the *Seanad* in the form of bills or motions. These must pass five readings in the relevant House: introduction of the bill; discussion of general principles; detailed consideration by a committee and proposal of amendments; report by the committee, including further amendments if necessary; and general debate on the bill. Once the bill is passed by one House, it must go through a similar process in the other House before finally going to the President for promulgation.

A bill that's rejected by the *Seanad* or not passed within 90 days (21 days in the case of financial bills) can still be enacted by the *Dáil*. The *Seanad* cannot enact amendments to the Constitution or financial bills and has only limited power to amend financial bills.

Voting & Elections

Only Irish citizens over 18 may vote in Presidential elections and referenda. Irish citizens and British citizens resident in Ireland may vote in general (i.e. *Dáil*) elections, which must be held at least once every five years. They and EU citizens resident in Ireland may vote in European Parliament elections. Anyone resident in Ireland who has his name on the electoral register may vote in local elections. To get on the register, you need to complete a form either at your local council office or at a post office. The register is updated once a year, in February, but only names added before the previous September are included.

☑ **SURVIVAL TIP**

To make sure your name is included on the electoral register, you can check the draft published on 1st November and available for inspection in post offices, libraries, *Garda* stations and local authority offices.

Since independence in 1922, Ireland has had a system of proportional representation (PR) under which each TD represents an average of approximately 22,000 people or 16,500 members of the electorate (i.e. those eligible to vote). However, the fact that there are 166 TDs and only 41 constituencies can lead to the curious situation where members of the same party are in competition with each other and have to spend much of their time 'wooing' constituents in order to retain their loyalty (as TDs are wont to complain).

Other systems are periodically considered, although none has yet been adopted. The most recent, a proposal by the current Minister for the Environment, Noel Dempsey, to reduce the number of TDs, so that there's only one per constituency, has aroused some controversy.

The advantage of the Irish system is that it keeps ministers in constant contact with their electorate; the disadvantage is that it can lead to parochial policy-making, and an inability to see the wood for the trees. TDs are expected to hold regular 'clinics' at weekends, when constituents ask them to raise a question in parliament on their behalf, even regarding 'trivial' matters such as a new roof for the village hall or a job for a relative; and TDs tend to spend much of their time dealing with such requests, rather than on a major policy. One effect of this is that parliamentary seats are often 'handed down' from one generation to the next – not literally, but in the sense that voters will naturally 'adopt' the son or daughter of their previous TD.

Political Parties

There's no strong left/right or lower/upper class political divide in Ireland, as in many other countries. The country was barely touched by Marxist or Fascist ideologies during the early and mid-20th century, and Irish government has been dominated by centre and centre-right parties for decades. There are 16 recognised political parties, but by far the most popular are *Fianna Fáil* and *Fine Gael*. One or other of these parties has been in power for most of the time since the 1940s, and between them they currently occupy 112 of the 166 seats in the *Dáil*, and 44 of the 60 in the *Seanad*.

Behind these two parties, in order of popularity, come the Labour Party, the Progressive Democrats, the Green Party, *Sinn Féin*, the Communist Party of Ireland, the Christian Solidarity Party, Independent *Fianna Fáil*, The National Party, The Natural Law Party, *Muíntít na hÉireann*, Republican *Sinn Féin*, the Socialist Party, the Socialist Workers' Party and The Workers' Party.

Fianna Fáil (meaning 'Soldiers of Destiny'!), which is currently in government with the Progressive Democrats, has around 81 seats in the *Dáil* and 29 in the *Seanad*. Founded in 1926 by Éamon de Valera, *Fianna Fáil* was responsible for drafting the Irish Constitution in 1937, for maintaining Irish neutrality during the Second World War, for bringing Ireland into the EEC in 1973, and for signing the Northern Ireland Good Friday Agreement in 1998. *Fianna Fáil* is essentially conservative though not right-wing, and is supported largely by farmers and tradesmen. It champions the underprivileged (believing in state subsidisation), and sees itself as the defender of nationalism (including the Irish language, Irish unity, and traditional beliefs and values).

Fine Gael, which was formed in 1933 and now has 31 *Dáil* and 15 *Seanad* seats, is rather more bourgeois, appealing more to business people. It is less nationalistic, more European in outlook than *Fianna Fáil,* and is committed to Constitutional change (it was responsible for legalising divorce in 1995). The Labour Party, which has 20 *Dáil* and five *Seanad* seats, is the oldest party in Ireland. It was founded in 1912 to 'establish a workers' republic founded on socialist principles', but has since adopted a more 'social democratic' stance.

The Progressive Democrats party, which was created in 1985 after a split in the *Fianna Fáil* party, is generally regarded as right-wing, and supports private enterprise rather than state intervention, although on moral issues it is fairly liberal. It has just eight *Dáil* and five *Seanad* seats, the Green Party has six seats in the *Dáil*, *Sinn Féin* five and the Socialist Party one (none of these has any *Seanad* seats). The remaining *Dáil* and *Seanad* seats are occupied by independent candidates. Left-wing parties generally share a mere 20 to 25 per cent of the vote, and the extreme left wing is represented mainly by the Socialist Workers' Party.

Local Government

Irish government is the most centralised of any EU country: 90 per cent of public spending is controlled from the capital, compared with the EU average of 70 per cent. Even local matters often have to be dealt with by central government, often at the expense of a national policy. As one commentator has put it, "Discussions in the *Dáil* tend to be taken up with the parish-pump issues."

The EU Commission has been encouraging Ireland to decentralise, as it offers aid to regions rather than to nations, and the Irish government has recently acknowledged the need for some regionalisation. Eight regional bodies have been created, as well as 35 City and County Enterprise Boards; but *Fianna Fáil* remains fundamentally opposed to decentralisation, and there is no great popular support for it either.

Theoretically, Ireland has a British system of county, borough and town councils, but in practice most local authority rests with central government. Some 65 per cent of local public spending comes from central government grants. The only source of local council income is a tax on business premises and, in some cases, charges for refuse collection and water and waste services. Education, health services and the police force are all funded by central government; local government controls only town planning, reconstruction and roads. There are no village or rural district councils, so country people can feel isolated from the mechanism of government, which increases the resentment they feel towards Dublin.

> As in the UK, mayors are elected only for one year, and have a mostly ceremonial function.

Real authority resides with the council manager, who isn't elected and has the power to overrule council decisions.

LEGAL SYSTEM & ADVICE

Just as the Irish parliamentary system is modelled on that of the UK, so the Irish legal system is based on English common law, though substantially modified by the Constitution, by acts passed by the *Oireachtas* and, recently, by EU law (which is now part of Irish law). The Constitution specifies that the Irish legal system is divided into three separate and distinct branches: the Executive (i.e. the 15 government ministers), the legislature (i.e. parliament) and the judiciary. The Constitution also sets out the fundamental rights of the individual in the State (e.g. free speech, privacy and the ownership of private property) and recognises the family as the primary and fundamental social unit. Any proposed changes to these basic rights must be agreed by the people, which is why there have recently been referenda on questions of divorce and abortion.

Under the Constitution, the Irish court structure has three levels: local courts (known as Circuit and District Courts), a High Court and a Supreme Court. Since Ireland's entry into the European Community (EC), a fourth tier has been added, consisting of the Court of Justice of the European Community and the European Court of Human Rights. There are also a number of special courts: Children's Courts, the Court of Criminal Appeal, the Special Criminal Court and a Small Claims Court. Ireland is divided into eight areas with regard to circuit courts (of which there are currently 56) and 23 districts with regard to district courts.

District Courts have what is known as summary jurisdiction, which means that they can deal with minor criminal and civil offences. There's no jury in District Courts, but defendants may elect to be tried in a Circuit Court, which has a jury. Circuit Courts deal with serious offences such as assault and robbery, and civil offences incurring significant damages.

The High Court (which is referred to as the Central Criminal Court when dealing with criminal matters) deals with serious offences such as murder, rape and treason. There's no limit to the fines or sentences it may impose. The Supreme Court is a court of appeal, as is the Court of Criminal Appeal. Children's Courts, as their name suggests, deal with cases involving minor crimes committed by children under 16. The Special Criminal Court was established for the trial of special cases, and normally deals with cases relating to the Offences against the State Act.

A Small Claims procedure has recently been set up along the lines of those in the UK, where claims for up to €2,000 can be dealt with quickly and cheaply (from the claimant's point of view) without the need for solicitors. Small Claims Courts normally deal with cases relating to defective goods or poor workmanship and don't consider claims for personal injury, damage resulting from road accidents or disputes over loans. To make a small claim (as around 3,000 people do every year), you must apply in writing to the Small Claims Registrar at your local District Court Office (you will be given a form and shown how to complete it) and pay a fee of €15.

Irish judges are appointed by the government on the advice of the Attorney General, and Supreme Court judges appointed by the President on the advice of the *Taoiseach* and his ministers. Judges apply common law, relying on earlier decisions on similar matters (legal precedent), which are recorded in the form of Law Reports.

Juries are supposed to consist of a typical cross-section of society and, as in the UK, most Irish citizens over the age of 18 and under 70 are liable to be called to sit on a jury, and are obliged to do so, if called. Some are fortunate enough never to be summoned, while others are called repeatedly (presumably because they're the most 'typical').

In Ireland, as in Britain, there are two types of lawyer: solicitors and barristers. Although they operate separately, their functions are complementary. Solicitors deal directly with the public; they can give general advice and may argue cases in court. As in all other parts of the world, they charge inordinate sums of money for their services. Where specialist opinion is required, solicitors will refer to a barrister; this is known as 'instructing counsel', and involves the client in even more astronomical costs (particularly if the barrister is a Senior Counsel or, in legal parlance, has 'taken silk'!). It isn't possible for members of the public to go directly to a barrister.

If you prefer to obtain free advice, you can turn initially to one of Ireland's Citizens' Information Centres. Details of your nearest centres and their opening hours are listed in the *Golden Pages* under *Citizens Information Centres*.

Ireland has a system of legal aid that provides assistance to those who cannot afford to pay a solicitor. The system is means tested on the 'disposable' income of the household (i.e. its income after the deduction of mortgage and other loan payments, income tax, health contributions, etc.), which must be less than €18,000 per annum; in addition, your 'disposable capital' must be less than €320,000. You're also entitled to legal aid if you're receiving Social Welfare payments. Means Test forms are available from any Legal Aid Board Law Centre (listed in the *Golden Pages* under Legal Aid). Even if you're receiving legal aid, you will still have to pay for legal advice and for legal representation: these cost a minimum of €10 and €50 (if your disposable income is less than €11,500) and a maximum of €150 and €1,675.

MARRIAGE & DIVORCE

Like many Western countries, Ireland has rising separation and divorce rates, but marriage is retaining its popularity nonetheless. The marriage rate (number of marriages per 1,000 population per year) peaked at 7.4 in the early '70s, then fell to an all-time low of 4.3 in 1995

and 1997 and has since risen to around 5. The average marrying age has risen to around 30 for men and 28 for women. Since 1996, the minimum legal age for marriage in Ireland has been 18 (until 1975 it was 14 for boys and 12 for girls!). Anyone under 18 wishing to marry must apply for special dispensation to the Circuit Family Court or the High Court Office.

Marriage is a civil contract, but certain religious ceremonies, including most Christian and Jewish, but not Muslim, ceremonies, are recognised by civil law. If the couple chooses not to have a church wedding, in which the clergyman acts for both church and state, they must marry in a register office or registered place of worship; no other venues are licensed for wedding ceremonies. Before 1970, fewer than 1 per cent of marriages took place in a register office. By 1995, the proportion had risen to 6 per cent, since when it has remained fairly constant.

The registrar for the area in which the wedding is to take place must be notified at least three months in advance of the ceremony. A list of registrars and an information leaflet entitled *On the Solemnisation (Celebration) and Registration of a Valid Marriage in Ireland* are available from the local Registrar-General of Marriages or the General Register Office, Government Offices, Convent Road, Roscommon (☎ 0906-632900 or ☎ 1890-252076, 💻 www.groireland.ie). Marriages outside Ireland aren't normally registered in Ireland. Irish weddings are big occasions, and the Irish spend a great deal on them. Further information about getting married in Ireland, including a list of Registrars, can be found on 💻 www.groireland.ie/getting_married.htm.

There are estimated to be 130,000 single parents in Ireland (25 per cent of births take place outside marriage, compared with the EU average of 23 per cent) and some 90,000 people who are separated or divorced (including the present *Taoiseach*, Bertie Ahern).

Divorce was legal in Ireland until 1925, when it was banned by a Conservative government. An attempt at reform in 1986 failed, and it was not until 1995 that a referendum was called and the Irish people voted, by the narrowest of margins, to lift the constitutional ban on divorce, clearing the way for its eventual legalisation. Since then, the number of applications for divorce has been relatively few, mainly because of the cost of legal proceedings – an average of €5,000 – although it's possible to 'do it yourself' for a tenth of this cost (see, for example, 💻 www.divorceinirelandforyou.com).

To 'qualify' for an Irish divorce, you and your spouse must have been living apart for a total of at least four of the last five years, and there must be 'no reasonable prospect of reconciliation'; in addition, 'proper arrangements' must have been made for dependants (including a non-working spouse). Provided these conditions are met, either party may apply to a court for a Decree of Divorce. It's possible to obtain a Separation Agreement (or Judicial Separation), regulating financial and other matters before applying for a Decree, which is irreversible.

A list of registered mediators, who can provide information on the financial and legal implications of separation and divorce, as well as helping with the divorce process itself, is available from the Mediators' Institute of Ireland (💻 www.mediationireland.com).

NATIONAL ANTHEM, ARMS, FLAG & HOLIDAYS

The Irish national anthem is *Amhrán na bhFiann* (The Soldier's Song), which was composed in 1907 by Patrick Heeney (music) and Peadar Kearney (words) and first published in 1912 in the newspaper *Irish Freedom*. Adopted initially by the Irish Volunteers, it was formally adopted as the national anthem in 1926, when it replaced God Save Ireland. The unofficial national arms (known as the Arms of State) are a gold harp with silver strings on a blue background. Although having no statutory significance, the harp symbol (which was modelled on the 14th century Brian Boru harp) forms the President's seal of office, as well as appearing on coins and bank notes (it continues to appear on euro coins, but not notes).

The Irish national flag, a tricolour of green, white and orange, dates from 1848, when Thomas Francis Meagher, a leading Nationalist and founder member of the Irish Federation, received it as a gift from the people of France, whose own flag has the same design. Originally the flag of the Young Ireland movement, of which Meagher was a prominent member, the tricolour came to be regarded as the national flag in 1916, when it was flown from the General Post Office in Dublin in the aftermath of the Easter Rising, and was officially adopted upon independence in 1922. The colours represent the union between Gaelic/Catholic Ireland (green) and Protestant Ireland (orange), the white band between them, in Meagher's own words, "signifying a lasting truce between the Orange and the Green".

An unofficial symbol of Irishness is the shamrock (the Irish word *seamróg* derives from *seamair* meaning clover and *óg* meaning young). The traditional act of 'drowning the shamrock', i.e. dropping a sprig of clover into the last pint you drink on St Patrick's Day, before throwing it over your shoulder, is supposed to guarantee you a year of good luck. St Patrick's Day, on March 17th, is a day of celebration not only throughout Ireland, but also for the 70m or so people throughout the world claiming Irish descent, who don the traditional green of Ireland for the day (and drink green beer!). It's one of Ireland's nine official public holidays, on which most companies and shops are closed.

The others are New Year's Day, Easter Monday, the first Mondays in May, June, and August, the last Monday in October, Christmas Day and St Stephen's Day (26th December). This last is traditionally celebrated with music and dancing, the performers dressed as 'wren boys' (recalling the days when wrens were hunted) with conical straw hats, their faces painted black and red; and going from house to house asking for 'donations' (of money, food or drink) in return for entertainment.

PETS

The Irish are generally fond of animals and many people keep dogs and cats in particular, and they're proud of the fact that the country has been rabies-free for over 100 years. If you plan to take a pet to Ireland, it's important to check the latest regulations. In mid-2004,

the European Union (EU) introduced a 'pet passport' system, based on the successfully piloted UK 'PETS' scheme; whereby animals can travel freely within the EU without the need for quarantine, provided certain conditions are met, namely that they're under three months old or:

♦ are microchipped;

♦ are vaccinated against rabies, and have been blood-tested at least six months before the date of entry;

♦ have been treated for ticks and tapeworm between 24 and 48 hours before arrival at the port or airport of departure.

In addition, pets must be transported by a company approved by the Department of Agriculture and Food (a list of approved companies can be found on its website (💻 www.agriculture.gov.ie). If you're travelling by sea, you should notify the shipping company, as some insist that pets are left in vehicles (if applicable), while others allow pets to be kept in cabins.

☑ SURVIVAL TIP

If your pet is of a nervous disposition or unused to travelling, it's best to tranquillise it on a long sea crossing.

The new system extends this permission to pets from certain non-EU countries: 'qualifying countries' in 2008 were Antigua and Barbuda, Andorra, Argentina, Aruba, Ascension Island, Australia, Bahrain, Barbados, Belarus, Bermuda, Canada, Cayman Islands, Chile, Croatia, Falkland Islands, Fiji, French Polynesia, Hong Kong, Iceland, Jamaica, Japan, Liechtenstein, Mauritius, Mayotte, Mexico, Monaco, Montserrat, Netherlands Antilles, New Caledonia, New Zealand, Norway, the Russian Federation, Saint Helena, Saint Kitts and Nevis, Saint Pierre et Miquelon, Saint Vincent and the Grenadines, San Marino, Singapore, Switzerland, Taiwan, Trinidad and Tobago, United Arab Emirates (UAE), the US (including Guam), Vanuatu, the Vatican City State, and Wallis and Futuna.

Animals that don't qualify for 'free' entry must be quarantined for six months on arrival in Ireland. There's only one approved quarantine centre in Ireland, Lissenhall Quarantine Kennels and Catteries, Lissenhall, Swords, County Dublin (☎ 01-890 0375, ✉ lissen hallvet@eircom.net). Quarantine fees for dogs vary (there are four size categories) between €2,250 and €2,850 for the statutory 26 weeks. There's a fixed fee for cats of €1,950. These fees don't of course include transport to Ireland, or to and from the quarantine centre, which must be arranged by owners; nor do they include heating, which costs €17 per week!

There's also a mandatory charge for vaccinations of €200 for cats and around €220 for dogs, **irrespective of your pet's vaccination history**. You must obtain an import licence; if your local embassy doesn't have the necessary forms, write to the Department of Agriculture, Veterinary Division, Kildare Street, Dublin 2. You will also need a Form of Declaration and Health (Form PQB), which must be completed by your vet and a magistrate, notary public or commissioner for oaths.

It's possible to quarantine your pet at home, but you must have plans for its accommodation approved three months before your arrival in Ireland, and the construction regulations are strict. Someone must be on the premises 24 hours a day, and anyone who looks after a quarantined animal must have a rabies vaccination. Even if you take this option, your pet must spend the first four to six weeks at Lissenhall.

Similar regulations apply to the import of other kinds of pets. Animals such as gerbils, guinea pigs, chinchillas and mice require an import licence, and must be quarantined for at least six months, unless they're imported from the UK. All birds imported into Ireland must have a health certificate in accordance with EU directives. Check the latest regulations with your local embassy or consulate, or directly with the Department of Agriculture's quarantine section in County Dublin (theoretically ☎ 01-607 2827 for cats and dogs or ☎ 01-607 2862 and ☎ 01-647 2412 for other animals – though staff don't seem sure which number applies to what) before making any arrangements.

In any case, you should contact the Department of Agriculture at least four months before your planned move to ensure that you obtain the necessary paperwork in good time. Further information is obtainable from the Department of Agriculture and Food (☎ 01-607 2000, 🖳 www.agriculture. gov.ie).

To obtain a pet passport in Ireland (i.e. in order to take a pet out of the country – irrespective of its destination), you must do the following:

◆ Have your pet microchipped by a vet.

◆ Ask a vet to complete a passport application form and send it off (the address is on the form). If you want your pet's photograph on its passport (optional), this should be no larger than 6cm by 4cm.

◆ Have your pet vaccinated against rabies.

◆ Approximately a month later, ask a vet to blood-test your pet to check that the vaccination has taken effect; if it hasn't, the pet must be vaccinated again.

◆ Collect your pet's passport from the vet, who must enter the details of its vaccinations and blood-test results.

♦ Wait until at least six months after the blood-test results before taking your pet abroad. (In fact, you may be allowed to take the pet out of the country, depending on your intended destination, but you won't be allowed to bring it back into Ireland until six months have elapsed, and then only if the pet hasn't been to any non-qualifying country (see above).

Thereafter, in order to maintain the validity of the passport, ensure that you have your pet re-vaccinated by the due date; in that way, your pet won't have to be blood-tested again. For further information contact the Department of Agriculture and Food's helpline (☎ 01-607 2827).

If you intend to live permanently in Ireland, you should have pets vaccinated against rabies (if they haven't already been vaccinated) and against the other most common contagious diseases, particularly if they're likely to spend some time in a cattery or kennels. You should obtain advice from your vet as to the best way to protect your pets. Note that there are no animal diseases which are peculiar to Ireland.

⚠ Caution

All dogs kept in Ireland must have a licence, which is available from a post office for €12.70 (you can be fined €30 for not having one).

Dogs (with the exception of guide dogs) are prohibited from entering certain public places, particularly restaurants and cafés. Some breeds must be muzzled and kept on a strong lead or chain (not more than a metre long) in public places, and accompanied by a person aged over 16, in addition to wearing a collar bearing the name and address of the owner. These include Bulldogs and Bull Mastiffs, Bull Terriers and Pit Bull Terriers, Rottweilers, Doberman Pinschers, German Shepherds (Alsatians), Rhodesian Ridgebacks, and Japanese Akitas, Bandogs and Tosas.

Note also that there may be discrimination against pets when renting accommodation, particularly if it's furnished. Many hotels accept pets such as cats and dogs, and the Irish Tourist Board's guides to hotels and bed & breakfast accommodation indicate whether pets are allowed.

POLICE

The Irish Constabulary was founded in 1822; but the present police force, the *Garda Síochána na hÉireann*, which is Irish for 'Peace Guard of Ireland' (commonly referred to simply as the *Garda*), was formed in the year of independence, 1922; and the Dublin Metropolitan Police (which had existed since 1836) was amalgamated with it three years later. The *Garda*, which has its headquarters in Phoenix Park in West Dublin, carries out all policing functions, from traffic control to state security. The total number of personnel currently stands at 12,265 (2,180 of them being female), including 1,700 plain clothes detectives, who are the only officers to carry guns (uniformed *gardaí* carry only wooden truncheons) and 1,645 civilian support staff.

The *Garda* commissioner is appointed by the government and is responsible to the Minister of Justice. There are two deputy commissioners, one of whom is responsible for crime, security, traffic and the six policing regions into which Ireland is divided. Below them are assistant commissioners, superintendents, inspectors, sergeants and *gardaí*.

The six Regions are broken down into 25 divisions, each commanded by a chief superintendent. Six of these divisions make up the Dublin metropolitan region, which is commanded by an assistant commissioner. Each division is further divided into districts, each under a superintendent (known as the district officer), and each district into sub-districts, each of which normally has only one station, with anything from 1 to 100 *gardaí*. Those with a single *garda* – in remote areas – are sometimes called sub-stations.

A number of specialist services, such as the National Bureau of Criminal Investigation, the *Garda* Bureau of Fraud Investigation and the *Garda* National Drugs Unit, are based in Dublin, but operate on a nationwide basis. The *Garda* also has a Mounted Unit, an Underwater Unit and an Air Support Unit; and each division operates a Traffic Corps, with responsibility for enforcing traffic regulation (in the Dublin metropolitan region it's known as the Traffic Department).

POPULATION

Ireland's long history as a country of mass emigration is well known. Between 1861 and 1961, emigration consistently exceeded immigration, and the natural increase in the Irish population shrank from around 4.5m (some estimates put the mid-19th-century population as high as 8m) to 2.8m. Mainly because of Ireland's sluggish economic development, net emigration was particularly high in the 'age of mass migration' (1871-1926) and the post-World War II period (1951-1961). As a result, an estimated 3m Irish citizens currently live abroad, of whom 1.2m were born in Ireland. The majority lives in the US and the UK.

From the '70s, the population began to increase again; but it was not until the '90s, when rapid economic growth created an unprecedented demand for labour, that the current surge began, although emigration has continued to be significant (around 17,000 people leave the country each year). While a large proportion of immigrants were Irish 'returners' (peaking at 27,000 in 2002), an increasing percentage were non-Irish (from around 35 per cent in the late '80s to almost 60 per cent today). The great majority of these have been workers, but over 10,000 asylum seekers have also settled in Ireland each year since 2000.

Many Africans and East Europeans, attracted by Ireland's new-found prosperity and generous welfare handouts, began knocking at her door and requesting asylum. Compared with a mere 39 applications for asylum in 1992, there were some 6,000 in 1998. The largest groups were Romanians, and other substantial contingents come from Algeria, Nigeria, Somalia and Zaire. Nine out of ten of these asylum seekers were illegal 'economic' immigrants, but were automatically eligible for a range of benefits until their status was decided, which could take up to three years. (Under the Dublin Convention, asylum seekers arriving in any EU country are entitled to have their applications considered although, if they're refused in one EU country, they cannot request asylum in another.)

The number of what the Immigration Office calls 'registered aliens' (i.e. immigrants from non-EU countries) also increased dramatically during this period: from 15,800 in 1996 to

Until the mid-'90s, the *Garda* was also responsible for clamping and towing away illegally parked cars, but these functions have now been hived off to private companies which, unlike the *Garda*, are in a position to exercise a total lack of discretion, and consequently have had a dramatic effect on parking behaviour, particularly in Dublin. Parking tickets (i.e. penalty notices) can also be issued by traffic wardens, of which there are around 100 in Dublin, but only one or two in other cities and towns.

The police have recently spent tens of millions of euros on a new centralised computer system, which is reputedly so complex and unwieldy that many *Garda* don't bother to record anything but serious crimes! A spate of scandals led the Minister for Justice, Equality and Law Reform, in August 2006, to draft a new police disciplinary code, as well as a 'whistleblowers'' charter. There's also a *Garda* Inspectorate and a *Garda* Ombudsman Commission (☎ 01-871 6727 or ☎ 1890-600800, 🖥 www.gardaombudsman.ie), which deals with complaints about the Garda from members of the public.

29,600 in 1999, the largest numbers coming from the US and China, with substantial numbers from Australia, India, Malaysia, Nigeria and Pakistan.

To control this growing problem, the government introduced a new system of dealing with asylum seekers in April 2000; and in May of the same year, came to an agreement with the Romanian government to 'exchange' illegal aliens (in practice, a Romanian repatriation programme, since it's unlikely that there are any Irish citizens living illegally in Romania!); similar agreements were subsequently negotiated with the governments of Bulgaria, Nigeria and Poland. By the end of 2004, there were 7,200 recognised refugees and 3,700 asylum seekers awaiting 'processing'.

Then, in March 2005, the government established the Irish Naturalisation and Immigration Service (within the Department of Justice, Equality and Law Reform) to deal with all aspects of immigration, including the processing of asylum applications; and an Immigration Integration Unit to foster the integration of migrants. The result has been a further reduction in the number of asylum-seekers, and an increased number of 'resettlements' to 200 per year.

Migration has obviously had a significant impact on the country's population. At the time of the last national census, in 2006, the Irish population was 4,239,848 (with some 2,500 more males than females), and rising at a rate of around 300,000 per year. There were at least 3,706,683 Irish nationals, 112,548 Britons, 163,277 citizens of other EU countries and 24,425 from non-EU European countries; 35,326 Africans, 46,952 Asians, 21,124 Americans (North and South), 16,131 from other parts of the world – 'at least', because 45,597 people failed to state their nationality on the census form.

> Ireland is the most sparsely populated country in Europe outside Scandinavia, with an average density of just 53 people per square kilometre compared, for example, with 245 in the UK.

Also, recent population increase has been confined to the towns and cities, principally Dublin and Galway, the latter having almost trebled in size in the last 50 years. By contrast, the population of the various islands off the coast of Ireland has shrunk by more than half. Well over half (58 per cent) of the population live in 'urban areas' (towns and cities with more than 1,500 inhabitants), of which there are around 150 in Ireland. Only 23 of these have populations of more than 10,000.

By far the largest city is the capital, Dublin, with an official population of 496,000, which is over 12 per cent of the country's total (although the figure is far higher when suburban areas are included). The next largest city is Cork, with a population of around 123,000, followed by Galway (which has moved into third place since 1996) with 65,800, Limerick with 54,000, Waterford with 44,600, Dundalk (in Co. Louth) with 30,000, Bray (just south of Dublin) with 27,000 and Drogheda (also in Louth) with 24,500. No other town exceeds 18,000.

The Irish population is the youngest in Europe. Around 21 per cent of the population is under 15 (compared with the EU average of 18.5 per cent). Only 11 per cent are aged 65 or over (compared with over 14 per cent in the EU as a whole), but the number of people aged 65 and over is set to double in the next 30 years, and 200,000 people will be aged 80 and over by 2031. Ireland is also a good place to go if you're a man looking for a female partner: females outnumber males by almost 25,000!

Racism

Ireland is one of the least multicultural countries in Europe; although in the last few decades, its population has become increasingly cosmopolitan (see statistics above), and with this change has come an increase in racism. In response to this, the government launched a National Plan of Action against Racism in January 2005. However, while there have been reports of racially motivated crimes and incidents, in particular at the time of the 2004 national referendum on citizenship, such reports remain low compared with other EU countries.

RELIGION

Ireland is a staunchly Catholic country, though adherence to the faith is gradually declining. According to the 2006 census (see above), 87 per cent of the population (92 per cent of native Irish people) is Roman Catholic – down from 89 and 93 per cent respectively in 2002. Less than 3 per cent (118,948 people) were classified as 'Church of Ireland, including Protestant'.

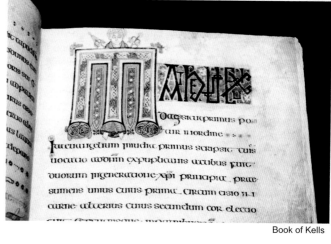

Book of Kells

Always a small minority in the Republic, Protestants have declined in both numbers (they comprised 10 per cent of the population as recently as 1991)' and influence, and the Church of Ireland is struggling – financially, as well as in its terms of attendance. The traditional antipathy of Catholics towards Protestants, which was a legacy of British rule, has now largely disappeared, however; there are both Protestants and Jews in positions of power and influence; and intermarriage, which was rare only 30 years ago, is now common.

Other Christians number a mere 28,028 (0.7 per cent), Presbyterians 21,496, Orthodox 19,994 and Muslims 31,779 (up from 19,147 in 2002). Those following other religions total 54,033 (Jews numbered 10,437 in 2002 but weren't allotted their own category in 2006), while 175,252 declared themselves as having no religion (up from 138,264 in 2002) and 66,750 didn't state their religious beliefs. There are mosques in Counties Cavan, Cork, Donegal, Dublin, Galway, Limerick and Mayo, and just three synagogues in the whole of Ireland.

As well as the official Catholic Church, represented by bishops and priests, there are hundreds of Catholic orders in Ireland (200 of them are grouped into the Conference of Major Religious Superiors of Men, which has 16,000 members), which tend to be more radical and vociferous than the official church.

Although some 80 per cent of Irish people still attend church regularly (more than in any other European country), the authority and control of the Church has diminished in recent years, particularly in urban areas.

Among younger people (18 to 25), regular church going is below 50 per cent. In some rural areas, church attendance is still as high as 90 per cent, but even in the villages the parish priest, who used to be the dominant figure in society, is less highly regarded (the many scandals that have recently hit the Catholic Church have eroded respect for its representatives), and many younger priests are quite liberal in their outlook.

Nevertheless, millions of Irish people still make regular visits to holy wells, and undertake pilgrimages to Knock, Croagh Patrick and Lough Derg (see below); nearly every Irish family has a close relative who is a priest or a nun; and even those who aren't practising Catholics somehow want the Church to retain its central position in Irish life – although cynics argue that church-going for many people has become little more than a habit based on fear and old-fashioned superstition.

Shrines

Knock, in County Mayo, is one of the world's foremost Marian shrines. On 21st August 1879, 20 villagers claimed to have seen an apparition of the Virgin Mary, accompanied by St John the Evangelist and St Joseph, hovering two feet above the ground for nearly two hours. Today, the tiny village draws vast crowds during the pilgrimage season (May to October), some spending their entire summer holiday there. Pilgrims participate in torch-lit, rosary processions and all-night vigils, and take communion in the huge Basilica of Our Lady, Queen of Ireland.

Some 50km (31mi) west of Knock, near the town of Westport, is Croagh Patrick, Ireland's 'holy mountain', where St Patrick is supposed to have spent 40 days and nights in 441 AD. On the last Sunday in July, known as Garland Sunday, around 50,000 people climb to the oratory at the 763m (2,503ft) summit, many of them barefoot.

But perhaps the most extreme Catholic pilgrimage is to St Patrick's Purgatory in County Donegal, known as 'Ireland's holy health farm'. Perched on an island in the middle of the remote Lough Derg (not to be confused with the lake of the same name in County Clare, where there are cosy pubs and expensive yacht clubs), St Patrick's Purgatory involves a three-day trial in pain and suffering, including clambering barefoot over the jagged remains of beehives, eating one meal a day consisting of dry toast and black tea, and going without sleep for 36 hours while chanting prayers. The only consolation is that pilgrimages take place in summer, between June and August.

SOCIAL CUSTOMS

All countries have their own particular (and peculiar) social customs, and Ireland is no exception. After 800 years of British rule, it's inevitable that many Irish social customs are modelled on British customs, with local influences that have become more pronounced over the years. In general, the Irish tend to be less reserved than the British, more relaxed and informal (the Irish would say, more friendly!). Nevertheless, people are punctual for appointments and social events. Business

is conducted in a cordial, not to say casual atmosphere, but it's customary to shake hands both when you meet and when you leave (though not in the case of colleagues) and to exchange business cards, although people will quickly switch from surname to first name terms.

Business dress is also quite formal, but in social situations the Irish tend to dress informally; only a few hotels and restaurants will insist on men wearing a jacket and tie to dinner.

TIME

Like the UK, Ireland is on GMT (i.e. five hours ahead of US eastern time and one hour behind standard European time) from late March until late October. For the rest of the year, Ireland is on GMT plus one hour, i.e. six hours ahead of US eastern time. Most published material (e.g. timetables) uses the 24-hour clock, but the am and pm system is still used in conversation (and in this book). The time in some major international cities, when it's noon in Dublin in January, is shown below.

TIPPING

Tipping isn't a habit in Ireland, other than in taxis, hotels and restaurants. Porters and doormen will expect €1 or €2, taxi drivers around 10 per cent of the fare (although some will even round the fare **down** to the nearest euro). A gratuity of 10 to 15 per cent is the norm in restaurants, unless a service charge has already been added to the bill – something that is becoming increasingly common. Some restaurants levy a service charge for parties over four, indicated on the menu, in which case tipping isn't necessary. It isn't usual to tip in pubs, but in hotel bars with waiter service you should leave a small tip. Women are expected to leave a tip of

SYDNEY	LONDON	CAPE TOWN	TOKYO	LOS ANGELES	NEW YORK
11pm	noon	2pm	9pm	4am	7am

around 10 per cent for their hairdresser – but not men!

TOILETS

Public toilets in Ireland usually leave something to be desired in terms of cleanliness and general upkeep. They're also less widespread than might be expected. The most sanitary toilets are to be found in hotels, restaurants, offices, shops, museums, galleries and airports. Pub toilets vary from acceptable to no-go areas. The good news is that public toilets are usually free.

Some toilets have facilities for nappy (diaper) changing, and for nursing mothers, and an increasing number also have special facilities for the disabled. Toilets are usually marked with the familiar male and female symbols, whereas disabled toilets are indicated by the international wheelchair sign, and generally used by both sexes.

19.
THE IRISH

Wherever in the world you live, you will almost certainly have encountered Irish people – or at least people who were born in Ireland or have Irish ancestors. Over a third of Irish-born people live outside Ireland (more than 10m Americans and one in three Australians claim Irish roots), and you may have formed an opinion about the Irish in general. Here are some of the most widely held beliefs about the Irish, some of which have more basis in fact than others: the Irish are proud of being Irish; the Irish constantly criticise themselves and their country; the Irish are garrulous and boastful; the Irish have an inferiority complex; the Irish are privately puritanical; the Irish are publicly permissive; the Irish are self-obsessed; the Irish aren't xenophobic; the Irish have a strong sense of national identity; the Irish are stupid; the Irish are astute, eloquent and witty; the Irish are deeply spiritual; the Irish have little thought for the future…

You may have noticed that the above list contains one or two contradictions, as does life in Ireland (the British, who ruled over the Irish for centuries, still refer to any apparently illogical statement as 'Irish'). It may be broadly true that the Irish are untidy and quarrelsome (they won't easily forget a wrong done to them), but they will quickly scotch any preconceptions you may have about them; there is, of course, no such thing as a typical Irish person and few people conform to popular stereotypes. For example, Irish men are reputed to be violent drunkards, yet teetotalism is more widespread in Ireland than elsewhere in Europe, and crime (particularly violent crime) less so.

The Irish reputation for being 'intellectually challenged' is a myth perpetuated (and probably invented) by the British, who are fond of telling jokes beginning 'There was an Englishman, an Irishman and a Scotsman…' (the Scots coming in for similar mockery for their supposed meanness). In reality, the Irish are at least as well educated as any other Europeans, and have produced far more than their share of world famous writers and musicians, among others.

People from the city and the country, from the east coast and from the west coast, are also supposed to have different characters (Connaught people, for example, are supposed to be especially hospitable, while Dubliners have a reputation for being know-alls), but such differences as there may once have been are becoming less pronounced, and foreigners may hardly even notice them. Besides, although the majority of Irish people now live in towns, even the most hardened city-dwellers retain links with their rural past.

Although Ireland is one of the least multicultural countries in Europe, that doesn't mean that people of different cultural and racial origins are discriminated against. On the contrary, the Irish are exceptionally tolerant of and well disposed towards 'foreigners' of all colours and creeds. Indeed, when asked why they visit Ireland, most foreigners put at the top of the list the warmth and friendliness of the people. The Irish are unstinting in their kindness, hospitality and generosity – they're among the most generous contributors to charities and appeals (it was an Irishman, Bob Geldof, who initiated Live Aid).

Instead of a Tourist Board, the Irish have a Welcome Board (*Bord Fáilte*), and Ireland is known as the land of *céad mile fáilte* – 'a hundred thousand welcomes'.

Eighty years after the end of British rule, the traditional antipathy towards Ireland's nearest neighbour has begun to fade. Relationships between the two countries are probably better than they have ever been, and the Irish are more inclined to look to the future than to dwell on the past. Nevertheless, eight centuries of oppression have inevitably left their mark, and a kind of inferiority complex persists. In some ways, the Irish share with the Jews a sense of long-term persecution, which they bear with a wry and self-deprecating humour.

Unlike their erstwhile oppressors, however, the Irish have embraced the idea of European unity and benefited immeasurably from the surrender of their insularity, emerging from centuries of poverty and suffering into a 'brave new world' of prosperity and contentment. Membership of the European Union and commitment to the single currency has at last enabled the Irish to break free of British influence (even after 1920, Ireland was reliant on Great Britain to buy its exports, and had an essentially British system of government and legal system). This new-found sense of 'Europeanness' was symbolised in the '90s by a boom in 'twinning' between Irish and European cities and towns, particularly those in Brittany, with which Ireland shares their Celtic heritage. Over 100 Irish towns are twinned with towns in Brittany – more than with the whole of the rest of the world!

The current Irish attempts to salvage the Gaelic language and Celtic folk music might also be seen as a reaction to British domination; a deliberate attempt to emphasise their dissimilarity to the British (some Irish people who normally converse in English will use Gaelic when abroad, so as not to be mistaken for Brits!). Yet even here there's a typically Irish irony: many communities in the *Gaeltacht* (Irish-speaking areas) are struggling to survive, and are more concerned with progress than folk culture. It's the educated urban classes (Galway is the self-styled Gaelic capital – it even has an Irish theatre) who don't want to let that culture die.

Ireland likes to regard itself as a classless society. Like any other country, it has extremes of rich and poor, but there's no 'ruling elite' (the British used to play that role). Status isn't conferred by family background or education, as in England, but by business and financial success, as in the US. There's what might be regarded as an urban working class, but it's small in comparison with those of other European countries. The cities have also recently witnessed the rise of enclaves of *nouveaux riches*, but generally, successful people are treated at worst with suspicion (particularly if they achieved their success in Ireland!), at best with indifference. The Irish are singularly unimpressed by stardom or status, which is the reason many film and pop stars have settled there (or is it because of the income tax benefits?). The Irish are fundamentally 'anti-individual'.

It is said that the promise of rewards in the next life has dampened the Irish spirit of enterprise, that the dominance in society of priests and bishops has suppressed the expression of individuality and the will to create secular organisations. Whatever the reason, the Irish generally aren't 'profit driven' (they take greater risks in property speculation and horse-trading than in business), and the national spirit of 'begrudgery' persists (a recent advertisement for a certain expensive make of sports car was headed "Enjoy the begrudgery").

The Irish are famous talkers (and singers) – supposedly because of their geographical isolation and their poverty: after all, words are free and can impress more than fancy clothes – Synge's *Playboy of the Western World* has become emblematic of this trait of Irishness. Or is it something to do with their bardic tradition, or kissing the Blarney Stone? Whatever the reason, the Irish share a delight in words and word-play, and love to exaggerate, although they're perhaps a little less boastful these days – now that they actually have more to boast about!

The Irish are also celebrated for their love of *craic*, meaning a good time. They will use almost any excuse to have a party: when a priest blesses a new house, for example, and even when someone dies – it isn't unusual for funerals to be attended by hundreds, even thousands of people who had only a passing acquaintance with the deceased; although the traditional Irish wake, complete with games, jokes and mock weddings, is seldom practised nowadays.

Although Ireland has one of the youngest populations in Europe, it isn't a 'youth culture', and there's still considerable respect for the older generation. The Irish are generally law-abiding people, yet there's often a distinction between what's officially allowed, by either the state or the Church, and what's actually practised (licensing hours are a notable example!). In Ireland, laws follow practice, not vice versa.

The Irish are passionate about sport, principally their own 'peculiar' sports of Gaelic football and hurling, which are very much family sports in that even women get quite excited about them and, if there's a big match on, such as the All-Ireland Final (of either game), houses everywhere sprout flags and banners, and normal life pretty much comes to a standstill.

When it comes to politics, the Irish seem more interested in the personalities than the policies of their politicians, who consequently spend much of their time 'wooing' their electorate. As regards the former 'troubles' in Northern Ireland, it's surprising how little the people of *Eire* discussed them or seemed to be affected by them. Although most Irish people may vaguely want the whole of Ireland to be united, they aren't impatient about it – any more than they're impatient about anything.

Irish society has changed more than almost any other Western country in the past 40 years; economic growth has brought with it social change, most dramatically in the position of women. As recently as 1977, female civil servants had to resign if they married. Now the Irish president is a woman (Mary McAleese was elected for a second seven-year term in 2004), there's a woman member of the Supreme Court, two female ministers, and 22 women in parliament – the *Dáil* – (13 per cent of the total number of members of parliament – RDs). The emergence of female politicians (there's even a Centre for Advancement of Women in politics), journalists such as Mary Kenny, Nell McCafferty and Maeve Binchy, and television and radio presenters such as Marion Finucane, has given a voice to women's views, and helped to liberate them from their traditional male subjugation.

Change has also challenged traditional religious taboos. Subjects such as contraception, divorce, abortion and suicide, which not long ago weren't even on the agenda as far as the Catholic Church was concerned, are now endlessly aired in the national media; and popular pressure has brought about liberalisation of the laws concerning birth control and homosexuality, although abortion remains illegal (at least in practice).

Not only do they have a more liberal outlook, but the Irish travel more than they used to, both for pleasure and on business, and have become more aware of the outside world. Where once they emigrated for good, nowadays they'll go and work abroad for a few months or years, return when it suits them, and go away again if a good opportunity arises. Nevertheless, with a population of just 4m,

Ireland remains a 'small' country. It almost seems as though everyone knows everyone else – and everyone else's business!

Of course, progress and prosperity have their drawbacks, and there are fears that the traditional features of Irish life and customs are under threat from, or even already succumbing to, the very different values of the modern global society. Traditional rural life has all but disappeared, particularly in the north-west, and country folk are increasingly being forced to adapt to new ways. There's less community spirit and people are increasingly left to 'make it' on their own. At times, Irish informality seems to sit uneasily with the efficiency demanded of modern business life; and certainly, the Irish face a challenge in coming to terms with the implications of their sudden emergence into the 21st century. In the words of Irish commentator John Ardagh, 'The challenge for the Irish today, and this is fundamental to their politics and society, is how to translate an old-style, nostalgic, narrow nationalisation into a modern, legitimate pride in their Irish culture and identity, within a wide European framework.'

When all is said and done, Ireland is one of the most open, liberal, stable and tolerant societies in the world. It has a strong economy, political stability, a good education system, a skilled workforce, a high standard of living, excellent health care services and a wealth of natural beauty. But perhaps, above all, the Irish are renowned for their relaxed way of life.

Put simply, Ireland is a great place in which to live, work and raise a family.

***Eireann go brách!* (Ireland for ever!)**

"When God made time, he made plenty of it," is a popular saying – and the Irish certainly seem to know how to make the most of it.

20.
MOVING HOUSE OR LEAVING IRELAND

When moving house or leaving Ireland, there are numerous things to be considered and a 'million' people to be informed. The checklists contained below are designed to make the task easier and may even help prevent an ulcer or nervous breakdown – provided of course that you don't leave everything to the last minute! See also Moving House on page 117.

MOVING HOUSE

When moving house within Ireland or abroad, the following items should be considered:

♦ If you're renting accommodation, you must give your landlord notice as per your rental contract and have your deposit refunded. Your notice letter should be sent by registered post.

♦ If you have an Irish driving licence or an Irish registered car, you must return your licence and car registration document, and have the address changed (see **Chapter 11**).

♦ Inform the following, as applicable:

– your employer;

– your present town hall and the town hall in your new municipality;

– your social security and income tax offices;

– your electricity, gas, telephone and water companies;

– your insurance companies (for example health, car, household, third party liability, etc.); hire purchase companies; lawyer; accountant; and local businesses where you have accounts. Take out new insurance, if applicable.

– your banks, and other financial institutions such as stockbrokers and credit card companies. Make arrangements for the transfer of funds, and for the cancellation or alteration of standing orders or direct debits (regular payments).

– your family doctor, dentist and other health practitioners. Health records should be transferred to your new practitioners.

– your family's schools. If applicable, arrange for schooling in your new community (see **Chapter 9**). Try to give a term's notice, and obtain copies of any relevant school reports and records from current schools.

– all regular correspondents, subscriptions, social and sports clubs, professional and trade journals, and friends and relatives. Arrange to have your post redirected.

– your local consulate or embassy if you're registered with them.

♦ Return any library books or anything borrowed.

♦ Arrange removal of your furniture and belongings, or hire transportation if you're doing your own removal.

♦ Ask yourself (again): 'Is it really worth all this trouble?'.

LEAVING IRELAND

Before leaving Ireland for an indefinite period, the following items should be considered **in addition to** those listed above under **Moving House**:

♦ Check that your family's passports are valid!

♦ Give notice to your employer, if applicable.

♦ Check whether any special entry require-ments are necessary for your country of destination, e.g. visas, permits or inoculations, by contacting the local embassy or consulate in Ireland. An exit permit or visa isn't required to leave Ireland.

♦ You may qualify for a rebate on your income tax and social security payments.

♦ Arrange to sell anything you aren't taking with you (house, car, furniture, etc.), and to ship your belongings. Find out the procedure for shipping your belongings to your country of destination. Check with the local embassy or consulate of the country to which you're moving. Special forms may need to be completed before arrival.

If you've been living in Ireland for less than one year, you're required to re-export all personal effects imported duty-free from outside the European Union (EU), including furniture and vehicles (if you sell them you may be required to pay duty).

♦ If you have an Irish registered car that you intend to take with you, you must have it re-registered in your new country of residence and inform the Irish authorities.

♦ Pets may require special inoculations or may have to go into quarantine for a period, depending on your destination.

♦ Arrange health, travel and other insurance (see **Chapter 13**).

♦ Depending on your destination, you may wish to arrange health and dental check-ups before leaving Ireland. Obtain a copy of your health and dental records.

♦ Terminate any loans, lease or hire purchase contracts, and pay all outstanding bills (allow plenty of time, as some companies are slow to respond).

♦ Check whether you're entitled to a rebate on your road tax, car and other insurance. Obtain a letter from your Irish insurance company stating your no-claims bonus.

♦ Make arrangements to sell or let your house or apartment, and other property in Ireland.

♦ Check whether you need an international driving licence or a translation of your Irish or foreign driving licence for your country of destination.

♦ Give friends and business associates in Ireland an address and telephone number where you can be contacted abroad.

♦ Finally, allow plenty of time to get to the airport or port, register your luggage, and clear security and immigration.

As they say in Ireland, 'May the road rise up to meet you, may the wind be always at your back, may the sun shine warm upon your face, and may God hold you in the hollow of his hand'!

Slán abhaile! (safe home!)

Molly Malone - 'the tart with the cart'

APPENDICES

APPENDIX A: EMBASSIES & CONSULATES

Foreign embassies and consulates in Ireland are located in Dublin and Cork, and are listed under Diplomatic and Consular Missions in telephone books. Note that business hours vary considerably and all embassies close on their national holidays, as well as on Ireland's public holidays. Always telephone to check the business hours before visiting. A list of Irish embassies and consulates abroad can be found at 🖳 www.dfa.ie/home/index.aspx?id=285. A selection of embassies and consulates in Dublin is listed below:

Argentina: 15 Ailesbury Drive, Dublin 4 (☎ 01-269 4603).

Australia: Fitzwilton House, Wilton Terrace, Dublin 2 (☎ 01-664 5300, 🖳 www.ireland. embassy.gov.au).

Austria: 15 Ailesbury Court, 93 Ailesbury Road, Dublin 4 (☎ 01-269 4577).

Belgium: 2 Shrewsbury Road, Ballsbridge, Dublin 4 (☎ 01-205 7100, 🖳 www.diplomatie.be/dublin).

Brazil: Harcourt Centre, 5th Floor, 41-54 Harcourt Street, Dublin 2 (☎ 01-475 6000, 🖳 www.brazil.ie).

Bulgaria: 22 Burlington Road, Dublin 4 (☎ 01-660 3293, 🖳 www.bulgaria.bg).

Canada: 7-8 Wilton Terrace, Dublin 2 (☎ 01-234 4000).

China: 40 Ailesbury Road, Dublin 4 (☎ 01-269 1707).

Czech Republic: 57 Northumberland Road, Dublin 4 (☎ 01-668 1135, 🖳 www.mzv.cz/dublin).

Denmark: 121 St Stephen's Green, Dublin 2 (☎ 01-475 6404, 🖳 www.denmark.ie).

Egypt: 12 Clyde Road, Ballsbridge, Dublin 4 (☎ 01-660 6718, 🖳 www.embegyptireland.ie).

Finland: Stokes Place, St Stephen's Green, Dublin 2 (☎ 01-478 1344, 🖳 www.finland.ie).

France: 36 Ailesbury Road, Dublin 4 (☎ 01-277 5000, 🖳 www.ambafrance.ie).

Germany: 31 Trimleston Avenue, Booterstown (☎ 01-269 3011, 🖳 www.germanembassy.ie).

Greece: 1 Upper Pembroke Street, Dublin 2 (☎ 01-676 7254).

Hungary: 2 Fitzwilliam Place, Dublin 4 (☎ 01-661 2902, 🖥 www.kum.hu/dublin/).

India: 6 Lesson Park, Dublin 6 (☎ 01-497 0843).

Iran: 72 Mount Merrion Avenue, Blackrock (☎ 01-288 5881).

Italy: 63 Northumberland Road, Dublin 4 (☎ 01-660 1744, 🖥 www.italianembassy.ie).

Japan: Merrion Centre, Nutley Lane, Dublin 4 (☎ 01-269 4244, 🖥 www.ie.emb-japan.go.jp).

Korea: 15 Clyde Road, Dublin 4 (☎ 01-660 8800, 🖥 www.mofat.go.kr/ireland).

Mexico: 19 Raglan Road, Dublin 4 (☎ 01-667 3105, 🖥 www.embamex.ie).

Morocco: 53 Raglan Road, Ballsbridge, Dublin 4 (☎ 01-660 9449).

Netherlands: 160 Merrion Road, Dublin 4 (☎ 01-269 3444, 🖥 www.netherlandsembassy.ie).

Nigeria: 56 Leeson Park, Dublin 6 (☎ 01-660 4366, 🖥 www.nigerianembassy.ie).

Norway: 34 Molesworth Street, Dublin 2 (☎ 01-662 1800, 🖥 www.norway.ie).

Poland: 5 Ailesbury Road, Dublin 4 (☎ 01-283 0855, 🖥 www.dublin.polemb.net).

Portugal: Knocksinna House, Foxrock, Dublin 18 (☎ 01-289 4416).

Russia: 184-186 Orwell Road, Dublin 14 (☎ 01-492 2048).

South Africa: Earlsfort Centre, Dublin 2 (☎ 01-661 5553).

Spain: 17a Merlyn Park, Dublin 4 (☎ 01-269 1640, 🖥 www.mae.es/embajadas/dublin).

Sweden: Iveagh Court, Harcourt Road, Dublin 2 (☎ 01-474 4400, 🖥 www.swedenabroad.com/dublin).

Turkey: 11 Clyde Road, Ballsbridge, Dublin 4 (☎ 01-668 5240).

United Kingdom: 29 Merrion Road, Dublin 4 (☎ 01-205 3700, 🖥 www.britishembassy.ie).

United States of America: 42 Elgin Road, Dublin 4 (☎ 01-668 8777, 🖥 http://dublin.us.gov).

Irish Government Departments

Central Bank & Financial Services Authority, PO Box 559, Dame Street, Dublin 2 (☎ 01-434 4000, 🖥 www.centralbank.ie).

Central Statistics Office, Skehard Road, Cork (☎ 021-453 5000 or ☎ 1890-313414, 🖥 www.cso.ie).

Citizens Information Board, George's Quay House, 43 Townsend St, Dublin 2 (☎ 01-605 9000, 🖥 www.comhairle.ie).

Collector General (Taxes), Sarsfield House, Francis Street, Limerick (☎ 061-310310 or ☎ 1890-203070).

Courts Service, Phoenix House, 15–24 Phoenix Street North, Smithfield, Dublin 7 (☎ 01-888 6000, 🖥 www.courts.ie).

Department of Agriculture and Food, Agriculture House, Kildare Street, Dublin 2 (☎ 01-607 2000 or ☎ 1890-200 510 , 🖥 www.agriculture.gov.ie).

Department of Communications, Marine and Natural Resources, 29–31 Adelaide Road, Dublin 2 (☎ 01-678 2000 or ☎ 1890-449900, 🖥 www.dcmnr.gov.ie).

Department of Education and Science, Marlborough Street, Dublin 1 (☎ 01-889 6400, 🖥 www.education.ie).

Department of Enterprise, Trade and Employment, 23 Kildare Street, Dublin 2 (☎ 01-631 2121 or ☎ 1890-220222, 🖥 www.entemp.ie).

Department of the Environment, Heritage and Local Government, Custom House, Dublin 1 (☎ 01-888 2000 or ☎ 1890-202021, 🖥 www.environ.ie).

Department of Finance, Government Buildings, Upper Merrion Street, Dublin 2 (☎ 01-676 7571 or ☎ 1890-661010, 🖥 www.finance.gov.ie).

Department of Foreign Affairs, 80 St Stephen's Green, Dublin 2 (☎ 01-478 0822, 🖥 www. dfa.ie).

Department of Health and Children, Hawkins House, Hawkins Street, Dublin 2 (☎ 01-635 4000, 🖥 www.dohc.ie).

Department of Justice, Equality and Law Reform, 94 St Stephen's Green, Dublin 2 (☎ 01-602 8202 or ☎ 1890-221227, 🖥 www.justice.ie).

Department of Social & Family Affairs, Store Street, Dublin 1 (☎ 01-704 3000 or ☎ 1890-662244, 🖥 www.welfare.ie).

Department of Enterprise, Trade and Employment, 23 Kildare Street, Dublin 2 (☎ 01-631 2121 or ☎ 1890-220222, 🖥 www.entemp.ie).

Department of Transport, Transport House, 44 Kildare Street, Dublin 2 (☎ 01-670 7444 or ☎ 1890-443311, 🖥 www.transport.ie).

Environmental Protection Agency, PO Box 3000, Johnstown Castle Estate, County Wexford (☎ 053-9160600 or (1890-335599, 🖥 www.epa.ie).

Garda Síochána (Police), Garda Headquarters, Phoenix Park, Dublin 8 (☎ 01-666 0000, 🖥 www.garda.ie).

Health and Safety Authority, Head Office, The Metropolitan Building, James Joyce Street, Dublin 1 (☎ 01-614 7000 or ☎ 1890-289389, 💻 www.hsa.ie).

Higher Education Authority, Brooklawn House, Crampton Avenue, Shelbourne Road, Dublin 4 (☎ 01-231 7100 or ☎ 1890-200637, 💻 www.hea.ie).

Irish Defence Forces, Parkgate, Infirmary Road, Dublin 7 (☎ 01-804 2690 or ☎ 1890-426555, 💻 www.military.ie).

Irish Tax & Customs, Apollo House, Tara Street, Dublin 2 (☎ 01-633 0600, 💻 www.revenue.ie).

Library Council, 53–54 Upper Mount Street, Mount Street, Dublin 2 (☎ 01-676 1167 or ☎ 01-676 1963, 💻 www.librarycouncil.ie).

National Roads Authority, St Martin's House, Waterloo Road, Dublin 4 (☎ 01 660 2511, 💻 www.nra.ie).

Passport Office (part of the Department of Foreign Affairs), 80 St Stephen's Green, Dublin 2 (☎ 01-478 0822, 💻 www.dfa.ie/home/index.aspx?id=253).

Revenue Commissioners, Apollo House, Tara Street, Dublin 2 (☎ 01-633 0600, 💻 www.revenue.ie**).**

Teagasc (Agriculture and Food Development Authority), Oak Park, Carlow (☎ 059-917 0200, 💻 www.teagasc.ie).

Miscellaneous

An Post, General Post Office, O'Connell Street, Dublin 1 (☎ 01-705 7600 or ☎ 1850 575859, 💻 www.anpost.ie).

Calor Gas, Long Mile Road, Dublin 12 (☎ 01-450 5000, 💻 www.calorgas.ie).

Chambers of Commerce of Ireland, 17 Merrion Square, Dublin 2 (☎ 01-661 2888, 💻 www.chambers.ie).

Companies Office, Parnell House, 14 Parnell Square, Dublin 1 (☎ 01-804 5200, 💻 www.cro.ie).

Construction Industry Federation, Construction House, Canal Road, Dublin 6 (☎ 01-406 6000, 💻 www.cif.ie).

Disability Federation of Ireland, Fumbally Court, Fumbally Lane, Dublin 8 (☎ 01-454 7978, 💻 www.disability-federation.ie).

Dublin Bus (Bus Átha Cliath), 59 Upper O'Connell Street, Dublin 1 ☎ 01-872 0000; passenger information ☎ 01-873 4222, 💻 www.dublinbus.ie).

Eircom, St Stephen's Green, Dublin 2 (☎ 01-671 4444, 💻 www.eircom.ie).

Electricity Supply Board, 27 Lower Fitzwilliam Street, Dublin 2 (☎ 01-852 9534 or ☎ 1850-372372, 🖥 www.esb.ie).

Enterprise Ireland, Head Office, Glasnevin, Dublin 9 (☎ 01-808 2000, 🖥 www.enterprise-ireland.com).

Gas Board (Bord Gáis), HR Department, Gasworks Road, Cork (☎ 01-453 4000, 🖥 www.bordgais.ie).

Irish Brokers' Association, 87 Merrion Square, Dublin 2 (☎ 01-661 3067, 🖥 www.iba.ie).

Irish Bus (Bus Éireann), Broadstone, Dublin 7 (☎ 01-830 2222, 🖥 www.buseireann.ie).

Irish Business and Employers Confederation, Confederation House, 84/86 Lower Baggot Street, Dublin 2 (☎ 01-605 1500, 🖥 www.ibec.ie).

Irish League of Credit Unions, 33/41 Lower Mount Street, Dublin 2 (☎ 01-614 6700, 🖥 www.creditunion.ie).

Irish Rail (Iarnród Éireann), Connolly Station, Dublin 1 (☎ 01-836 3333, 🖥 www.irishrail.ie).

Irish Tourist Board (Fáilte Ireland), Baggot Street Bridge, Dublin 2 (☎ 0800-039 7000, 🖥 www.discoverireland.com).

Land Registry, Nassau Building, Setanta Centre, Nassau Street, Dublin 2 (☎ 01-670 7500 or ☎ 1890-333001, 🖥 www.landregistry.ie).

Law Society of Ireland, Blackhall Place, Dublin 7 (☎ 01-672 4800, 🖥 www.lawsociety.ie).

National Disability Authority (Comhairle), 25 Clyde Road, Dublin 4 (☎ 01-608 0400, 🖥 www.nda.ie).

Pensions Board (An Bord Pinsean), Verschoyle House, 28–30 Lower Mount Street, Dublin 2 (☎ 01-613 1900 or ☎ 1890-656565, 🖥 www.pensionsboard.ie).

Radio and Television Ireland (Radio Telefís Éireann), Dublin 4 (☎ 01-208 3111, 🖥 www.rti.ie).

Royal Institute of the Architects of Ireland, 8 Merrion Square, Dublin 2 (☎ 01-676 1703, 🖥 www.riai.ie).

Society of Chartered Surveyors, 5 Wilton Place, Dublin 2 (☎ 01-676 5500, 🖥 www.scs.ie).

Training & Employment Authority (FÁS), 27/33 Upper Baggot Street, Dublin 4 (☎ 01-607 0500 or ☎ 1800-61116, 🖥 www.fas.ie).

VAT Enquiries, Apollo House, Tara Street, Dublin 2 (☎ 01-633 0600, 🖥 www.revenue.ie).

Vivas Health, Mountain View, Central Park, Leopardstown, Dublin 18 (☎ 1850-717717, 🖥 www.vivashealth.ie).

Voluntary Health Insurance Board (VHI), VHI House, Lower Abbey Street, Dublin 1 (☎ 056-775 3200 or ☎ 1850 444444, 🖥 www.vhi.ie).

APPENDIX B: NEWSPAPERS & MAGAZINES

Newspapers & Magazines

Image, Image Publications Ltd, 22 Crofton Road, Dun Laoghaire (☎ 01-280 8415, 🖥 www. image.ie).

Irish Examiner/Evening Echo, City Quarter, Lapps Quay, Cork (☎ 021-427 2722, 🖥 www. irishexaminer.com).

Irish Independent/Evening Herald, 27/32 Talbot Street, Dublin 1 (☎ 01-705 5333, 🖥 www. independent.ie)

Irish Property Buyer, Property Media Ltd, 16/17 College Green, Dublin 2 (☎ 01-612 1430, 🖥 www.irishpropertybuyer.com).

The Irish Times, The Irish Times Building, PO Box 74, 24/28 Tara Street, Dublin 2 (☎ 01-675 8000, 🖥 www.irishtimes.com).

Phoenix Magazine, 44 Lower Baggot Street, Dublin 2 (☎ 01-661 1062, 🖥 www.phoenix-magazine.com).

The Star, Star House, 62A Terenure Road North, Dublin 6 (☎ 01-490 1228, 🖥 www.thestar.ie).

Books

The books listed below are just a small selection of the many books written about Ireland. In addition to the general guides listed, there are many excellent regional guides available. Note that some titles may be out of print, but may still be obtainable from bookshops or libraries.

Food & Drink

The Complete Book of Irish Country Cooking, Darina Allen (Penguin USA)

Elegant Irish Cooking, Noel Cullen (Lebhar-Friedman)

Feasting Galore Irish Style, Maura Laverty (Hippocrene Books)

Festive Food of Ireland, Darina Allen (Roberts Rinehart)

Irish Food & Folklore, Clare Connery (Laurel Glen)

Irish Traditional Cooking, Darina Allen (K. Cathie)

The Joyce of Cooking, Armstrong et al. (Talman Co.)

Land of Milk & Honey, Brid Mahon (Irish Amer Book Co.)

A Little Book of Irish Baking, Marion Maxwell (Irish Books & Media)

The New Cooking of Britain & Ireland, Gwenda Hyman (John Willey & Sons)

Real Irish Cookery, Mary Caherty (Hale)

Splendid Food: Irish Country Houses, Gillian Berwick (Irish Amer Book Co.)

Taste of Ireland: In Food and Pictures, Theodora Fitzgibbon (Weidenfeld)

Traditional Irish Recipes, John Murphy (Irish Books & Media)

Wining and Dining at Home in Ireland, Sandy O'Byrne & Jacinta Delahaye (A&A Farmer)

World Food Ireland, Martin Hughes (Lonely Planet)

History

Home Away from Home: The Yanks in Ireland, Mary Pat Kelly (Stackpole)

Ireland: A Concise History, Maire O'Brien et al. (Thames & Hudson)

The Irish: Our History, John Leary (First Books Library)

The Oxford History of Ireland, R. F. Foster ed. (Oxford University Press)

That Was Then, This Is Now, ed. Adrian Redmond (Central Statistics Office)

Timetables of Irish History, Patrick Power (Black Dog & Lewenthal)

Property

150 Years of Architecture in Ireland, John Graby (Eblana Editions)

20th Century Architecture in Ireland, Annette Becker & Wilfred Wang (Prestel)

A Field Guide to the Buildings of Ireland, Sean Rothery (Lilliput)

A Guide to Irish Houses, Mark Bence-Jones (Constable)

Buildings of Irish Towns, Patrick & Maura Shaffrey (O'Brien Press)

Daily Telegraph Gardener's Guide to Britain and Ireland (Dorling Kindersley)

In the Houses of Ireland, Marianne Heron & Walter Pfeiffer (Thames & Hudson)

Irish Castles and Castellated Houses, Harold G. Leask (Dundalgan)

Irish Cottages, Joe Reynolds (Real Ireland Design)

Irish Country Houses, Terence Reeves-Smith (Appletree)

Irish Countryside Buildings, Patrick & Maura Shaffrey (O'Brien Press)

Irish Gardens, Terence Reeves-Smith (Appletree)

In an Irish House, David Davidson & Molly Keane (Weidenfeld & Nicolson)

Irish Houses and Gardens, Sean O'Reilly (Aurum Press)

New Irish Architecture, John Oregan (Gandon)

Travel

Baedeker's Ireland (Baedeker)

Berlitz Pocket Guides: Ireland (Macmillan)

Discover Ireland, Martin Gostelow (Berlitz)

Dublin: The Miniguide, Dan Richardson (Rough Guides)

Fodor's Exploring Ireland (Fodor)

Fodor's Ireland (Fodor's Gold Guides) (Fodor)

Frommer's Guide to Ireland from $50 a Day (Pocket Books)

Frommer's Ireland (Frommer)

Ireland, Catharine Day (Cadogan Books)

Ireland, a Bicycle and a Tin Whistle, David A. Wilson (Blackstaff)

Ireland: A Cultural Encyclopaedia (Thames and Hudson)

Ireland: A Travel Survival Kit, Tom Smallman (Vacation Work)

Ireland: The Rough Guide, Sean Doran (The Rough Guides)

Let's Go: Britain & Ireland (Pan)

Lonely Planet: Ireland, Tom Smallman & Sean Sheehan (Lonely Planet)

Michelin Green Guide to Ireland (Michelin)

Out and About in Dublin, Mary Finn (Irish Amer Book Co.)

Round Ireland in Low Gear, Eric Newby (Picador)

Round Ireland with a Fridge, Tony Hawks (Griffin)

The Time Out Guide to Dublin (Time Out)

Miscellaneous

Angela's Ashes, Frank McCourt (Scribner)

Enterprise Ireland: A Directory of Sources of Assistance for Entrepreneurs and Small Business Owners (Oak Tree Press)

Laying Down the Law, Olive Brennan (Oak Tree Press)

The Living Stream: Literature and Revisionism in Ireland, Edna Longley (Bloodaxe)

McCarthy's Bar, Pete McCarthy (St Martins)

The Truth about the Irish, Terry Eagleton (Griffin)

Your Guide to Irish Law, Mary Faulkner, Gerry Kelly & Padraig Turley (Gill Macmillan)

APPENDIX C: USEFUL WEBSITES

The general information websites listed below are only a selection of hundreds relating to Ireland. See also **Appendices A** and **B**, where the sites of government departments, publications and other organisations are listed. Websites about particular aspects of life and work in Ireland are mentioned in the relevant chapters.

General Information

Ask Ireland (💻 www.ask-ireland.com). Useful government website for anyone doing business with or visiting Ireland.

BASIS (💻 www.basis.ie). Business Access to State Information and Services (BASIS). Comprehensive Government information and services to business.

Breaking News (💻 www.breakingnews.ie). The latest Irish news.

Chambers (💻 www.chambers.ie). Chambers of Commerce in Ireland. Ireland's largest business network.

Citizens Information (💻 www.citizensinformation.ie). Government information on every conceivable topic – one of the most useful websites about Ireland.

Discover Ireland (💻 www.discoverireland.com/www.ireland.ie). Official government tourist website (Tourism Ireland).

DoChara (💻 www.dochara.com). General information for independent travellers.

Dublin City (💻 www.dublincity.ie). Dublin City Council site containing comprehensive information about the capital.

Enfo (💻 www.enfo.ie). Government information on environmental issues.

Enterprise Ireland (💻 www.enterprise-ireland.com). The government agency responsible for the development and promotion of the indigenous business sector.

ESRI (💻 www.esri.ie). Economic & Social Research Institute.

European Irish (💻 www.europeanirish.com). Information for Irish people working in Continental Europe.

Fáilte Ireland (💻 www.failteireland.ie). The National Tourism Development Authority of Ireland.

Finfacts (💻 www.finfacts.com). Business and finance portal.

Fix My Tax (💻 www.fixmytax.com). Offers 'tax solutions', but information isn't always reliable.

Forfas (💻 www.forfas.ie). National Economic Development Authority and Advisory Board.

Government (💻 www.irlgov.ie). The government of Ireland official website.

Guinness Storehouse (💻 www.guinness-storehouse.com). Everything you ever wanted to know about Guinness in five languages.

IDA Ireland (💻 www.idaireland.com). Website of the Industrial Development Agency (IDA), an Irish Government agency with responsibility for securing overseas investment. Contains a wealth of information about Ireland's economy, taxes, education system and infrastructure.

Ireland (💻 www.ireland.com). Travel and holiday information.

Ireland Information (💻 www.ireland-information.com). Culture and customs information and resources.

Ireland's Eye (💻 www.irelandseye.com). Information about Ireland's history, traditions and folklore.

Ireland Wide (💻 www.irelandwide.com). Business directory. Comprehensive information about each county.

Irish Culture & Customs (💻 www.irishcultureandcustoms.com). Irish Culture & Customs Newsletter and an email newsmagazine.

Irish News (💻 www.irishnews.com). Website of the Irish News newspaper.

Irish Post (💻 www.irishpost.co.uk). The voice of the Irish in Britain.

Jobs.ie (💻 www.jobs.ie). Job listings for Ireland.

Look Into Ireland (💻 www.lookintoireland.com). Extensive tourist and travel information.

NDP (💻 www.ndp.ie). Information about the National Development Plan – 'the roadmap to Ireland's future'.

Property Registration Authority (💻 www.landregistry.ie). The PRA is the Land Registry of Ireland.

Real Estate (💻 www.realestate.ie). Institute of Auctioneers and Valuers of Ireland (IAVI).

Recruit Ireland (💻 www.recruitireland.com). Job site.

Starting a Business Ireland (💻 www.startingabusinessinireland.com). Information about starting a business.

Visit Dublin (💻 www.visitdublin.com). Dublin Tourism.

Wikipedia (💻 http://en.wikipedia.org/wiki/ireland). The Ireland pages of Wikipedia, the online encyclopaedia.

APPENDIX D: WEIGHTS & MEASURES

Ireland uses the metric system of measurement. Those who are more familiar with the imperial system of measurement will find the tables on the following pages useful. Some comparisons shown are only approximate, but are close enough for most everyday uses. In addition to the variety of measurement systems used, clothes sizes often vary considerably with the manufacturer.

Women's Clothes									
Continental	34	36	38	40	42	44	46	48	50	52
UK		8	10	12	14	16	18	20	22	24	26
US		6	8	10	12	14	16	18	20	22	24

Pullover's												
	Women's						Men's					
Continental	40	42	44	46	48	50	44	46	48	50	52	54
UK	34	36	38	40	42	44	34	36	38	40	42	44
US	34	36	38	40	42	44	sm	med		lar	xl

Men's Shirts										
Continental	36	37	38	39	40	41	42	43	44	46
UK/US	14	14	15	15	16	16	17	17	18	-

Men's Underwear						
Continental	5	6	7	8	9	10
UK		34	36	38	40	42	44
US		sm	med		lar	xl

NB: sm = small, med = medium, lar = large, xl = extra large

Children's Clothes

Continental	92	104	116	128	140	152
UK	16/18	20/22	24/26	28/30	32/34	36/38
US	2	4	6	8	10	12

Children's Shoes

Continental	18 19 20 21 22 23 24 25 26 27 28 29 30 31 32
UK/US	2 3 4 4 5 6 7 7 8 9 10 11 11 12 13
Continental	33 34 35 36 37 38
UK/US	1 2 2 3 4 5

Shoes (Women's & Men's)

Continental	35	36	37	37	38	39	40	41	42	42	43	44
UK		2	3	3	4	4	5	6	7	7	8 9	9
US		4	5	5	6	6	7	8	9	9	10 10	11

Weight

Imperial	Metric	Metric	Imperial
1oz	28.35g	1g	0.035oz
1lb*	454g	100g	3.5oz
1cwt	50.8kg	250g	9oz
1 ton	1,016kg	500g	18oz
2,205lb	1 tonne	1kg	2.2lb

Area

British/US	Metric	Metric	British/US
1 sq. in	0.45 sq. cm	1 sq. cm	0.15 sq. in
1 sq. ft	0.09 sq. m	1 sq. m	10.76 sq. ft
1 sq. yd	0.84 sq. m	1 sq. m	1.2 sq. yds
1 acre	0.4 hectares	1 hectare	2.47 acres
1 sq. mile	2.56 sq. km	1 sq. km	0.39 sq. mile

Capacity

Imperial	Metric	Metric	Imperial
1 UK pint	0.57 litre	1 litre	1.75 UK pints
1 US pint	0.47 litre	1 litre	2.13 US pints
1 UK gallon	4.54 litres	1 litre	0.22 UK gallon
1 US gallon	3.78 litres	1 litre	0.26 US gallon

NB: An American 'cup' = around 250ml or 0.25 litre.

Length

British/US	Metric	Metric	British/US
1in	2.54cm	1cm	0.39in
1ft	30.48cm	1m	3ft 3.25in
1yd	91.44cm	1km	0.62mi
1mi	1.6km	8km	5mi

Temperature

°Celsius	°Fahrenheit
0	32 (freezing point of water)
5	41
10	50
15	59
20	68
25	77
30	86
35	95
40	104
50	122

Temperature Conversion

Celsius to Fahrenheit: multiply by 9, divide by 5 and add 32. (For a quick and approximate conversion, double the Celsius temperature and add 30.)

Fahrenheit to Celsius: subtract 32, multiply by 5 and divide by 9. (For a quick and approximate conversion, subtract 30 from the Fahrenheit temperature and divide by 2.)

NB: The boiling point of water is 100°C / 212°F. Normal body temperature (if you're alive and well) is 37°C / 98.6°F.

Power			
Kilowatts	**Horsepower**	**Horsepower**	**Kilowatts**
1	1.34	1	0.75

Oven Temperature		
Gas	**Electric**	
	°F	°C
-	225–250	110–120
1	275	140
2	300	150
3	325	160
4	350	180
5	375	190
6	400	200
7	425	220
8	450	230
9	475	240

Air Pressure	
PSI	**Bar**
10	0.5
20	1.4
30	2
40	2.8

INDEX

Q/R

S

Survival Books was established in 1987 and by the mid-'90s was the leading publisher of books for people planning to live, work, buy property or retire abroad.

From the outset, our philosophy has been to provide the most comprehensive and up-to-date information available. Our titles routinely contain up to twice as much information as other books and are updated frequently. All our books contain colour photographs and some are printed in two colours or full colour throughout. They also contain original cartoons, illustrations and maps.

Survival Books are written by people with first-hand experience of the countries and the people they describe, and therefore provide invaluable insights that cannot be obtained from official publications or websites, and information that is more reliable and objective than that provided by the majority of unofficial sites.

Survival Books are designed to be easy – and interesting – to read. They contain a comprehensive list of contents and index and extensive appendices, including useful addresses, further reading, useful websites and glossaries to help you obtain additional information as well as metric conversion tables and other useful reference material.

Our primary goal is to provide you with the essential information necessary for a trouble-free life or property purchase and to save you time, trouble and money.

We believe our books are the best – they are certainly the best-selling. But don't take our word for it – read what reviewers and readers have said about Survival Books at the front of this book.

Order your copies today by phone, fax, post or email from:
Survival Books, PO Box 3780, Yeovil, BA21 5WX, United Kingdom.
Tel: +44 (0)1935-700060, email: sales@survivalbooks.net,
Website: www.survivalbooks.net

Buying a Home Series

Buying a home abroad is not only a major financial transaction but also a potentially life-changing experience; it's therefore essential to get it right. Our Buying a Home guides are required reading for anyone planning to purchase property abroad and are packed with vital information to guide you through the property jungle and help you avoid disasters that can turn a dream home into a nightmare.

The purpose of our Buying a Home guides is to enable you to choose the most favourable location and the most appropriate property for your requirements, and to reduce your risk of making an expensive mistake by making informed decisions and calculated judgements rather than uneducated and hopeful guesses. Most importantly, they will help you save money and will repay your investment many times over.

Buying a Home guides are the most comprehensive and up-to-date source of information available about buying property abroad – whether you're seeking a detached house or an apartment, a holiday or a permanent home (or an investment property), these books will prove invaluable.

For a full list of our current titles, visit our website at www.survivalbooks.net

Living and Working Series

Our Living and Working guides are essential reading for anyone planning to spend a period abroad – whether it's an extended holiday or permanent migration – and are packed with priceless information designed to help you avoid costly mistakes and save both time and money.

Living and Working guides are the most comprehensive and up-to-date source of practical information available about everyday life abroad. They aren't, however, simply a catalogue of dry facts and figures, but are written in a highly readable style – entertaining, practical and occasionally humorous.

Our aim is to provide you with the comprehensive practical information necessary for a trouble-free life. You may have visited a country as a tourist, but living and working there is a different matter altogether; adjusting to a new environment and culture and making a home in any foreign country can be a traumatic and stressful experience. You need to adapt to new customs and traditions, discover the local way of doing things (such as finding a home, paying bills and obtaining insurance) and learn all over again how to overcome the everyday obstacles of life.

All these subjects and many, many more are covered in depth in our Living and Working guides – don't leave home without them.

The Expats' Best Friend!

Culture Wise Series

Our **Culture Wise** series of guides is essential reading for anyone who wants to understand how a country really 'works'. Whether you're planning to stay for a few days or a lifetime, these guides will help you quickly find your feet and settle into your new surroundings. **Culture Wise** guides:

- Reduce the anxiety factor in adapting to a foreign culture
- Explain how to behave in everyday situations in order to avoid cultural and social gaffes
- Help you get along with your neighbours
- Make friends and establish lasting business relationships
- Enhance your understanding of a country and its people.

People often underestimate the extent of cultural isolation they can face abroad, particularly in a country with a different language. At first glance, many countries seem an 'easy' option, often with millions of visitors from all corners of the globe and well-established expatriate communities. But, sooner or later, newcomers find that most countries are indeed 'foreign' and many come unstuck as a result. **Culture Wise** guides will enable you to quickly adapt to the local way of life and feel at home, and – just as importantly – avoid the worst effects of culture shock.

Culture Wise – The Wise Way to Travel

The essential guides to Culture, Customs & Business Etiquette

Other Survival Books

The Best Places to Buy a Home in France/Spain: Unique guides to where to buy property in Spain and France, containing detailed regional profiles and market reports.

Buying, Selling and Letting Property: The best source of information about buying, selling and letting property in the UK.

Earning Money From Your French Home: Income from property in France, including short- and long-term letting.

Investing in Property Abroad: Everything you need to know and more about buying property abroad for investment and pleasure.

Making a Living: Comprehensive guides to self-employment and starting a business in France and Spain.

Renovating & Maintaining Your French Home: The ultimate guide to renovating and maintaining your dream home in France.

Retiring in France/Spain: Everything a prospective retiree needs to know about the two most popular international retirement destinations.

Running Gîtes and B&Bs in France: An essential book for anyone planning to invest in a gîte or bed & breakfast business.

Rural Living in France: An invaluable book for anyone seekingthe 'good life', containing a wealth of practical information about all aspects of French country life.

Shooting Caterpillars in Spain: The hilarious and compelling story of two innocents abroad in the depths of Andalusia in thelate '80s.

**For a full list of our current titles, visit our website at
www.survivalbooks.net**

PHOTO

www.dreamstime.com

www.bigstockphoto.com

www.istockphoto.com

CREDITS

www.shutterstock.com

Pages 1 © Dario Sabljak, 19 © Cyril Hou, 20 © EML, 23 © Georgiy Pchemyan, 26 © EML, 28 © EML, 31 © kristian sekulic, 43 © Elena Ellisseeva, 44 © EML, 46 © EML, 49 © Vincent Giordano, 57 © Diego Cervo, 63 © EML, 64 © Maxim Kulemza & Alina Krashennikova, 74 © Adam Gryko, 87 © Mary E Cioffi, 99 © Jorge Pedro Barradas de Casais, 111 © Artur Bogacki, 112 © Jane McIlroy, 120 © Clara Natoli, 126 © igor terekhov, 135 © UltraOrto, S.A., 146 © Stillfx, 149 © Rui Vale de Sousa, 155 © Ronen, 156 © stocksnapp, 162 © Deborah Remy, 164 © xavier gallego morell, 172 © artproem, 174 © Factoria singular fotografia, 201 © EML, 211 © Zoran Tripalo, 213 © EML, 215 © Michael Fuery, 216 © Sergey Kolesnikov, 219 © Christine Gonsalves, 220 © EML, 223 © Donncha O Caoimh, 228 © EML, 260 © Thomas Barrat, 262 © Nanka (Kucherenko Olena), 291 © Leah-Anne Thompson, 298 © Mark Breck, 328 © Eoghan McNally, 332 © EML, 335 © EML, 343 © Artur Bogacki, 347 © Lucian Mares, 350 © Tolimir Miroslav, 356 © Victorian Traditions, 366 © vgstudio, 371 © EML, 378 © Stephen Coburn, 380 © Amra Pasic, 382 © Keith Levit, 386 © EML, 414 © Dmitry Pichugin, 415 © Zaporozhchenko, 415 © Colin & Linda McKie.

Peter Farmer

Pages 35, 52, 79, 105, 106, 132, 189, 193, 311, 312, 319, 354, 359, 364, 376, 385.

Survival Books

Pages 167, 169, 170.